D0850689

1969
The Supreme Court Review

1969

The

"Judges as persons, or courts as institutions, are entitled to
no greater immunity from criticism than other persons
or institutions . . . [J]udges must be kept mindful of their limitations and
of their ultimate public responsibility by a vigorous
stream of criticism expressed with candor however blunt."
—*Felix Frankfurter*

". . . while it is proper that people should find fault when
their judges fail, it is only reasonable that they should recognize the
difficulties. . . . Let them be severely brought to book,
when they go wrong, but by those who will take the trouble
to understand them."
—*Learned Hand*

THE LAW SCHOOL

THE UNIVERSITY OF CHICAGO

Supreme Court Review

EDITED BY

PHILIP B. KURLAND

 THE UNIVERSITY OF CHICAGO PRESS

CHICAGO AND LONDON

STANDARD BOOK NUMBER: 226-46420-2

LIBRARY OF CONGRESS CATALOG CARD NUMBER: 60-14353

THE UNIVERSITY OF CHICAGO PRESS, CHICAGO 60637

THE UNIVERSITY OF CHICAGO PRESS, LTD., LONDON

TO
KATE AND EDWARD

A la recherche du temps perdu

CONTENTS

KENNETH W. DAM

FORTNER ENTERPRISES v.

UNITED STATES STEEL:

"NEITHER A BORROWER,

NOR A LENDER BE"

The Supreme Court handed down an impressive number of important antitrust decisions in its 1968–69 Term. Some, such as the *Container* case,[1] will be remembered as major contributions to steadily evolving antitrust doctrine. *Fortner Enterprises, Inc. v. United States Steel Corp.*,[2] in contrast, was merely bizarre. But bizarre cases can be important.

The importance of *Fortner* rests more in the reasoning of the majority than in any positive contributions to antitrust doctrine. This reasoning permitted conventional legal principles to be used to reach an unexpected result. The decision cast a legal shadow on a practice that had not hitherto been thought subject to antitrust challenge—the provision of credit by a supplier on condition that

Kenneth W. Dam is Professor of Law, The University of Chicago.

[1] United States v. Container Corp. of America, 393 U.S. 333 (1969). The decision represents a further evolution of the rule against horizontal price-fixing and price-tampering agreements. The broadest reading of *Container* is that the exchange of current price information among competitors is illegal per se. Whether Mr. Justice Douglas' majority opinion announces a per se rule is an issue on which other Supreme Court Justices are divided. Compare Mr. Justice Fortas' concurring opinion with Mr. Justice Marshall's dissent.

[2] 394 U.S. 495 (1969).

the credit be used to purchase the supplier's goods. Not only the antitrust bar but the lower courts in the *Fortner* case were surprised by the Supreme Court disposition. The district court had decided for the defendant in an unhesitant, straightforward opinion. The court of appeals, affirming, had not even bothered to write an opinion. But Mr. Justice Black, speaking for a five-man majority, saw nothing unusual about the case. All that he found necessary to support reversal was the application of a short list of well-established antitrust principles.

Perhaps the most interesting question posed by *Fortner* is why the Supreme Court decision engendered surprise. Is it to be explained by the inability of the bar and the lower federal courts to reason logically from principle to result? Or is *Fortner* an example, par excellence, of a Supreme Court tendency to spawn simplistic rules—rules that increasingly permit a court so inclined to find antitrust violations at will in complex business arrangements, without the need to consider economic consequences?

If the second interpretation is correct, a number of implications command attention. When the courts have enough per se principles available to them to find both anticompetitive and procompetitive practices illegal, it is unlikely that all courts will readily use those principles on all occasions. Some judges will choose not to find illegality in arrangements that, to them, make sense for the economy as a whole. Decisions will thus become less predictable.

The Antitrust Division and the Federal Trade Commission will also have increased discretion. They will not be able to prosecute in every case, or indeed in any significant percentage of the cases, where illegality might be found. Such expanded prosecutorial discretion might be welcomed. Those who think that the purpose of the antitrust laws is to promote competition might be prepared to rely on the government (or at least the Antitrust Division) to prosecute only where a threat to competition actually exists.

So sanguine a view overlooks the rapidly expanding institution of the treble-damage antitrust action. A legal system that relies on prosecutorial discretion for the sensible application of overly stringent, undiscriminating prohibitions cannot function well when private attorneys-general are accorded massive financial incentives for not exercising equal restraint. The private treble-damage plaintiff has no interest in determining the impact on competition of the practices challenged. Indeed, where, as in the usual case, the defendant is a competitor or supplier, the plaintiff will often be seeking through litigation to offset the consequences of competition. Moreover, since the treble-damage plaintiff's transactions may be de minimis when viewed in the context of an industry as a whole, he will often have every incentive to direct the court's attention away from the underlying economic questions.

I. A LOOK AT THE RECORD

It is no coincidence that *Fortner* was a treble-damage action. The facts of the case throw light on the incentives of private plaintiffs and provide an essential background for an appreciation of how, as in *Fortner*, per se rules operate in private antitrust litigation.

The United States Steel Corporation had entered the business of manufacturing prefabricated houses. Through its Homes Division it sold house components in "home packages" to real estate builders and developers, who erected the houses on the home site for resale to the general public. In order to promote sales, like the vendors of many other products in the modern economy, U.S. Steel found it necessary to offer credit to purchasers. To that end in 1954 it created a wholly owned subsidiary, U.S. Steel Homes Credit Corporation. Since houses are located on land and the typical developer has to seek financing for the land during the period of construction, the Credit Corporation introduced the practice of financing not only the houses but also the land, pending sale of each house and lot.

U.S. Steel's venture into the housing market did not achieve unlimited success. For example, one of the markets where it was interested in establishing itself was Louisville, Kentucky, strategically located just across the Ohio River from the Homes Division plant in New Albany, Indiana. Despite the transportation cost advantages that such proximity might afford, however, the Homes Division had been singularly unsuccessful in penetrating the Louisville market. Although in 1957 it had succeeded in selling thirteen houses in Jefferson County (an area which included Louisville and environs), it had sold only two in 1958 and none at all in 1959.[3]

What the Homes Division obviously needed was a first-rate real estate developer in the Louisville area who could make a success

---

[3] Record, pp. 149a, 184a.

of a U.S. Steel homes subdivision. In late 1959 they thought they had located their man—A. B. Fortner, Jr., the president of Zettwoch Fortner Corporation and a successful real estate developer who had been in the business in Louisville since 1939.[4] Fortner not only had ability, but he also had the land on which to construct the homes. He held this land with a partner in another corporation, Iroquois Development, Inc. After negotiations between Homes Division salesmen and Fortner, it was decided that an appeal would be made to the Credit Corporation to finance the buying out of the partner's one-half interest in the land. Such financing would also help Fortner to realize, prior to sale of the completed homes to the public, at least part of the considerable increase in the value of the land in the five years since its purchase.[5]

Another Fortner corporation was to be the recipient of the loan and would use the proceeds to buy the land from Iroquois Development. This third Fortner corporation, Fortner Enterprises, Inc., was well suited to the purpose because it had an accumulated deficit for tax purposes of about $16,000.[6] Under the proposal made by the Homes Division sales department to the Credit Corporation, the latter would advance $151,950 of which $111,900 would be used to buy the land from Iroquois Development. Of the additional $96,000 that would be required to develop the yet undeveloped lots, the loan proceeds would cover $40,050 and the remaining $55,950 would be Fortner's equity in the land during the construction period.[7] This arrangement, in which the Credit Corporation would provide $151,950 of the $207,900 of the total purchase and development cost of the land, was somewhat in excess, but still within reach, of the 60 percent that was, under the Credit Corporation's announced policy, the maximum it would normally finance.[8]

---

[4] Id. at 385a–388a.

[5] The land had been purchased as farmland some five years previously at $1,100 an acre, but in the meantime the surrounding area had been partially built up by other developers, and utilities had been made available. Consequently, the still undeveloped land was now worth $1,100 a lot. The development averaged nearly four lots per acre. Id. at 313a–314a, 386a–387a, 392a.

[6] Id. at 295a. Fortner Enterprises, Inc., was inactive. The custom in the industry was to use a new corporation for each new subdivision, thereby limiting liability in the event of an unsuccessful project. Id. at 379a.

[7] Memorandum dated December 22, 1959. Id. at 385a–389a.

[8] Id. at 373a–379a.

Following the Homes Division recommendation on December 22, 1959, a meeting was scheduled for January 8, 1960, at which Fortner, Homes Division representatives, and Credit Corporation representatives were to discuss the loan. Fortner came to the meeting, however, with a totally new proposal. Whereas the original proposal had covered only 99 lots, Fortner's new proposal covered 186 lots, again all property of Iroquois Development. Fortner stated that he was prepared to proceed only if the Credit Corporation would finance the full cost of the 155 lots that were undeveloped ($170,500) plus the cost of their development ($139,500) and that, as his equity, he would put up 31 developed lots (valued at $62,000). In this version, as in the December version, it was assumed that the Credit Corporation would in addition finance Fortner's purchase of the home packages themselves.

Since Fortner's demands far exceeded the 60 percent guideline, Credit Corporation executives were unhappy. No final arrangements were made.[9] In March, moreover, Fortner demanded that the proposed land note bear a two-year maturity rather than the twelve-to-eighteen-month maturity theretofore discussed. When the Credit Corporation urged as an alternative a reduction of the number of lots to be covered by the financing, Fortner refused.[10] Further complications developed when Fortner's partner decided that the proposed transaction was too attractive for him to bow out. That hurdle was eventually surmounted, but the negotiations continued until September when the Credit Corporation finally agreed "to provide 100% financing for the purchase and development of the land in question."[11]

In October, 1960, the loan agreement was signed. It called for

---

[9] *Id.* at 634a. The president of the Credit Corporation complained to a subordinate that "the Fortner loan on the new basis is an extreme" and reminded him of the dangers involved: "With all our money out front, he has very little incentive to finish off a project. . . . In making this statement, it is not the financial risk aspects which are referred to, but rather the fact that the loan will not produce house sales. The worst thing that can happen is an unsuccessful development. This precludes, in most cases, any other house sales in that area, because the one we have there has been unsuccessful." Memorandum dated January 12, 1960. *Ibid.*

[10] *Id.* at 393a–394a.

[11] *Id.* at 290a. The language is the characterization given the transaction by Fortner in an affidavit.

land notes for $88,000 and $231,920 bearing 6 percent interest.[12] The loan agreement also called for construction notes for $373,200 and $1,362,180, also bearing interest at 6 percent.[13] Apparently neither of the latter two notes, which were to finance purchase of the house components from the Home Division and their subsequent erection on the land, represented "100% financing."

The following May, Fortner, having already sold at least 35 homes and having acquired additional land through his Iroquois Development corporation, sought an additional land loan for $54,000, to acquire 32 additional lots, and an additional construction loan of $462,000.[14] Since some $30,000 of the requested land loan was to be used to replenish working capital, the Credit Corporation representative explained to Fortner that "expenditures of this nature are normally borne by all builders and in many instances represents [sic] about the only risk capital a builder provides."[15] The Credit Corporation representative sought "to determine if there was a more conservative basis upon which we would provide financing on the lots in question and still be of assistance to him." But "Mr. Fortner's position was that he needed the financing as requested and felt that a loan similar to that which [the Credit Corporation] originally made was justified."[16] By August, 1961, the parties had agreed on a land loan of $59,000 (a total construction loan commitment of $403,400), again at a 6 percent rate.[17]

Fortner soon began to complain about the quality of the housing components delivered to him. Whether the frequency of complaints became significant before or after the second land loan is the subject of some ambiguity in the documents and affidavits,[18] but in

----

[12] The due dates were December 31, 1961, and December 31, 1962, respectively. Fortner thus got the better part of what he had asked with respect to his demand for a two-year maturity. *Id.* at 27a–37a, 47a–50a.

[13] *Id.* at 25a–26a, 50a–53a.

[14] *Id.* at 399a–401a, 407a–413a. The land had previously been sold by Iroquois Development but was reacquired. *Id.* at 408.

[15] *Id.* at 411a.

[16] The quotations are from a contemporaneous memorandum by the Credit Corporation representative. *Id.* at 409a.

[17] *Id.* at 243a–268a. All advances under both the 1960 and 1961 loan agreements were secured by mortgages.

[18] Plaintiff claimed that all of the 70 houses that had been delivered were defective. Many had been delivered prior to the completion of negotiations on the second loan agreement. *Id.* at 117a–118a.

any case the trickle of complaints soon became a flood. Windows leaked, exterior panels did not align, closet doors did not fit, and nails popped out. A contemporaneous Homes Division document suggests that Fortner's complaints were not exaggerated.[19]

Several meetings were held in late April and early May between Homes Division representatives and Fortner to discuss the complaints. It was apparently about this time that Fortner consulted his attorneys. A meeting was arranged with Homes Division and Credit Corporation representatives in the attorneys' offices on May 31, 1962. At that meeting Fortner or his attorneys proposed that the loans could be paid off if he were to complete the project with conventional housing. The representative of the Credit Corporation explained that so long as the loans were outstanding, Fortner had an obligation to construct only Homes Division housing on the land and that if Fortner wanted to construct other housing, he should first pay off the Credit Corporation. Fortner unsuccessfully requested the deletion of a loan agreement provision requiring the borrower "to complete the development of the Premises and to erect on each of said Lots . . . a prefabricated dwelling house manufactured by United States Steel Homes Division."[20]

Until this meeting the controversy between Fortner and U.S. Steel was a typical commercial dispute over the quality of goods, not greatly different from thousands of other disputes that are erupting and being resolved in the economy at any given time. Most lawyers consulted would probably have thought of the dispute in terms of warranties and other sales law concepts. But the explicit demand for the deletion of the clause in question suggested that Fortner had consulted uncommonly resourceful lawyers. Just how resourceful they were became clear a few weeks later when Fortner Enterprises filed an action under §§ 1 and 2 of the Sherman Act, alleging that the Homes Division and the Credit Corporation had conspired "to force corporations and individuals, including the plaintiff, as a condition to availing themselves of the services of United States Steel Homes Credit Corporation, to purchase at artificially high prices only United States Steel Homes."[21] The complaint further alleged that, after the construction of 70 houses,

---

[19] *Id.* at 116a–127a, 418a–422a.

[20] *Id.* at 26a, 292a–294a. This clause was somewhat reformulated in the second loan agreement. *Id.* at 245a.

[21] *Id.* at 21a.

Fortner Enterprises had not been able to complete the project because of the "faulty and defective" housing packages and that the defendants were effectuating the conspiracy by threatening to foreclose on the mortgage.[22] The plaintiff's principal theory was that the defendants had conspired to make a tie-in sale. In order to obtain the loan, the plaintiff had been compelled to take Homes Division houses. In the jargon of antitrust, the money was the tying product and the houses were the tied product.

After extensive interrogatories, depositions, and other pretrial proceedings lasting some four years (in the course of which the mortgages were foreclosed),[23] defendants moved for summary judgment. The motion was granted.

II. THE MAJORITY OPINION

Mr. Justice Black, writing for the majority, viewed the case as elementary. He had no doubt that the defendants had imposed a tying arrangement. It was, in fact, a "tying arrangement of the traditional kind."[24] Tie-ins are illegal per se. It suffices to bring a tie-in within the sphere of per se illegality that a significant volume of commerce is foreclosed in the tied product and that the seller has "sufficient market power" in the market for the tying product.[25] As to the foreclosure requirement, Mr. Justice Black could not say that the annual volume of sales of housing to the plaintiff, almost $200,000, "is paltry or 'insubstantial'" and, in any case, one must look to the volume of commerce foreclosed from all of the defendants' tie-in sales, not merely from sales to the plaintiff.[26] Sufficient market power is established whenever "the seller has the power to raise prices, or impose other burdensome terms such as a tie-in, with respect to any appreciable number of buyers within the market."[27] The implication left by Mr. Justice Black was that since the tie-in had been imposed, the defendants must have had the power to impose it. But he did not consider it necessary to state explicitly

---

[22] *Id.* at 21a–22a.

[23] The Credit Corporation's counterclaim sought foreclosure of the mortgages. Summary judgment for the Credit Corporation on the counterclaim was granted. The mortgages were foreclosed, and the secured property was sold. *Id.* at 52a–81a, 192a–200a, 229a–236a.

[24] 394 U.S. at 498.

[25] *Id.* at 498–99.

[26] *Id.* at 502.

[27] *Id.* at 504.

that the existence of the tie-in established the power to impose it since, in view of plaintiff's affidavits, the fundamental error had been to grant summary judgment.

Moreover, even if foreclosure and market power were not present, those two "standards are necessary only to bring into play the doctrine of *per se* illegality."[28] Even if plaintiff might fail to establish one or both of those two requisites, he "can still prevail on the merits whenever he can prove, on the basis of a more thorough examination of the purposes and effects of the practices involved, that the general standards of the Sherman Act have been violated."[29] Therefore, a trial would in any event be necessary on the plaintiff's "general allegations that respondents conspired together for the purpose of restraining competition and acquiring a monopoly in the market for prefabricated houses."[30]

The concluding paragraphs of the majority opinion are devoted to the rebuttal of several arguments made by the defendants and in the dissenting opinions of Justices White (with Harlan joining) and Fortas (with Stewart joining). Mr. Justice Black rejected the argument that the transaction should be treated as merely the "usual sale on credit" in which "the entire transaction could be considered to involve only a single product."[31] In the arrangement under challenge "the credit is provided by one corporation on condition that a product be purchased from a separate corporation" and "the borrower contracts to obtain a large sum of money over and above that needed to pay the seller for the physical products purchased."[32] Nor can credit be distinguished, ruled Mr. Justice Black, "from other kinds of goods and services, all of which may, when used as tying products, extend the seller's economic power to new markets and foreclose competition in the tied product."[33] Not only might credit tie-ins involve the same evils as other tie-ins but credit tie-ins might raise barriers to entry into the market for the tied product. An entrant into that market would have to have "sufficient financial strength to offer credit comparable to that provided by larger competitors under tying arrangements."[34] The argument of the majority opinion concludes with the observation that "it is easy to see how a big company with vast sums of money in its treasury could wield very substantial power in a credit market."[35]

---

[28] *Id.* at 499–500. [30] *Ibid.* [32] *Ibid.* [34] *Id.* at 509.

[29] *Id.* at 500. [31] *Id.* at 507. [33] *Id.* at 508. [35] *Ibid.*

On its face, Mr. Justice Black's opinion does not purport to bring anything fresh to the law on tie-ins. The standards are unchanged, he says, and credit tie-ins are not only subject to those standards but are tie-ins of the "traditional kind," creating dangers at least as grave as tie-ins involving two tangible products. That being so, there is no basis for summary judgment for the defendants where the plaintiff has any substantial evidence on the crucial issues of foreclosure and market power.

III. The Standards for Summary Judgment

In considering the importance of the *Fortner Enterprises* decision, it is worth asking whether this case can be viewed as dealing primarily with the standards for summary judgment in antitrust cases. Certainly every antitrust lawyer knows that the probability of a grant of certiorari following summary judgment against the plaintiff is high, whatever the importance to the economy or to antitrust doctrine of the case. *Fortner* may stand primarily for the proposition that it is per se erroneous to grant summary judgment against a plaintiff in any treble-damage action. The grant of certiorari and per curiam reversal without oral argument in a case decided only a few weeks after *Fortner* supports that view.[36]

The consequences of such a rule would be substantial. Although what little evidence is available suggests that juries can usually detect a meritless case,[37] a jury trial may be of considerable value to an antitrust plaintiff, if only because it improves his position in settlement negotiations. A rule guaranteeing every antitrust plaintiff the right to a jury trial, however groundless his case, would thus influence settlement practices, thereby increasing the cost of practices that engender litigation and, at the margin, altering the economic behavior of firms. The only matter for debate is the importance of this effect.

The fundamental case on the use of summary judgment in antitrust cases is *Poller v. Columbia Broadcasting Co.*[38] That decision

---

[36] Norfolk Monument Co. v. Woodlawn Memorial Gardens, Inc., 394 U.S. 700 (1969).

[37] Kalven & Zeisel, The American Jury 149–62 (1966). This product of the University of Chicago jury study was concerned with criminal cases only.

[38] 368 U.S. 464 (1962).

has frequently been cited for the language that Mr. Justice Black quoted in *Fortner Enterprises:*[39]

> We believe that summary procedures should be used sparingly in complex antitrust litigation where motive and intent play leading roles, the proof is largely in the hands of alleged conspirators, and hostile witnesses thicken the plot. It is only when the witnesses are present and subject to cross-examination that their credibility and the weight to be given their testimony can be appraised. Trial by affidavit is no substitute for trial by jury which so long has been the hallmark of "even handed justice."

Although the Supreme Court has put a good deal of energy into the enforcement of this procedural rule, it has on occasion, as in the 1967 Term's *Cities Service* decision,[40] conceded that not every complaint automatically entitles its draftsman to a jury trial. But Mr. Justice Black had heatedly dissented in the aberrational *Cities Service* case, arguing that "the best service that could be rendered in this field would be to abolish summary judgment procedures, root and branch."[41] In that dissent, in which Justices Warren and Brennan joined, he sought to make clear that his objection to summary judgment is that it "tempts judges to take over the jury trial of cases, thus depriving parties of their constitutional right to trial by jury."[42]

One may seriously doubt that the result in *Fortner* and similar antitrust cases is, as the *Cities Service* dissent suggests, compelled by the Constitution. Certainly the proliferation of per se rules militates against that view, for a per se rule has the effect and even the purpose of eliminating a trial in whole or in part. Mr. Justice Black made that very point in *Fortner*, where he observed that in the two principal Supreme Court tie-in precedents, *Northern Pacific*[43]

---

[39] *Id.* at 473, quoted 394 U.S. at 500.

[40] First National Bank of Arizona v. Cities Service Co., 391 U.S. 253 (1968).

[41] *Id.* at 304.

[42] *Ibid.* This dislike of summary judgment extends well beyond the antitrust area. Cases decided under the Federal Employees Liability Act are the leading example. The *Fortner* case thus provides an answer to Judge Aldrich's query in Dehydrating Process Co. v. A. O. Smith Corp., 292 F.2d 653, 656 n. 6 (1st Cir. 1961), whether FELA cases are to be considered "on their own bottom" or apply also to tie-in and other antitrust cases.

[43] Northern Pacific Railway Co. v. United States, 356 U.S. 1 (1958).

and *International Salt*,[44] the Court had "approved summary judgment against the defendants" because the standards "necessary . . . to bring into play the doctrine of *per se* illegality" had been satisfied.[45] Thus, the antitrust rule against summary judgment is a one-way street, benefiting plaintiffs but not available to defendants. No one has explained why the Constitution protects plaintiffs but not defendants. Since the coercive power of the state is brought to bear in a more direct manner when a defendant is ordered to pay than when the coercive resources of the judicial system are withheld from a plaintiff,[46] one might have thought that any constitutional bias would run the other way.

On a non-constitutional level, one might read some non-neutral principles of procedure into the Clayton Act's provision in § 5 for private actions. The Court did just that in *Radovich v. National Football League*[47] where, speaking of the standards for judging the sufficiency of a complaint, it condemned "technical objections" to a complaint on the ground that, in view of the general congressional policy embodied in the treble-damage provision of the antitrust laws, "this Court should not add requirements to burden the private litigant beyond what is specifically set forth by Congress in those laws."[48] That the Court reads this injunction to mean even more than that every plaintiff must have his day before a jury is suggested by the recent *Albrecht* case[49] where the Supreme Court set aside a jury verdict for the defendant and ordered not a new trial but rather judgment notwithstanding the verdict for plaintiff.

Whatever the doctrinal justification for this pro-plaintiff bias in treble-damage actions, one cannot put aside *Fortner* as no more than a further manifestation of it. If the Court wanted to leave the substantive reach of the Sherman Act undisturbed, it could merely have reversed on the authority of *Poller*. Although Mr. Justice Black's opinion does not purport to extend the substantive law on tie-ins, the opinion certainly calls into question a large number of

---

[44] International Salt Co. v. United States, 332 U.S. 392 (1947).

[45] 394 U.S. at 499–500.

[46] *Cf.* Shelley v. Kraemer, 334 U.S. 1 (1948).

[47] 352 U.S. 445 (1957).

[48] *Id.* at 454.

[49] Albrecht v. Herald Co., 390 U.S. 145 (1968).

credit practices not formerly thought subject to the Sherman Act. The summary judgment aspect of the case, although revealing the motivations of the Court, is a bit like the breakfast menu theory of jurisprudence. It may tell you why a particular judge decided as he did but it does not tell you what the precedent thus created will mean to cerebrally oriented lower-court judges in the future. It is not inappropriate, therefore, to turn to the implications of the discussion of the law on tie-ins in order to assess the full meaning of *Fortner*.

IV. What Is a Tie-In?

More complicated than the question whether the tying arrangement found in *Fortner* was illegal is the question whether there was any tie-in at all. A person untutored in antitrust law might find absurd the notion that a sale on credit was a tie-in. It warrants discussion whether, even assuming some sophistication in the mysteries of antitrust, that notion is not, at the very least, curious.

Mr. Justice Black had, as we have seen, no difficulty in finding a tie-in. As he quite properly observed, what was involved was technically more than a mere credit sale. The Credit Corporation had financed not only the home packages but also the land, which Fortner Enterprises bought from another Fortner venture. It is, of course, on such technical distinctions that antitrust law is built. But one may fairly ask whether the distinction does not distort the factual situation. The bulk of the advances (about $1,700,000 of the total of about $2,000,000) was to be disbursed against purchase and installation of the houses.[50] Financing exceeding the cost of the goods themselves is not at all unusual. As Mr. Justice Fortas observed, "It is common in our economy for a seller to extend financing to a distributor or franchisee to enable him to purchase and handle the seller's goods at retail, to rent retail facilities, to acquire fixtures or machinery for service to customers in connection with distribution of the seller's goods."[51] Where prefabricated houses are involved, the real estate builder is perhaps more in the retailing than the construction business. As a matter of fact, at the very outset of his relations with U.S. Steel, Fortner signed a "fran-

---

[50] 394 U.S. at 522.   [51] *Id.* at 524.

chise agreement."[52] But perhaps Mr. Justice Black sees such arrangements as tie-ins, too.[53]

Mr. Justice Black strongly suggests that credit would be a separate product even if it did not exceed the price of the goods. The methodology of this part of the opinion is particularly interesting for the light it throws on his judicial technique. He starts by conceding what would appear to be the decisive point, namely, that in the usual credit sale only a single product can be found because the so-called tying by the seller is nothing other than an "agreement determining when and how much he will be paid for his product."[54] But then he ominously adds a formula sometimes used by law-extending judges for distinguishing, while throwing a baleful shadow upon, a practice theretofore clearly legal: "It will be time enough to pass on the issue of credit sales when a case involving it actually arises."[55] After reminding his readers that *Fortner* did not involve the usual credit sale, he then waxes warm on the dangers of credit sales in the hands of large and competitively unscrupulous companies, concluding with a populist warning about the evils that may be perpetrated by "a big company with vast sums of money."[56] One is led to conclude that, so far as Mr. Justice Black is concerned, the usual credit sale, at least in the hands of big companies with vast sums of money, stands at the front lines of advancing per se illegality.

Whatever future tie-in battles may be fought in the Supreme Court, it is worth pondering whether the *Fortner* arrangement was a tie-in the sense that the other practices condemned as tie-ins by the Supreme Court have been. To be sure, there is nothing special about credit as such. For example, a refusal to sell automobiles to dealers who would not utilize the manufacturer's credit facilities,

---

[52] Record, pp. 922a–926a.

[53] One Federal Trade Commissioner immediately took the public position that the importance of *Fortner* lies precisely in its invalidation of "those franchise situations where a franchisor finances the purchaser of its franchisees on the condition that they purchase from suppliers approved by the franchisor." Address by Commissioner Everette MacIntyre, 5 CCH TRADE REG. REP. ¶ 50240, at p. 55489 (May 8, 1969). And Commissioner James M. Nicholson announced that under *Fortner* "the extension of valuable financial or management assistance on the condition that the franchisee agree to buy inferior ingredients at exhorbitant prices may establish . . . a tie." 5 CCH TRADE REG. REP. ¶ 50238, at p. 55481 n. 10 (April 26, 1969).

[54] 394 U.S. at 507.   [55] *Ibid.*   [56] *Id.* at 509.

as in the *GMAC* case,[57] can readily be said to be a tie-in of two products. *GMAC* was, of course, the opposite of *Fortner*, since in the former case, credit was the tied, not the tying product. But if the test is whether there are two products, then surely credit can be a product. Let us assume for the purposes of discussion therefore that, in this mechanical sense, two products can be said to be involved. The policy question still remains whether it makes antitrust sense to view the practice involved as a tie-in.

The relationship between the two products is different in *Fortner* than in the principal Supreme Court tie-in cases, *International Salt* and *Northern Pacific*. In both of those cases the tied product —salt and transportation—was purchased in quantities bearing no particular relation to the quantities of the tying product—salt machines and land. In the *Fortner* case, in contrast, the so-called tied and tying products were used in fixed proportions. A one-to-one relation existed between the provision of financing and the sale of houses. Not only was this true in the case of the construction loans that financed the purchase and erection of the houses, but it was also true in substance with respect to the land. Although the land was not acquired lot by lot, the total advance was calculated to equal the aggregate value of the lots. That was what was meant by "100% financing."

Moreover, unlike *International Salt* and *Northern Pacific*, the tied product was not used continuously following the purchase of the tying product. The proceeds of that portion of the loans represented by construction notes were disbursed as needed to purchase the houses and then to erect them.[58] Similarly, the advances under the land notes were to be made available as needed, first to acquire the land and later to improve it.[59]

The importance of these differences is not to be found in the mechanics of the present law on tie-ins but rather in the motives leading to different practices that the present law lumps together as tie-ins. Let us take the case where the two products are used in variable proportions, and particularly where sale of one unit of the tying product is followed by sale over time of a number of units

---

[57] United States v. General Motors Corp., 121 F.2d 376 (7th Cir. 1941).

[58] Record, pp. 34a–35a, 249a–251a.

[59] *Id*. at 30a–33a, 248a.

of the tied product. The tying arrangement in that situation serves as a counting device permitting a seller of the tying product to measure the intensity of its use. If the seller has some monopoly power in the tying product, price discrimination on sales of that product is facilitated by means of the tie-in. Price discrimination permits a monopolist to earn a greater return than he could earn by charging a uniform price. Differential pricing may take the form either of non-uniform prices for the tying product (based on marketing information obtained through prior tie-ins) or, if a uniform price is charged for the tying product, by a supracompetitive price for the tied product.[60] In *International Salt* the intensity of use for the salt machines could be measured by the volume of purchases of salt. It is less clear that this theory explains the tie-in in *Northern Pacific*, but the volume of transportation service required may be a measure of the intensity of use of land. If that was not the effect of the *Northern Pacific* tie-in, then its effect can be dismissed as de minimis.

Where, however, as in *Fortner*, the products are used in fixed proportions (and particularly where they are sold simultaneously), the purpose of any tie-in must be much different. Even if the seller had a monopoly in the tying product, he could achieve no greater supracompetitive profit through the tying arrangement than he could by selling the products separately.[61]

Two points should be observed. First, to assimilate the arrangement in *Fortner* to that in *International Salt* and *Northern Pacific* is to treat two economically different situations identically because, at a high level of abstraction, both involve "two products." Such mechanistic reasoning by a busy Court may be excused but hardly commended. Second, the evil involved in the price discrimination

---

[60] This explanation assumes that intensity of use provides a rough measurement of elasticity of demand. The use of a tie-in as a counting device to facilitate discrimination is considered in Bowman, *Tying Arrangements and the Leverage Problem*, 67 YALE L.J. 19 (1957). Bowman credits Professor Aaron Director with first formulating this explanation. In his dissent, Mr. Justice White picked up this point as part of a compendium of learning on tie-ins but apparently did not see its immediate relevance to the law on tie-ins. 394 U.S. at 515. This explanation, it should be noted, has nothing to do with popular leverage notions under which a monopoly in the tying product is supposedly extended to the tied product.

[61] See Bowman, note 60 *supra*, at 20–23. As Bowman points out, a tie-in in such a situation could be a technique for avoiding price regulation in the monopolized product.

explanation, if it is an evil,[62] is dependent upon monopoly power in the tying product. Although an economist would not be satisfied, a court might be justified in inferring that monopoly power in the tying product exists where the two products are used in variable proportions and hence the price discrimination explanation seems a priori plausible. On this ground, the determination concerning market power in the tying product in *International Salt* and *Northern Pacific* might be defended. But where, as in *Fortner,* no such explanation is possible, a deeper economic inquiry into the existence of market power in the tying product is essential, even if one believes that market power can somehow be transferred from the tying to the tied product. In the absence of market power in the tying product, there is nothing to transfer. Such a use of leverage is, of course, the evil that the courts have seen in tie-ins[63] and was decried by Mr. Justice Black once again in *Fortner* under the rubric of "barriers to entry": "[E]conomies in financing should not, any more than economies in other lines for business, be used to exert *economic power over other products* that the company produces no more efficiently than its competitors."[64]

The foregoing analysis suggests that the weakness of the "two products" approach is that it tends to sweep within the category of tie-ins many arrangements that are competitively benign. Mr. Justice Fortas suggested a technique for remedying this weakness in certain cases. He argued that no tie existed in *Fortner* because the "financing which [U.S. Steel] agrees to provide is solely and entirely ancillary to its sale of houses."[65] Mr. Justice Fortas' approach has much to recommend it. It affords the possibility of building on the ancillary restraints doctrine, which condemns only

---

[62] The output of the price discriminating monopolist may in certain circumstances exceed that of the monopolist charging a uniform price. Where that is so, the principal economic objection to monopoly—that it reduces output—becomes less forceful. ROBINSON, THE ECONOMICS OF IMPERFECT COMPETITION 188–95 (1933).

[63] "[T]he essence of illegality in tying agreements is the wielding of monopolistic leverage; a seller exploits his dominant position in one market to expand his empire into the next." Times-Picayune Publishing Co. v. United States, 345 U.S. 594, 611 (1953). "A tie-in contract may have . . . undesirable effects when the seller, by virtue of his position in the market for the tying product, has economic leverage sufficient to induce his customers to take the tied product along with the tying item." United States v. Loew's, Inc., 371 U.S. 38, 45 (1962). See Northern Pacific Railway Co. v. United States, 356 U.S. 1, 6 (1958).

[64] 394 U.S. at 509. (Emphasis supplied.)   [65] *Id.* at 521–22.

those restraints that are not ancillary to a lawful main transaction. Such a line of inquiry would permit more economic analysis than the intellectually sterile per se approach since a court would be forced to seek the purpose of the putative tie-in. Moreover, the ancillary doctrine would fit the facts of cases like *Fortner* well. As Mr. Justice Fortas observed, U.S. Steel was not "selling credit in any general sense."[66] All parties were agreed that the Credit Corporation made credit available only to purchasers of houses from the Homes Division.[67] Hence, the ancillarity approach expresses well the common-sense feeling that there is something wrong with saying that U.S. Steel was tying its credit to sales when the only purpose of making credit available at all was to promote the sale of houses. Finally, the ancillary restraints doctrine would distinguish most of the earlier tie-in cases, since, for example, it would be difficult to say that the lease of the patented salt machines was purely ancillary to the sale of salt in *International Salt*.

Although the ancillary restraints doctrine would thus provide a useful approach to the issue whether two products were tied, the underlying significance of the Credit Corporation's self-imposed restriction on the range of its money market activities is once more the light thrown on the issue of market power. It is difficult to believe that U.S. Steel could have any market power over an item so widely useful as credit if it made it available only in connection with sales of prefabricated homes. Whatever leverage advantages in the housing market it might be thought to gain through a tie-in could surely never compensate for the foregone supracompetitive profits it could secure, assuming it really had market power over credit, by making credit generally available to the public. When the point is put in those terms, the specter of U.S. Steel's market power in credit stemming from its "vast sums of money" dissolves. However "imperfect" credit markets may be, it is, Mr. Justice Black notwithstanding, far from "easy to see how a big company with vast sums of money in its treasury could wield very substantial power in a credit market."[68] If U.S. Steel had such power over credit, it could and surely would use it outside the narrow field of financing prefabricated houses.

---

[66] *Id.* at 521.

[67] The plaintiff's attorney went out of his way to establish this fact in the course of the depositions. *E.g.*, Record, pp. 838a–840a.

[68] 394 U.S. at 509.

Here again one is led to the conclusion that the definitional question is hard to separate from the question when tie-ins are harmful. Yet the decisions, in adopting the per se rule, have attempted to flee from that economic question by ruling that tying arrangements are presumptively harmful, at least whenever certain nominal threshold standards on power and foreclosure are met. The weakness of the per se methodology is that it places crucial importance on the definition of the practice. Once an arrangement falls within the defined limits, no justification will be heard. But a per se rule gives no economic standards for defining the practice. To treat the definitional question as an abstract inquiry into whether one or two products is involved is thus to compound the weakness of the per se approach.

V. THE REQUIREMENT OF ECONOMIC POWER

As the foregoing discussion has suggested at several points, any harm that can arise from a tie-in, whether as envisaged by the Court's leverage theory or through monopolistic price discrimination, requires market power in the market for the tying product. Aside from the cloud that *Fortner* throws on many financing arrangements in the economy, the practical importance of the case lies primarily in the further attenuation of the requirement of market power as a prerequisite to per se illegality.

A. ECONOMIC POWER FROM INTERNATIONAL SALT TO FORTNER

The attenuation of the market power requirement has been in process for some time. The Court has usually tended to view the market power requirement as a technicality to be manipulated in the particular case in such a way as to sweep the challenged practice within the sphere of the per se rule.

In *International Salt* the tying product, the salt machines, was patented. The Court, observing that patents confer "a limited monopoly of the invention they reward,"[69] failed to consider the possibility that legal monopoly might not correspond to an economic monopoly. In *Standard Stations*,[70] Justice Frankfurter noted that it had not been established in *International Salt* "that equivalent machines were unobtainable" or "what proportion of the business

---

[69] 332 U.S. at 395.

[70] Standard Oil Co. v. United States, 337 U.S. 293 (1949).

of supplying such machines was controlled by defendant."[71] But, he reasoned, a "patent, . . . although in fact there may be many competing substitutes for the patented article, is at least *prima facie* evidence of [market] control."[72] The *Times-Picayune* case[73] made clear that patents could indeed be taken, "on their face" and without further evidence, as conferring "monopolistic, albeit lawful, market control."[74] Whatever empirical justification there might be for assuming that economic monopoly was associated with patents, a line of patent cases treating tie-in clauses in patent licenses as a misuse of the patents made clear that a patent did not justify a tie-in.[75] *International Salt* might at the time have been read as saying that patent misuse was an antitrust violation whenever a substantial volume of commerce was involved.

The practice challenged in *Times-Picayune*, however, was a unit contract requiring advertisers in the city's sole morning paper to advertise in the same publisher's evening paper, which faced competition. No patent or copyright was involved. The question of requisite market power in the tying product therefore had to be faced, but the answer had two levels. Since advertising was not a "commodity" and hence the unit contract did not fall within the ambit of § 3 of the Clayton Act,[76] the Court treated that contract as subject only to the stricter standards of § 1 of the Sherman Act:[77]

> From the "tying" cases a perceptible pattern of illegality emerges: When the seller enjoys a monopolistic position in the market for the "tying" product, *or* if a substantial volume of commerce in the "tied" product is restrained, a tying arrangement violates the narrower standards expressed in § 3 of the

[71] *Id*. at 305.   [72] *Id*. at 307.

[73] Times-Picayune Publishing Co. v. United States, 345 U.S. 594 (1953).

[74] *Id*. at 608. See also *id*. at 611 n. 30.

[75] Morton Salt Co. v. G. S. Suppiger Co., 314 U.S. 488 (1942); Mercoid Corp. v. Mid-Continent Investment Co., 320 U.S. 661 (1944); Mercoid Corp. v. Minneapolis-Honeywell Regulator Co., 320 U.S. 680 (1944).

[76] Section 3 applies to leases and sales of "goods, wares, merchandise, machinery, supplies or *other commodities* . . . on the condition, agreement or understanding that the lessee or purchaser thereof shall not use or deal in the goods, wares, merchandise, machinery, supplies or *other commodities* of a competitor or competitors of the lessor or seller, where the effect . . . may be to substantially lessen competition or tend to create a monopoly in any line of commerce." 38 Stat. 731 (1944), 15 U.S.C. § 14 (1964). (Emphasis supplied.)

[77] 345 U.S. at 608–09.

Clayton Act because from either factor the requisite potential lessening of competition is inferred. And because for even a lawful monopolist it is "unreasonable *per se*, to foreclose competitors from any substantial market," a tying arrangement is banned by § 1 whenever *both* conditions are met.

In measuring control over the tying products, patent and copyright cases were to be distinguished: "Unlike other 'tying' cases where patents or copyrights supplied the requisite market control, any equivalent market 'dominance' in this case must rest on comparative marketing data."[78] The Court therefore examined the facts and found that the defendants did not have the market dominance required for a § 1 tie-in violation. Forty percent of the market did not in the circumstances confer the requisite dominance.[79]

Whether or not this disparity between Clayton and Sherman Act standards in *Times-Picayune* could be justified by the precedents, the gap was soon narrowed in the *Northern Pacific* case. Since neither the land nor the transportation service was a "commodity," the tie-in was again tested under the Sherman Act standards. In the hands of Mr. Justice Black, writing for the majority, the "monopolistic position" prerequisite to liability was watered down to "sufficient economic power": tie-ins "are unreasonable in and of themselves whenever a party has sufficient economic power with respect to the tying product to appreciably restrain free competition in the market for the tied product and a 'not insubstantial' amount of interstate commerce is affected."[80] The finding of "sufficient economic power" over the tying product was predicated not on "comparative marketing data" as in *Times-Picayune* but merely on the qualitative observations that the land was "strategically located," "within economic distance of transportation facilities," and "often prized by those who purchased or leased it and frequently essential to their business activities."[81] The only quantitative measurement was that "several million acres" were subject to the tie-in. No attempt was made to define any relevant market within which one could judge whether such an area could give rise to any market power in fact. Mr. Justice Black came close to saying that the

---

[78] *Id.* at 611.

[79] The percentage control of the market for the tying product was probably improperly defined. See Turner, *The Validity of Tying Arrangements under the Antitrust Laws*, 72 HARV. L. REV. 50, 55 n. 21 (1958).

[80] 356 U.S. at 6. See also *id.* at 11.   [81] *Id.* at 7.

requisite power was shown by the tie-in itself, particularly if many contracts contained the tying clauses: "The very existence of this host of tying arrangements is itself compelling evidence of the defendant's great power, at least where, as here, no other explanation has been offered for the existence of these restraints."[82] Mr. Justice Black made clear that he did not think it necessary to make a serious inquiry into the actual degree of market power in the tying product. After all, no such inquiry had been made in *International Salt.* And, *Times-Picayune* (in which Mr. Justice Black had dissented) to the contrary notwithstanding, the tie-in in *International Salt* was illegal "*despite* the fact that the tying item was patented, not because of it."[83]

The next step in the attenuation of the requirement of market power over the tying product was taken in 1962 in the *Loew's* case.[84] The Court there held block booking of copyrighted motion picture films for television exhibition to constitute an illegal tying practice. Again, since films are not "commodities," only the Sherman Act standards were in question. "Market dominance," in the sense of power in a significant economic market—that is, "some power to control price and to exclude competition"—became only one species of the "requisite economic power." Such power might also be "inferred from the tying product's desirability to consumers or from uniqueness in its attributes."[85] To emphasize that "uniqueness or consumer appeal" might be found in the absence of any power over price in the market for the tying product, Mr. Justice Goldberg added that "it should seldom be necessary in a tie-in sale case to embark upon a full-scale factual inquiry into the scope of the relevant market for the tying product and into the corollary problem of the seller's percentage share in that market."[86] And since, unlike *Northern Pacific,* industrial property rights were once

---

[82] *Id.* at 7–8. As the dissenting opinion of Mr. Justice Harlan pointed out, no substantial inference of power would be drawn from the existence of the clauses, since purchasers of the land were permitted to purchase transport service from other rail carriers "when offered either lower rates *or* lower rates or superior service." *Id.* at 13, 17. (Emphasis in original.)

[83] *Id.* at 9. The Government had argued that land could be analogized to patents or copyrights because it was unique. The Court did not fully accept that argument, but the idea had enough vitality to reappear in Justice Fortas' dissent in *Fortner.* 394 U.S. at 520, 523.

[84] United States v. Loew's, Inc., 371 U.S. 38 (1962).

[85] *Id.* at 45.   [86] *Id.* at 45 n. 4.

again involved, the Court stated that it would be appropriate to presume "sufficiency of economic power" from the fact that "the tying product is patented or copyrighted."[87] Moreover, with "uniqueness" now the test, the presumption could be reformulated. Just as the purpose of patents was to "reward uniqueness," so too was a copyrighted film unique. It did not matter that films might be "reasonably interchangeable"; they "varied in theme, in artistic performance, in stars, in audience appeal, etc.," and a copyright was by definition a species of monopoly.[88]

B. THE UNIQUENESS TEST APPLIED

Since even U.S. Steel has no patent or copyright on money, some ambiguity concerning the proper standard still remained in *Fortner*. To understand how the issue was treated by the Court, it is essential to understand the contention made by the plaintiff. On the motion for summary judgment, the plaintiff based its case on the economic power issue on two sentences in Fortner's affidavit:[89]

> Affiant states that to his knowledge no [100%] financial assistance was available to Fortner Enterprises, Inc. in 1959–1962 on the terms offered by the Credit Corporation from any other source. The offered financial assistance, particularly in terms of the 100% financing feature, was so unusual, unique as far as the Plaintiff was concerned, and attractive that the Plaintiff because of economic circumstances accepted the assistance offered, including conditions imposed by the Credit Corporation that prefabricated homes manufactured by the Homes Division would be built in the subdivision.

This affidavit was supplemented by the affidavit of the president of Louisville Mortgage Service Company, a local institutional lender, who stated that the Credit Corporation "financing package . . . was unusual and unique during the period from 1959 to 1962 in Jefferson County, Kentucky" and that "such a financing plan was not available to Fortner Enterprises or any other potential borrower from or through Louisville Mortgage Service Company or

---

[87] *Ibid.*

[88] The Court did not consider whether the difference between the legal rights accorded by a patent and a copyright might require a different result. A patent grants a monopoly in the sense of a right to exclude others even though they may independently have subsequently discovered the product. A copyright protects only against copying.

[89] Record, p. 290a.

from any lending institution or mortgage company to this affiant's knowledge during this period."[90]

In considering the plaintiff's theory of uniqueness, it is important to recognize the relationship between the amount advanced (measured as a percentage of value of the collateral) and the interest rate. The essential difference between the Credit Corporation's credit and institutional lenders' credit was that the Credit Corporation would advance Fortner more than institutional lenders against a given amount of collateral.[91] No assertion was made that the Credit Corporation charged a higher interest rate. The interest rate, however, tends to be an inverse function of the amount advanced (measured in terms of the collateral). Moreover, many institutional lenders make unsecured loans at a higher interest rate than secured loans. In view of this trade-off between the interest rate and the ampleness of the security, Mr. Justice White was surely correct in viewing the sole uniqueness of the Credit Corporation's loans as being their "low cost" to Fortner Enterprises.[92] U.S. Steel credit was unique because it was cheap.

The alternative theory of uniqueness, suggested by Mr. Justice Black but not argued by plaintiff, was that U.S. Steel may have had a legal advantage (presumably analogous to a patent or a copyright) because institutional lenders "may have been prohibited from offering 100% financing by state or federal law."[93] This theory is imaginative but questionable. The very affidavit of the mortgage company president relied upon by Mr. Justice Black states in the immediately following paragraph that after the Fortner transactions, Louisville institutional lenders "have been forced to offer their customers similar 100% financing for purchase and development of land."[94] In short, the amount of security required, like the interest rate, is determined by competition. Local Louisville lenders,

---

[90] *Id.* at 294a–295a, partially quoted, 394 U.S. at 504–05.

[91] This was not denied by defendants. On the contrary, it was explicitly stated to be against Credit Corporation policy to grant credit where institutional loans were available. Record, p. 857a.

[92] 394 U.S. at 515. Plaintiff's affidavits did not directly address themselves to the terms of credits made available by competing suppliers. The record suggests that the Credit Corporation's service fee of one-half point (that is, one-half percent of the loan) may have been less than that charged by other suppliers (Record, p. 377a), but the discounting of loan proceeds by such points is generally regarded as merely an adjustment of the interest rate.

[93] 394 U.S. at 506.   [94] Record, p. 295a.

perhaps in the face of competition from suppliers like U.S. Steel, found themselves willing to make equally "unique" loans when they found it in their self-interest to do so.

The district court, faced with the contention that the amount of the loan in relation to the amount of the collateral made the loan "unique" under the *Loew's* case, responded with two separate lines of argument. First, anyone could have provided "100% financing"; the Credit Corporation's generosity was thus not tantamount to economic power. Second, the test is not uniqueness for a particular customer; rather, the "test is universal compulsion not a peculiar attraction for one corporation as here."[95]

Mr. Justice Black opened his discussion of the economic power issue by attacking the latter argument. The earlier tie-in cases, he argued, "have made unmistakably clear that the economic power over the tying product can be sufficient even though the power falls far short of dominance and even though the power exists only with respect to some of the buyers in the market."[96] Then, perhaps lest it might appear that his definition of the relevant market was merely narrower than that of the court below, he quoted the language from *Loew's* permitting an inference of power "from the tying product's desirability to consumers or from uniqueness of its attributes."[97]

Thereafter, following an intricate discussion of the meaning of market power, he concluded that "the proper focus of concern is whether the seller has the power to raise prices *or* impose other burdensome terms such as a tie-in, with respect to any appreciable number of buyers within the market."[98] One important question in interpreting the *Fortner* decision is the meaning of this language. Taken out of context, it might be thought to mean that, just as the "host of tying arrangements" was "compelling evidence" of "great power" in *Northern Pacific*,[99] so the inclusion of tie-in clauses in contracts with "any appreciable numbers of buyers" establishes market power. But the passage read in context does not warrant this interpretation. For the immediately preceding sentence makes clear that market power in the sense of power over price must still

---

[95] *Id.* at 306a; 1968 Trade Cases ¶ 72576, at p. 85996.

[96] 394 U.S. at 502–03.

[97] *Id.* at 503, quoting from 371 U.S. at 45.

[98] *Id.* at 504.   [99] 356 U.S. at 8.

exist.[100] If the price could have been raised but the tie-in was demanded in lieu of the higher price, then—and presumably only
then—would the requisite economic power exist. Thus, despite the
broad language available for quotation in later cases, the treatment
of the law on market power is on close reading not only consonant
with the precedents but in some ways less far-reaching than *Northern Pacific* and *Loew's,* which could be read to make actual market
power irrelevant.

The interesting methodological question is therefore how Mr.
Justice Black, with a traditional reading of the law, could find the
requisite economic power here. There was no showing of any
power to raise price, that is, to charge higher interest rates or, the
functional equivalent, to demand greater security. U.S. Steel had
rather reduced its price on the credit. One might have thought such
evidence showed that U.S. Steel, which was using the Fortner
transaction to break into the Louisville market, had no power over
price in either homes or credit.

Mr. Justice Black's response to this difficulty was technically
careful and imaginative but, in part, hard to square with any traditional purpose of the antitrust laws. After observing that the procedural issue was whether the affidavits entitled the plaintiff to "its
day in court," he noted that the affidavit of a construction company
president that U.S. Steel's prices exceeded those of competitors by
at least $400.[101] This affidavit, which was apparently offered in sup-
port of the complaint allegation that the Homes Division and the
Credit Corporation had conspired to cause the plaintiff "[t]o purchase United States Steel Homes at unreasonably high prices"[102]
and in support of plaintiff's damage theory, was relied on by Mr.
Justice Black as tending to prove power over credit: "Since in a

---

[100] The preceding sentence reads: "In both instances [that is, 'regardless of whether the seller has the greatest economic power possible or merely some lesser degree
of appreciable economic power'], despite the freedom of some or many buyers from
the seller's power, other buyers—whether few or many, whether scattered throughout the market or part of some group within the market—can be forced to accept
the higher price because of their stronger preferences for the product, and the seller
could therefore choose instead to force them to accept a tying arrangement that
would prevent free competition for their patronage in the market for the tied
product." 394 U.S. at 503–04.

[101] 394 U.S. at 504. This "construction company president" was Fortner's general
contractor on the U.S. Steel project (Record, p. 349a) and was a former owner of
the land financed under the 1961 loan agreement. Record, pp. 638a–639a.

[102] Record, p. 22a.

freely competitive situation buyers would not accept a tying arrangement obligating them to buy a tied product at a price higher
than the going market rate, this substantial price difference with
respect to the tied product . . . in itself may suggest that respondents
had some special economic power in the credit market."[103] Since on
motion for summary judgment such an affidavit must be taken at
face value, this portion of the opinion would be convincing, were
it not for Mr. Justice White's point that the plaintiff had not in
fact made any "offer of proof that the seller has any market power
in the credit market."[104] Rather, as plaintiff's Supreme Court brief
indicates and as stated in unmistakable terms in oral argument, the
plaintiff relied solely on "the general uniqueness of the special financing plans offered by the Credit Corporation." That, argued the
plaintiff, under *Loew's* was all that it had to show.[105]

After this resourceful use of the construction company executive's affidavit, Mr. Justice Black adopted as the second part of his
reasoning the plaintiff's principal argument—that the terms of the
credit were unique. But he carefully explained that he was not accepting the argument as made to the Court:[106]

> We do not mean to accept petitioner's apparent argument
> that market power can be inferred simply because the kind
> of financing terms offered by a lending company are "unique
> and unusual." We do mean, however, that uniquely and
> unusually advantageous terms can reflect a creditor's unique
> economic advantages over his competitors.

The unique terms alone would not give rise to an inference of economic power. In the absence of a patent or copyright where competitors are "prevented from offering the distinctive product themselves," economic uniqueness could only prevent competitors from
offering the product if the seller had a "cost advantage in producing it."[107] Thus, it is not unique terms themselves but rather "unique
economic advantages" that, if present, would constitute the "sufficient economic power" that *Northern Pacific* made the prerequisite
to illegality. The plaintiff's affidavits could, and on motion for summary judgment should, be construed to mean that the Credit Corporation "had a unique economic ability to provide 100% financing
at cheap rates."[108] The unwillingness of local lenders to offer com-

---

[103] 394 U.S. at 504.

[104] *Id*. at 510.

[105] Petitioner's Brief, p. 29.

[106] 394 U.S. at 505.

[107] *Id*. at 505 n. 2.

[108] *Id*. at 505.

petitive terms "probably reflects their feeling that they could not profitably lend money on the risks involved."[109] U.S. Steel's ability to offer better terms might stem, speculates Mr. Justice Black, from "economies resulting from the nationwide character of their operations" or from legal prohibitions placed on institutional competitors.[110]

C. ECONOMIES AND COMPETITION "ON THE MERITS"

In suggesting that "economies" constitute a "competitive advantage" rendering conduct illegal that would otherwise be legal, the majority opinion returned to a theme that has appeared in a number of recent merger decisions.[111] No doubt cost advantages stemming from patents or economies of scale may lead to monopoly power and, if one adopts the leverage theory, one might be concerned with the transfer of that monopoly power in the market for the tying product to the market for the tied product. But despite Mr. Justice Black's language about market power permitting the seller to charge a higher price,[112] a reading of his opinion as a whole suggests that he was concerned more with U.S. Steel's competitive tactics than with the possibility that U.S. Steel had actual market power in the money market. It is surely difficult to see how evidence that U.S. Steel had to underbid its competitors in the credit market to get Fortner's business indicates that it had the economic power, even with respect to Fortner himself, to impose a supracompetitive price for U.S. Steel money and had merely traded off that possibility for the tying clause.

---

[109] *Ibid.* Mr. Justice Black did not consider the construction company president's statement that those lenders thereafter began to offer "100% financing." Surely it is equally plausible to infer that they could have offered such financing in the earlier period. In the absence of a study of competitive conditions in the Louisville area in the earlier period, it is difficult to make any inference. But it seems unlikely that Mr. Justice Black's conclusion would have been altered, even if he had considered this alternative inference to be drawn from the plaintiff's own affidavits, since on summary judgment a plaintiff's "claims . . . should be read in a light most favorable to [him]." *Ibid.*

[110] *Id.* at 506. Here, again, the fact that institutional lenders rather promptly began offering "100% financing" suggests that those legal impediments were minor or nonexistent.

[111] Brown Shoe Co. v. United States, 370 U.S. 294, 344 (1962); United States v. Aluminum Co. of America, 233 F. Supp. 718 (E.D. Mo. 1964), *aff'd per curiam*, 382 U.S. 12 (1965); *cf.* F.T.C. v. Procter & Gamble Co., 386 U.S. 568, 578 (1967).

[112] 394 U.S. 503–04. See text *supra*, at notes 97–103.

Far more likely, if one reads the affidavits and depositions as a whole, is that U.S. Steel had no such power but was merely competing vigorously.[113] The depositions and documents submitted by the plaintiff indicate that U.S. Steel began to give credit in order to meet terms offered by competitiors in the prefabricated and conventional housing markets. The Credit Corporation's policy was to provide credit when not available to the purchaser from institutional sources in order to make sales that would otherwise be lost to Homes Division competitors who did provide such credit.[114] The terms for such credit were dictated by commercial rather than strictly financial considerations. Thus it would be at least as plausible to infer that softer terms on credit were a reflection of intense competition in the housing market than that they were indicia of market power in the money market. Lower-priced credit was an alternative to lower-priced houses,[115] and U.S. Steel's competitive desire to establish itself in the Louisville market made it necessary to improve its original offer in the protracted negotiations with a hard-bargaining, sophisticated real estate operator like Fortner.

Mr. Justice Black appeared to recognize that soft credit terms were a competitive measure, particularly in the passage where he observed that "advantageous credit terms may be viewed as a form of price competition in the tied product."[116] Perhaps that is why he used "market power" and "competitive advantage" interchangeably.[117] Although he paid lip service to the leverage theory, he did not appear to be so concerned that U.S. Steel would trade market power in money for market power in goods as he was that U.S.

[113] Record, pp. 756a–758a, 828a, 851a–852a.

[114] *Id*. at 853a–854a.

[115] It is not clear why U.S. Steel preferred to cut the price of credit rather than the price of houses. If there had been a cartel in housing, offering better terms on credit might have been a means of covertly cheating on the cartel. But in view of the vast number of competitors and the nonstandardized form of the product in the housing market, this rationale is implausible. Another possibility is that the Robinson-Patman Act's prohibition against differential pricing made it legally risky to cut the price of housing components selectively to obtain new business.

[116] 394 U.S. at 508. The Court had previously, in *Brown Shoe*, recognized that the per se rule would not invalidate a tie-in when used "by a small company . . . to break into a market." 370 U.S. at 330. And see United States v. Jerrold Electronics Corp., 187 F. Supp. 545 (E.D. Pa. 1960), *aff'd per curiam*, 365 U.S. 567 (1961). It is not clear why, if a small company may use a tie-in for competitive purposes, a large company in similar circumstances should be encouraged not to compete.

[117] *Compare* 394 U.S. at 503 *with id*. at 506.

Steel would have an unfair advantage over competing sellers of
housing who did not provide credit. He was particularly concerned
that U.S. Steel, with "economies resulting from the nationwide
character of its operations" and with "vast sums of money in its
treasury" would be able to take business away from local competitors who did not have the same "financial strength."[118]

One might well ask whether it is not precisely the purpose of
competition to provide what the buyer needs, which in cases like
Fortner appears to be not only houses but also extensive credit. Under this view, if it is true that "larger companies have achieved
economies of scale in their credit operations,"[119] then the passing
of such credit economies on to buyers of those larger companies'
products, such as Fortner Enterprises, is a sign that competition is
working.

That view of competition is not, however, shared by Mr. Justice
Black. For him there can be competition only where each product
sells on its own merits. Houses must compete only against houses,
credit only against credit. That "economies" can be achieved
through provision of credit by suppliers or through the packaging
of diverse products is irrelevant in Mr. Justice Black's view of competition. This atomistic view of competition is a strong theme in
recent Supreme Court antitrust decisions. It is related to, but distinct from, the leverage theory. The latter requires economic power, whereas the atomistic view is that competition is distorted if
each product does not have its price.

The attraction of the atomistic view explains not only the attenuation of the market power requirement in tie-in cases where
Mr. Justice Black has twice stated that the vice of the tie-ins is that
"competition *on the merits* with respect to the tied product is inevitably curbed."[120] This notion is at the heart of the block-book-

---

118 *Id.* at 506, 509. Some basis for skepticism about the "vast sums of money" is
to be found in the record. The Credit Corporation's total paid-in capital was $2
million and the sums generated (including bank borrowings) apparently never exceeded $20 million for the country as a whole. Record, pp. 753a–759a. The district
judge found that the funds available in Louisville, Kentucky, from local sources
alone exceeded $160 million in 1960 and that in that year over $130 million in real
estate mortgages had been recorded in Jefferson County, Kentucky. Record, pp.
311a–312a; 1968 Trade Cases ¶ 72576, at p. 85993.

119 394 U.S. at 509.

120 *Northern Pacific*, 356 U.S. at 6, quoted in *Fortner Enterprises*, 394 U.S. at 508.

ing cases.[121] That reciprocal trading does not permit competition solely on the basis of "price, quality and service" appears to be the primary ground for challenging that practice.[122]

The atomistic view seems to be based on a dream of an ideal economy, filled with tiny firms, each selling a different product.[123] Whatever the legislative justification for this social objective,[124] it has little to do with competition in the economic sense. And at the doctrinal level, the weakness of this predominantly social view of antitrust when applied to tie-ins is that it presupposes that we know what a single product is. It is not readily apparent why in the ideal universe of small firms, each should not extend credit to purchasers.

D. THE SINCLAIR CASE

One residual doctrinal question created by the majority's treatment of price reduction as evidence of economic power is what effect the *Fortner* decision will have on the continued vitality of *F.T.C. v. Sinclair Refining Co.*,[125] a case relied upon by the defendants but ignored in the Court's opinion. The parallels between *Sinclair* and *Fortner* are striking. In *Sinclair* the defendant oil company provided gas pumps and storage tanks to service stations on condition that only defendant's gas be used in them. The terms in *Sinclair* were even better than in *Fortner*; the pumps and tanks were provided "at nominal prices."[126] In neither case was there any

---

121 In *Loew's*, Justice Goldberg was concerned that competition for "Gone With the Wind" would be distorted if that film was sold together with "Getting Gertie's Garter." See Stigler, *United States v. Loew's Inc.: A Note on Block-Booking*, 1963 SUPREME COURT REVIEW 152. In United States v. Paramount Pictures, Inc., 334 U.S. 131, 158 (1948), Mr. Justice Douglas argued that when films are block-booked, "[e]ach stands not on its own footing but in whole or in part on the appeal which another film may have."

122 F.T.C. v. Consolidated Foods Corp., 380 U.S. 592, 599 (1965) (quoting from F.T.C. opinion). One detects the same theme, somewhat muted, in the *TBA* cases: "The nonsponsored brands [of tires, batteries, and accessories] do not compete on even terms of price and quality competition; they must overcome, in addition, the influence of the dominant oil compan[ies]." F.T.C. v. Texaco, Inc., 393 U.S. 223, 230 (1968). See also Atlantic Refining Co. v. F.T.C., 381 U.S. 357 (1965).

123 *Cf.* Mr. Justice Black's attack on the disappearance of the family firm, in United States v. Von's Grocery Co., 384 U.S. 270 (1966).

124 *Compare* United States v. Aluminum Co. of America, 148 F.2d 416, 427–29 (2d Cir. 1945) *with* Bork, *Legislative Intent and the Policy of the Sherman Act*, 9 J. LAW & ECON. 7 (1966).

125 261 U.S. 463 (1923).   126 *Id.* at 465.

exclusive dealing provision. The service stations in *Sinclair* could accept additional pumps from other suppliers, and so also, according to the finding of the district court, could Fortner Enterprises deal freely with other purveyors of homes and credit.[127]

The *Sinclair* decision is often explained by saying that since the oil company was only in effect providing free financing for its distributors, it would be inappropriate to condemn the arrangement as a tie-in. Now, in *Fortner*, the provision of financing on favorable terms is treated as a suspect tie-in. Whether *Sinclair* can be distinguished as involving equipment rather than credit is questionable. Mr. Justice Fortas' analogy between extension of credit and "ancillary services," such as "delivery, installation, fixturing, servicing, training of the customer's personnel in use of the material sold, [and] furnishing display material and sales aids," suggests that such a distinction is not inevitable.[128]

The financing justification was more implicit than explicit in *Sinclair*. Emphasis was placed by Justice McReynolds on the importance of the practice to "preserving the integrity of . . . brands," to safety, and to the prevention of fraud. These and other distinctions between *Sinclair* and *Fortner* must be authoritatively rejected before it can be concluded that *Sinclair* has been overruled.

VI. The Two-Hurdle Doctrine

Although *Fortner* does not purport to introduce any new concepts into the law on the per se illegality of tie-ins, one more general portion of the opinion might be interpreted to introduce new dimensions into the use of the per se doctrine. Until *Fortner* the general understanding had been that once a particular practice became subject to the per se doctrine, the judicially announced prerequisite for per se illegality set forth the sole standards of illegality. Under that view, for example, a tie-in imposed by a firm not having economic power in the tying product not only would not be illegal per se but also could not be found to be unreasonable under the rule of reason.

The traditional interpretation is supported by *Northern Pacific* itself. Mr. Justice Black there explained that although § 1 of the Sherman Act "preclud[es] only those contracts or combinations

---

[127] Record, p. 313a; 1968 Trade Cases ¶ 72576, at p. 85994.

[128] 394 U.S. at 525.

which 'unreasonably' restrain competition," certain practices are "presumed to be unreasonable and therefore illegal without elaborate inquiry as to the precise harm they have caused or the business excuse for their use."[129] This presumption of unreasonableness was justified, he explained, on both substantive and procedural grounds. The "pernicious effect on competition and lack of any redeeming virtue of certain practices" warranted such out-of-hand condemnation.[130] And use of the per se doctrine "avoids the necessity for an incredibly complicated and prolonged economic investigation into the entire history of the industry involved, as well as related industries, in an effort to determine at large whether a particular restraint has been unreasonable—an inquiry so often wholly fruitless when undertaken."[131]

Language near the beginning of the *Fortner* opinion appears to reintroduce the possibility of such a thoroughgoing investigation where a tie-in is alleged but either the economic power or the foreclosure prerequisite is not established: "A preliminary error that should not pass unnoticed is the District Court's assumption that two prerequisites mentioned in *Northern Pacific* are standards that petitioner must meet in order to prevail on the merits. On the contrary, these standards are necessary only to bring into play the doctrine of *per se* illegality."[132] Although the presence of the two prerequisites justified summary judgment for plaintiff in *Northern Pacific* and *International Salt*, those decisions "by no means implied that inability to satisfy these standards would be fatal to a plaintiff's case," since the "general standards of the Sherman Act" remain.[133]

The conclusion that a challenged practice must clear two hurdles successively—first the per se and then the reasonableness test—cannot be said to be illogical. The basic test of § 1 is reasonableness, and the fact that a practice in some circumstances may be patently unreasonable does not mean that in other circumstances it may not prove to be, on close analysis, an unreasonable restraint.

Two practical objections to what might be called the "two-hurdle doctrine" may, however, be interposed. First, if the firm imposing a tie-in does not have economic power in the market for the tying product or if the foreclosure in the market for the

---

[129] 356 U.S. at 5.   [131] *Ibid.*

[130] *Id.* at 5.   [132] 394 U.S. at 499–500.   [133] *Id.* at 500.

tied product is not substantial, then surely one can conclude that the effect of the tie-in is de minimis. Since the rule-of-reason test is whether the restraint, and not merely the practice itself, is unreasonable, the Sherman Act should not be construed to invalidate a practice that has a negligible effect. Even under the now discredited "quantitative substantiality" test of *Standard Stations*,[134] for example, exclusive dealing practices are not illegal where the foreclosure is not substantial.

The second practical objection is that the two-hurdle doctrine is likely, wherever the trial court is unwilling to grant summary judgment for the plaintiff, to turn the trial into just that "so often wholly fruitless" and "incredibly complicated and prolonged economic investigation" that Mr. Justice Black decried in *Northern Pacific*. If there is a sufficient issue of fact about the economic power or foreclosure issues to warrant a trial, then the plaintiff will be inclined to introduce his evidence on the reasonableness of the restraint lest he abandon that second string in his antitrust bow. Although one could conceive of a bifurcated trial in which the per se prerequisite issue was tried first, and then, if necessary, the reasonableness issue was tried, such an alternative would involve covering much of the same ground twice. Not only would such a split trial be wastefully repetitious, but it would also not necessarily be justified under the existing patent infringement and negligence precedents, where the split is between liability and damages.[135]

If these practical objections to the two-hurdle doctrine are persuasive reasons for staying with the "per se or nothing" approach, then comfort may be found in the possibility that Mr. Justice Black did not mean to announce any such new doctrine. When the entire passage is read in context, particularly in the light of the complaint and the briefs, one may conclude that it is unlikely that Mr. Justice Black meant what the passages just discussed would appear on their face to say. After the language just discussed comes a sentence that suggests he was talking about applying a reasonableness test not to the tie-in allegation but rather to the conspiracy allegation: "[E]ven if we could agree with the District Court that the *Northern Pacific*

---

[134] Standard Oil Co. v. United States, 337 U.S. 293 (1949). And see Tampa Electric Co. v. Nashville Coal Co., 365 U.S. 320, 327 (1961).

[135] Cases permitting separate trials on affirmative defenses are also distinguishable. See generally 5 MOORE'S FEDERAL PRACTICE ¶ 42.03 (1968).

standards were not satisfied here, the summary judgment against petitioner still could not be entered without further examination of petitioner's general allegations that respondents conspired together for the purpose of restraining competition and acquiring a monopoly in the market for prefabricated houses."[136] The complaint, it may be noted, does not refer to the challenged clause as a tying arrangement. Rather it charges that the two defendants conspired to restrain trade under § 1 and to monopolize under § 2.[137] In the light of its defeat in both lower courts, the plaintiff made its principal point at the Supreme Court level that whatever the law on tie-ins might be, the two defendants had conspired with each other.[138] The defendants' brief led off with contention that the conspiracy theory was "a new theory . . . not urged below,"[139] a contention hotly denied in the reply brief.[140] This aspect of *Fortner* is largely ignored in the opinions, except for the passage here under consideration and Mr. Justice Black's statement that no conventional credit sale was involved, since one corporation provided the credit and the other sold the product. In the light of the complaint and the briefs, it may thus be concluded that Mr. Justice Black simply meant to say that even if the defendants should win on the tie-in issue, the plaintiff would still be entitled to a jury trial on the "general allegations that respondents conspired together for the purpose of restraining competition and acquiring a monopoly in the market for prefabricated houses."[141]

This attempt to explain away the two-hurdle doctrine may, however, render the passage subject to even more strenuous objection. Even if one ignores the special difficulties posed by this invocation of the intra-enterprise conspiracy doctrine,[142] one can nonetheless be surprised by the suggestion that two firms can conspire in violation of § 2 to commit an act which, if committed, is not illegal.[143]

---

[136] 394 U.S. at 500.

[137] Record, pp. 21a–22a.

[138] Petitioner's Brief, pp. 14–25.

[139] Respondent's Brief, p. 33.

[140] Petitioner's Reply Brief, pp. 4–6.

[141] 394 U.S. at 500.

[142] By citing the intra-enterprise conspiracy cases, 394 U.S. at 507 n. 4, Mr. Justice Black made *Fortner* an additional authority for that form-over-substance doctrine.

[143] The § 2 conspiracy-to-monopolize theory may also be subject to the somewhat different objection that the plaintiff did not offer to prove the existence of a dangerous probability that, if the conspiracy were successful, a monopoly would have resulted. American Tobacco Co. v. United States, 328 U.S. 781, 785 (1946). But see United States v. Consolidated Laundries Corp., 291 F.2d 563, 572–73 (2d Cir. 1961).

The intra-enterprise conspiracy cases to date have involved situations where related corporations were engaged in activity that would be illegal if engaged in by unrelated corporations. Among the practices thus potentially unlawful when engaged in by related corporations have been price-fixing[144] and allocation of territories.[145] Those are practices which are not illegal when only a single trader is involved. Therefore, a finding of multiplicity of actors via the intra-enterprise conspiracy doctrine is often the sine qua non of liability. A tie-in, on the other hand, is in substance a single-trader offense, the jurisdictional agreement being the agreement of sale itself. But if a credit sale does not constitute an illegal tie-in when imposed by a single firm, it is not clear why it should be illegal when two firms are involved, particularly if those two firms are not competitors. And if such a sale is an unlawful restraint of trade, then surely it is unlawful whether or not the defendants are related. One hesitates to conclude that Mr. Justice Black meant to suggest that independent lenders taking security in goods may not pass on the source of those goods.[146]

Thus, although the two-hurdle language in *Fortner* may be explained away as referring only to the intra-enterprise conspiracy doctrine, such an explanation would create new doctrinal difficulties not touched on by Mr. Justice Black.

VII. FORTNER AND THE PRIVATE ACTION

Although *Fortner* expresses great concern for U.S. Steel's competitors, who are said to be at a competitive disadvantage because they do not have its "vast sums of money," the ruling redounds directly to the benefit of one of the purchasers of U.S. Steel's products, Fortner Enterprises. Such a consequence is not surprising. In *Northern Pacific* Mr. Justice Black argued that tying arrangements harmed both competitiors and buyers. Tie-ins, he

---

[144] *E.g.*, Keifer-Stewart Co. v. Joseph E. Seagram & Sons, Inc., 340 U.S. 211 (1951).

[145] Timken Roller Bearing Co. v. United States, 341 U.S. 593 (1951).

[146] Certain facts in the record might distinguish the Credit Corporation's position from that of the typical independent lender. Certain Credit Corporation loans were guaranteed by the Homes Division pursuant to an underwriting agreement. Record, pp. 439a–442a, 764a. And although some residual control over source might be essential to assure the value of the collateral, the Credit Corporation insisted on Homes Division products in all cases. Thus, a conspiracy is easier to infer in *Fortner* than would ordinarily be true with independent lenders.

said, "deny competitors free access to the market for its tied product," and, at the same time, "buyers are forced to forego their free choice between competing products."[147] A paradox in *Fortner* is that Mr. Justice Black ignores the buyer justification in reaching a result directly benefiting a buyer while emphasizing at great length the competitor justification in a case where any harm to competitors is totally speculative.

Perhaps one of the explanations for this paradox is that when the market power criterion is watered down as far as it has been in *Fortner* and applied to as unusual a transaction as a credit sale, the buyer justification is hardly applicable. Certainly it is hard to believe that Fortner Enterprises was injured by accepting the tie-in. To be sure, it would have been better off with both the Credit Corporation credit and the right to pick and choose suppliers, but that choice would never have existed even if the result of the *Fortner* litigation had been known in advance. The Credit Corporation was not a bank. Furthermore, the Credit Corporation was only one of a great many sources of credit. The advantageous terms were not imposed on the plaintiff. It was Fortner himself who, throughout the extended negotiations, demanded easier terms than the Credit Corporation was offering. Moreover, having compromised his own freedom to buy competing products to the extent of the loan, Fortner sought a further loan on identical terms.[148] Certainly the plaintiff's assertion that it was only through "economic necessity" that Fortner accepted the tie-in is difficult to square with the history of the negotiations.[149]

Perma Life Mufflers suggests that Mr. Justice Black would see no anomaly in granting treble damages to one who had actively solicited the illegal transaction. In that case he sought to read the *in pari delicto* doctrine out of the antitrust laws on pragmatic law enforcement grounds:[150]

> The plaintiff who reaps the reward of treble damages may be no less morally reprehensible than the defendant, but the

---

[147] 356 U.S. at 6. The enchancement of freedom of choice of distributors through antitrust policy is an important theme in Supreme Court decisions, particularly in resale price-maintenance cases. See Albrecht v. Herald Co., 390 U.S. 145, 152–53 (1968); Kiefer-Stewart Co. v. Seagram & Sons, Inc., 340 U.S. 211, 213 (1951).

[148] See text *supra*, at notes 14–17.

[149] Petitioner's Brief, pp. 16–20; Record, p. 290a.

[150] Perma Life Mufflers, Inc. v. International Parts Corp., 392 U.S. 135, 139 (1968).

law encourages his suit to further the overriding public policy in favor of competition. A more fastidious regard for the relative moral worth of the parties would only result in seriously undermining the usefulness of the private action as a bulwark of antitrust enforcement.

Thus, even though Fortner aggressively sought precisely the contractual arrangement he obtained, his recourse to the court system is to be encouraged as a "bulwark of antitrust enforcement."[151]

The enthusiasm of the Supreme Court for the private action has been manifested in a number of decisions of procedural antitrust issues. The Supreme Court has uniformly decided these cases for plaintiffs, candidly offering the justification that private actions are to be encouraged. The cases on the standards for summary judgment, of which *Fortner* is one, are examples.[152] *Perma Life*, the *in pari delicto* decision, is another. Others include decisions limiting the "passing on" defense,[153] eliminating the public injury requirement,[154] and expanding the scope of the provision tolling limitations in § 5(b) of the Clayton Act.[155]

One can hardly deny that the private action plays a major, perhaps indispensable, role in the enforcement of the antitrust laws. The resources of the Antitrust Division are severely limited. So long as fines for criminal antitrust violations are subject to the present absurdly low maximum,[156] large corporations have more to fear from the private litigant than from the government.

---

[151] It is doubtful that an *in pari delicto* defense would have been available even before *Perma Life*, if for no other reason than that Fortner had not sought the tying clause itself. A motion to amend the answer to set forth an *in pari delicto* defense was held by the district court to have been filed too late. Record, pp. 320a, 927a.

A touch of irony may be detected in the Court's holding in a case decided only a few months after *Fortner* that a licensee may not challenge a package patent license (which bears a close analytical resemblance to a tying contract) where he did not demand individual patent licenses at the time of the original negotiations. Zenith Radio Corp. v. Hazeltine Research, Inc., 395 U.S. 100 (1969).

[152] See text *supra*, at notes 42–49.

[153] Hanover Shoe, Inc. v. United Shoe Machinery Corp., 392 U.S. 481 (1968).

[154] Klor's, Inc. v. Broadway & Hale Stores, Inc., 359 U.S. 207 (1959); Radiant Burners, Inc. v. People's Gas Light & Coke Co., 364 U.S. 656 (1961).

[155] Leh v. General Petroleum Corp., 382 U.S. 54 (1965); Minnesota Mining & Mfg. Co. v. New Jersey Wood Finishing Co., 381 U.S. 311 (1965).

[156] Violations of the Sherman Act are subject to a maximum fine of $50,000. 15 U.S.C. § 1. See discussion in the *Stigler Task Force Report*, 5 CCH TRADE REG. REP. ¶ 50250, at pp. 55521–22 (1969).

Fortner suggests, however, that enthusiasm for the private suit should not be unbounded. In the first place, it is far from clear that the case would have been brought by a rational enforcement agency. Certainly the odds are extremely slim that the Antitrust Division would have brought the case, even if its resources had been multiplied. U.S. Steel's attempt to establish itself in the Louisville market intensified competition in the housing market there and, insofar as one can judge from the record, in the local money market as well.[157] Any harm to competitors of the Homes Division is totally undocumented. And in this particular point in our national history, with mounting concern over the spiraling costs of housing, it might be thought to be in the public interest to encourage the introduction of factory-built houses in markets dominated by conventional construction methods.

Quite aside from doubts about the effect on competition of this species of private action, one may also have qualms about the relation between the antitrust laws and private law in the resolution of commercial disputes. This dispute was over the quality of goods. The plaintiff was not concerned about the effect of the loan agreement on competition until the deal went sour.[158] On the contrary, he sought an additional loan on identical terms some months after the first loan and after delivery of a number of houses. The private action was in *Fortner* simply what it has become with increasing frequency, an ace in the hand of a distributor in commercial disagreements with his manufacturer. Instead of being limited to the sales law measure of damages, the plaintiff was enabled to sue for three times its prospective profits plus attorney's fees and costs. The question of who was responsible for the failure of the housing project need never be litigated, except possibly in assessing the amount of damages.[159]

---

[157] See text *supra,* at notes 89–94.

[158] The record suggests that a slump in the Louisville new homes market may have contributed significantly to the plaintiff's difficulties. The rate of single-family dwelling completions in 1960–61 averaged less than 75 percent of the rate in the 1958–59 and 1963–65 periods. Record, p. 277a.

[159] The amended complaint sought "treble the sum of $249,837.31 . . . , a reasonable fee for the services of its attorneys in prosecuting this action, and its costs herein expended." Seventy houses were delivered at a price of about $3,000–$4,500 each plus tax and prepaid freight. Record, pp. 22a, 457a–632a. Sixty-two of the seventy houses had been sold to the public. *Id.* at 116a–118a.

The potential conflict between antitrust and private law policies has been considered by the Supreme Court in the context of antitrust defenses to actions for the price of goods sold. Such a defense was held improper on the ground that "the courts are to be guided by the overriding general policy, as Justice Holmes put it, 'of preventing people from getting other people's property for nothing when they purport to be buying it.' "[160] Although the contract defense cases can be distinguished, the treble-damage action nonetheless affords the purchaser the analogous possibility of waiting to see whether a transaction is profitable before deciding whether to pay or to sue.

It is probably no exaggeration to say that the private antitrust action has come to outweigh the Federal Trade Commission proceeding and the Antitrust Division action in practical importance.[161] The reasons for this development are complex, but surely one of the reasons is the steady expansion of the substantive law. In the area of manufacturer-distributor relations the trend of decisions has been toward protecting the distributor against unfair acts of the manufacturer rather than toward improving the allocation of resources and lowering prices to consumers, which are the economic *raisons d'être* of competition.[162] The emphasis on fairness suggests that the antitrust laws on vertical arrangements are coming increasingly to play for distribution agreements the role that the private law on contracts of adhesion has played for the insurance contract. The *Fortner* decision, while paradoxically relying solely on supposed harm to competitors, furthers this trend. Not only does it give franchisees and other distributors a new theory by which to challenge manufacturers wherever financing or other services are provided, but it also assures them a chance to appeal to the sympathy of a jury regardless of the substantiality of their offer of proof.

---

[160] Kelly v. Kosuga, 358 U.S. 516, 520–21 (1959).

[161] See A.B.A. Section on Antitrust Law, Antitrust Developments 1955–1968 274–75 (1968).

[162] See generally Bork, *The Rule of Reason and the Per Se Concept: Price Fixing and Market Division*, 74 Yale L.J. 775 (1965); 75 Yale L.J. 373 (1966).

FRANK R. STRONG

FIFTY YEARS OF "CLEAR AND PRESENT DANGER": FROM SCHENCK TO BRANDENBURG—AND BEYOND

The fiftieth anniversary of the "clear and present danger" test is not a happy one for it. Commentators no less than Justices have been undertaking to inter the test for some little time. Hailed at the outset as the interpretational device for effective realization of First Amendment liberties, the danger test has lost favor to the point where the Court only irregularly admits to its employment,[1] and there are few who would grieve at its total demise.[2]

Frank R. Strong is Professor of Law, University of North Carolina; Dean and Professor of Law Emeritus, The Ohio State University.

[1] See BERNS, FREEDOM, VIRTUE AND THE FIRST AMENDMENT 72 (1967); Krislov, *From Ginzburg to Ginsberg: The Unhurried Children's Hour in Obscenity Litigation*, 1968 SUPREME COURT REVIEW 153, 178–79. Cf. Karst, *The First Amendment and Harry Kalven: An Appreciative Comment on the Advantages of Thinking Small*, 13 U.C.L.A. L. REV. 1, 8–9 (1965); Van Alstyne, *First Amendment and the Suppression of War Mongering Propaganda in the United States*, 31 LAW & CONTEMP. PROB. 530, 546–47 n. 56 (1966).

[2] Among those on the non-mourners bench would be Corwin, *Bowing Out "Clear and Present Danger,"* 27 NOTRE DAME LAWY. 325 (1952); Emerson, *Toward a General Theory of the First Amendment*, 72 YALE L.J. 877, 910–12 (1963); FREUND, THE SUPREME COURT OF THE UNITED STATES 42–44 (1961); Kalven, *The New York Times Case: A Note on "The Central Meaning of the First Amendment,"* 1964 SUPREME COURT REVIEW 191; KRISLOV, THE SUPREME COURT AND POLITICAL FREEDOM 89–90, 122 (1968).

Brandenburg v. Ohio,[3] decided at the end of the last Term of the Warren era, is significant on the doctrine's current status among sitting Justices. The decision was announced in a per curiam opinion of a length and importance that in normal practice would be written for the Court and attributed to an individual Justice. In this opinion there is assiduous avoidance of any reference to, let alone admitted employment of, the "clear and present danger" test. Yet invalidation of the Ohio Criminal Syndicalism Act stems from the overruling of *Whitney v. California*.[4] Brandeis and Holmes, although technically concurring in *Whitney*, took strong exception to its thesis in the name of a virile formulation of the danger test. But *Whitney* was overruled because "thoroughly discredited by later decisions. See *Dennis v. United States*, 341 U.S. 494, at 507," the very decision in which a majority of the Court adopted Learned Hand's diluted reformulation of the test. The page citation provides the clue to reconciliation. The "clear and present danger" test, whatever its degree of potency, applies to all legislation, whether directly prohibitive of designated speech or indirectly restrictive of utterances through prohibition of acts capable of effectuation by speech. Nevertheless, "[t]hese later decisions have fashioned the principle that the constitutional guarantees of free speech and free press do not permit a State to forbid or proscribe advocacy of the use of force or of law violation except where such advocacy is directed to inciting or producing imminent lawless action and is likely to incite or produce such action."[5]

While this language appears to install as current doctrine the Holmes-Brandeis conception of the danger formula, a footnote assertion of its consistency with the holding in *Dennis* leaves open the interpretation that the test remains, but sapped of its earlier potency. We are left by *Brandenburg* with something seemingly akin to a definitional approach to constitutional determination:[6]

> As we said in *Noto v. United States*, 367 U.S. 290, 297–298, "the mere abstract teaching . . . of the moral propriety or even moral necessity for a resort to force and violence, is not the same as preparing a group for violent action and steeling it to such action." See also *Herndon v. Lowry*, 301 U.S. 242, 259–261 (1937); *Bond v. Floyd*, 385 U.S. 116, 134 (1966). A statute which fails to draw this distinction imper-

---

[3] 395 U.S. 444 (1969).

[4] 274 U.S. 357 (1927), see text *infra*, at notes 21–25.

[5] 395 U.S. at 447.

[6] *Id.* at 447–48.

missibly intrudes upon the freedoms guaranteed by the First and Fourteenth Amendments. It sweeps within its condemnation speech which our Constitution has immunized from governmental control.

Although concurring in reversal, Justices Black and Douglas wanted it clear that in their opinion the doctrine of "clear and present danger" "should have no place in the interpretation of the First Amendment." Mr. Justice Black was largely content to join in the views of Mr. Justice Douglas, who entered an extended caveat on this point. The Douglas position was stated this way:[7]

> Though I doubt if the "clear and present danger" test is congenial to the First Amendment in time of a declared war, I am certain it is not reconcilable with the First Amendment in days of peace. . . .
>
> In *Bridges* v. *California*, 314 U.S. 252, 261–263, we approved the "clear and present danger" test in an elaborate dictum that tightened it and confined it to a narrow category. But in *Dennis* v. *United States*, 341 U.S. 494, we opened wide the door, distorting the "clear and present danger" test beyond recognition. . . .
>
> When one reads the opinions closely and sees when and how the "clear and present danger" test has been applied, great misgivings are aroused. First, the threats were often loud but always puny and made serious only by judges so wedded to the *status quo* that critical analysis made them nervous. Second, the test was so twisted and perverted in *Dennis* as to make the trial of those teachers of Marxism an all-out political trial which was part and parcel of the cold war that has eroded substantial parts of the First Amendment. . . .
>
> The line between what is permissible and not subject to control and what may be made impermissible and subject to regulation is the line between ideas and overt acts.

The attitude of commentators has been equally unfriendly. "Today almost no one seems to believe that this formula can be very helpful in deciding concrete cases" is Professor McCloskey's verdict.[8] Kalven's is more extreme. In a tribute to the Warren Court he asserted that[9]

---

[7] *Id.* at 452–54, 456.

[8] McCloskey, *Reflections on the Warren Court*, 51 VA. L. REV. 1229, 1236 (1965).

[9] Kalven, *"Uninhibited, Robust, and Wide-Open"—A Note on Free Speech and the Warren Court*, 67 MICH. L. REV. 289, 297 (1968).

the most significant step [in] the abrogation of outmoded ideas
. . . has been the great reduction in the status and prestige of
the clear-and-present danger test. Immediately prior to the
advent of the Warren Court, this test had a considerable claim
as *the* criterion of the constitutionality of an exercise of governmental authority over communication. In limited areas the
test may still be alive, but it has been conspicuous by its
absence from opinions in the last decade. Since the test—
whatever sense it may have made in the limited context in
which it originated—is clumsy and artificial when expanded
into a general criterion of permissible speech, the decline in
its fortunes under the Warren Court seems to be an intellectual gain.

The weakness of the danger test is shown by attempted reliance
upon it as a complete constitutional solvent. No such role was originally conceived for it. In its beginning it scarcely purported to rise
to a constitutional level at all. For a unanimous Court in *Schenck v.
United States*,[10] Mr. Justice Holmes employed it essentially as a rule
of evidence. Under a statute prohibiting interference with war effort, speech could be punished only on evidence of clear and present danger that that speech would lead to the evil which Congress
had sought to forbid by the Espionage Act.

This technical usage of the test was turned against Holmes by
the majority in *Gitlow v. New York*,[11] involving the New York
statutory prohibition of advocacy of criminal anarchy:[12]

> It is clear that the question in such cases [as this] is entirely
> different from that involved in those cases where the statute
> merely prohibits certain acts involving the danger of substan-
> tive evil, without any reference to language itself, and it is
> sought to apply its provisions to language used by the de-
> fendant for the purpose of bringing about the prohibited re-
> sults. . . . In such cases it has been held that the general pro-
> visions of the statute may be constitutionally applied to the
> specific utterance of the defendant if its natural tendency and
> probable effect was to bring about the substantive evil which
> the legislative body might prevent. . . . [T]he general state-
> ment in the *Schenck Case* . . . was manifestly intended, as
> shown by the context, to apply only in cases of this class, and
> has no application to those like the present, where the legis-
> lative body itself has previously determined the danger of sub-
> stantive evil arising from utterances of a specified character.

---

[10] 249 U.S. 47 (1919).

[11] 268 U.S. 652 (1926).   [12] *Id.* at 670–71.

It is familiar knowledge that the distinction was washed out by *Dennis*:[13] the opinion for the Court elected the "Holmes-Brandeis rationale" despite *Gitlow*. Yet the distinction continued long enough into the period during which the danger test was used in an attempt to resolve issues of validity to produce the conflict, manifest in *Dennis* and later, between those insisting on jury determination of clear and present danger and those declaring that the making of that judgment was a question of law for the court. That the origin of the danger test was basically a rule of evidence must account for this conflict. For, as one acute commentator has observed: "Juries are not supposed to declare statutes unconstitutional. Such a practice (and it might have come about in the Dennis case if Douglas had had his way) would be consistent neither with practical wisdom nor with American judicial tradition."[14] It can be added that juries are not supposed to rule statutes (or other forms of governmental action) constitutional. This is the essential teaching of the Court's continued insistence upon the doctrine of constitutional fact.[15]

Professor Kalven recently observed that Holmes's attitude in *Debs*[16] "makes it evident that the clear-and-present-danger dictum did not in his mind become a constitutional test until sometime after *Schenck*," referring to Chafee's suggestion that Holmes "was waiting for *Abrams*."[17] Holmes's dissent in *Abrams v. United States*,[18] in which he was joined by Brandeis, contained the following familiar and substantiating language:[19]

> I wholly disagree with the argument of the Government that the First Amendment left the common law as to seditious libel in force. History seems to me against the notion. I had conceived that the United States through many years had shown its repentance for the Sedition Act of 1798, by repaying fines that it imposed. Only the emergency that makes it completely dangerous to leave the correction of evil counsels to time warrants making any exception to the sweeping command, "Congress shall make no law . . .

13 341 U.S. 494 (1951).   14 BERNS, note 1 *supra*, at 63.

15 See Brennan, *The Supreme Court and the Meiklejohn Interpretation of the First Amendment*, 79 HARV. L. REV. 1, 7–8 (1965); Strong, *The Persistent Doctrine of "Constitutional Fact,"* 46 N.C. L. REV. 223, 279–80 (1968).

16 Debs v. United States, 249 U.S. 211 (1919).   18 250 U.S. 616, 624–31 (1919).

17 Kalven, note 9 *supra*, at 291 n. 18.   19 *Id.* at 630–31.

abridging the freedom of speech." Of course I am speaking only of expressions of opinion and exhortations, which were all that were uttered here, but I regret that I cannot put into more impressive words my belief that in their conviction upon this indictment the defendants were deprived of their rights under the Constitution of the United States.

Elevated to constitutional level, the danger test, retaining much of its original evidentiary flavor, became a device whereby, for legislation to pass constitutional muster, it must be demonstrated that a permissible objective of government is imminently and substantially threatened. Permissible objectives were identified without analysis as "certain substantive evils" with respect to which government possessed some authority. Yet by the new test government was empowered to take action only on proof of the immediacy of serious peril to one or more of those substantive evils. The following paragraph from the *Abrams'* dissent specifies the reach of the test as a potent yet not total constriction on governmental power with respect to utterances:[20]

> I never have seen any reason to doubt that the questions of law that alone were before this Court in the cases of *Schenck, Frohwerk,* and *Debs,* 249 U.S. 47, 204, 211, were rightly decided. I do not doubt for a moment that by the same reasoning that would justify punishing persuasion to murder, the United States constitutionally may punish speech that produces or is intended to produce a clear and imminent danger that it will bring about forthwith certain substantive evils that the United States constitutionally may seek to prevent. The power undoubtedly is greater in time of war than in time of peace because war opens dangers that do not exist at other times.

The Brandeis concurrence in *Whitney v. California,*[21] in which Mr. Justice Holmes joined, is properly viewed as an invigorated articulation of their conception of the danger test as a measure of First Amendment freedom of speech. Early in this opinion this categorical assertion was made:[22]

> That the necessity which is essential to a valid restriction does not exist unless speech would produce, or is intended to produce, a clear and imminent danger of some substantive evil which the State constitutionally may seek to prevent has been settled. See *Schenck* v. *United States,* 249 U.S. 47, 52.

---

[20] *Id.* at 627–28.   [21] 274 U.S. at 372–80.   [22] *Id.* at 373.

At the same time:[23]

> This Court has not yet fixed the standard by which to
> determine when a danger shall be deemed clear; how remote
> the danger may be and yet be deemed present; and what
> degree of evil shall be deemed sufficiently substantial to
> justify resort to abridgement of free speech and assembly
> as the means of protection.

There followed the stirring Brandeis statement of the nature of the
nation sought to be created by "[t]hose who won our independence." "Believing in the power of reason as applied through public discussion, they eschewed silence coerced by law—the argument of force in its worst form."[24] As a consequence:[25]

> [N]o danger flowing from speech can be deemed clear and
> present, unless the incidence of the evil apprehended is so
> imminent that it may befall before there is opportunity for
> full discussion. . . .
>   Moreover, even imminent danger cannot justify resort to
> prohibition of these functions essential to effective democracy,
> unless the evil apprehended is relatively serious.

This potent formulation of the danger test received its most
clear-cut and continuing application in the line of cases involving
interference with the administration of justice. There was in these
cases such complete agreement on the legitimacy of protecting the
adjudicative function from disruptive forces that the permissibility
of this objective went unquestioned:

> We start with the premise that the right of courts to
> conduct their business in an untrammeled way lies at the
> foundation of our system of government and that courts
> necessarily must possess the means of punishing for contempt
> when conduct tends directly to prevent the discharge of their
> functions.[26]
>   . . . Among the "substantive evils with which legislation
> may deal" is the hampering of a court in pending controversy,
> because the fair administration of justice is one of the chief
> tests of a true democracy.[27]

The issue for the majority in this series of cases has been solely
whether a contempt citation can stand because of a clear and pres-

---

[23] *Id.* at 374.   [24] *Id.* at 375–76.   [25] *Id.* at 377.

[26] Wood v. Georgia, 370 U.S. 375, 383 (1962) (Warren, C. J.).

[27] Pennekamp v. Florida, 328 U.S. 331, 353 (1946) (Frankfurter, J., concurring).

ent danger that adverse comment on judicial behavior in pending cases or other judicial business imperils impartial administration of justice.

In the initial case involving Harry Bridges and the *Los Angeles Times*, Mr. Justice Black, after an interesting employment of the technical distinction taken in *Gitlow* to buttress support for the use of the danger test,[28] asserted: "What finally emerges from the 'clear and present danger' cases is a working principle that the substantive evil must be extremely serious and the degree of imminence extremely high before utterances can be punished."[29] By this test every one of the four challenges to state contempt citations has been sustained.

Yet in three of these four cases[30] vigorous dissents were registered, and the decision in the first was by a bare majority of one. Justice Frankfurter's powerful dissent in *Bridges* carried a paragraph that in retrospect presaged what was to happen to this formulation of the danger test a decade later in *Dennis*.[31]

> Comment however forthright is one thing. Intimidation with respect to specific matters still in judicial suspense, quite another. . . . A publication intended to teach the judge a lesson, or to vent spleen, or to discredit him, or to influence him in his future conduct, would not justify exercise of the contempt power. Compare Judge Learned Hand in *Ex parte Craig*, 282 F. 138, 160–161. It must refer to a matter under consideration and constitute in effect a threat to its impartial disposition. It must be calculated to create an atmospheric pressure incompatible with rational, impartial adjudication. But to interfere with justice it need not succeed. As with other offenses, the state should be able to proscribe attempts

---

[28] "For here the legislature of California has not appraised a particular kind of situation and found a specific danger sufficiently imminent to justify a restriction on a particular kind of utterance. The judgments below, therefore, do not come to us encased in the armor wrought by prior legislative deliberation. Under such circumstances, this Court has said that 'it must necessarily be found, as an original question,' that the specified publications involved created 'such likelihood of bringing about the substantive evil as to deprive [them] of the constitutional protection.' *Gitlow* v. *New York*, 268 U.S. 652, 671." Bridges v. California, 314 U.S. 252, 260–61 (1941).

[29] *Id.* at 263.

[30] The fourth case in the line, third in time of disposition, was Craig v. Harney, 331 U.S. 367 (1947).

[31] 314 U.S. at 291–92.

that fail because of the danger that attempts may succeed. The purpose, it will do no harm to repeat, is not to protect the court as a mystical entity or the judges as individuals or as anointed priests set apart from the community and spared the criticism to which in a democracy other public servants are exposed. The purpose is to protect immediate litigants and the public from the mischievous danger of an unfree or co-erced tribunal. The power should be invoked only where the adjudicatory process may be hampered or hindered in its calm, detached and fearless discharge of its duty on the basis of what has been submitted in court. The belief that decisions are so reached is the source of the confidence on which law ultimately rests.

Terminiello v. Chicago,[32] decided at the close of the 1940's, marked the apogee in the employment of the danger test under the *Abrams-Whitney* formulation. There all the Justices who addressed themselves to the merits agreed on the applicability of the test to the validity of conviction of a Chicago priest for a virulent address, before eight hundred persons, protested by an "angry and turbulent" crowd of "about one thousand persons" gathered immediately outside the auditorium. Reversing the conviction, Mr. Justice Douglas for the Court, explained that "a function of free speech under our system of government is to invite dispute," and declared:[33]

> That is why freedom of speech, though not absolute, *Chaplinsky* v. *New Hampshire* . . . is nevertheless protected against censorship or punishment, unless shown likely to produce a clear and present danger of a serious substantive evil that rises far above public inconvenience, annoyance, or unrest. See *Bridges* v. *California* . . . ; *Craig* v. *Harney*. . . . There is no room under our Constitution for a more restrictive view. For the alternative would lead to standardization of ideas either by legislatures, courts, or dominant political or community groups.

With this Mr. Justice Jackson took issue in a dissent (joined by Justice Burton and the views of which Justice Frankfurter declared he shared):[34]

> Rioting is a substantive evil, which I take it no one will deny that the State and the City have the right and the duty to prevent and punish. Where an offense is induced by speech, the Court has laid down and often reiterated a test of the

---

[32] 337 U.S. 1 (1949).   [33] *Id.* at 4–5.   [34] *Id.* at 25–26.

power of the authorities to deal with the speaking as also an offense. "The question in every case is whether the words *used are used in such circumstances* and are of *such a nature* as to create a *clear and present danger* that they will bring about the substantive evils that Congress [or the state or city] has a right to prevent." (Emphasis supplied.) Mr. Justice Holmes in *Schenck* v. *United States*, 249 U.S. 47, 52. No one ventures to contend that the State on the basis of this test, for whatever it may be worth, was not justified in punishing Terminiello. In this case the evidence proves beyond dispute that danger of rioting and violence in response to the speech was clear, present and immediate. If this Court has not silently abandoned this longstanding test and substituted for the purposes of this case an unexpressed but more stringent test, the action of the State would have to be sustained.

Familiar, yet sufficiently important for requotation, are the three paragraphs in Part III of the Vinson opinion for the Court in *Dennis* that embraced the Frankfurter-Jackson viewpoint. These rejected, at least in the context of international communism, the danger test as evolved by Holmes and Brandeis and applied in the contempt cases, all but the last of which were decided in the 1940's:[35]

In this case we are squarely presented with the application of the "clear and present danger" test, and must decide what that phrase imports. We first note that many of the cases in which this Court has reversed convictions by use of this or similar tests have been based on the fact that the interest which the State was attempting to protect was itself too insubstantial to warrant restriction of speech. In this category we may put such cases as *Schneider* v. *State*, 308 U.S. 147 (1939); *Cantwell* v. *Connecticut*, 310 U.S. 296 (1940); *Martin* v. *Struthers*, 319 U.S. 141 (1943); *West Virginia Board of Education* v. *Barnette*, 319 U.S. 624 (1943); *Thomas* v. *Collins*, 323 U.S. 516 (1945); *Marsh* v. *Alabama*, 326 U.S. 501 (1946); but cf. *Prince* v. *Massachusetts*, 321 U.S. 158 (1944); *Cox* v. *New Hampshire*, 312 U.S. 569 (1941). Overthrow of the Government by force and violence is certainly a substantial enough interest for the Government to limit speech. Indeed, this is the ultimate value of any society, for if a society cannot protect its very structure from armed internal attack, it must follow that no subordinate value can be protected. If, then, this interest may be

---

[35] 341 U.S. at 508-10.

protected the literal problem which is presented is what has been meant by the use of the phrase "clear and present danger" of the utterances bringing about the evil within the power of Congress to punish.

Obviously, the words cannot mean that before the Government may act, it must wait until the *putsch* is about to be executed, the plans have been laid and the signal is awaited. If Government is aware that a group aiming at its overthrow is attempting to indoctrinate its members and to commit them to a course whereby they will strike when the leaders feel the circumstances permit, action by the Government is required. The argument that there is no need for Government to concern itself, for Government is strong, it possesses ample powers to put down a rebellion, it may defeat the revolution with ease needs no answer. For that is not the question. Certainly an attempt to overthrow the Government by force, even though doomed from the outset because of inadequate numbers or power of the revolutionists, is a sufficient evil for Congress to prevent. The damage which such attempts create both physically and politically to a nation makes it impossible to measure the validity in terms of the probability of success, or the immediacy of a successful attempt. In the instant case the trial judge charged the jury that they could not convict unless they found that petitioners intended to overthrow the Government "as speedily as circumstances would permit." This does not mean, and could not properly mean, that they would not strike until there was certainty of success. What was meant was that the revolutionists would strike when they thought the time was ripe. We must therefore reject the contention that success or probability of success is the criterion.

The situation with which Justices Holmes and Brandeis were concerned in *Gitlow* was a comparatively isolated event, bearing little relation in their minds to any substantial threat to the safety of the community. Such also is true of cases like *Fiske* v. *Kansas*, 274 U.S. 380 (1927), and *De Jonge* v. *Oregon*, 299 U.S. 353 (1937); but cf. *Lazar* v. *Pennsylvania*, 286 U.S. 532 (1932). They were not confronted with any situation comparable to the instant one—the development of an apparatus designed and dedicated to the overthrow of the Government, in the context of world crisis after crisis.

Concurring separately, Justice Jackson was even more vigorous in his rejection of the test urged by petitioners. He first reinforced the assertions of the Chief Justice:[36]

---

[36] *Id.* at 570–71.

The authors of the clear and present danger test never applied it to a case like this, nor would I. If applied as it is proposed here, it means that the Communist plotting is protected during its period of incubation; its preliminary states of organization and preparation are immune from the law; the Government can move only after imminent action is manifest, when it would, of course, be too late.

The highest degree of constitutional protection is due to the individual acting without conspiracy. But even an individual cannot claim that the Constitution protects him in advocating or teaching overthrow of government by force or violence. I should suppose no one would doubt that Congress has power to make such attempted overthrow a crime. But the contention is that one has the constitutional right to work up a public desire and will to do what it is a crime to attempt. I think direct incitement by speech or writing can be made a crime, and I think there can be a conviction without also proving that the odds favored its success by 99 to 1, or some other extremely high ratio.

But more than this he then declared that Holmes's opinion for a unanimous Court in *Frohwerk*[37] demonstrated that "[t]he names of Mr. Justice Holmes and Mr. Justice Brandeis cannot be associated with such a doctrine of governmental disability."[38]

In the hour of its greatest test, against the tough opponent of national security at mid-twentieth century, the rule of clear and present danger lost its bid for general acceptance as a requirement that for state or federal restriction of speech to be valid it must be shown that a legitimate objective of government is imminently and substantially imperiled. Mr. Justice Black saw this clearly in his dissent. Even on the "radical assumption . . . that petitioners although not indicted for the crime of actual advocacy, may be punished for it . . . the other opinions in this case show that the only way to affirm these convictions is to repudiate directly or indirectly the established 'clear and present danger' rule."[39] In a separate dissent Mr. Justice Douglas made a case for the proposition that communism in this country is only a bogeyman. But the demonstration was unresponsive to the majority's position that the danger test in the formulation brought to the argument by petitioners was inapplicable.

---

[37] Frohwerk v. United States, 249 U.S. 204, 206 (1919).

[38] 341 U.S. at 571.   [39] *Id.* at 579–80.

In retrospect, *Dennis* has the dubious distinction of bringing to a head the paradox that the Holmes-Brandeis formulation of the danger test as a constitutional solvent would satisfy but few. To be sure, it is employed occasionally, as is attested by its reappearance in the last of the contempt cases. It will even turn up in surprising contexts, as where Mr. Justice Harlan, concurring in *Garner v. Louisiana,*[40] invoked it after explicit reference back to Holmes in *Abrams* and Brandeis in *Whitney.*[41] But to many it became, after *Dennis,* largely or wholly unsatisfactory because either too virile or overly weak. Extrajudicially, Mr. Justice Brennan not long ago limited it to the contempt cases and those involving subversive action.[42] Professor Freund had earlier thought even this went too far. Although finding the formulation "a useful criterion of illicit speech where the social harm apprehended from the speech would flow from the effect of the ideas conveyed," he regarded it as "not appropriate where the harm is such that a corrective could not be sought through countervailing speech: contempt of court, pornography, and political activities by civil servants are examples."[43]

In his monumental quest for a satisfactory theory of the First Amendment, Professor Emerson suggested that it was in dissent in *Scales v. United States*[44] that Mr. Justice Douglas abandoned the clear and present danger test which he, alone among the Justices, "made a serious attempt to apply" in *Dennis.*[45] The covert rejection clearly represented not delayed adherence to the *Dennis* majority view that the test was too strong, but embrasure of the quite opposite view that its unsatisfactoriness lay in its weakness. In Emerson's words: "To permit the state to cut off expression as soon as it comes close to being effective is essentially to allow only abstract or innocuous expression."[46] This is the absolutist theory in espousal of which Mr. Justice Douglas thus joined Mr. Justice Black, both undoubtedly influenced heavily by the views of Dr.

---

[40] 368 U.S. 157, 185–207 (1961).

[41] *Id.* at 201–03. "The life of the law can be full of surprises. One does not . . . hear much about clear and present danger these days under any circumstances; it is amazing to find the formula so seriously discussed in a case involving a sit-in." KALVEN, THE NEGRO AND THE FIRST AMENDMENT 132 (Phoenix ed. 1966).

[42] Brennan, note 15 *supra*, at 8.

[43] FREUND, note 2 *supra*, at 44.

[44] 367 U.S. 203 (1961).

[45] Emerson, note 2 *supra*, at 911 n. 35.

[46] *Id.* at 911.

Meiklejohn.[47] The judgment passed on the danger test is, however, the same as that of those concerned over its potency:[48]

> There is still some blood remaining in the doctrine, and it has continued to be used in certain types of situations [citing to *Wood v. Georgia*, the latest contempt case]. But, as a general test of the limits of the first amendment, the clear and present danger test must be regarded as unacceptable.

In the second *Konigsberg*[49] classic confrontation between absolutist and balancing theories of First Amendment interpretation, Mr. Justice Harlan for the majority sought to ground the latter partly on the proposition "[t]hat the First Amendment immunity for speech, press and assembly has to be reconciled with valid but conflicting governmental interests was clear to Holmes, J. (*Abrams v. United States* . . .); to Brandeis, J. (*Whitney v. California* . . .); and to Hughes, C. J. (*Near v. Minnesota* . . .)."[50] With the concurrence of Douglas, Mr. Justice Black assailed this bid for good paternity for the balancing test:[51]

> The Court attempts to justify its refusal to apply the plain mandate of the First Amendment in part by reference to the so-called "clear and present danger test" forcefully used by Mr. Justice Holmes and Mr. Justice Brandeis, not to narrow but to broaden the then prevailing interpretation of First Amendment freedoms. I think very little can be found in anything they ever said that would provide support for the "balancing test" presently in use.

Rather it was "the sudden transformation of the 'clear and present danger test' in *Dennis* v. *United States*" that equated it with the balancing test; "diluted and weakened by being recast in terms of this 'balancing' formula, there seems to me to be much room to doubt that Justices Holmes and Brandeis would even have recognized their test."[52]

---

[47] See Meiklejohn, *The First Amendment Is an Absolute*, 1961 SUPREME COURT REVIEW 245.

[48] Emerson, note 2 *supra*, at 912.

[49] Konigsberg v. State Bar of California, 366 U.S. 36 (1961).

[50] *Id.* at 50 n. 11.   [51] *Id.* at 62.

[52] *Id.* at 64. Contrast Mr. Justice Black's statement of the case in Martin v. City of Struthers, 319 U.S. 141, 143 (1943): "We are faced in the instant case with the necessity of weighing the conflicting interests of the appellant in the civil rights she claims, as well as the right of the individual householder to determine whether he

The Frankfurter concurrence in *Dennis* is clearly cast in terms of essential equivalency between "clear and present danger" and "careful weighing of conflicting interests." To be sure, he was dissatisfied with acceptance by others in the majority of Learned Hand's recasting of the danger test:[53]

> In all fairness, the [defendants'] argument cannot be met by reinterpreting the Court's frequent use of "clear" and "present" to mean an entertainable "probability." In giving this meaning to the phrase "clear and present danger," the Court of Appeals was fastidiously confining the rhetoric of opinions to the exact scope of what was decided by them. We have greater responsibility for having given constitutional support, over repeated protests, to uncritical libertarian generalities.

Yet his fulfilment of that "greater responsibility" led him, not into an attack on judicial balancing, but into an exposition and defense of it as "on the whole" the underlying rationale of the cases and the basis for resolving the issue in *Dennis*:[54]

> On the one hand is the interest in security. The Communist Party was not designed by these defendants as an ordinary political party. . . .
> On the other hand is the interest in free speech. The right to exert all governmental powers in aid of maintaining our institutions and resisting their physical overthrow does not include intolerance of opinions and speech that cannot do harm although opposed and perhaps alien to dominant, traditional opinion.

A full decade before the fateful decision in *Dennis* one of the ablest of commentators had sensed in the danger test a quality that would not make difficult its assimilation into the concept of balancing. Professor Wechsler observed:[55]

> Speech or assembly may be repressed or limited when it gives rise or is intended to give rise or may reasonably be thought by the legislature to give rise to a genuine danger of some substantive evil which the state has a right to prevent, unless the evil is not great enough to warrant the sup-

---

is willing to receive her message, against the interest of the community which by this ordinance offers to protect the interests of all of its citizens, whether particular citizens want that protection or not."

[53] 341 U.S. at 527.   [54] *Id.* at 546, 548.

[55] Wechsler, *Symposium on Civil Liberties,* 9 A. L. Sch. Rev. 881, 887 (1941).

pression of speech or assembly as a means to its prevention, or to say the same thing in a different way, unless the speech or assembly is justified by some end which outweighs the evil which it admittedly threatens. But if this is the clear and present danger test for which liberals have fought and bled, it needs no argument to show that the formula which it provides is only a formula; that it does little more than to state the general principle of justice which would be accepted in evaluating any legislation which interferes with individual freedom. The use to which freedom is put must threaten social interests; the danger inherent in the threat must not be outweighed by an affirmative good which the behavior entails. In short, what the clear and present danger test can do, and all it can do, is to require an extended judicial review in the fullest legislative sense of the competing values which the particular situation presents. And the scope of that judicial review may be limited by what is in effect a presumption of validity, or a deference to legislative judgment, at least where the legislation condemns specific doctrine or specifically described types of meetings.

Despite, therefore, employment of the Holmes-Brandeis brand of danger test from *Herndon v. Lowry*[56] through the 1940's to the very year of *Dennis*,[57] there was latent an element about it that would not make difficult its assimilation into the concept of balancing, as balancing came to be practiced and understood by Frankfurter in *Dennis* and by Harlan in *Konigsberg II*. Most commentators now assume a balancing role for the danger test. " 'Clear and present danger' is, to be sure, essentially a balancing formula," one has recently observed.[58] Professor Karst has insisted:[59]

> The clear-and-present-danger test, even with its original emphasis on the immediacy of the threatened harm, was always a "balancing" test. The Justices who used the language of clear-and-present-danger did not shrink from making the legislative judgments which are inescapable in our systems of judicial review.

Professor Kalven is the exception in continuing to distinguish "balancing [from] any form of clear and present danger."[60]

[56] 301 U.S. 242 (1937).

[57] In Niemotko v. Maryland, 340 U.S. 268 (1951); Kunz v. New York, 340 U.S. 290 (1951); Feiner v. New York, 340 U.S. 315 (1951).

[58] KRISLOV, note 2 *supra*, at 121.

[59] Karst, note 1 *supra*, at 10.   [60] KALVEN, note 41 *supra*, at 86, 121.

Metamorphosed into a balancing formula, "clear and present danger" fares no better as a test for satisfactory delineation of constitutional boundaries. Clearly unsatisfactory to the absolutists, it has, as well, deficiencies for those to whom balancing is necessary. Commentators are, for one, critical of it as an adequate vehicle for balancing. Paul Freund has often been quoted on this point:[61]

> Even where it is appropriate, the clear-and-present-danger test is an oversimplified judgment unless it takes account also of a number of other factors: the relative seriousness of the danger in comparison with the value of the occasion for speech or political activity; the availability of more moderate controls than those the state has imposed, and perhaps the specific intent with which the speech or activity is launched. No matter how rapidly we utter the phrase "clear and present danger," or how closely we hyphenate the words, they are not a substitute for the weighing of values. They tend to convey a delusion of certitude when what is most certain is the complexity of the strands in the web of freedom which the judge must disentangle.

Citing this passage, another commentator more recently observed that "to sophisticated balancers" clear and present danger as a balancing formula[62]

> suggests a simplification of the problem, an incomplete enumeration of the factors involved in balancing. This distortion is at a minimum in face-to-face situations. Yet, even there, external factors are not typically considered, and little play is given to a relative evaluation of the significance of the speech or the seriousness of the evil. In short, less freedom is given the judge than the balancers prefer.

The hazards of inadequate consideration of factors pertinent to the balancing operation are well illustrated by Mr. Justice Black's dissent in *Barenblatt*,[63] in which he was joined by Chief Justice Warren and Mr. Justice Douglas:[64]

> But even assuming what I cannot assume, that some balancing is proper in this case, I feel that the Court after stating the test ignores it completely. At most it balances

---

[61] FREUND, note 2 *supra*, at 44.

[62] KRISLOV, note 2 *supra*, at 121. To similar effect is McKay, *The Preference for Freedom*, 34 N.Y.U. L. REV. 1182, 1212, 1222 (1959).

[63] Barenblatt v. United States, 360 U.S. 109, 134 (1959).

[64] *Id*. at 144, 145.

the right of the Government to preserve itself, against Barenblatt's right to refrain from revealing Communist affiliations. Such a balance, however, mistakes the factors to be weighed. In the first place, it completely leaves out the real interest in Barenblatt's silence, the interest of the people as a whole in being able to join organizations, advocate causes and make political "mistakes" without later being subjected to governmental penalties for having dared to think for themselves. . . .

Moreover, I cannot agree with the Court's notion that First Amendment freedoms must be abridged in order to "preserve" our country. That notion rests on the unarticulated premise that this Nation's security hangs upon its power to punish people because of what they think, speak or write about, or because of those with whom they associate for political purposes. The Government, in its brief, virtually admits this position when it speaks of the "communication of unlawful ideas." I challenge this premise, and deny that ideas can be proscribed under our Constitution.

A further deficiency lies in the limitations of the type of balancing with which the diluted danger test has fused, even when that form takes into account all relevant factors of private right and public interest. This type, now known as ad hoc balancing, although ably defended,[65] has in the present decade come under growing criticism.[66] That criticism finds in ad hoc balancing a congenital infirmity. Because of the decisional character of the juristic process by which the weighing is done, no facet of speech, press, or assembly is protected if the intensity of the governmental interest is deemed "on balance" to override the private values in opposition. Mr. Frantz is mordaciously critical:[67]

If the arguments employed to justify balancing are carried to their logical conclusion, then the Constitution does not contain—and is not even capable of containing—anything what-

---

[65] Kauper, Book Review of MEIKLEJOHN, POLITICAL FREEDOM, 58 MICH. L. REV. 619 (1960); Karst, *Legislative Facts in Constitutional Litigation*, 1960 SUPREME COURT REVIEW 75; Karst, note 1 *supra;* see Morris & Powe, *Constitutional and Statutory Rights to Open Housing*, 44 WASH. L. REV. 1, 28–46 (1968), for employment of ad hoc balancing in an analysis at one of the cutting edges of constitutional litigation.

[66] Emerson, note 2 *supra*, at 912–14; Frantz, *The First Amendment in Balance*, 71 YALE L. J. 1424, 1441–45 (1962); Nimmer, *The Right to Speak from* Times *to* Time: *First Amendment Theory Applied to Libel and Misapplied to Privacy,* 56 CALIF. L. REV. 935, 935–47 (1968).

[67] Frantz, note 66 *supra*, at 1445.

ever which is unconditionally obligatory. Defendants in criminal cases can be tried in secret, or held incommunicado without trial, can be denied knowledge of the accusation against them, and the right to counsel, and the right to call witnesses in their own defense, and the right to trial by jury. Ex post facto laws and bills of attainder can be passed. Habeas corpus can be suspended, though there is neither rebellion nor invasion. Private property can be taken for public use without just, or any, compensation. Suffrage qualifications based on sex or race can be reinstituted. Anything which the Constitution says *cannot* be done *can* be done, if Congress thinks and the Court agrees (or is unwilling to set aside the congressional judgment) that the interests thereby served outweighed those which were sacrificed. Thus the whole idea of a government of limited powers, and of a written constitution as a device for attaining that end, is at least potentially at stake.

Unable on the other hand to accept in naked form Mr. Justice Black's absolutist approach to interpretation of the First Amendment,[68] these critics opt for what they describe as definitional balancing, some of them urging that this is actually what Mr. Justice Black is getting at in his rejection of ad hoc balancing.[69] In definitional balancing, weighing takes place, yet the juristic process is said to be significantly different:[70]

> To be sure, a judge who is obliged to formulate a new rule of law must consider what its advantages and disadvantages would be and weigh them against the advantages and disadvantages of the possible alternative rules which might be adopted. For example, if the judge is asked to decide whether the first amendment protects the refusal to state one's political affiliations, he must take into consideration the possible dangers to political freedom and other values of denying such protection. And he must also consider whether protecting that refusal would strip the government of power which may be needed for legitimate, non-repressive purposes. Mr. Justice Black provided an example of this type of "balancing" when, in order to decide whether the first amendment protects a right to anonymous publication, he took into consideration the possible social values of anonymous publication as indicated by the role such publications

---

[68] See, *e.g.*, Nimmer, note 66 *supra*.

[69] Emerson, note 2 *supra*, at 914–16; Frantz, note 66 *supra*, at 1433–38.

[70] Frantz, note 66 *supra*, at 1434–35.

have played in the past, and the danger of repressing con-
troversial views if identification of the proponents were required. But, though the mental process by which a judge
determines what rule to adopt can be described as "balancing," this does not make it the same as balancing, independently of any rule, to determine what is the best disposition to make of a particular case. Deciding the scope to be
accorded a particular constitutional freedom is different
from deciding whether the interest of a particular litigant in
freely expressing views which the judge may consider loath-
some, dangerous, or ridiculous is outweighed by society's
interest in "order," "security," or national "self-preserva-
tion."

In a concluding footnote Frantz leaves to others the major task
of determining "how constitutionally protected speech should be
defined," offering only the suggestion that the "starting point" be
the Meiklejohn thesis that "freedom of speech is essential to self-
government."[71] Professor Emerson laid the groundwork for this
task through his excellent formulation of the function of freedom
of expression in a democratic society.[72] Professor Nimmer's recent
article, following Emerson in embracing definitional balancing as
a viable theory of the First Amendment, finds it properly applied
by the Court in *Times* but not in *Time*.[73] In the present context
it is not necessary to stop to judge the validity of the Nimmer conclusions on either decision, in contrast with those of the Court majority or indeed of the Justices in dissent. The significant feature
is the intellectual process employed by both Court and commentator in defining the contours of the First Amendment.

The difference in approach to constitutional interpretation is
marked. Professor Kalven, who it will be recalled has not followed
others in viewing balancing as equivalent to any form of the danger test, immediately observed of the *Times* opinion: "There is not
a word of clear and present danger or of balancing."[74] Expanding
on the significance of these omissions, he subsequently said of the
danger test:[75]

Whether the rewriting of [the clear and present danger
test] by Judge Hand in the *Dennis* case or the persistent

---

[71] *Id.* at 1449–50 n. 105.   [72] Emerson, note 2 *supra*, at 878–86.

[73] Nimmer, note 66 *supra*, at 948–67; New York Times v. Sullivan, 376 U.S. 254
(1964); Time, Inc. v. Hill, 385 U.S. 374 (1967).

[74] KALVEN, note 41 *supra*, at 57.   [75] Kalven, note 2 *supra*, at 213–15.

attack on it as a constitutional formula by Mr. Justice Frankfurter or the perplexities of the newer speech issues or the sheer inadequacy of the formula itself caused its decline may be unclear. But it is clear that, as of the judgment in the *Times* case, it has disappeared. It did not occur to the Court to test the Alabama law before it in terms of clear and present danger, although barely a decade before, in *Beauharnais*, appeal to the test was the principal argument of the defendant. (It was one of the astute and successful gambles of the Wechsler brief that it did not argue the case in terms of clear and present danger.) The measure of the conceptual revolution promulgated by the *Times* case is that the Alabama law is found unconstitutional, not because there is no clear and present danger of a substantive evil in defendants' speech, but because the law looks too much like punishment for seditious libel.

There was one mention of the clear-and-present-danger test in the majority opinion. It occurred in a reference to *Pennekamp v. Florida* when the Court analogized the problem of defamation with that of contempt of court by publication. It would seem that the contempt problem is at least a sibling if not a twin to the one presented in the *Times* case. The former involves defamation of a specific public official, a judge. It might have been expected, therefore, that the same solution would fit both problems. But the modern Supreme Court decisions on the contempt problem—*Bridges*, *Craig* and *Pennekamp*—all rely for their disposition on the clear-and-present-danger test. And as recently as 1962, in *Wood v. Georgia*, the Court adhered to this approach in disposing of a contempt case. The contempt cases make the Court's silence in the *Times* case on the viability of the clear-and-present-danger test all the more deafening.

Immediately prior to the *Times* decision, the fashionable First Amendment test was what Professor Emerson called "ad hoc balancing." This formula, which he dates from the *Douds* case in 1950, has been the subject of several celebrated debates within the Court, especially between Justices Black and Harlan. The controversy has centered on large issues about absolutes and the proper role of judicial review. Professor Emerson, a critic of the balancing formula, has defined it: "The formula is that the court must, in each case, balance the individual and social interest in freedom of expression against the social interest sought by the regulation which restricts expression."

It is scarcely a novel suggestion that the law of defamation with its strict liability on the one hand and its complex of offsetting privileges on the other is a prime example

of balancing the interest in freedom against the social interest sought by inhibiting communication. It is this balancing that in fact generates the bulk of the law in this
area and the special fascination that it has derives from the
precision and detail with which the common law has struck
the balance in different situations. The issue before the
Court in the *Times* case, therefore, would have been peculiarly meet for the application of the balancing formula.
Again the failure to speak to the issue, either in the Court's
opinion or Mr. Justice Black's concurrence, suggests the
necessity for its re-evaluation.

The Court's contemporaneous opinion in *Garrison v. Louisiana*,[76]
extending the *Times* principle to criminal libel of public officials,
bears out the Kalven analysis. The judicial balancing is of the definitional, not the ad hoc, type:[77]

> Truth may not be the subject of either civil or criminal sanc-
> tions where discussion of public affairs is concerned. . . .
> [O]nly those false statements made with the high degree of
> awareness of their probable falsity demanded by *New York
> Times* may be the subject of either civil or criminal sanctions.
> For speech concerning public affairs is more than self-expres-
> sion; it is the essence of self-government.

On the other hand:[78]

> [T]he use of the known lie as a tool is at once at odds with
> the premises of democratic government and with the or-
> derly manner in which economic, social, or political
> change is to be effected. Calculated falsehood falls into that
> class of utterances which "are no essential part of any ex-
> position of ideas, and are of such slight social value as a
> step to truth that any benefit that may be derived from
> them is clearly outweighed by the social interest in order
> and morality. . . ." *Chaplinsky* v. *New Hampshire*, 315 U.S.
> 568, 572. Hence the knowingly false statement and the false
> statement made with reckless disregard of the truth, do not
> enjoy constitutional protection.

Advocates of definitional, as opposed to ad hoc, balancing can
find Court support for their views not alone in the line of libel
cases but, as well, in the longer line of obscenity decisions. The
unsatisfactoriness in results achieved from *Roth-Alberts*[79] to *Stanley*

---

[76] 379 U.S. 64 (1964).   [78] *Id.* at 75.

[77] *Id.* at 74–75.   [79] Roth v. United States, 354 U.S. 476 (1957).

v. Georgia[80] does not mitigate from the fact that the Court has been at work attempting to define the reach of First Amendment liberties in the morals area. And there is Chief Justice Warren's footnote disclaimer of ad hoc balancing at the close of his opinion for the Court in *United States v. Robel*:[81]

> It has been suggested that this case should be decided by "balancing" the governmental interests expressed in § 5(a)(1)(D) against the First Amendment rights asserted by the appellee. This we decline to do. We recognize that both interests are substantial, but we deem it inappropriate for this Court to label one as being more important or more substantial than the other. Our inquiry is more circumscribed. Faced with a clear conflict between a federal statute enacted in the interests of national security and an individual's exercise of his First Amendment rights, we have confined our analysis to whether Congress has adopted a constitutional means in achieving its concededly legitimate legislative goal. In making this determination we have found it necessary to measure the validity of the means adopted by Congress against both the goal it has sought to achieve and the specific prohibitions of the First Amendment. But we have in no way "balanced" those respective interests. We have ruled only that the Constitution requires that the conflict between congressional power and individual rights be accommodated by legislation drawn more narrowly to avoid the conflict. There is, of course, nothing novel in that analysis. Such a course of adjudication was enunciated by Chief Justice Marshall when he declared: "Let the end be legitimate, let it be within the scope of the constitution, and all means which are appropriate, which are plainly adapted to that end, *which are not prohibited, but consist with the letter and spirit of the constitution* are constitutional." *M'Culloch* v. *Maryland*, 4 Wheat. 316, 421 (1819) (emphasis added). In this case, the means chosen by Congress are contrary to the "letter and spirit" of the First Amendment.

Such trends in Court commitment and commentator critique would appear to spell the end of the line for "clear and present danger" after a half-century of vicissitudes. This, whether or not the weakened danger test was fully fused by *Dennis* into ad hoc balancing. It is therefore not surprising to find a funereal atmosphere permeating the fiftieth anniversary of "clear and present danger." But the current tearless farewells take no account of still another

---

[80] 394 U.S. 557 (1969).   [81] 389 U.S. 258, 268 n. 20 (1967).

facet in the life of "clear and present danger," a facet with a great potential future if definitional balancing is to be the standard approach to resolution of First Amendment boundaries. For, while definitional balancing draws the constitutional line generically, by determining the meaning of constitutional guarantees for different classes of situation (*e.g.*, price regulation, control of obscenity), another step is essential to disposition of any individual case. That step involves a judgment on whether legislation or other governmental action under challenge bears a sufficient nexus to objectives of government determined, through the definitional process, to be consistent with the reach of constitutional restriction. Clearly, the tightness of the nexus that is required will have a direct bearing on the outcome in a given context of validity or invalidity. Thus requirement of but a rational nexus would result in little invalidity. By a metamorphosis no more strained than those earlier experienced, "clear and present danger" could transform into a requirement in First Amendment litigation of a strong demonstration of constitutionality that would force governmental respect for the protected civil interests of the individual.

Although expressed in the conjectural, as a role that "clear and present danger" could play in the future, there is considerable basis in the decided cases for such a development. Origins can be traced back to the 1938 decision in the first *Carolene Products* case.[82] Congressional prohibition of the movement of filled milk in interstate commerce was sustained against Due Process challenge because "regulatory legislation affecting ordinary commercial transactions is not to be pronounced unconstitutional unless in the light of the facts made known or generally assumed it is of such a character as to preclude the assumption that it rests upon some rational basis within the knowledge and experience of the legislators."[83] But to this statement was appended what has become the famous "footnote four," the first two paragraphs of which, with omission of citations, read:[84]

> There may be narrower scope for operation of the presumption of constitutionality when legislation appears on its face to be within a specific prohibition of the Constitution, such as those of the first ten amendments, which are deemed

---

[82] United States v. Carolene Products Co., 304 U.S. 144 (1938).

[83] *Id.* at 152.   [84] *Id.* at 152–53 n. 4.

equally specific when held to be embraced within the Fourteenth. . . .

It is unnecessary to consider now whether legislation which
restricts those political processes which can ordinarily be expected to bring about repeal of undesirable legislation, is to
be subjected to more exacting judicial scrutiny under the
general prohibitions of the Fourteenth Amendment than are
most other types of legislation. . . .

Among numerous citations following the text of this second paragraph are "*Whitney* v. *California*, 274 U.S. 357, 373–378 . . . and
see Holmes, J., in *Gitlow* v. *New York*, 268 U.S. 652, 673." Significantly the page references are to the essence of the Holmes-
Brandeis dissent in *Gitlow* and of the Brandeis-Holmes concurrence in *Whitney*. The most immediate judicial consequence of
footnote four was the Court's probing of the ramifications of the
"political process" theory, wherein the two flag-salute decisions
figured so prominently.[85] With the vacating of the original judgment in *Opelika*,[86] Stone's reformulation of the footnote thesis in
terms of preferred freedom became majority doctrine in *Murdock
v. Pennsylvania*.[87] "Freedom of press, freedom of speech, freedom
of religion are in a preferred position."[88]

In *Barnette*'s repudiation of *Gobitis*,[89] which followed six weeks
after *Murdock*, Mr. Justice Jackson did not employ the new phrase.
But its essence pervaded his opinion and the tie with "clear and
present danger" was present, when he put the matter this way:[90]

Much of the vagueness of the due process clause disappears
when the specific prohibitions of the First become its standard. The right of a State to regulate, for example, a public
utility may well include, so far as the due process test is concerned, power to impose all of the restrictions which a legislature may have a "rational basis" for adopting. But freedoms
of speech and press, of assembly, and of worship may not be
infringed on such slender grounds. They are susceptible of restriction only to prevent grave and immediate danger to interests which the State may lawfully protect.

---

85 Minersville School District v. Gobitis, 310 U.S. 586 (1940); West Virginia
State Board of Education v. Barnette, 319 U.S. 624 (1943).

86 Jones v. Opelika, 319 U.S. 103 (1943), *vacating* 316 U.S. 584 (1942).

87 319 U.S. 105 (1943).   89 Note 85 *supra*.

88 *Id*. at 115.   90 319 U.S. at 639.

Three years later, at the hands of Justice Rutledge, although for a sharply divided Court, this distinction in judicial rule was explained explicitly in terms of the "preferred freedom" theory:[91]

> The case confronts us again with the duty our system places on this Court to say where the individual's freedom ends and the State's power begins. Choice on that border, now as always delicate, is perhaps more so where the usual presumption supporting legislation is balanced by the preferred place given in our scheme to the great, the indispensable democratic freedoms secured by the First Amendment. Cf. *Schneider* v. *State*, 308 U.S. 147; *Cantwell* v. *Connecticut*, 310 U.S. 296, *Prince* v. *Massachusetts*, 321 U.S. 158. That priority gives these liberties a sanctity and a sanction not permitting dubious intrusions. And it is the character of the right, not of the limitation, which determines what standard governs the choice. Compare *United States* v. *Carolene Products Co.*, 304 U.S. 144, 152–153.

The evolutionary relation between "clear and present danger" and the "preferred freedom" theory is thus quite clear. As Dean McKay has observed:[92]

> [I]t appears essential to recognize at least that the original formulation of the clear and present danger test by Justice Holmes in *Schenck* v. *United States* was a recognition that when first amendment values are involved, the otherwise permissible prohibitions which government might impose are to be examined in a different context and measured by a more critical standard. This, then, is the essence of the preferred position—the exercise of judgment to protect first amendment freedoms in a variety of ways.

On the other hand, it was not clear for a time that the theory of the preferred place of the First Amendment articulated a concept different from the Holmes-Brandeis formulation of the danger test as a full and distinct solvent for constitutional issues involving speech and related guarantees. This is evident from the passage in the Rutledge opinion in *Collins* which immediately follows the paragraph already quoted:[93]

> For these reasons any attempt to restrict those liberties must be justified by clear public interest, threatened not doubtfully

---

[91] Thomas v. Collins, 323 U.S. 516, 529–30 (1945).

[92] McKay, note 62 *supra*, at 1191.   [93] 323 U.S. at 530.

or remotely, but by clear and present danger. The rational connection between the remedy provided and the evil to be curbed, which in other contexts might support legislation against attack on due process grounds, will not suffice. These rights rest on firmer foundation. Accordingly, whatever occasion would restrain orderly discussion and persuasion, at appropriate time and place, must have clear support in public danger, actual or impending. Only the gravest abuses, endangering paramount interests, give occasion for permissible limitation.

Of those five sentences, the first, fourth, and fifth sound in terms of the Holmes-Brandeis test. Independently, they might be taken to imply the repudiation for First Amendment matters of the "any tendency" test of the *Gitlow* majority. Yet, linked by the second and third sentences a different meaning could be intended. These sentences place the concept of "clear and present danger" in an entirely new context. That context is an associational one, as is true under the Holmes-Brandeis view. But it is now a matter of essentially qualitative, rather than quantitative, connection.

For a Court again divided, Mr. Justice Black had three weeks earlier, in *Korematsu v. United States*,[94] made a direct linkage between the concepts of "clear and present danger" and nexus:[95]

> In the light of the principles we announced in the *Hirabayashi* case, we are unable to conclude that it was beyond the war power of Congress and the Executive to exclude those of Japanese ancestry from the West Coast war area at the time they did. True, exclusion from the area in which one's home is located is a far greater deprivation than constant confinement to the home from 8 P.M. to 6 A.M. Nothing short of apprehension by the proper military authorities of the gravest imminent danger to the public safety can constitutionally justify either. But exclusion from a threatened area, no less than curfew, has a definite and close relationship to the prevention of espionage and sabotage. The military authorities, charged with the primary responsibility of defending our shores, concluded that curfew provided inadequate protection and ordered exclusion. They did so, as pointed out in our *Hirabayashi* opinion, in accordance with Congressional authority to the military to say who should, and who should not, remain in the threatened areas.

---

94 323 U.S. 214 (1944).   95 *Id.* at 217–18.

The new function of the test is here clearer than in *Collins*. To withstand constitutional attack, the challenged governmental action must be shown to be closely and intimately connected with a permitted objective of government.

The requirement of an immediate or tight nexus for constitutionality dooms legislative restrictions and prohibitions cast in embracive terms. In this characteristic it contrasts with the rational nexus test, which because of its looseness ensures constitutionality on the meager showing of an iota of possible connection between the governmental action under attack and some permissible objective of government. Adoption of the test of "clear and present danger" nexus for First Amendment issues therefore requires that policy formulations, whether by court, city council, state assembly, or Congress, must be tightly drafted to guarantee that their thrust is confined to objectives that government is free to attain. The closing paragraphs of the Douglas opinion for the Court in *Murdock* bring this point to crystal focus, and relate it to what Edmond Cahn later aptly characterized as "the firstness of the First Amendment."[96] Excerpting from those paragraphs at once saves space and heightens effect:[97]

> Jehovah's Witnesses are not "above the law." But the present ordinance is not directed to the problems with which the police power of the state is free to deal. It does not cover, and petitioners are not charged with, breaches of the peace. . . . Furthermore, the present ordinance is not narrowly drawn to safeguard the people of the community in their homes against the evils of solicitation. See *Cantwell* v. *Connecticut*. . . . As we have said, it is not merely a registration ordinance calling for an identification of the solicitors so as to give the authorities some basis for investigating strangers coming into the community. . . . Nor can the present ordinance survive if we assume that it has been construed to apply only to solicitation from house to house. The ordinance is not narrowly drawn to prevent or control abuses or evils arising from that activity. . . .
> The judgment in *Jones* v. *Opelika* has this day been vacated. Freed from that controlling precedent we can restore to their high, constitutional position the liberties of itinerant evangelists who disseminate their religious beliefs and the tenets of their faith through distribution of literature.

---

[96] Cahn, *The Firstness of the First Amendment*, 65 YALE L.J. 464 (1956).

[97] 319 U.S. at 116–17.

Tight drafting as a constitutional necessity traces back to *Thornhill v. Alabama*[98] and *Cantwell v. Connecticut*,[99] decided a month apart in 1940. In each the requirement that the statute be "narrowly drawn" is associated with the danger test. The language used, however, is such that one cannot be sure the danger test had been disassociated from its formulation at the hands of Holmes and Brandeis. This is especially true of the *Cantwell* opinion, to which the Court referred in *Murdock*. With no dissent, Justice Roberts in *Cantwell* declared:[100]

> Although the contents of the [phonographic] record not unnaturally aroused animosity, we think that, in the absence of a statute narrowly drawn to define and punish specific conduct as constituting a clear and present danger to a substantial interest of the State, the petitioner's communication, considered in the light of the constitutional guarantees, raised no such clear and present menace to public peace and order as to render him liable to conviction of the common law offense in question [breach of the peace].

But the Murphy opinion in *Thornhill*, for all save Justice McReynolds, had been suggestive of the conception of "clear and present danger" as requiring a close connection between permitted objective of, and challenged action by, government:[101]

> The power and the duty of the State to take adequate steps to preserve the peace and to protect the privacy, the lives, and the property of its residents cannot be doubted. But no clear and present danger of destruction of life or property, or invasion of the right of privacy, or breach of the peace can be thought to be inherent in the activities of every person who approaches the premises of an employer and publicizes the facts of a labor dispute involving the latter. We are not now concerned with picketing *en masse* or otherwise conducted which might occasion such imminent and aggravated danger to these interests as to justify a statute narrowly drawn to cover the precise situation giving rise to the danger. Compare *American Foundries* v. *Tri-City Council*, 257 U.S. 184, 205. Section 3448 in question here does not aim specifically at serious encroachments on these interests and does not evidence any such care in balancing these interests against the interest of the community and that of the individual in freedom of discussion on matters of public concern.

98 310 U.S. 88 (1940).   100 *Id.* at 311.

99 310 U.S. 296 (1940).   101 310 U.S. at 105.

The years following were not propitious ones for further development in the transformation of the danger test into a strong nexus test for application in First Amendment and, as in *Korematsu*, related civil liberties cases. To adapt a favorite Frankfurter phrase, in the disposition of the bulk of litigation involving free speech and associated concepts of personal liberty, the thrust of judicial action was elsewhere—on the scope and application of the Holmes-Brandeis formulation, on the emergence and retirement of ad hoc balancing, and on the post-*Dennis* interrelationships between the danger test and that form of balancing.

The "preferred freedom" theory did not, as such, long survive the strictures leveled at it by Justice Frankfurter in his concurrence in *Kovacs v. Cooper*,[102] although its underlying philosophy of a "preference for freedom" did not abate. Where the Court's approach to constitutional resolution directly employed the nexus rationale, the connection required tended to be reduced to the substantial nexus level generally used by state courts to test the validity of exertions of governmental policy in the areas of both civil and economic liberty. The origin of this trend in *United Public Workers v. Mitchell*[103] may well explain it. Counsel for the Union had great difficulty identifying the constitutional protection allegedly breached by the Hatch Act's call for "political sterilization" of federal employees. In any event, a relaxed nexus test was employed in the earlier "membership list" cases. In *N.A.A.C.P. v. Alabama*,[104] invalidity followed from the absence of a demonstration of substantial connection between disclosure and legitimate objective. The language in *Bates v. Little Rock*[105] suggested an even less stringent test although perhaps unintentionally: "When it is shown that state action threatens significantly to impinge upon constitutionally protected freedom it becomes the duty of this Court to determine whether the action bears a *reasonable* relationship to the achievement of the governmental purpose [here license taxation] asserted as its justification."[106] Meantime in *Uphaus v. Wyman*,[107] involving legislative investigation, it was a dissenting Justice who insisted that "for an investigation in the field of the

---

102 336 U.S. 77, 95–96 (1949).

103 330 U.S. 75 (1947).

104 357 U.S. 449 (1958).

105 361 U.S. 516 (1960).

106 *Id.* at 525. (Emphasis added.)

107 360 U.S. 72 (1959).

constitutionally protected freedoms of speech and assemblage to be upheld by the broad standards of relevance permissible in a legislative inquiry, some relevance to a valid legislative purpose must be shown."[108]

The requirement that an ordinance or statute be "narrowly drawn," if there is threat of trespass upon First Amendment territory, fared better, thanks largely to its reciprocal. This reciprocal concept, that such legislation to be constitutional must avoid "overbreadth," can be taken to have had its origin in *Winters v. New York*.[109] There a section of the New York Penal Law, construed by the New York Court of Appeals to include within its prohibitions distribution of magazines in which stories of deeds of bloodshed "are massed so as to incite to violent crimes," was invalidated for vagueness and indefiniteness. Significantly, vagueness and indefiniteness arose not alone from uncertainty as to statutory coverage but also from the possibility that the section as officially construed could be restrictive of freedoms of the press guaranteed against abridgment by the First Amendment. The distinction between voidness for vagueness and voidness for overreach is now clear, with the latter concept standing firmly on its own constitutional feet. Thus in *Zwickler v. Koota*[110] there appears the following paragraph:[111]

> But we have here no question of a construction of § 781-b [the New York statutory prohibition on distribution of anonymous political handbills] that would "avoid or modify the constitutional question." Appellant's challenge is not that the statute is void for "vagueness," that is, that it is a statute "which either forbids or requires the doing of an act in terms so vague that men of common intelligence must necessarily guess at its meaning and differ as to its application. . . ." *Connally* v. *General Construction Co.*, 269 U.S. 385, 391. Rather his constitutional attack is that the statute, although lacking neither clarity nor precision, is void for "overbreadth," that is, that it offends the constitutional principle that "a governmental purpose to control or prevent activities constitutionally subject to state regulation may not be achieved by means which sweep unnecessarily broadly and thereby invade the area of protected freedoms." *N.A.A.C.P.* v. *Alabama*, 377 U.S. 288, 307. [Other citations omitted.] Appellee does not con-

---

[108] *Id*. at 100.

[109] 333 U.S. 507 (1948).

[110] 389 U.S. 241 (1967).

[111] *Id*. at 249–50.

test appellant's suggestion that § 781-b is both clear and precise; indeed, appellee concedes that state court construction cannot narrow its allegedly indiscriminate cast and render unnecessary a decision of appellant's constitutional challenge. See *Aptheker* v. *Secretary of State*, 378 U.S. 500.

In the 1960's, Court explanation of unconstitutionality in terms of overbreadth has become common. More and more, judicial references to statutory overbreadth and to lack of statutory narrowness are employed interchangeably. From among recent decisions the following are illustrative, both of these and of related developments toward the shaping of "clear and present danger" into a test of immediate nexus. In *Shelton* v. *Tucker*:[112]

> The scope of the inquiry required by Act 10 is completely unlimited. The statute requires a teacher to reveal the church to which he belongs, or to which he has given financial support. It requires him to disclose his political party, and every political organization to which he may have contributed over a five-year period. It requires him to list, without number, every conceivable kind of associational tie—social, professional, political, avocational or religious. Many such relationships could have no possible bearing upon the teacher's occupational competence or fitness.
>
> In a series of decisions this Court has held that, even though the governmental purpose be legitimate and substantial, that purpose cannot be pursued by means that broadly stifle fundamental personal liberties when the end can be more narrowly achieved. The breadth of legislative abridgment must be viewed in the light of less drastic means for achieving the same basic purpose. . . .
>
> As recently as last Term we held invalid an ordinance prohibiting the distribution of handbills because the breadth of its application went far beyond what was necessary to achieve

---

[112] 364 U.S. 479, 488–89 (1960). In both *Talley* and *Shelton* the opinions of the Court reach back for doctrinal basis to Lovell v. Griffin, 303 U.S. 444 (1938), the original decision invalidating a handbill ordinance unlimited in its embrasure. This momentous determination, rejecting the Holmesian proposition in Commonwealth v. Davis, 162 Mass. 510, *aff'd*, Davis v. Massachusetts, 167 U.S. 43 (1897), that a city has the same dominion over its streets, parks, and other public areas as does a private landowner over his property, precipitated a situation in which thousands of ordinances and hundreds of statutes from an earlier constitutional period became invalid for overbreadth and under the constitutional necessity of being "more narrowly drawn." During the thirty years since *Lovell*, the implications and ramifications of that revolutionary decision have grown steadily clearer to all involved in this phase of constitutional litigation.

a legitimate governmental purpose. *Talley* v. *California*, 362 U.S. 60. In that case the Court noted that it had been "urged that this ordinance is aimed at providing a way to identify those responsible for fraud, false advertising and libel. Yet the ordinance is in no manner so limited. . . . Therefore, we do not pass on the validity of an ordinance limited to prevent these or any other supposed evils. This ordinance simply bars all handbills under all circumstances anywhere that do not have the names and addresses printed on them in the place the ordinance requires." 362 U.S., at 64.

The *Button*[113] and *Cox*[114] decisions are especially instructive. The former has in it "something for everybody." For one thing, in a novel context the definitional approach to constitutional resolution is clear-cut in the majority opinion, while the dissent reflects continued adherence to ad hoc balancing. Having found the NAACP activities a protected form of "political expression," Mr. Justice Brennan for the majority went on to observe:[115]

> The objectionable quality of vagueness and overbreadth does not depend upon absence of fair notice to a criminally accused or upon unchanneled delegation of legislative powers, but upon the danger of tolerating, in the area of First Amendment freedoms, the existence of a penal statute susceptible of sweeping and improper application. Cf. *Marcus* v. *Search Warrant*, 367 U.S. 717, 733. These freedoms are delicate and vulnerable, as well as supremely precious in our society. . . . Because First Amendment freedoms need breathing space to survive, government may regulate in the area only with narrow specificity. *Cantwell* v. *Connecticut*, 310 U.S. 296, 311.

Mr. Justice White was forced to concur in part and dissent in part because:[116]

> If we had before us, which we do not, a narrowly drawn statute proscribing only the actual day-to-day management and dictation of the tactics, strategy and conduct of litigation by a lay entity such as the NAACP, the issue would be considerably different, at least for me; for in my opinion neither the practice of law by such an organization nor its management of the litigation of its members or others is constitutionally protected. . . .

---

113 N.A.A.C.P. v. Button, 371 U.S. 415 (1963).

114 Cox v. Louisiana, 379 U.S. 536 and 559 (1965).

115 371 U.S. at 432–33.   116 *Id.* at 447–48.

It is not at all clear to me, however, that the opinion of the majority would not also strike down such a narrowly drawn statute. To the extent that it would, I am in disagreement.

On the other hand the three dissenters, in an opinion by Mr. Justice Harlan, insisted that to[117]

declare that litigation is a form of conduct that may be associated with political expression does not resolve this case. Neither the First Amendment nor the Fourteenth constitutes an absolute bar to government regulation in the fields of free expression and association. . . . The problem in each such case is to weigh the legitimate interest of the State against the effect of the regulation on individual rights. . . .

So here, the question is whether the particular regulation of conduct concerning litigation has a reasonable relation to the furtherance of proper state interest, and whether that interest outweighs any foreseeable harm to the furtherance of protected freedoms.

In *Cox I* the Louisiana breach-of-peace statute went down because "unconstitutionally vague in its overly broad scope." But in *Cox II* the Louisiana statute modeled on 18 U.S.C. § 1507 itself passed muster:[118]

Here we deal not with the contempt power but with a narrowly drafted statute and not with speech in its pristine form but with conduct of a totally different character. Even assuming the applicability of a general clear and present danger test, it is one thing to conclude that the mere publication of a newspaper editorial or a telegram to a Secretary of Labor, however critical of a court, presents no clear and present danger to the administration of justice and quite another thing to conclude that crowds, such as this, demonstrating before a courthouse may not be prohibited by a legislative determination based on experience that such conduct inherently threatens the judicial process. We therefore reject the clear and present danger argument of appellant.

This language of Mr. Justice Goldberg cannot have been intended to reestablish the majority view in *Gitlow*. Yet it does reject the Holmes-Brandeis formulation of the danger test as fully and consistently applied in the contempt cases. What appears in evolutionary process is a reading of the test as requiring that legislation and equivalent forms of articulated governmental policy must, if they

---

[117] *Id.* at 453, 455.   [118] 379 U.S. at 566.

are to withstand constitutional scrutiny, bear such a close and immediate nexus to valid objectives beyond the reach of the First Amendment that there is no danger of jeopardy to the values protected by that amendment. This result is achieved by the Court's insistence that "the statute be narrowly drawn." The requirement is clearly more than one of relative narrowness, and certainly different in kind from the judicial requirement that policy formulation in the public sector satisfy the constitutional demand for reasonable certainty in meaning. It is a requirement that draftsmanship, whether by one or another branch of government, be such as to insure that the full scope of constitutional guarantees as demarcated by the Court is not weakened by laws so inclusively drawn that in administration they reach with civil or criminal sanctions territory determined to be off limits to government in the interest of individual civil liberty.

The two recent "burning" cases demonstrate the growing centrality in the Court's mind of the narrowness doctrine as thus understood. Concluding his sustainment in *United States v. O'Brien*[119] of the hotly disputed amendment of the Universal Military Service and Training Act, Chief Justice Warren for the Court found that[120]

> because of the Government's substantial interest in assuring the continuing availability of issued Selective Service certificates, because amended § 462(b) is an appropriately narrow means of protecting this interest and condemns only the independent noncommunicative impact of conduct within its reach, and because the noncommunicative impact of O'Brien's act of burning his registration certificate frustrated the Government's interest, a sufficient governmental interest has been shown to justify O'Brien's conviction.

Of the decision it has been said in the pages of this *Review:*[121]

---

[119] 391 U.S. 367 (1968).   [120] *Id.* at 382.

[121] Alfange, *Free Speech and Symbolic Conduct: The Draft-Card Burning Case,* 1968 SUPREME COURT REVIEW 1, at 18–19. Professor Alfange then continued with the assertion that "simply because overbroad statutes affecting speech are unconstitutional, it does not follow that narrow and specific statutes that limit speech only indirectly are valid as applied in all cases." *Id.* at 19. Later, *id.* at 21 n. 74, he demonstrated from both *Cox II* and *O'Brien* that the statutes there involved could be said to have overreached constitutional bounds. The footnote illustrations make clear, what is not clear in the text of the article, that Professor Alfange understands "narrowness" to be a word of art and not just a way of speaking comparatively with respect to the reach of various statutes.

The crucial factor in the Court's test is plainly the narrowness of the statute. If the statute is narrowly drawn, and is not on its face concerned with speech, courts are excused from the task of examining the degree of abridgment of expression that may be brought about by a particular application. In a sense, such a rule is the other side from the Court's repeated insistence that statutes having the effect of restricting speech in order to secure other social interests must not be vague or over-broad. "Because First Amendment freedoms need breathing space to survive," the Court has said [in *Button*, quoted earlier], "government may regulate in the area only with narrow specificity," and the constitutional requirement of narrowness has become the Court's most potent weapon in protecting freedom of expression against governmental incursion.

For the Court in *Street v. New York*,[122] Mr. Justice Harlan identified "four governmental interests" that inferentially he postulated to be constitutionally permissible objectives. The second of these was breach of the peace arising from physical retaliation against inflammatory words. Testing against this objective Street's conviction for flag burning under the New York statute, the majority could not[123]

> say that appellant's remarks were so inherently inflammatory as to come within that small class of "fighting words" which "are likely to provoke the average person to retaliation, and thereby cause a breach of the peace." *Chaplinsky* v. *New Hampshire*, 315 U.S. 568, 574 (1942). And even if appellant's words might be found within that category, § 1425, subd. 16, par. d, is not narrowly drawn to punish only words of that character, and there is no indication that it was so interpreted by the state courts. Hence, this case is again distinguishable from *Chaplinsky, supra,* in which the Court emphasized that the statute was "carefully drawn so as not unduly to impair liberty of expression. . . ."

Inasmuch as a "narrowly drawn" statute (or narrowly formulated common-law principle) is, in constitutional context, one so drawn (or formulated) as to foreclose attainment of impermissible objectives of government, it is but a different mode of expression to cast the functional concept into terms of close or immediate nexus. As earlier asserted, therefore, "there is considerable grounding in the decided cases" for the development of a new, and meaningful,

---

122 394 U.S. 576 (1969).   123 *Id.* at 592.

role for the "clear and present danger" test. The major "relic on the waters of the law," to adapt another Frankfurter phrase, is one of that Justice's own creation. This is his assertion in *Beauharnais*,[124] approvingly quoted by Mr. Justice Brennan in *Roth-Alberts*:[125]

> Libelous utterances, not being within the area of constitutionally protected speech, it is unnecessary, either for us or for the State courts, to consider the issues behind the phrase "clear and present danger." Certainly no one would contend that obscene speech, for example, may be punished only upon a showing of such circumstances. Libel, as we have seen, is in the same class.

Frankfurter may be excused for failing to anticipate *New York Times v. Sullivan*.[126] But the difficulty with the passage goes deeper. The assertion is correct only in terms of the Holmes-Brandeis formulation of the danger test. Under that formulation if the nature and circumstances of particular speech bring it under the First Amendment's protective mantle, the test applies. If not, then by definitional limitation the test has no relevancy to the constitutional question. Transformed into a requirement of immediate nexus for constitutionality, however, the danger test is always applicable where First Amendment rights are potentially in jeopardy. The only way to be certain that challenged governmental action will not invade protected freedoms is to ensure that it cannot, by subjecting it to the test of immediate nexus. Any less stringent requirement reduces pro tanto the certainty that that action, whatever its form, will not in its operation reach into areas that the Constitution has blocked off from intrusion by government. Thus reconceived, the test of "clear and present danger" has a vital role to play in future civil-liberty litigation.

Only the opinion, and not the result, would vary in such cases as *Roth*, *New York Times*, and *Brandenburg*. With *Roth*, reliance upon the *Beauharnais* assertion of the inapplicability of "clear and present danger" would have to be stricken, and the opinion rephrased to articulate the result as the consequence of the Court's satisfaction of the existence of a close nexus between the federal and state statutes as judicially construed and that obscenity which lies

---

124 Beauharnais v. Illinois, 343 U.S. 250, 266 (1952).

125 354 U.S. at 486–87.   126 376 U.S. 254 (1964).

beyond the protection of the First Amendment. In *Times*, the opinion would scarcely require alteration. Once the Alabama common law on libel was stated and the constitutional line drawn, it would be self-evident that no tight nexus could possibly be demonstrated between the applicable state law and a constitutionally permissible objective of the state. In *Brandenburg* it would be a matter of a short addendum to the opinion stating by way of summarization that the reach of the Ohio law, measured against the constitutional line separating the valid from the invalid, was such as to negate any close nexus between it and permissible objectives of government.

Significant as could be the role of "clear and present danger" in civil liberties litigation, there is an even greater place for the revamped danger test if Court orientation is to be one of neutral principle rather than preferred result. The point has been earlier made that the rational nexus test affords no protection whatever against governmental violation of constitutional rights, yet this is the controlling test long employed by the Court where the constitutional challenge is to governmental regulation in the economic sphere. *Carolene I*[127] is a classic illustration. *Collins*[128] is noteworthy as a case situation on the border line between the economic and the civil. Since *Nebbia v. New York*[129] installed as majority doctrine the classic dissent of Justice Holmes in *Lochner v. New York*,[130] American governments are essentially free to choose from among competing economic policies. "A constitution is not intended to embody a particular economic theory, whether of paternalism and the organic relation of the citizen to the State or of *laissez faire*."[131] Despite this fact, however, the Constitution of the United States has never been authoritatively interpreted as being devoid of constitutional protection for economic values. Decisions of Holmes and Brandeis in their time attest to this,[132] as do recent

---

[127] Note 82 *supra*.

[128] Note 91 *supra*.   [130] 198 U.S. 45, 74–76 (1905).

[129] 291 U.S. 502 (1934).   [131] *Id.* at 75.

[132] Pennsylvania Coal Co. v. Mahon, 260 U.S. 393 (1922) (Holmes and Brandeis dissenting); Louisville Joint Stock Land Bank v. Radford, 295 U.S. 555 (1935) (Brandeis); Thompson v. Consolidated Gas Utilities Corp., 300 U.S. 55 (1937) (Brandeis).

utterances of a current liberal Justice, Hugo Black.[133] The *Carolene* litigation is instructive on this score. Notwithstanding the ease with which the Court in *Carolene I* sustained the validity of the Filled Milk Act on demurrer to the indictment, the opinion in *Carolene II*[134] is careful to emphasize:[135]

> In the action of Congress on filled milk there is no prohibition of the shipment of an article of commerce merely because it competes with another such article which it resembles. Such would be the prohibition of the shipment of cotton or silk textiles to protect rayon or nylon or of anthracite to aid the consumption of bituminous coal or of cottonseed oil to aid the soybean industry.

Outright governmental product favoritism is constitutionally suspect despite *Powell v. Pennsylvania*.[136] *Carolene II*'s validation of the federal law on review of the conviction under the indictment is justified in terms of the concededly permissible objective of protection of the public from product misrepresentation:[137]

> Here a milk product, skimmed milk, from which a valuable element—butterfat—has been removed is artificially enriched with cheaper fats and vitamins so that it is indistinguishable in the eyes of the average purchaser from whole milk products. The result is that the compound is confused with and passed off as the whole milk product in spite of proper labeling.

So long as property interests enjoy some, although limited, constitutional protection, a strong nexus should be required between challenged governmental exertions and permissible objectives of government. It is a contradiction in terms for the Court to postulate the existence of areas of constitutional immunity while at the same time employing a rational nexus test, as was done in the *Carolene* cases. For the looseness of that test lays open to the government the indirect achievement of that which is directly

---

133 Bell v. Maryland, 378 U.S. 226, 318 (1964) (dissent); Amalgamated Food Employees Union Local v. Logan Valley Plaza, Inc., 391 U.S. 308, 327, 330 (1968) (dissent) ("I believe that, whether this Court likes it or not the Constitution recognizes and supports the concept of private ownership of property.") See also Adderley v. Florida, 385 U.S. 39 (1966).

134 Carolene Products Co. v. United States, 323 U.S. 18 (1944).

135 *Id*. at 31.

136 127 U.S. 678 (1888).   137 323 U.S. at 31.

denied to government. It is significant that the great majority of state supreme courts have never accepted, in interpreting their own constitutions, the Supreme Court's dichotomy. Rather, they have insisted upon demonstration of a substantial nexus regardless of the nature of the rights in litigation. A substantial nexus is one where there exists approximately as much evidence supporting, as disputing, connection between the challenged act of government and a permissible objective of government as determined by definitional balancing in constitutional interpretation. The usual state court approach has the merit of consistency, and the quality of the nexus required is a marked improvement over the mere demand for rationality.[138] Nevertheless, the substantial nexus test cannot guarantee that enclaves of constitutional immunity for the individual will not be invaded. From this it must be concluded that only the danger test as judicially redesigned can provide this assurance in optimum degree for all facets of constitutional litigation. If the first fifty years of "clear and present danger" prove to have brought this much of a contribution to the complexities of constitutional judicial review, the test's trials and tribulations of a half-century will have been worth the long period of gestation.

---

[138] Illustration may be found in STRONG, AMERICAN CONSTITUTIONAL LAW 688–96 (1950).

ROBERT A. BURT

MIRANDA AND TITLE II: A
MORGANATIC MARRIAGE

In *Katzenbach v. Morgan*,[1] the Supreme Court proclaimed that Congress had independent authority, to which courts would defer, to interpret the substantive provisions of the Fourteenth Amendment. Congress accepted the invitation at once. Several of the most important laws enacted during the Ninetieth Congress rest on the authority of *Morgan*. Title I (providing criminal sanctions for certain racially motivated private violence) and Title IV (fair housing) of the 1968 Civil Rights Act[2] used the newly revealed legislative power in ways clearly anticipated by the Court. Title II of the 1968 Omnibus Safe Streets and Crime Control Act[3] relied on *Morgan* in a way that Mr. Justice Harlan had foreseen in his dissent.[4] The congressional response to *Morgan* indicates its significant generative capacity. The readiness with which it was put to conflicting uses by the Ninetieth Congress suggests that the case warrants both close examination and some clarification. For the legislature in turn is generating litigation of no small constitutional significance.

Robert A. Burt is Associate Professor of Law, The University of Chicago.

[1] 384 U.S. 641 (1966).

[2] 82 Stat. 73 (1968). See S. Rep. No. 721, 90th Cong., 1st Sess. 6–7 (1967) (Title I); 114 *Cong. Rec.* 2273 (1968) (Title IV).

[3] 82 Stat. 197 (1968). See S. Rep. No. 1097, 90th Cong., 2d Sess. 53–63 (1968).

[4] 384 U.S. at 659, 665–71. He was joined in dissent by Mr. Justice Stewart.

I. Katzenbach v. Morgan and Its Lineage

Morgan was a declaratory action brought by New York voters joined by the state attorney general to challenge the constitutionality of § 4(e) of the Voting Rights Act of 1965.[5] Section 4(e) provided that no state could bar any person from voting solely on grounds of English illiteracy if that person could demonstrate that he had been educated in an American-flag school "in which the predominant classroom language was other than English." The sole practical effect of § 4(e) was to enfranchise Puerto Ricans living in New York[6] who had been barred from voting by that state's literacy requirement, enacted in its constitution in 1922[7]—two decades before any significant number of Puerto Ricans lived in the state.[8] The three-judge district court declared § 4(e) unconstitutional.[9] In an opinion by Mr. Justice Brennan, the Supreme Court

---

[5] 42 U.S.C. § 1973b(e) (Supp. IV, 1968).

[6] See 384 U.S. at 645 n. 3. "Our research indicates that it [the proposed § 4(e)] does not affect any other State [but New York]." 111 *Cong. Rec.* 16235 (1967) (Rep. Gilbert).

[7] Art. II, § 1, N.Y. Const.; New York Election Law §§ 150, 168.

[8] "[O]nly 7,700 people of Puerto Rican extraction lived in New York" in 1922. 111 *Cong. Rec.* at 11066. Following the Second World War, immigration from the island to the continental United States rose sharply. See Glazer & Moynihan, Beyond the Melting Pot 91-94 (1963). The 1960 Census showed 643,000 persons of Puerto Rican birth or parentage in New York State, of whom 613,000 lived in New York City. See Record, Morgan v. Katzenbach, p. 72; Glazer & Moynihan, *supra* at 94. Senator Kennedy, in the floor debate, stated that approximately 150,000 Puerto Ricans were registered voters in New York City. 111 *Cong. Rec.* at 11061. No one in Congress suggested any measure of the importance of the literacy test as a barrier to registration. Senator Javits said "[T]here has been considerable apathy about voting in this [Puerto Rican] community, and no figures are available on how many of these . . . [received] education in an American-flag school in Puerto Rico." 111 *Cong. Rec.* at 11066.

In 1969 it was estimated that Puerto Rican voter registration in New York City had risen to 250,000, an increase of 67 percent from Senator Kennedy's 1965 estimate. New York Times, Feb. 21, 1969, p. 46, col. 5; *id.*, May 11, 1969, p. 37, col. 1. According to a 1969 state survey, the city's Puerto Rican population had grown to 969,700. New York Times, June 8, 1969, p. 42, col. 3. Assuming that this population increase rose steadily from 1960, the city's Puerto Rican population would have grown by about 23 percent from 1965 to 1969. Thus it is possible that § 4(e) had a substantial impact in increasing voter registration, though perhaps only by stimulating greater organizational efforts to register Puerto Rican voters rather than by removing the literacy test, which in itself would have excluded the new registrants.

[9] 247 F. Supp. 196 (D.D.C. 1965). Judge McGowan dissented, on the ground that § 4(e) was an appropriate exercise of Congress' constitutional authority to make regulations for the territories.

reversed, reaching out to endorse a theory of congressional power to interpret § 1 of the Fourteenth Amendment that had been discussed as much in the brief congressional debates on § 4(e) as had the merits of the provision itself. The whole exercise thus had a self-consciously bookish quality, which heightened the doctrinal significance both Congress and the Court attached to it.

Though the Court endorsed the congressional theory, the terms of its endorsement are shrouded in ambiguity. It is unclear, for example, whether the Court deferred to the congressional judgment in § 4(e) or constructed a judgment of its own that it attributed to Congress. It is unclear whether the Court yielded to Congress even as much as a circumscribed and subordinated role in giving substance to the Equal Protection Clause. A cautious reading of the opinion could narrow it to traditional confines. But it is evident throughout *Morgan* that the Court is inviting a bolder reading and embracing an unaccustomed view of congressional relations with the Court in defining the substance of equal protection of the laws.

The boldness is evident at the outset of the opinion. The Court's characterization of the New York attorney general's argument, and its flat rejection of it, announced its intention to overturn the customary view of Court-Congress relationships in "enforcing" the Fourteenth Amendment. The Court stated:[10]

> The Attorney General of the State of New York argues that an exercise of congressional power under § 5 of the Fourteenth Amendment that prohibits the enforcement of a state law can only be sustained if the judicial branch determines that the state law is prohibited by the provisions of the Amendment that Congress sought to enforce. More specifically, he urges that § 4(e) cannot be sustained as appropriate legislation to enforce the Equal Protection Clause unless the judiciary decides—even with the guidance of a congressional judgment—that the application of the English literacy requirement prohibited by § 4(e) is forbidden by the Equal Protection Clause itself. We disagree. Neither the language nor history of § 5 supports such a construction.

The central premise here is that Congress has authority to define the substance of equal protection and that the courts will defer to a congressional judgment even if it is not persuaded that, acting independently, the court should have come to the same result. In effect, the Court is saying that—at least in some circumstances—

---

10 384 U.S. at 648.

where Congress and the Court disagree about the meaning of the Fourteenth Amendment, the Court will defer to Congress' version. The Court is suggesting that, to some extent at least, § 5 exempts the Fourteenth Amendment from the principle of Court-Congress relationships expressed by *Marbury v. Madison*,[11] that the judiciary is the final arbiter of the meaning of the Constitution.

To say that the framers of the Fourteenth Amendment intended this result—as the Court clearly claims—one must find some evidence that the framers addressed themselves explicitly or implicitly to the possibility of a Court-Congress disagreement about the meaning of § 1 of the Fourteenth Amendment. It is not surprising that, in common with many other interpretive problems that have emerged since 1866,[12] the debates in the Thirty-ninth Congress reveal very little consideration of this problem. What evidence there is favors the traditional position that the Court in *Morgan* pointedly rejected —that whenever disagreement appears, the Court will apply its own independent understanding and invalidate the contrary congressional judgment.

Section 5 provides: "Congress shall have power to enforce, by appropriate legislation, the provisions of this article." The language certainly does not exclude the reading urged by the New York attorney general. The "power to enforce" can be restricted simply to providing remedies—through assuring access to the courts, providing penal and civil sanctions, and commanding executive action. Clearly such power has broad substantive impact. To grant or withhold such remedies dictates the effective substance of the rights. In many matters—most notably, refusal of Congress to act—enforcement decisions may never reach the courts, but when those decisions do come before the courts their compatibility with the substance of the law can be a matter for independent judicial determination.

The Court's contrary reading is, of course, equally possible. The language of § 5 is simply fluid. Recognizing this, the Court puts primary reliance on the understanding of the framers of the Fourteenth Amendment and its early judicial interpretation. But examination of both historical sources cited by the Court and others suggests that the Court is not justified in relying on this history to support its view.

---

[11] 1 Cranch 137 (1803).

[12] See generally JAMES, THE FRAMING OF THE FOURTEENTH AMENDMENT 182–202 (1956).

The Court cites only one statement made in the Thirty-ninth Congress preceding passage of the amendment. That was a statement made in introductory remarks by Senator Howard of Michigan, who reported the amendment to the Senate from the Joint Committee on Reconstruction. Howard construed § 5 as a "direct affirmative delegation of power to Congress" and continued:[13]

> It casts upon Congress the responsibility of seeing to it, for the future, that all the sections of the amendment are carried out in good faith, and that no State infringes the rights of persons or property. I look upon this clause as indispensable for the reason that it thus imposes upon Congress this power and this duty. It enables Congress, in case the States shall enact laws in conflict with the principles of the amendment, to correct that legislation by a formal congressional enactment.

These remarks, read in the context of Howard's full speech, express a judgment that Congress will be the most important remedial agent in the enforcement of the Fourteenth Amendment, an eminently sensible proposition in view of the limited sanctions that the courts would be able to fashion for themselves in the absence of congressional action. But they do not readily connote an affirmative intent to exclude the judiciary from its ordinary dispositive role of interpreting the substance of the Constitution. Howard's statement that Congress can correct state legislation "in conflict with the principles of the amendment" need not mean that this congressional judgment would be final and unreviewable.

Strong contrary evidence that Howard expected the courts to predominate in determining the substance of § 1 is presented in an earlier portion of this same introductory speech. In describing § 1, Howard placed greatest importance on the Privileges and Immunities Clause, which he identified as drawn from Art. IV, § 2:[14]

> It would be a curious question to solve what are the privileges and immunities of citizens of each of the States in the several States. I do not propose to go at any length into that question at this time. It would be a somewhat barren discussion. But it is certain the clause was inserted in the Constitution for some good purpose. It has in view some results beneficial to the citizens of the several States, or it

---

[13] *Cong. Globe*, 39th Cong., 1st Sess. 2766, 2768 (1866) (hereafter cited as *Globe*), quoted 384 U.S. at 648–49 n. 8.

[14] *Id*. at 2765. (Emphasis added.)

> would not be found there; yet I am not aware that the
> Supreme Court have ever undertaken to define either the
> nature or extent of the privileges and immunities thus
> guarantied. . . . But we may gather some intimation of *what
> probably will be the opinion of the judiciary* by referring to
> a case adjudged many years ago in one of the circuit courts of
> the United States by Judge Washington. . . .

Howard then recited the passage, quoted numerous times by
others in the debates,[15] from Washington's opinion in *Corfield v.
Coryell*[16] enumerating personal rights that ranked among "the privileges and immunities." Howard thus clearly envisioned both that
the courts would be propounding further definitions of the "privileges and immunities of citizens" and that these future opinions
would be relevant to the future development of § 1 of the Fourteenth Amendment. His entire speech is clearly consistent with, if
it does not compel, the position that the Court rejected.

The relationship between the Civil Rights Act of 1866, enacted
over President Johnson's veto in April, and the virtually concurrent
consideration of the Fourteenth Amendment underscores the correctness of the New York attorney general's position. An important purpose of § 1 of the amendment was to remove doubts about
the constitutionality of the 1866 Civil Rights Act. That act provided that all citizens "shall have the same right . . . as is enjoyed by
white citizens" regarding enumerated civil rights and overrode "any
law, statute, ordinance, regulation, or custom, to the contrary."[17]
Congressional power to enact this legislation was claimed by its
proponents under § 2 of the Thirteenth Amendment, which provides, in language identical to § 5 of the Fourteenth Amendment,
"Congress shall have power to enforce this article by appropriate
legislation."

Representative Wilson of Iowa, chairman of the House Judiciary
Committee and floor manager of the 1866 act, gave a sweeping
interpretation to § 2:[18]

> Here, certainly, is an express delegation of power: How shall
> it be exercised? Who shall select the means through which

---

[15] See Harris, The Quest for Equality 41 (1960), Graham, Everyman's Constitution 307–11, 332–33 (1968).

[16] 6 Fed. Cas. No. 3230 (C.C. E.D. Pa.).

[17] 14 Stat. 27 (1866).   [18] *Globe* at 1118. (Emphasis added.)

the office of this power shall effect the end designed by the people when they placed this provision in the Constitution? . . .

Who will say that the means provided by this second section [of the act, providing penal and civil sanctions against anyone interfering with the civil rights denoted in the act's first section] are not appropriate for the enforcement of . . . the amendment abolishing slavery . . . ? The end is legitimate, because it is defined by the Constitution itself. *The end is the maintenance of freedom to the citizen.* . . . A man who enjoys the civil rights mentioned in this bill cannot be reduced to slavery. Anything which protects him in the possession of these rights insures him against reduction to slavery. This settles the appropriateness of this measure, and that settles its constitutionality.

Of the necessity of the measure Congress is the sole judge. . . .

If this bill shall pass both Houses and become a law, that fact of itself determines the question of necessity, and from this decision there is no appeal except to another Congress. This is the doctrine of the Constitution, as declared by the highest judicial tribunal known to our laws [citing *McCulloch v. Maryland*, 4 Wheat. 316 (1819)].

Wilson claims here not only broad authority to devise remedies to enforce the prohibition against slavery but apparently unreviewable discretion to define what the Thirteenth Amendment meant by "slavery" and "involuntary servitude." His argument runs this way. When the Thirteenth Amendment prohibited slavery, it did not simply negate a formal property relationship of one man to another. It also carried a guarantee of "freedom." The Congress that submitted the Thirteenth Amendment did not make this explicit and did not define the content of this "freedom," but subsequent Congresses can interpret the substance of the amendment and (here his argument stretches toward his conclusion) there is no appeal to the courts to review that congressional determination.

This is a stronger statement of the Court's thesis in *Morgan* than anything said regarding § 5 in the course of the debates on the Fourteenth Amendment—stronger not because of the breadth of congressional discretion claimed but because this claim is asserted in the context of a specific attempt to describe Court-Congress relationships.

Whatever the merits of Wilson's argument about the scope of § 2

of the Thirteenth Amendment,[19] it might appear tempting to transfer this understanding to the identical language of § 5, which was
considered in the same session of Congress. Professor tenBroek,[20]
a commentator relied on by the Court,[21] did just that. But this is a
mistake. It ignores the fact that, although the Supreme Court a
century later accepted Wilson's argument,[22] Representative John
Bingham of Ohio, the principal draftsman of § 1 of the Fourteenth
Amendment, at the time did not. Bingham viewed § 5 of that amendment as giving no independent interpretive authority to Congress,
and both in view of his central role in drafting § 1 and the context
in which that section was considered by the Thirty-ninth Congress,
it is most reasonable to consider this the "framers' intent."

Bingham, among those who were to support the Fourteenth
Amendment,[23] was particularly insistent that § 2 of the Thirteenth
Amendment did not authorize Congress to exercise the authority
claimed by proponents of the Civil Rights Act. Regarding § 1 of
the 1866 Civil Rights Act, he stated:[24]

> I say, with all my heart, that that should be the law of
> every State. . . . It is otherwise now . . . in many of the
> States. . . . I should remedy that not by an arbitrary as-
> sumption of power, but by amending the Constitution of the
> United States, prohibiting the States from any such abuse
> of power in the future.

Bingham displayed a clear recognition of the prerogatives of the
judiciary, both in general terms and in the context of § 2 of the
Thirteenth Amendment. In proposing an amendment to the proposed Civil Rights Act, which would reduce its coverage but not
resolve his constitutional doubts,[25] Bingham said:[26]

---

[19] See Note, *The "New" Thirteenth Amendment: A Preliminary Analysis,* 82
HARV. L. REV. 1294, 1295–1300 (1969), which suggests that Wilson was not accurately representing the understanding of the Thirty-eighth Congress.

[20] TENBROEK, THE ANTISLAVERY ORIGINS OF THE FOURTEENTH AMENDMENT 183–
86, 203, 219–20 (1951).

[21] 384 U.S. at 648 n. 7.

[22] Jones v. Alfred H. Mayer Co., 392 U.S. 409, 437–44 (1968). It is interesting
that Mr. Justice Stewart, who had joined Mr. Justice Harlan's dissent in *Morgan,*
wrote the Court's opinion in *Jones.* Mr. Justice Harlan, on the other hand, dissented
in both.

[23] See remarks of Shellabarger, *Globe* at 1293, and Raymond, *id.* at 2512–13.

[24] *Globe* at 1291.

[25] See Bickel, *The Original Understanding and the Segregation Decision,* 69 HARV.
L. REV. 1, 22–26 (1955).

[26] *Globe* at 1291.

> As I propose to take nothing for granted by favoring this amendment but to submit this proposition in the least objectionable form to the final decision of the Federal tribunals of the country, I beg leave to suggest to my honorable friend from Iowa, [Mr. Wilson] who knows me well enough to know that I make no captious objection to any legislation in favor of the rights of all before the law, if this bill be recommitted, the propriety of providing therein for a final appeal of all questions of law arising under it to the Supreme Court of the United States.

Bingham argued that § 2 of the Thirteenth Amendment essentially gave Congress nothing but power to devise remedies for guarantees whose substantive definition was committed for final determination to the courts. He voted against the 1866 bill in substantial part on the ground that it was unconstitutional. It is unlikely that Bingham would interpret the very same language in § 5 of the Fourteenth Amendment as conferring a broad, even unreviewable, discretion in Congress to determine the substance of § 1. Nor can it be assumed that the majority of the Congress that disagreed with Bingham's reading of the Thirteenth Amendment in enacting the Civil Rights Act also disagreed with his reading of the proposed § 5. The prime virtue of § 1 of the Fourteenth Amendment for many was that it explicitly authorized the Civil Rights Act and thus avoided the uncomfortable reading which had been given to § 2 of the Thirteenth Amendment.[27] Because of the great generality of the guarantees denoted in § 1 of the Fourteenth Amendment, as compared with the apparent specificity of the Thirteenth,[28] the need

---

[27] Following ratification of the Fourteenth Amendment, in deference to this uneasiness, the 1866 act was reenacted, in the Enforcement Act of 1870. 16 Stat. 140, 144 (1870).

[28] In opposing Senator Sumner's proposed substitute that the amendment should read, in part, "All persons are equal [or 'free'—there was some confusion when the Senate clerk read back the substitute] before the law, so that no person can hold another as a slave," Senator Howard said "I regard it as very immaterial whether the word 'free' or 'equal' is used in that connection. What I insist upon is this, that in a legal and technical sense that language is utterly insignificant and meaningless as a clause of the Constitution. I should like the Senator from Massachusetts, if he is able, to state what effect this would have in law in a court of justice. What significance is given to the phrase 'equal' or 'free' before the law in a common-law court? It is not known at all. . . .

". . . [T]he good old Anglo-Saxon language employed by our fathers in the ordinance of 1787 [repeated in the text of the Thirteenth Amendment as adopted], an expression which has been adjudicated upon repeatedly, . . . is perfectly well understood both by the public and by judicial tribunals. . . . I think it is well under-

for vesting broad substantive discretion in Congress did not appear necessary in order to accomplish any purpose to which the Fourteenth Amendment might be directed in the foreseeable future.[29]

In short, the choice presented to Congress in § 5 of the Fourteenth Amendment was between Bingham's restrictive reading and Wilson's permissive construction of § 2 of the Thirteenth Amendment. In the debate between them over the Civil Rights Act and the meaning of § 2 of the Thirteenth Amendment, Congress was vividly aware of the choices. Because of Bingham's dominant role in the formulation of § 1, it is plausible that in promulgating the Fourteenth Amendment, Congress was opting for the Bingham interpretation.

Other aspects of the legislative history of the Fourteenth Amendment support this conclusion. One important theme which ran through congressional debates on § 1 was that its substance was simply "declaratory" of existing constitutional law, that is, that nothing new in substance was added to the Constitution but that certain substantive provisions were now simply made binding on the states. Senator Howard stated this proposition in the remarks cited earlier. Representative Bingham stated this clearly both regarding the "first draft" of § 1 that the joint committee submitted to Congress in February, 1866,[30] and the "final draft" submitted in May.[31] As to the earlier draft, which gave Congress authority to legislate directly to "secure . . . all privileges and immunities of citizens . . . and . . . equal protection in the rights of life, liberty and property," Bingham stated:[32]

> Every word of the proposed amendment is to-day in the Constitution of our country, save the words conferring the express grant of power upon the Congress of the United

---

stood . . . by the people of the United States, and that no court of justice, no magistrate, no person, old or young, can misapprehend the meaning and effect of that clear, brief and comprehensive clause." *Cong. Globe,* 38th Cong., 1st Sess. 1488–89 (1864).

Sumner withdrew his substitute motion. *Id.* at 1489.

[29] See text *infra,* at notes 44–58.

[30] *Globe* at 1033–34.   [31] *Id.* at 2286.

[32] *Id.* at 1034. Bingham had been so eager to identify the substance of these guarantees with preexisting constitutional language that an earlier draft of § 1 he proposed in committee contained explicit parenthetical references to Art. IV, § 2, and the Fifth Amendment, in the text of the proposal. See FLACK, THE ADOPTION OF THE FOURTEENTH AMENDMENT 62–63 (1965 ed.).

States. The residue of the resolution, as the House will see
by a reference to the Constitution, is the language of the
second section of the fourth article, and of a portion
of the fifth amendment. . . .

Discussing the "final draft," Bingham repeated this theme:[33]

> [T]his amendment takes from no State any right that ever
> pertained to it. No State ever had the right, under the forms
> of law or otherwise, to deny to any freeman the equal
> protection of the laws or to abridge the privileges or im-
> munities of any citizen of the Republic, although many of
> them have assumed and exercised the power, and that without
> remedy.

The purpose of this characterization was not to fix the meaning of
the guarantees by reference to past case law. Senator Howard's specific envisioning of future substantive development made this clear.
The much-cited *Corfield v. Coryell* explicitly stated that its enumeration of privileges and immunities was not exhaustive. Rather,
the purpose appears to have been to offer assurances that the amendment was not revolutionary, that it had strong roots in constitutional tradition.[34]

The traditional cloak in which the proponents of § 1 draped its
substance would be inappropriate if they understood that the traditional role of the courts in defining existing constitutional guarantees
was to be displaced by an augmented congressional power in defining those same guarantees in the new amendment. Such a reading
might create a further problem. If the substance of the "old" and
the "new" guarantees were the same, but Congress had interpretive
authority regarding the "new," would that also augment Congress'
authority to interpret Art. IV, § 2, and the relevant portion of the
Fifth Amendment? Or would the substance of the "old" and the
"new" simply diverge after the amendment was adopted? If there
would be divergence, how could the proponents of § 1 argue that its
substance was identical to the "old" Constitution? But if Congress'
powers were augmented in interpreting both "old" and "new," it
would then be given authority to define the limitation on its own
powers, particularly under the Fifth Amendment, independent of
traditional judicial control.

No one in the congressional debates commented on these contradictions. That may be because—in common with other aspects of

---

[33] *Globe* at 2642.   [34] Bickel, note 25 *supra*, at 61–62.

the debate on the amendment—no one cared to make explicit that these contradictions existed. But it seems more plausible to explain silence on this matter as indicating a common understanding that the traditional notion of judicial supremacy in interpreting the substance of the Constitution was not meant to be displaced by § 5.

Five years later, Bingham repeated this "declaratory" view of § 1 in a Judiciary Committee report that he submitted to the House recommending that it reject a petition presented by a suffragette to enact legislation under § 5 proclaiming that state laws restricting the vote to men contravened the Fourteenth Amendment.[35] Bingham's argument was two-pronged. First, he argued, judicial opinions prior to the amendment's enactment had excluded suffrage from the "privileges and immunities" denoted by Art. IV and the Thirty-ninth Congress did not mean to alter this understanding.[36] Second, Congress had no "legislative power" to say "by a mere declaratory act, . . . that the construction claimed . . . is the true construction of the Constitution."[37] To buttress his second argument, Bingham stated: "If . . . as is claimed . . . the right to vote 'is vested by the Constitution in the citizens of the United States without regard to sex,' that right can be established in the courts without further legislation."[38] Though this second argument may be viewed as a mere tactic to dismiss a bothersome suitor, it would appear unlikely that Bingham in particular would so lightly have denigrated Congress' authority to impose its view of the substance of the Fourteenth Amendment on the judiciary, if that authority were really seen to rest in the amendment.

Finally, the crucial difference regarding the role of the judiciary should be noted in comparing the "first draft" of § 1 with the "final draft." The February draft provided:[39]

> ARTICLE——. The Congress shall have power to make all laws which shall be necessary and proper to secure to the citizens of each State all privileges and immunities of citizens in the several States, and to all persons in the several States equal protection in the rights of life, liberty, and property.

After some debate, the House voted to recommit this proposal.[40] Two distinct faults were found with it. The first, that it authorized

---

[35] *Victoria C. Woodhull*, H. Rep. No. 22, 41st Cong., 3d Sess. (1871).

[36] *Id.* at 1–3.   [38] *Ibid.*

[37] *Id.* at 4.   [39] *Globe* at 1033–34.   [40] *Id.* at 1095.

Congress to interfere too extensively with matters traditionally re-served to the states.[41] The second, that it failed to entrench the stated guarantees against a future unsympathetic majority in Congress.[42]

The May draft responded in particular to the second argument. It provided what now appears in § 1: "No state shall make or en-force any law which shall abridge the privileges or immunities of citizens of the United States . . . ," with § 5 providing enforcement powers in Congress. In order to overcome the difficulties identified by this second argument, this draft of the amendment virtually de-mands that the judiciary apply it, with whatever independent sanc-tions it can muster, irrespective of subsequent particularized en-forcement legislation (or substantive interpretations) proffered by future Congresses. Only in this way can Representative Garfield's ethereal purposes, revealed in debate on this provision, be realized:[43]

> [E]very gentleman knows [the Civil Rights bill] will cease to be a part of the law whenever the sad moment arrives when [the Democratic] party comes into power. It is pre-cisely for that reason that we propose to lift that great and good law above the reach of political strife, beyond the reach of the plots and machinations of any party, and fix it in the serene sky, in the eternal firmament of the Constitution.

Thus it is against future Congresses that the amendment must be protected. No one in these debates suggested that the amendment could not be trusted in the hands of the judiciary. However soon this belief was to appear, it was not voiced then. Again, silence seems the most reliable interpretive tool here. If the central role in protecting the amendment from future depredations is necessarily vested in the courts, and if that role was derived from an explicitly stated mistrust of future Congresses, where then does one find that the essence of the amendment was to enlarge the powers of Congress vis-à-vis the courts?[44]

---

[41] See remarks of Representative Rogers, *id.* at App. 133, Representative Hale, *id.* at 1063–66, Representative Davis, *id.* at 1083.

[42] Representative Hotchkiss stated this argument quite clearly. *Id.* at 1095.

[43] *Id.* at 2462.

[44] This is not to challenge the Court's conclusion in *Morgan* that the congression-al power to enact "all . . . necessary and proper" laws, conferred by the February draft, and the present § 5 language giving power to "enforce . . . by appropriate legislation" were equivalent formulations. 384 U.S. at 650, 650 n. 9. In 1871, debating the Ku Klux Klan Act, Bingham insisted the two formulations were identical. Representative Garfield replied that the form of the final version, as a direct limita-

The evidence cited to counter the Court's use of Senator Howard's remarks in *Morgan* is admittedly fragmentary. So far as has been revealed, no one in the debates proclaimed that the courts would have any authority to review congressional interpretations of the amendment. But the evidence to support the Court's position is even more fragmentary and less persuasive. When § 5 was described, by Howard and others, as enlarging congressional powers, the referent was always as against the states. The relationship between Congress and the courts in the "enforcement" of the Fourteenth Amendment was simply not directly considered in the Thirty-ninth Congress.

Nonetheless, in *Morgan* the Court ignored this silence or resolved its ambiguities by relying in part on the conclusion of several historical commentators that "the sponsors and supporters of the Amendment were primarily interested in augmenting the powers of Congress, rather than the judiciary."[45] Except that the support for this conclusion purports to rest on remarks such as Howard's, these commentators rely heavily on their belief that the dominant Republicans in the Thirty-ninth Congress had a deep-seated mistrust of the judiciary and that § 5 should thus be read as reflecting that mistrust. Professor Harris, in a passage to which the Court referred,[46] stated that the "Former Abolitionists" who ruled the Thirty-ninth Congress "had not forgiven the Court for its decision in the Dred Scott case."[47] Professor James, on whom the Court also relied,[48] said essentially the same thing:[49]

---

tion on states, limited congressional power to remedying "state action" in a manner that the earlier grant of direct legislative authority did not. But the absence of the "necessary and proper" language did not form the basis for Garfield's argument. *Cong. Globe*, 42d Cong., 1st Sess. App. 150–51 (1871). Given Bingham's general penchant for imprecise language, the identity of these two formulations for his purposes tells us nothing about the breadth of congressional discretion, as against the courts, in interpreting the substance of this amendment. It seems that in both versions of the section Bingham meant to preserve the traditional interpretive role of the courts. See text *supra*, at notes 30–34.

[45] 384 U.S. at 648 n. 7.

[46] *Ibid.*

[47] HARRIS, note 15 *supra*, at 54. Professor Harris also suggested: "The hostility of Radicals to the Court was intensified by Chief Justice Salmon P. Chase's refusal to hold circuit court in states under martial law, thereby preventing the trial of Jefferson Davis, and the fears that their reconstruction policies would be invalidated." *Ibid.*
But this overlooks both Chase's clear commitment to the antislavery cause before

It should be noted that decisions of courts had not normally favored abolitionists before the war. There was consequently little inclination to bestow new powers on the judiciary, but rather to lean on an augmented power of Congress, if it could be controlled.

But these assertions of the mood of the Thirty-ninth Congress are open to serious question.

In fact, in 1865 and 1866, there was every reason for the supporters of the Fourteenth Amendment to look confidently toward the judiciary. By that time, a majority of the Supreme Court—Chase, Davis, Field, Miller, and Swayne—had been appointed by President Lincoln and all "had played significant roles in antislavery politics and had loyally supported the war."[50] By 1866, Congress had reorganized the judicial circuits to end a major factor that had led to Southern dominance on the prewar Court—the fact that Justices were appointed from individual circuits and the circuits were so organized that the South had an assured majority of the Court.[51]

In a recent work, Professor Kutler offered a more persuasive view of the attitude of the sponsors of the Fourteenth Amendment to the judiciary:[52]

> The fact that Chase and some of the other Lincoln appointees proved disappointing to some Republicans after 1865 is immaterial here; *before* that disenchantment set in, it is clear that the Republicans respected the Court as an institution, recognized a place and function for it in the scheme of government, and seemed confident of the kind of role that it would play. When the Republican "ox" was gored—that is, when the optimism of 1864 was shattered by two decisions in [December] 1866 and 1867, many Republicans changed

---

his appointment and, more specifically, the contemporary role Chase was playing in privately circulating a draft of a proposed constitutional amendment promoting Negro suffrage and repudiating the confederate debt. JAMES, note 12 *supra*, at 118.

Chase's proposals were closely related to those favored by the Republican leadership in Congress on these issues, which were regarded a central elements in any Reconstruction program. Thus it is unlikely that Chase specifically was regarded with sudden mistrust by his previously outspoken Radical supporters in the Congress. See KUTLER, JUDICIAL POWER AND RECONSTRUCTION POLITICS 21–22 (1968).

48 The Court did not cite James directly, but instead referred to Franz, *Congressional Power to Enforce the Fourteenth Amendment against Private Acts*, 73 YALE L.J. 1353, 1356 and n. 18 (1964), which relies wholly on James and Harris.

49 JAMES, note 12 *supra*, at 184.   51 See *id.* at 48–63.

50 KUTLER, note 47 *supra*, at 90.   52 *Id.* at 26.

their tune. Then, admittedly, in some quarters it sounded like 1857 all over again; but surely there was no constant hostility, and there was no constant image of judicial disloyalty and inadequacy projected from 1857 through Reconstruction.

The Fourteenth Amendment, it should be noted, was submitted to the states in June, 1866.[53] In December, 1866, the Court published its opinions in *Ex parte Milligan*,[54] which first suggested to many in Congress that the Court intended to interfere extensively with Reconstruction legislation. A torrent of criticism erupted in the Thirty-ninth and Fortieth Congresses.[55] In 1868, the House passed a measure requiring two-thirds vote of the Court to invalidate any congressional act.[56] But nowhere in these debates did the Court's detractors, who had been the most active proponents of the Fourteenth Amendment, suggest that ratification of the amendment would bring, or was designed to bring, any measure of immunity from Court review of congressional reconstruction legislation, for which that amendment was intended to establish a basis.

Silence could of course have been merely tactical. Silence during the floor debates on the amendment, and in the Fortieth Congress while the amendment was pending before the states,[57] might have been calculated to mask a true, conspiratorial intent. But if there were such a conspiracy among the sponsors of the amendment, their success in keeping its existence from the majority of members of the Congress who voted for the amendment (or, if the entire Congress were implicated, its success in concealing this issue from the ratifying states) is surely a reason that the conspiracy should fail, that a court should refuse to read the cabal's intent into the amendment.

---

[53] *Globe* at 3149.   [54] 4 Wall. 2 (1866).

[55] 2 WARREN, THE SUPREME COURT IN UNITED STATES HISTORY 447–48 (rev. ed. 1937).

[56] *Cong. Globe*, 40th Cong. 2d Sess. 489 (1868). This measure was never brought to a vote in the Senate. See WARREN, *supra* at 471, KUTLER, n. 48 *supra*, at 74–77. Representative Bingham actively criticized the Court in these debates. In January, 1867, he suggested that Congress might find it necessary entirely to abolish the Court's appellate jurisdiction. *Cong. Globe*, 39th Cong., 2d Sess. 502 (1867). In 1868, he suggested that Congress might reduce the court to three members, thus necessarily insuring that no congressional act could be invalidated except by two-thirds vote of the Court. *Cong. Globe*, 40th Cong., 2d Sess. 483–84 (1868).

[57] The amendment was proclaimed in force on July 28, 1868. 15 Stat. 708–11 (1868).

The more plausible explanation for the silence in the Thirty-ninth Congress is that the supporters of the amendment were, in 1865 and 1866, not greatly concerned about the role that the judiciary would play in reviewing congressional legislation designed to implement § 1. They did not think it necessary to buttress congressional power under the Fourteenth Amendment against a hostile judiciary. They intended the Court to remain the final arbiter of the meaning of the Constitution.

In *Morgan* the Court also cited the early judicial construction of the Fourteenth Amendment to support its position. This evidence, too, is unpersuasive. In the initial cases construing the Fourteenth Amendment, disagreement appeared on the Court regarding the existence of judicial authority to strike down state acts in the absence of congressional legislation designating, if not specific state laws, at least the types of laws that came within the general prohibitions of § 1. But this dispute did not center on whether § 5 gave Congress a role independent of the judiciary in defining the substance of § 1. The Reconstruction Court appeared firmly agreed that the substance of § 1 was for the Court, and the Court alone, to determine. The controversy then concerned whether the rights conferred by §1, as defined by the judiciary, would remain wholly unenforceable—simply a "moral duty of the State"—without specific congressional remedial legislation.

Morgan referred to this controversy, but misconstrued it. The opinion quoted an excerpt from *Ex parte Virginia*:[58]

> It is the power of Congress which has been enlarged. Congress is authorized to *enforce* the prohibitions by appropriate legislation. Some legislation is contemplated to make the amendments fully effective.

But immediately preceding this cited language the following is to be found:[59]

> It is not said [in § 5] the *judicial power* of the general government shall extend to enforcing the prohibitions and to protecting the rights and immunities guaranteed. It is not said that branch of the government shall be authorized to declare void any action of a State in violation of the prohibitions.

---

[58] 100 U.S. 339, 345 (1880), quoted 284 U.S. at 648.

[59] 100 U.S. at 345.

At a later point in *Ex parte Virginia*, the Court continued: [60]

> Were it not for the fifth section of the amendment, there might be room for argument that the first section is only declaratory of the moral duty of the States. . . .

This same suggestion had appeared in a somewhat different guise in the *Slaughter-House Cases*,[61] the first in which the Supreme Court construed the Fourteenth Amendment. In discussing the scope of the Equal Protection Clause, and predicting that it was unlikely ever to be applied except to racial discrimination, Mr. Justice Miller said: [62]

> But as it is a State that is to be dealt with, and not alone the validity of its laws, we may safely leave that matter until Congress shall have exercised its power, or some case of State oppression, by denial of equal justice in its courts, shall have claimed a decision at our hands.

The Court here is suggesting that, by an unarticulated comity principle, Congress alone can administer the *coup de grâce* to state laws under the Fourteenth Amendment and that the Court is confined on its own authority to remedying violations by state judicial tribunals. This reading of the Fourteenth Amendment, like other Reconstruction Court interpretations of that amendment, is peculiarly inattentive to its legislative history and is disavowed by the four dissenters in the case, explicitly so by Justice Bradley.[63]

On the day of its unveiling, this bifurcated theory of enforcement was put to test and proved confusing, at the least. In *Bradwell v. Illinois*,[64] decided as a companion to the *Slaughter-House Cases*, the Illinois Supreme Court had refused bar admission to a woman applicant. A state statute vested discretion over admission in that court, but it construed the statute as intending to exclude women because the statute was silent on the question. In ruling that the Fourteenth Amendment was not violated, Justice Miller, again writing for the Court, spoke to the merits but simply failed to characterize the chal-

---

[60] *Id.* at 347.

[61] 16 Wall. 36 (1873).   [62] *Id.* at 81.

[63] "Very little, if any legislation on the part of Congress would be required to carry the amendment into effect. Like the prohibition against passing a law impairing the obligation of a contract, it would execute itself. The point would be regularly raised, in a suit at law, and settled by final reference to the Federal court." *Id.* at 123–24.

[64] 16 Wall. 130 (1873).

lenge as directed either to a state law or to "denial of equal justice in its courts."

In *Loan Association v. Topeka*,[65] the Court, without specific congressional legislation, held a state law invalid on its face, necessarily but not explicitly under the Fourteenth Amendment. There was impressive dicta anticipating this as a general result when the dissenters in the *Slaughter-House Cases* became spokesmen for a majority.[66] But when *Ex parte Virginia*[67] was decided, the point remained at least open to argument, and it was to this question that the proposition cited in *Morgan*—that § 5 enlarged legislative not judicial power—was directed.

In *Morgan* the Court also read *Strauder v. West Virginia*,[68] decided the same day as *Ex parte Virginia*, as giving support to its doctrine.[69] But that reading also appears strained. *Strauder* and its companion cases involved exclusion of Negroes from state juries. Strauder successfully sought removal of his criminal trial to the federal courts under legislation generally authorizing removal to protect "the equal civil rights of citizens of the United States."[70] West Virginia by law excluded Negroes from its juries. The Court relied on the language of the Fourteenth Amendment, the *Slaughter-House Cases*,[71] Blackstone,[72] and Bentham,[73] to establish that jury service was meant to be covered by the Fourteenth Amendment. Accordingly, the Court said, exclusion of Negroes violated equal civil rights, and the removal remedy was available.[74]

---

[65] 20 Wall. 655 (1875) (only Clifford, J., dissented).

[66] Writing for the Court in the Civil Rights Cases, 109 U.S. 3, 20 (1883), Justice Bradley stated: "This Amendment [the Thirteenth], as well as the Fourteenth, is undoubtedly self-executing without ancillary legislation. . . ."

[67] 100 U.S. 339 (1880).

[68] 100 U.S. 303 (1880).   [71] *Id.* at 306.

[69] 384 U.S. at 650–51.   [72] *Id.* at 308.

[70] 100 U.S. at 311.   [73] *Id.* at 309.

[74] In Virginia v. Rives, 100 U.S. 313 (1880), it was alleged that jury exclusion would be practiced by the state tribunals though no state law authorized this. The Court ruled that removal was not available under the statute in this circumstance, but suggested in dicta, *id.* at 332, that in the event such exclusion took place, a judicial remedy would be available even though not specifically authorized by Congress. Subsequently in Neal v. Delaware, 103 U.S. 370 (1881), this suggestion was

In *Ex parte Virginia*, a criminal prosecution had been brought against a state official who had allegedly excluded Negroes from a state jury. The Civil Rights Act of 1875 specifically provided criminal penalties for any state officer who excluded jurors on grounds of race. The Court cited *Strauder* for the proposition that such jury exclusion violated the Fourteenth Amendment,[75] and cited § 5 of the amendment to denote Congress' authority to punish the violation by penal sanction.[76] It is certainly possible to read the cases together for the proposition that the Court would not have found a violation of the Fourteenth Amendment in jury exclusions had Congress not specifically dealt with jury exclusions in the 1875 act. The argument runs that there is strong evidence from the Thirty-ninth Congress' debates on the amendment that jury service was not meant to be covered,[77] and that the Court in these cases relied heavily on the Forty-third Congress' interpretation of the amendment in the 1875 act.[78]

But if we are reading *Strauder* and its companions to discern the Reconstruction Court's attitude toward congressional power, it seems much more significant that the Court chose to structure its argument so as to denigrate—virtually to the vanishing point—any substantive role that might be ascribed to Congress. In *Strauder*, the Court cited every conceivable source for its reading of the Fourteenth Amendment but the 1875 act. Whatever the Court's hidden motive may have been, its presentation clearly indicates that it was elaborately careful to reassert its role—claimed earlier in the *Slaughter-Houses Cases*—as final arbiter of the substance of the amendment. That is what *Strauder* and its companions stand for, not the contrary proposition for which they are used in *Morgan* by the Court.[79]

---

put into effect. The bifurcated theory of enforcement under the amendment, suggested in the *Slaughter-House Cases*, can be seen as an operative assumption in these cases.

[75] 100 U.S. at 345.

[76] *Id.* at 347–48.

[77] See Bickel, note 25 *supra*, at 56, 64–65; Frank & Munro, *The Original Understanding of "Equal Protection of the Laws,"* 50 COLUM. L. REV. 131, 145 (1950).

[78] The Solicitor General's brief in *Morgan* set out this argument. Brief for the Appellants, pp. 37–39.

[79] See Mr. Justice Harlan dissenting, 384 U.S. at 666.

II. Congress as Liege to the Court

This review of the debates on the Fourteenth Amendment and its early judicial construction suggest that based solely on the "language [and] history" of § 5 New York was correct in arguing, as the Court paraphrased it, that congressional invalidation of a state law under § 5 "can only be sustained if the judicial branch determines that the State law is prohibited by the provisions of the Amendment that Congress sought to enforce."[80]

It has been observed, however, that the Court frequently seems to rely on assertedly "plain language" and equally plain "aboriginal history" when it wishes, for extrinsic but unarticulated reasons, to manipulate ambiguous language and cloudy history to reach a result that confounds contemporary understanding.[81] Those reasons must now be sought in the interstices of the *Morgan* opinion.

Morgan sustained § 4(e) on two different grounds. The first was this:[82]

> [Section] 4(e) may be viewed as a measure to secure for the Puerto Rican community residing in New York nondiscriminatory treatment by government—both in the imposition of voting qualifications and the provision or administration of governmental services, such as public schools, public housing and law enforcement.
>
> Section 4(e) may be readily seen as "plainly adapted" to furthering these aims of the Equal Protection Clause. The practical effect of § 4(e) is to prohibit New York from denying the right to vote to large segments of its Puerto Rican community. . . . This enhanced political power will be helpful in gaining nondiscriminatory treatment in public services for the entire Puerto Rican community. Section 4(e) thereby enables the Puerto Rican minority better to obtain "perfect equality of civil rights and equal protection of the laws."

Seen in this way, § 4(e) expresses no legislative variant of the Equal Protection Clause. The provision is instead a remedy, perhaps simply prophylactic, to achieve ends clearly within judicial construction of the clause—"nondiscriminatory treatment in public

---

[80] 384 U.S. at 648.

[81] See Kelly, *Clio and the Court: An Illicit Love Affair*, 1965 Supreme Court Review 119; see also Casper, *Jones v. Mayer: Clio, Bemused and Confused Muse*, 1968 Supreme Court Review 89.

[82] 384 U.S. at 652–53.

services." Mr. Justice Harlan, in his dissent, objected that "[t]here is simply no legislative record supporting such hypothesized discrimination of the sort we have hitherto insisted upon when congressional power is brought to bear on constitutionality reserved state concerns."[83] But it is not inappropriate for the Court to sustain legislation on the premise that Congress based its judgments on facts outside the legislative record.[84] To insist, as a precondition for sustaining § 4(e), that the legislative record contain facts to support the judgment that future discrimination may result from voting exclusion is an artificial requirement. However hospitable the State or City of New York may have been in the past to its partially disenfranchised Puerto Rican minority, surely it is not unreasonable to fear that future discrimination may occur, particularly in a national climate of increasing hostility among racial and ethnic groups. On this issue, it is impossible to imagine that the Court would ever be willing to assert that Congress could not have concluded rationally that danger of future discrimination existed and that increasing the voting population among the threatened minority would be a useful protective device. To require ritual incantation of "facts" that would "prove" future danger seems unnecessary.

The absence of any legislative record suggesting past or future discrimination might indicate, however, that Congress never intended to make the judgment that the Court ascribes to it. A fair reading of the floor debates, particularly in the Senate where § 4(e) received its only extended consideration,[85] does suggest that this remedial view of the provision was not relied on by its proponents or considered by its opponents. But using this silence as a grounds for refusing to view § 4(e) as a remedy seems inappropriate. There are many reasons—unwillingness to rile local officials or to provoke perhaps exaggerated concern in minority or majority groups—that members of Congress might choose not to charge state or local authorities with discriminatory conduct, and even stronger reasons that one elected official would choose not to charge that other offi-

---

[83] Id. at 669.

[84] See Katzenbach v. McClung, 379 U.S. 294, 301, 304–05 (1964); Dennis v. United States, 341 U.S. 494, 547–48, 562–66 (1951). Cf. Cox, Constitutional Adjudication and the Protection of Human Rights, 80 HARV. L. REV. 91, 105 (1966).

[85] The provision was introduced as a floor amendment and was debated under a one-hour time limitation. There had been no hearings on it. 111 Cong. Rec. 11027–28, 11060–74, and 28368 (1965).

cials will engage in future discrimination, though he cannot conclusively document such past actions. Thus Congress' failure to articulate a remedial motive should not be given undue weight. That it might have had such motive is quite plausible.

To uphold § 4(e) on this ground would be to reaffirm the Court's rationale earlier in the Term in *South Carolina v. Katzenbach*.[86] In that case, sustaining the provisions of the Voting Rights Act primarily designed to suspend literacy tests in southern states, the legislative record was much more substantial and persuasive than in *Morgan* that remedial action was needed to extirpate past discrimination and to prevent future discrimination. But under the logic of the *South Carolina* opinion, giving broad remedial discretion to Congress under the enforcing section of the Fifteenth Amendment, which is identical to § 5 of the Fourteenth, extension of the doctrine to uphold § 4(e) would be quite natural and, indeed, would indicate why the *South Carolina* case may properly be regarded as "germinal."[87]

But the Court was not content to rest its validation of § 4(e) on this ground. It put forward another, independent ground, and it was here that the Court set out the constitutional theory that followed from its disagreement with New York:[88]

> The result is no different if we confine our inquiry to the question whether § 4(e) was merely legislation aimed at the elimination of an invidious discrimination in establishing voter qualifications. We are told that New York's English literacy requirement originated in the desire to provide an incentive for non-English speaking immigrants to learn the English language and in order to assure the intelligent exercise of the franchise. Yet Congress might well have questioned, in light of the many exemptions provided [primarily a "grandfather clause" exempting previously registered voters], and some evidence suggesting that prejudice played a prominent role in the enactment of the requirement, whether these were actually the interests being served. Congress might also have questioned whether denial of a right deemed so precious and fundamental in our society was a necessary or appropriate means of encouraging persons to learn English, or of fur-

---

[86] 383 U.S. 301 (1966).

[87] Cox, *Constitutional Adjudication and the Promotion of Human Rights*, 80 HARV. L. REV. 91, 102 (1966).

[88] 384 U.S. at 653–56.

thering the goal of an intelligent exercise of the franchise. Finally, Congress might well have concluded that as a means of furthering the intelligent exercise of the franchise, an ability to read or understand Spanish is as effective as ability to read English for those to whom Spanish-language news-papers and Spanish-language radio and television programs are available to inform them of election issues and govern-mental affairs. Since Congress undertook to legislate so as to preclude the enforcement of the state law, and did so in the context of a general appraisal of literacy requirements for voting, see *South Carolina v. Katzenbach* . . . , to which it brought a specially informed legislative competence, it was Congress' prerogative to weigh these competing con-siderations. . . . [I]t is enough that we perceive a basis upon which Congress might predicate a judgment that the appli-cation of New York's English literacy requirement to deny the right to vote to a person with a sixth grade education in Puerto Rican schools in which the language of instruction was other than English constituted an invidious discrimination in violation of the Equal Protection Clause.

It is not inconceivable that a majority of the Court, in the absence of any congressional legislation, could have independently con-cluded that New York's literacy requirement for voting denied equal protection to foreign-literate citizens. Two members of the *Morgan* Court, Justices Douglas and Fortas, indicated in a com-panion case, *Cardona v. Power*,[89] that they were prepared to reach this result independently. But five members of the Court[90] must be considered to have affirmed a contrary proposition in *Morgan*—that the Court, acting independently, was reluctant to reach this result under the Equal Protection Clause but was eager to defer to a contrary congressional judgment construing the clause. The Court insisted on this interpretation, first, by its stark characterization of its disagreement with the constitutional theory put forward by New York and, second, by reaching out to assert this additional independent ground for affirmance when it could easily have rested on the ground first stated. The Court was not purporting to defer to Congress from politeness. It clearly meant to assert a new consti-tutional theory of Court-Congress relationships under the Four-teenth Amendment.

---

[89] 384 U.S. 672, 675 (1966).

[90] Mr. Justice Brennan, joined by Chief Justice Warren and Justices Black, Clark, and White.

As has been stated, the Court's explicit historical justification for propounding a new theory is unpersuasive. But the weakness of the historical support cannot conclude the argument. *Morgan* can be premised not simply on the Fourteenth Amendment as its framers understood it but also on a century's experience in the application of it. Section 1 of the amendment was clearly designed for organic growth by the generality of its commands. The institutional processes by which that growth takes place might similarly admit development in light of changed circumstances, for good cause shown. Regrettably, the Court, by relying on a reconstructed history, did not show good cause. But if a more persuasive justification for this doctrinal development is to be found within the corners of the opinions, it must be sought in the paragraph from the *Morgan* opinion quoted above.[91]

Some commentators have found the Court's rationale there to indicate a willingness to defer to Congress' judgment where Congress has greater capacity than the Court to "gather and evaluate facts."[92] The paragraph does support this interpretation. It contains a litany of disputed factual issues which, at various times, the Court has indicated reluctance to determine and rely on as bases for invalidating a state law: whether the legislature had an invidious motive in adopting a measure that could be construed as nondiscriminatory on its face,[93] whether different means to pursue a legitimate legislative purpose should have been chosen,[94] whether the legislature was correct in thinking that it should have been pursuing this clearly legitimate purpose.[95]

The argument that this was the Court's rationale would appear strengthened by its reference to Congress' "specially informed legislative competence" in appraising voting requirements. This competence could be seen to arise both from contemporary congressional investigation of the uses of voting literacy tests generally and from

---

[91] See text *supra*, at note 88.

[92] Cox, note 87 *supra*, at 107. See also S. Rep. No. 1097, 90th Cong., 2d Sess. 55, 60–61 (1968), discussed in the text *infra*, at notes 156–63.

[93] See Gomillion v. Lightfoot, 364 U.S. 339 (1960).

[94] *Cf.* Shelton v. Tucker, 364 U.S. 479 (1960); United States v. Robel, 389 U.S. 258 (1968).

[95] *Cf.* Southern Pac. Co. v. Arizona, 325 U.S. 761 (1945); Bibb v. Navajo Freight Lines, 359 U.S. 520 (1959).

the unique experience legislators secured in their own perennial attempts to inform voters of their own merits. In support of this proposition, the Court cited the "testimony" offered during the floor debates by Senators Long of Louisiana, Young of Ohio, and Holland of Florida, "drawing on their [affirmative] experience with voters literate in a language other than English."[96] Thus the Court may well have intended to rely on Congress' purported fact-finding capacity to justify its deferential posture.

Unless more can be shown, however, this rationale is unpersuasive. Accepting the premise that the kinds of disputed factual issues noted by the Court are best resolved by legislative rather than judicial tribunals, it need not follow that the national legislature is better fit to resolve those issues than a state legislature. All that can be asserted with confidence is that, on many issues, the national legislature is likely to differ from a state legislature in its perception and evaluation of facts.

It might be argued that the superiority of congressional judgment has itself become an operative assumption of the constitutional scheme because of the current vast reach of Congress' commerce, taxing, spending, and other constitutional powers over every facet of national life. And that may indeed be the whole of the Court's implicit argument. But before joining the Court in that leap of faith, it would be useful to test the proposition that Congress' resolution of disputed facts on a given subject matter is more likely to be consonant with the "fundamental national values" than a state resolution, that where states and Congress differ, Congress is likely to have considered factors that the states improperly failed to weigh.

The subject matter of *Morgan* itself suggests the weakness of this proposition. In deciding that certain citizens literate in Spanish should not, on literacy grounds alone, be barred from voting, Congress' judgment must be considered restricted, first, by a parochial vision leading it to give insufficient weight to the different, quite legitimate perspective of the state legislature, and, second, by a a narrow partisanship that led it to act for political advantage at the

---

[96] 384 U.S. at 656 n. 17. The Court also cited an affidavit in the record "from Representative Willis of Louisiana expressing the view that on the basis of his thirty years' personal experience in politics he has 'formed a definite opinion that French-speaking voters who are illiterate in English generally have as clear a grasp of the issues and an understanding of the candidates, as do people who read and write the English language.' " *Ibid.*

expense of contrary party interests of the dominant groups in the
state legislature.

First, the Court's reliance on senatorial experience with "well-
informed" foreign language voters overlooked the important differences between mass media and voter interest in national candidates and state and local candidates. It is likely to be more difficult
for a candidate to the state senate to obtain coverage by the mass
media, whether the language be English or Spanish, than a candidate
for the United States Senate. And there are thus likely to be peculiar
burdens—both in diminished voter receptivity and in added expense
that local candidates cannot so easily bear—that fall on an English-
speaking local candidate trying to reach a Spanish-speaking group
within his electoral district. Legislators with perspectives shaped by
national political experience may well lack sensitivity to such local
concerns. New York's legitimate interest in assuring that state and
local candidates have equal chances of communicating with all their
constituency, and thus be able to counteract mindless bloc or ethnic
group politics, is for this quite prosaic reason in danger of not receiving a fully sympathetic hearing from the national legislature.[97]

Second, in reviewing state-imposed voter qualifications, the Congress stands preeminently as a judge in its own cause. Section 4(e)
did not simply alter state-imposed voting qualifications. It changed
Congress' own voting constituency. Section 4(e) was regarded in
Congress as addressed exclusively to New York State, and was
designed particularly to enlarge the Puerto Rican voting popula-

---

[97] Because New York has been the center of mainland migration for Puerto
Ricans in the past twenty-five years, national representatives of other states also
may not be expected to appreciate the unique problems that New York has confronted in breaking through the Spanish-language barrier to provide services to,
and generally to foster some degree of assimilation into the external community by,
Puerto Ricans. In 1960, the New York City Board of Education reported that some
56,000 elementary school children (of a total city-wide enrollment of 558,000) were
"of Puerto Rican ancestry whose lack of ability to speak or understand English
represented a considerable handicap to learning." Citing this report, Glazer and
Moynihan note that the "shift to a new language has been particularly difficult for
the Puerto Ricans." Note 8 *supra*, at 127. They point to many difficulties this language issue presented for local officials and note the strong resistance generally
within the Puerto Rican community willingly "to relegate the immigrant tongue to
a minority position." *Id.* at 101. Precisely because the franchise is regarded as a
fundamental instrument for any group seeking political power, the voting literacy
requirement could serve as a powerful ally in any state effort to enlist the leaders
of the Puerto Rican community in campaigns to increase English language facility
within that community generally.

tion in New York City.[98] Its principal Senate proponents were
Senators Robert Kennedy and Jacob Javits of New York, both
of whom—particularly Kennedy—had substantial political interest
in enlarging the liberal-minded voting population in New York City
and thus diminishing the importance of the upstate conservative
voters in statewide elections. Senator Javits noted, in the floor debates, that the Democrats were most assured to gain from increased
Puerto Rican voting rolls because of the traditionally heavy support that Democratic candidates had received from bloc voting
among Puerto Ricans.[99]

The competing partisan interests swirling about the congressional
deliberation on § 4(e) were most graphically demonstrated in the
House, where its most vociferous opponents were upstate Republican congressmen.[100] The provision was offered as an amendment to
the Voting Rights Act and defeated in the House.[101] But Representative Celler, Democrat of New York City, floor manager of the
bill, supported adoption of § 4(e), and he was chairman of the House
conferees on the bill. Not surprisingly, the House conferees accepted § 4(e) as passed by the Senate. When the conference report
was returned to the House, it could then only approve or disapprove
the entire Voting Rights Act as a package.[102]

This is not a tale of corruption. The simple mathematics of constituency voting dictates that national legislators—particularly senators—often must have a political perspective radically different
from those legislators who dominate state legislatures. From the
perspective of the leaders of the New York legislature, no matter
how many Puerto Ricans, living in any particular New York City
legislative district, vote for the Democratic candidate, that district

---

[98] See note 6 *supra*.   [99] 111 *Cong. Rec.* 11066.

[100] Representative Fino of New York was particularly acid in his criticism, stating
that the provision "represents legal irrelevancy and political opportunism." 111
Cong. Rec. 19196. Representative McCulloch, ranking Republican on the House
Judiciary Committee opposed the provision, stating, "The motive of some people,
Mr. Speaker, is purely political." *Id.* at 19194. See also the editorial in the New York
Times, July 30, 1965, describing § 4(e) as "a pure concession to political dema-
goguery."

[101] The vote was 202 to 216. 111 *Cong. Rec.* 16282.

[102] In debating the conference report Representative Fino repeated his denunci-
ation of § 4(e) and announced that he would vote against adoption of the report
to defeat this section. 111 *Cong. Rec.* 19196–97. The House agreed to the report, by
a vote of 328 to 74. *Id.* at 19201.

will still have only one Democratic representative. But for the United States senator from New York, it matters intensely how many Puerto Ricans in that district are qualified to vote. If he can assume that 80 percent of all who vote in that district will vote for him, enlarging the voter population there will give him added strength in prevailing against the upstate and suburban conservative voters. He cannot afford to disregard the peculiar interests of the Puerto Ricans in his constituency, as the New York legislature can.

The need to secure concurrence of a majority in both houses of Congress introduces no significant counterweight to these pressures in the consideration of § 4(e). Because the legislation was drawn only to affect New York, the congressional allies of the New York senators were willing to defer to their interests,[103] and many senators were delighted to see a provision included in the Voting Rights Act that was directed at a northern state.[104] The tactic to avoid the adverse House vote on § 4(e) is a common ploy.[105]

Section 4(e) is not an isolated legislative event. The "liberal" coalition that coalesced around it, to override a contrary state legislative judgment, is precisely the group that is more substantially represented in the Senate than in most state legislatures—precisely because, unlike state legislatures, each senator is elected by statewide constituencies that in most states tends to give greater weight to single-minded interest groups in urban areas.[106] Because their constituencies differ fundamentally, and the interests to which they are most responsive thus also differ, the Senate and, though to a lesser extent, the House are likely to "perceive and evaluate facts" from a perspective quite different from the dominant forces in most

---

103 A practiced view of the matter was offered by Representative Dowdy of Texas, commenting on proposed § 4(e): "[T]his bill is a local bill, and should be considered as such.

"If the delegation from New York considers the State legislature of New York is incompetent to legislate on this matter, and if they want the Members of Congress from New York to do so, our New York colleagues ought to get together and write the bill the way they think it ought to be, as applicable only to New York. That is the way local bills are written, and is the way they should be written." 111 Cong. Rec. 16245.

104 See remarks of Senators Long of Louisiana, 111 Cong. Rec. 11061, and Holland of Florida, id. at 11064, supporting the provision.

105 See generally FROMAN, THE CONGRESSIONAL PROCESS: STRATEGIES, RULES AND PROCEDURES 141–68 (1967).

106 See FROMAN, CONGRESSMEN AND THEIR CONSTITUENCIES 80–84 (1963).

state legislatures. I see no self-evident reason that the courts, in these circumstances, should ascribe any greater objective fact-finding capacity to Congress than to state legislatures.[107]

There is a different, much firmer, rationale for *Morgan*. The Court did not directly articulate it, but it can be seen implicitly operative not only in that case itself but in several cases that immediately preceded *Morgan* dealing with discrimination against Negroes. Mr. Justice Black, dissenting in *Bell v. Maryland*,[108] sounded a cautious opening note for the *Morgan* doctrine. Joined by Justices White and Harlan, Mr. Justice Black denied that "Section 1 of the Fourteenth Amendment, standing alone," prohibited private restaurants from excluding patrons on racial grounds. But he explicitly expressed "no views" regarding the power of Congress "acting under one or another provision of the Constitution" to legislate this end.[109] Mr. Justice Black again brought the *Morgan* proposition forward in his dissent in *Harper v. Virginia Board of Elections*.[110] Though *Harper* was decided a month before argument in *Morgan*, Mr. Justice Black's dissent clearly appears written in anticipation of it. In denying that the Court could properly apply § 1 of the Fourteenth Amendment to proscribe the use of the poll tax as a voting prerequisite, he wrote: "I have no doubt at all that Congress has the power under § 5 to pass legislation to abolish the poll tax in order to protect the citizens of this country if it believes that the poll tax is being used as a device to deny voters equal protection of the laws."[111]

---

[107] Professor Wechsler gave insufficient weight to the critical role of the differing constituencies within the same state to which national and state legislators are responsible, when he asserted without qualification that "the Court is on weakest ground when it opposes its interpretation of the Constitution to that of Congress in the interest of the states, whose representatives control the legislative process and, by hypothesis, have broadly acquiesced in sanctioning the challenged Act of Congress." Wechsler, *The Political Safeguards of Federalism*, 54 COLUM. L. REV. 543, 559 (1954). Senator Sam Ervin raised a similar objection to Wechsler's proposition in an interesting exchange with Professor Paul Mishkin. *Hearings on the Supreme Court before the Subcommittee on Separation of Powers, Senate Committee on the Judiciary*, 90th Cong., 2d Sess. 198–99 (1968).

[108] 378 U.S. 226, 318 (1964).

[109] *Id.* at 343.   [110] 383 U.S. 663, 670 (1966).

[111] *Id.* at 679. Premised on a theory similar to that which underlay enactment of § 4(e), the House had proscribed imposition of a poll tax as a voting prerequisite as a means of "enforcing" the substance of both the Fourteenth and the Fifteenth

In *United States v. Guest*,[112] decided four days after *Harper*, Mr. Justice Brennan developed the point in the context in which Mr. Justice Black had first advanced it—reaching private discrimination under the Fourteenth Amendment. Fully rehearsing the arguments to be presented later in *Morgan*, including an appeal to the same historical sources,[113] Mr. Justice Brennan stated that Congress could proscribe private discriminatory acts under § 5, even if the courts could not do so independently. A contrary reading of § 5, he said, "reduces the legislative power to enforce the provisions of the Amendment to that of the judicary; and it attributes a far too limited objective to the Amendment's sponsors."[114]

In the immediate context of *Guest*—imposition of criminal sanctions—the judiciary is of course powerless to act without legislation. But the *Morgan* doctrine has important relevance to the broader question that the majority addressed in its *Guest* opinion—the power of Congress to forbid private acts of discrimination under the Fourteenth Amendment. The Court had itself been seeking a means to devise remedies for private discriminatory acts since *Shelley v.*

Amendments. The final version of this provision, however, simply expressed a congressional finding that poll taxes abridged "the constitutional right of citizens" because they imposed "unreasonable financial hardship," had no "reasonable relationship to any legitimate State interest in the conduct of elections," and "in some areas [have] the purpose or effect of denying persons the right to vote because of race or color." § 10(a), Voting Rights Act of 1965. But, after making this "finding," Congress went no further than to direct the Attorney General "forthwith" to test the constitutionality of poll taxes in the courts. § 10(b).

It may be that the conferees who favored abrogation of the poll tax agreed to deletion of the House version of § 10 because they were uncertain that the Court would sustain the novel constitutional theory underlying it and § 4(e). See the remarks of Representative McCulloch, 111 *Cong. Rec.* 19194. They might have been unwilling to risk judicial rejection of a congressional enactment voiding the poll tax, while they were willing to risk a test of the constitutional theory in the nationally less sensitive context of Puerto Rican voting rights. If the theory passes muster there, it would be available for later use against the poll tax.

The Justice Department's unwillingness to press Congress to apply its § 4(e) theory to the poll tax issue has been explained by Professor Cox, who was solicitor general during congressional consideration of the act, as "reluctance to add to the constitutional hurdles" in defending the act generally, and concern about "the injustices and confusion that would result if citizens failed to pay their poll taxes in reliance upon a federal enactment" later held invalid by the courts. Cox, note 87 *supra*, at 96 n. 37.

The litigation in *Harper* had been instituted before enactment of the Voting Rights Act and, in holding the poll tax unconstitutional, the Court's opinion by Mr. Justice Douglas did not refer to the congressional finding in § 10.

[112] 383 U.S. 745 (1966).   [113] *Id.* at 783 n. 7.   [114] *Id.* at 783.

Kraemer.[115] But difficulties derived from the fact that the Court could not independently proscribe some private discrimination without its proclaimed principle expanding to proscribe all discrimination. As Mr. Justice Black stated in his *Bell* dissent, embracing such a principle would wholly sacrifice the competing values involved in "a storekeeper's right to choose his customers or . . . a property owner's right to choose his social or business associates."[116]

But clearly Congress is less burdened by the principled constraints under which courts labor. Congress, using no principle but fiat by majority vote, could act, for example, to permit Mrs. Murphy to turn away black lodgers so long as she lived with her other lodgers in a house that could accommodate no more than four families.[117] Congress could easily conclude that in Mrs. Murphy's case, but not in others closely analogous, the values involved in free choice of companions should predominate. The Court would have much greater difficulty independently constructing an exemption for Mrs. Murphy, no matter how important some such exemption might be, in order to mediate the clashing principles and political pressures at stake. The Mrs. Murphys of the country are more likely to find spokesmen in the legislature than in the courts, and the Murphy voices or silences can be noted by the legislature, which then is able to make a reliable decision about where it might be politic to temper the application of proscription against private discrimination.[118] In this context—devising appropriate adjustment of directly conflicting principles—the legislative mechanism is greatly superior to the courts.

The thorny issue whether, or to what extent, *Brown v. Board of Education*[119] forbids "beneficent" racial discrimination similarly may not successfully yield to judicial line-drawing. Congress can, however, examine the problem context by context and need give no precedential effect to its decisions from one to the next. It can consider whether publicly funded black studies programs, limited

---

[115] 334 U.S. 1 (1948).   [116] 378 U.S. at 343.

[117] 42 U.S.C. § 3603 (b) (2) (Supp. IV, 1968).

[118] The Court had surprising difficulty, however, in finding a way to defer to this congressional judgment when it construed the 1866 Civil Rights Act to ban all private discrimination in the sale or rental of housing. Jones v. Mayer, 392 U.S. 409 (1968). See Casper, note 81 *supra*, at 129–32.

[119] 347 U.S. 483 (1954).

to blacks, should exist in public universities—and then wait to see what impact that decision will have. It can examine "beneficent" residential housing quotas, supported by public funds or enforced by zoning practices, and decide whether they are indeed beneficent, without then having to explain why it might reach a contrary decision regarding the beneficence of separate black studies in university education. Unlike at least the lower federal courts, Congress has no institutional obligation to explain why it withholds relief from any applicant who presents a claim.[120]

Morgan presented a similar problem for the Court. As Professor Cox has observed, for the Court independently to hold—as Mr. Justice Douglas argued in *Cardona*—that English literacy cannot be a prerequisite to voting would suggest that it is prepared to proscribe all literacy tests and go beyond to resolve, on the basis of its equal protection criteria, such issues as whether the voting age should be eighteen or twenty-one.[121] But Congress could decide in § 4(e) where it believed the practical injury existed, and it need go no further to strike at more speculative harms merely because they were analogous.

This, then, could be the peculiar legislative capacity to which the Court was willing to defer. Congress can make distinctions

---

120 It is particularly interesting that a faint anticipation of *Morgan* can be seen in *Brown*. The famous questions the Court posed to the parties in ordering reargument contained a suggestion, at least inferentially, that under § 5 Congress might have a role independent of the Court in interpreting the substance of the Fourteenth Amendment. The Court's second question was, in relevant part: "[W]as it . . . the understanding of the framers of the Amendment (*a*) that future Congresses might, in the exercise of their power under section 5 of the Amendment abolish [public school] segregation, or (*b*) that it would be within the judicial power, in light of future conditions, to construe the Amendment as abolishing such segregation of its own force?" 345 U.S. 972 (1953).

Almost none of the lengthy historical arguments that the Court subsequently received addressed itself to developing this inference, though it might have been put to tactical advantage by the respondents. Indeed, this argument in 1954 could only have been seen to aid the respondents. The apparent invincibility of the filibuster in the Senate and the southern grip on congressional committees through seniority assured that any deference by the Court to Congress on the segregation issue would effectively end the matter. And the Court in the *Brown* opinion did not allude to congressional power under § 5, while dismissing the other historical evidence compiled by the parties as "inconclusive." 347 U.S. at 489.

The end of the filibuster's unshakable reign, and the passage of the civil rights legislation of 1964 and 1965 were the political conditions precedent for the *Morgan* opinion.

121 Cox, note 87 *supra*, at 96–97.

among classes that the Court would itself be hard put to explain on principled grounds both because Congress is more sensitively tuned to the competing social interests that demand accommodation and because the institutional legitimacy of a legislative act depends not so much on the rational persuasiveness of its decisions as on the simple fact that a majority of "responsible" elected officials were willing to vote for the proposition.

But can it be said that Congress is more generously endowed with this capacity than state legislatures? Can the Court justify congressional supremacy over state legislation to make distinctions among groups different from those the state had proscribed, where the Court would itself defer to the state judgment? The *Morgan* opinion, closely read, does yield a justification for this congressional "supremacy" which, if not irrebuttable, is at least arguable.

The limitations, explicit and implicit, with which *Morgan* hedged its conferral of interpretive authority on Congress suggest that it intended to approve Congress' use of this authority only to serve as an adjunct to the purposes the Court itself had been pursuing under the Fourteenth Amendment, to reach state laws or private conduct that the Court in effect would itself like to reach but, because of its principled constraints, cannot quite bring itself to do so. Thus the *Morgan* Court could argue that it does not authorize Congress to impose its value preferences on the states, but rather that Congress "enforces" the Court's value preferences, under the Fourteenth Amendment, on the states in circumstances where the Court does not feel able to do so itself.

The building blocks for this argument can be seen in the limits that *Morgan* places on the congressional power it finds in § 5. The Court sets out two explicit limitations. The first is quite permissive. The Court must be able to "perceive a basis upon which Congress might predicate [its] judgment" in interpreting the Fourteenth Amendment.[122] This is simply the test of rationality, with implications of even greater deference to Congress than that ordinarily deferential standard would itself suggest.[123]

The second limitation was framed seemingly as an afterthought in response to Mr. Justice Harlan's dissent. To the textual statement, derived from *McCulloch v. Maryland*, that § 5 legislation must be "plainly adapted to that end [enforcing the Equal Protection

---

[122] 384 U.S. at 656.   [123] Cox, note 87 *supra*, at 104.

Clause]" and "not prohibited by but . . . consistent with 'the letter and spirit of the Constitution,'" the Court appended footnote 10: "Contrary to the suggestion of the dissent . . . , § 5 does not grant Congress power to exercise discretion in the other direction and to enact 'statutes so as in effect to dilute equal protection and due process decisions of this Court.'. . . § 5 grants Congress no power to restrict, abrogate, or dilute these guarantees."[124]

The most revealing limitation is a third, which is even more restrictive than the footnote 10 limitation and which at least implies that the Court would strike down § 5 legislation even though no equal protection rights, as the Court has interpreted them, would be directly abrogated. Appellees in *Morgan* and New York raised an equal protection objection to § 4(e) itself on the ground that it discriminated invidiously between foreign language literates who had been educated in American-flag schools and those who had not. Their argument was in effect that there is no rational difference between the voting capacities of a Spanish-literate citizen who had been educated in Puerto Rico and one who had been educated in Mexico. The Court rejected this argument, but in a way that establishes an additional limitation on Congress' exercise of § 5 authority.

The straightforward way to handle the objection would have been to discern rational differences between the two classes. In enacting § 4(e), Congress did not intend to proscribe all voting literacy tests but only to enfranchise foreign language literates. It might have required all states that insist on literacy to administer foreign language literacy tests, but it did not do so, arguably on grounds of administrative convenience. Instead, § 4(e) permits a state simply to require a certificate of education from a foreign language applicant, and Congress could be seen to have more confidence in the worth of such certificates from American-flag schools conducted under its territorial authority than it had in foreign schools. In addition, although the existence of Spanish or other foreign language media might give much information about immediate political issues, Congress might reasonably conclude that a citizen literate only in Spanish who had been educated in foreign schools would lack familiarity with basic characteristics of American political institutions. The civics courses in American-flag school curriculums, however, with which Congress was familiar, would equip

---

[124] 384 U.S. at 651 and n. 10. See part III of the text.

the Spanish-speaking Puerto Rican with this necessary background.[125] These distinctions may seem strained, but surely they pass muster under the permissive rationality test against which *Morgan* had proclaimed it would test congressional action.

A more important distinction could be drawn, however, a distinction which congressional sponsors of § 4(e) clearly embraced and to which the Court would seem to owe deference consistent with its proclaimed purpose to respect Congress' independent judgment in defining equal protection. Put simply, the sponsors believed that a special debt was owed, as a matter of "fundamental justice," only to those foreign-literate citizens who were educated in American-flag schools. To refuse them special treatment, the sponsors argued, was to deny them equal protection of the laws.

Thus Senator Kennedy stated, in the floor debate, that the disenfranchisement of the Spanish-speaking Puerto Rican "exists because of the policy of cultural autonomy for Puerto Rico which we in the Congress have fostered" and that the Puerto Rican's "schooling takes place in Spanish is not up to him, but is due to the fact that the U.S. Government has chosen . . . to make Puerto Rico a showcase for all of Latin America."[126] Similarly, Senator Javits said, "There is a feeling of injustice on the part of those from Puerto Rico who were educated in American-flag schools. . . . [T]hey did not choose that system. The fact I emphasize is that the Federal Government allows the instruction there to be in Spanish."[127] These statements, and similar ones by House proponents of the measure,[128] were directed specifically to the argument that the *Morgan* respondents raised, that § 4(e) invidiously discriminated against the foreign-educated. This perception of the demands of justice was one of the important steps in Congress' interpretation of the Equal Protection Clause in § 4(e).

But *Morgan* did not make this congressional judgment controlling. The Court cited the administrative convenience argument and the "unique historic relationship between the Congress and the

---

[125] In the floor debate, Senator Kennedy stated: "For the educated Puerto Rican . . . this [literacy test] barrier is completely arbitrary. He has learned about American Government in school and he can keep up with current events through a very articulate Spanish language press." 111 *Cong. Rec.* 11061.

[126] *Id.* at 11060.   [127] *Id.* at 11066.

[128] See remarks of Representatives Gilbert, 111 *Cong. Rec.* 16235, and Scheuer, *id.* at 16238.

Commonwealth of Puerto Rico"[129] only after it had independently determined that § 4(e) was a "reform" measure rather than a "restrictive" one. The Court reasoned that if § 4(e) contracted, rather than expanded, the number of eligible voters, the distinction drawn between those educated in American-flag schools and others might well invalidate the measure. But as it was, the distinction was "only . . . a limitation on a reform measure aimed at eliminating an existing barrier to the exercise of the franchise."[130] Citing *Williamson v. Lee Optical Co.*,[131] the Court concluded, "reform may take one step at a time, addressing itself to the phase of the problem which seems most acute to the legislative mind."[132]

The Court's characterization of § 4(e) as a reform is interesting. By what standard did it purport to recognize a "reform" rather than a "restriction of existing rights"? The appellees in *Morgan* clearly contended that their existing rights, as competent voters, to influence elections were restricted by enfranchising incompetents. Congress regarded § 4(e) as a reform, but by hypothesis would consider any of its enactments that change existing entitlements as reforms. Given the Court's reading of § 5 to give "independent" interpretive authority to Congress, on what basis did it refuse to defer to this congressional judgment?

The Court seems to place special weight on the "fundamental" character of the right to vote. But unless it were willing itself to assert that all foreign literates had a constitutional right to vote—which, by hypothesis, the Court was unwilling to do—it is difficult to understand why the Court would not simply defer to Congress' judgment regarding the justice of the matter. The Court clearly retains its option to pass on any § 5 legislation that touches on "fundamental"—though not, as such, constitutional—rights. By this standard, there is no exercise of "independent" congressional authority under § 5 that is independent of the Court's final arbitration.

Accepting the premise that the Court intended § 5 power to be exercised by Congress to draw distinctions that the Court was itself unwilling to draw, it is apparent that such "judicial indistinguishability" is precisely the predicate that will trigger the Court's independent judgment whether the congressional act is a "reform" or not. *Morgan* thus appears to confer independent power on Congress

---

[129] 384 U.S. at 658.

[130] *Id.* at 657.

[131] 348 U.S. 483, 489 (1955).

[132] 384 U.S. at 657.

with one hand and then not even bother to switch hands to retake that power.

At this point, the *Morgan* opinion appears a *tour de force.* To regulate activities that the Court wishes to reach under the Fourteenth Amendment, but cannot itself justify regulating, the Court has enlisted congressional assistance. But the Court will set the basic terms. Congress can only fill in the blanks.

This novel amalgam of judicial and congressional powers under § 1 might be considered a misuse of the Fourteenth Amendment. As § 1 has been applied by the judiciary, state legislation has been struck down generally only when clearly inconsistent with "fundamental" principles that could be stated and applied with sweeping generality. *Morgan* poses the question whether this restricted use must inhere in the substance of § 1 itself, or whether the restriction arose as an institutional consequence of the fact that the judiciary acted alone in applying the section and could not comfortably justify any use but a restricted and highly generalized one.

To raise this question is not to suggest that it can be readily answered. Following *Morgan*'s appeal to the framers' intent, it might be said that notwithstanding the ambiguous language of § 5, it was intended that the courts independently ratify every application of the substance of § 1. But the breadth of intervention the framers envisioned regarding state legislation—to protect "the privileges and immunities of citizens," "due process," "equal protection"—may be so extensive that the Court has no choice but to enlist the assistance of the national legislature to carry out the intent of § 1, irrespective of what the framers may have intended by § 5. Section 1 was designed to grow, and if that growth now requires legislative assistance to tailor its application, in some circumstances, to accommodate competing though subordinated interests, then the *Morgan* doctrine can be justified.

III. TITLE II: THE BANNS ARE PROCLAIMED

This central use of the *Morgan* doctrine, as thus described here, suggests that the Court was wrong to erect its apparently rigid footnote 10 limitation on § 5 legislation. The Court resisted Mr. Justice Harlan's suggestion that, under its doctrine, "Congress would be able to qualify this Court's constitutional decisions,"[133] but it may have done so too hastily.

---

[133] *Id.* at 667.

The justification for a relaxation of footnote 10 and for extension of *Morgan* to permit Congress to "restrict, delete, or abrogate" Court-proclaimed constitutional doctrine can perhaps most graphically be illustrated in the context of the reapportionment cases. Here the Court has clearly decided that one particular value should predominate and that all other competing values should be decisively subordinated. As the variations in population between districts in cases before the Court grow smaller,[134] as the units of government appear less important,[135] the single-minded and relentless character of the Court's "one-man one-vote" touchstone becomes more evident. But, as early critics of *Baker v. Carr* suggested,[136] the Court sees no alternative for itself but to march forward to the ends of the logic of its proclaimed principle.

Congressional intervention might, in some contexts and to some degree, be welcomed by the Court to permit some variations on the theme. The Ninetieth Congress attempted such an intervention regarding standards that should govern state legislatures in fixing congressional districts. House and Senate conferees were unable to resolve differences between the measures passed by each chamber and the bill died. It was nonetheless an instructive enterprise for present purposes.

The House-passed bill provided in part that congressional districts, for the 1968 and 1970 elections, be permitted to vary in population up to 30 percent between the largest and smallest districts.[137] After 1970, the permitted variance would drop to 10 percent. The bill seemed directly responsive to painful political pressures under which many congressmen found themselves as their districts were reshaped.[138] To its opponents, the bill was clearly contrary to the

---

[134] See Kirkpatrick v. Preisler, 394 U.S. 526 (1969); Wells v. Rockefeller, 394 U.S. 542 (1969).

[135] See Kramer v. Union Free School Dist. No. 15, 395 U.S. 621 (1969).

[136] See BICKEL, THE LEAST DANGEROUS BRANCH 192-97 (1962); Neal, *Baker v. Carr: Politics in Search of Law,* 1962 SUPREME COURT REVIEW 252, 284-86.

[137] H.R. 2508, 90th Cong., 1st Sess. (1967). It was never made clear—and perhaps purposely obscured—whether the bill authorized a 30 percent variance with no further justification, or whether that figure was simply an upper limit but affirmative justification must be shown within that limit. Nor was the character of the measure, as "suggestive guidelines" or as "mandatory legislation" for the courts ever resolved. See 113 *Cong. Rec.* 11077 (1967).

[138] For example, the 30 percent figure was not selected at random. Chairman Celler, of New York, who sponsored and managed this bill, observed during House

most recent Supreme Court decisions which appeared to suggest that population variances "far below" 30 percent were per se invalid.[139]

From the Court's perspective, however, surely it would have been useful to have had Congress enact this measure even with its apparent inconsistency with Court-proclaimed doctrine. In substantial ways, the bill would have assisted the Court in carrying out the essential purposes of its "one-man one-vote" principle. By simply opting for a percentage figure, Congress could relieve the Court of its embarrassment in stating that mathematical precision is not always a realistic or necessary goal, but never quite finding a population variance above zero that the Court could comfortably embrace.[140] More important, perhaps, the legislation would have clearly conveyed a congressional legitimization of the basic purposes of the reapportionment decisions—a quite substantial virtue for the Court's work in this highly charged political area.

The Senate passed a substitute measure proposed by Senator Edward Kennedy which, on this issue, insisted that a 10 percent population variance was the immediate maximum allowable and made clear that, within that limit, affirmative justification for any variance from zero must be shown.[141] At the time, no Supreme Court decision had appeared hostile to the 10 percent variation as such, though subsequently contrary suggestions have appeared.[142] Surely, in this

---

debates that the "spread" between the largest and smallest districts in New York was 29.5 percent. With admirable candor, he told the House, "It is very important that these figures be correct." 113 *Cong. Rec.* 11082 (1967). After the bill passed the House, new calculations were made which indicated that the variation in New York state was 34.5 percent. (See Appendix A to Minority Views on H.R. 2508, S. Rep. No. 291, 90th Cong., 1st Sess., 21.) The Senate Judiciary Committee obligingly amended the House-passed bill to increase the permissible variation to 35 percent.

[139] *Minority Views on H.R. 2508*, S. Rep. No. 291, 90th Cong., 1st Sess. 13 (1967). In the first Kirkpatrick v. Preisler, 385 U.S. 450 (1967), and Duddleston v. Grills, 385 U.S. 455 (1967), the Court invalidated congressional districting in which the population variations were 21.9 percent and 22.9 percent, respectively, between the largest and smallest districts. See also *Minority Views of Representative Conyers*, H. Rep. No. 191, 90th Cong., 1st Sess. 9–11 (1967).

[140] See generally Kirkpatrick v. Preisler, note 134 *supra*.

[141] The text of the substitute adopted by the Senate appears as Appendix E to the minority views, note 139 *supra*, at 25–26.

[142] In Kirkpatrick v. Preisler, note 134 *supra*, the Court invalidated congressional districting in which the largest and smallest districts varied, on the calculus pre-

context at least, the question whether Congress was speaking before or after the Court had carried forward the logic of its prior decisions hardly rises to the dignity of a constitutional principle limiting congressional power. That is, however, the effect of the footnote 10 limitation.

Population variation is not the only part of the reapportionment imbroglio in which the Court might find congressional assistance useful. Should multimember districts in any particular context be proscribed or permitted?[143] Does weighted voting in unequally populated districts serve important purposes in any particular context?[144] Do some particular units of local government so directly impinge on the interests of a particular segment of the voting population, and so speculatively on the rest, that a special case can be made for setting aside "one-man one-vote" in those situations?[145] Congressional action on these questions would have considerable worth to the Court in assisting its resolution of them. And, unlike exceptions to the general rule that the Court might itself be tempted to carve out of "one-man one-vote," congressional exceptions have no necessary, self-contained logic of expansion.

The scope of this congressional revisory authority, as it arises from the logic of *Morgan*, would be "around the edges" of the Court's proclaimed doctrine. As in *Morgan*, the Court would independently characterize the measure as a "reform" that it approved or a "restriction" that it did not. Using these flexible notions, the Court could approve congressional action that reshaped Court doctrine to make it responsive to conflicting interests in a manner that the Court itself might not comfortably be able to reach.

---

scribed by H.R. 2508, by 6.1 percent. Though the Court did not explicitly state that this variance per se invalidated the plan, it held out little hope that such variance would ever be accepted. As Mr. Justice Fortas observed, the Court "proceeds to reject, *seriatim*, every type of justification that has been—possibly, every one that could be—advanced." 394 U.S. at 537.

143 See Fortson v. Dorsey, 379 U.S. 433, 439 (1965); Burns v. Richardson, 384 U.S. 73, 88 (1966); Jewell, *Local Systems of Representation: Political Consequences and Judicial Choices*, 36 GEO. WASH. L. REV. 790, 798–807 (1968).

144 See Iannucci v. Board of Supervisors, 20 N.Y.2d 244 (1967); Banzhaf, *One Man, ? Votes: Mathematical Analysis of Voting Power and Effective Representation*, 36 GEO. WASH. L. REV. 808 (1968).

145 See Avery v. Midland County, 390 U.S. 474, 483–84 (1968). *Cf.* Mr. Justice Fortas' dissent in *Avery*, 390 U.S. at 495, and Mr. Justice Stewart's dissent in *Kramer*, note 135 *supra*, 395 U.S. at 634.

It might not appear essential for the Court explicitly to extend *Morgan* to bring these advantages to it. In the situations described, one might simply say that Congress was in effect petitioning the Court to overrule itself in some particular application of its doctrine. But the same reasons that led the Court to reach out to a novel doctrine in *Morgan,* when the case could have been resolved on narrower grounds, would lead to embracing this explicit extension. First, the extension would affirmatively invite congressional action to assist the Court for the purposes described.[146] Second, if the Court has the option only of overruling its previous decision when confronted by variant congressional legislation, it must then enunciate new doctrine of its own to make room for the congressional act. It must thus give independent life, and growth potential, to whatever doctrine it distills from the congressional act, a possibility that by hypothesis *Morgan* is designed to avoid.

Finally, relaxation of footnote 10 would eliminate a practical problem that now attends it. A Congress eager to play a significant interpretive role under *Morgan,* with its present limitation, would be greatly tempted to legislate quickly and at large when the first suggestion of new applications of the Fourteenth Amendment appeared in a Court opinion. The interval between *Baker*[147] and *Reynolds*[148] or *Escobedo*[149] and *Miranda,*[150] for example, or the time between suggestions of constitutional doctrine in some lower courts and its ratification by the Supreme Court, would be seen as Congress' only real opportunity to avoid the strictures of footnote 10. The possibility of a congressional race against the Court's docket, if *Morgan*'s use becomes increasingly attractive to Congress, might tempt the Court to prematurely sweeping doctrinal statements. And, perhaps more significantly, generous time lags between Court enunciation of doctrine and congressional response appears important to accomplish the Court's purposes in *Morgan.* Congress' capacities in accommodating clashing principles depend for their successful invocation on the clarity and precision with which that

---

146 The risks that attend this invitation are discussed in the text *infra,* following note 171.

147 Baker v. Carr, 369 U.S. 186 (1962).

148 Reynolds v. Sims, 377 U.S. 533 (1964).

149 Escobedo v. Illinois, 378 U.S. 478 (1964).

150 Miranda v. Arizona, 384 U.S. 436 (1966).

clash can be seen in practice. It takes time for practical experience to accumulate, for Congress to hear from "the folks back home," and that time should not be unduly foreshortened by Congress' feeling obliged to leap before the Court looks.

The Court may soon find itself confronted with an opportunity to endorse the extension of *Morgan* discussed here. Enactment of Title II of the 1968 crime bill[151] was heralded by its proponents as at least a partial reversal of *Miranda v. Arizona.*[152] With some skillful reading of Title II, the Court could readily fit it into the *Morgan* mold. It might want to do so because in the criminal justice area, as in reapportionment, the Court has expansively applied its own conceptions of fairness to subordinate competing considerations, and the Court might welcome some assistance from Congress in striking somewhat different accommodations of the competing interests involved.

The difficulties, and opportunities, presented by Title II deserve detailed examination. As it was reported to the Senate by an evenly divided vote of the Judiciary Committee, Title II was a wide-ranging attempt to undo much of the Court's recent work in the criminal justice area.[153] Title II contained four sections: the first was aimed at reinstating, in federal criminal prosecutions, the "voluntariness" test, based on the trial court's examination of "all the circumstances" as the exclusive test of a confession's admissibility under the Fifth Amendment, displacing the ritual invariably prescribed by *Miranda.* The second denied federal jurisdiction "to review or to reverse" a state court ruling in any criminal prosecution admitting a confession in evidence "as voluntarily made." The third, though drafted with particular obscurity, appeared intended to reverse, in federal criminal prosecutions, the Court's decision in *United States v. Wade,*[154] which required opportunity for counsel's presence at a police lineup as a requisite for admitting testimony in court that an eyewitness to the crime had identified the defendant at the lineup. This section also denied federal jurisdiction to review state court decisions admitting eyewitness testimony in any crimi-

---

151 18 U.S.C. §§ 3501–02.

152 Note 150 *supra.*

153 The text of Title II as reported out by the Senate Judiciary Committee appears in S. Rep. No. 1097, 90th Cong., 2d Sess. 9–10 (1968).

154 388 U.S. 218 (1967).

nal prosecution. The fourth section sharply reduced the availability
of federal habeas corpus for review of state criminal convictions.

After extended debate, the Senate rejected the second and fourth
sections and that part of the third section which would have denied
federal jurisdiction to review state court decisions admitting eyewitness testimony. Thus Title II, as approved by the Senate and
enacted by the House with virtually no debate, deals only with the
Miranda and *Wade* rules in federal criminal prosecutions. For present purposes, the relevant portions of Title II, as enacted, are as
follows:[155]

§ 3501. *Admissibility of confessions*
   (a) In any criminal prosecution brought by the United
States or by the District of Columbia, a confession . . . shall
be admissible in evidence if it is voluntarily given. . . .
   (b) The trial judge in determining the issue of voluntariness
shall take into consideration all the circumstances surrounding
the giving of the confession, including (1) the time elapsing
between arrest and arraignment of the defendant making the
confession, if it was made after arrest and before arraignment,
(2) whether such defendant knew the nature of the offense
with which he was charged or of which he was suspected at
the time of making the confession, (3) whether or not such
defendant was advised or knew that he was not required to
make any statement and that any such statement could be
used against him, (4) whether or not such defendant had
been advised prior to questioning of his right to the assistance
of counsel; and (5) whether or not such defendant was
without the assistance of counsel when questioned and when
giving such confession.
   The presence or absence of any of the abovementioned
factors to be taken into consideration by the judge need not
be conclusive on the issue of voluntariness of the confession. . . .

§ 3502. *Admissibility in evidence of eyewitness testimony*
   The testimony of a witness that he saw the accused commit
or participate in the commission of the crime for which the
accused is being tried shall be admissible in evidence in a
criminal prosecution in any trial court ordained and established under article III of the Constitution of the United States.

Section 3501 appears on its face in direct conflict with *Miranda*,
which specified at least that the absence of "circumstances" (3) and
(4) must be conclusive to bar admission of the confession in evi-

---

[155] Note 151 *supra*.

dence. Section 3502 would similarly appear in direct conflict with *Wade*. Must one then conclude that Congress has strayed beyond its permitted interpretive role under the Fourteenth Amendment into the forbidden gardens of the *Morgan* footnote 10?[156]

The proponents of Title II, in part at least, sought to justify reshaping *Miranda* by developing the warning posed in Mr. Justice Harlan's *Morgan* dissent. In the Judiciary Committee report, *Morgan* was interpreted as permitting Congress to review constitutional rulings if Congress "made *its* appraisal of the facts and reached a different factual conclusion than the Court had."[157] The central factual premise that Title II proponents saw underlying *Miranda* was that "custodial interrogation was inherently coercive . . . without the [*Miranda*-required] safeguards." But, the report continued, "if, *in fact*, custodial interrogation is not inherently coercive, how does the constitutional basis of the decision fare? With its underpinning removed, it would seem that the Court would be compelled to retreat to its past standard—the standard of voluntariness."[158] Congress could, it was then asserted, make the contrary factual conclusion and the Court would under *Morgan* defer to that legislative judgment.

There are many difficulties with these propositions. It is not at all clear that the "inherently coercive atmosphere" of custodial questioning was the only or the central factual underpinning for *Miranda*. The Court was clearly concerned with the ineffectiveness of the traditional voluntariness test as a means for judicial protection of Fifth Amendment rights.[159] Even conceding that not all custodial interrogation is necessarily coercive, the Court found itself unable to distinguish satisfactorily between coercive and noncoercive interrogation using the traditional test. Indeed, the Court's willingness to permit waiver of the warned rights suggests it had not concluded that custodial interrogation was "inherently coercive."[160]

More significantly, the committee report misstates the central

---

[156] The relevance of the *Morgan* doctrine to constitutional limits on congressional powers is discussed in the text *infra*, at notes 170–71.

[157] S. Rep. No. 1097, note 153 *supra*, at 61.

[158] *Id*. at 60.

[159] 384 U.S. at 445–48.   [160] *Id*. at 475–76.

premise of *Morgan*. As discussed earlier, *Morgan* did not (or cannot) suggest deference to Congress because it can gather and evaluate facts better than courts. The institutional biases that necessarily made suspect the "facts" perceived by Congress in considering § 4(e) of the Voting Rights Act are equally pronounced in congressional consideration of Title II. As a general matter, it can be said that entire congressional debate on all sides of Title II was notably devoid of anything but the most speculative assertion of facts.[161] And even among these factual speculations, both the proponents and opponents of Title II were far from objective observers. Thus one "fact" about *Miranda* that common sense would suggest, and that was explicitly supported by the most satisfactory empirical research then available on the practical impact of the case, was that the *Miranda* warnings, when given, "had little impact on suspects' behavior"[162] and "are almost wholly ineffective"[163] to assist a suspect in understanding his right to remain silent and have legal assistance. But both proponents and opponents of Title II studiously avoided any hint of this proposition. It served no partisan purpose for the proponents who wanted to prove that *Miranda* destroyed effective law enforcement or for the opponents who wanted to prove that *Miranda* was the most important protection for criminal suspects since abolition of the thumbscrew.

Refusal to argue that the *Miranda* warnings were virtually ineffective deprived the proponents of a strong argument that Title II was wholly consistent with *Miranda* and *Wade*. The Court had said this in its opinion:[164]

---

[161] Compare the conclusion, published four days before the Senate Judiciary Committee reported out Title II, by the Reporters for the American Law Institute's *Model Code of Pre-Arraignment Procedure*. Indicating why they were not prepared to recommend any legislation in response to *Miranda*, the Reporters stated: "[I]t cannot be overemphasized that the state of empirical research work to date does not permit even a start at answering most of the difficult questions underlying the development of legislation in this field." A.L.I., MODEL CODE OF PRE-ARRAIGNMENT PROCEDURE, STUDY DRAFT No. 1 107 (1968).

[162] Note, *Interrogation in New Haven: The Impact of Miranda*, 76 YALE L.J. 1519, 1563 (1967).

[163] Note, *A Postscript to the Miranda Project: Interrogation of Draft Protesters*, 77 YALE L.J. 300, 318 (1967).

[164] 384 U.S. at 467.

It is impossible for us to foresee the potential alternatives for protecting the privilege [against self-incrimination] which might be devised by Congress or the States in the exercise of their creative rule-making capacities. Therefore we cannot say that the Constitution necessarily requires adherence to any particular solution. . . . We encourage Congress and the states to continue their laudable search for increasingly effective ways of protecting the rights of the individual while promoting efficient enforcement of our criminal laws. However, unless we are shown other procedures which are at least as effective in apprising accused persons of their right of silence and in assuring a continuous opportunity to exercise it, the [Court-imposed] safeguards must be observed.

If Congress could conclude, and the Court could be persuaded, that the *Miranda* ritual was no more "effective" than the previous voluntariness test, it could sensibly be argued that Title II was wholly consistent with *Miranda*. But that argument would have defeated another clearly apparent partisan purpose of the Title II proponents. They wanted to dispute the Court, not comply with its strictures. Title II was, to an important degree, a gesture of defiance at a Court which protected criminals and Communists, and attacked traditional religious, political, and social institutions. To bring Title II into explicit harmony with *Miranda* would have defeated its symbolic value for its proponents.

At this point, the invitation to congressional action issued by the Court, in the passage quoted above, warrants close attention. In central ways, it and the invitation to Congress expressed in *Morgan* arise from the same premise and are, indeed, the same invitation. First of all, they are similar in their cloudiness. The *Morgan* invitation to interpret the substance of equal protection is as open-textured as the *Miranda* invitation to devise "procedures . . . as least as effective" as the Court's. One might design elaborate empirical studies to quantify the comparative "effectiveness" of the Court's procedures and some other—measured, perhaps, by suspects' professed comprehension of their rights under both procedures, or simply the tenacity with which rights are asserted under both. But it is unlikely the Court would insist on this effort at precise measurement to uphold congressional action. Rather it is a rough equality, a good-faith effort, some indication that Congress has accepted the spirit of *Miranda* and is working to implement it, that the Court is asking. The first *Morgan* test describes it well. The Court needs to

"perceive a basis on which Congress could have predicated its judgment" that its procedures and the *Miranda* rules were equivalent
protection for suspects.

Second, the controls that the Court clearly retained in *Miranda*
as the basis for reviewing any congressional action displacing its
procedures are directly parallel to the controls retained explicitly
and implicitly by the Court in *Morgan*. Both leave to independent
judicial scrutiny the question whether congressional action is a "reform" to which deference is due or a "restriction on fundamental
rights" to be viewed with hostility. Clearly the Court can, and has
virtually given notice that it intends to, manipulate these tests at
will according to standards that it cannot precisely articulate.

Third, both *Miranda* and *Morgan* turn to Congress because it
can operate with greater flexibility than the Court and can balance
competing objectives with a more sensitive touch than the Court
can apply. In the *Miranda* context, Congress' greater capacity
springs more directly from its ability to appropriate new funds, to
create new officers, to use new techniques such as televised taping
of interrogations, than from the doctrinal flexibility which *Morgan*
found useful (though doctrinal flexibility might have some uses in
reshaping the demands of the self-incrimination clause as well).[165]
The Court in both cases invites congressional action not because
Congress sees facts more clearly but because it can react to the same
facts more resourcefully than the Court to accommodate conflicting interests.

One difference between *Morgan* and *Miranda* should be noted.
In *Morgan*, Congress was not invited to revise a specific judgment
that the Court had already articulated. The Court instead approved
congressional action in a context which the Court had not directly
addressed—the exclusion of foreign language literates from voting—
though it had spoken in an analogous context approving exclusion
of illiterates[166] which suggested that the Court would probably not
reach the congressional result in § 4(e). In *Miranda*, however, the
Court explicitly invited Congress to revise specific procedures
that it regarded as necessary to protect constitutional rights.

---

[165] See, *e.g.*, Schaefer, *Police Interrogation and the Privilege against Self-Incrimination*, 61 Nw. U. L. Rev. 506, 519–21 (1966); Friendly, *A Postscript on Miranda*,
in Benchmarks 266 (1967); Traynor, *The Devils of Due Process in Criminal Detection and Trial*, 16 Cath. U. L. Rev. 1, 17–22 (1966).

[166] Lassiter v. Northampton Bd. of Election, 360 U.S. 45 (1959).

The strictures of *Morgan*'s footnote 10 injunction are avoided by the Court's insistence in *Miranda* that "the Constitution [does not] necessarily require adherence to any particular [procedural] solution." But this seems a formalist point. As noted above, the Court seems quite prepared to ratify congressional procedures that would, to some degree, facilitate interrogation more than the *Miranda* procedures and thus would, to some degree, "restrict, dilute or abrogate" the ability of some to insist on their right to silence. The Court, in *Miranda*, was really inviting Congress to revise its constitutional doctrine "around the edges," so long as the congressional procedures would most likely work in most cases to achieve the Court's general protective purposes.

An argument is readily available that Title II, on the face of its language, does no more than that. Section 3501(b) does not provide that no suspect shall be warned of his right to silence or "of his right to the assistance of counsel," or that no suspect is entitled to "the assistance of counsel when questioned." Instead it provides that the "presence or absence" of these "factors . . . need not be conclusive on the issue" of the admissibility of the confession. The section does not wholly sweep aside *Miranda* and its immediate ancestor *Escobedo v. Illinois*, to restore pristine the prior federal law. In particular, Title II explicitly recognizes that "prior to questioning" there is "a right to the assistance of counsel," a right that was not clearly established until *Escobedo*.[167]

In addition, the legislative enumeration of factors arguably gives them a special status, a particular importance, that did not necessarily obtain when the courts fashioned for themselves the all-circumstances test for voluntariness. Thus one can discern a congressional intention that, in the ordinary case, all of these factors would be satisfied—the time between arrest and arraignment would be limited,[168] the suspect would know "the nature of the offense," he would have received the silence warnings and been advised of his right to counsel, and counsel would be present during questioning—

---

[167] 378 U.S. at 490–92.

[168] Section 3501(c) provides, with limited exceptions, that any confession, to be admissible, must be "given . . . within six hours immediately following . . . arrest or other detention" and that within the six-hour period no confession shall "be inadmissible solely because of delay." This designation of the delay factor as one that cannot be the "sole" ground for exclusion might suggest that any of the other factors enumerated in subsection (a) could be "sole" grounds for exclusion.

unless some affirmative explanation for the absence of any one of these factors were brought forward.

Miranda itself indicates that the absence of counsel can be satisfactorily explained by showing "knowing and intelligent waiver," and § 3501 can be regarded as having codified that proposition. Delay between arrest and arraignment can be explained in a number of ways, two of which are specifically enumerated in subsection (c): distance to be traveled from the place of arrest "to the nearest available" commissioner and "means of transportation" at hand.[169]

One strains to imagine satisfactory explanations for failures to give the warnings. Congress did not mean to prohibit such warnings, and one must presume that Congress had some touchstone for distinguishing between circumstances when a court should and should not insist upon them. But the primary argument articulated by the proponents of Title II—that *Miranda* hamstrung effective law enforcement—was made with little specific consideration of how the various elements of the *Miranda* requirements might individually affect enforcement. This general theme might, however, be applied to identifying a circumstance when the warnings might not be insisted upon—that is, when such insistence would hamper law enforcement without producing any discernible advantage to the rights of criminal suspects generally. Thus if failure to give the warning in a particular case was clearly accidental, nothing more than an individual "constable's blunder," rather than evidence of a systematic police practice, it could be argued that only the individual policeman would be "punished" by excluding the confession, that one essential purpose of the exclusionary rule—to influence general police practice—would not be advanced, and that *Miranda* was unnecessarily rigid in insisting that, in all circumstances, exclusion for failure to give warnings was necessary to provide effective protection to the rights of criminal suspects generally.[170] Indeed,

---

[169] Whether delay solely in order to interrogate within the six-hour limit would be a satisfactory explanation is not explicitly resolved, but it would be excessively disingenuous to suggest that, in no circumstances, could such an explanation suffice, in view of the history of the *Mallory* rule, 354 U.S. 449 (1957), in the District of Columbia which immediately provoked subsection (c). See Sen. Rep. No. 1097, note 153 *supra*, at 38–41; Title III of the 1968 District of Columbia Omnibus Crime Act, 81 Stat. 735 (1968).

[170] The Department of Justice is now apparently prepared to argue for a similar interpretation of Title II—that a confession obtained without *Miranda* warnings

by excusing a particular failure to give warnings only on proof that the failure reflected no general police practice, the generality of police interrogation practices becomes relevant in every case. This may be a more effective mode for judicial protection of self-incrimination rights for all criminal suspects than the *Miranda* scheme, which permits the courts only to examine isolated, episodic instances of police interrogation practices.

There is a somewhat fictitious air about this congenial reading of Title II.[171] But its draftsmanship is less than pellucid, and its supporters and opponents both described it typically in grandiose assertions quite unencumbered by any consideration of the manner in which those assertions related to the specific provisions of the Title. Indeed, one can conclude that the heart of Title II for its proponents was contained in those sections, rejected by the Senate, which denied federal court jurisdiction to review testimonial admissions in state court criminal prosecutions and restricted federal habeas corpus jurisdiction over state criminal convictions. The specific provisions that survived were relatively unimportant, given the comparative narrowness of federal criminal jurisdiction and the likelihood that the *Miranda* procedures were not really relevant to the success of significant federal prosecutions, particularly those involving organized crime, except in the District of Columbia.

Even under the suggested reading of Title II, it is clear that in some circumstances the interrogation procedures that *Miranda* prescribed need not be observed, and these circumstances can be described as a "dilution" of *Miranda*. Assuming that the Court wants to uphold Title II, and that it frankly acknowledges even a limited inconsistency with *Miranda*, there are two options before it. One is to characterize the legislation as within the broad terms of the invitation that *Miranda* extended to Congress. The second is to take

---

may be admissible "if a Federal official inadvertently fails to give a full warning." New York Times, Aug. 1, 1969, p. 16, col. 6. It has been reported that the department, under former Attorney General Clark, had instructed U.S. attorneys to "ignore" Title II and only to offer confessions where the *Miranda* prerequisites had been satisfied. New York Times, July 28, 1969, p. 21, col. 4.

171 Section 3502, dealing with *Wade*, which required the *Miranda* warnings before the conduct of a police lineup, can be given the same reading as is given to § 3501. In fact, the draftsmanship of § 3502 is so obscure that it can be given any reading. See United States v. Kinnard, 297 F. Supp. 786, 791 n. (D. D.C. 1968), that § 3502 "cannot be given literal application."

Morgan one step further, giving circumscribed authorization to Congress to revise the constitutional judgments of the Court. Whichever characterization is chosen, the grounds for the Court's acceptance of the differences between *Miranda* and Title II would be the same: those differences are limited in scope, and do not entrench upon the basic purposes which the Court was pursuing but instead make a more finely tuned and more flexible adjustment of competing interests in the conduct of custodial interrogation derived from Congress' appreciation of practicalities.

The choice between the two characterizations is prudential. To rely on the *Miranda* invitation alone would submerge the significance of the congressional action and would merely be a technique by which the Court could gracefully overrule *Miranda pro tanto* without directly admitting it. To rely on the *Morgan* ground is to acknowledge the logical reach of its already proclaimed doctrine in altering the relationship between Court and Congress on constitutional issues. Considering both the proper rationale for the *Morgan* opinion and the practical artificiality of the footnote 10 limitation, the *Morgan* doctrine with that limitation strikes an unstable equilibrium that invites this further extension.

It should not matter that Title II deals only with *Miranda* in the federal courts. If the Court is willing to cede revisory authority to Congress, in the terms and for the purposes described, regarding limitations on state power, there is no substantial reason that Congress should not play a similar role regarding its own powers. Congressional capacities for sensitive adjustments of competing interests would be equally useful to the Court in its efforts to shape fully responsive constitutional doctrine regarding both federal and state power. The objection that Congress would be biased in its own favor in reviewing its constitutional authority would not appear a compelling distinction in view of Congress' clear bias in its own favor, discussed above, in reviewing limits on state power. No matter how its authority is sliced, Congress is not an impartial tribunal. For the Court thus to acknowledge that Congress has some role in defining the constitutional imperatives that limit its own authority is truly to turn *Marbury v. Madison* on its head, but that somersault was implicit in *Morgan* itself.

Relaxation of footnote 10 and extension of the *Morgan* doctrine would not necessarily be more attractive to an "active" or to a "restrained" Court. Each would find different uses for it. An activist

Court could use the doctrine to justify extending constitutional doctrine in response to pressing immediate problems without great concern that the proclaimed doctrine inappropriately subordinates legitimate interests. If that be so, the Court might say, let Congress unravel this problem which is marginal to our central concern. For a restrained Court, intent perhaps on undoing the work of its active predecessors, the doctrine would permit a graceful and selective retreat limited to those areas where the political branch gives an explicit contrary judgment.

Morgan with footnote 10 retained is equally available for competing uses. The activist could similarly ignore necessary future implications—implicit, perhaps, rather than explicit—of the extension of doctrine proclaimed to meet an immediately pressing problem. For the restrained, a stronger argument would be available to work against expansion of constitutional doctrine to limit state power. Prior to *Morgan*, to assert that an issue was properly left to legislative discretion meant simply that the Court should defer to the judgment of whatever legislature—state or national—was challenged before it. Now *Morgan* gives the argument that, though an issue is best left to legislative judgment and the Court should not interfere with a particular exercise of state power, Congress will be able—without being forced to mask the exercise in its commerce, or some such, power—directly to impose national values on the states by superseding their judgment on that issue. Mr. Justice Black's anticipation of the *Morgan* doctrine in his dissent in *Harper v. Board of Elections* reflects precisely this argument.[172]

One might expect that a doctrine with so many uses for such varied temperaments was predestined to grow. But there are substantial risks for the Court that run with this doctrine. Though the role *Morgan* and its extension approve for Congress is narrowly circumscribed and the Court retains ample doctrinal handles to disapprove congressional action, nonetheless its presentational rhetoric—that Congress has, to whatever degree, an "independent" role in interpreting the Constitution—is likely to remove an important restraint on Congress which has, in the past, usually counseled great wariness in trespassing on the Court's prerogatives. The *Morgan* invitation, however carefully hedged, weakens that constraint, and might in itself provoke strenuous Court-Congress conflict. To pro-

---

172 See also Fay v. New York, 332 U.S. 261, 282–84 (1947).

tect its prerogatives, the Court must then be prepared to do battle. But *Morgan* will have surrendered, in part at least, one of the Court's most potent institutional weapons: the authoritative tone of its constitutional *ipse dixit*.

But these dangers may be overstated. The Court might expect Congress to read its *Morgan* doctrine with the same care and respect—whatever that may be—that Congress gives its other constitutional pronouncements. And rather than provoking Court-Congress conflict, *Morgan* and its extension can instead be viewed as a mediating response to present conflict that has come from the wide-ranging activities of the Court in the past fifteen years. As the Title II exercise was meant to demonstrate, Congress has become less wary about contesting the Court. For its part, the Court has shown less reluctance to use its constitutional weaponry against Congress, and might be relied on to defend itself.[173]

Particularly if the Court intends not to abandon its active role, it would appear desirable to design a mechanism by which the national legislature, at least, can discuss and attempt to refine the Court's interpretations of the Constitution without necessarily precipitating a constitutional crisis, in which the felt need to defend or attack the Court generally takes precedence over the merits of the particular issue at hand (as in the Title II debate). *Morgan* and its extension might yield such an ordered dialogue between Court and Congress on the detailed application of constitutional doctrine. It seems worth a try.

---

[173] See, *e.g.*, Powell v. McCormack, 395 U.S. 486 (1969); Shapiro v. Thompson, 394 U.S. 618 (1969); Leary v. United States, 395 U.S. 6 (1969).

MARTHA ANDES ZISKIND

JUDICIAL TENURE IN THE AMERICAN CONSTITUTION: ENGLISH AND AMERICAN PRECEDENTS

When the representatives of the several States met to revise the Articles of Confederation in May, 1786, they brought to bear a substantial knowledge of political theory and broad experience in the political process. In their speeches and their writings they drew lessons from the political history of Greece and Rome. Nor were they ignorant of contemporary political thought, especially the works of Blackstone and Montesquieu. Most were familiar with the workings of the English government, and many had held responsible positions in colonial and early state governments.

The delegates all agreed on the philosophical superiority of a balanced constitution, but they were far from clear about the details of such a system. They repeatedly expressed fear that a strong executive would exert too much power over the other branches of government. Among the sins of George III catalogued in the Declaration of Independence was his habit of making judges "dependent on his will alone, for the tenure of their offices, and the amount & paiment of their salaries,"[1] a power which he could not exercise over the English bench. At the same time, experience with state governments had shown that an unbridled legislature led to corrup-

---

Martha Andes Ziskind is a Ph.D. candidate in history at The University of Chicago.

[1] See BECKER, THE DECLARATION OF INDEPENDENCE 178 (1942).

tion and paralysis of governmental functions. The delegates agreed on the importance of an independent judiciary, but they differed on the degree of this independence and on whether the judiciary were to be ultimately responsible to the executive, to the legislature, or only to the people themselves. Arguments over the length of judicial tenure and the method of removal essentially concerned this fundamental issue.

The major judicial question confronting the Constitutional Convention was the relationship between the proposed federal judiciary and the state courts. Some attention, however, was given to problems of tenure and removal. The Articles of Confederation had authorized Congress to set up courts for "the trial of piracies and felonies committed on the high seas," and to establish "courts for receiving and determining, finally, appeals in all cases of captures," but with the limitation that no member of Congress could sit as a judge.[2] The articles stipulated neither length of office nor method of removal for judges. Article 9 also provided for special judges to settle disputes between states over territorial jurisdiction or landownership, but these men would be appointed to sit as each case arose.

The Constitutional Convention ultimately settled on the following provisions for the new federal judiciary:

> Article III. Section 1. The judicial Power of the United States, shall be vested in one supreme Court, and in such inferior Courts as the Congress may from time to time ordain and establish. The Judges, both of the supreme and inferior Courts, shall hold their Offices during good Behaviour, and shall, at stated Times, receive for their Services, a Compensation, which shall not be diminished during their Continuance in Office.

Article III does not specify a method for removing judges, but Article II, § 4, provides that the "President, Vice President and all civil Officers of the United States, shall be removed from Office on Impeachment for, and Conviction of, Treason, Bribery, or other high Crimes and Misdemeanors." Article I, § 2, gives the House of Representatives the sole power of impeachment; § 3 gives the Senate the sole power to try impeachments. Interpreters of the Constitution, from the time of its ratification, have understood the impeach-

---

[2] Article 9, quoted from the text in JENSEN, THE ARTICLES OF CONFEDERATION 266 (1963).

ment provisions to include federal judges as "civil Officers of the United States." Such an understanding is historically valid. Colonial and state constitutional experiments are far more important precedents than references to English practice in establishing the governing rules.

I. ENGLISH AND COLONIAL EXPERIENCE

For much of England's history, judges held their offices during the king's pleasure. The dismissal of Sir Edward Coke by King James in 1616 is the most famous example of judicial displacement by the Crown.[3] To remove judges from just such political pressure, Parliament provided in the Act of Settlement in 1701 that "judges commissions be made *quamdiu se bene gesserint*, and their salaries ascertained and established; but upon address of both houses of parliament it may be lawful to remove them," and that "no pardon under the great seal of *England* be pleadable to an impeachment by the commons in parliament."[4] No clearer statement could be made of Parliament's desire for supremacy within the British constitution. Whereas the judges had formerly been responsible to the king, they were now to answer for their actions to Parliament. Their tenure was more secure than it had been under the Stuarts, but they enjoyed at best a limited independence.

A. J. Carlyle has suggested that the provision for tenure during good behavior in the American Constitution "derived immediately" from the Act of Settlement,[5] but the Constitutional Convention specifically rejected removal by joint address.[6] In England, impeachment of judges had not been discontinued. Impeachment remained the method for removing judges for misconduct, while removal on joint address of both houses could be used for any reason whatsoever.[7]

Before the Act of Settlement, judges holding office during good behavior could be removed by a writ of *scire facias* from the King's

---

[3] See PLUCKNETT, A CONCISE HISTORY OF THE COMMON LAW 239–45 (5th ed. 1956); 5 HOLDSWORTH, A HISTORY OF ENGLISH LAW 351–52 (1937).

[4] 12 & 13 Will. III, c. 2 (1701); quoted in WILLIAMS, THE EIGHTEENTH CENTURY CONSTITUTION, 1688–1815 59 (1960).

[5] CARLYLE, POLITICAL LIBERTY 160 (1941).

[6] See text *infra*, at notes 77–83.

[7] CARPENTER, JUDICIAL TENURE IN THE UNITED STATES 125 (1918).

Bench. In his article on federal judges, Burke Shartel maintained that judicial removal of lower level judges continued even after the eighteenth century.[8] But he did not substantiate his position. His cases, even for the Tudor period were weak: they dealt with removals of court officials, not of judges.[9] Blackstone, the principal source of English law for eighteenth-century Americans, did not mention judicial removal by *scire facias*. He stated only that "in order to maintain both the dignity and independence of the judges in the superior courts, it is enacted by the statute 13 W. III c. 2 that their commissions shall be made (not as formerly, *durante bene placito*, but) *quamdiu se bene gesserint*, and their salaries ascertained and established; but that it may be lawful to remove them on address of both houses of parliament."[10]

The clearest rejection of Shartel's argument lies in the fact that no colonial or state constitution provided for such a use for the *scire facias*, nor was a proposal made to include it during the Constitutional Convention. Even in the unreformed common law, there was a distinction between precedents and fossils.

During the colonial period, for the most part judges held their offices during the pleasure of the royal governor. With the exception of Pennsylvania, colonial assemblies were unable to assert the right to impeach judges.[11]

II. EARLY STATE CONSTITUTIONS

Drafters of early state constitutions, determined to remedy this defect in the governmental balance of power, disagreed over the best way to control judges. Some gave state legislatures almost unlimited power to select and remove judges.[12] Others restricted

---

[8] Shartel, *Federal Judges—Appointment, Supervision, and Removal—Some Possibilities under the Constitution*, 28 MICH. L. REV. 870, 882 n. 33 (1930).

[9] See Appendix *infra*. Impeachment was not used during the later Middle Ages. It was revived when Parliament began its attack on Stuart favorites in the seventeenth century, based largely on the researches of John Selden.

[10] I BLACKSTONE, COMMENTARIES ON THE LAWS OF ENGLAND 267 (1774 Phila. ed.). The American editions of Blackstone do not gloss this passage.

[11] CARPENTER, note 7 *supra*, at 101.

[12] 2 CHROUST, THE RISE OF THE LEGAL PROFESSION IN AMERICA 46 (1965).

the legislatures to impeachment for misconduct.[13] Several states did not substantially change their governmental structure at independence. Connecticut simply added a declaration of rights to its 1662 charter, which was based on the articles of incorporation of a trading company. It provided for a governor, deputy governor, and twelve assistants chosen from the free men of the company. These men carried on the functions of government.[14] Rhode Island retained its charter of 1663 until 1846. Under this charter, the legislature was given the power to set up courts and determine their powers.[15]

The colonies that drafted constitutions on becoming independent affirmed no uniform pattern in their provisions for a judiciary. Article 12 of the Delaware constitution empowered the governor and the general assembly to appoint three justices of the state supreme court, a judge of admiralty, and four justices of the courts of common pleas and orphans' courts for each county. The constitution also provided for a special appeal court of seven, one of whom was to be the governor. The tenure of all judges was to be during good behavior.[16] Like other government officials they could be removed on impeachment by the house of assembly before the legislative council for "offending against the state . . . by maladministration, corruption, or other means, on conviction of misbehaviour at common law, . . . or upon address of the general assembly."[17] In 1792 the governor was given power to remove justices for "reasonable cause" even though sufficient grounds for impeachment were lacking, provided he acted on the "address of two-thirds of all the members of each branch of the legislature."[18] In Delaware the legislature kept firm control over the judiciary; removal by joint address was instituted as a supplement to impeachment.

The New Jersey constitution made the legislature, composed of an elected assembly and council, the dominant branch of government. The council and assembly chose the governor, who served

---

[13] For some of the political considerations in constitution making at this time, see MAIN, THE ANTI-FEDERALISTS: CRITICS OF THE CONSTITUTION, 1781–1788 (1961).

[14] 1 POORE, FEDERAL AND STATE CONSTITUTIONS, COLONIAL CHARTERS, AND OTHER ORGANIC LAWS OF THE UNITED STATES 253 (2d ed. 1878). Hereinafter referred to as POORE.

[15] 2 POORE 1598.

[16] Arts. 12 and 17, 1 POORE 275.

[17] Art. 23, 1 POORE 276–77.

[18] Art. 6, § 2, 1 POORE 283.

as chancellor as well as chief executive. The governor and council were to serve as the court of appeals in last resort in all cases of law, much as they had when New Jersey was a royal colony. The judges of the state supreme court were appointed for seven-year terms by the governor and assembly. Lesser judicial officers were appointed for five years. Reappointment was possible. Judges could be removed before the expiration of their term of office when found guilty of misbehavior by the council or on impeachment by the assembly.[19] Here again, the ultimate responsibility of the judiciary was to the legislature. The New Jersey constitution of 1776 was not revised until 1844.

New York, on the other hand, provided tenure during good behavior or until age sixty for the chancellor, the judges of the supreme court, and for the judges of the county courts. Judges were to be appointed by a council composed of one senator from each county. Like other state officials, they could be impeached on action of two-thirds of the assembly present for "mal and corrupt conduct in their respective offices."[20] The constitution did not stipulate the composition of the impeachment tribunal for trial of a judge.[21] There was no provision for removal on direct address, perhaps because only two-thirds of the members present in the assembly could initiate an impeachment. Both the New Jersey and the New York constitutions may be considered conservative. Neither was submitted to the people for ratification.

The Pennsylvania constitution of 1776 was the most radical of the early state constitutions. It is often contrasted by historians with the Massachusetts constitution of 1780, whose evolution will be examined later. Dominated by a democratic minded group of Philadelphia artisans and western farmers and influenced by Tom Paine, the Pennsylvania constitutional convention created a unicameral legislature whose members were elected annually by all taxpayers. The assembly was the dominant element in government. The executive was composed of an elected council and a president and vice-president chosen annually by joint ballot of the assembly and coun-

---

[19] Art. 12, 2 Poore 1312.   [20] Art. 33, 2 Poore 1337.

[21] Provision was made for the trial of impeachments of other government officials. The accused was given the right to counsel and was tried before a court composed of the president of the senate, the senators, the chancellor, and the judges of the supreme court. Art. 32, 2 Poore 1337.

cil. Judges were appointed by the president and five councilmen for seven-year terms. Reappointment was possible. Every executive and judicial officer was open to impeachment by the assembly, "either when in office, or after his resignation or removal for maladministration."[22] Even the Pennsylvania constitution of 1776 did not provide for an annually elected judiciary, but through limited terms and a simple removal process, the judges were rendered less than independent.

A conservative reaction brought about a revision of the Pennsylvania constitution in 1790. The balance of power within the government was weighted less heavily in favor of the legislature. Judges of the supreme court and of the courts of common pleas were awarded tenure during good behavior. Nevertheless, they were subject to impeachment and to removal by the governor on the address of two-thirds of each branch of the legislature for a "reasonable cause" which need not be sufficient for impeachment.[23]

Vermont did not enter the Union until 1791, but a constitution was drafted in 1777 and again in 1786. The first constitution provided that local and lower court judges were to be elected by the freemen of the state. They were to hold their offices during good behavior but could be removed by the assembly on proof of maladministration.[24] Although a supreme court was mentioned in the constitution, no term of office for its judges was specified. Impeachments were to be tried before the governor and council.[25] The 1786 constitution provided for annual election of all judges by the house of representatives and council.[26] The earlier provisions for impeachment by the general assembly were retained.[27] Vermont, like the other northern states, created a judiciary heavily dependent on the legislature.

In the southern colonies, before the Revolution judicial functions were exercised by the governor and his council, who were appointed either by the officers of a trading company, by a proprietor, or by the king. The elected colonial legislatures had little control over royal nominees.

After concluding that control of judicial salaries was insufficient restraint on the judiciary, the colonial assembly of North Carolina

---

22 § 22, 2 POORE 1545.

23 Art. 5, § 2, 2 POORE 1552.

24 § 27, 2 POORE 1864.

25 § 20, 2 POORE 1863.

26 Ch. 2, § 9, 2 POORE 1870.

27 Ch. 2, § 21, 2 POORE 1872.

made an unsuccessful claim of the power to appoint judges. Under Governor Marten, the conflict over the judicial system "was the most troublesome of all the grievances and turned against the royal party the lawyer and officeholding classes."[28] When North Carolina drew up its first constitution, the delegates empowered the general assembly, by joint ballot of both houses, to appoint judges of the supreme courts of law and equity, judges of admiralty, and the attorney general. The judges were then to be commissioned by the governor and to hold their offices during good behavior.[29] Article 23 of the constitution provided that the governor, and other officers offending against the state, by violating any part of the constitution, by maladministration, or by corruption, could be prosecuted on impeachment by the general assembly, or on presentment of the grand jury of any court of supreme jurisdiction in the state.[30] North Carolina, like the other states, was determined to control the kind of corruption in office that had prevailed during the colonial period.

The conservative Maryland constitution established good behavior as the duration of judicial tenure, but it left the judges far from independent. The chancellor and common-law judges could be removed for misbehavior on conviction in a court of law, or by the governor, upon the address of the general assembly, provided that two-thirds of all members of each house concurred in such an address.[31]

Direct address also appeared in the South Carolina constitution, the most conservative in the South. While judges held their office during good behavior, they could be removed on the address of the general assembly and legislative council, who also elected them.[32] Legislative control of the judiciary went further. The governor and council served as the court of chancery. In 1778, the general assembly framed a new constitution, which authorized the senate and house of representatives to elect all major judicial officers except for chancery judges and to remove them on joint address of both houses.[33]

[28] Green, Constitutional Development in the South Atlantic States, 1776–1860 25 (1930).

[29] Art. 13, 2 Poore 1412.

[30] 2 Poore 1413.   [32] Art. 20, 2 Poore 1619.

[31] § 30, 1 Poore 819; Art. 40, 1 Poore 826.   [33] Art. 27, 2 Poore 1625.

The Georgia constitution was the most radical in the South. It provided for a one-house legislature and gave the vote to all white taxpayers. It even stipulated voting by written ballot.[34] The 1777 constitution did not make specific provisions for the appointment, tenure, or removal of judges except by stipulating that every officer of the state was to be held to account by the house of assembly.[35] The Georgia constitution of 1787 gave judges three-year terms.[36] The judges were again responsible to the state legislature.

The constitutional experiments in Madison's own state, Virginia, and in Massachusetts are especially important because delegates from these states dominated the Constitutional Convention. Just after independence, the Virginia legislature appointed a committee headed by George Mason to draft a constitution. Rumors of Pennsylvania's radical constitution had reached Virginia and alarmed the tidewater aristocracy. Two committee members, Arthur Lee and George Wythe, wrote to John Adams for a conservative answer. Adams' reply, later published as *Thoughts on Government*, was circulated widely in the South.[37] According to Adams, judges should be elected by the legislature, serve during good behavior, and be removable only by impeachment. The two plans drawn by Adams and Patrick Henry, then a radical in local politics, most influenced the convention.[38] Jefferson's plan arrived too late to be considered. His proposed reforms of the 1780's did not envision a structural modification of the judicial system, though he criticized the dependence of the executive and judiciary on the legislature.[39]

The Virginia constitution as adopted in 1776 stood midway between Adams' conservatism and the radicalism of Pennsylvania, Georgia, Vermont, and the farmers of western Massachusetts. It provided for an extremely powerful legislature which chose the governor and delegates to the Continental Congress. In addition, the legislature appointed by joint ballot of the two houses, "Judges of the Supreme Court of Appeals, and General Court, Judges in Chan-

---

34 MAIN, note 13 *supra,* at 17.

35 Art. 49, 1 POORE 383.   36 Art. 3, § 5, 1 POORE 386.

37 ALDEN, THE SOUTH IN THE REVOLUTION, 1763–1789 308 (1957).

38 GREEN, note 28 *supra,* at 64–65.

39 JEFFERSON, NOTES ON THE STATE OF VIRGINIA 114 (Torchbook ed. 1964). See, especially, Query XIII, "The Constitution and the State" and Query XIV, "The Administration of Justice."

cery, Judges of Admiralty, Secretary, and the Attorney-General, to be commissioned by the Governor, and continue in office during good behaviour."[40] The governor, when out of office, and other officers of the state were subject to impeachment by the House of Delegates for offending against the state by maladministration, corruption, or other means that endangered the state.[41] These impeachments were to be tried in the General Court. If all or any of the judges of the General Court "should on good grounds (to be judged by the House of Delegates) be accused of any of the crimes or offences above mentioned," the House of Delegates could impeach the accused judge. The proceedings were to take place in the Court of Appeals. On conviction the judge could be removed from office or disabled for life from holding government office, or subject to such penalty "as the laws shall direct."[42] Clearly, the legislature set itself up as arbiter of correct judicial conduct. The vagueness of the legislature's powers in the constitution left that body the strongest branch of government. The legislature was left to determine on what grounds a judge was to be impeached.

The dominance of the government by the legislature remained the greatest weakness of the northern as well as the southern state constitutions. American political leaders were well aware of this difficulty. At the Philadelphia convention, Madison remarked that "experience in all States has evinced a powerful tendency in the legislature to absorb all power into its vortex. This was the real source of danger to the American Constitutions; and suggested the necessity of giving every defensive authority to the other departments that was consistent with republican principles."[43]

The experience of Massachusetts showed that creating a practical government based on "republican principles" and acceptable to the majority was a difficult task indeed. The citizens of Massachusetts did not ratify a constitution until 1780. Drafts prepared in Boston were unacceptable to the townspeople of western Massachusetts. These democratic minded men insisted on special constitutional conventions and ratification by town meetings. In 1777 the legislature and council were elected with the power to become a constitutional convention. The plan they submitted in 1778 was rejected because of objections to its provisions for representation, for con-

---

40 2 POORE 1911.

41 2 POORE 1912.

42 Ibid.

43 Quoted in GREEN, note 28 supra, at 103.

trol of the militia, and because of a lack of a bill of rights, the exclusion of Negroes from the suffrage, and the inadequacy of the protection of property.[44] In other words, it satisfied neither radicals nor conservatives, neither religiously motivated idealists nor less devout men of affairs.

A second convention met in September, 1779. Among the participants were John and Samuel Adams, John Hancock, James Bowdoin, Benjamin Lincoln, Theophilus Parsons, James Sullivan, and Caleb Strong, representatives of all shades of political opinion. The second constitution was ratified by the towns in 1780. The amendments proposed by the towns indicate that the main issues debated were the suffrage, the relation of church and state, the nature and power of the legislature, control of the militia,[45] frequency of elections, and in a few cases, the tenure of judges.[46]

The rejected constitution of 1778 awarded judges tenure during good behavior.[47] Impeachments of all officers of state for malconduct were to be tried before the governor and senate on initiation by the house of representatives. A provision limiting the ages of judges did not pass the convention.[48] The *Journal of the Convention* from June 17, 1777, through March 6, 1778, reveals no debate over tenure or impeachment,[49] but returns of the towns indicate some dissatisfaction with the judicial system. A few towns wanted the local election of justices of the peace, the men who really controlled local government.[50]

Impeachment was criticized on several grounds. The townspeople of Sutton thought impeachment involved double jeopardy, since the impeached official could subsequently be tried in a court of law.[51] Boothbay also objected to the impeachment clause because it denied a man trial by his peers in a regular court of law.[52] Lenox feared that impeachment would be used primarily as a political weapon.[53]

---

44 HANDLIN & HANDLIN eds., THE POPULAR SOURCES OF POLITICAL AUTHORITY: DOCUMENTS ON THE MASSACHUSETTS CONSTITUTION OF 1780 22 (1966).

45 *Id.* at 34 *et seq.*

46 *Id.* at 50.

47 *Id.* at 199.

48 *Id.* at 183.

49 *Id.* at 177–93.

50 *Id.* at 216, 219.

51 *Id.* at 236.

52 *Id.* at 250.

53 *Id.* at 256.

Tenure during good behavior was unacceptable to a number of towns. Sutton criticized the vagueness of the term "good behavior." They suspected that *"Good Behaviour* will be judged according to disaffection on the one Hand; or Favour on the other."[54] New Salem preferred direct election of justices by the people for a fixed term.[55] Boothbay thought one-year terms were more democratic,[56] as did Shelburne.[57] Lenox, located in the radical western part of the state, objected to tenure during good behavior because judges were made independent both of the legislature and of the people. They argued that the people "have an undoubted right to be pleased with those officers who are to be their judge in all cases both of Life and Property, if they are not pleased with them, the wheels of Government must move very heavily and the laudable ends of the Legislature rendered abortive."[58] At the other end of the political spectrum and of the state, one town thought that the constitution limited the independence of the judges too severely. The *Essex County Result,* probably written by the conservative lawyer Theophilus Parsons, suggested that the judges be appointed by the executive and assured fixed salaries. Essex wanted the good behavior tenure limited only by impeachment by the house and trial by the senate.[59]

In September, 1779, James Bowdoin headed a committee to draft a second constitution. The constitutional convention did not substantially alter the draft clauses relating to the judiciary.[60] Addressing the convention, the committee noted that "[y]ou will readily conceive it to be necessary for your own Safety, that your Judges should hold their offices during good behaviour; for men who hold their places upon so precarious a Tenure as annual or other frequent Appointments will never so assiduously apply themselves to study as will be necessary to the filling their places with dignity. Judges should at all Times feel themselves independent and free."[61] In

---

54 *Id.* at 237.   57 *Id.* at 286.

55 *Id.* at 244.   58 *Id.* at 256.

56 *Id.* at 251.   59 *Id.* at 363–64.

60 The draft, similar to the text of the constitution of 1780, is set out in THE JOURNAL OF THE CONVENTION FOR FRAMING A CONSTITUTION FOR THE STATE OF MASSACHUSETTS BAY 211 (1832).

61 *Id.* at 220.

effect, the committee was trying to answer the objection of the democratic towns to removal of the judges from their control.

The Massachusetts constitution of 1780 stipulated tenure during good behavior for all judges, but the governor, with the consent of the council, could remove them upon the address of both houses of the legislature.[62] Bowdoin's draft also referred to the judiciary in its declaration of rights,[63] and this paragraph was incorporated without change into the constitution. The text explains why many political leaders thought secure tenure for judges was essential to the maintenance of political freedom:[64]

> It is essential to the preservation of the rights of every individual, his life, liberty, property and character, that there be an impartial interpretation of the laws, and administration of justice. It is the right of every citizen to be tried by judges as free, impartial and independent as the lot of humanity will admit. It is therefore not only the best policy, but for the security of the rights of the people, and of every citizen, that judges hold their offices as long as they behave themselves well; and that they should have honourable salaries ascertained and established by standing laws.

This is the philosophy that was to be embodied in the provisions of the national constitution of 1787.

The New Hampshire constitution, ratified in 1783, contains the same clause in its declaration of rights. The provisions with regard to the tenure of judges[65] were probably also copied from the Massachusetts constitution. New Hampshire was strongly anti-Federalist, but it did not object to the Constitution's provision for judicial tenure.

III. Constitutional Convention

The spectrum of views on the judiciary in the town responses to the two Massachusetts constitutions[66] also obtained in other sections of the country in the years before the Constitutional

---

62 Ch. 3, Art. 1, 1 Poore 968.   64 Art. 29, 1 Poore 960.

63 Journal, note 60 *supra*, at 197.   65 2 Poore 1290.

66 The towns returns to the Massachusetts constitution of 1780 indicate that not everyone was persuaded by the arguments in the declaration of rights. Some towns

Convention. The variation in practice among the several states meant that the question of the judiciary's relation to the other branches of government would certainly arise in Philadelphia. Since the Articles of Confederation had not provided for a national judiciary, the debates were primarily over the relationship between the state and federal courts. Nevertheless, some attention was given to the problem of judicial terms of office and removal.

Representatives of every state but Rhode Island met in Philadelphia at the end of May, 1787. A quorum of seven states was reached on May 25, and on May 29, Governor Edmund Randolph presented the Virginia Plan to the assembled delegates. Section 9 of his draft resolved "that a national judiciary be established to consist of one or more supreme tribunals, and of inferior tribunals to be chosen by the National Legislature, to hold their offices during good behaviour."[67] This was the arrangement in Virginia that continued the dominant role of the legislature. Randolph did not specify a method of removal in this clause, but his plan provided for impeachment of national officers to take place in the inferior and then supreme courts. In Virginia, a judge was subject to impeachment by the lower house and trial by the court of appeals.

Charles Pinckney of South Carolina offered a plan on the same day, by which the national legislature would establish courts of law, equity, and admiralty, whose judges would enjoy tenure during good behavior. One of these courts was to be a supreme court. Within its competence would be cases arising under the laws of the United States, or affecting ambassadors or other public ministers and consuls, and the trial of impeachments of officers of the United States.[68]

---

retained the position that the best security for liberty lay in the responsibility of the judges to the people. The town of Adams preferred annual elections. HANDLIN & HANDLIN, note 44 *supra*, at 475. Richmond argued that the "Continuance of Persons in Office for a long or unlimited Term makes them too independent of their Constituents, exposes them to negligence and haughtiness and endangers the Rights of the People and may deprive the State of the benefit of persons better Qualified." *Id.* at 489. Other towns suggested annual appointments or appointments for a short term of years. *Id.* at 540, 785, 803, 839, 868. The voters of Medfield suggested that the governor, with the consent of the senate, should remove judges upon the address of the house of representatives. *Id.* at 783. Boston, the commercial and legal center, accepted the judiciary provisions without dissent. *Id.* at 754–55.

[67] 1 FARRAND, THE RECORDS OF THE FEDERAL CONVENTION OF 1787 21 (rev. ed. 1966).

[68] 3 *id.* at 600.

Sitting as a committee of the whole, the convention debated the Virginia resolutions of May 29 until June 13. During this time, there was some argument over judicial appointments. The Virginia Plan provided for election by the legislature. James Wilson argued for appointment by the President. Madison favored appointment by the senate, and the convention accepted his view. The major debates, however, were over the jurisdiction of the inferior national courts.

The Virginia resolutions were reported out by the convention on June 13. On June 15, William Paterson offered the New Jersey Plan, under which the judges of the supreme court were to be appointed by the President and to hold their offices during good behavior. The supreme court was to decide all impeachments of federal officers.[69]

Alexander Hamilton of New York read to the convention a plan of government "meant only to give a more correct view of his ideas, and to suggest the amendments which he should probably propose to the plan of Mr. R[andolph] in the proper stages of its future discussion."[70] Among Hamilton's amendments was a judiciary article that provided for a supreme court whose justices were to hold their offices during good behavior and were to be removable only by conviction on impeachment for some crime or misdemeanor.[71]

The convention continued debates until June 19, when it rejected the New Jersey Plan and began discussions of the nationalist resolutions offered June 13. Resolution 11 provided for a national judiciary, to consist of one supreme tribunal, the judges of which were to be appointed by the second branch of the national legislature and to hold their offices during good behavior. No provision for removal was specified. Debate continued throughout July. During a discussion on impeaching the executive, Rufus King of New York distinguished between officials holding their places for a term of years and those, like judges, having tenure during good behavior. He thought only the latter could be impeached.[72]

Late in July the resolutions of the convention were turned over to the five-man committee of detail, composed of Rutledge of South Carolina, Randolph of Virginia, Wilson of Pennsylvania, Ellsworth

---

[69] 1 *id*. at 244.

[70] 3 *id*. at 617.

[71] 3 *id*. at 625.

[72] 2 *id*. at 66–67.

of Connecticut, and Gorham of Massachusetts. On August 6 they brought in a draft constitution of three articles, divided into forty-one sections. Sources for this draft were the plans submitted to the convention, its resolutions, state constitutions, and the Articles of Confederation.[73] Their draft was considered for over a month and then referred to a committee of style and revision, whose most important member was Gouverneur Morris. The committee on style reported on September 12.

Article XI, § 2, of the August 6 draft awarded judges of the supreme court and inferior courts tenure during good behavior. The draft did not specify a method for removal. During the discussions following its presentation, Gouverneur Morris submitted a list of members for the President's council of state. Among them was the chief justice of the supreme court, who, with the other ministers, would be removable from office for "neglect of duty, malversation, or corruption."[74] Gerry of Massachusetts moved that the Committee of Five be given the responsibility of devising a mode of trying the supreme court judges in cases of impeachment.[75] The August 6 draft had provided for trial of impeachments in the supreme court. Two days later, on August 22, Rutledge suggested an amendment to Article XI, § 2, to provide for trial of supreme court judges by the Senate on impeachment by the House of Representatives.[76] The report on this resolution was postponed.

Serious consideration of Article XI was resumed on August 27. Dickinson of Pennsylvania moved that the article be amended to include removal by the executive on the application of the Senate and House of Representatives.[77] This, in effect, was removal by joint address. Gerry seconded the motion. Gouverneur Morris objected that it was a contradiction in terms to give judges tenure during good behavior and then leave them open to removal without a trial. In addition, he thought it was wrong to subject judges to so arbitrary an authority.[78] Sherman of Connecticut answered that there was no contradiction or impropriety and observed that Great

---

[73] JENSEN, THE MAKING OF THE AMERICAN CONSTITUTION 72 (1964).

[74] 2 FARRAND, note 67 supra, at 344.

[75] Ibid.

[76] 2 id. at 367.

[77] 2 id. at 428.

[78] Ibid.

Britain had a similar procedure.[79] Rutledge countered that the supreme court's position as judge between the United States and the several States precluded such removal.[80]

Wilson, who came from a state where the legislature had long dominated the government, maintained that removal by direct address was less dangerous in England than in the United States because the Lords and Commons were less likely to concur on removal than the House and Senate. He reminded the convention of Chief Justice Holt, who had managed to alienate both the Commons and Lords, but not at the same time. Wilson was convinced that political factions in the House and Senate would try to remove unfriendly judges.[81] Dickinson answered rather lamely that it was unlikely that the House and Senate would unite to displace a judge for purely political reasons.[82] Nevertheless, Dickinson's motion was voted down seven to one, with three abstentions.[83] Significantly, several states whose constitutions provided for removal on direct address voted against such a provision in the national constitution.

The next day, Madison noted that no mode of impeaching the judges was established.[84] The convention apparently preferred to let the committee on style, composed of King, Johnson, Hamilton, Morris, and Madison, settle the issue. Madison and King were the leading advocates of a strong executive to counteract legislative irresponsibility,[85] and they could be expected to provide security for the judiciary against legislative domination. On September 12, when the committee reported, the problem was still not clearly resolved. During the discussion of this draft, judicial tenure was not questioned. The constitution was adopted, subject to state ratification, with no provision for removal in the judiciary article. There is a legitimate textual question whether judges were included in the impeachment provisions of Article II. On the basis of state constitutional practice and the rejection by the convention of removal on direct address, it is more than likely that they were.

---

[79] *Ibid.*

[80] *Ibid.*

[81] 2 *id.* at 429.

[82] *Ibid.*

[83] *Ibid.*

[84] 4 *id.* at 56.

[85] JENSEN, note 73 *supra*, at 111.

IV. Post-Convention Views

Few records of the debates which occurred in the state ratifying conventions survive, and those extant reveal little discussion
of the tenure of federal judges or of the congressional power of
impeachment.[86] During the Virginia debates, Pendleton maintained
that the independence of the judges was upheld through tenure
during good behavior.[87] There was no argument over removal. In
none of the amendments that Virginia submitted to the constitution
was there a change in judicial tenure or in the method of removal.[88]

Historians usually look to the *Federalist Papers* for elucidation of
the terse clauses of the Constitution. In Number 78, Hamilton argues
that tenure during good behavior "is conformable to the most approved of the State constitutions."[89] In Number 79, he clearly
limits the independence of judges by impeachment. "They are
liable to be impeached for malconduct by the House of Representatives, and tried by the Senate; and, if convicted, may be dismissed
from office, and disqualified for holding any other. This is the only
provision on the point which is consistent with the necessary independence of the judicial character."[90] The only other excuse he
would accept for removing a judge was insanity.[91]

In these two *Federalist* numbers, Hamilton was a truthful propa-
gandist. In all but a few states, judges held office during good
behavior and could be removed only by impeachment.[92] The Constitutional Convention, at which Hamilton had been present, decisively rejected removal on joint address and refused to consider

---

[86] See, *e.g.*, Debates and Proceedings of the Constitutional Convention of the
State of New York, 17 June 1788 16–60, 138–40 (facsimile repr. 1905).

[87] Debates and Other Proceedings of the Convention of Virginia, June 2, 1788
367 (2d ed. 1805).

[88] *Id.* at 471–77.

[89] The Federalist 503 (Mod. Lib. ed. 1941).

[90] *Id.* at 513.

[91] *Id.* at 514.

[92] A worthwhile study of local records could be made to determine how often
and in what circumstances the states resorted to impeachment. A similar study might
be undertaken of the states that provided for removal on joint address of the legislature.

an elective judiciary. They hoped to make the judges free from popular pressure and from legislative control. Their purpose was to create a truly independent judiciary limited only by the cumbersome process of impeachment.

APPENDIX*

1. *Vaux v. Jefferson*, 73 Eng. Rep. 251 (K.B. 1555).
   Vaux was a filazer dismissed by Common Pleas. The King's Bench upheld his removal because he was absent from his post for two years.
2. *Rex v. Toly*, 73 Eng. Rep. 436 (K.B. 1561).
   In this case *scire facias* issued to repeal the patent of auditorship because the auditor did not pass in his accounts according to statute.
3. *Rex. v. Blage*, 73 Eng. Rep. 436 (K.B. 1561).
   Here *scire facias* issued to repeal the patent of office of the king's remembrancer in the Exchequer because the remembrancer had lost his estate in the office when he was made a baron of the Exchequer.
4. *Rex v. Eston*, 73 Eng. Rep. 437 (K.B. 1562).
   A *scire facias* was sent to repeal the patent of the office of the serjeant at arms for not attending his office.
5. *Sir Robert Chester's Case*, 73 Eng. Rep. 465 (K.B. 1562).
   Chester was granted a patent by Edward VI to hold as receiver of the Court of Augmentations and Revenues of the Crown, but with the condition of forfeiture and loss of office for failure to enter his account annually before the end of Hilary Term. He failed to do this and thus forfeited his patent.
6. *Earl of Shrewsbury's Case*, 77 Eng. Rep. 798, 804–05 (K.B. 1610).
   Coke refers to clerks of the court necessary to the operation of the court. He lists three means to lose office: abuse, non-use, refusing to hold it.
7. *Harcourt v. Fox*, 89 Eng. Rep. 680, 720 (K.B. 1692).
   A custos rotulorum must appoint a clerk of the peace for life *quamdiu se bene gesserint* by 1 W. & M., c. 21, § 5 (1688). The court decided that the clerk does not lose his place by removal of the custos.
   On writ of error to the House of Lords, Harcourt was upheld. He could be removed only if he did not perform his office. *Fox v. Harcourt*, 1 Eng. Rep. 107 (H.L. 1693).

---

* These are the cases relied upon by Shartel, see text at notes 8–10 *supra*, to support his argument that the English common law experienced removal of judges by *scire facias*.

8. *Reg. v. Bailiffs of Ipswich,* 91 Eng. Rep. 378 (1706).
   A recorder forfeits his office for failure to attend sessions of the corporation because his office is a public office relating to justice.
9. *Lord Bruce's Case,* 93 Eng. Rep. 870 (K.B. 1728).
   A *quo warranto* will not be issued against a recorder for a forfeiture by non-attendance.
10. *Rex v. Richardson,* 97 Eng. Rep. 426 (K.B. 1758).
    A *quo warranto* was issued against Richardson to show by what authority he claimed to be one of the postmen of the borough of Ipswich. This was another case in which the court held that absence was not sufficient cause for removal.
11. *Rex v. Wells,* 98 Eng. Rep. 41 (K.B. 1767).
    The tenure of a recorder was *quamdiu se bene gesserint.* The court held the absence of the recorder from one session was not sufficient cause for forfeiture for nonfeasance.

EDMUND W. KITCH

THE SUPREME COURT'S CODE OF

CRIMINAL PROCEDURE:

1968–1969 EDITION

It is asserted, with only random empirical support, that legal doctrines carefully built, which fit mortise and tenon to the structure
of our law and the history of our people, will survive long and serve
well. Those speedily built and ill fit must soon decay and, becoming
unusable, will be abandoned.[1] The quality of the work of the
Supreme Court during the 1968 Term in the area of criminal procedure betokens yet another example of jerry-building. The pomp
offered by instant commentators to mark the end of the Warren
Court took no notice of this potential debris. The activist approach
of the Warren Court toward criminal procedure had been quietly
overtaken by events.

One objective has dominated the work of the Warren Court in
the area of criminal procedure: to fashion a constitutional code that
will effect basic constitutional values in both state and federal courts.
In the two great cases of the criminal due process revolution, *Mapp
v. Ohio*[2] and *Miranda v. Arizona*,[3] the Court emphasized the need
for effective enforcement of constitutional rights. In *Mapp* the
Court extended the Fourth Amendment's exclusionary rule to the

---

Edmund W. Kitch is Associate Professor of Law, The University of Chicago.

[1] See LEVI, INTRODUCTION TO LEGAL REASONING (Phoenix ed. 1961).

[2] 367 U.S. 643 (1961).　　　　　　　　[3] 384 U.S. 436 (1966).

states for the reason it was applied in the federal courts. Without the exclusionary rule "the assurance against unreasonable . . . searches and seizures would be 'a form of words,' valueless and undeserving of mention in a perpetual charter of inestimable human liberties. . . . [T]he purpose of the exclusionary rule 'is to deter—to compel respect for the constitutional guaranty in the only effectively available way—by removing the incentive to disregard it.' "[4] In *Miranda*, the Court fashioned its fourfold warning procedure for in-custody interrogation as a safeguard against the inherently coercive nature of interrogation and to give suspects full opportunity to exercise the privilege against self-incrimination.[5] Nor have the Court's decisions been directed solely at the police. The Court has also created a new guarantee of access to appellate and post-conviction remedies designed to force the trial courts to adhere more closely to the commands of the Constitution.[6]

In the 1968 Term the Court continued to expand its control over the police and the trial courts. Increasingly the Court is designing its code of procedure on the premise that the officers of the criminal justice system—policeman, lawyer, and judge—cannot be trusted to respect the Constitution. This premise—which may concede the Court's own lack of power, since its authority must ultimately rest on the respect accorded to the Court as a constitutional institution—leads to procedures that make compliance in good faith, by responsible officers, increasingly demanding. At the same time the complexity and difficulty of the task of formulating a procedural code on a case-by-case basis is undermining the ability of the Court effectively to declare a coherent body of law capable of guiding the operation of the criminal process. The Court's distrust of the inferior agencies of criminal law has led it to invalidate codes of criminal procedure other than its own. But after powerful assertions of authority in *Mapp* and *Miranda*, the Court has itself been unable to articulate and enforce an operable and coherent code of criminal procedure. This has followed not so much from the public outcry against the Court's decisions as from inherent limitations of the

---

[4] 367 U.S. at 655–56, quoting from Elkins v. United States, 364 U.S. 206, 216 (1960).

[5] 384 U.S. at 457–58, 467.

[6] The leading cases are Douglas v. California, 372 U.S. 353 (1963), holding that an indigent has a right to be represented by counsel on appeal on the same conditions that a non-indigent appellant might hire counsel, and Fay v. Noia, 372 U.S. 391 (1963), expanding the availability of federal habeas corpus.

judicial institution to perform the task. The Court has been unable to innovate processes to carry out the responsibility it has assumed. The result is an unsatisfactory division of responsibility between the Supreme Court and the other courts of the land.

The casual reader of the opinions of the 1968 Term will not be alerted to the Court's difficulties in the area of criminal procedure. The opinions read bravely in a business-as-usual way. But careful examination shows that the Court is in retreat from implementation of its system of constitutional criminal procedure.

I. CONTROL OF THE POLICE

When the Court extended the Fourth Amendment exclusionary rule to the states in *Mapp*, its rationale was the need to deter police from making unconstitutional searches and seizures. The conceptual structure of this deterrence mechanism is simple. If the police fail to comply with the Constitution in making searches, the courts "punish" them by refusing to admit the seized items into evidence. In fact, the exclusionary rule has led to a more complicated interaction between the Court, the Constitution, and the police.

First, it is not clear what type of law enforcement officer will be affected by this deterrence mechanism. The target of the deterrence rule appears to be the basically honest policeman who desires to obtain legal convictions. The exclusionary rule provides a remedy for his errors in judgment or zeal. But if one assumes that the real problem is dishonest police who have no qualms about violating the Constitution in order to deal with crime, the deterrent force of the rule is dissipated. Police can conduct illegal searches for the purpose of harassment or to obtain information without seeking prosecution. Searches can be made without the knowledge of the suspect and the information obtained used to provide leads to other evidence. Only procedures that force the police to divulge the complete background of their evidence can make the exclusionary rule effective in this situation. The Court, in dealing with the procedures surrounding the administration of the Fourth Amendment, has not yet confronted the issue whether it is fashioning a device to deal with the good-faith policeman who errs or one to keep dishonest policemen in line. Increasingly, however, the Court seems to be assuming that it is dealing with the second problem, a concept of the function of the exclusionary rule that carries within it the seeds of its own failure.

Second, the exclusionary rule has not only made the police more directly subject to the Constitution; it has also taken the Court into the business of police administration. In the process, demands of administrative reasonableness have begun to make significant inroads on formerly rigid constitutional prohibitions. The exclusionary rule has had an effect not only on the police but on the Court and the Constitution as well.

In *Spinelli v. United States*,[7] the Court was concerned with the warrant procedure under the Fourth Amendment. The Court has long accorded the warrant procedure a central place in its scheme of administration of the Fourth Amendment. *Chimel v. California*[8] —the bright spot in the Court's criminal procedure work this Term —overruled *United States v. Rabinowitz*[9] and limited the scope of warrantless search incident to an arrest. In *Chimel*, the Court quoted at length from an earlier decision:[10]

> We are not dealing with formalities. The presence of a search warrant serves a high function. Absent some grave emergency, the Fourth Amendment has interposed a magistrate between the citizen and the police. This was done not to shield criminals nor to make the home a safe haven for illegal activities. It was done so that an objective mind might weigh the need to invade that privacy in order to enforce the law. The right of privacy was deemed too precious to entrust to the discretion of those whose job is the detection of crime and the arrest of criminals. . . . And so the Constitution requires a magistrate to pass on the desires of the police before they violate the privacy of the home.

The issue in *Spinelli* was whether the affidavit submitted to the commissioner issuing the warrant was sufficient to support a finding by the commissioner of probable cause. The Court reversed the court of appeals and held five to three, with Mr. Justice White writing a separate, enigmatic, concurring opinion,[11] that the affidavit was insufficient. The affidavit, signed by an agent of the FBI, was detailed but worded in a stilted and technical way. In substance it alleged that the FBI had observed the defendant driving into St. Louis, Mis-

---

[7] 393 U.S. 410 (1969).   [8] 395 U.S. 752 (1969).   [9] 339 U.S. 56 (1950).

[10] 395 U.S. at 761, quoting McDonald v. United States, 335 U.S. 451, 455–56 (1948).

[11] 393 U.S. at 423.

souri, on five different days, that on four of those days Spinelli had gone to a particular apartment building about 4:00 P.M., and one of those days he was seen entering a particular apartment. An informer, said to be known by the agent to be reliable but otherwise unidentified, had informed the FBI that Spinelli was carrying on bookmaking operations at telephone numbers WY 4-0029 and WY 4-0136. A check with the telephone company revealed that there were two phones in the apartment, listed in the name of Grace P. Hagen, with these same numbers.

The opinion of the Court, written by Mr. Justice Harlan, was cautious, focusing largely on the specific factual statements of the affidavit. The problem for the Court was to reconcile two lines of cases. One line stressed the problem of relying on unverified information from unidentified informants.[12] How can a magistrate make an objective determination of probable cause if he knows nothing about the informer and how his information was obtained? No such information was contained in the *Spinelli* affidavit. Another line of cases acknowledged this problem but emphasized that information, insufficient in and of itself, could be adequate if officers found that it checked out with other information about the defendant.[13] Did not the fact that Spinelli was making daily trips to an apartment, not his home, where phones with the very numbers provided by the informant were installed, verify the informant's information?

The affidavit in *Spinelli* suffers from curious omissions. Where did Spinelli live? Did he have any employment or regular activity in St. Louis? Who is Grace P. Hagen? Was she the lessee of the apartment Spinelli visited each day? If there was an owner other than Spinelli, did he live there? Why didn't the officers call the number and place a bet? In addition, the affidavit contained a statement that "William Spinelli is known to this affiant and to federal law enforcement agents and local law enforcement agents as a bookmaker, an associate of bookmakers, a gambler, and an associate of gamblers."[14] This statement bothered the Court. In another context, the Court observed that "it is especially important that the tip describe

---

12 Aguilar v. Texas. 378 U.S. 108 (1964); Nathanson v. United States, 290 U.S. 41 (1933).

13 United States v. Ventresca, 380 U.S. 102 (1965); Draper v. United States, 358 U.S. 307 (1959).

14 393 U.S. at 422.

the accused's criminal activity in sufficient detail so that the magistrate may know he is relying on something more substantial than a
casual rumor circulating in the underworld or an accusation based
merely on an individual's general reputation."[15] "[T]he allegation
that Spinelli was 'known' to the affiant and to other federal and local
law enforcement officers as a gambler and an associate of gamblers,"
said the Court, "is but a bald and unilluminating assertion of suspicion that is entitled to no weight in appraising the magistrate's
decision."[16]

Although the Court's opinion is less than clear, the heart of the
decision seems to be that the informer's tip cannot be afforded any
credibility unless details of the tip and the information in the affidavit about the informer and how he obtained his information entitle the tip to credibility without regard to whether the tip is cor-
roborated by further investigation:[17]

> [T]he standards enunciated in *Aguilar* [holding that an affi-
> davit setting forth undetailed conclusions based on "reliable
> information from a credible person" was insufficient] must
> inform the magistrate's decision. He must ask: Can it fairly
> be said that the tip, even when certain parts of it have
> been corroborated by independent sources, is as trustworthy
> as a tip which would pass *Aguilar*'s tests without independent
> corroboration?

The clarity of this holding is muddied by the fact that the Court
distinguished but did not overrule cases which appear to hold the
opposite. But why did the Court follow this line of reasoning?

The Court explained its position in terms of the need for the
magistrate to make an independent factual determination. But this
seems unpersuasive. Should not a fact-finder consider the evidence
as a whole and doesn't the identity of the informer's telephone numbers and the actual telephone numbers add force to the tip? More
important, the Court's frequent language about the objective, detached magistrate has no correspondence to reality. In fact, warrants
are for the most part issued routinely by magistrates in a mechanical
fashion,[18] and the first real exploration of the probable cause issue

---

[15] *Id.* at 416.   [16] *Id.* at 414.   [17] *Id.* at 415.

[18] The perfunctory role of the magistrate in the issuance of a search warrant has
been documented by the American Bar Foundation in three states: Kansas, Michigan, and Wisconsin. LaFave, Arrest: The Decision to Take a Suspect into Custody 30–36 (1965); Miller & Tiffany, *Prosecutor Dominance of the Warrant Deci-*

comes when the search is challenged at trial. In the context of a motion to suppress, the affidavit serves two important functions. First, it has pinned the government down at an early stage to specific allegations so that the facts cannot be altered to fit the results of the search. Second, it acts as a discovery device, giving the defense some information about the way in which the government built its case. But if "reliable information from a credible person" can be used to build the chain of inference on which a finding of probable cause is based, the defense is denied any such information. To illustrate by means of a hypothetical in the context of the *Spinelli* case. Suppose that the FBI, suspecting that Spinelli was a bookmaker, followed him and found that he was visiting a particular apartment each day. The FBI wondered what was going on there, so it put a tap on the phones in the apartment. From the tap the agents learned that Spinelli was carrying on a bookmaking operation. Unfortunately, however, the tap was illegal under § 605 of the Federal Communications Act,[19] and a warrant based on such a tap would be illegal as a fruit of the tap.[20] So, instead of stating that the information that Spinelli was accepting wagers and disseminating wagering information on the two telephones came from a tap, the agent swore that it came from "a confidential reliable informant."[21] This of course need not even be untrue, since the "confidential reliable informant" may be the FBI agent who listened to the tap—confidential because further information about him would reveal the existence of the illegal tap.

The Court did not say that this was the rationale for its decision.

---

sion: *A Study of Current Practices*, 1964 WASH. U. L. Q. 1. Donald McIntyre, Jr., however, in TIFFANY, McINTYRE, & ROTENBERG, DETECTION OF CRIME 119 (1967), concludes that "generally magistrates give more attention to requests for search warrants than they do requests for arrest warrants, which are often signed by the judge's clerk." No supporting evidence is adduced for this conclusion. The basic problem is one of numbers and McIntyre concludes from the study of Kansas, Michigan, and Wisconsin that search warrants are rarely used. *Id.* at 100. But the Court's decision in *Chimel*, narrowing the scope of a search incident to an arrest, should increase the use of search warrants and diminish the magisterial time available for passing on them.

19 47 U.S.C. § 605 (Supp. IV, 1968).

20 Nardone v. United States, 302 U.S. 379 (1937).

21 For a similar situation see United States v. Pearce, 275 F. 2d 318 (7th Cir. 1960), where "confidential information from a source which in the past has proven reliable" was received from the affiant's superior.

This is understandable, since the explicit statement of such a rationale would require the Court to spell out an unproved suspicion that agents of the FBI were intentionally dishonest. In a suggestive passage, however, the Court observed:[22]

> The tip does not contain a sufficient statement of the underlying circumstances from which the informer concluded that Spinelli was running a bookmaking operation. We are not told how the FBI's source received his information—it is not alleged that the informant personally observed Spinelli at work or that he had ever placed a bet with him. Moreover, if the informant came by the information indirectly, he did not explain why his sources were reliable.

On the facts of *Spinelli* the need for disclosure is a more persuasive rationale for the decision than the need for an independent, objective determination of probable cause.

The rationale proffered for the *Spinelli* decision raises serious questions. If the Court believes that agents are willing to mislead the courts as to the source of their information, why shouldn't those same agents be willing to go further and fabricate more details about the informer? Perhaps this is a line some wouldn't cross, since the statement in the *Spinelli* affidavit might be rationalized as a "white lie" while an entirely fabricated story would be a bald lie. But it is hard to believe that a person who is willing to sign a misleading affidavit would be affected by such nice distinctions. If *Spinelli* forces such agents to fabricate at greater length, what is gained? Because the Court has held that the defense is not entitled to the name of the informant,[23] it will be difficult to attack such stories. Perhaps in a few cases the fabrication will be inconsistent with other facts in the case, and the exposure of the inconsistency will throw doubt on the whole affidavit. But in the process, how many common-sense affidavits of honest policemen will fall afoul the technicalities of *Spinelli?*

The Court touched on the problem of enforcing the exclusionary rule more dramatically in *Alderman v. United States*,[24] decided together with *Ivanov v. United States* and *Butenko v. United States*. In these cases the solicitor general conceded that the defendants' conversations had been monitored illegally. The defendants argued

22 393 U.S. at 416.

23 McCray v. Illinois, 386 U.S. 300 (1967).   24 394 U.S. 165 (1969).

that they were entitled to see the transcripts of the illegally monitored conversations to ascertain whether any of the Government's evidence against them was a fruit of the illegal surveillance. The Government argued that the transcripts should first be turned over to the trial judge for in camera inspection, and only if he found them "arguably relevant" should they be given to the defendants. The Court rejected the Government's procedure, emphasizing the importance of adversary procedure in a matter of such factual complexity. Mr. Justice White, writing for the Court, said:[25]

> Adversary proceedings are a major aspect of our system of criminal justice. Their superiority as a means for attaining justice in a given case is nowhere more evidenced than in those cases, such as the ones at bar, where an issue must be decided on the basis of a large volume of factual materials, and after consideration of the many and subtle interrelationships which may exist among the facts reflected by these records. . . .
>
> Adversary proceedings will not magically eliminate all error, but they will substantially reduce its incidence by guarding against the possibility that the trial judge, through lack of time of unfamiliarity with the information contained in and suggested by the materials, will be unable to provide the scrutiny which the Fourth Amendment exclusionary rule demands.

The apparent clarity of the opinion, however, was obscured by a footnote in which the Court seemed to reject the solicitor general's concession that the surveillance had been illegal. "In all three cases," said the Court, "the District Court must develop the relevant facts and decide if the Government's electronic surveillance was unlawful."[26] But the discussion in the opinion on the procedure to be followed was apparently directed to the situation where the illegality of the surveillance was clear. What procedure was to be followed on the equally important question of the legality of the surveillance?

The Court spoke briefly to this problem two weeks later in *Giordano v. United States*[27] a per curiam opinion remanding a large number of cases in which allegations of illegal surveillance had been made by defendants for disposition in light of *Alderman*. Quoting *Alderman*, the Court said:[28]

---

[25] *Id.* at 183–84.

[26] *Id.* at 170 n. 3.

[27] 394 U.S. 310 (1969).

[28] *Id.* at 312–13. (Emphasis added.)

"[T]he District Court must develop the relevant facts and decide if the Government's electronic surveillance was unlawful." Of course, a finding by the District Court that the surveillance was lawful *would make disclosure* and further proceedings unnecessary.

Mr. Justice Stewart, in a concurring opinion, offered an interpretation of *Alderman* without objection from the majority. "We did not in *Alderman* . . . and we do not today, specify the procedure that the District Courts are to follow in making this preliminary determination [of legality]. We have nowhere indicated that this determination cannot approximately be made in ex parte, in camera proceedings."[29] And in his own footnote Mr. Justice Stewart practically urged the Government to argue that the surveillance in all the cases was legal.[30] And lest anyone think that the virtues of adversary proceedings praised so highly in *Alderman* would require such a procedure on the issue of legality, he added:[31]

> One might suppose that all of this should be entirely clear to any careful reader of the Court's opinion in *Alderman, Butenko,* and *Ivanov.* Perhaps so, and perhaps, therefore, what I have said is quite unnecessary. But 10 years of experience here have taught me that the most carefully written opinions are not always carefully read—even by those most directly concerned.

The Court's failure to provide any guidelines for the procedure to be followed on the surveillance issue was a serious abdication of judicial responsibility.[32] The issue was bound to be raised, at the Court's own invitation, in the proceedings below. Surely the Court should have given some indication of how to proceed.

---

[29] *Id.* at 313–14.

[30] *Id.* at 313–14 n. 1: "In oral argument of the *Butenko* and *Ivanov* cases, the Solicitor General, mystifyingly, sought to concede that the surveillances there *were* in fact unconstitutional, although he was repeatedly invited to argue that they were not. . . . In deciding those cases [including *Alderman?*], the Court declined to accept the Solicitor General's proffered concession."

[31] *Id.* at 315.

[32] The grant of certiorari in *Ivanov* and *Butenko* was limited to the procedural questions "on the assumption that there was electronic surveillance of petitioner or a codefendant which violated the Fourth Amendment." 392 U.S. at 924. By rejecting the concession of illegality, the Court itself breached the limits of its grant of certiorari. The limited grant can, therefore, hardly justify the Court's failure to address the problem.

Does the government have a duty to disclose illegal surveillance? Does it have to disclose the facts surrounding legal surveillance? Arguably illegal surveillance? Can the Department of Justice reach its own conclusions about legality? For instance, can the Department of Justice take the position in these proceedings as it long has for internal purposes that wiretapping is not in violation of § 605 so long as the department has not divulged the contents of the communication and that, therefore, there is no obligation to disclose?[33] Can the department unilaterally decide on its own that the surveillance was within its "inherent power" and therefore legal, and therefore not necessary to disclose?

The Court is faced with a hard problem. At root, if the Department of Justice cannot be trusted to make a good-faith effort to comply with the law, there is little the Court can do about it unless the facts are uncovered by the defendants. But the contrast between the Court's quiet avoidance of the procedural problems in determining legality of surveillance and its proud trumpeting about the adversary process in *Alderman* smacks of hypocrisy. On the one hand, the Court orders all transcripts of any illegal taps, no matter what their degree of relevance to the case, spread across the public record. On the other, the Court refuses even to specify the procedures to be followed in making the determination of legality. Won't one effect of the *Alderman* case be to make the Department of Justice and other law enforcement agencies less likely to admit illegal surveillance in the future? Doesn't the *Alderman* procedure unduly embarrass and penalize the good-faith prosecutor who attempts to comply with the Court's rulings on electronic surveillance while protecting the prosecutor who refuses to make any disclosures about surveillance? The fashioning of appropriate procedures for the administration of the deterrent mechanism of the exclusionary rule in this secrecy-prone area is a difficult task. Abstract paeans to the adversary system are of little help.

Strangely enough, the Court has, in other opinions, been sensitive to the problems raised by use of the exclusionary rule as a deterrent. But the Court has revealed such awareness not in cases involving the appropriate procedures under the exclusionary rule but in cases extending the scope of the Fourth Amendment to new areas. There

---

[33] See, *e.g.*, Brownell, *The Public Security and Wire Tapping*, 39 CORNELL L. Q. 195, 197–99 (1954); Rogers, *The Case for Wire Tapping*, 63 YALE L. J. 792, 793 (1954).

have been a number of these cases because the Court has consistently disregarded illogical, historic limitations on the scope of the Fourth Amendment and held that a search is a search is a search. The most notable example of a case recognizing the limits of usefulness of the exclusionary rule is *Terry v. Ohio*,[34] holding a police "stop and frisk" constitutional when based on reasonable suspicion. Chief Justice Warren discussed the limits of the exclusionary rule in these terms:[35]

> [T]he issue is not the abstract propriety of the police conduct, but the admissibility against petitioner of the evidence uncovered by the search and seizure. Ever since its inception, the rule excluding evidence seized in violation of the Fourth Amendment has been recognized as a principal mode of discouraging lawless police conduct. . . .
>
> The exclusionary rule has its limitations, however, as a tool of judicial control. It cannot properly be invoked to exclude the products of legitimate police investigative techniques on the ground that much conduct which is closely similar involves unwarranted intrusions upon constitutional protections. Moreover, in some contexts the rule is ineffective as a deterrent. Street encounters between citizens and police officers are incredibly rich in diversity. . . . Doubtless some police "field interrogation" conduct violates the Fourth Amendment. But a stern refusal by this Court to condone such activity does not necessarily render it responsive to the exclusionary rule. Regardless of how effective the rule may be where obtaining convictions is an important objective of the police, it is powerless to deter invasions of constitutionally guaranteed rights where the police either have no interest in prosecuting or are willing to forego successful prosecution in the interest of serving some other goal.
>
> Proper adjudication of cases in which the exclusionary rule is invoked demands a constant awareness of these limitations. . . . [A] rigid and unthinking application of the exclusionary rule, in futile protest against practices which it can never be used effectively to control, may exact a high toll in human injury and frustration of efforts to prevent crime.

It is all a bit backward. The exclusionary rule was adopted to enforce the Fourth Amendment, which defined the legality of government conduct. But now we are told the issue is what the scope of the exclusionary rule should be, not "the abstract propriety of the police conduct."

---

[34] 392 U.S. 1 (1968).   [35] *Id.* at 12–15.

In *Terry,* the Court rejected the argument that a "stop and frisk" was not a "search and seizure" within the Amendment and also rejected the necessary consequence of such a holding, that probable cause was required to "stop and frisk." Instead the Court discussed at length the various "interests" involved and concluded that "stop and frisk" is legal if the officer has "reasonable suspicion."

The Court first used this type of analysis in *Camara v. Municipal Court,*[36] and *See v. City of Seattle.*[37] At first, these cases seem of relatively minor importance for the administration of the criminal justice system because they deal with the problem of searches by nonpolice officials for fire, housing, and health code violations. They may yet prove to be among the most important Fourth Amendment cases ever decided. In *Frank v. Maryland*[38] the Court, in an opinion by Justice Frankfurter, held that such searches were not within the Fourth Amendment because historically such "civil" searches were outside the scope of the protection. In *Camara* and *See* the Court reversed *Frank* and held that a search is a search. Having done so, it proceeded to deal with the problem whether its holding would make systematic area enforcement searches illegal. In its discussion, the Court specifically equated the problem of probable cause for a search with the question whether a search is "reasonable":[39]

> In determining whether a particular inspection is reasonable —and thus in determining whether there is probable cause to issue a warrant for that inspection—the need for the inspection must be weighted in terms of [the] reasonable goals of code enforcement.
> There is unanimous agreement among those most familiar with this field that the only effective way to seek universal compliance with the minimum standards required by municipal codes is through routine periodic inspections of all structures. It is here that the probable cause debate is focused, for the agency's decision to conduct an area inspection is unavoidably based on its appraisal of conditions in the area as a whole, not on its knowledge of conditions in each particular building. Appellee contends that, if the probable cause standard urged by appellant is adopted, the area inspection will be eliminated as a means of seeking compliance with code standards and the reasonable goals of code enforcement will be dealt a crushing blow.
> . . . The . . . argument is in effect an assertion that the

---

[36] 387 U.S. 523 (1967).

[37] 387 U.S. 541 (1967).

[38] 359 U.S. 360 (1959).

[39] 387 U.S. at 535–37.

area inspection is an unreasonable search. Unfortunately, there can be no ready test for determining reasonableness other than by balancing the need to search against the invasion which the search entails. But we think that a number of persuasive factors combine to support the reasonableness of area code-enforcement inspections. First, such programs have a long history of judicial and public acceptance. . . . Second, the public interest demands that all dangerous conditions be prevented or abated, yet it is doubtful that any other canvassing technique would achieve acceptable results. . . . Finally, because inspections are neither personal in nature nor aimed at the discovery of evidence of crime, they involve a relatively limited invasion of the urban citizen's privacy.

The balancing approach to the legality of Fourth Amendment searches has a certain ominous ring. It is always the reasonable demands of the public interest that are used to justify incursions on civil liberties. Suppose a child is kidnapped.[40] Can the police search every home in town because the interest in saving the child's life is greater than the "relatively minor" inconvenience of having a policeman in your house? Because experts say the fastest way to find the child is to look everywhere? Because the search is aimed at finding the child, not aimed personally at the occupants of the homes?

The quoted language was greeted by commentators with relative calm.[41] Both cases involved the problem of extending the Fourth

---

[40] "[I]f we are to make judicial exceptions to the Fourth Amendment for these reasons [of practical necessity], it seems to me they should depend somewhat upon the gravity of the offense. If we assume, for example, that a child is kidnapped and the officers throw a roadblock about the neighborhood and search every outgoing car, it would be a drastic and undiscriminating use of the search. The officers might be unable to show probable cause for searching any particular car. However, I should candidly strive hard to sustain such an action, executed fairly and in good faith, because it might be reasonable to subject travelers to that indignity if it was the only way to save a threatened life and detect a vicious crime." Brinegar v. United States, 338 U.S. 160, 183 (1949) (Jackson, J., dissenting).

[41] LaFave, *Administrative Searches and the Fourth Amendment: The Camara and See Cases,* 1967 SUPREME COURT REVIEW 1, 20: "[T]he Court has taken the view that the evidentiary requirement of the Fourth Amendment is not a rigid standard, requiring precisely the same quantum of evidence in all cases, but instead is a flexible standard, permitting consideration of the public and individual interests as they are reflected in the facts of a particular case. This is an extremely important and meaningful concept, and one which may well prove most useful in reshaping some rather shaky Fourth Amendment doctrine." See also Kitch, *Katz v. United States: The Limits of the Fourth Amendment,* 1968 SUPREME COURT REVIEW 133, 142–43.

Amendment to new areas where as a matter of historic custom standards less rigorous than probable cause had prevailed. Surely these cases had nothing to say about the probable cause requirement of the Fourth Amendment in the context of police searches for the purpose of obtaining evidence to convict a person of a crime.

Last Term, in *Davis v. Mississippi*,[42] the Court gave that sanguine reaction a sharp jolt. The script for *Davis* reads like that of many a classic civil rights case:[43]

> The rape occurred on the evening of December 2, 1965, at the victim's home in Meridian, Mississippi. The victim could give no better description of her assailant than that he was a Negro youth. Finger and palm prints found on the sill and borders of the window through which the assailant apparently entered the victim's home constituted the only other lead available at the outset of the police investigation. Beginning on December 3, and for a period of about 10 days, the Meridian police, without warrants, took at least 24 Negro youths to police headquarters where they were questioned briefly, fingerprinted, and then released without charge. The police also interrogated 40 or 50 other Negro youths either at police headquarters, at school, or on the street. Petitioner, a 14-year-old youth who had occasionally worked for the victim as a yardboy, was brought in on December 3 and released after being fingerprinted and routinely questioned.

The defendant was also taken to the victim's hospital room but she did not positively identify him as her assailant. On December 12 the police took the defendant out of town to Jackson and incarcerated him overnight. The next day the defendant signed a statement and took a lie detector test, neither of which were used at the trial. He was returned to Meridian, fingerprinted again, and the new prints along with the prints of twenty-three other Negro youths were sent to the FBI for analysis. The FBI reported that the defendant's prints matched those on the window. This fingerprint evidence was used against the defendant at trial.

Before the Supreme Court, the state conceded that the second set of prints was illegally obtained because the arrest of the petitioner was without probable cause and illegal. But the state argued that the prints taken on December 3 were taken legally and that it didn't make any difference which set of prints had actually been sent to

---

42 394 U.S. 721 (1969).   43 *Id*. at 722.

the FBI.[44] The state argued that the December 3 prints were obtained legally because the detention occurred at the investigatory rather than the accusatory stage, and because detention for taking fingerprints is not an arrest subject to the Fourth Amendment. The Court, in an opinion by Mr. Justice Brennan, rejected both arguments on the ground that the Fourth Amendment applies to all searches for any evidence of crime at any stage of the proceeding. Mr. Justice Stewart in dissent offered a reinterpretation of the majority's opinion, as he had in *Giordano*, again without objection from the Court. The opinion didn't mean, said Mr. Justice Stewart, that Mississippi couldn't go out and get another set of prints from the defendant and prosecute him again. After all, "We deal . . . with 'evidence' that can be identically reproduced and lawfully used at any subsequent trial."[45] In a footnote, he explained that the testimony of the victim who had identified the defendant at the trial would provide probable cause for a legal arrest.[46] But since the victim apparently had not identified the defendant until after the investigation by the police[47] her identification might possibly be a tainted fruit of the improperly obtained prints or statement. Mr. Justice Brennan failed to say anything that would undermine Mr. Justice Stewart's interpretation of the decision.[48] Mr. Justice Stewart dissented because he could not "believe that the doctrine of *Mapp* . . . requires so useless a gesture as the reversal of this conviction."[49]

Mr. Justice Brennan seemed to go out of his way to confirm that the Court was indeed more concerned about "gestures" than about the substance of what the police had done:[50]

---

[44] Brief for Respondent, pp. 7–8.   [45] 394 U.S. at 730.   [46] *Id.* at 730 n.

[47] The identification of the defendant by the victim, an eighty-seven-year-old woman, was ambiguous. Record A. 22. The cross-examination of the victim did not explore the way in which she had become sure of her identification. The police conducted their diligent investigation as if they had no reliable identification. The victim, in her hospital bed, was unable positively to identify the defendant as her assailant. *Id.*, A. 51. The victim seemed to be made certain in her identification by her belief that the defendant had confessed. *Id.*, A. 29. But no confession was introduced at trial. The Mississippi Supreme Court held that defense counsel had not preserved any objection to the mention of the confession. Davis v. Mississippi 204 So.2d 270 (Miss. 1967). But the admissibility of any such confession and the source of the identification are questions that can be raised in subsequent proceeding.

[48] He acknowledged by implication in a footnote the possibility of a retrial. 394 U.S. 725–26 n. 4.

[49] *Id.* at 730.   [50] *Id.* at 727–28.

> It is arguable . . . that, because of the unique nature of the fingerprinting process, such detentions [for the purpose of taking prints] might, under narrowly defined circumstances, be found to comply with the Fourth Amendment even though there is no probable cause in the traditional sense. See *Camara* v. *Municipal Court*. . . . Detention for fingerprinting may constitute a much less serious intrusion upon personal security than other types of police searches and detentions. Fingerprinting involves none of the probing into an individual's private life and thoughts which marks an interrogation or search. Nor can fingerprint detention be employed repeatedly to harass any individual, since the police need only one set of each person's prints. Furthermore, fingerprinting is an inherently more reliable and effective crime-solving tool than eyewitness identifications or confessions and is not subject to such abuses as the improper line-up and the "third degree." Finally, because there is no danger of destruction of fingerprints, the limited detention need not come unexpectedly or at an inconvenient time. For this same reason, the general requirement that the authorization of a judicial officer be obtained in advance of detention would seem not to admit of any exception in the fingerprinting context.

In other words the real objection to the procedure followed in *Davis* was that the police did not ask the courts to approve of it in advance. Mr. Justice Brennan seems to have forgotten that the Fourth Amendment was written to ban that most odious of all oppressive instruments, the general warrant.[51] The general warrant did, after all, produce reliable evidence and the inconvenience to the householder was a passing one. But the experience of history has shown that it was subject to gross abuse.

The Court will some day repudiate this dictum. But in the mean-

---

[51] See the discussion in Boyd v. United States, 116 U.S. 616 621–33 (1886); LANDYNSKI, SEARCH AND SEIZURE AND THE SUPREME COURT 21–42 (1966); LASSON, THE HISTORY AND DEVELOPMENT OF THE FOURTH AMENDMENT TO THE UNITED STATES CONSTITUTION 13–78 (1937). The objections to a general warrant developed in England in response to efforts to enforce the criminal libel laws through indiscriminate seizures of a man's papers and in the colonies in response to the use of writs of assistance empowering revenue officers to make indiscriminate searches for smuggled goods. Resentment of the substantive laws being enforced was an important factor in the development of opposition to the practice. But the common theme was the general search on suspicion that indiscriminately affected the innocent as well as the guilty. The Court seems insensitive to the substantial difference between being subjected to an area housing code search, authorized in *Camara*, and being taken to the police station for compulsory fingerprinting in a murder investigation.

time it will be used as a justification by thousands of lower courts for procedures that are unconstitutional under the Fourth Amendment.

II. CONTROL OF THE COURTS

The thrust of the Warren Court's work in the area of police investigation has been to create barriers to the adjudication of guilt by inquisitorial methods at the investigatory stage, thereby shifting the focus of adjudication to the courts with their accusatorial procedures. The problem here is that of preserving free and open access to the courts for all defendants. The growing recognition of the overwhelming importance of the guilty plea for the administration of criminal justice and the existence in some jurisdictions of policies of differential sentencing designed to induce guilty pleas[52] are at the frontiers of this problem.

In *Boykin v. Alabama*[53] the Court reversed a death sentence for armed robbery imposed by a jury after a plea of guilty. The common-law record in the case showed the following:[54]

> This day in open court came the State of Alabama by its District Attorney and the defendant in his own proper person and with his attorney, Evan Austill, and the defendant in open court on this day being arraigned on the indictment of these cases charging him with the offense of Robbery and plead guilty.

Mr. Justice Douglas, writing for the Court, held: "It was error, plain on the face of the record, for the trial judge to accept petitioner's guilty plea without an affirmative showing that it was intelligent and voluntary."[55] He added:[56]

> A plea of guilty is more than a confession which admits that the accused did various acts; it is itself a conviction; nothing remains but to give judgment and determine punishment. . . . Admissibility of a confession must be based on a "reliable determination on the voluntariness issue which satisfies the constitutional rights of the defendant." . . . The requirement that the prosecution spread on the record the prerequisites of a valid waiver is no constitutional innovation.

---

[52] See Alshuler, *The Prosecutor's Role in Plea Bargaining*, 36 U. CHI. L. REV. 50 (1968); Scott v. United States, No. 20,954 (D.C. Cir. 1969).

[53] 395 U.S. 238 (1969).

[54] Record, A. 4.

[55] 395 U.S. at 242.

[56] *Id.* at 242–44.

In *Carnley* v. *Cochran* . . . we dealt with a problem of waiver of the right to counsel, a Sixth Amendment right. We held: "Presuming waiver from a silent record is impermissible. The record must show, or there must be an allegation and evidence which show, that an accused was offered counsel but intelligently and understandingly rejected the offer. Anything less is not waiver.

We think that the same standard must be applied to determine whether a guilty plea is voluntarily made. For, as we have said, a plea of guilty is more than an admission of conduct; it is a conviction. Ignorance, incomprehension, coercion, terror, inducements, subtle or blatant threats might be a perfect cover-up of unconstitutionality. . . .

. . . We cannot presume a waiver . . . from a silent record.

What is at stake for an accused facing death or imprisonment demands utmost solicitude of what courts are capable in canvassing the matter with the accused to make sure he has a full understanding of what the plea connotes and of its consequence. When the judge discharges that function, he leaves a record adequate for any review that may be later sought . . . , and forestalls the spin-off of collateral proceedings that seek to probe murky memories.

The reasoning seems to be that a plea of guilty is a waiver of all constitutional rights. Therefore the procedure for a valid waiver of these rights must be at least as rigorous as that required for waiver of any constitutional right. Presuming waiver of the right to counsel from a silent record is impermissible; therefore, presuming waiver of any constitutional right from a silent record is impermissible. But the "silent record" the Court was discussing in *Carnley v. Cochran*[57] was the record in a post-conviction proceeding. The silent record in *Boykin* was the record on the plea itself. If the state has a burden to "spread on the record the prerequisites of a valid waiver," should it not have the opportunity to do so in a post-conviction proceeding when the question is raised?

Procedures and standards for the waiver of constitutional rights raise important and difficult issues. The Court has seldom discussed them except in terms of the overly general concepts: voluntary, knowing, and intelligent.[58] It is unfortunate that the Court once again passed up an opportunity to discuss these issues. The scope of

---

[57] 369 U.S. 506 (1962).

[58] Chief Justice Warren's oft-repeated triad in Miranda v. Arizona, 384 U.S. 436 (1966).

a constitutional right is not fully defined until the conditions under which it can be waived have been delineated. When the Court thinks seriously about the problem, it will discover that standards and procedures for the waiver of a constitutional right must be delineated in relation to the nature and function of that right.[59] What did the Court in fact mean by the requirement "that the prosecution spread on the record the prerequisites of a valid waiver"? Must the judge hear evidence on the matter? Does the state have the burden of an evidentiary presentation relating to all the facts surrounding the plea of guilty? Must the defendant take the stand and be interrogated at length about his understanding of his rights? It is clear from the footnotes to the opinion that the Court had none of these things in mind.[60] Instead, the Court meant that the record must show that the trial judge had followed a procedure like that required by Rule 11 of the Federal Rules of Criminal Procedure.

Rule 11 provides: "The court . . . shall not accept such plea [of guilty] . . . without first addressing the defendant personally and determining that the plea is made voluntarily with understanding of the nature of the charge and the consequences of the plea." The significance of Rule 11 was dramatized last Term in *McCarthy v. United States.*[61] McCarthy was convicted of willful income tax evasion on a plea of guilty. His counsel entered the plea, assuring the court that his client understood the consequences of a plea. The trial judge personally inquired only whether or not the plea was the product of any threats or promises. At the subsequent sentencing hearing defendant's counsel unsuccessfully argued that a suspended sentence should be imposed because the defendant's failure to pay taxes had been accidental and unintentional.

---

[59] The rule that a defendant may be tried again after reversal of his conviction has long been justified on the ground that by appealing the defendant has waived his right to be protected against double jeopardy. But such a "waiver" is hardly voluntary, knowing, and intelligent. In discussing the rule last Term in North Carolina v. Pearce, 395 U.S. 711, 720–21 (1969), the Court was more precise: "Although the rationale for this 'well-established part of our constitutional jurisprudence' has been variously verbalized, it rests ultimately upon the premise that the original conviction has, at the defendant's behest, been wholly nullified and the slate wiped clean. . . . A new trial may result in an acquittal. But if it does result in a conviction, we cannot say that the constitutional guarantee against double jeopardy of its own weight restricts the imposition of an otherwise lawful single punishment for the offense in question."

[60] 395 U.S. at 243–44 nn. 5, 6.   [61] 394 U.S. 459 (1969).

The Court reversed the conviction and held that the defendant had the right to plead anew because the trial court had not complied with Rule 11. The court had not personally addressed the defendant to ascertain whether he understood the nature of the charge and the consequences of his plea. The Court observed that the record in *McCarthy* illustrated the problems that can arise when a trial judge fails clearly to establish on the record that the defendant understood the nature of the charge and the consequences of his plea. The fact that counsel had argued at the sentencing hearing that the tax evasion was inadvertent, said the Court, casts "considerable doubt on the Government's assertion that petitioner pleaded guilty with full awareness of the nature of the charge."[62] Although this argument is at the least oversimplified and probably specious, given the instructions on the presumption of intent from the act of nonpayment of taxes which the government would probably be able to get at trial,[63] it does suggest that the Court viewed the central problem as one of incompetence of counsel. Counsel's argument at the sentencing hearing suggested to the Court that counsel did not understand the elements of the offense. If one has confidence in counsel, he can be counted on to inform the defendant about the nature of the charge and ascertain whether the defendant is in fact likely to be convicted.

But can interrogation by the trial judge really operate to ensure that a plea is knowing, voluntary, and intelligent? The record in *McCarthy* itself suggests that interrogation by the trial judge cannot protect against involuntary pleas. McCarthy was charged with three different offenses in his indictment: income tax evasion in 1959, 1960, and 1961. When he entered his plea of guilty the Government "informed the court that if petitioner's plea of guilty to

---

[62] *Id.* at 470.

[63] Holland v. United States, 348 U.S. 121, 139 (1954): "A final element necessary for conviction is willfulness. The petitioners contend that willfulness 'involves a specific intent which must be proven by independent evidence and which cannot be inferred from the mere understatement of income.' This is a fair statement of the rule. Here, however, there was evidence of a consistent pattern of underreporting large amounts of income, and of the failure on petitioners' part to include all of their income in their books and records. Since on proper submission, the jury could have found that these acts supported an inference of willfulness, their verdict must stand." *Cf.* United States v. Mitchell, 271 F. Supp. 858, 863 (N.D. Ill. 1967): "Though consistent substantial understatement of income is highly persuasive evidence of intent to defraud, I do not believe that such understatement in and of itself is proof enough."

count 2 [1960] were accepted, the Government would dismiss counts 1 and 3."[64] This certainly looks like a plea bargain. Can it be argued that this bargain made McCarthy's plea involuntary—the result not of a free decision but of government-created inducements to plead? But when the judge asked McCarthy if any promises had been made to induce a plea of guilty he answered no. This is no surprise. Any promise to induce a plea of guilty is going to be made on condition that the defendant correctly answer such questions. It is not without significance that the prosecutor in *McCarthy* specifically requested the judge to ask the defendant whether the plea had been induced by any threats or promises. He wanted to make a record that would bar any subsequent attack on the plea based on the existence of the plea bargain.

Can interrogation by the judge operate to make a plea knowing and intelligent? Experience indicates that the interrogation by the trial judge will usually be conducted in abstract terms of deceptive simplicity. The defendant, having already consulted his counsel, is unlikely to insist on a full explanation of simple sounding but highly technical concepts. To illustrate from the facts of *McCarthy*. Suppose the trial judge had personally told McCarthy that the charge required proof of a "willful failure" to pay taxes and asked whether McCarthy understood that. Wouldn't McCarthy have probably answered yes because the concept of willfulness is one which a layman is likely to feel he understands, even though it has confused lawyers for centuries? Or take a defendant charged with murder. Is the judge going to explain the problems of the required mens rea, the degrees of the crime, and the scope of all available defenses? Perhaps the procedure of Rule 11 provides some protection against incompetent counsel who has given his client grossly erroneous advice about the crime charged or the range of penalties, but it cannot insure that a plea is knowing, voluntary, and intelligent.

In this light, the Court's insistence in *McCarthy* and *Boykin* that such a procedure bars further attack on the plea is troubling. "Our holding," wrote Chief Justice Warren in *McCarthy*, "will help reduce the great waste of judicial resources required to process the frivolous attacks on guilty plea convictions that are encouraged, and are more difficult to dispose of, when the original record is inadequate."[65] "When a judge," wrote Mr. Justice Douglas in *Boykin*,

---

[64] 394 U.S. at 461.   [65] *Id*. at 472.

"discharges that function [of canvassing the matter with the accused], he leaves a record adequate for any review that may be later sought . . . , and forestalls the spin-off of collateral proceedings that seek to probe murky memories."[66] In other words, once the defendant has answered all the proper questions, it will be almost impossible for him successfully to contend that he was coerced, or that he really didn't understand the nature of the charge and the consequences of his plea, even if he had been coerced and he had not understood.

That these very real problems in the administration of guilty pleas are not impossible of solution is illustrated by the procedure actually followed by the Alabama courts on Boykin's guilty plea. For under Alabama procedure, unlike that of most other states, when a man pleads guilty to a capital offense that is not the end of the matter.[67] In Boykin's case the Court proceeded to have an abbreviated jury trial with testimony from the witnesses, submission of the issue of guilt and innocence to the jury, and determination by the jury of the sentence to be imposed. This procedure, to be sure, does not offer the same safeguards as a trial, because the cross-examination and argument by the defense counsel are pro forma only. It does, however, provide two important protections. First of all, it forces the state to put in actual eyewitness testimony of the crime. This provides a basis independent of the plea for concluding that the defendant has in fact committed the crimes charged. Second, because the jury imposes the ultimate penalty, it protects against any form of bargaining over the penalty. This is a particularly serious problem in capital cases because a promise from a trial judge or a prosecutor that the death penalty will not be imposed if a defendant pleads guilty creates substantial coercive pressures so to plead. But if the penalty is imposed by a jury, impaneled after the plea and informed as to the full range of penalties that can be legally imposed, then neither the judge nor the prosecutor has effective control over the disposition. Therefore, a defendant will plead guilty only when he feels there is no advantage to a trial, not because he knows that he can save his life by so pleading.

---

[66] 395 U.S. at 244.

[67] Ala. Code, tit. 30, § 70 (1958): "[I]f the defendant enters a plea of guilty . . . such plea of guilty . . . shall be entered of record . . . the trial of the cause shall be had and the question of the degree of guilt must be ascertained and the punishment fixed by a jury."

The Supreme Court, however, treated these additional procedural protections as irrelevant. Ironically, there is reason to suppose that had Boykin not formally pleaded guilty his conviction would have been sustained. Examination of the record shows that the state put in eyewitness testimony to each of the five armed robberies charged in the indictment. Defense counsel did not object to the introduction of hearsay evidence and confined his cross-examination to the two witnesses who testified that the defendant had fired his gun. The purpose of the cross-examination was to establish that the gun was not discharged in order to injure anyone and that the one injury actually inflicted was not serious.[68]

In many cases there are good tactical reasons for the defendant neither to plead guilty nor to make a defense. For instance a defendant who has lost a motion to suppress critical evidence will not be able to raise this question in the appellate courts if he pleads guilty. But if he has no other defense there is every reason to simplify the presentation of the case so that the defendant can in substance be in the position of a defendant who has pleaded guilty and thrown himself on the mercy of the court. Such bench trials are not very different from the hearing actually held in *Boykin*. But in these cases the defendant waives numerous substantial constitutional rights without the benefit of any interrogation by the judge. Are such convictions now invalid under *Boykin?*

In contrast to the generalities of *Boykin*, the Court was able last Term to fashion specific procedural protection against differential sentencing designed to penalize resort to the appellate courts. In *Benton v. Maryland*[69] the Court overruled *Palko v. Connecticut*[70] thus extending the federal double-jeopardy rule to the states. Then in *North Carolina v. Pearce*[71] the Court confronted the question whether the double-jeopardy provision or the Equal Protection Clause bars a trial judge from imposing a heavier sentence after a retrial following appellate reversal. The Court held that they did not. But it proceeded to rule that the Due Process Clause requires that there be a valid reason for any increased sentence. Mr. Justice Stewart wrote:[72]

> It can hardly be doubted that it would be a flagrant violation of the Fourteenth Amendment for a state trial court

---

[68] Record, A. 15–16, 20–21.

[69] 395 U.S. 784 (1969).

[70] 302 U.S. 319 (1937).

[71] 395 U.S. 711 (1969).

[72] *Id.* at 723–24.

to follow an announced practice of imposing a heavier sentence upon every reconvicted defendant for the explicit purpose of punishing the defendant for his having succeeded in getting his original conviction set aside. Where, as in each of the cases before us, the original conviction has been set aside because of a constitutional error, the imposition of such a punishment, "penalizing those who choose to exercise" constitutional rights, "would be patently unconstitutional." *United States* v. *Jackson*. . . . And the very threat inherent in the existence of such a punitive policy would, with respect to those still in prison, serve to "chill the exercise of basic constitutional rights." *Id.* See also *Griffin* v. *California* . . . ; cf. *Johnson* v. *Avery*. . . . But even if the first conviction has been set aside for a nonconstitutional error, the imposition of a penalty upon the defendant for having successfully pursued a statutory right of appeal or collateral remedy would be no less a violation of due process of law. "A new sentence, with enhanced punishment, based upon such a reason, would be a flagrant violation of the rights of the defendant." . . . "This Court has never held that the States are required to establish avenues of appellate review, but it is now fundamental that, once established, those avenues must be kept free of unreasoned distinctions that can only impede open and equal access to the courts. . . ."

If there is no constitutional right to appeal, what right is being "chilled" by the increased sentence? The precedents which the Court cites for its conclusions deal with different problems. *United States v. Jackson*[73] held unconstitutional a statutory scheme that imposed the risk of the death penalty only on those who insisted on jury trial. But the Court has repeatedly held that there is a due process right to a jury trial. *Griffin v. California*[74] dealt with comments by the prosecutor on the failure of the defendant to testify. The reference to *Johnson v. Avery*[75] is most curious. In that case, decided last Term, the Court held that jail-house lawyers must be permitted to pursue their trade because otherwise their fellow inmates would be effectively deprived of the federal right to habeas corpus.

Perhaps the Court is groping toward a general concept that every federal constitutional right carries with it the right to an effective remedy for the vindication of that right. But even that would not explain the Court's actions because presumably trial courts are designed to be an effective forum for the vindication of constitutional

---

[73] 390 U.S. 570 (1968).   [74] 380 U.S. 609 (1965).   [75] 393 U.S. 483 (1969).

rights. The Court seems to go farther and say that there is a right to have a right not recognized by a trial court vindicated by an appellate court.[76] And a right not recognized by an appellate court vindicated in a post-conviction proceeding.[77] And, for state defendants, a right not recognized in a post-conviction proceeding vindicated on federal habeas corpus.[78] In short, maybe there is a constitutional right to appeal, not once but ad infinitum.

In analyzing a policy of more severe penalties on retrial, the Court is insensitive to the problem of channeling appellate resources to the review of cases where there is a real possibility of righting injustice. For appellants who pay their own expenses there is a financial sanction to deter the pursuit of meaningless appeals. But for indigent appellants, the Court has declared unconstitutional any channeling devices which operate unequally on the poor.[79] Continuing that tradition, the Court last Term held improper a rule of the Ninth Circuit that, in substance, required indigent petitioners in federal post-conviction proceedings who allegedly had been deprived of their right of appeal to disclose, without the assistance of a lawyer, the errors they would have raised and to demonstrate that denial of the appeal had caused prejudice.[80] And in *Williams v. Oklahoma City*[81] the Court extended *Griffin v. Illinois*[82] to petty offenses, holding that a free transcript must be provided to an indigent appealing a drunken driving conviction. But a more severe sentence after retrial is a resource channeling device that affects rich and poor alike. Someone who stands reconvicted after an appellate reversal is someone who was legally guilty. Should he not have been discouraged from pursuing his appeal simply to force the state to try him again?

---

[76] Douglas v. California, 372 U.S. 353 (1963).

[77] In Case v. Nebraska, 379 U.S. 958 (1964), the Court granted certiorari to determine "whether the Fourteenth Amendment requires that the States afford state prisoners some adequate corrective process for the hearing and determination of claims of violation of federal constitutional guarantees." 381 U.S. 336, 337 (1965). When Nebraska passed a post-conviction act, the case was remanded. *Ibid.*

[78] Johnson v. Avery, 393 U.S. 483 (1969).

[79] The leading case is Griffin v. Illinois, 351 U.S. 12 (1956), holding that all indigents must be furnished a free stenographic transcript—or its equivalent—so that they may prepare their appeals.

[80] Rodriquez v. United States, 395 U.S. 327 (1969).

[81] 395 U.S. 458 (1969).   [82] Note 79 *supra.*

The reasoning of the Court in *Pearce* requires a similar procedure to protect against differential sentences designed to chill assertion of the constitutional right to trial. Whether or not there is a constitutional right to appellate review, the right to a trial is the most fundamental due process right. But such a procedure is much easier to fashion in the context of appellate review. The first sentence is established in the record, whereas the sentence the judge would have imposed on a plea of guilty is not on the record and is known only to the participants in a bargaining conference. The only way bargaining and differential sentencing can ever be supervised is by devising procedures to make plea discussions a matter of record, fully disclosed. Unfortunately, the Rule 11 procedure imposed by the Court in *Boykin* has the effect of driving plea bargaining underground, since any promises must always be denied for purposes of the record.

The Court's intensive concern with barriers to appellate and post-conviction remedies, and a willingness to shape in detail the access channeling mechanisms, contrasts sharply with its treatment of the access problem in the trial courts in terms of general, vacuous abstractions. This is a curious inversion of what would seem to be the sensible priority. Shouldn't full and effective access at the trial level come first, and shouldn't the Court be more willing to tolerate limitations on access at the secondary and really less important appellate level? This inversion probably reflects the natural orientation of a court without trial experience but a court with day in and day out experience with appellate procedures. The Court's preference for appellate as opposed to trial remedies was sharply illustrated last Term by the contrast between *Kaufman v. United States*[83] and *Alderman v. United States*.[84] In *Kaufman* the Court held that a federal defendant could raise the issue of an unlawful search and seizure in a post-conviction proceeding even though the issue had not been raised at trial or on appeal. The Government argued that the deterrent function of the exclusionary rule "is adequately served by the opportunities afforded a federal defendant to enforce the exclusionary rule before or at trial, so that the relatively minimal additional deterrence afforded by a post-conviction remedy would not seem to justify, except in special circumstances, the collateral release of guilty persons who did not raise the search

---

[83] 394 U.S. 217 (1969).   [84] 394 U.S. 165 (1969).

and seizure issue at trial or on direct appeal."[85] This argument, first advanced by Professor Anthony Amsterdam[86] was rejected by the Court. "The provision of federal collateral remedies rests more fundamentally upon a recognition that adequate protection of constitutional rights relating to the criminal trial process requires the continuing availability of a mechanism for relief."[87] But in *Alderman v. United States*, the Court, contrary to the expectations of many commentators,[88] reaffirmed the standing rule requiring that a motion to suppress be made by a person whose rights were violated by the search. The argument against the standing rule is that it decreases the deterrent force of the exclusionary rule. The Court answered:[89]

> The deterrent values of preventing the incrimination of those whose rights the police have violated have been considered sufficient to justify the suppression of probative evidence even though the case against the defendant is weakened or destroyed. . . . [W]e are not convinced that the additional benefits of extending the exclusionary rule to other defendants would justify further encroachment upon the public interest in prosecuting those accused of crime and having them acquitted or convicted on the basis of all the evidence which exposes the truth.

If the objective is effective vindication of constitutional rights, however, wouldn't it make more sense to make the exclusionary rule broadly available at the trial level but limit its availability at subsequent procedural levels, more distant from the law enforcement process? What is gained by allowing a defendant who has not raised the search and seizure issue at trial to raise it in a subsequent proceeding? The only possible explanation is that the Court is concerned about the effectiveness of defense counsel and the trial courts to vindicate constitutional rights. Therefore, it is led to devise more effective appellate and post-conviction remedies to act as a

---

[85] 394 U.S. at 224–25.

[86] Amsterdam, *Search, Seizure, and Section 2255: A Comment*, 112 U. Pa. L. Rev. 378 (1964).

[87] 394 U.S. at 226.

[88] See Comment, *Standing to Object to an Unreasonable Search and Seizure*, 34 U. Chi. L. Rev. 342 (1967), and authorities cited in the dissenting opinion of Mr. Justice Fortas, 394 U.S. at 206 n. 8.

[89] 394 U.S. at 174–75.

check on the trial courts. As Mr. Justice Harlan, dissenting last Term in *Desist v. United States*,[90] expressed it: "[T]he threat of habeas serves as a necessary additional incentive for trial and appellate courts throughout the land to conduct their proceedings in a manner consistent with established constitutional standards." But it is a hopeless task. For the post-trial proceedings are administered by those same judges and those same lawyers and there is no reason to expect that they will do any better the second time around. Indeed, post-conviction proceedings, lacking clear procedural rules[91] or rules of evidence, seem a particularly inadequate forum to correct the defects of trial procedures.

III. THE COURT'S CONTROL OF THE LAW

The most important innovation of the Warren Court in the area of the conventions governing its own work has been the prospective application of new constitutional decisions. Although prospective overruling undermines the symbolic status of the Constitution as permanent, fundamental law, it has been attractive for the Warren Court because it makes the process of constitutional change less difficult, sparing the Court the public outcry that would surely follow a general jail delivery.

From its announcement in *Linkletter v. Walker*[92] the doctrine has given the Court difficulty. First of all, which new rules should be announced prospectively and which apply to all cases, past and present? Surely most constitutional rules are of such fundamental importance that all defendants should be entitled to their protection. The Court has attempted, following a suggestion by Professor Paul

---

[90] 394 U.S. 244, 262–63 (1969).

[91] In Harris v. Nelson, 394 U.S. 286 (1969), the Court held that the discovery provisions of the Federal Rules of Civil Procedure were inapplicable to habeas corpus. But the Court went on to observe: "Where specific allegations before the court show reason to believe that the petitioner may, if the facts are fully developed, be able to demonstrate that he is confined illegally and therefore is entitled to relief, it is the duty of the court to provide the necessary facilities and procedures [unspecified] for an adequate inquiry." *Id.* at 300. In a footnote, the Court left open the question of the applicability of other civil rules to habeas corpus. *Id.* at 294–95 n. 5. In still another footnote, the Court indicated that special rules should be drafted for habeas corpus. *Id.* at 301 n. 7.

[92] 381 U.S. 618 (1965).

Mishkin,[93] to distinguish between rules relating to the reliability of the guilt-determining process and rules designed to advance other objectives, such as the exclusionary rule designed to enforce the Fourth Amendment. The distinction is, however, a difficult one to apply.[94]

Second, what events constitute a cut-off for the assertion of a prospective rule? In *Linkletter v. Walker*, the Court held that *Mapp* applied only to cases that had not become final as of the date of *Mapp*. But if the purpose of the exclusionary rule is deterrence, then why should the rule apply to any search that occurred before the date the rule was announced? Responding to this question, the Court has moved the relevant date, first to the date of trial in *Johnson v. New Jersey*[95] and then to the date of the regulated conduct itself in *Stovall v. Denno*.[96] The Court has continued to apply the rule in the case in which it is announced, however, ostensibly to keep the new rule from being dictum but probably to preserve an incentive for counsel to argue for new constitutional rules.

Last Term the prospective overruling doctrine began to run amuck. In *Desist v. United States*, the Court held that the rule of *Katz v. United States*[97] extending the Fourth Amendment to non-trespassory surveillance, would apply only to surveillance conducted after the date of *Katz*. And in *Halliday v. United States*[98] the Court held that the interpretation of Rule 11 in *McCarthy* should be applied only to pleas entered after the date of the decision. Prior to last Term, the prospective overruling doctrine had been confined to cases of major constitutional significance announc-

---

[93] Mishkin, *The High Court, the Great Writ, and the Due Process of Time and Law*, 79 HARV. L. REV. 56 (1965).

[94] See Schwartz, *Retroactivity, Reliability, and Due Process: A Reply to Professor Mishkin*, 33 U. CHI. L. REV. 719 (1966).

[95] Johnson v. New Jersey, 384 U.S. 719 (1966), held that the rules of Escobedo v. Illinois, 378 U.S. 478 (1964) and Miranda v. Arizona, 384 U.S. 436 (1966), relating to police interrogation procedures, applied only in trials after the date of the decisions. Last Term the Court held that the rules do not apply to retrials after the date of the decisions, if the first trial predated the decision. Jenkins v. Delaware, 395 U.S. 213 (1969).

[96] 388 U.S. 293 (1967). It held that the identification procedure of United States v. Wade, 388 U.S. 218 (1967), and Gilbert v. California, 388 U.S. 263 (1967), applied only to confrontations for identification conducted after the date of the decisions.

[97] 389 U.S. 347 (1967).   [98] 394 U.S. 831 (1969).

ing the extension of additional provisions of the Bill of Rights to the states. Last Term the doctrine was quietly extended to cases both constitutional and nonconstitutional whose "new" rule simply represents an extension of established principles in the traditional, case-law manner. Unless this development is quickly checked, it will have a lasting impact on the process of case-by-case development of the law and the ability of the Court effectively to declare the content of that law.

In *Desist* the defendant argued that the extension of the Fourth Amendment to nontrespassory searches should not be applied prospectively because the extension had been clearly foreshadowed by *Silverman v. United States*.[99] The Court held that the rule should be applied prospectively. "Because the deterrent purpose of *Katz* overwhelmingly supports nonretroactivity, we would reach that result even if relatively few convictions would be set aside by its retroactive application."[100] The Court is once again determining the scope of the Fourth Amendment by considerations based on the existence of the exclusionary rule. The defendant argued that even if *Katz* were held to be prospective, it should, like *Mapp* apply to all cases pending on direct review at the time of the decision because both cases involved the Fourth Amendment. The Court rejected that argument. "Both the deterrent purpose of the exclusionary rule and the reliance of law enforcement officers focus upon the time of the search, not any subsequent point in the prosecution, as the relevant date."[101]

The most serious problem raised by the decision is the scope of the doctrine. Almost every case decided by the Supreme Court involves in some sense the announcement of a "new" rule, and most rules in the criminal procedure area are designed to shape the conduct of the police or the courts. It is possible to dismiss *Desist* as an atypical case, reflecting the special pressures on the Court last Term in the electronic surveillance area. It is said that electronic surveillance has been most frequently used in national security cases. The Court may not want to be responsible for reversing the convictions of foreign spies on the basis of procedural protections not available to our spies in other countries. Both *Desist* and the discussion of standing in *Alderman* show a desire on the part of the Court

---

[99] 365 U.S. 505 (1961).

[100] 394 U.S. at 251–52.			[101] *Id.* at 253.

to bring the constitutional doctrine within the scope of Title III of the Crime Control Act[102] both in time and coverage,[103] thereby shifting from the Court to Congress the responsibility for prohibitions against electronic surveillance. But *Halliday v. United States*[104] makes it clear that *Desist* was more than a pragmatic reaction to an intense political problem. In holding that the rule of *McCarthy* should be applied prospectively, the Court said:[105]

> [A] defendant whose plea has been accepted without full compliance with Rule 11 may still resort to appropriate post-conviction remedies to attack his plea's voluntariness. Thus, if his plea was accepted prior to our decision in *McCarthy*, he is not without a remedy to correct constitutional defects in his conviction. . . . In *McCarthy* we noted that the practice we were requiring had been previously followed by only one Circuit; that over 85% of all convictions in the federal courts are obtained pursuant to guilty pleas; and that prior to Rule 11's recent amendment, not all district judges personally questioned defendants before accepting their guilty pleas. Thus . . . we decline to apply *McCarthy* retroactively.

Mr. Justice Harlan, concurring, argued that since *McCarthy* turned on the meaning of Rule 11 it should be applied from July 1, 1966, the date when Rule 11 was amended by the addition of the phrase "address personally." Mr. Justice Black, in dissent, argued that Rule 11 had always required the judge to determine that the plea was made voluntarily with understanding and that therefore *McCarthy* should be applied to all pleas entered since Rule 11 became effective.[106] Both of these positions are oversimplified. The real issue in *McCarthy* was not the meaning of Rule 11 but the sanction that should be used to enforce Rule 11. The Court held that where a plea has been entered without compliance with Rule 11, a defendant should be permitted to withdraw his plea in order to insure compliance with the requirements of Rule 11. Rule 11 does not say

---

[102] 18 U.S.C. §§ 2510 *et seq.*

[103] In *Alderman* the Court observed: "Of course, Congress or state legislatures may extend the exclusionary rule and provide that illegally seized evidence is inadmissible against anyone for any purpose. . . . Congress has not done so." 394 U.S. at 175 and n. 9.

[104] 394 U.S. 831 (1969).

[105] 394 U.S. at 833.

[106] The plea in *Halliday* was entered in 1954. Rule 11 became effective on March 21, 1946.

what consequences will follow from a failure to comply, although it is a reasonable implication that pleas in violation of the rule are not binding.

The meaning of *Halliday* became somewhat more confused when a month later the Court announced its opinion in *Boykin*. *Boykin* held that Rule 11 procedures were constitutionally required. Furthermore, it held not that this new constitutional requirement was to be enforced by permitting defendants to plead again, but that a plea so obtained was invalid.[107] After *Boykin*, Rule 11 procedures can no longer be viewed as designed to prevent unconstitutional pleas. Their absence makes a plea unconstitutional.

Mr. Justice Harlan in dissent in *Boykin* argued that the case was an application of the *McCarthy* rule to the states and that since the *McCarthy* rule had been held to be prospective in *Halliday*, it should not be extended to *Boykin*. This argument has two serious defects. First, it is not clear why a rule of criminal procedure cannot be applied at different times to the federal government and the states. Thus in *Linkletter* the Court did not apply *Mapp* prospectively as of the date of the 1914 *Weeks*[108] case, which adopted the exclusionary rule in federal cases. Second, certiorari had already been granted in *Boykin*[109] at the time of the *McCarthy* opinion, and unless the Court wished to move to an even more overtly random process of selecting the defendants who will benefit from retroactive application of a new rule, it should extend the rule to all defendants in cases before the Court for direct review at the time the rule is announced. For instance, in *Miranda* the Court did not limit retroactive application of the *Miranda* rules to *Miranda* but extended them to all the companion cases. *Halliday* on the other hand came to the Court on collateral attack and certiorari was not granted until after the *McCarthy* opinion.[110]

---

[107] In *McCarthy*, the Court held that the defendant should have the opportunity to plead anew and remanded the case. In *Boykin*, the Court held the conviction itself unconstitutional and reversed. Thus, after *McCarthy* the burden was on the defendant to reopen the proceeding while after *Boykin* the burden was on the state to reprosecute the defendant.

[108] Weeks v. United States, 232 U.S. 383 (1914).

[109] 393 U.S. 820 (1968).

[110] Certiorari was granted and the opinion issued on the same day, May 5, 1969, after *McCarthy*. This enabled the Court to indicate immediately the nonretroactive

Although *Boykin* casts doubt on *Halliday* because it elevates the Rule 11 procedure from a rule of court to a constitutional mandate, it seems clear that *Halliday* will control the retroactivity of *Boykin* for the same reasons that the Court chose nonretroactive application of the *Katz* rule in *Desist*. The *Boykin* rule is a prophylactic rule designed to improve the procedures for entering guilty pleas. It can only affect these procedures in the future. But what other "new" rules adopted by the Court this Term will be held to be prospective? Of the cases discussed above, *Spinelli v. United States, Davis v. Mississippi*, and *North Carolina v. Pearce* would all appear to be prospective under the standards of *Desist* and *Halliday*. In addition, *Orozco v. Texas*,[111] extending the application of *Miranda* to interrogation in the suspect's home, and *Chimel v. California*,[112] narrowing the scope of a search incident to an arrest, should be prospective.

The fact that the "rule" of an opinion is declared to be prospective has an impact on the way in which that opinion can be read and interpreted. In the normal case a Court's opinion speaks in the context of a line of cases and the language of the Court can be interpreted in light of that tradition. But when the Court declares an opinion to be prospective it clearly states that the rule of this opinion is different from the rule of prior cases and that those cases are not to be controlling in the application of the new rule. In *Desist*, Mr. Justice Stewart described the rule of his own *Katz* opinion as follows:[113]

> [W]e held that the reach of the Fourth Amendment "cannot turn upon the presence or absence of a physical intrusion into any given enclosure." . . . Noting that the "Fourth Amendment protects people, not places," . . . we overruled cases holding that a search and seizure of speech requires some trespass or actual penetration of a particular enclosure. We concluded that since every electronic eavesdropping upon

---

impact of *McCarthy*. The use of pending cases on the miscellaneous docket for this purpose seems an unnecessary formality which leads the Court to decide the case without any opportunity given to the petitioner for the appointment of counsel or the argument of the case. It might be better if the Court would simply indicate in each of its opinions whether or not the opinion applies retroactively.

111 394 U.S. 324 (1969).

112 395 U.S. 752 (1969).   113 394 U.S. at 246.

private conversations is a search or seizure, it can comply with constitutional standards only when authorized by a neutral magistrate upon a showing of probable cause and under precise limitations and appropriate safeguards.

There are at least three different rules that can be drawn from Mr. Justice Stewart's opinion in *Katz*:[114]

1. Henceforth, the Fourth Amendment will apply to all surveillance of conversations conducted by a means that relies on the transmission of sound or electronic impulses through a solid in direct contact with a protected area.

Comment: This rule would apply to bugs attached to walls or other objects in direct contact with the protected area. It would not apply to parabolic microphones pointed through open windows. It would apply to wiretaps. This rule removes technical distinctions based on property rights from the law of the Fourth Amendment.

2. Henceforth, the Fourth Amendment will apply to surveillance of all conversations conducted by means of electronic devices where the person who is the object of the surveillance has a reasonable expectation of privacy.

Comment: This rule is the same as that of Title III of the Crime Control Act[115] and is designed to serve the purpose of the Fourth Amendment: the protection of privacy. It represents a sharp break with the cases because it extends to conversations conducted in areas such as parks and restaurants that have normally not been protected. It is inconsistent with the opinion in *Katz* because a limitation on the scope of the Fourth Amendment based on the means of surveillance, a distinction inconsistent with the wording of the Fourth Amendment, was not discussed by the Court in *Katz* and has never been defended in any opinion of the Court.[116]

3. Henceforth, the Fourth Amendment will apply to surveillance of all conversations conducted by any means including the human ear where the participants in the conversation have a reasonable expectation of privacy.

Comment: This is the same rule as 2 but the distinction between electronic and other forms of surveillance is eliminated. Most important, it extends the application of the

---

[114] My own reading is to be found in Kitch, note 41 *supra*.

[115] See 18 U.S.C. § 2511, § 2510(2), § 2510(4).

[116] Mr. Justice Brennan has argued for the distinction. Lopez v. United States, 373 U.S. 427, 465–66 (1963).

Fourth Amendment to any use of informers. It is supported but not required by recent decisions of the Court in the informer area.[117]

There is even a fourth rule, apparently rejected by Mr. Justice Stewart in *Desist,* that can be drawn from *Katz.*

> 4. Henceforth, the Fourth Amendment will apply to all surveillance, visual or aural, where the effect of the surveillance is to offend the society's notions of privacy.
>
> *Comment:* This rule responds to the inherent inconsistency of distinguishing between things that can be seen and things that can be heard.

Mr. Justice Stewart seems extremely proud of his phrase: "The Fourth Amendment protects people and not places." But it is difficult to deduce a rule from it.

If *Katz* is interpreted in light of the case-by-case development that precedes it, it announces rule 1 but foreshadows the future development of rule 3.[118] In *Desist,* however, the Court, by emphasizing the "newness" of the *Katz* rule and its application exclusively to electronic surveillance, seems to have reinterpreted *Katz* to stand for rule 2.

The Court's problem of effectively establishing its new rules is compounded by the spongy quality of its opinions. The opinions typically tend to speak in public relations jargon with little discussion of how those generalities would be applied to different facts. Precedents are cited not as examples of applications of those generalities but as examples of earlier expressions by the Court of the same generalities. As long as one could assume that the "rule" being applied in the case at hand was the same or at least related to rules earlier announced, then the precedents of the Court could be examined in order to determine the implications of the new "rule." A good-faith judge, using the body of the Court's decisions as a reference point, could then hope to do a reasonably craftsmanlike job of interpreting and applying the law. But when that body of decisions has explicitly been declared "different," how is this job to be done?

Part of the problem for the Court is that the convention of a judicial opinion does not lend itself to a clear statement of the "new

---

[117] Particularly Osborn v. United States, 385 U.S. 323 (1966).

[118] As I argued extensively in Kitch, note 41 *supra.*

rules." The new rule and the reasons for that rule (or in other terms, its legislative history) are stated together and the problem for the interpreter is to separate them. One solution, of course, would be for the Court to abandon the present convention and explicitly have three sections: in one, the new rule would be announced; in another the reasons for the rule would be discussed; in the third the application of the rule to the particular facts of the case would be made. The Court's style has in fact been moving in this direction; it is particularly noticeable in the opinions of Chief Justice Warren in *Miranda v. Arizona*[119] and *Terry v. Ohio*.[120] But do such general, legislative pronouncements bind the Court for the future? The convention of *stare decisis* is built around the concept that the Court is bound only by the holding of a case, that is, by the narrow application of the rule to the particular facts. Do the general rules announced in these opinions really reflect the enthusiasm of the opinion writer rather than a future commitment of the Court as an institution? To make such general pronouncements binding the Court will have to strengthen the convention of *stare decisis*. The whole thrust of its work, however, points in the opposite direction. The Court might solve this problem by making more frequent use of its power to amend the Federal Rules of Criminal Procedure. But the Rules, at least in theory, are not binding on the states, and the amendment procedure is subject to explicit congressional check.[121]

The frequent use of prospective overruling of prior doctrine dramatizes the equal protection problem inherent in any change of law. Whenever a new rule is announced by a court it is denied to those who have no present means of obtaining judicial relief. This problem is substantially mitigated where the change takes place in a gradual manner over a long period of time. But where a new rule is announced to apply only for the future because it reflects policy considerations of a constitutional magnitude, why should it be denied to defendants affected by conduct one week earlier in time? The Court's answer is that since retroactive application of the rule cannot affect past conduct there is no constitutional purpose to be served by it. This provides a reasonable basis for the classification.

---

[119] 384 U.S. 436 (1966).

[120] 392 U.S. 1 (1968).   [121] 28 U.S.C. § 2072.

The Court, then, is like a legislature, declaring new guidelines for conduct for the future.

But there are two problems of equal protection that arise in the judicial system but do not arise in a legislative system. First is the de minimis but aesthetically offensive problem that the Court applies the new rule retroactively to the defendant in the case in which the new rule is announced. Why should he get the benefit of the rule? How is he chosen? It is sometimes said that if the rule is not applied in the case in which it is announced it will be dictum. That may be so, but the Court could deal with that problem by acknowledging the binding quality of a rule so announced and actually following it in future cases. The more serious problem is the lack of incentive for counsel to argue for new rules if they would not be extended to their clients. It is doubtful, however, that extension of the rule to the one case in which it is announced is really sufficient to preserve a flow of cases presenting "new" questions for resolution to the Court. The decision to present a new constitutional issue is often made not before the Supreme Court but at trial, where the factual underpinnings for a constitutional issue must be laid. When a defense counsel faced with a trial strategy choice knows that an anticipated rule can help his client only if the case is the lucky one that actually goes to the Supreme Court, he must prefer strategies that do not rely on such rules.

An even larger problem of equal protection is the problem of geographic discrimination. For instance, on November 2, 1965, the Ninth Circuit had already applied the interpretation of Rule 11 adopted by the Court in *McCarthy*.[122] Foreshadowing *Halliday*, the Ninth Circuit applied its decision prospectively to all pleas entered after the date of the decision.[123] Since that date, defendants in the Ninth Circuit have had the benefit of Rule 11. In other circuits, defendants did not have advantage of the rule until the date of *McCarthy*, April 2, 1969. Why should they be denied the rule because they were convicted in a different circuit? In some circuits, they are denied the rule because the court of appeals decided the question erroneously, contrary to *McCarthy*.[124] But weren't those

---

[122] Heiden v. United States, 353 F.2d 53 (9th Cir. 1965).

[123] Castro v. United States, 396 F.2d 345 (9th Cir. 1968).

[124] Kennedy v. United States, 397 F.2d 16 (6th Cir. 1968); United States v. Del

courts wrong? Or were they right because *McCarthy* retroactively validated their rule for pleas before April 2, 1969? In other circuits defendants are denied the rule because no one has made the argument for a *McCarthy* rule.[125] Suppose a circuit should decide that, had it been presented with the question at any time after the Ninth Circuit decision adopting the *McCarthy* rule, it would have followed the Ninth Circuit.[126] Should defendants in that circuit then get the benefit of the November 2, 1965, date? The problems are compounded if one brings the state and district courts into the picture, greatly increasing the number of jurisdictions.

The most important consequence of the rise of the nonretroactivity doctrine is its deeply conservative impact on the lower courts. It was formerly thought that when a lower court was faced with an unresolved question of constitutional law, it should ask: How would the Supreme Court decide the question if it were deciding it now? But that can no longer be the appropriate question, because if the Supreme Court were deciding the question today it would also decide that the rule should not be applied to the case before the lower court. Rather, the lower court must now ask, what is the "old" rule that will be applicable in these cases until the Supreme Court has clearly announced the "new" rule? For instance, last winter the Seventh Circuit in *United States v. White*,[127] followed the hints of the Court in *Katz* and other cases and held that *Katz* stood for rule 2, as described above, extending the Fourth Amendment to a "wired for sound" informer. The case was decided prior to *Desist* and applied to conduct prior to *Katz*. The Supreme Court

---

Piano, 386 F.2d 436 (3d Cir. 1967); Halliday v. United States, 380 F.2d 270 (1st Cir. 1967); Stephens v. United States, 376 F.2d 23 (10th Cir. 1967); Lane v. United States, 373 F.2d 570 (5th Cir. 1967); Brokaw v. United States, 368 F.2d 508 (4th Cir. 1966).

[125] Apparently this is true in the District of Columbia, Second, and Seventh Circuits.

[126] The Eighth Circuit rejected a collateral attack based on the pre-1966 Rule 11 on the ground that Rule 11 had been complied with. Bartlett v. United States, 354 F.2d 745 (8th Cir. 1966). Did this imply that if the rule were not complied with, the plea was subject to collateral attack? And in Halliday v. United States, 380 F.2d 270 (1st Cir. 1967), and United States v. Del Piano, 386 F.2d 436 (3d Cir. 1967), both dealing with pre-1966 Rule 11, the courts made passing references to amended Rule 11 suggesting that the result under the amended rule might be different. 386 F.2d at 437 n. 2; 380 F.2d at 272. Should the *McCarthy* rule apply in these circuits as of the effective date of amended Rule 11, July 1, 1966?

[127] 405 F.2d 838 (7th Cir. 1969).

has granted certiorari in the case.[128] Should the Court hold that the decision is in error because *Katz* applies only prospectively? Should it hold that the application of the Fourth Amendment to informers is a new rule that should apply in the case in which it is announced? Should it hold that the Seventh Circuit's interpretation of the Fourth Amendment is correct, or that that question is not before the Court because the case involves only the application of old "trespass" Fourth Amendment law? Or should it hold that the case is rightly decided under Seventh Circuit law because it was decided by the Seventh Circuit before notice was given in *Desist* that *Katz* was only prospective?

The rise of retroactivity, freeing the lower courts from an obligation to carry out the implications of contemporary Supreme Court law, was paralleled by the sudden re-emergence of the harmless error doctrine last Term—in the very class of cases where the retroactivity doctrine does not apply. Shortly after the Court's due process revolution was announced in *Mapp*, the Court proceeded to limit this threat to its control mechanism. If prosecutors continued to win cases on appeal even though unconstitutionally seized evidence had been admitted at trial because there was enough other evidence in the record to sustain the conviction, they would not be sufficiently inconvenienced to put pressure on the police to comply with the Fourth Amendment. In *Fahy v. Connecticut*,[129] a search and seizure case, Chief Justice Warren wrote:[130]

> [In deciding whether the error was harmless] we are not concerned . . . with whether there was sufficient evidence on which the petitioner could have been convicted without the evidence complained of. The question is whether there is a reasonable possibility that the evidence complained of might have contributed to the conviction.

The Court strengthened the limitations on the harmless error doctrine in *Chapman v. California*,[131] a case involving the no-comment rule of *Griffin v. California*,[132] held prospective in *Tehan v. Shott*.[133] "We, therefore," wrote Mr. Justice Black, "do no more than adhere

---

[128] 394 U.S. 957 (1969).

[129] 375 U.S. 85 (1963).

[130] *Id.* at 86–87.

[131] 386 U.S. 18 (1967).

[132] 380 U.S. 609 (1965), holding that a prosecutor may not comment to the jury on the fact that a defendant has exercised his right not to testify.

[133] 382 U.S. 406 (1966).

to the meaning of our *Fahy* case when we hold, as we now do, that before a federal constitutional error can be held harmless, the court must be able to declare a belief that it was harmless beyond a reasonable doubt."[134]

The first case in which the Court applied the harmless error doctrine last Term was *Foster v. California*.[135] *Foster* was a pre-*Wade* identification case. In *Stovall v. Denno*[136] the Court held that the rule of *United States v. Wade*,[137] requiring an attorney for the suspect to be present at a lineup, was prospective. The Court acknowledged in *Stovall*, however, that identification procedures judged by the "totality of the circumstances" may be "so unnecessarily suggestive and conducive to irreparable mistaken identification" as to be a denial of due process of law.[138] In *Foster*, the Court applied this rule and found that the identification procedures denied due process. Foster was convicted on the basis of identification by the victim and the testimony of his accomplice. The Court held that the identification procedures used with the victim, who had been unable to identify the defendant until after a lineup and a one-to-one confrontation, violated due process. But the Court then remanded the case to the state courts to determine whether the error was harmless. It is difficult to see how identification by the victim in a criminal case could be harmless error. But Mr. Justice Black, the author of the *Chapman* opinion, enthusiastically supported the remand even in dissent. "[T]he question whether an error in a particular case is harmless is an issue peculiarly for the lower not the highest appellate courts. . . . This Court was not established to try such minor issues of fact for the first time."[139] In light of *Chapman* this is nonsense. The only obvious reason for the remand seems to be to avoid the need to overrule *Chapman* even though mitigating the effects of the pre-*Wade* rule announced in *Stovall*.

The Court also apparently applied a kind of harmless error doctrine in *Boulden v. Holman*,[140] a case involving the rule of *Witherspoon v. Illinois*.[141] *Witherspoon* held that a jury, chosen under a rule that gave the state the right to challenge veniremen for cause

---

[134] 386 U.S. at 24.

[135] 394 U.S. 440 (1969).

[136] 388 U.S. 293 (1967).

[137] 388 U.S. 218 (1967).

[138] 388 U.S. at 302.

[139] 394 U.S. at 452.

[140] 394 U.S. 478 (1969).

[141] 391 U.S. 510 (1968).

for having an opinion against the death penalty, could not constitutionally impose the death penalty because the jury was biased on that issue. Such a rule is applied retroactively because its rationale is based on the integrity of the penalty determining process. Alabama statutes give the state a challenge for cause as to veniremen who have "a fixed opinion against capital or penitentiary punishment."[142] Such challenges were exercised at Boulden's trial. Mr. Justice Stewart, writing for the Court in *Boulden*, held:[143]

> It appears, therefore, that the sentence of death imposed upon the petitioner cannot constitutionally stand under *Witherspoon* v. *Illinois*. We do not, however, finally decide that question here, for several reasons. First, the *Witherspoon* issue was not raised in the District Court, in the Court of Appeals, nor in the petition for certiorari filed in this Court. [The Court of Appeals decision had been rendered prior to *Witherspoon*.] A further hearing directed to the issue might conceivably modify in some fashion the conclusion so strongly suggested by the record now before us. Further it is not clear whether the petitioner has exhausted his state remedies with respect to this issue. Finally, in the event it turns out, as now appears, that relief from this death sentence must be ordered, a local federal court will be better equipped than are we to frame an appropriate decree with due regard to available Alabama procedures.

The last reason for the remand is clearly specious, since the district court could just as easily frame the decree after the Court determined the *Witherspoon* issue. The first reason is Kafkaesque. Why should the defendant, after having arrived at the highest court in the land, be forced to go back to the bottom of the judicial system in order to argue an issue on which the highest court says he is right but which he didn't know about at the time he initially sought relief? The second reason is inexplicable, since neither the *Boulden* nor *Witherspoon* opinions give any hint of what other evidence might be relevant. Is the Court inviting the district court, as the Illinois Supreme Court did in *People v. Speck*,[144] another pre-*Witherspoon* trial, to find by some mysterious process that the particular questions asked and challenges exercised in *Boulden* did not have any effect on the jury?

---

[142] Ala. Code, tit. 30, § 57 (1958).

[143] 394 U.S. at 484.

[144] 41 Ill. 2d 177 (1968). See also People v. Mallett, 244 N.E. 2d 129 (Ill. 1969).

The Court faced the issue of the present scope of the *Chapman* rule directly in *Harrington v. California*.[145] Harrington had been tried with three co-defendants. Each of the other co-defendants confessed and their confessions were introduced into evidence at the trial in violation of the rule of *Bruton v. United States*,[146] holding that such a procedure violated the Sixth Amendment right to confrontation even when the jury was instructed that each confession was admissible only against the defendant who made it. The petitioner argued that the conviction should be reversed whether or not the error was harmless. The Sixth Amendment right to confrontation, he argued, is a right "of the first magnitude" whose violation requires automatic reversal. The rules involved in *Fahy* and *Chapman*, on the other hand, were "secondary" rules designed to implement major constitutional rights. Thus, the exclusionary rule in *Fahy* was designed to prevent unreasonable searches and seizures. And the no-comment rule in *Chapman* was designed to prohibit prosecution tactics which capitalize on the defendant's exercise of his right not to testify. But in *Harrington*, the constitutional requirements of the Sixth Amendment had themselves been violated. Indeed, the Court had spoken of the *Bruton* rule in this way when, in *Roberts v. Russell*,[147] it held the rule retroactive. "The retroactivity of the holding in *Bruton* is . . . required; the error 'went to the basis of fair hearing and trial because the procedural apparatus never assured the [petitioner] a fair determination' of his guilt or innocence."[148] How can a denial of a right essential to a fair hearing and trial be held harmless? For instance, could a denial of the right to appointed counsel be held harmless error because the evidence against the defendant was overwhelming and the presence of counsel couldn't have made any difference? Under *Gideon v. Wainwright*,[149] rejecting the actual prejudice standard of the earlier cases,[150] clearly not.

The entire Court, however, treated the question as if there were a single unitary standard of "constitutional harmless error," the standard of the *Fahy* and *Chapman* cases. Mr. Justice Douglas, writing for the Court, found that the error was harmless because apart from the confessions "the case against Harrington was so

---

[145] 395 U.S. 250 (1969).

[146] 391 U.S. 123 (1968).

[147] 392 U.S. 293 (1968).

[148] *Id.* at 294.

[149] 372 U.S. 335 (1963).

[150] *E.g.*, Betts v. Brady, 316 U.S. 455 (1942).

overwhelming that we conclude that this violation of *Bruton* was harmless beyond a reasonable doubt."[151] Mr. Justice Brennan, dissenting with the Chief Justice and Mr. Justice Marshall, argued:[152]

> The Court today by shifting the inquiry from whether the constitutional error contributed to the conviction to whether the untainted evidence provided "overwhelming" support for the conviction puts aside the firm resolve of *Chapman*. . . . As a result, the deterrent effect of [our constitutional rules] . . . on the actions of both police and prosecutors, not to speak of trial courts, will be significantly undermined.

The record reveals that *Harrington* might well present an example of harmless error even under the test of *Chapman* and *Fahy* as interpreted by the dissenters. But the test requires a more complex and speculative analysis than Mr. Justice Douglas cared to indulge. The four defendants had attempted to rob a small grocery and liquor store in southern Los Angeles with a blinding incompetence that would be comic if a clerk had not been shot dead by one of them in the course of the attempt. With brash self-confidence, when arrested each admitted participation in the events to the police but attempted to avoid responsibility for the murder itself. None had anticipated, however, the operation of the felony-murder rule and all four were convicted of murder. The case against Harrington, even apart from the confessions, was overwhelming. He admitted that he had gone to the scene with the other three but denied planning or participating in the robbery.[153] His story was that he was just an honest dupe along for a ride who walked into the store to buy cigarettes as the shot rang out. The testimony of two of the store personnel and a customer placed Harrington inside the store throughout the robbery and shooting.[154] Harrington's only possible line of defense was to argue that although he was there, he had not been a co-conspirator to the robbery and therefore was not vicariously liable for the shooting under the felony-murder rule. On this issue the three confessions were cumulatively quite important in establishing that the four had indeed planned the robbery before they entered the store.

It seems highly unlikely that Harrington would have done any better with his defense had he had a separate trial. There was some

---

[151] 395 U.S. at 254.

[152] *Id.* at 255.

[153] Record, A. 363–64.

[154] *Id.* at A. 56–138.

confusion about his identification in the store because the witnesses had originally reported the robbers as four colored men. Harrington was white.[155] Particularly damning for Harrington would be the testimony of a resident of the neighborhood that she had seen four men, three colored and one white, changing from two cars to a single car several blocks from the grocery store shortly before the robbery.[156] But it is difficult to tell what would happen in such a trial from the record in the case because counsel's knowledge that the three confessions would be admitted may have made it pointless for him to pursue lines of inquiry and argument that would otherwise have been available.

Mr. Justice Douglas' analysis is particularly deficient in its treatment of the confession of one of the co-defendants, Rhone. Rhone's confession was the most damaging to Harrington because it placed him by name in the store with a gun at the time of the murder. But after the state's case was in, Rhone took the stand in his own defense to testify that he was not a party to the robbery attempt. Harrington's lawyer then cross-examined him. Neither Rhone's testimony nor the cross-examination were helpful to Harrington. Mr. Justice Douglas assumed that the introduction of Rhone's confession did not violate the *Bruton* rule. He apparently took the position that the cross-examination satisfied the confrontation requirement of the Sixth Amendment. But the admission of the confession was error. How was the error cured by the subsequent examination? Suppose Rhone felt forced to take the stand because the admission of his confession left him with no other workable defense strategy. In *Bruton* the Court had observed that the violation of the right of confrontation was particularly serious in cases where the co-defendant whose confession was admitted did not testify.[157] But that observation did not justify holding the *Bruton* rule inapplicable where the co-defendant did testify. Is it now constitutional for a prosecutor to introduce a confession in violation of *Bruton* in the hope that the confession will "flush out" the confessor and force him to testify?

---

[155] *Id.* at A. 88–90, A. 120–21, A. 138.

[156] *Id.* at A. 140–45.

[157] "The unreliability of such evidence is intolerably compounded when the alleged accomplice, as here, does not testify and cannot be tested by cross-examination." 391 U.S. at 136.

Although the record in *Harrington* might support a finding of harmless error even under the "contributed to" standard of the dissenters, the style of Mr. Justice Douglas' opinion suggests that the Court is turning back toward an "untainted overwhelming evidence" approach rather than a "what might have happened if there had been no error" approach. Particularly troubling is the Court's apparent assumption that the standard of harmlessness for all constitutional errors is the same. Surely some constitutional requirements are such that their violation requires automatic reversal. Is the *Bruton* rule, so fundamental that it must be applied retroactively, one of them?

The explanation for this approach to harmless error may be that the Court wishes to preserve *Chapman* as a precedent in order to enforce its criminal procedure rules in the future while at the same time using the harmless error rule to avoid the retroactive effect of rules that are not limited to prospective application. It is probably not without significance that in *Harrington* the State of California, joined by Arizona, Arkansas, Colorado, Connecticut, Delaware, Illinois, Kentucky, Minnesota, Montana, New Mexico, New York, North Carolina, South Carolina, South Dakota, Utah, Virginia, and Washington as amici curiae, urged the Court to overrule *Roberts* and apply *Bruton* prospectively.

IV. Conclusion

The Warren Court in the last Term of its existence was retreating from implementation of the system of control over criminal procedure it had so forcefully built. In characteristic fashion, it did not retreat by limiting the procedural system it had created while more strongly integrating its essential features into the body of our constitutional law. Rather, it retreated by creating a new set of doctrines which substantially undermine the ability of the Court to declare and enforce the law. It is ironic that a Court that has built a complex system of rules based in part on the implicit assumption that the officials of the criminal justice system cannot be trusted should at the same time create doctrines that increase their discretionary power.

The rapid development of the doctrines of retroactivity and harmless error does not seem to be the result of a desire to bend to the shifting winds of public opinion. Mr. Justice Black has become remarkably more conservative. There does seem to be some desire on the part of the three critical swing voters, Mr. Justice Brennan, Mr. Justice Stewart, and Mr. Justice White, to moderate the impact of the Court's decisions. But the more important factor seems to be an institutional one. The system of rules the Court has created in the area of criminal procedure has become extremely complex. The Court has been able to simplify it somewhat, at the expense of meaningful control over the lower courts, by the convenient fiction that waiver and harmless error are unitary doctrines. Because of the complexity, the Justices are having trouble agreeing on a majority opinion. If the cases are disposed of without a majority opinion, then the Court announces no law at all.

This fate actually overtook the Court last Term in *Spinelli*, where Mr. Justice White finally concurred with the majority in order to prevent a four-to-four deadlock. "I join the opinion of the Court and the judgment of reversal, especially since a vote to affirm would produce an equally divided Court."[158] *Spinelli* must be one of the few cases in the history of the Court decided the way it was because otherwise it would have been decided differently. But a case decided on such a basis declares no law at all. The institution of an opinion makes it difficult for the Court to declare a system of procedural rules because each opinion must in a sense "re-enact" the applicable rules. But if no majority of the Court favors the application or result of the rule in the case at hand, the existing rules can be preserved only by creating some exception in order to form a majority opinion. Since almost all members of the Court now seem to feel that it is important to uphold the decisions of the past ten years lest the authority of the Court be weakened, this strategy can lead to an almost unanimous opinion. The original dissenters from the rule sign an opinion upholding the rule in exchange for a new rule that undermines its impact. For instance, it is hard to believe that the language of Mr. Justice Brennan in *Davis* authorizing a general fingerprinting warrant was not essential in order to frame an opinion of the Court. Yet the opinion, as finally written, was supported by seven Justices. Similarly in *Boulden*, it is hard to believe that there were five members of the Court who supported disposition of the case without a remand. Yet the opinion as written on the *Witherspoon* issue was supported by all members of the Court.

---

[158] 393 U.S. at 429.

The alarming aspect of this development is its inherent danger to the preservation of civil liberties. A relatively minor aspect is a doctrine like the general fingerprinting warrant of the *Davis* case, announced as a Court, cut off from history and *stare decisis*, gropes for good policy in a changing political climate. More important is the fact that the Court, having taken on itself the primary burden for the protection of the integrity of the American criminal justice system, has substantially undermined the ability of the state courts to do the job. The state courts reacted to the criminal due process revolution at first with anger and then with sullen resentment. They have now discovered the new nullification doctrines, and many are applying them with a vengeance. But they are trapped in a reactive system of law; their decisions must be framed in relation to the Supreme Court's decisions. In this climate there is a tendency to choose sides, to support or to reject the Supreme Court, rather than to attempt to articulate and enforce a system of justice responsive to the state courts' norms of procedural fairness. This problem is in part the result of petty pique, and perhaps it could be avoided if judges were better men. But it is hard for a state court that does not share the Supreme Court's norms to avoid using the new doctrines to undermine the Court's procedural law. This leaves the jurisdiction with no real system of procedural law at all. The Supreme Court's rules are not abandoned, only sapped.

If these developments during the final Term of the Warren Court are not checked, they will substantially undermine the ability of the courts to protect the integrity of the American system of criminal justice. The challenge to the "new" Court is to prevent that from happening.

AL KATZ

PRIVACY AND PORNOGRAPHY:

STANLEY v. GEORGIA

What is most intriguing about *Stanley v. Georgia*[1] is neither the Supreme Court's decision to reverse a state court conviction for mere possession of obscene materials nor the unanimous agreement of the Justices in the conclusion reached, if not in the reasons given therefor. The case is significant for its revelation of the difficulty that the Court has in shaping a conceptually defensible rationale for its judgments in the obscenity area. As written, the majority opinion casts a curious light on *Griswold v. Connecticut*[2] and weakens, if it does not destroy, the theoretical premises and doctrinal content of *Roth v. United States*.[3]

The relevant facts of the case are quickly stated. Stanley's home was searched under authority of a warrant particularly describing certain items related to alleged bookmaking activities. In the course of the search, officers "found three reels of eight-millimeter film" in one of the upstairs bedrooms, a room transmogrified by the Court's opinion into a "library." Using Stanley's projector, the officers viewed the films, seized them, and arrested Stanley for possession of obscene materials.

The Court might have characterized the case in any of several ways: like *Mapp v. Ohio*,[4] as a search and seizure problem; like

Al Katz, now Assistant Professor of Law at the State University of New York at Buffalo, was at the American Bar Foundation when this was written.

[1] 394 U.S. 557 (1969).   [3] 354 U.S. 476 (1957).

[2] 381 U.S. 479 (1965).   [4] 367 U.S. 643 (1961).

Roth v. United States, as an obscenity problem; like *Redrup v. New York,*[5] as an obscenity case concerned with the audience reached; or, like *Griswold v. Connecticut,* as a question of privacy. A strong minority chose the first reading. The majority chose the last. The Court preferred to see the case as presenting the privacy issue, thus getting into the deepest morass of its own making. By characterizing the case in this way, the Court managed to avoid dealing directly with the question of *Roth's* continuing vitality. But it clearly enervated the *Roth* doctrine, for the privacy approach affords a distinction that, of necessity, severely limits *Roth's* ken. The Court employed much rhetoric about the power of the states to control obscenity while analytically rejecting almost every premise for the exercise of such power. *Stanley* may well prove a classic example of destruction by distinction.

The Court's opinion, by Mr. Justice Marshall, can be outlined as follows: The case is one of first impression because it raises the question whether the state can punish mere private possession of (what is assumed to be) obscene material. Even though the state retains broad power to regulate obscenity, the valid justifications that explain the state's interest make it clear that the power is limited to instances of commercial distribution, not mere private possession. Furthermore, the interests underlying the state's regulation of obscenity are insufficient to justify intrusion into the privacy of one's home and inspection of the content of one's library.

Why is an allegation of obscenity an insufficient justification for the conduct of a reasonable search? Why is the invasion of privacy to search for obscenity invalid although the right to receive commercially distributed obscene materials is not protected? What is the nature of the unique danger of commercial distribution that is absent from noncommercial distribution or mere private possession? How wide a net may the states cast in order to reach the evil of commercial distribution? These are a few of the questions raised by *Stanley* which the Court could be expected to consider.

According to Mr. Justice Marshall's opinion for the Court, mere private possession is a crucial constitutional fact because there is a fundamental "right to be free, except in very limited circumstances, from unwarranted governmental intrusion into one's privacy."[6] But it is clear that the Court did not mean to characterize this as an ordi-

---

[5] 386 U.S. 767 (1967).   [6] 394 U.S. at 564.

nary Fourth Amendment case. It was not concerned with the first aspect of the law of search and seizure, the technical requirements of a warrant, and the reasonableness of searches without a warrant. It was somewhat concerned with the second aspect, the requirement that what is sought bear some relation to a criminal offense. It was primarily concerned with the notion that some conduct may not be made criminal because its discovery depends wholly on intrusions into some "sanctuary" to search for "particularly private" things.

The second aspect of search and seizure doctrine, the requirement that what is sought bear some relation to a criminal offense, leads into the *Stanley* problem as fashioned by the Court. "There must, of course, be a nexus . . . between the item to be seized and criminal behavior."[7] This follows from the premise that the Fourth Amendment protects privacy[8] and the security of one's personal effects, an interest that may be overcome only by the assertion of some serious governmental need.[9] Since the governmental interest in searching for and seizing the fruits and instrumentalities of crime is clear, and since there is "nothing in the nature" of "mere evidence" that "renders it more private"[10] than instrumentalities, the same governmental interest that justifies seizure of the latter may justify seizure of the former.

There may be items, however, that, unlike mere evidence, are so private that they may not be sought even through a reasonable search. If a particular mode of criminal conduct cannot be discovered except by the invasion of a "sanctuary" in order to seize some particularly private item—like birth control devices—the procedural bar operates to invalidate the substantive crime in the absence of a sufficiently strong governmental interest for invasion of the sanctuary. This seems to be the meaning of *Griswold v. Connecticut* that the Court had in mind in *Stanley*. If the criminal conduct (possession of obscene material) requires for its enforcement governmental inquiry into the contents of one's library, a particularly private res by definition, the criminal statute is itself unconstitutional because of the absence of a sufficiently strong countervailing state interest. All that *Stanley* actually held was that possession of obscene matter

---

[7] Warden v. Hayden, 387 U.S. 294, 307 (1967).

[8] *Id*. at 304.

[9] *Cf*. Camara v. Municipal Court, 387 U.S. 523 (1967).

[10] 387 U.S. at 302.

"is [an] insufficient justification for such a drastic invasion of personal liberties."[11]

In effect, however, the Court gave prima facie First Amendment protection to a person's library. It takes as the relevant question not whether the item seized is constitutionally protected but whether the state interest in conducting a search for pornography outweighs the constitutional protection given the library as library, thereby establishing a form of "locus" test rejected in *Katz v. United States*.[12] But there is no reason why a personal library needs special constitutional protection if it contains only written or filmed material otherwise protected by the First Amendment. To justify a search of a library the government should only have to show reason to believe that it contains material not protected by the First Amendment—like an unregistered sawed-off shotgun—and that a sufficient nexus exists between the material and criminal behavior. This would have been a simpler way of answering the question presented with fewer ramifications.[13]

An allegation of obscenity is an insufficient justification for the conduct of a reasonable search, according to the Court in *Stanley*, because "the right to be free, except in very limited circumstances, from unwanted governmental intrusions into one's privacy" is not outweighed by the state's interest in suppressing pornography. In brief, a state's interest in general regulation is confined to four bases: children must be protected; the general public must be protected both from intrusions upon their sensibilities and from incitements to antisocial conduct; individual minds must be protected both from intrusions upon their sensibilities and from incitements to antisocial conduct; individual minds must be protected from degenerate influ-

---

[11] 394 U.S. at 565.

[12] 389 U.S. 347 (1967).

[13] *Stanley* also casts a shadow on the government's subpoena power. If the government alleges that books or films privately possessed are evidence of a crime, does this interest justify a search of one's library? Would an allegation that subversive literature is privately possessed justify such a search? Can individuals be required to produce such items, for purposes of congressional investigation, under threat of contempt? Is not the use of the contempt power here merely a formality to avoid directly searching some "sanctuary"? Professor Kalven raised with me the interesting question whether a search for illegally possessed literature of the type involved in Schenck v. United States, 249 U.S. 47 (1919), would justify a result different from *Stanley*.

ences. According to the Court, none of these claims justified the "inquiry into the contents of [Stanley's] library."[14]

The Court considered concern for the protection of minors to be irrelevant here, since it found no inherent danger that juveniles would be exposed. The Court distinguished *Stanley* from *Roth* because the latter case involved commercial distribution where some of the "material might fall into the hands of children."[15] But that is not a persuasive argument for according greater constitutional protection to possession over distribution. First, the possessor of such films could very well invite all the juveniles in his neighborhood to a showing of them. Whether or not this would constitute a criminal offense is beside the point. Short of distributing his own film commercially, the private possessor retains considerable freedom to "expose" (through invitation) a significant number of people, not excluding juveniles. The Court has denied that concern for the protection of minors is a sufficient justification for general regulation,[16] and has sanctioned such concern only when reflected in narrowly drawn statutes.[17] To the extent that it is not clear that private possession presents less of a danger to juveniles than commercial distribution, the "protection of minors" argument does not go far in sustaining a constitutional difference between commercial distribution and private possession.

Commercial distribution, unlike private possession, might indeed present the risk that an unwilling public will be exposed to offensive sexual material. There was no allegation in *Roth*, however, of offense to a captive audience. *Redrup v. New York*[18] strongly suggested that to make out a constitutional case for suppression it was necessary specifically to allege some offense to an unwilling audience. Commercial distribution per se did not suffice, as was evident from the fact that all the material involved in *Redrup* was commercially distributed.[19] In *Stanley* the Court cited *Redrup* for the cap-

---

14 394 U.S. at 565.

15 *Id.* at 567. This is the classic "trickle" principle. See Book Review of Kuh, *Foolish Figleaves?* 56 CALIF. L. REV. 555, 561 (1968).

16 Butler v. Michigan, 352 U.S. 380 (1957).

17 Interstate Circuit, Inc. v. Dallas, 390 U.S. 676, 690 (1968).

18 386 U.S. 767 (1967).

19 See also Fort v. City of Miami, 389 U.S. 918 (1967), *cert. den.*, Justices Stewart, Black, and Douglas, dissenting.

tive audience point but ignored the clear distinction *Redrup* implies between mere commercial distribution and distribution accompanied by actual offense to an unwilling recipient-observer. In sum, the interest in protecting an unwilling public cannot, as the Court said in *Stanley*, justify seizure of privately possessed materials. By the same token that interest does not perforce bring all commercially distributed material within the ambit of legal regulation. The majority opinion in *Stanley* by dichotomizing commercial and noncommercial in order to distinguish *Roth* implies the contrary.

The Court's handling of the assertion that the states have an interest in regulating obscenity because such material may incite antisocial conduct was equally unsatisfactory. The Court seemed to dismiss it entirely, because "[t]here appears to be little empirical basis for that assertion."[20] The Court expressed the view that the appropriate way to handle this danger, if it be such, is through "education" and the ordinary processes of the criminal law.[21] If the state is to justify regulation on this basis it has the burden of proving a "clear and present danger" of incitement to illegal action from pornography. *Roth*'s rejection of the "clear and present danger" test is unaffected by this ruling because "that case dealt with public distribution of obscene materials and such distribution is subject to different objections."[22] Those objections are the twin dangers of exposure to juveniles or to an unwilling public.

The Court's argument here is entirely sophistical. The incitement claim has nothing to do with the state's interest in protecting an unwilling public. Protection of that audience is rational and defensible whether the material will harm the audience or not. As the Court says, it is really a matter of the "privacy of the general public."[23] The interest in protecting juveniles, furthermore, is a man of straw, for no one contends that with respect to them the state must show a clear and present danger of harm. The incitement claim is not relevant to either of these groups; it is intended as a justification for keeping obscenity away from willing adults.

The Court's handling of this issue gives rise to two possible interpretations. (1) The incitement claim is rejected, subject to the "clear and present danger" test, so long as one is dealing only with willing adults. Thus, the incitement claim does not help the state in the *Stan-*

---

[20] 394 U.S. at 566.

[21] *Id.* at 566–67.

[22] *Id.* at 567.

[23] *Ibid.*

ley case and probably will be of no avail in most obscenity cases. To this extent *Roth* really is disapproved. (2) The incitement claim may support the state's interest in commercial distribution cases because commercial distribution is an undifferentiated phenomenon: by definition it endangers juveniles and may offend the privacy of an unwilling public. This second reading of *Stanley* keeps *Roth* alive but is subject to the criticisms mentioned above, and it seriously cripples *Redrup*.

The Court also seemed to reject outright the state's claim that society has an interest in protecting individual minds from the degenerate influences of obscenity, thus protecting the moral qualities of social life. "We are not certain that this argument amounts to anything more than the assertion that the State has the right to control the moral contents of a person's thoughts."[24] The Court refused to consider whether the material involved was obscene, whether or not it contained any ideas,[25] an inquiry central to *Roth:*[26]

> Nor is it relevant that obscenity in general, or the particular films before the Court, are arguably devoid of any ideological content. The line between the transmission of ideas and mere entertainment is much too elusive for this Court to draw, if indeed such a line can be drawn at all.

Taken out of context this statement again reads like an open rejection of *Roth*, for the opinion in that case depended upon the possibility of drawing the precise line the existence of which the Court now doubts. But the Court said that it intended no such general rejection of *Roth:* in commercial distribution cases the irrelevance of ideological context becomes relevant, the "much too elusive" line must be drawn,[27] and the state then apparently retains the right to control the moral content of a person's thoughts. The reason for the distinction between the two types of situations remains the same. The right of the willing adult to receive commercially dis-

---

[24] *Id.* at 565.

[25] Katz, *The "Tropic of Cancer" Trials: The Problem of Relevant Moral and Artistic Controversy,* 9 MIDWAY 99 (Spring, 1969).

[26] 394 U.S. at 566.

[27] It is important to note that if the Court meant to insist on a clear distinction between the commercial and the serious, the factor of ideological content becomes even more central than it was in *Roth.* This is particularly true if the Court drew a silent analogy to the distinction between advertising and communication of ideas found in Valentine v. Chrestensen, 316 U.S. 52 (1942).

tributed material is sacrificed to protection of the sensibilities of the unwilling and the sensitivities of the young.

One is tempted to argue that the Court's opinion would have been stronger resting on *Griswold* alone. But the majority opinion already suggests that the notion of privacy cannot stand alone. The Court cannot designate a particular locus or res as private without either holding that the privacy may not be invaded for any reason, or explaining why the specific grounds for invasion alleged in the case at hand are insufficient. This means that in *Stanley* the Court had to say either one's bedroom drawers or books or library are absolutely private, or that an allegation of obscenity is an insufficient justification for invasion. While the latter is clearly the more reasonable course, it would entail two interesting consequences. To the extent *Griswold* is controlling, it would mean that the state's interest in preventing the use of contraceptives is an insufficient justification for invading the bedroom sanctuary, which invasion wasn't involved in *Griswold* in any event. Having found a particular place to be private, the Court would be bound to consider the constitutional implications of the government's reason for invading it. The second consequence of this approach would be that in *Stanley* itself the Court necessarily had to venture into the First Amendment and find that Stanley's primary interest was in the "right to receive information and ideas, regardless of their social worth," a right that receives the *"added dimension"* of privacy.[28] In turn, this approach would place an unbearable burden on *Roth* and the significance of commercial distribution.

Although *Roth* was concerned with commercial distribution, it is clear that the Court there did not frame the question as whether the fact of distribution adversely affected the constitutional protection otherwise accorded the material. *Stanley* suggests that *Roth* was dead wrong in its approach: obscenity is protected speech subject only to regulation in the interest of protecting the unwilling and the young.[29] Rather than state openly that *Roth* was wrong, *Stanley* confines the premise that obscenity is not protected as free speech or press to the context of commercial distribution. The Court here plays a dangerous jurisprudential game. It is equating a general

---

[28] 394 U.S. at 564. (Emphasis added.)

[29] But *cf.* Ginsberg v. New York, 390 U.S. 629, 635 (1968): "Obscenity is not within the area of protected speech or press."

rule subject to qualification (obscenity is not protected speech unless privately possessed) with a qualification of a contrary general rule (obscenity is protected speech unless commercially distributed). For First Amendment purposes it makes a great deal of difference which form the general principle takes. Under the *Roth* formulation, as a practical matter, the burden is on the defense to snatch the item out of the obscenity bag by proving ideological content or some other sort of value. Under the *Stanley* formulation the burden would be on the state to prove offense to an unwilling audience or exposure to juveniles. The theoretical difference is analogous to the effect of saying libelous utterances are protected speech if they relate to matters of public concern rather than holding that libelous utterances are protected speech unless communicated with a malicious intent to harm.[30] The effect of *Stanley* is to substitute a First Amendment analysis for the much criticized "double level" approach of *Roth*.[31]

Having held that an allegation of obscenity was insufficient to justify an otherwise reasonable search, the Court seemed to say that such an allegation was sufficient to justify interference with the "right to receive" the products of commercial distribution. While the Court did not make the connection clear, apparently the reason, again, was the possible exposure of juveniles and unwilling adults. If this be so, the Court should have noted that the precedents it cites for the "right to receive" doctrine are founded on a concern about getting willing speakers and recipients together without offending a captive audience, not on simple commercialism.

As authority for the "right to receive" doctrine the Court first cited *Martin v. City of Struthers*,[32] the case involving door-to-door distribution of religious literature. The relevant language in *Martin* was: "This freedom [of speech and press] embraces the right to distribute literature . . . and necessarily protects the right to receive it."[33] There appears to be no suggestion in *Martin* that the right to receive is superior to the right to distribute (particularly since the appellant in *Martin* was the distributor not the recipient). But at

---

[30] See Kalven, *The New York Times Case: A Note on "The Central Meaning of the First Amendment,"* 1964 SUPREME COURT REVIEW 191.

[31] Kalven, *The Metaphysics of the Law of Obscenity*, 1960 SUPREME COURT REVIEW 1.

[32] 319 U.S. 141 (1943).   [33] *Id.* at 143.

the heart of that case was an issue crucial to the problem underlying *Stanley:* the potential conflict between the desire of distributors to distribute and the desire of some recipients to be left alone, not to receive. As interpreted in *Kovacs v. Cooper*,[34] *Martin* struck down the ordinance prohibiting door-to-door distribution because "the home owner could protect himself from such intrusion by an appropriate sign."[35] In *Kovacs* the potential recipient of sound truck distribution had no such ready protection.[36] In short, as used in *Martin* the "right to receive" is only the reciprocal of the right to distribute, and reflects the problem of getting willing hearers and speakers together without offending the rest of the community.

The same principle informs *Lamont v. Postmaster General*,[37] the concurring opinion of which was cited in *Stanley* for the "right to receive" proposition. A post office regulation required that Lamont specifically request certain politically questionable material addressed to him before it would be delivered. The opinion of the Court there held this placed too great a burden on the exercise of First Amendment rights, without mentioning the "right to receive." The concurring opinion of Mr. Justice Brennan did indeed discuss the "right to receive."[38] It began by noting that the case would have been difficult if Lamont had asserted the First Amendment rights of the distributors, for that would present problems of standing, of constitutional *jus tertii*. Lamont avoided this problem by asserting his own right, the right to receive, which Mr. Justice Brennan regarded as equally sacred. (Since the material was addressed to him and Lamont interposed no objection to receiving it, willing hearer and speaker were brought together without offense to a captive community.) In *Stanley* the Court cited the Brennan concurring opinion rather than the majority in *Lamont* because the latter would have required it to decide whether the material before the Court was constitutionally protected, as was the case in *Lamont*. Therefore, it would seem that the elevation of the "right to receive" over the right to distribute is more apparent than real. Relying on the "right to receive" doctrine was simply another way of avoiding direct confrontation with *Roth*.

The "right to receive" doctrine is consistent with the Court's

[34] 336 U.S. 77 (1949).

[35] *Id.* at 86.

[36] *Id.* at 87.

[37] 381 U.S. 301 (1965).

[38] *Id.* at 308.

concern about getting distributors and willing recipients together without offending an unwilling public. In this respect the fact of private possession is crucial. Private possession indicates that the recipient is willing to hear, and a pure possession case involves no questions about possible exposure of those who are unwilling.[39] The upshot of the *Stanley* approach is a sharp constriction of the so-called "broad power [of the states] to regulate obscenity,"[40] and a disapproval of *Roth* to the extent that content becomes irrelevant to the inquiry.

The "broad power" to regulate obscenity is confined by *Stanley* to instances of commercial distribution. The question is whether the Court meant to allow the states to cast even so broad a net. Need the government only show that the material was commercially distributed? Or must it show that the manner of distribution presented a "clear and present danger" that the unwilling or the young will be exposed? Or need the state only show a probability of such exposure? Or must the government prove that in fact these groups were exposed? These questions are unanswered in *Stanley*, and even *Redrup* is unclear on the nature of the required allegation. If the government need only plead and prove commercial distribution, then *Stanley* becomes an intellectually silly case. Stanley himself probably bought his film through some sort of commercial distributor. If so, and if the act of distribution may be proscribed, then Stanley had no "right to receive," only a right to keep whatever he can manage to find. The right to receive, if there be such in this context, is implied from the right to distribute. If there is a right to receive "information and ideas, regardless of their social worth," then commercial distribution per se is not proscribable.

---

[39] Making mere possession criminal is not common to criminal codes, but it is not unknown. Perhaps one reason for the relative scarcity of this type of crime is the potential problem of proving mens rea, and possible constitutional barriers to shifting the burden of proof to the defendant. United States v. Romano, 382 U.S. 136 (1965). But it is more likely that the relative infrequency of the crime of possession indicates an unwillingness to "overcriminalize" in the interest of eliminating a substantive evil. Thus prostitution is a crime but the "possession" of a prostitute is not. Since the matter is relative, a particularly serious substantive evil may justify making possession criminal, *e.g.*, dangerous weapons. Looking at *Stanley* from this perspective, it may be that the Court does not regard the evil of obscenity as serious enough to justify making criminals of its possessors. In doctrinal terms one reaches this result by combining the "less onerous alternative" test with a "balancing" approach.

[40] 394 U.S. at 568. "*Roth* and the cases following that decision are not impaired by today's holding." *Ibid.*

Beyond this the nature of the state's burden is unclear, but a good case can be made for requiring the government to produce a victim. We have had enough experience with victimless crimes in other areas, and with allegations of probable offense in obscenity cases, to have learned that sound administration of legal regulation requires the narrowest possible definition of the protected social interest, and real rather than opinion evidence of violation. These principles demand that regulation of commercially distributed pornography require an allegation of actual exposure of unwilling adults or juveniles. Trial courts, as well as the Supreme Court, will have the unenviable task of deciding when the audience is "captive," whether the communication was sufficiently offensive to be an intrusion into the "captive's" privacy, and in the case of juveniles, of formulating some criteria for review of state determinations of what is unsuitable for the young.

Implicit in this analysis is the view that "pandering" is a totally useless concept that should (and probably will) be considered an ill-begotten child of hard cases. No interest is invaded by pandering that is not covered by the two other arms of *Redrup*. The evil of pandering has never been clearly identified; one can only suppose it presents the possibility that the unwilling will be enticed. But if the unwilling are truly so, they can have the protection of appropriate legislation.[41] The same is true with respect to juveniles. The lack of clear definition of harm exacerbates the difficulties inherent in the pandering notion. Can "stag movies," for example, be sold commercially if they are not publicly displayed or sold to minors? After *Stanley*, what constitutes the offense of pandering? Advertising motion pictures as "stag movies"? What are the elements of the offense of pandering? Clearly the test can no longer be "appeal to the prurient interest." After *Stanley*, could the Court rationally accept Richard Kuh's proposed pandering statute:[42]

Any person shall be guilty of a misdemeanor who, in any capacity, knowingly distributes, leases, sells, or otherwise com-

---

[41] "The only valid purpose of obscenity law is to prevent public offense. It should be viewed, purely and simply, as the proscription of nuisance. People who do not wish to have erotic or other material that they find offensive foisted upon them are entitled to protection from it, just as they are arguably entitled to be protected against having to witness the real-life conduct of which pornography is the simulacrum." PACKER, THE LIMITS OF THE CRIMINAL SANCTION 324 (1968).

[42] KUH, FOOLISH FIGLEAVES? 297 (1967).

mercially markets or rents any book . . . [etc.], or who possesses such item for purposes of so disposing of it, under circumstances demonstrating his intention to exploit commercially a morbid interest in sadomasochistic abuse, sexual conduct, sexual excitement, defecation, or urination.

If the buyer has the right to include whatever he likes in his private library, if the state has no interest in protecting his morals or in protecting him from these kinds of "incitements" to antisocial conduct, if he is an adult, and if there are no complaints from citizens whose privacy has been offended, what state interest could justify this statute?[43]

The concurring opinion of Mr. Justice Stewart,[44] joined by Justices Brennan and White, characterized *Stanley* as a search and seizure problem of the first aspect. The Stewart opinion was careful to point out that this was "not a case where agents in the course of a lawful search came upon contraband, criminal activity, or criminal evidence in plain view."[45] The crucial constitutional fact was that the officers went so far as to run the film through Stanley's home projector, which was, of course, the only way they could discover whether the films were obscene.

For reasons not at all clear from a reading of the concurring opinion alone, the majority chose not to respond to it apart from footnoting the fact that in *Mapp v. Ohio*, where the "mere private possession" issue was also raised, Mr. Justice Stewart would have reached the merits and held that the proscription of mere possession was "not 'consistent with the rights of free thought and expression assured against state action by the Fourteenth Amendment.' "[46]

The search in *Stanley* was authorized by a warrant particularly describing certain materials which would be used in a bookmaking

---

[43] It is interesting that the Court cites both the *Model Penal Code* and Packer's *The Limits of the Criminal Sanction* for the proposition that obscenity regulation should be "limited to cases of commercial dissemination." 394 U.S. at 567, n. 10. In the paragraph immediately following that quoted in note 41 *supra*, Professor Packer wrote: "In this view of the proper function of obscenity law, the *Ginsburg* decision is precisely wrong, as is the Model Penal Code legislation addressed to the advertising and promotion of obscenity. The more clearly the package advertises its contents, the more effectively the unwary consumer will be protected from exposure to what he is likely to find distasteful. Nor need it be feared that the advertising itself be likely to give offense. No seller in his right mind is going to give away free what he wants to induce people to buy."

[44] 394 U.S. at 569.   [45] *Id*. at 571.   [46] *Id*. at 560 n. 3.

operation, or which would be evidence of such an operation. In the course of searching for these items the officers found the alleged obscene films in "a desk drawer in an upstairs bedroom."[47] In Mr. Justice Stewart's opinion the controlling cases were *Marron v. United States*[48] and *Rabinowitz v. United States*,[49] from which the conclusion in *Stanley* followed in fashion.

Both *Marron* and *Rabinowitz* raised the question of the proper scope of search either incident to a lawful arrest or incident to the execution of a lawful search warrant. These cases are relevant because the concurring opinion takes as the crucial datum the fact that the officers in *Stanley* took the film out of a desk drawer, found a projector, and proceeded to run the film. Characterizing the facts differently would have led the minority Justices into the question whether, prior to running the film, there was probable cause to believe the film was an instrumentality of, or evidence of, a crime, or into the question whether the film might be seized at all under a warrant authorizing a search for bookmaking materials. The latter question would have required Mr. Justice Stewart to deal with *Harris v. United States*: "If entry upon the premises be authorized and the search which follows be valid, there is nothing in the Fourth Amendment which inhibits the seizure by law-enforcement agents of government property *the possession of which is a crime*, even though the officers are not aware that such property is on the premises when the search is initiated."[50]

The quoted paragraph from *Harris* suggests a possible explanation why the majority chose to ignore Mr. Justice Stewart's opinion, and why that opinion was careful to focus on the fact that the officers ran the film through Stanley's projector. Perhaps the Court ignored the search and seizure issue because it realized that to deal fully with the search and seizure problem it would have to distinguish *Harris*. On the other hand, to deal with the search and seizure problem and avoid the possession question, Mr. Justice Stewart needed to focus on the fact that the agents ran the film through Stanley's projector. *Harris* and the possession question could only be avoided by holding that merely finding the reels of film in a desk drawer gave the offi-

---

47 *Id.* at 558.

48 275 U.S. 192 (1927).   49 339 U.S. 56 (1950).

50 331 U.S. 145, 155 (1947). The case was cited with apparent approval in Alderman v. United States, 394 U.S. 165, 177 n. 10 (1969).

cers no probable cause to believe they were obscene, and that to put
the film through Stanley's projector constituted a search beyond
the scope permissible under the authority of the original search warrant. Unfortunately the minority did not deal with the former proposition, and the cases it relied on for the latter proposal are readily
distinguishable.

Considering *Stanley* from the viewpoint of the Court's avowed
practice to decide cases on the narrowest grounds possible under the
facts,[51] both the majority and the minority selected imprudent characterizations. The "private sanctuary" approach of the majority
requires a complex doctrinal analysis that creates more problems
than it solves. Likewise, the minority characterization of the case
as presenting an "incidental search" question was ill-advised if only
because of the almost ad hoc quality of the cases decided between
Agnello v. United States[52] and *Cooper v. California.*[53]

The *Stanley* case could have been decided on the narrow ground
that the statute in question did not reflect "a specific and limited
concern for juveniles," and there was no evidence of pandering.[54]
Since *Redrup* was decided, these matters have been taken as demark-
ing the limit of judicial concern with content. *Stanley* presented the
Court with an opportunity to make it clear that this reading of
Redrup is correct. By indirection *Stanley* does just that: obscenity is
"vested" with constitutional protection subject to divestment upon
a finding of distribution to minors or exposure to an unwilling (captive) audience. The majority opinion also casts doubt on the future
of the pandering notion, but such indirection and questioning were
unnecessary. *Stanley* was one of those few occasions when a per
curiam reversal without opinion would have been most welcome.

---

[51] Garner v. Louisiana, 368 U.S. 157, 163 (1961).   [53] 386 U.S. 58 (1967).

[52] 269 U.S. 20 (1925).   [54] 386 U.S. at 769.

ROBERT G. DIXON, JR.

THE WARREN COURT CRUSADE

FOR THE HOLY GRAIL OF

"ONE MAN–ONE VOTE"

> *"But my dear, we never compromise on virtue,"*
> *quoth the Queen.*
> *"Horrors, no," exclaimed Alice, "but what is*
> *virtue? That is the question."*
> (With apologies to Lewis Carroll)

I. Representation and the Warren Court Style

A. ABSOLUTISM VERSUS POLITICAL REALITY

In *Baker v. Carr*[1] in 1962 the Supreme Court cut a wide swath through the political thicket. In the recent companion cases, *Kirkpatrick v. Preisler*[2] and *Wells v. Rockefeller*[3] in 1969, the Court majority apparently forgot that the problem was political and that the issue was political representation, not numbers. It ordered an unqualified absolute population equality rule for congressional districts, and presumably for other kinds of districts as well.[4] The new

---

Robert G. Dixon, Jr., is Professor of Law, George Washington University.

[1] 369 U.S. 186 (1962).   [2] 394 U.S. 526 (1969).   [3] 394 U.S. 542 (1969).

[4] It has become common to speak of revision of state legislative districts as "reapportionment" and revision of congressional districts inside a state as "redistricting." Logically, however, the "one man–one vote" upheaval has made it improper to use the term "reapportionment" regarding state legislative seats, because the tight population equality now required makes it impossible to "apportion" state legislative seats

rule leaves little or no room for recognition of traditional political subdivision lines—county lines, city lines—and the communities of interest they tend to contain, except on a fortuitous basis. It may reduce creativity in those districting arrangements by which we seek to achieve the ever elusive goal of fair and effective representation. It may even foster gerrymandering.

Just as the political system seemed to need some Court help in 1962, it now is becoming obvious that the Court needs help from the political system in managing the equality concept in apportionment-districting. The result in *Preisler* and *Wells* gives pause even to firm friends of "one man—one vote," as elaborated below.

Moreover, the Court achieved this result in cases in which one of the sets of challenged congressional districts had a maximum deviation from the ideal of only 3.1 percent, and the other only 6.6 percent. The Missouri 3.1 percent plan was a court-impelled replacement of a prior 9.9 percent deviation, the invalidation of which had already raised some eyebrows in 1967.[5] The New York 6.6 percent plan replaced a prior 15.1 percent deviation. It was bipartisan rather than partisan in the sense of being the product of a split legislature, each party controlling one house.[6] Neither appeal was taken by any political party or other significant organized group of voters. Rather, each was almost a solo appeal. In this field, any voter has standing to maintain a suit. Each state was told that it must devise yet one more congressional districting plan, to achieve absolute equality on the basis of the 1960 census figures, for a single use in the 1970 congressional election. Other states, with less vigorous plaintiffs, will

---

to existing units such as counties or cities. With no fixed districts, the whole process of creating and revising state legislative seats is simply redistricting. The process of revising state legislative seats will, however, continue to be referred to here as "reapportionment" whenever it is needed for clarity. "Apportionment-districting" will denote both state legislative district revision and congressional district revision.

[5] Kirkpatrick v. Preisler, 385 U.S. 450 (1967).

[6] The vote was 126 to 19 in the Democratic-controlled assembly and 51 to 5 in the Republican-controlled senate. Strangely, this point was not mentioned either by the district court or the Supreme Court, nor was it stressed sufficiently in the State's brief and argument in support of the plan's political fairness. Brief for Appellees, p. 30, *Wells v. Rockefeller*.

Even more strange, by the time of the Supreme Court's decision in April, 1969, the Republicans had captured both legislative houses. The Court, therefore, was overturning a bipartisan plan and ordering a partisan replacement.

hold their 1970 congressional election in districts having greater deviations than either of the invalidated plans.[7]

Mr. Justice Brennan, speaking for the Court, said that the Constitution "requires that a State make a good-faith effort to achieve precise mathematical equality."[8] To Mr. Justice Fortas, concurring only in the result and rejecting the rationale, this approach ignored the "boundaries of common sense."[9] He hypothesized the *reductio ad absurdum* of "running the congressional district line down the middle of the corridor of an apartment house, or even dividing the residents of a single-family house between two districts."[10] With an eye on gerrymandering possibilities, Mr. Justice White noted: "If county and municipal boundaries are to be ignored, a computer can produce countless plans for absolute population equality, one differing very little from another, but each having its own very different political ramifications."[11] And in similar vein Mr. Justice Harlan, joined by Mr. Justice Stewart, predicted that legislatures, freed of the traditional public opinion–enforced duty to follow county and regional lines, would gain enhanced gerrymandering freedom: "Even more than in the past, district lines are likely to be drawn to maximize the political advantage of the party temporarily dominant in public affairs."[12]

In *Wesberry v. Sanders* in 1964 the Court, in somewhat ambiguous terms, had required for congressional districts only a rule that districts be equal "as nearly as is practicable."[13] At the same time, in the group of state legislative apportionment rulings headed by *Reynolds v. Sims,* the Court announced a rule of "substantial equality."[14] Technically the *Wesberry* ruling was based on Art. I, § 2 of

---

[7] A 1968 tabulation for the 1968 congressional election showed that districts in at least twenty-seven states (most of them revised since *Baker v. Carr*) exceeded Missouri's 3.1 percent deviation. Dixon, Democratic Representation: Reapportionment in Law and Politics 632 (1968) (hereinafter referred to as Dixon). Additional citations for many of the points covered in this article may be found in that book.

[8] 394 U.S. at 530–31.   [10] *Ibid.*   [12] *Id.* at 552.

[9] *Id.* at 538.   [11] 394 U.S. at 556.   [13] 376 U.S. 1, 7–8 (1964).

[14] 377 U.S. 533, 579 (1964). See also *id.* at 568 and 578. In *Reynolds,* the Court indicated that the equal "as is practicable" test was also appropriate for state legislatures. *Id.* at 577.

For contemporary discussion see Auerbach, *The Reapportionment Cases: One Person, One Vote–One Vote, One Value,* 1964 Supreme Court Review 1; McKay, Reapportionment: The Law and Politics of Equal Representation (1965); Dixon, Kauper, & McKay, *Reapportionment Symposium,* 63 Mich. L. Rev. 209 (1964).

the Constitution, which speaks not of intrastate congressional districting but of apportionment of seats among the states. The *Reynolds* ruling was based on the Equal Protection Clause of the Fourteenth Amendment. But it has never been apparent that the Court sees these two clauses as producing different yardsticks for districting matters.

To be sure, in *Reynolds*, Chief Justice Warren, after noting that normally there were more state legislative seats than congressional seats to be distributed within a state, said: "Somewhat more flexibility may therefore be constitutionally permissible with respect to state legislative apportionment than in congressional districting."[15] But he made this comment in the context of the possibility of its being more feasible to use "political subdivision lines" in state legislative districting than in congressional districting. In any event, there was no indication in the 1964 opinions that a rigid rule of arithmetic population equality would be applied either in congressional districting or state legislative districting. More significantly, in the avalanche of lower court decisions following 1964, and in occasional Supreme Court opinions, congressional districting precedents and state legislative apportionment precedents were cited interchangeably on all questions including the population equality question.[16]

The Court in *Reynolds* was divided 8 to 1, with only Mr. Justice Harlan dissenting on the ground that he could find no applicable

---

[15] 377 U.S. at 578.

[16] For example, in 1967 the Court nullified a 12.8 percent congressional districting plan in Indiana. Concurrently, in the case destined to come back again as the 1969 *Kirkpatrick v. Preisler* case, the Court sustained a federal district court's invalidation of a 9.9 percent congressional districting plan in Missouri. See Duddleston v. Grills, 385 U.S. 455 (1967); Kirkpatrick v. Preisler, 385 U.S. 450 (1967). The rulings were per curiam orders in which the Court merely cited as authority the contemporaneous 1967 Florida apportionment case in which it had invalidated an 18.3 percent deviation plan. In this case the Court said that only de minimis deviations were permissible unless special justification were shown. Swann v. Adams, 385 U.S. 440, 444 (1967).

Some may see in these 1967 rulings, which did tighten the "substantial equality" concept, a way-stop toward the 1969 *Preisler* and *Wells* absolute equality standard. But it was Mr. Justice White who wrote the opinion for the Court in the Florida case, *Swann v. Adams*, and he dissented vigorously in *Preisler* and *Wells*. And in neither case did he indicate he was making any distinction in equality rules between congressional districting and state legislative apportionment.

or manageable constitutional standards.[17] But when the Court also voided the Colorado plan, which had far more modest population deviations and had been approved by a 2 to 1 vote in a statewide popular referendum, the margin dropped to 6 to 3, with Justices Clark and Stewart joining Mr. Justice Harlan in dissent.[18] It was this ruling, and not *Reynolds*, that provided the main push for the drive in 1965–66 to amend the Constitution to confirm the "one man–one vote" principle but to modify it to make room for Colorado-type apportionments, when approved by popular vote.[19]

If as Mr. Justice Stewart said, with some hyperbole, the Colorado ruling was an exercise in "sixth-grade arithmetic,"[20] then the *Preisler* and *Wells* absolute population equality ruling of 1969 almost seems to be playing with blocks, and faceless blocks at that. Forgotten was the *Reynolds* statement that "[m]athematical exactness or precision is hardly a workable constitutional requirement"; and the accom-

---

[17] There were five sets of cases decided with *Reynolds:* Alabama cases, Reynolds v. Sims, Vann v. Baggett, McConnell v. Baggett, 377 U.S. 533 (1964); New York case, WMCA, Inc. v. Lomenzo, 377 U.S. 633 (1964); Virginia case, Davis v. Mann, 377 U.S. 678 (1964); Delaware case, Roman v. Sincock, 377 U.S. 695 (1964); Colorado case, Lucas v. Colorado General Assembly, 377 U.S. 713 (1964). Cases from Michigan, Washington, Oklahoma, Illinois, Idaho, Connecticut, Florida, Ohio, Iowa were disposed of with brief statements a week later. 378 U.S. at 553, 554, 556, 558, 560, 561, 563, 564, 565.

[18] An alternative straight population plan had been defeated, also by a 2 to 1 popular vote. No other case presented this popular referendum feature.

In population terms the invalidated Colorado plan had a population variance ratio of 3.6 to 1 for the senate and 1.7 to 1 for the house (the latter figure not being challenged by the parties was left open by the Court as possibly permissible). Of the fourteen additional state plans invalidated contemporaneously by the Court in June, 1964, only one had a figure for one house close to 1.7 to 1 (Ohio, 1.9 to 1), but for Ohio's other house the figure was 9.4 to 1. DIXON 266.

Significantly, United States Solicitor General Archibald Cox, in his amicus curiae brief, sought only some changes in the senate, not a "one man–one vote" principle across the board. And he argued that if the Court could not adopt his halfway house position the equity factors, including the referendum vote, indicated that the Court should stay its hand. *Id.* at 246.

[19] DIXON 385–435; *Reapportionment Symposium*, note 14 *supra*; Dirksen, Ervin, Kauper, Carsen, Dixon, Bonfield & McCloskey, *Symposium on the Article V Convention Process*, 66 MICH. L. REV. 837 (1968).

[20] 377 U.S. at 750. Professor Auerbach, note 14 *supra*, at 84, felt that under specified conditions (not all of which in his view were clearly satisfied in the Colorado case) plans adopted by the popular initiative process should be "recognized as a valid, constituent act of the people," even if the plans departed from the equal population principle to some degree.

panying comment quoted from Holmes that the machinery of government will not work if "not allowed a little play in its joints."[21]

Baker v. Carr can be justified without jumping all the way to arithmetic absolutism. In a dozen states in 1962 at least one state legislative district was more than 500 percent deviant. Congressional district deviations were somewhat less extreme, but exceeded 50 percent in a dozen states. This is hardly justifiable even if the extent to which the political process was distracted by this factor, and the boons which reapportionment brings, are still debatable—for we have lost our innocence and idealism in these matters. Malapportionment was undermining popular faith in our system. As was noted at the time, political avenues for change had become dead-end streets; some judicial intervention in the politics of the people seemed necessary to have an effective political system.[22]

The proposition that in a democratic system a "population base" must be the dominant feature in apportionment-districting merely states the obvious. But some sense of "community" is relevant too. Anyone familiar with the suburbs of Washington, D.C., knows there is a world of difference between the adjacent Maryland counties. Prince Georges is southern-oriented, with a slave tobacco culture just emerging into the twentieth century; Montgomery County is northern-oriented, with a family farm culture being replaced by vibrant middle-class suburbia. Similar examples abound in all states. A maximum allowable deviation of 10 or 15 percent, which was all that anyone sought in the era of *Baker v. Carr*, would terminate egregious population disparities while leaving room for accommodation of such "communities." The true question is: *what* population—*what* people—*what* spokesmen for *what* interests? Our decade of romancing with numbers has not touched these basic questions in any significant way. They remain for the seventies, albeit the *Preisler* and *Wells* ruling may make solutions more difficult than if the Warren Court had left a little more "play in the joints."

B. ANALOGOUS RULINGS

"One man—one vote" thus may turn out to be one of the greatest successes if one of the most Sisyphean ventures of the so-called Warren era. In some aspects it may be the prototype of the Warren

---

[21] 377 U.S. at 577.

[22] Dixon, *Legislative Apportionment and the Federal Constitution*, 27 LAW & CONTEMP. PROB. 329, 346, 350 (1962).

Court in action. Motivated by the best of ideals, unchained to the past, the Court broke new ground in numerous fields with the abandon of a western settler exploiting virgin territory. But it seldom tarried to tidy up. More seriously, it sometimes did not pause to think through the implications of its pronouncements before plunging ahead.[23]

In a way, this is traditionally the pathway of change. But in some other noteworthy fields touched by the Warren Court—racial equality, criminal procedure, and review of the internalities of congressional operation—the Court often did leave various options open. Despite all the drama surrounding *Brown v. Board of Education*[24] and the sequence of suits following it, school integration has in fact moved very slowly. Doctrinally, it appears that we have a color-blind Constitution for some purposes; a color-conscious Constitution for other purposes. The choice in a given situation remains unclear.[25] Perhaps that is as it should be in this complex and tragic field, where the problems sometimes seem less soluble with the passing of time.

In the field of criminal procedure despite the intrinsic rigidity of the rules in some areas—for example, in a given situation the right of counsel either exists totally or not at all—the Court has left options open at crucial points. Best known to the public may be the Court's rulings in the confession cases headed by *Miranda v. Arizona.*[26] The warnings which the Court said must be given in order to validate a confession were all prefaced by the statement "unless other fully effective means"[27] are available to dispel the presumption of undue police coercion during in-custody interrogation.

---

[23] An early comment on *Baker v. Carr*, and the opinions insufficiently delineating its scope, referred to the case as a better "example of the role of fiat in the exercise of judicial power" than of the rule of law. Neal, *Baker v. Carr: Politics in Search of Law*, 1962 SUPREME COURT REVIEW 252, 327. And *Baker* was referred to by one commentator, who was attempting to support it, as "merely a call for action." Katzenbach, *Some Reflections on Baker v. Carr*, 15 VAND. L. REV. 829, 832 (1962).

[24] 347 U.S. 483 (1954).

[25] See Kaplan, *Equal Justice in an Unequal World: Equality for the Negro—the Problem of Special Treatment*, 61 Nw. U. L. REV. 363 (1966); Hellerstein, *The Benign Quota, Equal Protection and "The Rule in Shelley's Case,"* 17 RUTGERS L. REV. 531 (1963); Bittker, *The Case of the Checker-Board Ordinance: An Experiment in Race Relations*, 71 YALE L. J. 1387 (1962). And see Green v. County School Board, 391 U.S. 430 (1968).

[26] 384 U.S. 436 (1966).   [27] *Id*. at 444.

In *Powell v. McCormack*[28] on almost the last day of its last Term the Warren Court seemed to be asserting, if one saw only the headlines, a broad power of scrutiny of the internal operations of Congress. Actually, the Court managed to avoid such difficult issues as its power to order the seating of Adam Clayton Powell despite the vote of the House of Representatives denying him a seat, the power to restore his seniority, and the right of his Harlem constituents to complain about loss of political representation. Only the issue of back salary remained, and this point the Court remanded to the district court with something less than clear-cut guidance on how to effectuate the presumably valid claim.

In the field of "one man–one vote," by contrast, the Warren Court in another of its terminal acts handed down a rule so absolute and uncompromising as to make difficult if not impossible—short of constitutional amendment—the needed process of articulation of more refined rules responsive to the fresh set of "one man–one vote" problems which will be spawned by the 1970 census. The crucial problems are political and racial gerrymandering and reapportionment method.

On the new absolute rule the decision was only 5 to 4, with dissents or caveats from Justices Fortas, Harlan, White, and Stewart. More significantly, many knowledgeable loyal partisans of "one man–one vote" are puzzled, if not dismayed, by the inflexible and doctrinaire quality of Mr. Justice Brennan's opinion for the Court in *Preisler* and *Wells*. Even plaintiff David Wells in the New York case has remarked in jocular vein: "Can we appeal from a decision that we won?"[29]

We have known doctrinaire jurisprudence before. The 1930's when the Hughes Court was invalidating New Deal legislation with dogged persistence is of recent memory. The judicial activism of the sixties, however, is less easily ameliorated than the judicial activism of the thirties, for one simple reason. The Hughes Court was saying no to new legislation, thus leaving the status quo unchanged. Only a yes vote was needed to start a new direction. The Warren Court by announcing new constitutional rights not only added to the constitutional edifice, thereby creating new sets of affirmative governmental duties, but also impelled major social and political change. A vote to change a right created by the Warren

---

[28] 395 U.S. 486 (1969).   [29] Correspondence, author's files.

Court can be met by the opponents' charge–"They're going to take it away!" A vote to change an anti–New Deal decision on the Hughes Court merely conferred on the receptive political branches power previously withheld under such provisions as the Commerce Clause. I propose, therefore, to include here a discussion of the question whether we now need a constitutional amendment in the legislative districting field and, if so, what kind. I do so with much trepidation because traditionally the only thing more sacred than our written Constitution is the institution of judicial review as the preferred mode for interpretation and modification.

II. OF PREMISES AND PRINCIPLES

A. THE COURT'S LOGIC

Inadequacies in perception of basic premises and principles– what lawyers call deficiencies in characterization of the issue–commonly produce insufficient or misguided remedies for the wrongs brought to judicial attention. The Supreme Court's latter-day apportionment-districting rulings fit this mold all too well. After an auspicious beginning in *Baker v. Carr,* the Court has proceeded logically and inexorably from a defective major premise to a questionable conclusion concerning the population role in districting and apportionment. It has centered on something called "equality"; it has never come to grips with "representation."

Its very terminology is confusing and self-defeating. It talks of "equal representation for equal numbers of people" as the goal.[30] Functionally, however, there is no such thing as "equal representation" in a district system of electing legislators. There may be "equal population" districts, which is an objectively verifiable concept. But with a district basis there never can be "equal representation" because all districting discriminates by discounting utterly the votes of the minority voters. This is the well-known, simple plurality rule and it operates district by district as a winner-take-all rule. In this precise sense all districting is gerrymandering, both in single-member districting and in multimember districting, although the effect is more dramatic in the latter instance.[31]

---

30 376 U.S. at 18; 377 U.S. at 559–60.

31 For example, if Group X has at least 51 percent of the vote in a given area, and six legislators are elected at large, Group X will elect all six and Group Y, the opposition, will elect none. If there is a conversion to six single-member districts, Group X

A goal of "equal representation" can be approximated only through abolishing districts and using proportional representation, such as the party list form used in Europe, or some version of the Hare system.[32] Such proportionalization, whereby all the votes cast in the area covered by the legislature are pooled and contending groups achieve legislative representation closely proportional to their total popular vote, does represent voters equally in proportion to their numbers. In short, "equal representation" is generically a proportional representation concept.[33]

Apparently not realizing this, the Court fallaciously equated "equal population" districting with "equal representation." It further seems to assume that the more equal the population among districts, the more equal the representation. It is this equation of the objective population equality concept with the subjective fair representation goal that seems to have led the Court to move logically from the "substantial equality" language of the 1964 cases to the arithmetic absolute of the *Preisler* and *Wells* decisions in 1969.

Along the way the Court has shown some uneasiness, evidencing perhaps an instinctive feeling that "one man–one vote" when placed in legislative representation context has more complexities than appear at first glance. Both in *Wesberry v. Sanders* and *Reynolds v. Sims* in 1964 the Court discounted the feasibility and wisdom of "mathematical precision."[34] Several caveats are sprinkled through Chief Justice Warren's opinion in *Reynolds*. He referred favorably to the claim of "political subdivisions" to having some voice in at least one body of the legislature[35] and to following principles of compactness and contiguity in districting. Significantly, he said: "[I]ndiscriminate districting, without any regard for political subdivisions or natural or historical boundary lines, may be little more than an open invitation to partisan gerrymandering."[36]

-----

again will capture all seats *if* its strength is spread evenly. Only if the weaker group's voters are fortuitously concentrated geographically, will it have a chance of electing some spokesmen. Under either system, Group X will tend to be overrepresented even if its voting strength is not fully cohesive.

[32] MacKenzie, Free Elections (1958); Ross, Elections and Electors (1955).

[33] Of course there are a number of reasons for preferring a district system to a proportional representation system for purposes of governmental stability and discouraging narrow factionalism among the voters, but that is a separate issue.

[34] 376 U.S. at 18; 377 U.S. at 577.

[35] 377 U.S. at 577–81.   [36] *Id.* at 578–89.

Here and also in some later cases there was language that went beyond the concept of equal numbers and focused on the realities of representation of groups and partisans in the legislature where the crucial public policy decisions are made. After all, most of the plaintiffs in most of the apportionment-districting cases have sought district equalization, not as an end in itself, but to vindicate the legitimate aspirations for a fairer share of legislative seats. In *Reynolds*, there is a reference to the goal of "full and effective participation by all citizens in state government."[37] A few lines later there is the statement that "fair and effective representation for all citizens is concededly the basic aim of legislative apportionment."[38] In considering multimember districting in 1965 and 1966, the Court made the following statement, which looks beyond numbers to the question of an effective individual or group voice in the legislature:[39]

> It might well be that, designedly or otherwise, a multimember constituency apportionment scheme, under the circumstances of a particular case, would operate to minimize or cancel out the voting strength of racial or political elements of the voting population. When this is demonstrated it will be time enough to consider whether the system still passes constitutional muster.

All these considerations and others are now subordinated to the driving force of the fallacious equation of "equal population" with "equal representation." In *Preisler* and *Wells* Mr. Justice Brennan, the author of the 1965 and 1966 statement quoted above, wrote:[40]

> Equal representation for equal numbers of people is a principle designed to prevent debasement of voting power and diminution of access to elected representatives. Toleration of even small deviations detracts from these purposes. Therefore, the [constitutional command] permits only the limited population variances which are unavoidable despite a good-faith effort to achieve absolute equality, or for which justification is shown.

But with computers, or even a desk calculator in nonpopulous states, there are no "unavoidable" variances. It is possible to achieve exact equality, and with many different sets of districts, subject only to possible dispute over how to compute zero.

Mr. Justice Brennan went on, as Mr. Justice Fortas noted, to rec-

---

[37] *Id.* at 565.   [39] Fortson v. Dorsey, 379 U.S. 433, 439 (1965).

[38] *Id.* at 565–66.   [40] 394 U.S. at 531.

ognize and forthrightly reject virtually every conceivable "rational" basis for stopping short of an arithmetic absolute. First, the Court rejected Missouri's contention that the minor deviations (3 percent or under in this plan) were justifiable in order to "avoid fragmenting areas with distinct economic and social interests,"[41] thus diluting the effective representation of those interests. Second, it disallowed any room for "legislative interplay,"[42] *i.e.*, the argument that there must be a little room for legislative negotiation and compromise on practical political problems affecting districting. As Dean Edward L. Barrett, Jr., noted before the decision, the political process of legislative districting is not likely to appear "rational," and yet "some room must be left for it to operate if redistricting is to be a legislative rather than a judicial function."[43]

Third, the Court rejected the State's argument that some minor deviations produced by attempting to follow existing county, municipal, or other boundaries are justifiable because they "minimize opportunities for partisan gerrymandering."[44] Rejection of this argument is especially interesting because it was simply a paraphrase of Chief Justice Warren's statement in *Reynolds* that ignoring such boundaries would be an open invitation to partisan gerrymandering.

Fourth, the Court rejected Missouri's argument, not well supported by the record in the case, that some deviations were a product of the legislature's taking into account the fact that in some of the congressional districts there was a large nonvoting population—military personnel and college students. It left open the question whether, on a more consistent record, "eligible voter population"[45] rather than total population could be used. Fifth, the Court disallowed taking into account projected population shifts unless the shifts could be predicted with a "high degree of accuracy," an element not found in the case. Finally, the Court rejected geographical

---

[41] *Id.* at 533.   [42] *Ibid.*

[43] Dean Edward L. Barrett, Jr., of the University of California, Davis. Correspondence in author's files.

[44] 394 U.S. at 534.

[45] *Ibid.* In a case from Hawaii involving state legislative apportionment, the Court approved, on the record before it, use of eligible voter population rather than total population. Burns v. Richardson, 384 U.S. 73 (1966). *Quaere,* whether the Art. I, § 2, foundation for congressional districting would prevent similar flexibility and compel use of total population for intrastate districting as well as interstate apportionment of seats? See Wilkins v. Davis, 205 Va. 803 (1965).

compactness as a justification for the minor deviations presented by the case.

The trouble with this latest word from the Court on the equal population principle is not that it raises more questions than it answers but that it gives too clear an answer, under an invalid major premise of what the "one man–one vote" struggle is all about. Unlike some of the earlier orders, it seems destined to cause major redistricting upheavals without any measurable gain in terms of political representation. Nor is there any assurance that the door is not being opened to more sophisticated forms of planned political unfairness in the districting process.

B. THE SURPRISED FRIENDS OF "ONE MAN–ONE VOTE"

"One man–one vote" is beginning to resemble an army which has outrun its organizers and generals. A surprising number of respected supporters both of this principle and the Supreme Court find dangerous, if not wholly unacceptable, the newly formulated absolute equality rule. The plaintiff himself, in one of the cases, is disturbed by the implications. In this sense the *Preisler* and *Wells* majority opinion may be a unique addition to our constitutional history; certainly it is highly unusual.

Plaintiff David Wells in the New York case, was not seeking absolute population equality. His own tentative, alternative plan offered deviations of 4.7 percent.[46] This figure exceeded the 3.1 percent deviation of the challenged Missouri plan, and now is presumptively unconstitutional under the Supreme Court majority's new approach to the "equal as is practicable" idea. He agrees with the thought expressed here that the new rulings, "unless subsequently altered or refined or clarified in some way, can indeed open the way to egregious gerrymandering."[47]

---

[46] For example, he pointed out that some additional tinkering would reduce population disparities in some areas without breaking any additional county lines. Also, some whole county transfers would better equalize populations of adjacent districts. These were examples, however, designed to support a primary reliance on a rigid equality–burden of proof rule phrased as follows: "Except for inconsequential population variations, all deviations from the districting norm must be justified by the state on some rationally permissible principle other than 'deference to area and economic or other group interests,'" Brief for Appellant, p. 16, *Wells v. Rockefeller.* This is not very far from the phrasing of the new standard used by Mr. Justice Brennan in his opinion for Court.

[47] Correspondence with author. Quotations and summaries of views in the following paragraphs are similarly based on correspondence in May–September, 1969.

William J. D. Boyd, assistant director of the National Municipal League, an organization that has staunchly supported the "one man–one vote" efforts and provided a valuable information service, finds acceptable the Court's decision, but not the majority rationale. He noted that the plans could have been made more equal by the simple device of shifting whole units of government from one district to another. But he also has a worried reaction: "Unfortunately, the Court seems to be saying that no social, economic or political data of any type may be used as a criteria for districting and that city and county boundaries are pretty much irrelevant. It should be carte blanche for the gerrymanderers until the day the Court rules."

William M. Beaney wrote in a letter: "I think your solution of a presumption of constitutionality using a *de minimis* figure makes sense, and I wish the Court would veer back in that direction." And he added the thought that "anyone familiar with the realities of the legislative process recognizes that any attempt at precise equality accomplishes nothing that goes significantly beyond the accomplishment of substantial equality—i.e., 5–10 per cent deviation from the average."

Two well-known political scientists, close students of reapportionment-redistricting, share these views. Professor Malcolm E. Jewell observed that the census figures are neither accurate enough nor recent enough "to justify this kind of passion for mathematical perfection" and agrees that gerrymandering will be easier if political subdivision boundaries become wholly irrelevant under an absolute equality rule. He asserted that "existing political subdivisions do have some sense of community and community interest" and added this hypothesis: "It can also be argued that legislators are less likely to be visible and identifiable to their constituents if legislative district boundaries are completely independent of other existing city and county boundaries."

Professor Gordon E. Baker was equally puzzled and concerned about prospects for achieving fair and effective representation under an absolute population equality rule. He expressed the hope that the opinion will be found "somewhat ambivalent," that in any event it will be "narrowly construed so that the extent to which equality may practicably be achieved both in state legislative and congressional districting may differ from state to state and from district to district." And he feels that a possible constitutional amendment as outlined in the next section is now "worth thinking about."

Some of the reservations of the plaintiff in *Wells v. Rockefeller* were shared by his counsel, Dean Robert B. McKay of the New York University Law School. Dean McKay and I, in a jointly written short comment, observed that "one is left with an uneasy feeling that the majority has settled too quickly for a simplistic formula based on numbers alone. The prospects are not entirely encouraging."[48]

Obviously, *Preisler* and *Wells* is not just one more apportionment-districting ruling. It takes us back to first premises about democratic representation and to the continuing confusion between "equal population" and "equal representation." To be sure, as Chief Justice Warren wrote in 1964, "legislators represent people, not trees or acres."[49] But how slippery are the terms "represent" and "people":[50]

> The distinctive thing about people, in contrast to trees or acres, is that *people* are *not fungible*. Failure to perceive this leads to the "identity of interest" fallacy which underlies such simple arithmetic measures as the electoral percentage . . . and which is the central fallacy of a rigid, simplistic "one man–one vote" theory. Although legislators are elected "by voters," as Chief Justice Warren said, they are elected by voters who have interests which lead them to organize for group political action.

It is the Court's lack of attention to this "equal population–equal representation" distinction, perhaps more than any other factor, which seems to underlie the various expressions of concern over the *Preisler* and *Wells* absolute population equality rule.

---

[48] *Election Districts, Substantial Population Equality, and Exceeded Expectations,* 1 HUMAN RIGHTS (1969) (in press).

[49] 377 U.S. at 562.

[50] DIXON 272. The "electoral percentage" is one of three commonly used arithmetic analyses of districting plans on a gross population basis. The other two are the percentage by which the most deviant district's population deviates from the ideal or average population ("maximum percentage deviation"), and the "population variance ratio" which is computed by comparing the largest and smallest district. The "electoral percentage" (more appropriately called the fictional electoral percentage because it has no necessary relation to actual control) is computed by cumulating the total population represented by the half of the legislature (plus one district) which comes from the smaller districts. These measures are readily computed, but they tend to focus attention only on the extremes and of course do not involve the actualities of political representation.

III. The Case for a New Kind of Reapportionment
Amendment

Few things are less common—or less popular—in American
constitutional law than constitutional amendments. Except for the
Civil War Amendments, and the Bill of Rights which was part of
the original arrangement, few have really amounted to very much.
In particular, the idea of a Reapportionment Amendment has become somewhat shopworn in the past few years. Some versions
were flatly misconceived;[51] improved versions were misreported in
the press and hence popularly misunderstood.[52]

Preisler and *Wells* cast the matter in an entirely new light. The
appropriate response to *Preisler* and *Wells* may be a constitutional
amendment of a very simple type. It should confirm the aims and
expectations of supporters of *Baker v. Carr*, while curing the mis-
direction of the Court majority in *Preisler* and *Wells* before it aborts
the drive for fair and effective representation.[53]

The majority opinion in *Preisler* and *Wells* is so forthright and
uncompromising that the prospects are not encouraging for its being
satisfactorily "distinguished" or "narrowed" in future applications.[54]

---

[51] See, *e.g.*, the December, 1962, proposal of the sixteenth Biennial General Assembly of the States to reverse *Baker v. Carr* as quoted in Shanahan, *Proposed Constitutional Amendments: They Will Strengthen Federal-State Relations*, 49 A.B.A.J.
631 (1963). The opening sentence of Senator Dirksen's initial draft could have been
construed to limit court jurisdiction on reapportionment, S.J. Res. 2, 89th Cong.,
1st Sess., introduced January 6, 1965. For detailed discussion, see Dixon 398–403.

[52] See, *e.g.*, the Dirksen final draft, S.J. Res. 66, 89th Cong., 1st Sess., as amended
July 22, 1965, and the Javits draft, proposed as an amendment to the revised Dirksen
draft. 111 Cong. Rec. 19042 (1965). Both would have permitted deviations from the
equal population principle in one house of a bicameral legislature *provided* the plan
was approved in a popular referendum and *provided further*, that the plan would
have to be reapproved by popular referendum after each census, to avoid a political
freeze.

In the press, however, all efforts were generally reported as attempts to repeal
totally "one man–one vote," with intimations of a conspiracy. See, *e.g.*, Sorenson &
Simon, *The Quiet Campaign*, 50 Sat. Rev. 17, 20 (July 15, 1967).

[53] The proposal made in the succeeding pages has no relation to the still-contin-
uing campaign to achieve what is popularly called the Dirksen Reapportionment
Amendment by the device of state petitions for a federal constitutional convention.
See note 68 *infra*, and accompanying text.

[54] The developing "one man–one vote" principles apparently apply in full also to
conventional local bodies such as city councils and county boards. Avery v. Midland County, 390 U.S. 474 (1968). Unresolved questions remain, however, regard-

But the possibility should not be discounted, and the reasons listed below in support of the amendment idea can be read also as arguments for revision of the *Preisler* and *Wells* ruling by the judicial process of reevaluation and reinterpretation. In one respect, however, even a major judicial reevaluation may not be the "solution" to placing "one man–one vote" on a viable foundation. We are dealing in part with a problem of population arithmetic, and the question of the allowable range of percentage deviation from the "average" district size indicated by the best population count available, the most recent federal census. Any percentage figure picked will be arbitrary and hence a matter for political-legislative determination (including the constitutional amendment process as our highest form of political-legislative determination), rather than for Court determination.

From this perspective, we have failed to give the Court adequate support by not achieving an amendment before now which would undergird "one man–one vote" constitutionally by using language not appropriate for judicial proclamation. To put the problem differently, the Court may well feel that it is not a judicial function to pick out of the air a given arithmetic percentage figure of maximum allowable deviation and undergird it with the general language of the Fourteenth Amendment (or Art. I, § 2) as a judicially created constitutional rule. The constitutional amendment process is well suited to such proclamations.

Although the thought might seem startling, some recent Supreme Court opinions may support the idea that Congress might give some direction to this field merely by statute. The Voting Rights Act of 1965 rests on a broad view of congressional remedial power under the Fifteenth Amendment.[55] In cases involving voting and other civil rights matters, opinions of various Justices have suggested that Congress has broad power under § 5 of the Fourteenth Amendment to implement the substantive guarantees of equality and fairness in § 1 of the Fourteenth Amendment—broader power indeed than that

---

ing a "special-purpose unit of government," *id*. at 483–84; bodies that are primarily "administrative" in function or of an "appointive" nature, Sailors v. Board of Education, 387 U.S. 105 (1967); and use of unequal candidate residence districts which are part of unusual local governments elected at large, Dusch v. Davis, 387 U.S. 112 (1967).

[55] South Carolina v. Katzenbach, 383 U.S. 301 (1966).

possessed by the Court acting without the aid of legislation.[56] Thus Congress, by use of theories expressed in these opinions, might have authority to "interpret" the Fourteenth Amendment (and Art. I, § 2, for congressional districting) as being presumptively satisfied when a given level of arithmetic equality has been achieved in legislative districting. A constitutional amendment, however, would be a more forthright approach.

Unless there can be valid congressional legislation of this sort, what seems to be needed is a constitutional amendment that will establish a *presumption* of constitutionality—but no more than a presumption—for districts within a selected de minimis figure of percentage deviation from the average or "ideal" district population. It could read as follows:

> The districts within any state for the election of members of the House of Representatives of the Congress of the United States, or for the election of members of either house of the state legislature or of the single house of a state unicameral legislature, shall be deemed constitutional if the population of any district does not deviate by more than 15 percent (or 10, or 5) from the arithmetic mean computed by dividing the population of the state by the number of districts; and the districts within any state for the election of local government bodies or any other bodies whose districts are subject to the restraint of the Fourteenth Amendment shall be deemed constitutional if the population of any district does not deviate by more than 15 percent (or 10, or 5) from the arithmetic mean computed by dividing the population of the area to be served by the number of districts; *Provided,* that the presumption of constitutionality created by the foregoing provisions may be overcome in a suit by any voter in the area concerned by demonstrating that the districts, although within the allowable percentage deviations stated, operate unreasonably to minimize the voting strength of racial or political elements of the voting population.

Such an amendment would yield many benefits. First, it would provide just as much assurance as do the present extreme Supreme Court decisions that egregious population malapportionment would not recur. It must be remembered that of the thirty legislative houses in the fifteen bicameral state legislature cases decided in

---

[56] United States v. Guest, 383 U.S. 745 (1966); Katzenbach v. Morgan, 384 U.S. 641 (1966). See Cox, *Constitutional Adjudication and the Promotion of Human Rights,* 80 HARV. L. REV. 91 (1966).

1964, when the Court for the first time announced a "substantial equality" rule, only three had population variance ratios between largest and smallest district of less than 3 to 1. In fifteen houses the population variance ratio exceeded 10 to 1; and it was 20 to 1 or higher in seven houses.[57] It was this evil against which "one man–one vote" was originally aimed. In most instances the suburbs and in an occasional instance the large central cities, had fewer seats than their population justified.[58]

Second, an amendment of this kind would ease the path to achieving a prompt redistricting, whether the task be handled by the traditional legislative process, or by some nonlegislative agency. Those charged with redrawing district lines need a fixed target. In California, for example, there were many months of shilly-shallying until the state supreme court laid down specific guidelines. The court directed that for each house no district could deviate by more than 15 percent from average size districts; the electoral percentage had to be at least 48 percent.[59] Within a month and a half reapportionment resulted.

Under an inexact "substantial equality" rule, or perhaps even under the new "absolute equality rule" (for how many ways are there to figure "zero deviation"), there is no firm basis for planning or bargaining. Incumbents and interest groups keep slipping in to suggest that their position can be saved or improved merely by this or that minor adjustment which would cause only a de minimis increase in population disparity. All lines remain fluid, tentative agreements are undercut as soon as they are made, and apportionment districting becomes worse than a game of musical chairs. By contrast, objective guidelines provide a basis on which even the regular legislative process can revise districts.

Third, the proposal would at last provide a basis for achieving intercensus finality in apportionment districting, by clarifying the role of judicial review. During the 1960's nothing was less final than a legislatively enacted revision of legislative districts. Each legislative vote was followed by a prompt return of the litigants to the courts and a resultant judicial revision or order directing the legis-

---

[57] Tabular material is presented in Dixon 266, 590–628.

[58] Boyd, *Suburbia Takes Over*, 54 Nat. Civ. Rev. 294 (1965).

[59] Silver v. Brown, 46 Cal. Rptr. 308 (1965).

lature to try again.[60] The draft amendment preserves the role of the courts but gives automatic finality once the specified de minimis deviation standard is met, subject to an occasional gerrymandering challenge directed to demonstrable political or racial inequities. Such challenges as resulted would at last be directed to the realities of representation; they would not be shadowboxing over population percentage points and district shape in the abstract.

Fourth, the amendment, by incorporating language from the Supreme Court's opinion in *Fortson v. Dorsey*, would make gerrymandering challenges justiciable.[61] It would open the way to case-by-case development, without attempting the impossible task of reducing to a rule what is generically a general question of due process. Furthermore, it would not dictate any required degree of judicial vigor or overload the Court's docket. Nonmeritorious, or nontimely challenges still could be deflected for "want of equity."[62]

---

[60] *E.g.*, Preisler v. Secretary of State of Missouri, 238 F. Supp. 187 (W.D. Mo. 1965); Preisler v. Secretary of State of Missouri, 257 F. Supp. 953 (W.D. Mo. 1966); Kirkpatrick v. Preisler, 279 F. Supp. 952 (W.D. Mo. 1967).

[61] The proposed amendment in its "Provided" clause quotes almost directly from the language of the Court's opinion in *Fortson* regarding the doubtful constitutionality of districts that "operate to minimize or cancel out the voting strength of racial or political elements of the voting population." 379 U.S. at 439. Although stated in multimember district context, it would make no sense to confine the *Fortson* thought to multimember districts, because the interest of given political or racial elements of the voting population are tied to representation results in the legislature, not to district form.

The word "unreasonably" is inserted in the *Fortson* language as adapted for the proposed amendment in deference to the fact that perfect racial or political representation is impossible in a district system (unlike a proportional representation system). The constitutional aim is to achieve as fair representation as is possible under a district system. Although no single "right" set of districts can be identified, extremes can be challenged and nullified, just as unfair trade practices can be tested case by case by the Federal Trade Commission.

In short, gerrymandering presents a due process-reasonableness kind of question, and the draft amendment reflects this thought. Indeed, it can be argued that our whole "one man–one vote" development since *Baker v. Carr* would have a better constitutional foundation if grounded either on the Due Process Clause or on the Guarantee Clause. See Dixon, *supra* note 22, at 381–83; Auerbach, *supra* note 14, at 84–87. The equal protection concept, on which the Court has relied so far, makes difficult both the avoidance of arithmetic absolutism and the creation of a concern for the operating fairness of representation systems.

[62] Although the Court has been less than clear in its writings on justiciability, there is a meaningful distinction between matters deemed intrinsically nonjusticiable and matters potentially justiciable but not ripe or timely on the record presented. In Colegrove v. Green, 328 U.S. 549 (1946), Justice Rutledge's opinion ex-

It simply would be made clear that such challenges were "within *Baker v. Carr*," when appropriately presented, and not *generically* outside federal judicial review.

Fifth, the amendment would make possible the preservation of a substantial number of political subdivision lines in the districting both for state legislatures and for Congress. With a de minimis figure of 10 or 15 percent maximum deviation from average, less cutting would be necessary than at 5 percent. And yet Missouri in the *Preisler* case, in part because it had a fairly large number of counties to use as building blocks, managed even at 3.1 percent deviation to avoid cutting county lines in seven of the ten congressional districts created.[63] A rule of absolute population equality would seem to require cutting county lines in the formation of most districts, with the result that the residents of the area sliced from a county to serve as a district "equalizer" might be in a congressional district serving a community of interest they did not share.

Sixth, the proposal would bring us into line with the districting practice in England and West Germany, where similar objective percentage deviation targets are set as ways of channeling and rendering final the districting process. The 25 percent deviation rule of thumb followed in these countries, however, is higher than would be acceptable here.[64]

Seventh, the proposal would leave more than is now apparent under the emerging absolute equality rule for experimentation and creativity in devising new representation forms. This consideration is especially relevant at the local government level, where much

---

presses the latter idea, Justice Frankfurter's opinion the former. See also the several opinions in Poe v. Ullman, 367 U.S. 497 (1961).

[63] Brief for Appellant, p. 12, Kirkpatrick v. Preisler.

[64] BUTLER, THE ELECTORAL SYSTEM IN BRITAIN, 1918–1951 (1953); Pollock, *The Electoral System of the Federal Republic of Germany–a Study in Representative Government*, 46 AM. POL. SCI. REV. 1056 (1952).

In Great Britain dissatisfaction with the rigidity of the 25 percent ceiling as used in 1944 led to its abolition in 1947. In 1958 the rules were loosened still further. House of Commons (Redistribution of Seats) Act, 1958, 6 & 7 Eliz. II, ch. 26, § 2 (a).

The last British redistribution of parliamentary seats occurred in 1954, and a new redistribution is due. As of this writing Great Britain is embroiled in a proposal by the Labour Government to postpone redistribution of most seats pending a new regional map, which may be implemented in five years. The proposals for some seat changes which accompanied the postponement bill were met by gerrymandering charges from the Conservative party. New York Times, July 14, 1969, p. 9, cols. 1–5.

overhauling is needed and under way, but where a rigid rule may force upheaval not commensurate with resulting benefits. For a general-purpose city government, or county government, there is no reason to allow more deviation from population equality than for congressional or state legislative districts. Special-purpose local units raise more subtle "one man–one vote" issues, and the Court itself is not yet fully committed here. Some perhaps should be wholly exempt from the "one man–one vote" principle, under knowledge now available to us. For this reason, the draft amendment applies only to those local government bodies "subject to the restraint of the Fourteenth Amendment." It thus preserves to the Court through case-by-case elaboration the meaning of the possible "special-purpose unit" exemption from the equal population rule which was mentioned in *Avery v. Midland County*[65] but not explained. A case challenging the representation system in Missouri junior college boards, now pending in the Supreme Court, may throw more light on this question.[66]

The most important unresolved issue may be the applicability of the "one man–one vote" rule to the now local councils of governments movement, *i.e.*, the voluntary councils of delegates from the various local governments in a given urban area. Well-known examples include the Metropolitan Washington Council of Governments, covering the District of Columbia and parts of surrounding Maryland and Virginia, and, in California, the Association of Bay Area Governments covering a far-flung area around San Francisco. It is unlikely that these voluntary councils can emerge into true regional governments, even on a single-purpose basis, without provision for some representation on a "one unit–one vote" basis rather than a straight population basis. Such a proposal has been made for the Association of Bay Area Governments.[67] But a "federal plan"

---

65 390 U.S. at 483–84.

66 Hadley v. Junior College Dist. of Kansas City, 432 S.W.2d 328 (Mo. 1968), *prob. juris. noted,* 393 U.S. 1115 (1969). The representation system is based on school age population and is inexactly proportioned because certain district seats are allocated by a fixed scale, depending on whether a subunit has one-third, one-half, or two-thirds of the total school age population.

67 This proposal, and an alternative plan for a directly elected, multipurpose organization, were pending in the California legislature in 1969. 2 REGIONAL REV. Q. 1 (July, 1969). See also Jones, *Metropolitan Detente: Is It Politically and Constitutionally Possible?* 36 GEO. WASH. L. REV. 741 (1968).

concept of this kind would be unconstitutional, if this type of government were deemed fully subject to the equal population rule under the Fourteenth Amendment. This problem, also, is not touched by the draft amendment. Should it become a matter of national concern, it ought to be handled separately.

Eighth, the draft amendment would not relate to the issue of the 1964 Colorado case, which was the focus of the Reapportionment Amendment controversy in 1965 and 1966. The present proposal seeks only to define arithmetic equality in terms slightly less stringent than that indicated by the *Preisler* and *Wells* cases. The earlier proposal, with which the name of the late Senator Dirksen is prominently associated, has the different goal of allowing the people of the state, by popular referendum, to choose to have one house of their bicameral state legislature deviate from the equal population principle. The two proposals are essentially independent of each other, and the draft on de minimis deviations now being suggested could be amended to accommodate the one-house-referendum proposal should the latter gather popular favor in the future.[68]

And finally, the proposal would "bring back into the fold" this area of constitutional litigation and apply to it conventional canons concerning burden of proof and presumptions of constitutionality. For some, this may be a touchy issue. As every attorney knows, "happiness" lies in enshrouding oneself in a favorable presumption, and casting the burden of proof on one's opponent. In some areas of constitutional litigation something like a presumption of unconstitutionality has arisen to protect certain interests against governmental infringement. In the area of the First Amendment freedoms,

---

[68] Although this Dirksen proposal failed by seven votes to achieve the needed two-thirds vote for initiation in the Senate in 1965 and 1966, the idea might be proposed by a future Congress, or by the process of a federal constitutional convention. A campaign to have two-thirds of the states petition Congress under Art. V of the Constitution to call a convention for reapportionment purposes dates from 1963. A recent count indicates that thirty-three states have petitioned Congress, with only one more needed to bring the total to the thirty-four required by the Constitution. Some states, however, have been considering withdrawing their petitions; not all petitions are similarly worded; and a bill proposed by Senator Ervin would bar counting petitions more than seven years old. This last provision, if enacted, would apply as of spring, 1970, to two state petitions enacted in 1963, cutting the number of petitions back to thirty-one. S.J. Res. 623, 91st Cong., 1st Sess. (1969). See also status report, Washington Post, July 10, 1969, p. H1, col. 1; *Symposium on the Article V Convention Process,* note 19 *supra.*

the clear and present danger doctrine is essentially a burden of proof rule. Freedom of expression has almost trump card status in the dichotomy between order and liberty. Hence, peaceful expression not in violation of valid permit statutes is immune to suppression, even if the crowd grows restive, unless there is a clear and present danger of serious disorder.[69] If the government fails to meet this burden of proof, its case against the speaker fails. But no government program falters, nor is government structure put in question.[70]

By contrast, in apportionment-districting, neither is there need to bolster every plaintiff's case with a presumption of unconstitutionality of the challenged plan, nor is the result restricted to personal effect; a part of the governmental structure is in question. All votes are being counted, and voting is in districts that are at least "substantially equal." Nevertheless the Court majority in *Preisler* and *Wells* continues to favor even the casual challenger to a statewide districting system with a burden of proof rule under which the state's case is almost foredoomed to failure. It says that the "State must justify each variance, no matter how small."[71] Although the point is not explored, earlier rulings suggest that the justifications, assuming them to be possible at all, must take the form of showing all districts to be the product of a "rational state policy."[72] And by "rational" is meant logical, internally consistent rules consistently applied, not merely a rule of reason grounded on general considerations of fair representation.[73] Hence, plans in

---

[69] Tinker v. Des Moines Independent Community School District, 393 U.S. 503 (1969); Cox v. Louisiana, 379 U.S. 536 (1965); Edwards v. South Carolina, 372 U.S. 229 (1963); Terminiello v. Chicago, 337 U.S. 1 (1949).

[70] See generally on proof and burden of proof problems Karst, *Legislative Facts in Constitutional Litigation*, 1960 SUPREME COURT REVIEW 75; Alfange, *The Relevance of Legislative Facts in Constitutional Law*, 114 U. PA. L. REV. 637 (1966).

[71] 394 U.S. at 531.

[72] 377 U.S. at 579, and see 385 U.S. at 444.

[73] This point seems to have its origin in the argument of the solicitor general as amicus curiae in *Baker v. Carr*, as adopted in the concurring opinion of Mr. Justice Clark, and accepted implicitly if not expressly in most reapportionment-redistricting cases ever since, including *Preisler* and *Wells*. See Brief for the United States as Amicus Curiae on Reargument, 28, 45–47, *Baker v. Carr*; 369 U.S. at 251–52, 258; and statements quoted *supra* at notes 71, 72.

Dean Neal early implied that this process was "an example of winning without actually cheating." Neal, *supra* note 23, at 287.

which particular population deviations could be linked to any of the following features would be "irrational" and unacceptable: cutting some city and county lines but not cutting others; some symmetrical and some asymmetrical shapes; linking of a small county to a large county in one area to reduce a deviation, while ignoring deviation elsewhere by leaving another small county linked to similar small counties.

Such a rigid burden of proof rule flies in the face of life and the legislative process. Whenever a legislature seeks to incorporate competing values, it is foredoomed to be "irrational," *i.e.*, inconsistent and lacking in full logical symmetry either in design or operation. Yet it may well produce a reasonable accommodation which is far more satisfying than pushing a single value to its logical conclusion. This is so regarding tax legislation, the selective service system, zoning legislation with its variances and exceptions, and many other areas. It is so regarding the "population equality" value in constructing a fair representation system in a modern democracy.

In short, there is no longer any reason to "stack the deck" in apportionment-districting litigation so that a challenger with a plan more equal than equal, or with deviations more zero than zero, will always win. The known inaccuracies in the decennial census, even ignoring the degree of population shift within a single year, make this approach counterproductive.

With an amendment of the type proposed here, in the seventies legislatures would have an objective population equality target but would be forewarned that they faced gerrymandering challenges if they played too fast and loose with political equities. Challengers to enacted plans that satisfied the de minimis population deviation test would have to do their homework and could no longer win with a mere burden of proof ploy—a ploy that has no exact counterpart in other constitutional litigation and is no longer needed here. The resulting careful attention in apportionment-districting litigation to factors other than bare population would at last bring the reapportionment revolution above the level of ninth-grade civics. In short, such an amendment would incorporate all the major gains since *Baker v. Carr*, would avoid the arithmetic straitjacket of *Preisler* and *Wells*, and would lay a firm foundation for an informed, case-by-case elaboration of the detailed, practical issues of fair representation.

IV. Apportionment-Districting Method: Key to Achieving Fair and Effective Representation

The "equality" syndrome focusing narrowly on arithmetic population deviations has overly dominated the reapportionment revolution. The long-run prospects for achieving fair and effective representation are tied not to numbers but to apportionment-districting method. This is so whatever the arithmetic equality ground rules may be, and with or without the reapportionment amendment proposed above, which ties a presumption of constitutionality to a de minimis deviation figure. Equally important, the methodology suggested below is the answer to those who are concerned about the Court's headlong rush to arithmetic absolutism but fear the consequences of greater judicial involvement if courts try to police gerrymandering in fine detail.[74]

In a phrase, the solution is to devise procedures for openly bipartisan apportionment procedures, plus a provision for breaking ties if necessary. With methodology of this sort, designed to build fairness into the process of districting itself, the presumption of constitutionality in favor of a plan with de minimis deviation would be further strengthened. Furthered also would be the laudable goal of minimizing litigation and conserving the courts for occasional intrusions into the political thicket in pursuit of larger issues of representational equality.

Traditionally, apportionment districting has been a legislative function, dominated by the party in power at the moment. But this leaves political equity to the uncertain factor of conscience as prompted by public opinion, or to the chance factor of a split in party control of the two houses or the governorship. The latter factor fortuitously did operate to produce informal bipartisan apportionment in several states, and avoidance of partisan excesses, after the Supreme Court demanded "substantial equality" in 1964. The problem is how to institutionalize avoidance of partisan excesses.

All apportionment is political, because every line drawn wittingly or unwittingly will have a political effect different from another

---

[74] See, e.g., Professor Alfred H. Kelly, who refers to the Court's "tunnel vision on 'one man–one vote'" but wonders if the "remedy for the present failure of judicial-political policy-making is even more judicial-political policy-making." Kelly, Book Review, 15 Wayne L. Rev. 568, 571 (1968).

equally "equal" and equally available line. For this reason the solution does not lie in the direction of so-called nonpartisan apportioning agencies, although the idea has superficial appeal. In addition to such overt policy choices as single-member versus multimember districts, and degree of concern for preserving political subdivision lines, there are a number of crucial hidden policy choices. They include: swing districts versus safe districts and the number controlled by each party; homogeneous suburban districts versus mixed suburban and central city districts; safe Negro or other ethnic districts versus spreading the minority over many districts where it may be submerged or may occasionally have a balance of power. The list could be expanded in the context of special factors in each state. Every district line makes one or more of these policy choices, whether the draftsmen are aware or unaware of them. Attempted "nonpartisanship" only heightens the prospect that the considerations will not be carefully evaluated. Nonpartisan politics is a contradiction in terms.[75] As one experienced draftsman has observed:[76]

> Every plan has a political effect, even one drawn by a seventh grade civics class whose parents are all non-partisans and have only the United States census data to work with. Even though they drew such a plan with the most equal population in districts, following the maximum number of political subdivision boundaries and with the most regular shapes, it could very well result in a landslide for a given political party.

The apportionment-districting task calls for philosopher-kings, but they are notoriously in short supply. Nevertheless, in the post-1964 period, at least one judge, Chief Judge William J. Campbell of the United States District Court for the Northern District of

---

[75] It may be observed that "nonpartisanship" suggestions come most frequently from some members of the press and some academicians—groups not known for nonpartisanship despite their vigor and popular respect. In one plan submitted to the 1967 New York constitutional convention a prominent role would have been played by university presidents, a group whose image has now been considerably tarnished by ineptness in handling the mixed political-legal problem of student disorder. New York Constitutional Convention, Proposal No. 452, introduced May 23, 1967.

In support of the nonpartisan commission idea, see McKay, REAPPORTIONMENT REAPPRAISED 25–28 (1968).

[76] A. Robert Kleiner, Democratic Member, Michigan Bipartisan Apportionment Commission, in paper at National Municipal League annual meeting, 1966.

Illinois, did rise to the occasion and effectuate a well-received re-vision of the Illinois state legislative and congressional districts. The device was bipartisan, pretrial conference, with a commitment from the representatives of each political party that any non-negotiable deadlocks would be broken by the judge—operating in a politically informed but balanced fashion. His resulting comment is a model of frankness, and a model of political representation wisdom:[77]

> I certainly did [consider political realities]; it's a necessary part of trying to work out a fair and balanced set of districts from the standpoint of the interests of each political party, but there is a crucial difference between considering political factors in an attempt to do justice to each party in regard to provision of safe and swing districts, and a one-sided partisan political gerrymander for the advantage of one party alone.

The problem is how to institutionalize a process for avoiding one-sided partisanship at the outset of redistricting, while preserving political realism. The answer is the bipartisan commission with a provision for breaking the tie vote, which has been considered or adopted by several states since 1966. New Jersey (1966),[78] Penn-sylvania (1968),[79] and Hawaii (1968)[80] have amended their state constitutions in this way for state legislative apportionment. Draft constitutions for Maryland[81] and New York,[82] and the now-pend-ing Oklahoma revision to be acted on in 1970[83] proposed use of bipartisan commissions with a tie breaker for congressional district-ing as well as for state legislative apportionment.[84] The New York

---

[77] Press conference comment, as related in interview with author, Washington, D.C., September, 1965. The litigation was in a three-judge federal district court, and concurrently in the state courts. The arrangement included agreement of the other judges to have Chief Judge Campbell take the lead in pretrial to see what could be accomplished. The full three-judge federal bench, and the state supreme court, endorsed the outcome. Germano v. Kerner, 247 F. Supp. 141 (N.D. Ill. 1965). See also People ex rel. Scott v. Kerner, 33 Ill.2d 460 (1965), and Kirby v. Illinois State Electoral Board, 251 F. Supp. 908 (N.D. Ill. 1965).

[78] N.J. Const. Art. XI, § 5.

[79] Pa. Const. Art. II, §§ 16, 17.

[80] Hawaii Const. Art. III, §§ 2, 4, as amended.

[81] Proposed Constitution (defeated May, 1968), Art. III, § 3.05-3.08.

[82] Proposed Constitution (defeated November, 1967), Art. III, § 2.

[83] Special Committee on Constitutional Revision (Oklahoma), Report and Rec-ommendations, 10-11 (1968), pending for action in state senate in 1970, as HJR 1022.

[84] There is no federal obstacle to shifting the congressional districting function

and Maryland draft constitutions were defeated at the polls, but the defeats were not attributable to the bipartisan commission provisions.

The use of a bipartisan commission for the redistricting function may solve several problems at once. The commission device permits a focus on the political representation realities of all proposed plans, thus avoiding a process of shadowboxing with pseudo-standards such as contiguity and compactness. Redistricters will know, or have access to, the relevant political and social data bearing on representation needs, and the degree of satisfaction of these needs by alternative redistricting plans. The unavoidable element of partisanship will be recognized, and by being recognized will be contained and ameliorated institutionally in the redistricting agency itself. Invidious gerrymandering detrimental to either party may be checked at the outset, instead of being left to uncertain correction in the judicial process. Burden of proof problems may prevent correction of all except the more egregious instances of gerrymandering, if the sole reliance is the judicial process. A bipartisan commission plan, although still subject to judicial review, could be supported by a strong presumption of fairness and constitutionality, subject to proof of particularized "unrepresentativeness." The judiciary could serve as an ultimate safeguard but would not have to attempt an affirmative definition of political fairness on an uncertain record.

Although the basic pattern is the same, bipartisan commissions may vary in details of their structure and operation. The partisan members of the bipartisan commission can be majority and minority party leaders in each house of the legislature, or persons appointed by them, or perhaps by the state central committee of each party. To curb self-interest, a provision may be included, as in Hawaii, barring from election within a specified period any person who has served on the commission.

The tie breaker may be appointed in various ways. He serves also as chairman in Pennsylvania and Hawaii and is appointed at the outset by the entire bench of the state's highest court if the par-

---

in a state from the legislature to a bipartisan commission. The federal statute speaks simply of redistricting "in the manner provided by the law" of the state. 2 U.S.C. § 2a(c) (1964). In the past congressional redistricting legislation has been subjected, by state law, to popular referendum and to gubernatorial veto. Ohio *ex rel.* Davis v. Hildebrant, 241 U.S. 565 (1916); Smiley v. Holm, 285 U.S. 355 (1932).

tisan commissioners fail to agree on a choice. He is appointed by the chief justice of the state supreme court in New Jersey, but only after the partisan commissioners have deadlocked on competing plans. Conceivably he could be appointed by the governor, as in Maryland's defeated plan. The first device, appointment by the entire bench of the state's highest court, may have the special merit of being less partisan than gubernatorial appointment, while at the same time blunting the political onus that might attach to the state's chief justice if he were solely responsible for this appointment function.

The bipartisan commission device does not touch the problem—if indeed it be a problem in view of our traditional commitment to a two-party system—of third-party interests or intraparty factional interests. But neither does our present practice of vesting districting power in the current majority party in the state legislature. The commission device is an improvement over straight partisan apportionment, which may sacrifice many interests, major party as well as minor party.

Even in states dominated by one party the bipartisan commission device would have the merit of easing the transition to two-party politics, or of arresting a trend toward one-party status. Of the states listed above which have considered or adopted the bipartisan commission device, three have been strongly Democratic, especially in their legislative politics: Hawaii, Maryland, Oklahoma. In such states in the normal course of events the tie breaker would be from the dominant party anyway, thus preserving the legitimate interests of that party. Alternatively, and certainly preferable to straight partisan apportionment, strongly one-party states could utilize a modified bipartisan commission formula in which the majority party would appoint more commissioners than the minority party.

If the trend to bipartisan commissions with tie breakers continues, the question is certain to be raised whether minor parties have a constitutional right to representation on apportionment commissions. In support of such a contention litigants might cite the Supreme Court's order that Ohio place George C. Wallace and his American Independent party on that state's 1968 presidential ballot.[85] At least two rebuttals could be offered. The Wallace case involved access to the ballot in order to run for public office, where-

---

[85] Williams v. Rhodes, 393 U.S. 23 (1968).

as an apportionment commission is a nonelective device to discharge a special pre-election function. Further, a plea of constitutional right to special-interest representation on an apportionment commission would raise the larger question of a right to such representation on administrative bodies generally.[86]

A. NOTE ON DISTRICTING STANDARDS

Either in conjunction with provision for a bipartisan commission, or separately, attempts are sometimes made to specify some districting criteria in advance,[87] in the hope of limiting or channeling partisan discretion. The *Preisler* and *Wells* majority opinion, with its single-minded stress on absolute population equality and its discounting of virtually every relevant nonpopulation consideration, may make passé any further attempts to detail districting standards in advance. At least in this respect, the *Preisler* and *Wells* ruling should not be decried. Districting "standards" have been notoriously ineffectual anyway—a fact that makes institutionalization of bipartisanship in the very process of districting all the more important.

The reasons for inability to articulate and enforce objective criteria for districting are several. The primary difficulty is that in a generic sense *all districting is gerrymandering*. A near-infinite number of sets of "equal" districts may be drawn in any state, each set, however, having a quite different effect in terms of overall party balance and minority representation. Another difficulty is that the criteria, even including the equal population requirement, tend to fail at the outset by not recognizing that the ultimate aim is political representation—fair and effective political representation responsive to the group dynamics of American politics.

For example, contiguity and compactness, which often are viewed as touchstones of proper districting whether specifically required or not, are really pseudo-standards. Given the realities of modern communication and of anomie with one's neighbors, particularly in metropolitan areas, modest departures from contiguity pose no intrinsic representation problems unless gross partisan purpose be present. At the same time, a requirement of contiguity does not block gross partisan purpose.

---

[86] Witherspoon, *The Bureaucracy as Representatives,* in NOMOS X, REPRESENTATION ch. 17 (Pennock & Chapman, eds. 1968).

[87] Hawaii Const. (1968): Art. III, §§ 2 and 4 as amended; Mich. Const. (1968): Art. IV, §§ 2–5.

The requirement of compactness is usually interpreted as meaning that districts be as symmetrical as practicable. (An alternative approach would be to stress the population center of gravity—drawing the lines so as to minimize the distance of each citizen from the district center—which could be quite asymmetrical.) As a practical matter, absolute symmetry would require that all districts be perfect circles, which is an impossibility. A district pattern of symmetrical squares, while practicable, could well operate to submerge significant elements of the electorate. More important, a benign gerrymander, in the sense of some asymmetrical districts, may well be required in order to assure representation of submerged elements within a larger area. This same consideration casts doubts also on overly rigid requirements of adherence to natural or political subdivision boundaries.[88]

Further, an attempt to delineate districting standards in advance may run into a further possible requirement of uniformity of application, judicially imposed whether or not specified in the statute. This is the so-called rational plan idea (*i.e.*, internal consistency), which is truly the bête noire of apportionment-districting litigation since Mr. Justice Clark first mentioned the idea in *Baker v. Carr*. For example, a congressional districting bill introduced by Senator Edward Kennedy in January, 1969, suggested the following qualification on the equality concept:[89]

> A State may make reasonable deviations from numerical equality in order to take into consideration the factors of contiguity, compactness, extraordinary natural boundaries, and a maintenance of the integrity of political subdivision lines, *but only if such criteria are uniformly applied.*

---

[88] A rule of compactness and contiguity, if used merely to force an explanation for grossly unusual district shape, can have some merit provided the Court is willing to entertain a political explanation. Perhaps in this spirit, the Rhode Island Supreme Court has referred to the state constitutional requirement of "compactness" as being "peripheral in its thrust," forbidding a "complete departure" but leaving to legislative determination the degree of compactness which is "possible" in the total representation picture. Opinion to the Governor, 221 A.2d 799, 803 (R.I. 1966).

[89] S. 10, 91st Cong., 1st Sess. (1969). (Emphasis added.) Although the equality definition has now been overtaken by the *Preisler* and *Wells* decision in April, 1969, the bill still is illustrative of the point discussed in the text. A bill introduced by seventeen New York congressmen, after the *Preisler* and *Wells* ruling, specified a maximum deviation of 2.5 percent for the 1972 and subsequent congressional elections, but did not attempt to specify additional standards, other than compactness and contiguity. H.R. 11817, 91st Cong., 1st Sess., introduced June 3, 1969, by Congressman Dulski for himself and sixteen others.

On its face the italicized uniformity phrase seems innocuous. But in terms of representation realities, and particularly minority representation, it may be advisable to treat political subdivision lines nonuniformly in different parts of the state, depending upon the residence relationship to the lines in question of the persons whose representation needs are to be served. Further, any requirement of uniformity of application of standards as vague as these poses two additional problems. One is the difficulty of proving compliance or noncompliance. The other is total inconsistency with the decisional process in all legislatures. The legislative process is a matter of compromise and adjustment, not a matter of uniform, logical derivation from agreed principles. To paraphrase Walter Bagehot's comment, it may be said of political districting that neat appearances conceal gross realities.[90]

Other districting variables, such as the factor of safe versus swing districts for the two major parties, and the corollary factor of homogeneity versus heterogeneity generally, have already been mentioned. All persons receive some general representation whether their district be swing or safe. Only in swing districts, however, do the members of both opposing parties have an opportunity for "control representation," *i.e.*, the election of a member of their own party. Our system now grossly overweighs the voters who are members of the majority party in safe districts. Ideally, there should be a large number of swing districts, in order that both parties be responsive to a broad spectrum of interests. Further, the safe districts for each party ideally should be scattered, rather than grouped in regional patterns, in order to maximize opportunities for political expression on the part of all voters. A commission, specifically a bipartisan commission, may work toward this ideal. But it can be guaranteed to fail if it is tied to detailed pseudo-standards specified in advance and uniformly followed.

B. NOTE ON COMPUTERS

Whether the redistricting function be handled by a bipartisan commission or otherwise, use of a computer may be helpful as a tool for the decision-makers. But it must ever be stressed that a computer is only a tool; it makes the analyses and correlations it is asked to make. It offers no solution in districting impasse situations. A com-

---

90 See BAGEHOT, THE ENGLISH CONSTITUTION 242 (1900).

puter reports back the biases ("parameters" in computer terms) of the master who feeds it. It can incorporate political data; or it can fly blind with only population data and perhaps some sort of "compactness" instruction (of which several alternatives are available). In both instances, and especially the latter, it can report back *many* alternative plans—in a large state hundreds or thousands—which satisfy simple criteria.

It is "almost an abuse of a computer not to take advantage of its great versatility."[91] There should be data on a wide variety of political, social, and economic aspects of community. The availability of politically meaningful social science data with which to "feed" computers has improved markedly in recent years.[92] Computer printouts showing political and social profile information on each of the arithmetically similar districts from which a final districting choice is to be made should be generally available. Especially provocative is a technique combining a television screen and a computer. Plans may be displayed and can be modified according to suggestions made by on-the-scene participants. Prospective political performance of the districts can be shown if adequate data are in the computer.[93]

By contrast the experimental program of a National Municipal League–sponsored organization—Computer Research on Nonpartisan Districting, Inc. (CROND)—eschews political data, and indeed all data, except population and special "compactness" and "contriguity" considerations.[94] Although all experimentation is to be encouraged in this new field, it is unfortunate to have it presented under the misleading label "nonpartisan districting." A more descriptive term would be: "Computer Research on Districting with Unrefined Population Figures." It may be appealing to those courts who do not like to admit that they are indeed deep in the political thicket. But those who use it will do so at their peril, because it has

---

[91] Nagel, *Simplified Bipartisan Computer Redistricting*, 17 STAN. L. REV. 863, 898 (1965).

[92] See, *e.g.*, COUNCIL OF SOCIAL SCIENCE DATA ARCHIVES, SOCIAL SCIENCE DATA ARCHIVES (1967).

[93] Steven, "On the Screen: Man-Machine Interaction," paper at National Municipal League annual meeting, November, 1967.

[94] NATIONAL MUNICIPAL LEAGUE (CROND), REDIST VERSION 3.3; PROGRAM DESCRIPTION AND USER MANUAL (1969).

no planned relevance to any consideration of fair and effective political representation, for either majorities or minorities. It does use gross population, but we all start at this point. Nor does the new *Preisler* and *Wells* ruling necessarily point in the CROND direction. It seems to mandate absolute population equality. It does not reach the question of making a fair representation choice among the several equally equal "equal population" plans which can be devised.

The CROND compactness measure is not geographic in the conventional sense. It seeks to minimize the distance each person is from his district center, the "center" itself being an artificial arithmetic concept based on working only with the population of the state and the number of districts to be created.[95] The program had its origin in one designed to yield optimum location (centers) of regional warehouses to minimize freight costs on nationwide orders.[96] A comment made in 1965 still seems to apply to the latest version of the CROND program:[97]

> [It] does not consider equality and compactness simultaneously, it does not guarantee contiguity, and it has no political features. The . . . program is thus nonpartisan only in the sense that it is unpredictable as to which party it will favor.

Computers undoubtedly will be used frequently as legislators, commissions, and courts grapple anew with revision of all districts in the seventies. Computers can be very helpful, indeed suggestive, when used as analytical tools. But it would be unfortunate if the final result of the reapportionment revolution would be to replace the question "Who controls the redistricting committee?" with the question "Who devised the program the computer used?" Computers may achieve their highest, and safest, utility in conjunction with bipartisan apportionment agencies.

V. Gerrymandering: A Sanctuary in the Thicket?

Incredible as it may seem, although almost eight years have elapsed since the political thicket was first entered in *Baker v. Carr* in 1962, the most important issue of all—the gerrymandering prob-

---

[95] *Id.* at p. 1.2.2.

[96] Weaver & Hess, *A Procedure for Nonpartisan Districting: Development of Computer Techniques*, 73 Yale L.J. 288, 301 (1963).

[97] Nagel, note 91 *supra*, at 874 n. 12.

lem—is still unresolved. Although raised in *Wells v. Rockefeller*,[98] albeit on a meager record, it was not reached by the Court. Thus, as we move into the 1970's our present learning must be gleaned from lower court cases, and by reasoning by analogy from the racial gerrymandering rulings.

Arguably, *Baker v. Carr* itself resolves in the affirmative the question of justiciability of political gerrymandering, even though the issue was not squarely presented in that case. After all, the central goal of the *Baker* plaintiffs, and of plaintiffs in reapportionment and redistricting cases generally, is a political representation goal. The goal is to modify the legislative districts so that plaintiffs will have a better opportunity of electing partisan legislators in sympathy with their goals than is possible under the system being attacked. There is nothing illegitimate about such a partisan goal: fair representation of partisans so that all interests may have an adequate voice is what democracy is all about.

A. GERRYMANDERING DEFINED

Conventional definitions of gerrymandering focus too much on shape, too little on substance. Whenever legislators are elected from districts there is seldom—except by accident—exact correlation between the percentage of popular votes gained by a political party and the percentage of seats captured by the party. Only a pure proportional representation system produces a near-exact correlation. In this functional sense, all districting is gerrymandering. A certain amount of inexactness in political representation is the price paid in order to achieve certain important advantages that go along with a district system, such as achievement of a broader popular consen-

---

[98] Brief for Appellant, 35–38, Brief for Appellees, 27–32, Wells v. Rockefeller, 394 U.S. 542 (1969). The appellant's argument on this point simply noted that there was some evidence of subdistricting (particularly the counties of Queens and Kings-Richmond in New York City) so as to give the minority party some representation rather than a freeze-out. For example, the four districts in Queens as drawn yielded one seat to the Republican minority (43 percent of the vote); but the seven districts in Kings-Richmond yielded no seat to the Republican minority (28 percent of the vote). The city of Rochester and environs as divided yielded two Republican seats rather than a 1 to 1 split.

But such choices as these are the essence of bipartisan apportionment. The alternative is blind chance or a possible statewide partisan plan. In the state as a whole under the one-time use of this plan in 1968 (permitted by the district court pending the appeal), the result was twenty-six congressmen for the Democrats, fifteen for the Republicans.

sus and a greater governmental stability. But when districting becomes unduly discriminatory, either by conscious design of the political cartographers or as an unforeseen operating result, we commonly call it gerrymandering. Most attempted definitions of gerrymandering are too precise and hence too narrow. Gerrymandering is simply discriminatory districting which operates to inflate unduly the political strength of one group and deflate that of another. It may be associated with oddities in the shape of districts but has no necessary relationship to distorted shapes of districts.

B. SUPREME COURT AMBIGUITIES

There has as yet been no Supreme Court ruling on the justiciability of political gerrymandering, and the lower courts are divided. In a statement attached to one Supreme Court per curiam ruling[99] in the complex New York state legislative apportionment litigation, speaking only for himself, Mr. Justice Harlan expressed the view that political gerrymandering should not be justiciable. He thus remained consistent with his opposition to justiciability of any legislative apportionment question expressed in his dissents to *Baker v. Carr* and *Reynolds v. Sims*. In the New York muddle there were four different reapportionment plans, and attacks by various parties in the state courts as well as in the federal district court. The one plan which the latter court had found acceptable, after brushing aside a Democratic charge of gerrymandering as being nonjusticiable, was concurrently nullified by the state courts on nongerrymandering grounds.[100] The per curiam opinion was not a full review on the merits after briefing and oral argument. It came on the eve of a special election and is best viewed as putting the Supreme Court's blessing on a temporary accommodation to keep the state government functioning.

In 1966 the Supreme Court refused to review a Michigan case in which political gerrymandering was one of the issues. After the Republican plaintiffs had been denied relief in the Michigan state courts, the Supreme Court dismissed their attempted appeal "for want of a substantial federal question," without citing any authority or attaching any explanation.[101]

---

[99] WMCA, Inc. v. Lomenzo, 382 U.S. 4 (1965).

[100] WMCA, Inc. v. Lomenzo, 238 F. Supp. 916 (S.D. N.Y. 1965); *In re* Orans, 15 N.Y.2d 239 (1965). For full discussion see DIXON 349–62.

[101] Badgley v. Hare, 385 U.S. 114 (1966).

Under present Supreme Court practice a pseudo-mandatory "appeal" from a state court may be handled in three ways: full review by vote of four or more Justices; summary affirmance or reversal of the lower court judgment; or summary dismissal for want of a substantial federal question. Mr. Justice Brennan has said that the votes by which the court chooses between the latter two courses are "on the merits."[102] Following this lead, a district court judge said that an insubstantial federal question dismissal "amounts to an affirmance of the case on the merits."[103] If this be so, however, the Court should abolish the "insubstantial federal question" category and dispose of "appeals" in only two ways; on full review, or by summary affirmance or reversal of the lower court judgment.[104] The problem lies in the "appeal" concept itself. It originated at a time when there was a substantial part of American jurisprudence beyond the pale of national cognizance. More and more the dismissal for want of jurisdiction category has come to be treated as the equivalent of a denial of certiorari.

In any event the Michigan reapportionment case is an especially inappropriate basis for asserting that this "insubstantial federal question" dismissal placed political gerrymandering in the nonjusticiable category. The Michigan supreme court's handling of the matter was confused by a welter of opinions, the record was meager, and the issue presented was a novel and crucial one in the area of constitutional law.

C. "BACKDOOR" INVALIDATIONS OF POLITICAL GERRYMANDERING

Despite these negative intimations from the Supreme Court on the justiciability of political gerrymandering which have induced some lower courts to back away,[105] lower courts also have achieved

---

[102] Ohio *ex rel.* Eaton v. Price, 360 U.S. 246, 247 (1958).

[103] Port Authority Bondholders Protective Committee v. Port of New York Authority, 270 F. Supp. 947, 950–51 (S.D. N.Y. 1967).

[104] Dismissal for want of jurisdiction may properly occur, of course, where the technicalities of the "appeal" statute are not satisfied. But it has long been obvious that "insubstantial federal question" dismissals cover a far broader range than that. See WOLFSON & KURLAND, ROBERTSON & KIRKHAM, JURISDICTION OF THE SUPREME COURT OF THE UNITED STATES 101 *et seq.* (1951); STERN & GRESSMAN, SUPREME COURT PRACTICE 81 *et seq.* (2d ed. 1954).

[105] See Meeks v. Avery, 251 F. Supp. 245 (D. Kan. 1966); Bush v. Martin, 251 F. Supp. 484 (S.D. Tex. 1966); Sims v. Baggett, 247 F. Supp. 96 (M.D. Ala. 1965);

what might be called "backdoor" invalidations of political gerrymandering. They have granted relief on extratight population equality grounds, after denying it on gerrymandering grounds. In some
of these cases it does not take much reading between the lines to see
that the real reason for the "nitpicking" arithmetic was to invalidate
a gerrymander without saying so. The New Jersey supreme court,
for example, wrote as follows:[106]

> [A] limited deviation may be acceptable if it is needed to
> stay with the lines of political subdivisions and thus to
> avoid the spectre of partisan gerrymandering. . . . But . . . if
> equality would be more nearly achieved by shifting whole
> municipalities to a contiguous district, the draftsman has not
> achieved equality "as nearly as practicable," unless some other
> constitutionally tenable reason (if there is any) can be shown
> to justify the disparity.

Thus, an alleged gerrymander is presumptively unconstitutional *if*
another plan cutting fewer subdivision lines would produce the same
degree of population equality.

Attorneys faced with the task of constructing a political gerrymandering challenge would be well advised to look at the Delaware
reapportionment case, *Sincock v. Gately*,[107] in which varied and
fairly massive proof of partisan gerrymandering was presented and
well summarized in the lengthy opinion of the federal district court.
The plaintiffs amassed detailed party election performance data, and
were aided by the fact that an election already had occurred under
the challenged plan. The proof convinced the entire three-judge
court that some gerrymandering had occurred. But doubting the
justiciability of gerrymandering, the court found for the plaintiffs
on the alternative ground of population inequality. Objecting to this

---

Newbald v. Osser, 425 Pa. 478 (1967); Jones v. Falcey, 48 N.J. 25 (1966); Sincock
v. Gately, 262 F. Supp. 739 (D. Del. 1967). In several of these, however, the matter
of justiciability was not extensively discussed and the courts indicated that the
gerrymandering charge was not adequately proved.

106 Jones v. Falcey, 48 N.J. at 37. The court did allow one-time-only use of the
plan in 1966 and it did produce a Democratic 9 to 6 margin in congressional seats,
even though the Republican popular vote exceeded the Democratic vote 1,045,641
to 1,020,779. Other apparent examples of "backdoor" invalidations of gerrymandering include Long v. Avery, 251 F. Supp. 541 (D. Kan. 1966); Drum v. Seawell, 250
F. Supp. 922 (M.D. N.C. 1966); and the *Sincock* case discussed below.

107 262 F. Supp. 739 (D. Del. 1967).

pussyfooting on the gerrymandering issue, District Judge Caleb M. Wright added a forthright comment on the justiciability of political gerrymandering:[108]

> Concededly, gerrymandering is fairly deep in the "political thicket." Nevertheless, to allow a legislature to deprive any group of fair representation in any manner would be to condone invidious discrimination. . . . Since the discrimination worked by partisan gerrymandering is as sinister as that worked by malapportionment—both operate to nullify the voting power of certain elements of the citizenry—it would seem that the rationale of Baker v. Carr requires that those whose votes are debased by partisan gerrymandering be afforded the protection of the Fourteenth Amendment.

D. GERRYMANDERING IN MULTIMEMBER DISTRICT CONTEXT

In sharp contrast to this unsatisfactory state of the record concerning gerrymandering challenges to single-member districting, the Supreme Court seems to have conceded the justiciability of gerrymandering challenges to multimember districting, although there have been no actual invalidations. In *Fortson v. Dorsey*, less than a year after *Reynolds v. Sims*, the Supreme Court reviewed a case from Georgia challenging the mixed use of multimember and single-member districts for the Georgia senate. Arithmetic equality (really proportionality with the varying sized districts in the multimember arrangement) was not at issue. Nor was the obvious line of proof made that racial or political minorities were unjustly submerged in the large multimember districts. Rather the attack focused on the alleged representation disparity between Fulton County (Atlanta), where seven senators were elected at large, and a small rural county. Although elected at large, the Fulton County senators were required to reside in, and in this sense to "represent," seven subdistricts within the county. The population of these seven subdistricts was roughly equivalent to at least one rural county which was a single-member district by itself. It was argued that this arrangement created a disparity in representation in the sense that the voters in the single-member rural county "controlled" their legislator, whereas the voters in the equivalent-sized subdistricts within Fulton County had no similar man "controlled" by them.

Finding the asserted discrimination "highly hypothetical," the Supreme Court brushed aside the challenge. But the opinion for

---

[108] *Id.* at 857.

the Court, written by Mr. Justice Brennan, went out of its way to keep alive a possible gerrymander challenge to a multimember district system by asserting that "our opinion is not to be understood to say that in all instances or under all circumstances such a system as Georgia has will comport with the dictates of the Equal Protection Clause." And he added that a multimember district system might not be constitutional if it operated "to minimize or cancel out the voting strength of racial or political elements of the voting population."[109]

In 1967 Mr. Justice Douglas, joining in the Court's invalidation of a Texas legislative apportionment on arithmetic equality grounds, added:[110]

> I reserve decision on one aspect of the problem concerning multimember districts.
> Under the present regime each voter in the district has one vote for each office to be filled. This allows the majority to defeat the minority on all fronts. . . .
> I am not sure in my own mind how this problem should be resolved.

Attempts to implement these ideas in state court litigation have had a mixed reception. A multimember district plan was invalidated in Iowa in 1966,[111] but not specifically on grounds of political discrimination, although such proof was part of the record. One wing of the Court (five Justices) was impressed with the thought that a multimember district resident has more legislative spokesmen, and hence more effective representation, than residents of a single-member district. This view makes mixed use of multimember and single-member districting almost per se unconstitutional unless specially justified. The other wing of the Court (four Justices) was more concerned with the lack of "identifiable constituencies" and the length of the ballot in multimember districts, thus making intelligent voting more difficult and representation more impersonal.

A recent attempt in *Rockefeller v. Smith* to use the Iowa ruling as a basis for invalidating a similar mixed multimember and single-

---

109 378 U.S. at 439. The same thought was repeated by Mr. Justice Brennan for the Court and amplified in his opinion in another unsuccessful challenge to a mixed multimember and single-member districting system in the Hawaiian reapportionment case. Burns v. Richardson, 384 U.S. 73, 88 (1966).

110 Kilgarlin v. Hill, 386 U.S. 120, 126 (1967).

111 258 Iowa 1121 (1966), *cert. den.,* Kruidenier v. McCulloch, 385 U.S. 851 (1966).

member districting system in Arkansas succeeded in the lower court but was then dismissed by the state supreme court on a jurisdictional technicality.[112] In the lower court plaintiffs alleged—and supported with substantial unrebutted evidence—a number of representational inequalities between the single-member districts and the multimember districts, the largest of which was Pulaski County with thirteen legislators elected at large for the lower house and five for the senate. The alleged inequalities included: lack of "identifiable constituencies"; "bloc voting" and hence submergence of "minority groups" in multimember districts; the large number of points of influence in the legislature accruing to residents of multimember districts.[113] For the reapportionment to take effect with the 1970 census, the court ordered: use of single-member districts unless valid and compelling reasons are shown for use of multimember districts in certain areas; grouping of traditionally Republican counties together, instead of linking to more populous counties; confining floterial districts to groups of small counties, instead of linking small counties to large counties.[114]

The burden of proof point is interesting, and perhaps crucial. If we are to resolve cases largely by presumptions, why does not a presumption against multimember districts, unless specially justified, make more sense than a presumption that they are constitutional unless particular political or racial inequity be proved? The former presumption, although contrary to the dictum of the Supreme Court in *Fortson v. Dorsey*, is more responsive to normal representation needs, and to the interest in maintaining viable party competition. Indeed, a presumption in favor of single-member districts makes more sense, in representation terms, than the new *Preisler* and *Wells* presumption in favor of absolute population equality unless all deviations are somehow "justified." In short, from the standpoint

---

[112] 440 S.W.2d 580 (Ark. 1969). The court, although expressing some sympathy for the arguments in favor of single-member districting, said the case was in the wrong court. It construed a state statute to vest exclusive jurisdiction in the state supreme court to hear challenges to the work of the state apportionment board. The court also cited *Preisler* and *Wells* as possibly rejecting some of plaintiff's arguments, but *Preisler* and *Wells* does not touch at all the multimember district issue.

[113] Smith v. Rockefeller, Circuit Court of Pulaski County, Ark., July 17, 1968, unreported, pp. 2-3 of manuscript opinion.

[114] As summarized in state supreme court opinion, note 112 *supra*.

of representation realities, we not only have had decisions in too many cases by use of presumptions; the presumptions themselves have been too casually chosen.

E. THE 1969 INDIANA CASE

In an interesting but somewhat difficult to classify ruling, an Indiana federal district court in *Chavis v. Whitcomb*[115] in July, 1969, nullified on two or possibly three grounds a mixed single-member and multimember legislative apportionment plan for the state legislature. Racial gerrymandering, excessive population deviations, and a possible theory of per se invalidity of mixed single-member and multimember districting all entered into the opinion.

The primary attack by the predominantly Negro plaintiffs was on the Marion County (Indianapolis) multimember districts in which fifteen state representatives and eight state senators were elected at large. Slate voting is the practice, and since 1920 only slightly more than 1 percent of the General Assembly candidates from Marion County have been elected from the political party that did not generally prevail. Inadequate Negro representation on the party slates was indicated by proof showing that a principal "ghetto area" with 17.8 percent of the county population elected only 4.75 percent and 5.97 percent, respectively, of the house and senate members from the county in 1960–68. One predominantly white middle-class area with 13.98 percent of the population elected 47.52 percent and 34.33 percent. Under subdistricting, this principal ghetto area would elect approximately two members of the house and one senator. There was also extensive proof of the distinguishing characteristics of the ghetto in terms of social and economic indices, and an allegation that because of its "cognizable minority characteristics" the ghetto area has an "unusual interest in specific areas of substantive law."[116]

Although rejecting some special theories of the invidious effect of the Marion County multimember district on Negroes,[117] the

---

[115] As of the time this volume went to press, the case was still unreported.

[116] See note 115 *supra*.

[117] The special plea of plaintiff Chavis himself was rejected. He was neither a voter nor a resident of the ghetto area (although his law practice and political activities including a ward chairmanship were centered there) but a resident of an area where Negroes were too few to achieve political influence by bloc voting. Nevertheless he claimed an interest in having Marion County subdistricted so as to

Court found that the *Fortson* dictum as amplified in *Burns v. Rich-ardson*[118] concerning the possible invidious effect of multimember districts on minorities had been satisfied. And on this ground alone the entire state plan was held unconstitutional because redistricting Marion County alone would create impermissible population varia-tions between Marion districts and other districts.

The Court also found that the population deviations in the chal-lenged Indiana plan, which had been approved in 1965 under the "substantial equality" principle,[119] were now too extreme under the tightened standards of the Supreme Court in *Swann v. Adams* and *Preisler* and *Wells*. The deviations above and below the ideal were for the house 11.1 percent and 13.6 percent, and the senate 13.67 percent and 14.52 percent.

More significantly, the Court received and reacted to argument that any legislative districting system which mixes single-member and multimember districts, or mixes different sizes of multimember districts, can be shown on mathematical grounds alone to overrep-resent the residents of the larger districts in terms of ability to influ-ence policy outcomes in the legislatures.[120] The analysis turns on the fact that residents of the larger districts have a larger number of representatives who may be in a position to cast a deciding vote in the legislature. And the exaggerated influence may occur even if the populations of the different-sized districts are arithmetically propor-

---

yield ghetto area seats, because his true (Negro) representation could come only from there. It was an ingenious theory which if accepted would logically give any minority Republican or Democrat a claim also to have the areas of his party's strength subdistricted.

Also rejected was the special plea of a Negro in Lake County, a multimember district somewhat less populous than Marion and hence with fewer legislators. He pointed out that the Negro populations of Marion and Lake were similar in size but that the Marion Negroes, because of the at-large voting feature, could vote for and possibly influence more legislators than Lake Negroes could.

[118] See text *supra*, at note 109.

[119] Stout v. Bottorff, 249 F. Supp. 488 (S.D. Ind. 1965).

[120] This can be called the "higher math" of "one man–one vote" to distinguish it from the "sixth grade arithmetic" of merely equalizing (or proportionalizing) gross population figures. See Banzhaf, *Multi-member Electoral Districts—Do They Violate the 'One man, One Vote' Principle*, 75 YALE L.J. 1309 (1966); Riker & Shapley, *Weighted Voting: A Mathematical Analysis for Instrumental Judgments*, in NOMOS X, note 86 *supra*, at 211–16; DIXON 535–43.

tional, *e.g.*, a 10,000 population district with one representative and a 90,000 population district with nine representatives.[121]

If this "higher math" analysis of "one man–one vote" be adopted, the mixed or "disuniform" districting system would not only be presumptively unconstitutional, but irrebuttably unconstitutional. The impact would be nationwide. The Indiana federal district court chose not to grant relief to the plaintiff who had made this challenge, desiring "stronger evidence of dilution." But at the same time in a strong advisory opinion to the Indiana legislature, which was ordered to revise the Indiana districts by October 1, 1969, the court said: "We believe that the Indiana General Assembly if it does the apportionment found to be needed here, should give consideration to the uniform district principle in making its apportionment."[122]

From the standpoint of representation theory in regard to minorities, and the proper content of constitutional rules concerning representation generally, these recent cases in Iowa, Arkansas, and Indiana would provide a better basis than *Preisler* and *Wells* for exposing the issues and forcing Supreme Court consideration of some political realities on a meaningful record.[123] The Supreme Court has yet to give full review to such a case. Had the Court

---

[121] The total or over-all influence on legislative outcomes of the voter in a multimember district (or his "effective representation") has been shown to be proportional to the square root of the population of the district, and thus increases with district size in comparison to smaller districts. DIXON 541.

[122] See note 115 *supra*.

[123] The Indiana case contained still another interesting plaintiff demand for relief. One plaintiff was a white Republican from the Marion County suburbs, containing less than one-third of the county population but almost half of the regular Republican voters. Her complaint was that people like her are "deprived of a proportionate voice as to who their Republican state legislators shall be in years of Republican victory in Marion County." In other words, she apparently wanted sub-districting so as to elect more suburban Republicans and fewer city Republicans to the state legislature. But the Court said there was a failure to prove that her interests "are significantly different from those of other Republican voters in years of Republican victory." And the Court added the thought that her complaint was an intraparty issue and so "does not in our opinion rise to the degree of a constitutional deprivation of equal protection by reason of the statutes here under attack."

Although not mentioned by the Court, her cause probably was not aided by the fact that Republican slates had won in Marion County in 1956, 1960, 1962, 1966; Democrats had won in 1958 and 1964. For this point, and a seven-state survey of districting effects, see JEWELL, METROPOLITAN REPRESENTATION: STATE LEGISLATIVE DISTRICTING IN URBAN COUNTIES (1969).

entertained such cases as these earlier, ideally with even more ample records, it perhaps would not have painted itself so quickly into an arithmetic absolutism corner.

F. RACIAL GERRYMANDERING

In a functional sense racial gerrymandering may be classified as simply a special instance of political gerrymandering. Where race, rather than partisan affiliation alone, is the basis for the gerrymandering allegation, however, courts have found no difficulty in treating the issue as justiciable. Once over the justiciability hurdle, they have been faced with difficult questions of burden of proof and standards of proof.

In the leading Supreme Court case, *Wright v. Rockefeller*,[124] concerning the three predominantly white congressional districts and the one predominantly Negro–Puerto Rican congressional district in Manhattan, the gerrymander argument was unsuccessful. The *Wright* case leaves in doubt the relative importance of the following possible components of a successful gerrymandering case: (1) proof of racial intent in the construction of districts; (2) proof of invidious racial result in the election outcome produced by the districts; (3) shifting of the burden of proof to the state to justify the districts, after proof either of racial motive or racial effect, or both, has reached a certain level of plausibility. In *Wright* there was no direct proof at all on the question of intent. In the Supreme Court a question of racial effect became intertwined with the larger issue of what is "fair representation" for a racial minority which may have one safe seat if its votes are massed, or no safe seat but a possible balance of power in several districts if its votes are spread.

This issue split the Negro community itself, and there were Negro parties on both sides of the *Wright* case, as Mr. Justice Black noted in his opinion for the Court rejecting the racial gerrymandering argument:[125]

> As the majority below pointed out, the concentration of colored and Puerto Rican voters in one area in the county made it difficult, even assuming it to be permissible, to fix districts so as to have anything like an equal division of these voters among the districts. Undoubtedly some of these voters, as shown by this lawsuit, would prefer a more even distribution of minority groups among the four congressional dis-

---

[124] 376 U.S. 52 (1964).   [125] *Id.* at 57–58.

tricts, but others, like the intervenors in this case, would argue strenuously that the kind of districts for which appellants contended would be undesirable and, because based on race or place of origin, would themselves be unconstitutional.

As might be expected, some racial gerrymandering challenges have been successful in the Deep South where past patterns of racial discrimination may make it easier to reach a conclusion of either racial intent or racial effect, and on a more meager record than in the North.[126] Even in the South, however, the road to proving a racial gerrymander is not easy. The Supreme Court refused in 1967 to review a federal district court dismissal of a challenge to Mississippi's all-white congressional delegation, despite the fact that under the 1960 census Mississippi was 42 percent Negro.[127] And in Virginia, paintiffs were unsuccessful in challenging a reapportionment plan that combined the city of Richmond and Henrico County into one eight-man multimember district.[128] Negroes constituted only 29 percent of the enlarged district population but 42 percent of Richmond's population and arguably would have been assured of one or two seats under a single-member district system. The 1969 federal district court invalidation of the Marion County (Indianapolis) multimember district, primarily on racial discrimination grounds, may presage greater Negro success in the North as well as the South. But it is worth noting that this ruling, like all other successful pleas of racial gerrymandering, was in the context of multimember or at-large voting, not single-member districting.

G. STANDARDS FOR A GERRYMANDER CHALLENGE

Both the logic of *Baker v. Carr* and the realities of effective political representation through a district system dictate that political gerrymandering, with or without accompanying racial allegations, be deemed justiciable. The Supreme Court's new absolute population equality ruling of April, 1969, adds a further push in this direction. For one predictable result of this ruling is to open up further

---

[126] Sims v. Baggett, 247 F. Supp. 96 (M.D. Ala. 1965); Smith v. Paris, 257 F. Supp. 901 (M.D. Ala. 1966); Smith v. State Exec. Comm. of Democratic Party of Georgia, 288 F. Supp. 371 (N.D. Ga. 1968).

[127] Connor v. Johnson, 386 U.S. 483 (1967).

[128] Mann v. Davis, 245 F. Supp. 241 (E.D. Va. 1965), *aff'd per curiam sub nom.*, Burnette v. Davis, 382 U.S. 42 (1965).

opportunities for gerrymandering in the process of ignoring all traditional restraints in pursuit of the arithmetic equality goal. The racial gerrymandering precedents indicate some of the proof problems which will be presented in political gerrymandering litigation.

1. Would a demonstrably unfair *partisan result* be unconstitutional?

2. Would a demonstrably *partisan purpose* be unconstitutional even if the proof showed simply a purpose to get all of the facts out in the open in order to achieve a fair partisan balance—in short a consideration of political data in districting in order to assure that the resultant districts would provide a basis for equitable party competition? If this be the rule, bipartisan apportionment commissions are doomed and blind apportionments are mandated, with fair representation being left to chance.

3. Would demonstrable unfair *partisan purpose* (assuming it could be proved) be unconstitutional,[129] even if the plan in operation actually boomeranged against its designers and turned out to be fair or to favor the opposition party?[130]

----

[129] For example, one Republican redistricting expert saw in *Wells v. Rockefeller* an opportunity for six to eight additional Republican congressmen from New York and added the comment: "Now it's just a question of slicing the salami, and the salami happens to be in our hands." New York Times, April 8, 1969, p. 34, col. 4. He referred to the fact that the Court-rejected plan was the product of a split legislature but that the new plan would be drawn by a legislature now Republican-controlled in both houses.

Similarly, the new 1969 Louisiana congressional districting by a legislature dominated by Democrats markedly strengthened the Democratic vote in the district of Representative Hale Boggs, majority whip in the House of Representatives. All of the new districts are within a 1 percent deviation from ideal population. All eight Louisiana congressmen are Democrats, and the Boggs district is the only one in which Republicans had a strong chance of winning. 27 CONG. Q. WEEKLY REP. 1462–63 (1969).

Hawaii, which has elected both its congressmen at large since 1962, was required by a 1967 federal statute to redistrict by 1970 and did so in 1969. The plan places Hawaii's two incumbent Representatives, Spark M. Matsunaga and Patsy T. Mink, in separate urban and rural districts. The plan is based on registered voters, not population, and the figures are respectively 139,819 and 134,380. 27 CONG. Q. WEEKLY REP. 1570 (1969). The question whether a congressional districting plan, in contrast to a state legislative apportionment plan, may utilize a base other than total population has not been judicially determined. See note 45 *supra*.

[130] For example, the New York 1961 congressional districting plan modified Democratic Representative Samuel Stratton's district to make it stretch narrowly for 200 miles through traditionally Republican territory in upstate New York. But Representative Stratton has won reelection in this district in every congressional election since then, and in 1969 he expressed "a very real affection" for it at a hear-

The first possibility listed, *i.e.*, demonstrated partisan result, seems to be the only sound basis for erecting a workable jurisprudence of gerrymandering for several reasons. Questions of intent, or purpose, are notoriously difficult to prove. In *Wright v. Rockefeller*, for example, because Negroes are not only a racial classification but also are primarily Democrats, some of the racial allegations foundered because alternative political motivations were equally plausible, *i.e.*, to preserve one Republican district on Manhattan Island while conceding three to the Democrats.[131]

More critically, political data must be considered if there is any hope of achieving fair and effective representation for all, via a districting system. A rule elevating "partisan intent" or purpose to the level of automatic unconstitutionality might mean that those who openly considered political data would put their plan in peril. Even so-called nonpartisan apportionment agencies, if they are to discharge their tasks effectively, must consider political data. All agree that no district line is neutral. This being so, some advance knowledge of possible outcomes is essential. We did not put a man on the moon by closing our eyes to possible consequences. Similarly, we cannot "fly blind" toward the actually more difficult goal of representation fairness.

The basic premise should be that political gerrymandering, like racial gerrymandering, is justiciable, subject to a reasonably heavy burden of proof on the challenger. In making the proof, evidence of adverse political result should be far more probative than allegations of invidious partisan purpose. Most relevant will be detailed party election performance data, comparing party votes cast and party seats gained. The "best evidence" of course is how a plan actually works in a given election. Such evidence cannot be gleaned until one "government" has been elected under the challenged gerrymandered plan.

This would be a high price to pay for the "best evidence" available. It would deny the plaintiffs immediate relief. A burden of proof rule may help to solve this problem. Timely challenge before

---

ing before the committee preparing a new set of districts for 1970 under the *Preisler* and *Wells* ruling. New York Times, Aug. 10, 1969, § 1, p. 80, col. 1. And see CONGRESSIONAL DIRECTORY FOR 87TH CONGRESS 2D SESS. 114, 818 (1962); CONGRESSIONAL DIRECTORY FOR 88TH CONGRESS 1ST SESS. 120, 848 (1963).

131 211 F. Supp. 460, at 470, 473.

a plan is put in effect could be allowed, but a somewhat higher level of proof could be required than in those situations where actual performance data are available. The surprising thing is not that substantive rules for judicial review of political gerrymandering are difficult to articulate but that the needed case-by-case process of detailed litigation to produce them has not yet begun.

VI. Conclusion

The unfinished agenda of the "one man–one vote" revolution is long and prickly. Heading the list is a critical need to clarify our basic premises as to what the struggle is all about. "Equal population" districting is an objective concept. But it has no necessary relation to any particular quality of political *representation*. "Equal representation" is a misnomer. Even as translated into the functional concept of fair and effective representation, it has no necessary relation to mere "equal population districting" once egregious population disparities are eliminated, as they now have been. Failure to realize this may lead us to fasten on ourselves a majoritarian, numbers-dominated, representation system which tends to "pay off" only for large groups.

The history of America, far more than the history of any Communist nation, has been to a surprising extent a long romance with an egalitarian ideal. Egalitarianism was bolstered considerably by the exigencies of frontier life. It is nourished also by our still-developing national moral sense and the exigencies of twentieth-century mass democracy. "One man–one vote" should be perceived as the symbol of an aspiration for fairness, for avoidance of complexity, for intelligibility in our representational process—indeed, for a sense of meaningful membership in the *polis*. These are legitimate aspirations; but there is no single, simple formula for their accomplishment.

Centering as it does on the equality concept, "one man–one vote" is a powerful engine for overturning accepted practices in many areas. But by its very surface simplicity "equality" often does not allow us to ask the right questions, or even to gather the right data for an intelligent evaluation. For a general election in a single constituency, voter equality of course must be the rule.[132] And racial

---

[132] Gray v. Sanders, 372 U.S. 368 (1963).

discrimination in form or in substance is forbidden.[133] As soon as we move into a district system for electing a general legislature, and use a winner-take-all rule inside each district, equality fails as a tool for analyzing effectiveness of representation.[134] "Black Power" demands for proportional legislative power now highlight the issue in some areas, but the problem is as old as apportionment.

The utility of a simple "equality" concept diminishes further as we move toward some newly developing issues. Should we exempt some special local government districts from the equal population rule?[135] What of regulation of political party leadership,[136] and of the presidential national nominating conventions?[137] What of the extraordinary majority requirements we traditionally have had for bond issues, which affect future generations;[138] and for initiation or ratification of constitutional amendments, which affect basic political norms? How can the committee and seniority systems for allocation of power inside legislatures be squared with "one man–one vote," if it be defined in simple "equality" terms?

---

[133] Harper v. Virginia Board of Elections, 383 U.S. 663 (1966).

[134] See, *e.g.*, Burns v. Richardson, 384 U.S. 73 (1966), and especially the following per curiam comment of the three-judge federal district court on a multimember district situation: "While there perforce must be some overlap of representation with the several senate and house districts, that overlap must not be such as to concentrate and intensify the voting power of a single senatorial-representative district to the point that the voters therein have a built-in disproportionate representational advantage over any other voters of the State. . . . Such artificially concentrated political power negates any notion of equality of representation for the minorities entrapped therein, as well as for all other electors of the State outside such a monolithic political unit." Holt v. Richardson, 240 F. Supp. 724, 729–30 (D. Hawaii 1965).

[135] Avery v. Midland County, 390 U.S. 474 (1968). See *Symposium on One Man One Vote and Local Government*, 36 GEO. WASH. L. REV. 689 (1968). And see Hadley v. Junior College of Kansas City, 432 S.W.2d 328 (Mo. 1968), *prob. juris. noted*, 393 U.S. 1115 (1969).

[136] Smith v. State Exec. Comm. of Democratic Party of Georgia, 288 F. Supp. 371 (N.D. Ga. 1968).

[137] Note, *Regulation of Political Parties: Vote Dilution in the Presidential Nomination Procedure*, 54 IOWA L. REV. 471 (1968); Irish v. Democratic–Farmer Labor Party of Minn., 399 F.2d 119 (8th Cir. 1968).

[138] Lance v. Board of Education (W.Va. Sup. Ct., No. 12809, July 8, 1969); Bogert v. Kinzer (Idaho Sixth Jud. Dist., Memorandum Decision and Order, No. 26864, *appeal pending*, Idaho Supreme Court, 1969); Larez v. Shannon (Superior Court of Sutter County, California, Aug. 8, 1969, *appeal pending*); Preisler v. City of St. Louis (E.D. Mo. No. 69C 250 [1], filed Aug. 1, 1969).

Perhaps some of our traditional practices in these fields should be changed.[139] The wand of "equality" may achieve change; it will not tell us why.[140] Concededly a two-thirds majority requirement is not "equal." But that is not the question. The issue is whether or not in certain fields an extraordinary majority requirement makes sense as a way of ensuring a broader consensus than a bare majority, and of avoiding precipitate action. Mass-meeting democracy, of course, has no such defenses. But mass-meeting democracy—"participatory democracy" in modern parlance—has not been our governmental model before. If it is to become our model, it should be discussed in these terms, not stumbled into in pursuit of an abstract "equality" goal. Judicial review itself cannot be squared with a simple equality concept, yet it is one of our most revered institutions for high policy making.

The essential contribution of the "one man–one vote" concept is this. We must now face regularly those elemental questions which even a democratic people tend to ignore. Who is represented? How? For what purpose? With what result? When do we want simple majorities? When do we need consensus? Where does "one man–one vote" properly apply? Where is it irrelevant? The revolution has barely begun.

---

[139] See, *e.g.*, the Court's recent nullification of restricted electorate laws for such special purposes as school board elections and bond issues. Kramer v. Union Free School District, 395 U.S. 621 (1969); Cipriano v. Houma, 395 U.S. 701 (1969).

[140] Contrast, *e.g.*, the inadequately rationalized results in two cases in April–May, 1969, in which the Court nullified an Illinois geographic spread requirement for nominating petitions but refused to intervene in behalf of two unsentenced Chicago jail inmates awaiting trial who could not vote because they constituted one of a number of classes for whom no provisions for absentee voting had been made. One was being held on a nonbailable charge (murder); the other (robbery charge) was unable to post a $5,000 bond. Moore v. Ogilvie, 394 U.S. 814 (1969); McDonald v. Bd. of Election Com'rs of Chicago, 394 U.S. 802 (1969).

GERHARD CASPER

WILLIAMS v. RHODES AND PUBLIC FINANCING OF POLITICAL PARTIES UNDER THE AMERICAN AND GERMAN CONSTITUTIONS

In the autumn of 1966, Congress enacted the Presidential Election Campaign Fund Act.[1] The act is still the law of the land, in a manner of speaking. But since the legislature can undo what is done and can, like the courts, accomplish such a feat without admitting it, Congress got rid of the act seven months after it was passed by making it "inoperative."[2]

The first of these two statutes is popularly known as the Long Act. It was adopted as an amendment to the "Christmas Tree" bill, *i.e.*, the Foreign Investors Tax Act of 1966. Along with other nongermane matters the campaign financing measure had been added to the Foreign Investors Tax Bill and, on October 22, 1966, passed the Senate in the very last hours of the Eighty-ninth Congress, with half the senators already away campaigning. Herbert E. Alexander attributes the enactment to the "persuasive, skilled, determined and powerful" advocacy of Senator Russell Long, chairman of the Sen-

Gerhard Casper is Professor of Law and Political Science, The University of Chicago.

[1] 80 Stat. 1587 (1966).   [2] 81 Stat. 57 (1967).

ate Finance Committee and then assistant majority leader.[3] More-over, the Johnson administration gave it last-minute support, al-though Senator Long's bill had taken precedence over an adminis-tration scheme to grant tax incentives for political contributions. According to Alexander, Congressman Wilbur Mills, chairman of the House Ways and Means Committee, was also persuaded of the desirability of approving some legislation to help cope with prob-lems of political finance.[4]

There was much public and congressional dissatisfaction with the manner in which this important measure had been pushed through Congress, as well as with its substance. Senators Gore and Williams led the opposition forces and, despite heavy White House pressure, in May, 1967, the statute died as it was born, by an amend-ment to the Investment Credit Act of 1967 which provided that the Long Act should become effective only after adoption by law of guidelines for the distribution of funds that would accumulate by its provisions. Senate debates on the matter were lengthy and bitter. Although Senator Gore had failed to achieve repeal of the Long Act, the final vote was 93 to 4 for the amendment. Senator Long himself voted "yea."[5]

After narrowly avoiding repeal (the penultimate vote on that amendment required the Vice-President to cast the tie-breaking "nay"), Majority Leader Mansfield said he hoped to establish "the congressional view"[6]

> that public funds can provide at least part of the solution to the dangerous dilemma which is posed to popular govern-ment by the skyrocketing costs of modern political campaign-ing. Put bluntly, it will remind all who were not born yester-day, that the millions of dollars which go into campaigns must come from somewhere and the question of who pays for campaigns and why is not academic but vital in a modern democratic state. The retention of the reminder will compel us in the Congress—I repeat, will compel us in the Congress to ask ourselves again and again: Shall the piper be the whole of the American people through a system of public partici-pation in campaign financing? Or shall the tune be called more and more in the beat of special interests and great

---

[3] Alexander, *Financing Presidential Elections*, New Series 17 JAHRBUCH DES ÖFFENT-LICHEN RECHTS DER GEGENWART 573, 597 (1968).

[4] *Id.* at 598.

[5] 113 CONG. REC. 12169 (1967).   [6] *Id.* at 12165.

wealth? The retention of that reminder will keep before us the implications of these questions which go to the very heart and structure of the Government of the Republic.

Although Senator Mansfield's theories about the relationship between money and politics seem simplistic, it is difficult to disagree with his assertion that the question of political finance "goes to the very heart and structure of the Government of the Republic." Yet Mansfield hardly succeeded in establishing on the record what might be called "a congressional view."

Given the fact that the Republican administration will have little reason to revive the legislation, perhaps, one should let it rest in peace. Neither the problems stated by Mansfield, however, nor the constitutional questions that any method of public financing of political parties would raise are likely to disappear. Previously existing doubts about the constitutionality of the law[7] have been greatly strengthened by the Supreme Court decision last Term in *Williams v. Rhodes.*[8] I will examine some of the constitutional problems created by such legislation as the Presidential Campaign Fund Act. I propose to do this by way of comparison with the constitutional jurisprudence on the subject in, to use Senator Mansfield's expression, another "modern democratic state."

The German *Bundesverfassungsgericht* has had to decide a series of challenges brought against various schemes of public financing of political parties, most recently in December, 1968.[9] In my opinion these cases yield a wealth of data about certain aspects of the political culture of postwar Germany and, simultaneously, highlight problems connected with the role played by political parties in the democratic process. If one accounts for differences in historical origins, institutional techniques, attitudes, and legal theories of the American and German polities, a limited comparison of the type envisaged here may even be fruitful for American constitutional law.[10]

---

[7] In the Senate most eloquently stated by Senator Gore. 112 CONG. REC. 28783 (1966).

[8] 393 U.S. 23 (1968).

[9] BVerfGE 24, 300 (1968). In citing German cases I shall follow the German tradition of citation. Solely for the sake of simplicity, all mention of Germany herein refers only to the Federal Republic, unless otherwise specified.

[10] *Cf.* Riesenfeld & Casper, *Public Law: Comparative Public Law*, 13 INT. ENCYC. Soc. Sci. 183 (1968).

Before I describe the German developments, however, I want to establish more clearly what I am comparing. The Presidential Election Campaign Fund Act was the first national direct-subsidy measure to be enacted in the United States.[11] Its most important features may be summarized:

1. Every taxpayer was given the right to designate annually that $1.00 of his income taxes be paid into the Presidential Election Campaign Fund. What Senator Mansfield euphemistically called "citizen participation in campaign financing" consisted simply of granting the taxpayer the right to determine directly on his tax return how a small portion of his tax money should be spent. Though this device may in itself constitute a dangerous precedent,[12] it has the advantage of making it possible for the taxpayers to control the total amount of public funds to be spent by political parties. In Germany, on the other hand, this amount was and is determined by parliament, thus by the political parties themselves.[13]

2. Payments out of the Fund are to be made into the treasuries of political parties running presidential candidates, upon certification by the party treasurer to the comptroller general of campaign expenditures. In short, payments would go to the *national* party treasury.

---

[11] On the history see Alexander, note 3 *supra;* and ALEXANDER, REGULATION OF POLITICAL FINANCE (1966). Considering the statute as innovation, I can understand the interest of those supporting some form of public financing, like Senator Mansfield, to "preserve the principle" by strenuously fighting formal repeal of the law. *Cf.* remarks of Senator Mansfield, 113 CONG. REC. 12160.

[12] See the remarks by Senator Lausche, 112 CONG. REC. 28783 (1966).

[13] In July, 1966, the *Bundesverfassungsgericht* outlawed annual subsidies to political parties, but suggested that reimbursement for campaign expenditures would be considered constitutional by the court. In the fall of that year the Allensbach Institute asked the public whether they agreed that political parties should receive public contribution toward their campaign expenditures. Sixty-nine percent said they disagreed; 18 percent agreed; 13 percent had no opinion. NOELLE, DIE POLITIKER UND DIE DEMOSKOPIE 34 (1968). A Gallup poll released August 7, 1966, showed a plurality (48 percent) of Americans favored tax deductions for campaign contributions up to $50 (41 percent were opposed). A majority (57 percent) thought it was a good idea to have the government print and mail pamphlets in which candidates state their position on public issues. Unfortunately, these German and American opinions are not really comparable, since the German public, two to three months after the *Bundesverfassungsgericht* decision, must have been impressed by the magnitude of the amount the parties had previously allocated to themselves. Also, while the Gallup questions referred to specific and limited proposals, the Allensbach question was quite general.

3. The Fund would be distributed in the following manner:
   a) Each political party whose candidate obtained more
      than 15 million votes at the preceding election (*i.e.*,
      the Republican and Democratic parties abstractly de-
      fined), would share the sum arrived at by multiplying
      the total number of votes cast for those parties by
      $1.00 and subtracting $5 million per party from the total.
      Thus the act would give the same amount of money
      to each major party. If the Long Act were to be
      revived in time for the 1972 election, each major
      party would receive approximately $26 million.[14]
   b) If, in the preceding election, a party obtained less than
      15 million but more than 5 million votes, it would be
      paid $1.00 multiplied by the number of votes in excess
      of 5 million. This would give the American Independent
      party approximately $5 million.
   c) A party that received less than 5 million votes would
      get nothing.
   d) A new party would get nothing.
   e) Any surplus would revert to the general fund of the
      Treasury.
4. The Fund is to be administered by the comptroller general
   with the advice of a board composed of two representatives
   from each of the major parties and three additional
   members selected by them.

Senator Mansfield suggested that the Presidential Campaign Fund
Act aimed at making the parties more independent of special interests.[15] Although political theory has in the past and present confidently generalized about political influence, linking political power

---

[14] Whatever else might be the consequences of the statute, it would considerably
increase the money available to the major parties and probably send campaign costs
skyrocketing. This seems to have been the German experience, though it obviously
is difficult to establish firmly a causal link between public financing and rising campaign costs. The cost of the 1957 Bundestag campaign was approximately DM 40
million. No direct public financing was then available. In 1959 modest public subsidies in the amount of DM 5 million were paid. The cost of the 1961 campaign was
approximately DM 57 million. By 1965, the parties were receiving DM 38 million
from the public treasury. The election campaign of that year cost DM 83 million.
See Der Spiegel No. 31, p. 18 (1966). In the 1964 election the Republican party, the
only party for which we have reliable figures, spent approximately $15 million for
its presidential campaign. See Alexander, Financing of the 1964 Election 48 (1966).

[15] Other goals were to be achieved by it as well. One of those was quite candidly
admitted by Senator Long during the Senate debates: "The Democratic Party finds
itself in the position of being for the poor man, the common man—so that it does not
always have sufficient funds. . . ." 112 Cong. Rec. 28766.

to the resources available to an individual, group, or nation,[16] the consequences of money, either in directing party policy or in effecting elections, remain hard to evaluate.[17] To be sure, systematic data are now available,[18] and muckraking, of course, has always linked campaign contributions to governmental decision making.[19] Yet it remains exceedingly difficult to develop generalizations.[20] For instance, even the relatively small amount of approximately $60 million of public funds that the Long Act would have made available every four years could have an impact not only on the financial position of political parties relative to one another[21] but also on their internal structure. The national committees could become more independent of state and local committees which, at present, can use

---

[16] It is always appropriate to remember that money is only one kind of political resource. This is particularly true for political campaigns where skill or, given the mass communications, appeal of the candidate's position on the issues or his "charisma" constitute resources in themselves. See DAHL, PLURALIST DEMOCRACY IN THE UNITED STATES: CONFLICT AND CONSENT 374 (1967).

[17] Schlesinger, *Parties, Political: Party Units*, 11 INT. ENCYC. Soc. Sci. 428, 435 (1968). A more optimistic view is taken by Heard, *Political Financing*, 12 *id.* at 235.

[18] Data for the United States are assembled in HEARD, THE COSTS OF DEMOCRACY (1960). For Germany, Norway, and Japan there is now available the excellent study, HEIDENHEIMER & LANGDON, BUSINESS ASSOCIATIONS AND THE FINANCING OF POLITICAL PARTIES (1968).

[19] See, *e.g.*, the classic case of the oil industry and the 1952 Eisenhower campaign, referred to in HEARD, note 18 *supra*, at 105. For a current example see Representative Patman's remarks about the banking lobby, in his words "the single most potent lobby that operates year-round in Washington": "While I do not intend to name names here today, it is an open secret on Capitol Hill that many campaign chests are swelled by the contributions from the banks." Banks "have been known to flood their stockholders and others with thousands of pieces of mail to help in the election campaigns of some public officials." New York Times, Aug. 1, 1969. On campaign contributions by banking interests and how they tend to favor the Republican party, see HEARD, note 18 *supra*, at 123–26. Heard remarks: "Campaign donors, at least, seem to think the parties stand for something." *Id.* at 124.

[20] See Heidenheimer, *Comparative Party Finance: Notes on Practices and Toward a Theory*, 25 J. POL. 790, 796 (1963).

[21] "During the period of Democratic ascendancy from 1932 to 1952, the Republicans consistently spent more money in presidential campaigns than did the Democrats. During the Eisenhower campaigns, the pattern of greater Republican spending continued. In 1960, the Democrats went deeply into debt to spend as much as the Republicans spent, though the G.O.P. also incurred a small deficit. In 1964, the Republicans surged ahead again while reporting a surplus; the Democrats went into debt though they raised more money than ever before." Alexander, note 3 *supra*, at 576.

the threat of withholding financial support to influence national policies.[22] The Fund might enable national committees to rely on their increased purse as leverage for influencing local organizations.[23] None of these questions was adequately examined before passage of the legislation, nor was it very likely that such examination would have got very far. The main reason for the "repeal" of the Long Act may well have been the fear that the Fund might have upset the delicate system of internal party pressures and relations. Faced with uncertainty, Congress preferred the status quo.

In addition, it would seem that providing public funds for political parties presupposes some concept of what political parties are. That concept, and in particular one linking political parties and political representation, is lacking in the United States.[24] The Madisonian belief that, in a country as large as the United States, somehow the mere multitude of represented interests provides checks and balances that work out in the public interest[25] seems to be vaguely accepted. Yet, attitudes toward the use of private power to influence government remain very ambivalent.[26]

If political theory affords little guidance, the same is true for constitutional law, even if we take this term to refer to all of constitu-

---

[22] See HEARD, note 17 supra, at 290.

[23] Id. at 291. For congressional expressions of such fears, see Alexander, note 3 supra, at 603.

[24] "[T]heory about representation has not moved much beyond the eighteenth-century formulation of Edmund Burke." Prewitt & Eulau, Political Matrix and Political Representation: Prolegomenon to a New Departure from an Old Problem, 63 AM. POL. SCI. REV. 427 (1969). The notable exception is Hanna Pitkin's recent book THE CONCEPT OF REPRESENTATION (1967). And yet, Miss Pitkin's excellent analysis, too, devotes very little attention to the relation of political parties to representation. For a summary of whatever theory there is, see FRIEDRICH, CONSTITUTIONAL GOVERNMENT AND DEMOCRACY 430–53 (4th ed. 1968).

[25] See THE FEDERALIST No. 10; cf. PITKIN, note 24 supra, at 191–97; McCONNELL, PRIVATE POWER AND AMERICAN DEMOCRACY 102–07 (1966).

[26] McCONNELL, note 25 supra, at 25. The ambivalence is well expressed in survey responses reported by McClosky, Consensus and Ideology in American Politics, 58 AM. POL. SCI. REV. 361, 370 (1964). The following percentages of (I) the general electorate and (II) the political influentials agree (1) that "most politicians are looking out for themselves above all else": (I) 54.3 and (II) 36.3; (2) "many politicians are bought off by some private interest": (I) 65.3 and (II) 43.0; (3) "most politicians can be trusted to do what they think best for the country": (I) 58.9 and (II) 77.1; (4) "I usually have confidence that the government will do what is right": (I) 89.6 and (II) 81.6.

tional law, the "living constitution," not merely the judgments of the Supreme Court.[27] The written constitution was adopted before the emergence of political parties in the United States.[28] Certain institutions, like the electoral college, were even hostile to the idea of political parties. As a matter of fact, the extent to which the modern state can be truly characterized as a *Parteienstaat*[29] may be judged by the fact that American political parties were able to make the electoral college serve their purposes.

Short of constitutional amendment, there is no other way to determine the constitutional status of political parties in the United States, except by the "neglected" method advocated by Professor Black: that is, by drawing inferences from the structure of the Constitution.[30] That job, however, has been done neither by theorists nor by the Court. In the huge house of constitutional jurisprudence political parties occupy but a tiny closet from which they emerge only occasionally when it is difficult to ignore them because a party has either managed to monopolize elections (the "white primary" cases)[31] or sought to subvert the government (the Communist party

---

[27] The latter notion of constitutional law continues to prevail in spite of, or more likely because of, so-called legal realism. The legal realists' theoretical fascination with prediction made them concentrate on the courts, which were also those governmental agencies they knew best. Unfortunately, here too Holmes provided an easy formula: "The prophecies of what the courts will do in fact and nothing more pretentious are what I mean by the law." HOLMES, COLLECTED LEGAL PAPERS 173 (1920). This notion was very unpretentious. On the prediction theory, see CASPER, JURISTISCHER REALISMUS UND POLITISCHE THEORIE IM AMERIKANISCHEN RECHTSDENKEN 56–64 (1967).

[28] They really date no further back than the Jacksonian period. See NICHOLS, THE INVENTION OF THE AMERICAN POLITICAL PARTIES 294 (1967).

[29] See LEIBHOLZ, STRUKTURPROBLEME DER MODERNEN DEMOKRATIE (3d ed. 1967); see also LEIBHOLZ, POLITICS AND LAW 35 (1965). Although Huber may be overstating the point when, writing about political parties in the German Empire, he says that any system of representative government conceptually presupposes free political parties, it nevertheless is true enough that there exists not a single such system in the modern world without political parties. See HUBER, 4 DEUTSCHE VERFASSUNGSGE-SCHICHTE SEIT 1789 3 (1969).

[30] See BLACK, STRUCTURE AND RELATIONSHIP IN CONSTITUTIONAL LAW ch. 1 (1969). Casper, *Jones v. Mayer: Clio, Bemused and Confused Muse*, 1968 SUPREME COURT REVIEW 89, 100.

[31] The crucial case is Smith v. Allwright, 321 U.S. 649 (1944), where Justice Reed, who delivered the opinion of the Court, argued that certain state statutes providing for the organization of primary elections made the party an agency of the state. He then continued by saying that the right to vote "is not to be nullified by a State

cases).[32] The Supreme Court's lack of experience in dealing with political parties and their constitutional status is well illustrated by the 1968 decision in *Williams v. Rhodes.*

To bring the Long Act more sharply into the focus of that case I should like to stress the distinction the legislation makes between major, minor, minimal, and new parties. While the latter two categories of political parties are left out in the cold, exclusively dependent on private money tainted by special interests (the language used by supporters of the Long Act), the former two categories are considered worthy of public funds, though again different degrees of worthiness are distinguished. Which leaves us with the question whether government may validly draw such distinctions among political parties.

Williams v. Rhodes raised a host of constitutional problems that I shall not attempt to resolve here. Instead, I should like to emphasize the question of discrimination. The state of Ohio had sought to keep off the ballot for the 1968 presidential election two parties that had failed to fulfill various state requirements. The parties concerned were an old party, the Socialist Labor party, which in 1964 had been on the ballot in sixteen states, and a new party, the Ohio American Independent party, which supported George Wallace for President. Both parties had brought suit in a three-judge district

---

through casting its electoral process in a form which permits a private organization to practice racial discrimination in the election." *Id.* at 664. Although political parties may, indeed, have become "agencies" of the state, this is due more to the actual role they play in the representation of the people than to any state statutes. See Terry v. Adams, 345 U.S. 461 (1953). Nevertheless it is quite unclear what follows from such characterization, except that it makes it possible to apply the restraints of the Fourteenth Amendment. That *Smith v. Allwright* may have created more problems than it resolved is illustrated by the criticism Wechsler made in the course of his vain search for "neutral principles," when he said that the regulation of party membership found in *Smith v. Allwright* could be read to prohibit religious parties. Wechsler, *Toward Neutral Principles of Constitutional Law*, 73 HARV. L. REV. 1, 29 (1959). I always found this hard to understand, since the Constitution may have different principles for different categories of party membership. The real question *Smith v. Allwright* poses is whether its prohibition of racially organized parties is not too sweeping. What happens if blacks in America decide that the only way to be politically effective is to organize a black party? On *Smith v. Allwright* and also the Communist party cases, *cf.* Deutsch, *Neutrality, Legitimacy, and the Supreme Court: Some Intersections between Law and Political Science*, 20 STAN. L. REV. 169, 192–97 (1968).

[32] *E.g.*, Dennis v. United States, 341 U.S. 494 (1951). In these cases, however, emphasis is on the individual members charged with guilt by association.

court which declared unconstitutional the burdensome Ohio requirements and ruled that the parties were entitled to write-in space; estoppel by laches prevented the court from providing for a ballot position.[33] The American Independent party immediately asked Mr. Justice Stewart for interlocutory relief, which he granted them but refused to the Socialist Labor party, which had requested it a couple of days later, too late, in Justice Stewart's opinion, not to disrupt the election machinery. Although the full Supreme Court reversed the district court only in the case of the American Independent party, it seems (at least, as the Court's opinion written by Mr. Justice Black is understood by Justices Douglas and Harlan)[34] that the Court gave declaratory relief to the Socialist party as well.

The requirements stipulated by Ohio law were summarized by Judge Kinneary in the trial court:[35]

> To engage in the primary electoral process a new political party must first comply with Section 3517.01, which defines "political party." In its essential provisions it defines a political party to be: (1) any group of voters which polled ten (10) per cent of the vote in the last preceding election for its candidate for governor, or (2) any group of voters who have filed with the secretary of state, at least ninety (90) days before an election, a petition signed by not fewer than fifteen (15) per cent of the total number of voters in the last preceding regular state election. This year the required number of signatures is 433,100. In 1953, 540,766 signatures would have been required.
>
> However, even filing a petition with the number of signatures required by the statute is not sufficient to obtain a position on the ballot for the candidates of a new political party. Inextricably interwoven with Section 3517.01 are many provisions regulating the organization and procedures of political parties in this state. *First*, at the primary election, the new party, or any political party, is required to elect a state central committee consisting of two members from each congressional district and county central committees for each county in Ohio. *Second*, at the primary election the new party must elect delegates and alternates to a national convention. Since Section 3513.19.1, Ohio Rev. Code, prohibits a candidate from seeking the office of delegate to the national convention or committeeman if he voted as a member

---

[33] 290 F. Supp. 983 (S.D. Ohio 1968).

[34] 393 U.S. at 40, 46.   [35] 290 F. Supp. at 994.

of a different party at a primary election in the preceding four
year period, the new party would be required to have over
twelve hundred members who had not voted in another
party's primary, and who would be willing to serve as com-
mitteemen and delegates. *Third*, the candidates for nomination
in the primary would have to file petitions signed by qualified
electors. The term "qualified electors" is not adequately defined in the Ohio Revised Code, but a related section, provides
that a qualified elector at a primary election of a political
party is one who, (1) voted for a majority of that party's
candidates at the last election, or, (2) has never voted in any
election before. Since neither of the political party plaintiffs
had any candidates at the last preceding regular state election, they would, of necessity, have to seek out members
who had never voted before to sign the nominating petitions,
and it would be only these persons who could vote in the
primary election of the new party.

The Socialist Labor party in 1968 had 108 members in Ohio.[36] It
could not dream of obtaining the 15 percent quota. Wallace's forces
had secured more than the required 433,100 signatures, but since
the Ohio American Independent party had been formed only in
January, 1968, it could not possibly meet a February 7 deadline for
filing the petitions.

The Supreme Court, over the dissent of Chief Justice Warren
and Justices Stewart and White, ordered the Independent party on
the ballot holding that the state had violated the Equal Protection
Clause of the Fourteenth Amendment by invidiously placing unequal burdens on the freedom of association and the right to vote.
Mr. Justice Douglas agreed with Mr. Justice Black but emphasized
that it was the First Amendment that "lies at the root of these
cases."[37] Mr. Justice Harlan concurred only in the result, since he
would have rested the decision "entirely on the proposition that
Ohio's statutory scheme violates the basic right of political association assured by the First Amendment which is protected against
state infringement under the Due Process Clause of the Fourteenth
Amendment."[38] Justices Stewart and White thought Ohio had
ample power to pass the challenged legislation under Art. II, § 1,

---

[36] 393 U.S. at 28.

[37] *Id*. at 38. It is also the right to vote that lies "at the root of the present controversy."

[38] *Id*. at 41.

of the Constitution, since the legislation did not discriminate invidiously and since there was no constitutional right to vote for presidential electors to begin with.[39] Chief Justice Warren, finally, though not without sympathy for the plaintiffs, found that the case in which the district court had rendered its opinion on August 29, 1968, and which the Court decided on October 15, 1968, called for "unhurried deliberation which is essential to the formulation of sound constitutional principles."[40]

I should like to sketch here only a few reactions to the majority opinions. For this, I assume that there is a constitutionally protected right to vote in presidential elections. Whatever the difficulties created by Art. II, § 1, and the narrow scope of the Fourteenth, Fifteenth, Nineteenth, and Twenty-fourth Amendments may be, it strikes me as academic to emphasize, as did Mr. Justice Stewart,[41] that the states have the right to choose their electors by methods other than popular election. Since popular election is the only method at present adopted by the states, it stands to reason that states cannot arbitrarily determine who may participate in the process, as Mr. Justice Stewart conceded.[42]

This much said, I find it very difficult to see how the right "to vote effectively" (the Court and Douglas) or the right "to associate effectively" (the Court, Douglas, and Harlan) can be the heart of the matter. Granted, Mr. Justice Black found the Ohio statutes to be in violation of the Equal Protection Clause. Granted, too, that he spoke about equal opportunities for political parties.[43] Still, the crucial point, as seen by the Court, was the fact that Ohio placed burdens on the freedom of association and the right to vote.[44] Although the Court and Mr. Justice Harlan expressed the position somewhat more moderately, Mr. Justice Douglas' words can stand for the direction of the majority's thinking: "I would think that a State has precious little leeway in making it difficult or impossible for citizens to vote for whomsoever they please and to organize campaigns for any school of thought they may choose, whatever part of the spectrum they reflect."[45] Unless the Court wanted to

---

39 *Id.* at 48.

40 *Id.* at 63.   43 *Id.* at 31.

41 *Id.* at 48.   44 *Id.* at 30.

42 *Id.* at 50.   45 *Id.* at 39.

say that the right to associate and vote effectively calls for the maxim "one man–one party" or "two men–one party," the question of which requirements may be imposed on political parties seems to be one of degree, and essentially a problem of equal political opportunities.

I find unpersuasive Mr. Justice Harlan's argument that it is the Due Process Clause rather than the Equal Protection Clause that governs the case.[46] Although it is correct that the Constitution makes exceptions to the "one man–one vote" principle in presidential elections, none of these exceptions is at stake in *Williams v. Rhodes*. I find it somewhat surprising, too, that, of all the Justices, Mr. Justice Harlan should equate the Equal Protection Clause with the "one man–one vote" principle. But more important, in the last analysis his contention that denial of participation in presidential elections violates due process is no more than an equal opportunity argument in disguise. To be sure, the right freely to form political parties as well as their constitutional status derives from a systematic interpretation of the various political rights guaranteed in the Constitution bulwarked by the fact that only political parties can provide effective representation. Yet, once this has been established, the most important question remaining is how much equality? For instance, Ohio's 15 percent requirement seems indeed aimed at depriving parties other than the two established parties of an opportunity to participate equally in the struggle for votes. Where, along the scale from one man–one party to a 15 percent requirement, invidious discrimination can be found is extremely difficult to determine, as is any measure of what will constitute equality.[47]

Mr. Justice Black considered the cumulative effect of the Ohio provisions as too burdensome for dissident voters and new political parties.[48] Although he may implicitly have recognized the right of

---

[46] *Id.* at 43. I concede that emphasis on one Clause rather than the other has, for some time, been a matter of aesthetics.

[47] Forty-two states require third parties to obtain the signatures of only 1 percent or less of the electorate to appear on the ballot. *Id.* at 33 n. 9. The German *Bundesverfassungsgericht* justifies such quotas as ways to establish that a party is a "serious" enterprise. From the vantage point of equal opportunity it will, however, not permit requirements which go beyond approximately one-quarter of 1 percent. See BVerfGE 3, 19 (1953); 4, 375 (1956). One must admire the mathematical precision with which German judges know what is required by the principle of equality.

[48] 393 U.S. at 25.

a state to protect itself against the evils of party proliferation,[49] a
system creating a monopoly for the two established parties is unconstitutional:[50]

> The fact is, however, that the Ohio system does not merely
> favor a "two-party system"; it favors two particular parties—
> the Republicans and the Democrats, and in effect tends to
> give them a complete monopoly. There is, of course, no
> reason why two parties should retain a permanent monopoly
> on the right to have people vote for or against them. Compe-
> tition in ideas and governmental policies is at the core of
> our electoral process and of the First Amendment freedoms.
> New parties struggling for their place must have the time and
> opportunity to organize in order to meet reasonable require-
> ments for ballot positions, just as the old parties have had in
> the past.

Mr. Justice Black, in effect, points to what Professor Lowi called
"the oligopolistic character of the interest-group liberal's mechanisms of representation,"[51] achieved in part through deliberately
reducing the number of competitors to the most interested and best
organized. Mr. Justice Black is well aware of the fact that this involves, to use Lowi's words once more, "some exchange of legitimacy for the false comfort of stability."[52] Preceding his condemnation of oligopoly, the Justice quoted his own observation in
Wesberry v. Sanders[53] about the link between representation and
obedience to the law: "No right is more precious in a free country
than that of having a voice in the election of those who make the
laws under which, as good citizens, we must live."[54] The language
used by Mr. Justice Black makes me doubt that the Supreme Court,
as now constituted, would consider constitutional the advantages the
two major parties provided for themselves in the Long Act. The
exclusion of minimal and new parties from a share in the presidential
campaign fund seems clearly in danger under *Williams v. Rhodes.*

---

[49] In Germany, with essentially a system of proportional representation, the
Bundesverfassungsgericht has held valid a rule excluding from representation in state
or federal parliaments parties which had not obtained at least 5 percent of the popular vote. See BVerfGE 1, 208 [256] (1952).

[50] 394 U.S. at 32.

[51] Lowi, The End of Liberalism 96 (1969).

[52] *Ibid.*

[53] 376 U.S. 1, 17 (1963).   [54] 393 U.S. at 31.

Unfortunately, because the Court relied on the cumulative effect of the Ohio provisions, it did not provide an analysis of the "democratic party structure" requirement in Ohio law which, in turn, is intimately linked to the period of time a party has to be in existence before an election. The Court found early registration objectionable. On this latter point Mr. Justice Black made a subtle argument that reveals the nonideological nature of American political parties:[55]

> Since the principal policies of the major parties change to some extent from year to year, and since the identity of the likely major party nominees may not be known until shortly before the election, the disaffected "group" will rarely if ever be a cohesive or identifiable group until a few months before the election. Thus, Ohio's burdensome procedures, requiring extensive organization and other election activities by a very early date, operate to prevent such a group from ever getting on the ballot and the Ohio system thus denies the "disaffected" not only a choice of leadership but a choice on the issues as well.

In spite of its failure to confront the problems of internal party rule,[56] this passage revealed the most serious attempt by the Court to understand the difficult question of the relationship between political parties and political representation.

In Germany, to which I now turn, such attempt has been made by the constitution itself. Art. 21 of the 1949 Basic Law provides:[57]

1. The political parties participate in the forming of the political will of the people. They may be freely established. Their internal organization must conform to democratic principles. They must publicly account for the sources of their funds.
2. Parties which, by reason of their aims or the behavior of their adherents, seek to impair or abolish the free democratic basic order or to endanger the existence of the

---

[55] *Id.* at 33.

[56] On this subject, see HORN, GROUPS AND THE CONSTITUTION 100–10 (1956).

[57] Where suitable, in translating from the German, I have retained the present tense indicative of the German original, rather than use the imperative that would be employed in English. A historical and psychological study of linguistic differences in legislation might be rewarding.

Federal Republic of Germany, are unconstitutional. The
Federal Constitutional Court decides on the question of
unconstitutionality.

3. Details will be regulated by federal laws.

Although Art. 21 has frequently been celebrated as a major innovation, it does hardly anything more than "constitutionalize" an
existing phenomenon.[58] (In view of the one-party state of the
Third Reich this is, of course, not without historical, political, and
normative significance of its own.) In addition, Art. 21 spells out
a couple of meager and vague principles at which one could have
arrived quite independently through systematic interpretation of
the constitution, with the possible exception of § 2, though American experience would deny even that. It is hard to believe that Art.
21 turns political parties into "organs of the state," and even if this
were so, nothing would follow automatically from such characterization.[59] The principle of the free establishment of parties in connection with Art. 38 (guaranteeing "general, direct, free, equal,
and secret" elections) and Art. 3 (the general principle of equality)[60] does, however, provide the constitutional bases for the mandate that political parties should have equal opportunities.[61]

On the question of political finance, Art. 21 says very little. From
the last sentence in § 1, Professor Ridder has concluded, in my view
correctly, that the drafters of the Basic Law had only conventional
methods of party finance in mind when they formulated Art. 21.[62]
Incidentally, it took the political parties until 1967, that is, almost
twenty years, to agree on legislation concerning public accounting
for funds. This came as part of the Political Parties Act of 1967

---

[58] Cf. Ridder, *Grundgesetzwidrige Wettbewerbsbeschränkungen im politischen
Prozess durch staatliche Direktfinanzierung der Parteien?* in COING, KRONSTEIN,
MESTMÄCKER (eds.), WIRTSCHAFTSORDNUNG UND RECHTSORDNUNG 21, 27 (1965). See
also HUBER, note 29 *supra.*

[59] Cf. note 31 *supra.*

[60] Art. 3 Basic Law:

"(1) All men are equal before the law.

"(2) Men and women have equal rights.

"(3) No one may be prejudiced or favored because of his sex, his descent, his race,
his language, his homeland and origin, his faith or his religious or political
opinions."

[61] Cf. Häberle, *Unmittelbare staatliche Parteienfinanzierung unter dem Grund-
gesetz,* 1967 JURISTISCHE SCHULUNG 64, 72.

[62] Ridder, note 58 *supra,* at 27–28.

(*Parteiengesetz*)[63] after the *Bundesverfassungsgericht*, in the Subsidies case,[64] had mildly censored parliament for its inaction[65] and after the entire question of public disclosure had become somewhat less relevant because, through generous public financing, the parties had become less dependent on outside sources. Earlier, legislation had been made impossible by the insistence of the Social Democrats that individual donors be named, a requirement that the business-dependent Christian Democrats and Free Democrats found all too burdensome.[66] The solution finally adopted was the result of concessions made by the Social Democrats in the era of the Great Coalition. Section 25 of the Political Parties Act called for disclosure of donors only if an individual had given more than DM 20,000 in any one year, or a corporation more than DM 200,000. Heidenheimer, in his excellent study of political finance in Germany, has accurately characterized the effects of this provision: "Under this fantastically generous formula, which all but made a mockery of the disclosure provision as a whole, just about none of the contributions even of the very largest corporate donors would need to be publicized."[67]

In 1968, in the Campaign Expenditures case, the *Bundesverfassungsgericht* reasserted that Art. 21 aimed at informing the voter about the forces "which determine party policy." The voter "shall be given the opportunity to examine the agreement existing between political platforms and the behavior of those who seek to influence political parties through financial means."[68] The reader of this highly laudable political theory is, however, considerably let down when, two paragraphs later, economic theory leads a unanimous court to the conclusion that DM 20,000 was indeed the correct limit since any lesser amount would not yield significant polit-

---

[63] 1967 Bundesgesetzblatt I 773.

[64] Hereafter I shall refer to the three major decisions of the *Bundesverfassungsgericht* in this area as the Tax Deduction case (1958), the Subsidies case (1966), and the Campaign Expenditures case (1968).

[65] BVerfGE 20, 56 [106] (1966).

[66] *Cf.* Heidenheimer, *Germany*, in Heidenheimer & Langdon, Business Associations and the Financing of Political Parties 14, 76 (1968).

[67] *Id.* at 87.

[68] BVerfGE 24, 300 [356] (1968).

ical influence. The court, although divided 5 to 3, went on to strike down the DM 200,000 limit for corporate donors with the exceedingly formal argument that the differentiation made by § 25 between natural and legal persons was arbitrary under Art. 21 and Art. 3, § 1, of the Basic Law.[69]

The intriguing story of public financing of German political parties and the courts[70] began in 1952 with an advisory opinion the *Bundesfinanzhof* (Federal Tax Court) rendered upon request of the federal minister of finance.[71] The *Bundesfinanzhof* held that business contributions to political parties were not tax deductible under existing law. Trade associations, however, could make such contributions without losing their tax-exempt status on the strikingly simple ground that representing the political interests of their members was part of their *raison d'être*. They would retain their tax-exempt status as long as contributing to political parties did not turn the business association itself into a political association (in practice this meant that an association could spend 25–30 percent of its budget for contributions). Membership fees paid by business organizations to their associations were, of course, deductible as business expenses. In short, businesses could make tax-free contributions only if they were indirect (through their association). This ingenious ruling gave business leaders the added advantage of centralizing and streamlining political support and thus creating more power than individual donors might have been able to generate. The ruling led to the immediate establishment of a tight net of conveyer organizations which controlled most political finance in the crucial early years of the Bonn Republic.[72]

The development reached its peak when, in 1954, the governing coalition (the most important members of which were the Christian

---

[69] *Id.* at 357. For the text of Art. 3, see note 60 *supra*. *Cf.* the $100-disclosure rule, the $5,000-ceiling on individual donations, and the prohibition of corporate and labor union contributions in the United States. The latter two prohibitions continue to be strongly supported by the American public. See Gallup poll of August 7, 1966 (62 percent and 57 percent, respectively). I need say nothing here about the ineffectiveness of the American law.

[70] I restrict myself to the major cases.

[71] BFHE 56, 591 (1952).

[72] For details, and in particular, for the way business leaders exercised this political power, see Heidenheimer, note 66 *supra*, at 43–71.

Democrats and the Free Democrats), over the strenuous opposition of the Social Democrats, amended the tax law to permit tax-deductible contributions for "staatspolitische Zwecke."[73] The deductions permitted were very large indeed. Individuals could deduct up to 10 percent of their income, corporations up to 5 per cent.[74] The legislation did not bring about a more direct channeling of political finance; rather, it led to further tightening of the conveyor system through the founding of the *Staatsbürgerliche Vereinigung* (Civic Association) in Cologne which served as the central collecting agency for the fifty or sixty largest firms and which also maintained branches in the *Länder*. The *Staatsbürgerliche Vereinigung* was controlled by the executives of the leading business associations.[75]

The Social Democrat most adamantly opposed to any public financing of political parties was the minister president (governor) of the SPD controlled state of Hessen, Zinn. Fighting for principle and the interests of the Social Democrats, the state of Hessen requested the *Bundesverfassungsgericht* to review the constitutionality of the tax legislation.[76]

---

[73] "Zweck" means purpose. One cannot translate "staatspolitisch" without destroying the peculiar, at the same time "principled" and "Machiavellian," flavor of the term.

[74] 1954 BUNDESGESETZBLATT I 373.

[75] Heidenheimer, note 66 *supra*, at 52.

[76] So-called abstract judicial review. Under German law (see Art. 93 Basic Law), the federal government, or a state government, or one third of the *Bundestag* have standing per se to ask for review of the constitutionality of legislation. I cannot here discuss jurisdictional and procedural details. English language literature on the *Bundesverfassungsgericht* is copious and easily available. For a legal introduction see Kauper, *The Constitutions of West Germany and the United States: a Comparative Study*, 58 MICH. L. REV. 1091, 1162–81 (1960). A recent overview by a member of the Second Senate which decided the cases here discussed, can be found in Rupp, *The Federal Constitutional Court in Germany: Scope of Its Jurisdiction and Procedure*, 44 NOTRE DAME LAW. 548 (1969). Judge Rupp is also professor of law at the University of Tübingen. Another member of the Second Senate, who has written widely in English, is Judge Leibholz, professor at the University of Göttingen. See note 29 *supra* and in particular, his *Politics and Law*, at 271–332. Judges of the court are permitted to continue as academic teachers; however, they may keep only one-third of their academic salaries (§ 101 *Bundesverfassungsgerichtsgesetz*). In Judge Leibholz' case a conflict arose between his judicial and professorial role in the Subsidies case. I shall return to the problem in my discussion of that case. An overall characterization of the Second Senate has been attempted by Kommers, *The Federal Constitutional Court in the West German Political System*, in GROSS-MAN & TANENHAUS (eds.), FRONTIERS OF JUDICIAL RESEARCH 73, 109 (1969).

The Second Senate of the *Bundesverfassungsgericht*[77] declared the tax-deduction scheme unconstitutional.[78] The decision followed one handed down the previous year by the First Senate, which had struck down a tax ordinance excluding deductions of gifts to parties not represented in the federal or a state parliament. The court held that such exclusion violated a party's basic right to equal opportunity.[79] In the Tax Deduction case the court essentially followed the arguments advanced by the government of Hessen.[80] The court said that a party's right to equal opportunity was not protected when a law guaranteed mere formal equality while its actual operation resulted in substantive inequality. Aggravation of existing inequalities had to be justified by a "compelling reason." While the state is not obliged to do anything about existing inequalities between parties, it must not act in a manner which enhances such inequalities. This, however, the 1954 tax statute did, since it favored parties which appealed to capital. "This factor becomes relevant only when the political parties clearly differ as to their goals and the means by which to achieve them, *i.e.*, when the donor who wants to protect his interests has to decide in favor of one party (or group of parties) and against another party (or group of parties)."[81]

The court's argument, based on its conception of the German party system as consisting of parties which represent clearly distinguishable interests (interests of the wealthy as against interests of the working class), is characterized by an appealing straightforwardness. And no doubt, to some extent the opinion accurately reflected the realities. In the 1957 election campaign the parties of the governing coalition were given about DM 20 million in tax-deductible business contributions while the Social Democrats re-

---

[77] The court is divided into two panels with eight judges each who, alternately, are elected by a committee of the *Bundestag* or by the *Bundesrat*, the chamber in which the *Länder* governments are represented.

[78] BVerfGE 8, 51 (1958). The judges' individual votes are not disclosed. Since 1967, the Second Senate has, however, indicated by what majority a decision had been reached.

[79] Constitutional complaint of the *Gesamtdeutsche Volkspartei*, BVerfGE 6, 273 (1957).

[80] *Cf.* Rupp, note 76 *supra*, at 554.

[81] BVerfGE 8, 51 [66].

ceived virtually nothing.[82] On the other hand, while the Christian Democrats and the Free Democrats are loosely organized parties with relatively few members and little property of their own, the SPD, the only postwar party with a prewar history, has approximately 700,000 well-organized members (1965) who are mostly industrial workers, low civil servants, and other salaried employees. In addition, the party possesses business enterprises such as large publishing houses.[83]

Although any application of the principle of equality must look at the realities, in particular the actual effects of a law, the court, unfortunately, was satisfied with an assertion about the effects, while putting its emphasis on a dubious model of German political parties. The court need not have looked beyond the flow of indirect government subsidies in one direction. Instead, the court suggested that this was due to different views held by bourgeois and socialist parties about the relationship between the individual and society,[84] surely a thicket which it was dangerous and probably illegitimate for the court to enter. In addition, the court overemphasized ideological differences as they existed then[85] and was made inaccurate only one year later by the adoption of the Bad Godesberg platform of the SPD which consciously discarded most of the Socialist past of that party.[86]

---

[82] DER SPIEGEL, note 14 *supra*, at 21.

[83] On the nature of German political parties, see EDINGER, POLITICS IN GERMANY ch. viii (1968). Membership figures and dues income of the three major parties for 1965 were estimated as follows (party, membership, income from membership dues): SPD 700,000, DM 16.2 million; CDU 300,000, DM 3.4 million; FPD 100,000, DM 1.5 million. See DER SPIEGEL, note 14 *supra*, at 21. SPD membership constituted about 7 percent of its voters, whereas the figure was only 3 percent for the CDU; EDINGER, *supra*, at 255.

[84] BVerfGE 8, 51 [66].

[85] The CDU was and is, to use Edinger's characterization, "a relatively amorphous alliance of quite heterogeneous groups. . . . The party counts among its members and leaders representatives of the Roman Catholic Church as well as prominent Protestants; it had a right wing with close ties to conservative business and agricultural interests and a left wing associated with the trade unions. It includes spokesmen for the expellees and refugees . . . and groups representing the interests of various occupational and socio-economic subsectors of German society." EDINGER, note 83 *supra*, at 240.

[86] The Bad Godesberg platform also "omitted the section of the original 1958 draft which had denounced 'the granting of huge financial resources by powerful interest groups for propaganda which befuddles the voter as to where his interests

The court was on firmer ground when it held that the incremental
provisions violated the principle of equality as it applied to individual citizens. Under a system of progressive taxation, which the
court found required by Art. 3, § 1, Basic Law, wealthy citizens
benefited from the tax deduction to the extent that some could
double their political contributions without spending more of their
own money. The governmental scheme was unconstitutional, since
it gave the wealthy an inordinate opportunity to influence politics.[87]

The tax-deduction decision of the *Bundesverfassungsgericht* displayed considerable independence. It came one year after the only
election in which the Christian Democrats obtained a popular majority of the vote and the majority of *Bundestag* seats. It had the
immediate effect of bringing a sharp decline in the income of the
Staatsbürgerliche Vereinigung and the contributions that group
could make.[88] Yet, the court had substantially sweetened the pill
which it forced the majority parties to swallow, by unnecessarily
(or compromisingly) opening its opinion with a general statement
of principles: "Since the conduct of elections is a public task, and
since the constitution assigns political parties a decisive role in its
implementation, it must be permissible to provide public funds not
only for the election campaigns, but for the parties themselves."[89]
The majority parties decided to take the hint.[90] For the first time
in 1959, the federal budget included DM 5 million for party efforts
in the area of "political education." In 1962 the amount was raised
to DM 20 million to be spent "for the tasks of political parties according to Art. 21 Basic Law." By 1964 the amount had increased

really lie.' Starting with the Hessen *Landtag* campaign of 1959, the SPD also began
to devote large resources to utilizing expensive professional methods, while by 1961,
it actually sent letters to corporations asking for the same kind of financial contributions which it had bitterly denounced only four years earlier." Heidenheimer,
note 66 *supra*, at 75–76.

[87] BVerfGE 8, 51 [68–69]. Almost identical reasoning was used by Senator Long
when he explained why he did not support President Johnson's $100 tax-deduction
proposal. 112 CONG. REC. 28765.

[88] Heidenheimer, note 66 *supra*, at 71.

[89] BVerfGE 8, 51 [63].

[90] The adoption of public financing as a means to decrease conveyer power and
its effects are considered in Heidenheimer, note 66 *supra*, at 70–71.

to DM 38 million, which was also the amount shown in the 1965 Budget Appropriations Act. In addition, some DM 12 million were distributed through *Land* and communal budgets.[91] The allocations were made over the objections of the Social Democrats. The basic key for distribution of the subsidies was the percentage of seats a party held in the *Bundestag*. Parties not represented in parliament were excluded from the subsidies in violation of the *Bundesverfassungsgericht* decision of 1957.[92]

The subsequent history of litigation about the subsidies is extremely complicated and, at stages, almost weird.[93] Except for one episode, I cannot attempt to reconstruct it here. It must suffice to mention that the litigation included suits brought by various political parties (among them the *Nationaldemokratische Partei Deutschlands*, popularly assumed to be a neo-Nazi organization). The *Bundesverfassungsgericht* hesitated to decide these cases.[94] Finally, another request for "abstract judicial review" by the minister president of Hessen, Zinn, brought a court response. After the court had first announced that it would make public its decision on July 30, 1965, the deadline was postponed several times, hearings were reopened, and the final pronouncement did not come until one year later (July 19, 1966). It has been suggested that this was because the Second Senate was evenly split and influenced by the impending election campaign of 1965.[95] There is some circumstantial evidence that the court was indeed split. Since this would normally have led to dismissal of the various suits,[96] one may assume that the Second Senate continued to seek a compromise. Rather than add guesswork of my own to the various conjectures about the court's "internal dynamics,"[97] however, let me just state the facts which have become

---

[91] *Id.* at 79.

[92] See text *supra*, at note 79.

[93] For an account see Laufer, Verfassungsgerichtsbarkeit und politischer Prozess 512–34 (1968).

[94] *Id.* at 514.

[95] *Id.* at 515.

[96] See § 15 *Bundesverfassungsgerichtsgesetz.* In the *Spiegel* case which the First Senate decided three weeks after the Subsidies case, § 15 caused the dismissal of the *Spiegel*'s constitutional complaint. See BVerfGE 20, 162 (1966).

[97] See Kommers, note 76 *supra*, at 128.

part of the public record. In view of the present American discussion about "outside" activities of judges, the case possesses more than ordinary charm.

In October, 1965, Judge Leibholz, who is also a professor of law at Göttingen University and one of the principal analysts of the *Parteienstaat*[98] read a paper, "The State and Associations," at a meeting of German professors of constitutional law in Würzburg. As Leibholz had done previously in his writings, he supported public financing of political parties. In the course of his paper, as published later, he made the following remark: "In the conflict about the financing of political parties it has become apparent how groups with a negative attitude toward our present form of democracy, have aligned themselves with liberal critics."[99] The *Nationaldemokratische Partei Deutschlands*, probably rightly so, thought that Leibholz had made reference to it. It alleged that in his oral presentation Leibholz had even spoken of an "unholy alliance," a version which Leibholz essentially confirmed in a statement to the court.[100] The NPD, along with the *Bayernpartei*,[101] which also had a suit pending, asked the court to disqualify Judge Leibholz from all further proceedings because he was "prejudiced" in the matter ("befangen," § 19 *Bundesverfassungsgerichtsgesetz*).

The *Bundesverfassungsgericht*, sitting without Leibholz, disqualified a judge for the first time in its history.[102] Potentially, such a decision can have a far-reaching impact, since a judge disqualified from a panel of the *Bundesverfassungsgericht* will not be replaced; the bench will have seven judges only. There was immediate speculation that four opponents of party financing had availed themselves of an opportunity to create a majority for their view.[103] Whether

---

[98] See note 76 *supra*.

[99] Leibholz, *Staat und Verbände*, 24 Veröffentlichungen der Vereinigung deutscher Staatsrechtslehrer 5, 19 (1966).

[100] See BVerfGE 20, 1 [4] (1966).

[101] A regional Bavarian party which, as one commentator remarked, nobody had ever suspected of being either liberal or antidemocratic. Sarstedt, *Anmerkung*, 1966 Juristenzeitung 314, 315.

[102] BVerfGE 20, 1 and 9 (March 1966).

[103] See remarks by and references in Friesenhahn, *Anmerkung*, 1966 Juristenzeitung 704, 706.

this interpretation is correct or not, the decision was extraordinary. Granted that Leibholz did not act wisely, an exclusion on the ground that such remarks created the appearance of prejudice seems unprecedented in German law.[104] Leibholz' remark, made in passing, was descriptive of only one group of many actors in an extremely complex litigation. And, as concerns the extent to which, again unwisely, Leibholz expressed legal views on party financing, he did nothing very extraordinary for, at least, the professors among German judges.

The decision to disqualify was even more intricate. The suits brought by the NPD and the *Bayernpartei* were so-called *Organstreitigkeiten*. For procedural purposes the *Bundesverfassungsgericht* considers political parties to be "constitutional organs" for which the constitution provides special proceedings (see Art. 93 Basic Law). Here certain political parties were "suing" parliament. The remedy available in such cases is a declaratory judgment that parliament had violated the constitution.[105] In the "abstract judicial review" proceedings, on the other hand, the validity of the 1965 Budget Appropriations Act itself was at stake. In the latter type of proceedings there are no official "parties to the suit." Nevertheless, in a letter, Hessen suggested that the court should bar Judge Leibholz from participating in the abstract review proceedings, so that the same bench would decide the various cases the subjects of which were undoubtedly related. The Second Senate asked Judge Leibholz for his reaction. The judge answered with a memorandum in which he stated that the government of Hessen evidently did not consider his participation in the abstract judicial review proceedings desirable. Since the court had confirmed the possibility that he might be prejudiced against the NPD and the *Bayernpartei* and since Hessen might also fear prejudice, he was prepared to withdraw from further participation in the proceedings.[106] The court chose to treat this somewhat sibylic statement as a "self-disqualification" ("Selbstablehnung," § 19 *Bundesverfassungsgerichtsgesetz*), though Leibholz had not used the term "Selbstablehnung" and in spite of the fact that a judge cannot withdraw from a proceeding if he him-

---

104 *Cf.* Sarstedt, note 101 *supra.*

105 See, *e.g.*, BVerfGE 20, 119 (1966).   106 BVerfGE 20, 26 [28–29].

self does not think he is prejudiced, which Leibholz obviously did not.[107]

Thus, after one additional hearing, the court was ready to make its decision. On July 19, 1966, it declared the subsidies provisions of the Budget Appropriations Act unconstitutional and void. It goes without saying that the court could not do this without abandoning some of the principles it had announced at the opening of its opinion in the Tax Deduction case.[108] Yet, it would be all too easy to point to the apparent contradiction between the 1958 decision and the Subsidies case which is not free of its own inconsistencies. Reading the opinion one is left with the very strong impression that doctrinal purity was sacrificed on the altar of judicial compromise.

The opinion started out, quite accurately, by disqualifying the principles announced in 1958 as mere dicta.[109] It then conceded that the federal and state parliaments had enacted their subsidy schemes in good faith since the decision in the Tax Deduction case could be understood as permitting subsidies. The court said, on the basis of the hearings in the case at bar, it had reached the conclusion that public subsidies for party activities violated Art. 21 and Art. 20, § 2, of the Basic Law.[110] Nevertheless, as in the Tax Deduction case, the Senate opened its opinion by announcing a compromise: it would be constitutional, the court said, to reimburse political parties for the necessary costs of reasonable election campaigns ("die notwendigen Kosten eines angemessenen Wahlkampfes").[111]

The reasoning behind this ruling was essentially based on the nineteenth-century distinction between state and society.[112] The court argued that the forming of the political will of the people must take place free from government influence (the term used was "staatsfrei"). Although the opinion did not show that the subsidies

---

[107] For a sharp criticism of the court by a former member of the Second Senate and professor at the University of Bonn, see Friesenhahn, note 103 *supra*. For Leibholz' own reaction see LEIBHOLZ & RUPPRECHT, BUNDESVERFASSUNGSGERICHTSGESETZ 68 (1968).

[108] See text *supra*, at note 89.

[109] BVerfGE 20, 56 [86].

[110] Art. 20, § 2 Basic Law: All state authority emanates from the people. It is exercised by the people by means of elections and voting and by specific legislative, executive, and judicial organs.

[111] BVerfGE at 20, 56 [97].

[112] For one comprehensive critique, see Häberle, note 61 *supra*.

did in fact permit government influence, the court may have had a point which, unfortunately, it expressed rather awkwardly. The court objected to creating a system of state care ("staatliche Vorsorge") for political parties since this would imply doubts about the capacity and willingness of citizens to support political parties. The argument would have been more rational had the court put forward the proposition that "forming of the political will of the people" presupposed actively involved citizens and that involvement might atrophy even further if the government financed political parties. Even if difficult to verify empirically, such argument would at least have made some sense. Yet, it could not have resolved the basic contradiction in the court's opinion, which on the one hand seemed to deny any special constitutional status of practical consequence to political parties,[113] while on the other hand permitting reimbursement of campaign costs because in a democracy elections are the decisive act of "politische Willensbildung" which cannot take place without political parties.

The distinction seems highly artificial and unmanageable. First, it is fair to assume that parties are always campaigning. Second, it should be almost impossible to distinguish between campaign expenses and running expenses (in particular, if reimbursement of the former may be staggered over several years, as provided for in § 20 Political Parties Act of 1967 which was upheld by the court in the Campaign Expenditures Case of 1968). Finally, the court will be hard put to enforce its standard of "necessary costs of a reasonable campaign." This is borne out by the court's 1968 review of the Political Parties Act which, on the basis of the costs of the 1965 election campaign, set as the standard for reimbursement DM 2.50 per qualified voter, which will be distributed in proportion to the votes obtained (§ 18 *Parteiengesetz*). This flat rate will make available approximately DM 100 million for the 1969 election campaign. The court's discussion of the flat rate in the Campaign Expenditures case is characterized by much judicial restraint and little consideration.[114] One might say, of course, that, at least for the time being,

---

113 Admitting that Art. 21 made a constitutional "institution" of political parties, the court nevertheless emphasized that they were rooted in "the social-political sphere." BVerfGE 20, 56 [101]. The court used some other arguments to distinguish sharply between state organs and political parties, governmental decision making and societal decision making. Those arguments are of no interest here.

114 BVerfGE 24, 300 [336–39].

the decision in the Subsidies case has had a moderating influence, if one assumes the *Bundestag* had continued to allocate DM 38 million annually, as it had first done in 1964. For a four-year period this would have amounted to DM 152 million; the 1969 flat rate thus represents a saving of at least DM 50 million. The only question is whether this is a constitutionally required difference and whether this price was worth the court's excursion into a political thicket from which it did not emerge unscratched.

The *Bundesverfassungsgericht* concluded its opinion in the Subsidies case with some unclear advice on how to draft constitutional legislation. The court said the principle of equal opportunities called for including all political parties participating in an election in a scheme for reimbursing campaign expenditures except that parliament might provide for a minimum vote quota (which had to be less than 5 percent, because otherwise the effect of the 5 percent exclusionary rule would be "doubled")[115] in order to prevent small groups from participating in an election merely because they would receive reimbursement of their expenditures. The court also said that it would not violate a political party's right to equal opportunities if the reimbursement rate would take into consideration "size, political importance and capacity" of a political party, since campaign expenditures were related to these factors. To give all parties the same amount of money would "distort" the actual competitive situation.[116]

The remaining developments are anticlimactic. The parties (CDU and SPD then precariously united in the Great Coalition)[117] immediately went ahead to draft and enact the Political Parties Act[118] so that they could continue to receive government subsidies in the form of "reimbursements." The statute led to an *Organstreit*[119] by the NPD[120] which here as previously effectively utilized the prop-

---

[115] *Cf.* note 49 *supra*.

[116] BVerfGE 20, 56 [117–19]. On the latter point, *cf.* the Tax Deduction case, text *supra*, at note 81.

[117] On the gradual change of Social Democratic attitudes toward public financing of political parties, which actually put the SPD leadership in opposition to Zinn's request for judicial review of the subsidies legislation, see Heidenheimer, note 66 *supra*, at 86.

[118] On the act, see text and notes following note 61 *supra*.

[119] See text *supra*, at note 105.

[120] And some other minute parties as well.

aganda potential of constitutional litigation on a highly political matter where public attitudes were opposed to the established parties.[121] The bench was differently composed this time. Judge Leibholz was participating; two other judges had been replaced.[122]

In the end, the combination of relentless party efforts to realize the *Parteienstaat* by making the state pay for the parties, with the judges' own uncertainty and conflict about the constitutional status of political parties under an ambiguous constitutional provision, proved to be too much for the court. Its attempt to develop a consistent theory of political parties and the role assigned to them in a democracy failed. The court legitimized all the important provisions of the act while, in a weak and unpersuasive gesture, by a vote of 6 to 2 it declared unconstitutional the 2.5 percent exclusionary vote quota, and by 5 to 3 struck down the DM 200,000 nondisclosure limit for corporations.[123]

These are the main features of the campaign expenditures provision in the otherwise not very innovative Political Parties Act:

1. Reimbursement for campaign expenses will be based on a flat rate of DM 2.50 per qualified voter (§ 18).[124]

2. Section 18 also provided that parties which had received less than 2.5 percent of the popular vote, were not entitled to be reimbursed for their campaign expenditures. The court admitted that its advisory remarks in the Subsidies case[125] could be interpreted so as to permit such a quota. The court, using a method it had previously employed, however,[126] translated this percentage into the *number* of votes needed and found that 835,000 was too high a figure to establish that a party had seriously campaigned. Instead, the court said, that 167,000 or 0.5 percent would be about right.[127] Although the court's approach is characterized by some subtlety, one of its problems is that it may not be subtle enough, since the opinion made the 0.5 percent quota applicable to the states as well[128] without

---

121 *Cf.* note 13 *supra.*

122 For a profile of the new judges, see DER SPIEGEL No. 31, 35 (1967).

123 On the disclosure question see text and notes following note 61 *supra.* The court also declared unconstitutional a retrospective, partial reimbursement for 1965 campaign expenses. The Political Parties Act was amended on July 22, 1969, to conform with the decision. See 1969 BUNDESGESETZBLATT I 925.

124 See text *supra,* at note 114.

125 See text *supra,* at note 115.

126 See cases cited note 47 *supra.*

127 BVerfGE 24, 300 [339–43].

128 *Id.* at 353.

translating 0.5 percent into numbers of votes needed. In Nordrhein-Westfalen, the largest state, the percentage would amount to approximately 57,000 votes, while in Bremen, the smallest state, only 2,265 votes would constitute the quota. It is an open question how much serious campaigning it takes to persuade 2,265 Bremen voters to vote for one's party in a state election. The *Bundesverfassungsgericht* may have come very close to a "two men–one party" principle of its own.

3. Section 18 *Parteiengesetz* determined the key for the distribution of public funds to be the proportion of votes received. The court, over one dissent, accepted this key, though it indicated some misgivings in view of its decisions concerning the distribution of radio and television time[129] where it had permitted differentiations according to the relative "importance" of parties but had also warned against perpetuating the status quo and suggested that a common minimum of free time was constitutionally desirable, if not required.[130] The court overcame these misgivings by referring to legislative discretion without explaining where the constitutional structure yields a "compelling reason" which would justify the aggravation of existing inequalities[131] by giving a greater share of public funds to the strongest in the struggle for votes. The court never discussed whether the perpetuation of the status quo through governmental means, which the distribution key may involve owing to the marginal utility of additional funding, constitutes such aggravation or not. Instead, the court reiterated the guidelines provided in the Subsidies case[132] and found that the truest measure of a party's significance was the number of votes received. This had the advantage of making the voter decide which party should receive what reimbursement. Whether a party's "significance" constitutes a constitutionally sufficient reason seems highly doubtful. To be sure, to give every party the same amount of money would "distort the actual competitive situation,"[133] but an *argumentum ad absurdum* can hardly be sufficient to justify the specific mode of differentiation

---

[129] The German broadcasting industry is owned by government corporations.

[130] *Cf., e.g.,* BVerfGE 14, 121 (1962).

[131] For these standards, see BVerfGE 6, 273 [280] (1957); 8, 51 [67], and text *supra,* following note 80.

[132] See text *supra,* at note 116.   [133] BVerfGE 24, 300 [344].

adopted by parliament. Most certainly, it is not an excuse to abandon the search for a constitutionally satisfactory solution for public financing that does not raise serious problems under the equal opportunities standard.

The reasoning that under the § 18 distribution key the voter decides what is the true importance of a party misses the question whether the voter may discriminate against smaller parties the way parliament permits him to. The effect of the voter's retrospective "judgment" is compounded by the scheme of staggered advances under which parties which participated in the last election will receive 60 percent of the reimbursements they may be entitled to in the three years preceding the election (§ 20 *Parteiengesetz*). This key seems seriously to impair the equal opportunities of parties which did not do well or did not participate at all in the previous election. The Political Parties Act does not even display the minimum sense of fairness that characterized the Long Act. The Long Act treated at least the two most serious competitors for governmental power equally. Under the German scheme the Social Democrats will receive approximately DM 5.5 million less in advances than the Christian Democrats. I do not know the marginal utility of that amount, but the added advantage of advances generally is obvious when one compares the advances for the Christian Democrats and Social Democrats (DM 28.8 million and DM 23.4 million, respectively; DM 52.2 million combined) with the advance of some DM 6 million which the only opposition party in the pre-election *Bundestag*, the Free Democrats, will receive. The *Bundesverfassungsgericht* approved this scheme with no detailed analysis. The doctrinal arguments made in upholding a system of staggered advances as such, on which the court spent most of its labors, constitute a direct reversal of the theories about the role of political parties developed in the Subsidies case of 1966. The court reached its decision on § 20 *Parteiengesetz* by a vote of 5 to 3. Very likely the three dissenters were part of the 1966 majority.[134]

Reading the court's opinion, I am left with a sense of great unease about the discrepancy between the court's lofty rhetoric on how equal opportunities for the parties and the "existing competitive situation" must not be distorted by governmental action, and the court's failure to examine reimbursements critically as to their polit-

---

[134] *Id.* at 347–53.

ical effects.[135] Seen in terms of the dynamics of the German political system, it may simply be the case that the court had deprived itself of an opportunity to consider seriously the "establishing" effects of §§ 18 and 20 *Parteiengesetz* because of the erratic manner, characterized by compromising obiter dicta, in which it had decided the earlier cases. But it may be equally true that, with respect to public financing of political parties, the court merely desired to rejoin the mainstream of the *Parteienstaat,* which turned out to be a very powerful stream indeed. I, of course, do not want to belittle the court's success in at least securing *unequal* opportunities for all political parties.

---

[135] It is ironic that the court, in the Campaign Expenditures case, also upheld §§ 34 and 35 *Parteiengesetz* which made contributions to political parties in the amount of up to DM 600 annually by individuals and corporations (DM 1,200 for married couples filing joint returns) *tax deductible.* The court considered the amount insignificant and also found, that the tax deduction would not operate in a discriminatory manner because the parties had become more alike. *Id.* at 357–61. However this may be (and it is doubtful), granting tax relief of up to DM 300, according to the court's own computation, most certainly means providing a subsidy, not reimbursement for campaign expenditures.

MARGARET K. ROSENHEIM

SHAPIRO v. THOMPSON:

"THE BEGGARS ARE COMING

TO TOWN"

> Hark! Hark! The dogs do bark;
> The beggars are coming to town.
> Some gave them white bread;
> And some gave them brown,
> And some gave them a good horsewhip,
> And sent them out of town.[1]

The nursery jingle puts the problem: the public is—and has been—divided and ambivalent about the proper response to dependent persons. Beggars, paupers, public assistance recipients—call them what we may—sorely tax both public purse and private conscience. In the 1968 Term the Supreme Court of the United States issued its first opinion on the constitutionality of a condition of eligibility for public assistance. My aim in discussing *Shapiro v. Thompson*[2] is to relate it to welfare policy for, though I was trained in law, my professional experience is limited to study of social legislation and administration. Analysis of *Shapiro*'s contribution to constitutional doctrine must await another author.

Margaret K. Rosenheim is Professor in the School of Social Service Administration, University of Chicago.

I wish to acknowledge the assistance and support of the Center for the Study of Welfare Policy in the School of Social Service Administration, University of Chicago, during the period of preparation of this article.—M. K. R.

[1] As quoted in 2 TREVELYAN, HISTORY OF ENGLAND 32–33 (Anchor ed. 1952).

[2] 394 U.S. 618 (1969).

If any aspect of the American public aid scene had seemed to be permanent, it was the durational residence requirement. Like the means test, this feature derived from the Elizabethan Poor Law. It had been part of the states' poor relief laws from the beginning.[3] Only once, for the brief period of the Federal Emergency Relief Administration during the Great Depression, had the burden of meeting a residence requirement been lifted in a means-test program.[4] To be sure, there had been a liberalizing trend since 1935.[5] Now, as a result of *Shapiro v. Thompson* and companion cases, the durational test has been shot down, an early casualty in what promises to be an extended campaign against conditions on public assistance.

I. Background of Shapiro

The programs immediately affected by *Shapiro* share a common denominator. Heir to the Poor Law tradition, they are characterized by assessment of need (as defined by locality or state) and payment of variable amounts dependent upon case-by-case determination of the gap between need and available resources. Discretion heavily infuses the administration of these programs. As compared to the objective entitlement conditions and detailed benefit schedules of social insurance, public assistance calls for subjective deter-

---

[3] Abbott, Public Assistance 133–55 (1940). Nearly one-half of Miss Abbott's introduction to documents on the old poor law was devoted to the evils of settlement and removal provisions.

[4] Report of the Select Committee of the House of Representatives Investigating the Interstate Migration of Destitute Citizens, H.R. Rep. No. 369, 77th Cong., 1st Sess. 592–606 (1941).

[5] In order to participate in the federal-state categorical assistance titles, most states had to liberalize their residence requirements. A few states have abolished or modified waiting-period tests since World War II. See Note, *Residence Requirements in State Public Welfare Statutes*, 51 Iowa L. Rev. 1080, 1082 (1966). The latest needs-related title to be added to the Social Security Act, Medicaid (title XIX), prohibits "any residence requirement which excludes any individual who resides in the State." 42 U.S.C. § 1396a(b)(3) (Supp. IV, 1968). It is not an income-maintenance program, of course, but bears intimate relationship to the cash payment titles insofar as medical care is a prime factor generating indigency. Prior to Medicaid, a study conducted in New York State of public assistance recipients who had lived in the state less than one year revealed that 60 percent required only hospitalization. Note, *Residence Requirement for Public Relief: An Arbitrary Prerequisite*, 2 Colum. J. Law & Soc. Prob. 133, 135 (1966).

mination of status and for continuing review of both need and other aspects of eligibility.[6]

Specifically, the opinion deals with two of the four income-maintenance categorical assistance titles established by the Social Security Act—Aid to Families with Dependent Children (AFDC)[7] and Aid to the Permanently and Totally Disabled (APTD).[8] The remaining programs, Aid to the Blind (AB)[9] and Old Age Assistance (OAA),[10] round out the income-maintenance categories for which federal matching funds are available.[11] Combined, they account for most of the "residual" poor in receipt of public income support, and of the four AFDC is the dominant category. Relatively few indigents are relegated to the wholly nonfederal program of general assistance (GA) maintained in every state.[12]

I shall ordinarily use the term "welfare" to mean public assistance. But these so-called categorical aids do not exhaust the range of what is conveniently (though inaccurately) termed the welfare "system." At a minimum, that phrase connotes a heterogeneous collection of social insurance and public assistance programs disbursing cash, health, and medical benefits "in kind," as well as such direct service programs as child welfare, vocational rehabilitation, and school meals (to cite a few examples).[13] The dominant elements in the panoply of welfare benefits, whether measured by expenditures or persons affected, are the several social insurances. Public assistance occupies a small corner of this untidy and by no means comprehensive "system." In 1966–67, for example, public aid expenditures approached $9 billion; social insurance benefits exceeded $37 billion.[14] The beneficiaries of the social insurance and veterans' pro-

---

6 tenBroek & Wilson, *Public Assistance and Social Insurance—a Normative Evaluation,* 1 U.C.L.A. REV. 237 (1954).

7 42 U.S.C. §§ 601–09 (1964).   9 *Id.* at §§ 1201–06.

8 *Id.* at §§ 1351–55.   10 *Id.* at §§ 301–06.

11 Title XVI, the so-called combined category, authorizes a state's combining aid in the three adult categories for administrative simplicity. *Id.* at §§ 1381–85. It does not create a new class of recipients. The combination is feasible because of the similarity in plan requirements and matching formulas applicable to the adult categories. AFDC is very much in a class by itself.

12 As of January, 1969, there were 850,000 GA recipients; there were 600,000 in 1950.

13 See Soc. SEC. BULL. ANNUAL STATISTICAL SUPPLEMENT, Table 3, p. 14 (1967).

14 *Id.,* Table 1, p. 13.

gram—over thirty-three million—outnumbered public aid recipients, the latter then totaling less than ten million persons of whom over one-half were under AFDC (and four-fifths of these were children).[15]

Nonetheless, it is public assistance that attracts heated criticism. The social insurances are relatively immune from controversy and dissatisfaction. Such contests as do arise appear to be containable within the established internal adjustment procedures. Such discontent as relates to benefit level typically finds expression through organized interest groups. On the whole, Congress and the state legislatures have responded to complaints with steady, if slow and modest, increases in persons and conditions covered and in average benefits. Social insurance is an entrenched "middle-class" program, based on "right." Public assistance is "charity."[16] Whatever terminology is used does not disguise the fact that it is the last resort of the poor.[17] Nor does it alter the ambiguous position of those who partake thereof. In America: "Poverty itself is slightly disreputable, and being on welfare somewhat more disreputable . . . [and] the 'hard core' [of demoralized and immoral poor] is further along on a range of disrepute."[18]

The most recent rediscovery of poverty[19] in the United States has coincided with the civil rights movement. The poor are seen as victims of fate or active prejudice, as are minority groups. In

---

15 *Id.*, Table 9, p. 18, and Table 128, p. 124. This is the crudest kind of count. A number of public assistance recipients get social insurance benefits; some insurance beneficiaries, also, are entitled to payments under more than one program. Comparable data as of January, 1969, reveal a substantial increase in AFDC, but the proportion of child to adult recipients remains the same. WELFARE IN REVIEW 51 (May–June 1969).

16 Friedman, *Social Welfare Legislation: An Introduction*, 21 STAN. L. REV. 217, 228–29 (1969).

17 Organized charity's role in providing financial aid has atrophied since 1935. See STEINER, SOCIAL INSECURITY 8–17 (1966). It is charged that these voluntary agencies increasingly serve a middle-class clientele. Cloward & Epstein, *Private Social Welfare's Disengagement from the Poor: The Case of Family Adjustment Agencies*, in ZALD, ed., SOCIAL WELFARE INSTITUTIONS 623 (1965).

18 Matza, *Poverty and Disrepute*, in MERTON & NISBET, eds., CONTEMPORARY SOCIAL PROBLEMS 620 (2d ed. 1966). Oscar Wilde identified the difficulty some years ago: "As for the virtuous poor, one can pity them, of course, but one cannot possibly admire them." WILDE, SOUL OF MAN UNDER SOCIALISM (1910) (unpaged).

19 Matza, note 18 *supra*, at 637, referring to Pitirim Sorokin's statement about the "Columbus complex" of rediscovery.

fact, of course, many of the poor (though not the majority)[20] are
members of racial minorities. Economic dependency exacerbates the
vulnerability of persons who rely on public agencies for help. The
poor are not the only citizens who depend on the discretionary
judgment of officials, but the poor are dependent for the necessities
of life. It is said, moreover, that the lack of resources heightens their
sense of grievance and increases the potential for injustice which
inheres in these relationships. Advocates of improved life situations
for the poor see at least a partial solution in transforming benefit
programs into "rights," using the social insurance approach of entitlement. Such a drive offers fertile soil for the talents of lawyers,
and in the welfare rights movement, spin-off of contemporary concern for the dispossessed and disadvantaged, the adversary methods
of the lawyer have been creatively exploited.[21] *Shapiro v. Thompson* and *King v. Smith*[22] are evidence that the welfare woes of the
indigent can compel even the attention of the United States Supreme Court.

II. RESIDENCE AND SETTLEMENT TESTS UNDER THE POOR LAW

The Poor Law was of parochial origin. It was locally devised, supported, and administered. It evolved from a well-articu-
lated body of canon law and centuries of church experience in dispensing relief.[23] The landmark statute of 1601,[24] traditionally identified as the beginning of public responsibility for relief of the
destitute, is more accurately characterized as a consolidating act.
But even if some of the rhetoric is inaccurate, its importance is
undeniable:[25]

> Through it, the final step was taken, permanently shifting a
> part of the burden to relieve economic distress from the
> ecclesiastical, private, and voluntary, to the civil, public, and
> compulsory. The assumption of responsibility, moreover, was
> made by the nation, and its application was nationwide.

---

[20] Orshansky, *The Shape of Poverty in 1966*, Soc. SEC. BULL. 3, 4 (March, 1968).

[21] See Sparer, *The Role of the Welfare Client's Lawyer*, 12 U.C.L.A. L. REV. 361
(1965); Reich, *Individual Rights and Social Welfare: The Emerging Issues*, 74
YALE L.J. 1245 (1965).

[22] 392 U.S. 309 (1968).

[23] TIERNEY, MEDIEVAL POOR LAW (1959).   [24] 43 Eliz. 1, c.2 (1601).

[25] tenBroek, *California's Dual System of Family Law: Its Origin, Development,
and Present Status*, 16 STAN. L. REV. 257, 262 (1964).

Consistent with the Tudor method of extending central governmental powers, local officials (principally the unpaid justices of the peace) were used for administration. They were vested with the power to assess and collect taxes in support of the poor of the parish. In tenBroek's words:[26]

> One immediate and long-range consequence of this distribution of authority, administration, and cost was that great reliance was placed on settlement and removal provisions. These served to identify the community responsible for providing support in each case and to keep down relief expenditures. Only those who had been born in a community or had long lived there were eligible. . . . The size of the taxing and paying unit thus was determinative.

There are obvious similarities with the welfare structure we have today. Yet we should not be beguiled by historical parallels into overlooking differences in social and economic conditions to which residency and settlement laws[27] make response, both in terms of formal coverage and of administrative implementation.

The germ of present legislation is to be found in a fourteenth-century enactment proscribing begging by the able-bodied. It ordered an able-bodied person to remain and labor "in the hundred, rape or wapentake where he is dwelling."[28] The impotent poor were to remain where resident or born. Two centuries later, in the germinal period of poor relief legislation, no special note was taken of settlement. It was assumed that eligibility would ordinarily be lim-

---

[26] Id. at 265.

[27] Settlement is the older term referring to acquisition of domicile in a locality. See Riesenfeld, *The Formative Era of Public Assistance Law*, 43 CALIF. L. REV. 175, 181–98 (1955). Residence, the newer concept in public welfare law, refers to the establishment of a place of abode with intent to remain in a state. Categorical assistance waiting-period requirements are phrased in terms of state residence. The usual controversy today concerns a contest over nonresponsibility between states, as the Court noted in *Shapiro*, 394 U.S. at 628 n. 7. Nevertheless, settlement remains, in many state welfare programs which are financed partially out of local taxation, an important concept; the distinction, not always drawn in the literature, lies between settlement as "a prerequisite for relief" and as a means to determine "only the ultimate allocation of the burden." Riesenfeld, *supra*, at 227–28.

[28] 12 Rich. 2, c.3, c.7 (1388). Poor relief legislation has been closely related to that which regulates begging and vagabondage. Indeed, in the early periods of development they are inseparable. See LEONARD, THE EARLY HISTORY OF ENGLISH POOR RELIEF 64–66 (1900); Rosenheim, *Vagrancy Concepts in Welfare Law*, 54 CALIF. L. REV. 511 (1966).

ited to long-time residents. The innovations of the Elizabethan era concerned other targets—relatives' responsibility (including that of fathers for their illegitimate offspring) and productive activity for the able-bodied.[29]

The next phase of settlement legislation dates from 1622, with the famous Act of Settlement[30] setting a stringent financial test for residence and initiating the oppressive practice of removal. For the first time[31] prohibition of population mobility was combined with the principle of conveying back. The result was "the most extreme and cruel form of localism that England had known previously or has known since."[32] Of great significance is the fact that no longer was the stranger—the lone predator of earlier unsettled times —the target of legislation. Parliament was instead concerned with the mobility of whole families and the consequent burden of their relief, a burden that was unevenly distributed among the parishes.

The preamble to the act of 1662 notwithstanding,[33] historians of the period generally agree that the acute relief problem was concentrated in a few cities, and most particularly in the London region. Unsettled paupers were the flotsam in a growing pool of non-agricultural labor drawn to the cities by the prospect of better employment and the associated lures of housing and livelier social intercourse. Modification of the harshness of the 1662 provisions is suggestive that Parliament had overreached its target. Full enforcement of the law would have prohibited change in residence, by Marshall's estimate, of the greater part of the lower working

---

29 WEBB & WEBB, ENGLISH LOCAL GOVERNMENT: ENGLISH POOR LAW HISTORY, PART I: THE OLD POOR LAW 54–65 (1927).

30 13 & 14 Chas. 2, c.12 (1662).

31 More accurately, the act of 1662 "is a curious instance of the adoption by statute of a custom which had long existed. The custom had been enforced without statutory authority while the town government continued to possess semi-independent powers, but it could not be enforced without statutory authority in later times. . . . This practice of preventing settlement has a far closer connection with the social order of the reign of Elizabeth than with that of Charles II. It was a great hardship to the poor, but it was hardship to which they had long been partially accustomed and which fitted in with the economic policy of the towns." LEONARD, note 28 *supra*, at 109.

32 DE SCHWEINITZ, ENGLAND'S ROAD TO SOCIAL SECURITY 39 (1943).

33 "Whereas . . . poor people . . . do endeavor to settle themselves in those parishes where there is the best stock, the largest commons or wastes to build cottages and the most woods for them to burn and destroy. . . ." 13 & 14 Chas. 2, c.12 (1662), quoted in DE SCHWEINITZ, note 32 *supra*, at 39–40.

class as well as those who were actually chargeable.[34] The amendatory provisions of 1696–97, therefore, excused entrants bearing certificates of legal settlement from their "home" parishes. Application for aid—a claim on public authorities for relief of destitution —was necessary before the removal process could be set in train.[35]

We are handicapped in our judgment of the purposes served by settlement provisions by lack of information. We suffer from inadequate knowledge of poor law administration. Reliant, perforce, upon a small body of statutory materials supplemented with fragments of contemporary and historical writing, we can only hazard a guess as to the effect and broad social consequences of particular measures. Even so, this exercise raises doubts as to the validity of a single thesis about the function of residency or settlement tests. Holdsworth pointed out their relationship to other economic conditions:[36]

> It is clear that the evil effects of these restrictions will be more and more severely felt as the number of wage earners, and the fluctuations of trade, increase with the growth of the capitalistic organization of industry, and the greater freedom of trade which resulted therefrom. Moreover, the fact that the poorer classes were put under these disabilities tended to give them a peculiar status; and . . . this strengthened existing tendencies to regard those in receipt of parish relief, not as a class which was receiving a benefit to which it had a legal right, but as a class to which the stigma of disability was attached.

A final effort to tie the laboring class to the land, a means of restricting begging, indirect restraints on strangers, limitation of the parish relief burden—these are some of the purposes attributed to the tests. There is an additional function in a federal system, where residency tests serve to allocate fiscal responsibility within a three-tiered governmental structure.

Understandably, the importance of the last-named function has increased concurrently with the rise in federal welfare responsibilities, i.e., since 1935. Prior thereto, developments in the relief laws of the states generally paralleled the English experience. The original colonies found a model in 43 Elizabeth I.[37] tenBroek commented: "In a land where free movement and the open frontier

---

[34] MARSHALL, THE ENGLISH POOR IN THE EIGHTEENTH CENTURY 1–2 (1926).

[35] 6 HOLDSWORTH, A HISTORY OF ENGLISH LAW 352 (1924).

[36] Id. at 353.   [37] RIESENFELD, note 27 supra, at 176–77.

were determinative forces in shaping the nation, the poor were still bound to the places of their misfortune, held immobile by rigid rules of settlement and removal, and locked in poorhouses, attempted escape from which resulted in solitary confinement on bread and water."[38]

It could be argued that "free movement and the open frontier" were the very factors which in America materially altered the significance of similar statutory provisions. Indeed, public aid measures were not perceived as national problems until the twentieth-century depression. Nor is there much evidence of sustained concern in either state or local government before the 1920's.[39] It was the immigrant, more than the pauper (settled or not), who was the focus of public alarm. Provision for bonding of shipmasters and deportation of aliens were among the statutory responses to the specter of invasion by the diseased, criminal, and improvident.

Within the states, attention centered on "rationalization" of public welfare administration. The movement away from local toward state administration began in the early 1800's. It was vastly expedited by the rise of modern technology and the eruption of social problems in the aftermath of the Civil War. The era of public institutionalization commenced with state provision for those wards thought peculiarly its responsibility (juvenile offenders, the mentally ill and deficient, the unsettled poor, and criminals, among

---

[38] tenBroek, note 25 *supra*, at 297–98.

[39] To the extent that settlement was at issue it resulted from the fact that poor relief was local relief, without significant exception, until well into the nineteenth century, when state institutions and private charity began to take part of the burden off of towns and cities. Even so, state institutions often were required to charge back the cost of institutional care to the county, a practice which sometimes deterred the county from removing indigents in need of specialized treatment from the local almshouse and sending them to the more expensive state institution. See, *e.g.*, the account of continued use of county almshouses for the mentally ill after the establishment of state hospitals in New York. Deutsch, The Mentally Ill in America 252–54 (2d ed. 1949).

I do not intend to suggest that settlement provisions were unimportant, or that litigation thereunder was not extensive, costly, and focused on issues some of which appear incredibly arcane to modern eyes. See generally Mandelker, *The Settlement Requirement in General Assistance*, 1955 Wash. U. L.Q. 355, 1956 Wash. U. L.Q. 21. I would venture to suggest, however, that the evils have been exaggerated, see Hampson, *Settlement and Removal in Cambridgeshire, 1662–1834*, 2 Cam. Hist. J. 273, 289 (1928), and that criticism directed solely at the abuses revealed in the records of denials and removals missed an important target, viz., the repressive effects of settlement laws on persons who did not move.

others). The larger cities also established congregate facilities, usually for an undifferentiated population of the poor and "nuisance" deviants. President Pierce's 1854 veto of an act of Congress to allocate federal land for care of the mentally ill, the culmination of hard-fought campaigning by the indefatigable Dorothea Dix,[40] forestalled federal participation in welfare efforts, save for persons who were unquestioned obligations of the national government. It guaranteed a growing role for the states.

Settlement and removal laws were old themes running along in counterpoint to the dominant themes of a maturing welfare system. The pressing welfare issues of the nineteenth century were flagrant corruption, competition among the emerging professions for the public accolade of expertise in welfare, and adaptation of social institutions to the novel demands of life in the city. Work opportunity could generally be found; the relief "problem" centered on those identified by Sophonisba Breckinridge, even as recently as 1927, as "individuals who labor *under some special disadvantage*, in whose behalf recognized principles of relief have been developed."[41]

The welfare problem, as she stated it, arose because:[42]

> [As between social and other public services it could be said that] in addition to the principles of efficient economical administration that should characterize all public organization, in the case of each of these groups there is a body of professional practice to be acquired and applied. At the same time that this is true, it must also be recognized that the nature of the service—institutional care; relief in the home; care and treatment of children, of the aged, and of the mentally deficient—offers a great number and variety of opportunities for dishonest and corrupt practices.

In summary, settlement and removal procedures appear to have occupied American relief agencies relatively less than in England. There are exceptions clustered in the records of New England and the Middle Atlantic states. Nor is this surprising in light of their strategic location as prime ports of entry from abroad and populous centers of industry whose need for a mobile, increasingly skilled labor force would have the natural effect of attracting people to jobs.

---

[40] See DEUTSCH, note 39 *supra*, at 176–79.

[41] Preface to First Edition, BRECKINRIDGE, PUBLIC WELFARE ADMINISTRATION vii (2d ed. 1938). (Emphasis supplied.)

[42] *Ibid.*

A changing perception of state responsibility toward the poor—
and the depression—altered welfare patterns. The plight of the
Okies generated a reaction of shock and shame that the suffering
of children in North Carolina textile mills had failed to stimulate
some years earlier. Newspapers, weekly magazines, and radio joined
the nation in a common experience of suffering with victims of
bank failures in Florida, apple-sellers on Wall Street, and dispossessed mortgagors in North Dakota.

The public assistance titles of the 1935 Social Security Act were
as much intended—then—for the "submerged middle-class" as were
the titles authorizing state unemployment compensation plans and
creating a national social security system. In fact, it was precisely
the submerged middle class for whom categorical assistance was
meant.[43] It, alone, promised short-run relief from destitution, since
the maturity of the social insurances lay in the future. Is it accidental
that Title I of the act is Old Age Assistance? Statutes are designed
to present politically attractive features first. OAA introduced the
act, Old Age Insurance was second, and Unemployment Compensation third. Aid to Families with Dependent Children then appeared fourth. Reaction in state legislatures to enactment of the
federal statute was swift. OAA was quickly enacted by the states
and AFDC, while slower to gain public acceptance, was in effect
by 1945 in every jurisdiction but Alaska and Nevada.

The congressional scheme contemplated continuation of the residence test, authorized in the relief laws of nearly all jurisdictions
at the time, but with an important change: the maximum durational
periods were lowered well below those generally prevailing.[44] This
period was limited, in AFDC, to one year immediately preceding
application,[45] and to five out of the last nine years in the adult cat-

---

[43] And specifically the aged. Steiner, note 17 *supra*, at 18–21.

[44] Hearings on S. 1130, Economic Security Act, before the Senate Committee on
Finance, 74th Cong. 1st Sess., Table 15, facing p. 50 (1935).

[45] 42 U.S.C. § 602(b) (1964). The one-year maximum waiting period, while lower
than that allowed under the adult categories, conformed to laws existing at the
time in twenty-seven of the forty-nine jurisdictions which had mothers' aid laws
on the books. Only two states had durational periods in excess of three years. In
testimony before the House Ways and Means Committee, the executive director
of the Committee on Economic Security, Edwin Witte, explained: "[W]e have
never started in this country with long residence requirements, because these families, wherever they are, obviously must be taken care of. The point to be kept in
mind is that this not really a mothers' pension [*sic*]. It is aid toward the care of

egories.[46] This was only one of the significant changes between the federal legislation and that generally prevailing in the states. Another—of greater immediate budgetary impact, it may be supposed[47]—was the requirement that a categorical program for which the state sought federal matching funds be in effect throughout all political subdivisions of the state.[48] This banned the use of "local option" in the federal categories. No longer could assistance for the aged, for example, be available in a few of the most populous counties of the state but not elsewhere. Nor could program standards vary within a state.[49] Uniformity of policy within a state was a cardinal (though implicit) principle underlying the "state plan" requirements.

There were several courses of action that Congress did not pursue. It did not establish a federal obligation to relieve indigency per se. It did not establish assistance for the employable. It authorized a national social insurance system for persons who were already outside the labor market (or whose exit was desired). Wage-related, with benefits tied to a statutory schedule, it was intended to deal with presumptive need. The act also encouraged establishment by the states of a social insurance program for the victims of unemployment. Otherwise, federal assumption of responsibility for in-

---

these unfortunate children who have been deprived of a father's support. . . . They must be taken care of, regardless of residence requirements." Hearings on H.R. 4120, Economic Security Act, before the House Ways and Means Committee, 74th Cong. 1st Sess., 161 (1935).

[46] 42 U.S.C. § 302(b) (OAA); 42 U.S.C. § 1202(b) (AB). Subsequently, APTD was added as a fourth income-maintenance category with a similar five-out-of-nine maximum. 42 U.S.C. § 1351(b) (1964).

[47] Testimony before the Senate Committee on Finance by Edwin Witte revealed that, in all of the twenty-eight states then having what were known as old-age pension laws, "only some of the counties actually are paying old-age pensions." Hearings on S. 1130, note 44 supra, at 61. Most old people at the time were being assisted under general relief provisions. It should be recalled that old age assistance was a method of categorizing the aged for better treatment than that available through ordinary relief channels. Even the administrative structure was separate in a number of states, e.g., county judge, old-age pension commission, trustees of old-age assistance fund. Id. Table 15, facing p. 50.

[48] "A State plan . . . must (1) provide that it shall be in effect in all political subdivisions of the State, and, if administered by them, be mandatory upon them." 42 U.S.C. § 602(a) (1964) (AFDC). Identical provisions are found in the adult categories.

[49] Note that this means uniformity within a category as administered in a state. Differentials among states and between categories have long existed, of course.

digents was limited to three categories of the prima facie unemployable:[50] the aged, the blind, and children dependent because of the
"death, continued absence from the home, or physical or mental
incapacity of a parent."

Thus, there was no "relief" for intact families headed by unemployed adults. Nor did Congress authorize supplementation of
wages in behalf of families of extraordinary size or need, or families
whose income was unusually small. In fact, the adult caretaker of
qualified dependent children was originally excluded from coverage
under AFDC.[51] The only destitute adults for whose support federal
funds were authorized in 1935 were the blind and the aged, though
the indirect benefit of AFDC payments to adult caretakers must
have been clear to legislators and administrators of the time.

Residency was a factor of administration in all but one program
of the act and in all the newly established categories. As a national
system, Old Age Insurance established certain conditions of entitlement, but state residency or settlement was not among them. It
was intended to create vested rights, portable throughout the economy, in persons working in "covered" employment. The remaining
titles, however, were permissive with respect to state requirements
on residence. The categorical assistance titles set a durational period,
albeit a greatly liberalized one, within which states were free to use
a residency test or not. Similarly, with respect to unemployment
compensation, the states were granted latitude in establishing the
conditions of entitlement: length of time worked in covered employment, type of employment covered, amount of wages earned,
class of beneficiaries, length of time within the state. The analogue
of certain of these entitlement conditions to a test for residence is
apparent. They have not yet been challenged.

III. THE "BEGGARS" STAY IN TOWN: SHAPIRO,
     WASHINGTON, AND REYNOLDS

The three cases consolidated for decision by the Court arose
under similar statutes. Each conformed to the "state plan requirements" of the Social Security Act,[52] and each jurisdiction's "state

---

[50] STEINER, note 17 *supra*, at 5–6.   [51] *Id*. at 25.

[52] The applicable statutory language directs the Secretary of HEW not to approve
any plan with a residence requirement which, in the case of AFDC, "denies aid with
respect to any child residing in the State (1) who has resided in the State for one

plan" for the categories at issue had secured approval of the Department of Health, Education, and Welfare. Probable jurisdiction was noted,[53] and the cases were initially argued during the 1967 Term. Reargument followed in October, 1968, and the decision was rendered April 2, 1969. Affirming the judgment below in each of the three cases, the Court found unconstitutional relevant statutory provisions that denied assistance to residents of the jurisdiction who had not resided therein for one year preceding application. The provisions were held to violate the Equal Protection Clause of the Fourteenth Amendment or the Due Process Clause of the Fifth Amendment.

In the title case Vivian Thompson, a nineteen-year-old pregnant unwed mother of one child, an erstwhile recipient of AFDC in Boston, had moved from that city to Hartford, Connecticut, to be near her mother. Upon arrival in June, 1966, she lived with her mother, moving into her own apartment in August when her mother could no longer support her and her son. At that time she filed for assistance. It was denied in November solely because of the residence requirement. The Connecticut statute provided for the usual one-year waiting period. Temporary relief, however, was available to "any person [who] comes into this state without visible means of support for the immediate future." But this form of relief was contingent on the recipient's acceptance of a plan for "voluntary return" to the last prior place of residence.[54] By regulation applicants "without visible means of support for the immediate future"

---

year immediately preceding the application for such aid, or (2) who was born within one year immediately preceding the application, if the parent or other relative with whom the child is living has resided in the State for one year immediately preceding the birth." 42 U.S.C. § 602(b) (1964).

The statute, in the case of adult categories, withholds approval of a plan which "excludes any resident of the State who has resided therein five years during the nine years immediately preceding the application for old-age assistance and has resided therein continuously for one year immediately preceding the application." *Id.* at § 302(b)(2).

[53] 389 U.S. 1032 (1968) in Shapiro v. Thompson, 390 U.S. 940 (1968) in Washington v. Legrant and Reynolds v. Smith. The cases were argued May 1, 1968, 36 U.S. L. Week 3421 (1968), restored to the calendar for reargument, 390 U.S. 920 (1968), and reargued October 23–24, 1968, 37 U.S. L. Week 3153 (1968).

[54] 1 Conn. Welfare Manual Ch. II, § 219.3, set forth in Appellant's Brief in *Shapiro* at 9, 23. See also Amicus Brief, Legal Aid Society of Alameda County, 15; Amicus Brief, Center on Social Welfare Policy and Law, 7, 15; Mandelker, *Exclusion and Removal Legislation,* 1956 Wis. L. Rev. 57.

are those who arrive with neither specific employment prospects nor a cash stake sufficient to meet their needs for a period of three months.[55] She sued to establish her right to AFDC benefits. The district court held the residence requirement to be unconstitutional on grounds of its "chilling effect on the right to travel" and denial of equal protection of the law.[56]

Washington v. Legrant arose in the District of Columbia.[57] This was a class action involving four plaintiffs, applicants in three instances for AFDC and, in the fourth, for Aid to the Permanently and Totally Disabled. In each case denial turned on failure to meet a one-year residence test. The claimant for APTD failed to qualify by virtue of institutionalization in St. Elizabeth's Hospital, where she had been a patient since 1941. Under local regulation "time spent in the hospital did not count in determining compliance with the one-year requirement."[58] The decision of the trial court in favor of plaintiff rested on the claim to equal protection, secured by the Due Process Clause of the Fifth Amendment.[59]

Reynolds v. Smith was also a class action. One appellee, Juanita Smith, had moved with her five children from Delaware to Philadelphia to live with her father, who supported her and her family for several months until he lost his job. The second appellee had returned with her children to Pennsylvania after briefly living in the South in order to care for invalid relatives. She returned to the state in which she had resided for twelve years prior to the temporary absence. Both parties had applied for AFDC. Again, the Pennsylvania statute was held unconstitutional below as a violation of the Equal Protection Clause.[60]

---

[55] Appellant's Brief in *Shapiro* at 20, 22.

[56] 270 F. Supp. 331 (D. Conn. 1967).

[57] Harrell v. Tobriner, 279 F. Supp. 22 (D.D.C 1967).

[58] 394 U.S. at 624. See 279 F. Supp. at 23 n. 2, pointing out that "residence could not be 'gained' while one was confined to a public institution." Neither the district court, 279 F. Supp. at 30 n. 19, nor the Supreme Court reached the question whether such a provision would be invalid under other circumstances. Mr. Justice Harlan, finding the durational test constituional, would have remanded for consideration of this question, 394 U.S. at 656 n. 1.

It has been common practice, by regulation or statute, to disregard time spent as a public charge (or even as a recipient of charity or of a relative's help, Brief for Appellees in *Shapiro* at 25) in computing the durational period needed to acquire settlement or residence. See Mandelker, note 39 *supra*, at 25-33.

[59] 279 F. Supp. at 25.   [60] 277 F. Supp. 65 (E.D. Pa. 1967).

Measured by the number of briefs filed, these cases attracted an unusual amount of attention. Not only did several state attorneys general record their interest, but a variety of groups was represented in the amicus briefs.

A. THE MAJORITY OPINION

The central contention of those attacking the residence provisions was "that the statutory prohibition of benefits to residents of less than a year creates a classification which constitutes an invidious discrimination denying them equal protection of the laws."[61] With this, a six-man majority was in agreement, holding that the "interests . . . promoted by the classification either may not constitutionally be promoted by government or are not compelling governmental interests."[62]

The principal defense of the waiting period related to protection of state fiscal integrity. It was alleged that those who became dependent early in a period of residence within a state were likely to remain continuing burdens on the public treasury. Their demands could be met only to the detriment of long-term residents.

The Court met this argument head on:[63]

> We do not doubt that the one-year waiting-period device is well suited to discourage the influx of poor families in need of assistance. An indigent who desires to migrate, resettle, find a new job, start a new life will doubtless hesitate if he knows he must risk making the move without the possibility of falling back on state welfare assistance during his first year of residence, when his need may be most acute. But the purpose of inhibiting migration by needy persons into the State is constitutionally impermissible.

Since the purpose of deterring immigration was constitutionally impermissible, the further question arose whether the "mere showing of a rational relationship between the waiting period and . . . four admittedly permissible state objectives will suffice to justify the classification."[64] The asserted objectives foundered, however, on the failure to establish a *"compelling* governmental interest" that

---

61 394 U.S. at 627.

62 *Ibid.*

63 *Id.* at 629. In support of this proposition the Court cited United States v. Guest, 383 U.S. 745 (1966), which acknowledges that the right to travel interstate is not grounded in an identifiable provision of the Constitution.

64 394 U.S. at 634.

would counterbalance exercise of a constitutional right or to demonstrate the link between a valid objective and the waiting period.

Thus, we were told that "the argument that the waiting-period requirement facilitates budget predictability is wholly unfounded."[65] Likewise, the Court rejected the contention that a durational period "serves as an administratively efficient rule of thumb for determining residency." The eligibility process currently in use undercut that argument, since detailed investigation of each application is mandated to establish both facts and amount of need. The process can be—and is—used to determine residence, as well.[66] Similarly, the investigative process can be relied upon as a safeguard against fraudulent receipt of assistance. Blanket denial of aid to all newcomers for "an entire year" was held an unwarranted "blunderbuss method" for meeting this hazard. The fourth argument, that a waiting period encourages prompt entry into the labor force, was rejected out of hand.[67]

All asserted justifications failed. Significantly, the Court noted that "even under traditional equal protection tests a classification of welfare applicants according to whether they have lived in the State for one year would seem irrational and unconstitutional."[68]

---

[65] *Ibid.* Note that the Court concedes that state departments of public welfare have been "exceptionally accurate" in their estimates of the cost of changes in regulations. *Id.* at 635. It is not clear why the Court accepts the departments' accuracy in some respects but denies them the ability to forecast the additional burden which would flow from addition of new residents to caseload. Neither is it clear exactly what the states have in mind when they advance the argument of budget predictability in support of residence requirements. In fact, one suspects that the ability to predict accurately may produce a higher estimate of anticipated assistance costs than many a state legislature cares to learn about. In some states it is generally believed that the legislature would rather be "surprised" by a rise in public assistance costs than receive an estimate, and approve a budget, for the full amount which reasonable men would reasonably anticipate.

[66] *Id.* at 636. Were the eligibility process to be simplified, as so many have urged, what would be the consequence for determination of residence? According to the majority: "Presumably the statement of an applicant that he intends to remain in the jurisdiction would be accepted under a declaration system." *Id.* at 637 n. 17. Two points deserve comment. The Court apparently assumed that intent is an intrinsic aspect of residency determination. Compare Mandelker, note 39 *supra*, at 366–77, arguing against importing an intent element into the concept of settlement. Moreover, the costs of establishing residence, mentioned by some writers as a reason for elimination of the requirement, are neither reduced by elimination of a *durational* requirement (with retention of an "intent-to-reside" test) nor clearly separable from the costs of other aspects of the eligibility process.

[67] 394 U.S. at 637–38.   [68] *Id.* at 638.

But traditional criteria were not applicable. "Since the classification here touches on the fundamental right of interstate movement, its constitutionality must be judged by the stricter standard of whether it promotes a *compelling* state interest. Under this standard, the waiting period requirement clearly violates the Equal Protection Clause."[69] In so concluding, the Court was quick to note that it implies no judgment on the validity of either waiting period or residence requirements for "determining eligibility to vote, eligibility for tuition-free education, to obtain a license to practice a profession, to hunt or fish, and so forth."[70]

By the very nature of the state legislation under attack, the Court was also bound to consider the relationship of the Social Security Act to the constitutional arguments being urged upon it. In each case the constitutionality of a state or District of Columbia statute was at issue. But these local enactments must conform to certain provisions of the federal statute in order to secure federal approval of the assistance plan. Absent such approval, federal matching funds would be withheld.

It was appellants' contention that the "constitutional challenge to the waiting period requirements must fail because Congress expressly approved the imposition of the requirement by the States as part of the jointly funded AFDC program."[71] The majority's rejoinder was less than convincing. It argued that "the statute does not approve, much less prescribe, a one-year requirement."[72] It relied on legislative history to show that meeting so limited a durational test depended on "repeal or drastic revision"[73] of requirements then existing in forty-one jurisdictions.[74] But this did not reach the issue whether, in the resulting compromise, Congress conferred its approval upon minimal requirements. Moreover, however one reads the legislative history surrounding the 1935 enactments, the fact remains that the original formulas—one year for AFDC and not more than five out of nine in the adult categories—have withstood criticism and successive efforts to repeal the relevant provisions.[75]

---

[69] *Ibid.*

[70] *Id.* at n. 21. See text *infra*, at note 158.

[71] *Id.* at 638.

[72] *Id.* at 639.   [73] *Id.* at 640.

[74] SOCIAL SECURITY BOARD, SOCIAL SECURITY IN AMERICA 235–36 (1937); STEINER, note 17 *supra*, at 132–40. Efforts to deal with the problem of persons who fail to meet a durational test through an interstate compact or reciprocal laws have been less than successful.

[75] See dissenting opinion of Chief Justice Warren, 394 U.S. at 647.

There remained the issue of the constitutionality of relevant federal statutes. In *Shapiro* and *Reynolds* the sole section to be considered was § 402(b), stating the maximum durational period permitted under a state plan. The Court disposed of the states' argument that striking down residence requirements would jeopardize the entire scheme of categorical assistance by indicating that it is the "responsive *state* legislation which infringes constitutional rights."[76] It added, however, that were § 402(b) dispositive of the cases before the Court, it would hold that section unconstitutional.[77] In *Washington* the waiting period requirement was embodied in the District of Columbia Code. It, too, was found unconstitutional. The discrimination, under familiar doctrine,[78] violated the Due Process Clause of the Fifth Amendment.

B. THE CHIEF JUSTICE'S DISSENT

For Chief Justice Warren (joined by Mr. Justice Black), the properly framed issue in *Shapiro* was: "may Congress, acting under one of its enumerated powers, impose minimal nationwide residence requirements or authorize the States to do so?"[79] He sought his answer in both the legislative history of the Social Security Act and prior interstate travel decisions.

The Chief Justice's reading of legislative history is persuasive, though, it should be noted, not necessarily inconsistent on specific points with the reading offered by the majority. Both opinions agreed to the magnitude of the changes in state programs of income maintenance that Congress sought—and that were shortly accomplished. The difference between them turns on a narrower point: whether the act was a statute of authorization or of limitation. As to the purpose underlying the state plan requirements, however, Chief Justice Warren stressed that the act was intended as a major experiment in "cooperative federalism":[80]

---

[76] *Id.* at 641.

[77] *Ibid.* The Court is sharply criticized for reaching that constitutional question by the Chief Justice. *Id.* at 653–54.

[78] *Id.* at 642, citing Schneider v. Rusk, 377 U.S. 163, 168 (1964); Bolling v. Sharpe, 347 U.S. 497 (1964).

[79] 394 U.S. at 644.

[80] *Id.* at 645, citing King v. Smith, 392 U.S. 309, 317 (1968). The Chief Justice had written the Court's opinion in that case, which turned on the interpretation of the Social Security Act. See text *infra*, at note 136.

> The primary purpose of the categorical assistance programs was to encourage the States to provide new and greatly enhanced welfare programs. . . . Federal aid would mean an immediate increase in the amount of benefits paid under state programs. But federal aid was to be conditioned upon certain requirements so that the States would remain the basic administrative units of the welfare system and would be unable to shift the welfare burden to local governmental units with inadequate financial resources.

In considering the wisdom of residency requirements, Congress had confronted the "competing claims of States who feared that the abolition of residence requirements would result in an influx of persons seeking higher welfare payments" and those of "organizations which stressed the unfairness of such requirements to transient workers forced by the economic dislocation of the depression to seek work far from their homes."[81] Section 402(b) (and comparable sections of the other titles) evidenced a compromise: a reduction in residence requirements but retention of the principle. That this course was acceptable to most states may be inferred from the speed with which they sought to take advantage of federal funds.

The Chief Justice also emphasized one additional aspect of the legislative history. Reviewing evidence in support of the beneficial impact of the Social Security Act upon state assistance programs, he noted that the states have continued to respond to[82]

> the federal stimulus for improvement in the scope and amount of categorical assistance programs. . . . [Yet] Congress has adhered to its original decision that residence requirements were necessary in the face of repeated attacks against these requirements. The decision to retain residence requirements, *combined with Congress' continuing desire to encourage wider state participation in categorical assistance programs,* indicates to me that Congress has authorized the imposition by the States of residence requirements.

In short, Congress had not been disposed to eliminate durational requirements in these categories, although it had significantly liberalized the programs in other respects.[83]

---

[81] 394 U.S. at 646.   [82] *Id.* at 647. (Emphasis added.)

[83] A few examples of liberalization of AFDC may be offered: Elevation of the age of eligible children successively from sixteen to eighteen and now to twenty-one (if attending school); addition of the adult caretaker to the grant; creation of the subcategories of AFDC-U (unemployed parent) and AFDC-F (foster care of

The Chief Justice also rejected the majority's analysis of the right-to-travel cases. They were distinguished on the ground that, with few exceptions, the cases did not present the question whether Congress had unduly burdened this right. State authority to deter interstate travel, absent congressional authorization, was not at issue under the facts in *Shapiro*.[84] Nor was Congress' power to "remove impediments to interstate movement," the decisive question in *United States v. Guest*.[85] Upon review of the few cases[86] which dealt with Congress' power to inhibit the right to travel, he found the burden upon a potential welfare recipient one of "uncertain degree"[87] and he relied on appellee's assertion that "there is evidence that few welfare recipients have in fact been deterred by residence requirements."[88]

Implicit in the Chief Justice's thesis, that congressional power derived from the Commerce Clause, was the need to show a rational basis for the conclusion that residence requirements furthered interstate commerce. He contended that it was reasonable for Congress to conclude that improvement in the conditions of welfare recipients would enhance the flow of commerce. The familiar negative argument was, in any event, dispositive: "I cannot say that Congress is powerless to decide that residence requirements would promote this permissible goal [removal of an impediment to the commercial life of the nation] and therefore must conclude that such requirements cannot be termed arbitrary."[89]

The Chief Justice concluded his dissent on a note further developed by Mr. Justice Harlan. This related to an implication in the majority's opinion that other types of state residence requirements

---

children). The proportionate effect of these changes greatly exceeds that of adding residents who cannot meet a durational test (estimated at between 0.5 and 2 percent of caseload). See notes 103–06 *infra*.

[84] 394 U.S. at 647–48.   [85] *Id*. at 649.

[86] Kent v. Dulles, 357 U.S. 116 (1958); Zemel v. Rusk, 381 U.S. 1 (1965); Aptheker v. Secretary of State, 378 U.S. 500 (1964).

[87] 394 U.S. at 650. Warren noted that all the claimants in the cases found alternative means of support. In the case of Vivian Thompson a private charity contributed $31.60 a week, "a sum considerably less than what the appellee would have received from the Connecticut Welfare Department as an AFDC recipient." Brief for Appellee in *Shapiro* at 3.

[88] 394 U.S. at 650.   [89] *Id*. at 653.

may not present constitutional questions. He failed to discover an adequate rationale for the dichotomy the Court had created and uttered a warning:[90]

> The Court's decision reveals only the top of the iceberg. Lurking beneath are the multitude of situations in which States have imposed residence requirements including eligibility to vote, to engage in certain professions or occupations or to attend a state-supported university. Although the Court takes pains to avoid acknowledging the ramifications of its decision, its implications cannot be ignored.

C. MR. JUSTICE HARLAN'S DISSENTING OPINION

These implications became explicit grounds of dissent for Mr. Justice Harlan. But he reached them via consideration of the burden on interstate travel and the assertedly novel equal protection doctrine, which he claimed the Court here applied.[91] Reiterating his previously stated objections to extension of the "compelling interest" test on which the majority's opinion was rested, Harlan identified two troublesome branches of that theory. One is that of "suspect" criteria which have now been extended, he feared, to prohibit classifications based on interstate movement or "perhaps those based upon the exercise of *any* constitutional right."[92] Even more alarming was that branch of doctrine that suggested "that a statutory classification was subject to the compelling interest test if the result of the classification may be to affect a 'fundamental right,' regardless of the basis of the classification."[93] These fears were based on[94]

> the Court's cryptic suggestion . . . that the "compelling interest" test is applicable merely because the result of the classification may be to deny the appellees "food, shelter, and other necessities of life," as well as in the Court's statement . . .

---

[90] *Id.* at 655.

[91] Mr. Justice Stewart, in a separate concurring opinion, took issue with Harlan's assertion that the Court had accomplished an expansion of the "compelling interest" doctrine in its *Shapiro* holding. *Id.* at 642–44.

[92] *Id.* at 659.   [93] *Id.* at 660.

[94] *Id.* at 661–62. Parenthetically, it may be noted that two amicus briefs supporting affirmance rested their arguments upon due process grounds, Amicus Brief, American Jewish Congress; Amicus Brief, City of New York. The majority of amici relied on equal protection.

that "[s]ince the classification here touches on the fundamental right of interstate movement, its constitutionality must
be judged on the stricter standard of whether it promotes
a *compelling* state interest."

I think this branch of the "compelling interest" doctrine
particularly unfortunate and unnecessary. It is unfortunate
because it creates an exception which threatens to swallow
the standard equal protection rule. Virtually every state
statute affects important rights. . . . Rights such as [pursuit
of an occupation, receipt of more or less wages, right to
inherit property] are in principle indistinguishable from those
involved here, and to extend the "compelling interest" rule
to all cases in which such rights are affected would go far
toward making this Court a "super-legislature." This branch
of the doctrine is also unnecessary. When the right affected
is one assured by the Federal Constitution, any infringement
can be dealt with under the Due Process Clause.

Harlan concluded that under traditional equal protection criteria,
or the analogous standard of due process, the residence requirement
will withstand constitutional attack. Not only might a legislature
rationally identify valid government objectives to be gained in its
imposition but, further, it "might also find that residence requirements have advantages not shared by other methods of achieving
the same goals."[95]

Harlan treated the interstate travel issue extensively. After consideration of the possible sources of a right to travel interstate, for
him grounded in the Due Process Clause of the Fifth Amendment,[96]
Harlan weighed the extent to which a welfare residence requirement interfered with that right and the governmental interests
which can be urged in support of the requirement. He noted appellees' assertion that "only a minuscule increase in the number of
welfare applicants" would result from abolition of residence requirements.[97] Hence, it cannot be said that the requirements deter
appreciable numbers of persons from moving interstate. He acknowledged—as the authors of the other opinions did not—that we
do not know the "number or proportion of persons who are actually
deterred from changing residence by the existence of these provisions."[98]

---

95 *Id.* at 663. He cited administrative simplicity and relative certainty as two virtues not necessarily present under alternative ways of identifying eligibles.

96 *Id.* at 671.   97 *Id.* at 671–72.   98 *Id.* at 671.

Also placed in the scale on the side of constitutionality were four governmental interests to be served by imposition of residence tests. These interests coincided with those identified (and rejected) by the majority. The first, denial of benefits to persons who move primarily to receive them, did not offend Mr. Justice Harlan:[99]

> This seems to me an entirely legitimate objective. A legislature is certainly not obliged to furnish welfare assistance to every inhabitant of the jurisdiction, and it is entirely rational to deny benefits to those who enter primarily in order to receive them, since this will make more funds available for those whom the legislature deems *more worthy* of subsidy.

The additional three purposes were familiar from the Court's opinion. Mr. Justice Harlan saw the residence requirement as providing an "objective and workable means" of identifying those applicants who plan to remain in the jurisdiction, thus a preventive for fraud. While conceding that the collected data were insufficient to support precise budgetary predictions, he nonetheless concluded that the residence requirement "may" help in forecasting budgetary amounts in the future. And, finally, he conceived legislative efforts to relate welfare payments to what persons have contributed to the state economy to be a valid goal.[100] His inquiry also went beyond identification of the aforementioned legitimate governmental interests to deal with the effect of the residency requirement on freedom to travel interstate ("indirect" and "insubstantial"),[101] and he cited evidence that the legislatures, having been fully exposed to contrary arguments, had rejected them.

Appellees' contention that lesser remedies were at hand to reach the governmental interest was rejected as a matter of judgment on which reasonable men may differ. Mr. Justice Harlan's general position was, of course, that the judiciary should be cautious not to fetter the judgment of the legislature in choice of methods. This was exposed plainly in his concluding comment:[102]

---

[99] *Id.* at 672. (Emphasis supplied.) The very concept of persons being "more worthy of subsidy" is anathema to many of the critics of contemporary public welfare. The idea, of course, undergirds the act's categorical divisions; it also crops up in unexpected places. See text *infra*, following note 158.

[100] 394 U.S. at 673.   [101] *Id.* at 674.

[102] *Id.* at 677. Demonstrating his concern for the effect of *Shapiro* on innovative approaches to the problems of welfare, Mr. Justice Harlan remarked that "the field of welfare assistance is one in which there is a widely recognized need for

Today's decision . . . reflects to an unusual degree the current notion that this Court possesses a peculiar wisdom all its own whose capacity to lead this Nation out of its present troubles is contained only by the limits of judicial ingenuity in contriving new constitutional principles to meet each problem as it arises. . . . [I]t is an essential function of this Court to maintain the constitutional divisions between state and federal authority and among the three branches of the Federal Government. . . . This resurgence of the expansive view of "equal protection" carries the seeds of more judicial interference with the state and federal legislative process, much more indeed than does the judicial application of "due process" according to traditional concepts. . . . I consider it particularly unfortunate that this judicial roadblock to the powers of Congress in this field should occur at the very threshold of the current discussions regarding the "federalizing" of these aspects of welfare relief.

IV. Welfare Policy in the Wake of Shapiro: A Few Unanswered Questions and Unquestioned Answers

The *Shapiro* holding, especially since it was grounded on the Equal Protection Clause, radiated a host of equality questions into the welfare field. These questions reach deeply into fundamental assumptions about the nature of society and the role of government. It has often been asserted that the character of a society may be measured by its response to the problem of poverty. In our own day, in sharp contrast to earlier ages, we confront "the paradox of poverty in the midst of plenty." We are consequently challenged to defend the reach and efficacy of policies of income redistribution. And in the process comes the painful discovery of how little factual data we possess, how deep-rooted are our assumptions, and how limited our imagination on the subject of reform.

An obvious initial question concerns the immediate effect of the Court's holding. Estimates offered at trial[103] and in briefs submitted

---

fresh solutions and consequently for experimentation. Invalidation of welfare residence requirements might have the unfortunate consequence of discouraging the Federal and State Governments from establishing unusually generous welfare programs in particular areas on an experimental basis, because of fears that the program would cause an influx of persons seeking higher welfare payments." *Id.* at 674–75.

103 See, *e.g.*, testimony of Deborah Davis, director of the Bureau of Assistance Policies and Standards, Office of Public Assistance, Commonwealth of Pennsylvania, in Appendix in *Reynolds* at 84a–85a. The number denied aid on grounds of a durational test has been steady over the years. *Id.* at 83a.

to the Court[104] suggest that it will be modest. The increase in assistance caseloads that will result from abandonment of durational tests has been estimated at between 0.5 percent and 2 percent of caseload.[105] The increases appear, moreover, to be fairly evenly distributed among the assistance categories, judging from limited returns to date.[106] These are affected, however, by the litigation on residency tests within the states. Continuance of the tests was enjoined only in the programs that were the subject of suit by rejected applicants.[107] In very few states do we have information on all programs: the four federally funded categories and general assistance. And of course the data cover a brief span of time, hardly long enough to separate the impact of the newly eligible class of recipients from that of seasonal and other factors.

Contrary to the arguments of residence requirement advocates,[108] there is no reason, from preliminary impressions, to suspect that newly arrived residents applying for assistance differ in social characteristics from the pool of applicants who would satisfy a dura-

---

[104] Brief for Appellees in *Shapiro* at 12 n. 12; Amicus Brief, Center on Social Welfare Policy and Law, pp. 27–29.

[105] Note, note 5 *supra*, at 135; MORELAND COMMISSION ON WELFARE, PUBLIC WELFARE IN THE STATE OF NEW YORK 27–28 (1963); Smith v. Reynolds, 277 F. Supp. at 66–67; Harrell v. Tobriner, 279 F. Supp. at 29.

[106] Data supplied by Washington, D.C., reveal that recipients who have resided in that jurisdiction less than one year range, by category, between 2.8 and 6.4 percent. As of April, 1969, 3.9 percent of AFDC recipients would not have been eligible under a durational test. Data Sheet, "Status of 1217 nonresident applications received through period: January 2, 1968 through March 31, 1969," District of Columbia Department of Public Welfare. During a comparable period (February 1, 1968–May 31, 1969) in Cook County, Illinois, similar results obtained (based on unpublished data supplied to the author by the Illinois Department of Public Aid). These data should not be interpreted in terms of an increase in caseload over time. Caseload fluctuations are normally expressed in terms of the net increase or decrease, the difference between new applications and case closings in a given period. The percentages reported above are based on new applications only. They do not reflect movement off assistance by persons who would fail, as well as those who can meet, a durational test.

[107] In the District of Columbia, for example, the injunction against enforcement of durational requirements affected AFDC, AB, APTD, and general assistance. OAA was not covered. As a result, the welfare agency is referring every OAA applicant of less than one year's residence to the medical review team which reviews eligibility for APTD. This team usually finds the applicant qualified for APTD. Letter from Gerard M. Shea, Program Analyst, Department of Public Welfare, District of Columbia, dated August 18, 1969.

[108] As reported in 394 U.S. at 627–28.

tional qualification.[109] But certainly this is a crucial issue deserving of close investigation. If the recent immigrant who experiences destitution differs in some important way from other indigents who apply for aid, this might well argue for a special kind of crisis service or relief.[110] It might throw further light on policies which influence interstate migration and suggest better ways of indirectly stimulating or inhibiting population movement among groups atypically vulnerable to economic disaster.[111]

At present, we are consigned to the realm of speculation. Residence requirement controversy has centered, almost exclusively, for centuries on the "sturdy beggar." Debate has been cast into the narrow mold of arguing whether employable persons move to claim

---

[109] A sample of 177 cases was drawn from a population of 1,775 (AFDC, OAA, and APTD) formerly ineligible applicants approved for assistance between February 1, 1968, and May 31, 1969. These cases involved persons who had resided in Illinois for less than one year at the time of application and were approved in Cook County during the above period (excluding 88 AFDC-U and 7 AB cases). During the same period applications from 24,010 persons who had met the old residency requirements were approved; data were supplied to the author on a sample of 2,000 drawn from this population. From this sample, another of 190 was drawn, again excluding AFDC-U (90 cases) and AB (8 cases). My comparisons relate to a sample of 190 "residents" and 177 persons with less than a year's residence. For these data and aid with their interpretation I gratefully acknowledge the assistance of Wayne Epperson of the Illinois Department of Public Aid and Walter Hudson of the Cook County, Illinois, Department of Public Aid.

It appears, from the limited data pertaining to AFDC cases in both samples, that the individuals who would not qualify under residence requirements have less work experience or somewhat more marginal skills than those who meet the old requirements. Twice as many persons in the newly eligible class have no previous work experience whatsoever. While the individuals in both groups are mainly categorized as laborers, service workers, or operators, the heretofore ineligible group includes fewer persons whose previous job experiences were of a clerical nature. (The percentages were approximately 5 percent in the previously ineligible, and 20 percent in the eligible, groups.) With respect to other characteristics (e.g., marital status, place of previous residence) the two groups are similar.

[110] Cf. Simons, *Services to Uprooted and Unsettled Families*, in NATIONAL CONFERENCE ON SOCIAL WELFARE 1962 SOCIAL WELFARE FORUM 169. See also Fried, *The Role of Work in a Mobile Society*, in WARNER, ed., PLANNING FOR A NATION OF CITIES 81, 101–04 (1966).

[111] These policy considerations appear to be very much on the minds of those concerned with labor mobility and manpower requirements, see Manpower Report of the President pp. 127–66, 1968. It has been suggested that a guarantee of general assistance, or some equivalent form of income aid, without a durational residence requirement would increase labor mobility toward high-demand markets. Kasper, *Welfare Payments and Work Incentive: Some Determinants of the Rates of General Assistance Payments*, 3 J. HUMAN RESOURCES 86 (1968).

relief. Studies of migration show that the age group of highest mobility is that of twenty to thirty years.[112] Most within it are, presumably, employable and their moves relate either to employment or to schooling. But older adults also move, and some communities (and some regions of the country) experience high immigration of persons in their sixties or older.[113] It is not necessarily inconsistent to assert that most people do not move for welfare benefits but that some take the availability of such benefits very much into account.[114] If it is true, as studies of assistance caseload repeatedly conclude, that over three-fourths of all recipients are unemployable,[115] then it is not illogical to claim that the recent migrants among them have not moved to secure employment.

The argument falters for lack of facts. The judgment of unemployability is itself a difficult one. What renders the aged classifiable this way is likely to be ill health; for the AFDC mother, or AFDC-U father, it may be a combination of labor market conditions, personal qualifications, child-care responsibilities, and racial discrimination.[116]

Some writers have asserted that movement to benefit from welfare can be demonstrated. The case traditionally is offered by advocates of residence tests. More recently, opponents of the present welfare system have suggested this possibility to buttress their drive for reform. Cloward and Piven, for instance, interpret the rise in welfare rolls of northern cities in terms of a "geography of welfare eligibility."[117] People have moved from areas of harsh welfare rules to areas of greater leniency and higher benefits. But, they say, to what extent welfare is a *cause* of this population movement or an *effect* of a movement generated by different factors cannot be determined upon information now available. History warns us, how-

---

[112] STOCKWELL, POPULATION AND PEOPLE 160 (1968).

[113] *Ibid.*

[114] *Cf.* Note, note 5 *supra*, 51 IOWA L. REV. at 1085, citing Select Committee report, note 4 *supra*, at 2.

[115] *E.g.*, GREENLEIGH ASSOCIATES, ADDENDA TO FACT, FALLACIES AND FUTURE: A STUDY OF THE AID TO DEPENDENT CHILDREN PROGRAM OF COOK COUNTY, ILLINOIS 101 (1960).

[116] See Carter, *The Employment Potential of AFDC Mothers*, WELFARE IN REVIEW 1 (July–August 1968).

[117] Cloward & Piven, *Migration, Politics, and Welfare*, 51 SAT. REV. 31 (Nov. 16, 1968).

ever, that welfare is too easy an explanation. Hindsight usually rejects it.

Given the shaky basis for past judgments of welfare's relationship to population movement, it would be foolhardy to state assuredly the long-term implications of *Shapiro*. It may significantly alter caseload composition on the point of length of residence; it may not. So far, at least, the effects have been within the predicted range, though this is probably small comfort to administrators and legislators who strain to meet the program's escalating costs. And fears of uncontrollable escalation have had the consequence of directing national attention to the welfare system.[118] What kind of system will we have by 1975, forty years after the initial venture in "cooperative federalism"? What "Stop" or "No entry" signs are posted in the Court's decision?

Shapiro, it should be noted, differed in a fundamental respect from earlier equal protection decisions. It relied neither upon "suspect" criteria, such as race, to find unconstitutionality nor upon "a notion of the minimum decencies demanded by our ideals of a fair trial," which was offered to explain the stream of cases affecting administration of criminal justice.[119] Rather, *Shapiro* struck to the core of the equality theory in relying upon poverty—absence of "the very means to subsist"[120]—as the major premise by which to evaluate the classification of residents according to durational periods in the jurisdiction. To be sure, the Court avoided comments that might undermine the whole categorical scheme. It did not dispute the fact that public assistance benefits are usually regarded as a "privilege," not a right, though it is well established that this will not justify an improper classification.[121] It confines its holding to discrimination only among residents, on durational grounds, though the plight of migrants was also brought to its attention during argument[122] and is usually more dismal than that which a short-term

---

[118] The immediate reaction of big-city mayors and other political figures in urban areas to *Shapiro* was to emphasize the need for federalization of the assistance burden. As subsequent developments indicate, there is less agreement on how to do this. See, *e.g.*, proposals adopted by the National Governors' Conference on Welfare, New York Times, Sept. 3, 1969, p. 1, after the Nixon welfare message.

[119] See Kurland, *Equal Educational Opportunity: The Limits of Constitutional Jurisprudence Undefined*, 35 U. Chi. L. Rev. 583, 587 (1968).

[120] 394 U.S. at 627.   [121] *Id.* at 627 & n. 6.

[122] 37 U.S. L. Week 3153, 3155 (Oct. 29, 1968).

resident faces. Basic revision of income-maintenance programs, an explicit objective of many commentators on welfare law, was adverted to only in dissent by Mr. Justice Harlan,[123] as he alluded to the need for a fresh approach by Congress and the state legislatures.

Yet, unless the Court has silently given decisive weight in these cases to the fact of destitution, the outcome is hard to understand. And if it has, the potential of *Shapiro* for redistribution of resources by judicial indirection is great—greater than that involved in the criminal justice cases, comparable only perhaps to that which would result from a constitutional requirement of equal educational opportunity or equal distribution of funds among custodial institutions,[124] contrary to local "tastes" and historic patterns. As Professor Kurland asserted in another (though related) connection: "Statewide equality is not consistent with local authority; national equality is not consistent with state power."[125]

But "national equality" is precisely what the welfare rights movement is all about. At least this is its "middle-range" target; the present mood of the movement suggests that equal treatment for the destitute at too low a level would fail to satisfy the rising demands of the increasingly organized poor.[126] And the level at which income maintenance shall be provided, which I believe lies at the core of agitation in the welfare field, is an issue under any system that is cast into a parochial mold.

Even under the Social Security Act, with admittedly high proportions of federal funds being channeled into state treasuries, the quintessential parochialism of public assistance remains intact. Commentators who favor the extension of equal protection doctrine to various aspects of welfare administration have said as much.[127] The

---

[123] 394 U.S. at 674–75, 677.

[124] Is it defensible that a person experience different levels of custodial care, depending on whether he is committed to a county jail or a state penitentiary, a county home for the aged or a state hospital for the senile aged? In the former instance, the crime can scarcely serve as the principle of differentiation, for those incarcerated in jails are usually either awaiting trial or confined for minor offenses. Yet they are more poorly housed and have fewer amenities than offenders sentenced to imprisonment for felonies.

[125] Kurland, note 119 *supra*, at 590.

[126] See report of the Welfare Rights Organization activities, New York Times, June 1, 1969, § 4, p. 2.

[127] *E.g.*, Horowitz & Neitring, *Equal Protection Aspects of Inequalities in Public Education and Public Assistance Programs from Place to Place within a State*, 15

judicial rulings they seek would attack at the heart of theories which have, in the past, rationalized both local prejudice and local experimentation. Ironically, the plea for expansion of equal protection doctrine is heard at the same time that loud claims are asserted in behalf of decentralization and increase in the power of local groups. These are particularly prominent themes in welfare. "Maximum feasible participation of the poor" in control of neighborhood institutions is urged. Relaxation of requirements for statewide uniformity in public assistance is advocated to permit experimentation, thus to thwart a stultifying tendency toward mediocrity.

Why should the parochial spirit persist in the administration of the categorical assistances? Even if general assistance, still a permissive program for local jurisdictions within many states, is significantly—if not wholly—subject to local control,[128] how can it be that the experiment in "cooperative federalism" represented by the categorical aid titles is dominated by state and local interests? I will simply refer to two aspects of these state-federal programs.

First, as Professor Handler has pointed out,[129] there is the fact that public assistance is suffused with discretionary determinations at numerous strategic points of program administration. In an important sense, the client of public assistance is at the mercy of local, lower-level officials. They are hard to supervise (even if their superiors attempt it) in their everyday client dealings, no matter how objective the standards stated in the regulations they are charged to implement. Besides, many aspects of the program import delicate judgmental determinations on matters which, it seems fair to say, resist both identifiable consensus and objective formulation. The official is often free to go either way.

Second, there is the fact that financing arrangements do not relieve local taxpayers of the oppressive awareness of a welfare "burden," regardless of the proportion of federal funding that a particular state receives.[130] This is because state expenditures trigger fed-

---

U.C.L.A. L. Rev. 787 (1968); Harvith, *Federal Equal Protection and Welfare Assistance*, 31 Albany L. Rev. 211 (1967).

[128] Wedemeyer & Moore, *The American Welfare System*, 54 Calif. L. Rev. 326, 334 (1966).

[129] Handler, *Controlling Official Behavior in Welfare Administration*, 54 Calif. L. Rev. 479 (1966). See generally Davis, Discretionary Justice (1968).

[130] Critics of the welfare system have pointed out that federal funds supply more than half the national expenditures for public assistance. Under existing formulas, in fact, the lower a state's benefits under a particular category, the higher the pro-

eral reimbursement. Therefore, state "generosity" is, up to the statutory ceiling, determinative of the size of federal grants. Given the well-known fact that the revenue base of state and local governments has relatively little growth potential, resting heavily as it does on property and sales taxation, increases in expenditure within these units call for conscious acts to elevate tax rates, a process of which the propertied and relatively affluent members of the jurisdiction cannot but be painfully aware. By comparison, expenditure increases at the national level have a less immediate impact on the personal (though not necessarily the corporate) taxpayer.

Taxpayers naturally take a keen interest in local expenditures which, from their vantage point, appear to account for rising rates. In municipal government the best example of citizen "watch-dogging" is the monitoring of educational costs. In state government, where welfare ranks among the two or three largest budget items (and unlike highway construction, welfare lacks a natural "users" population to bear the costs), it is little wonder that the welfare item is highly visible and vulnerable to attack. In fact, some of the most persuasive arguments for federalizing public assistance cite the unenviable position of the public assistance programs in state government to strengthen their assertions that a better-tolerated, and therefore better-funded, scheme would be one wholly administered and paid for in the relative darkness of a nationalized administration. That the correctness of such arguments may be doubted appears from comparative study of "residual" welfare programs, akin to public assistance, which have been nationalized in other countries.[131]

---

portion of cost borne by federal contributions. The federal share of all public assistance programs (excluding general assistance) is 79 percent in Mississippi, only 45 percent in New York. Soc. Sci. Bull, note 13 *supra*, at Table 133, p. 127. In the period July, 1958–July, 1968, the AFDC caseload shifted dramatically from the fifteen lowest grant states (with proportionately high federal contribution), which carried 43.5 percent of the recipients in 1958, to the fifteen highest grant states. By July, 1968, the latter group of states had 50.9 percent of the caseload, an increase of 163.1 percent. Population increase was about the same in both groups of states: 11 percent. Information supplied by Mary-Claire Johnson, supervisor of legislative research, Illinois Department of Public Aid.

[131] Commentators on the residual welfare schemes of countries abroad have noted the difficulty of providing "adequate" income under dignified circumstances even in nations whose social welfare systems are more fully developed than in the United States. See ROSENTHAL, THE SOCIAL PROGRAMS OF SWEDEN 150 (1967); RODGERS, COMPARATIVE SOCIAL ADMINISTRATION 260–61 (1968). British journals contain an abundant

There is a related point that bears on discussion of the parochial influence in welfare administration. It cannot be doubted that particular localities, at a given time, hold a special attraction for potential welfare recipients. Dispute over the cause for this is ancient, though one may question whether benefit level has as much to do with rising caseloads as a locality's appeal as job market or otherwise superior place to live. Nonetheless, welfare populations bunch in certain areas; so far as records reveal, large cities are relatively more vulnerable to this phenomenon. In consequence, costs of public aid —even if steady over time or over the nation as a whole—may be felt unevenly, with resulting pressures on state and local jurisdictions, according to the structure of the assistance program and the assignment of responsible units of taxation.

Everyone presumably knows that New York City—to cite one instance—has experienced a disproportionate growth in welfare costs.[132] Its welfare budget, further, is only one measure of the total fiscal burden produced by an increase in indigent populations.[133] This particular hazard is well documented in the annals of welfare administration. What critics of relief are less likely to recognize is that the innovations introduced by the Social Security Act, while undeniably shifting some of the costs, have not materially reduced the taxpayer's sense of incidence of costs. Moreover, when combined with the discretionary authority inherent in the very conception of a means-tested, needs-relieving program, the local awareness of burden is likely to produce restrictive or uneven applications of policy in order to keep "the county free."

All of this is simply to say that *Shapiro v. Thompson* must be appraised in the context of welfare programs that are still, public opinion to the contrary notwithstanding, parochial in orientation and discretionary in administration. From this vantage point, how-

polemical literature on Great Britain's Supplementary Benefits scheme that reads very much like American diatribes against public assistance.

132 See Horowitz, *A Portrait of New York's Welfare Population—in One Month, 50,000 Persons Were Added to the City's Welfare Rolls,* New York Times Magazine, Jan. 26, 1969, at 22.

133 Immigration of low-income groups produces great strains on public education, public housing, law enforcement, and criminal justice. This generalization scarcely needs documentation, though it is amazing how often such pertinent data as are gathered are treated as "privileged." Disciplined inquiry and criticism are thereby inhibited. That this may be "functional" for the public agency in question, *cf.* Cahn & Cahn, *The New Sovereign Immunity,* 81 Harv. L. Rev. 929, 960 n. 110 (1968).

ever, *Shapiro* gives greater promise of benefiting would-be recipients than may be expected from most welfare litigation.

Usually two conditions must be met for the rise of litigation—or the threat of litigation (which may equally well serve to get the client what he wants).[134] There must be a willing litigant, one who knows his rights and concludes on balance that the costs of litigation are worth taking. There must be "bad" law to attack. The law is either flawed on its face or discriminatory in application. The adversary techniques of lawyers are not even called into play when the first condition does not prevail and they will be of limited usefulness when the target of attack is the arbitrary action of officials in administering the program.

Adequate protection of welfare clients' rights may well be thought to entail broad-scale monitoring, yet neither lawyers nor lay advocates can easily inspect the decisions of authorities. Discretionary power is diffuse and pervasive throughout the welfare hierarchy. It is difficult to encapsulate its exercise under prevailing program concepts. It pervades all assistance programs, all levels of administration, all crucial decisional points. This is not to say that all decisions are discretionary. On the contrary, many—perhaps far more than we would like—are cut and dried. But the potential for introducing a discretionary determination is ever present. In some categories possibly, it does not "feel" this way to clients.[135] It may not appear this way to the public. Yet the containment of discretion in these instances says more for the spirit in which the program is administered (which in turn reflects public attitudes about the "worthiness" of that particular category) than it says about formal differences in rules and regulations.

King v. Smith[136] offers an instructive illustration of the difficulties of first securing, then implementing, a welfare "victory." At issue was Alabama's "substitute father" regulation. It denied AFDC to

---

[134] Much of the following discussion derives from the work of Joel F. Handler. See Handler, note 129 *supra;* Handler, *Justice for the Welfare Recipient: Fair Hearings in AFDC—the Wisconsin Experience,* 43 Soc. Serv. Rev. 12–15 (1969). Publication is expected in 1970 of Handler's empirical study of AFDC administration and client attitudes in six counties of Wisconsin; I have had the benefit of seeing parts in draft form.

[135] Cf. Briar, *Welfare from Below: Recipients' Views of the Public Welfare System,* 54 Calif. L. Rev. 370, 375 (1966).

[136] 392 U.S. 309 (1968).

the children of a mother who "cohabits" with such a man. A "substitute father" was an "able-bodied"[137] man who either lived in the home, visited the home frequently, or was with the mother outside the home, for purposes of cohabitation. Whether he was the father of the children, legally obligated to support them, or actually contributing to their support was irrelevant. The significance of the regulation derived from the federal act's provision that aid be granted only if a parent of a needy child is absent from the home.[138] Under this regulation a "substitute father" was considered a non-absent parent and, accordingly, aid was denied. Only if the mother successfully discharged the obligation to show that her relationship with the man had been discontinued (or was wrongly alleged) would AFDC be granted.

It followed from the nature of the Alabama regulation that a test case would require an applicant and "substitute father" willing to expose their impropriety and bear the risk of criticism. Even harassment might be anticipated as a result of this kind of litigation, for it has been claimed that the regulation under attack (as well as others like it) had overtones of racial discrimination.[139]

Given willing litigants and a successful outcome, will these ingredients produce the desired changes in administration? It is not enough to declare the "substitute father" regulation invalid under the Social Security Act. It is also necessary to guard against expansion of other regulations that will permit the states to accomplish much the same purpose.[140] Moreover, as the Court acknowledged in *King*, "there is no question that regular and actual contributions to a needy child, including contributions from the kind of person Alabama calls a substitute father, can be taken into account in determining whether the child is needy."[141] A state bent upon keeping program costs low (and confining payments as much as possible to "worthy" recipients) has at hand techniques of low-level harassment. For example, an isolated contribution can be construed as evidence of continuing benefit, throwing the burden (even more heavily than usual) upon the indigent to establish need.

The *Shapiro* case entailed a different kind of rule, a one-time determination. Applicants must establish intent to reside, a relatively

---

[137] *Id*. at 311.   [138] *Id*. at 313.

[139] BELL, AID TO DEPENDENT CHILDREN 181–86 (1967).

[140] *Ibid*.   [141] 392 U.S. at 319.

objective condition. Factors that might inhibit potential recipients from availing themselves of the assistance to which they are now entitled would be ignorance of the Court's action or failure to establish the requisite intent. But there are—once again, relatively speaking—mechanical devices for minimizing both of these hazards and narrowing the range of administrative freedom.

The newly promulgated HEW regulation on residency,[142] in direct response to *Shapiro*, addresses both client ignorance and proof of residence. It demands of states that previously had durational tests the formulation of "effective methods" (to be approved by HEW) of publicizing the invalidation of the tests. Where records permit identification of rejected applicants who were otherwise eligible, the state "must give prompt written notice" to such persons concerning the change in requirement. The regulation further calls for states to notify potential applicants and "other interested persons."

States are also circumscribed as to the factors from which intent to reside is established. The regulation specifically provides that a child's residence flows from the mere fact of his "making his home in the State."[143] It expressly states that temporary absence "shall not interrupt continuity of residence." And the regulation forecloses inquiry into the purpose for which a person entered the state, "except insofar as it may bear upon whether he is there for a 'temporary purpose.'" The last provision is directed against statutory attempts to curtail receipt of assistance by short-term residents. A well-known example is New York's so-called Welfare Abuse Law,[144] which denies assistance to applicants found to have entered

---

[142] 34 FED. REG. 8715 (June 3, 1969), superseding Handbook of Public Assistance Administration, Pt. IV, §§ 3600–3665.

[143] This would obviate some of the present absurdities. A child is eligible for foster family or institutional care without a waiting period or residence test. His eligibility for AFDC, however, may turn upon the ability of the relative with whom he lives to conform to the durational requirement. This may lead to splitting up the family unit in order to obtain aid for the child with an eligible relative, *e.g.*, a grandmother. See example cited in Supplemental Brief for Appellees in *Shapiro*, at 37–38 (typescript). The impediments to assistance for indigent children which are erected by the notion of derivative settlement in general assistance programs are noted in Mandelker, note 39 *supra*, at 42–48.

[144] *N.Y. Soc. Welfare Law* § 139(a), discussed in Sparer, *The New Public Law: The Relation of Indigents to State Administration*, in THE EXTENSION OF LEGAL SERVICES TO THE POOR 3–314 (1964); Note, note 5 *supra*, 2 COLUM. J. L. & SOC. PROB. at 140–42.

the state for the purpose of receiving assistance. This is now an impermissible reason for denial under the HEW regulation.[145]

Clearly the purpose of the regulation, which goes beyond literal conformity with the Court's decision, is to push the states toward a more liberal view of their duty to aid the indigent. It may fall short of the mark, given the difficulties of overseeing welfare administration to which I have already alluded. But I think it significant that the potential applicant who challenges an official's decision on the matter of residency is differently positioned from the recipient who is already party to a continuing caseworker-client relationship. When a recipient objects to an adverse decision—on rent or a special allowance request or the treatment of resources in computing need —he is questioning a facet of a relationship upon which he depends for subsistence.

Even with claimants who face the alternatives of acceptance or rejection, distinctions are possible. The claimant asserting residence is contesting a one-time determination. He either succeeds or loses. And he does not confront the necessity of giving something up. In *King*, by contrast, Mrs. Smith's eligibility turned on her willingness to abandon her relationship of cohabitation. In other welfare contests, too, the "choice" that the client faces lies between enduring destitution or making changes to conform to eligibility conditions. The AFDC-U father or the seventeen-year-old school dropout can accept a job or training referral—or challenge it. The AFDC mother likewise. The client may tolerate the caseworker's regular home visit—or protest it, as a violation of privacy perhaps.[146] But in *Shapiro*-like situations the client does not, by his own immediate actions, improve or jeopardize his prospects for receipt of welfare.

Besides, a test of residence does not involve a moral issue. If applicants are sometimes inhibited from aggressive pursuit of their just deserts by fear of stigma, of exposing themselves to public scorn, then they will be more reluctant to contest a determination of fitness to work or the contribution of income by a paramour than to challenge a finding on residency. At least, this position can be argued.[147]

---

[145] Note 142 *supra*.

[146] See James v. Goldberg, No. 69 Civil 2448 (S.D. N.Y. Aug. 18, 1969), permanently enjoining termination of assistance to an AFDC recipient who refused to permit home visits required by statute, reported in C.C.H. Pov. L. Rep. ¶ 10262.

[147] For fuller exposition of the argument, see Handler & Rosenheim, *Privacy in*

In short, *Shapiro* is distinctive among welfare cases. It deals with the legitimacy of a long-accepted statutory classification. That classification turns on fairly easily determined factual grounds. The decision is made once. Under these conditions it is reasonable to anticipate the rapid translation of the Court's holding into action, namely, an increase in persons accepted into the assistance programs. But this prediction does not reach the heart of the welfare problem.

Attacking the "illegality" of the welfare system is like doing battle with a feather pillow. Probably this is why critics speak in despair of the welfare "mess." Parochialism and discrimination are the major evils, as yet eluding fundamental cure. Periodic waves of public interest in the system typically leave minor imprint; the contours of the programs are rarely affected in any basic sense. The states are still the chief builders and maintainers.

It is doubtful whether the present programs will be permitted to continue, for signs of discontent are rapidly accumulating. Congress now demands a certain showing of state investment, an addition to the lengthy string of quids for quos. Levels of assistance are required to be adjusted to living costs;[148] the old flexibility of periodic percentage cuts is doomed. States no longer enjoy as many options as formerly, and they are required to institute specific programs in which Congress has confidence[149] (though in some cases its judgment might well be faulted). Proposals for significant changes in funding formulas are pending, and "federalization" of public assistance appears to be imminent.[150]

Welfare: Public Assistance and Juvenile Justice, 31 L. & CONTEMP. PROB. 377 (1966). But see findings from Handler's Wisconsin AFDC study relating to client feelings of stigma, HANDLER & HOLLINGSWORTH, STIGMA, PRIVACY, AND OTHER ATTITUDES OF WELFARE RECIPIENTS (1969).

[148] 42 U.S.C. § 602(a)(23)(Supp. IV 1968). This addition in the 1967 amendments has already generated litigation. See Rosado v. Wyman, No. 69 Civ. 355 (E.D. N.Y. July 29, 1969), reported in C.C.H. Pov. L. REP., ¶ 10086.

[149] E.g., foster care for AFDC-eligible children who require care out of their homes, and the so-called WIN (Work Incentive) program under which both AFDC mothers and AFDC-U fathers (in states having the AFDC-U program) are to be referred for employment or training. See generally *The Welfare and Child Health Provisions of the Social Security Amendments of 1967: Legislative History and Summary*, WELFARE IN REVIEW 1 (May–June 1968). For a critical account of the WIN program see *Compulsory Work for Welfare Recipients under the Social Security Amendments of 1967*, 4 COLUM. J. L. & SOC. PROB. 197 (1968).

[150] Address of President Nixon on welfare reform, New York Times, August 9, 1969, p. 10.

Yet, so long as certain principles underlie the programs skepticism is warranted in judging the impact of various reforms. Both parochialism and state power to discriminate survive as cardinal aspects of those contemporary proposals which command a respectable amount of political support. Thus, proposals for changing the matching formulas do not destroy the importance of parochial influences. They may reduce the range of average payments by elevating the bottom tier. This would not be an inconsequential achievement, I gladly admit, but its long-term value would depend on what happened at the top.[151] If Congress responded slowly with adjustments in the federal contribution, during a time of rising prices, the spread of average payments might soon again become as large as it was prior to elevation of the floor. The generosity of benefit, under most politically viable plans, is still state-determined.

Furthermore, many contemporary suggestions for change in public assistance do not destroy the principle of categorization. Today, Congress wields decisive influence over the choice of categories; the options available to the states are more theoretical than real. And such modest choices as they once controlled have gradually been foreclosed. Until the 1967 amendments the states could institute AFDC-U or AFDC-F if so inclined. Now the latter is a mandatory subprogram of AFDC. While the AFDC-U remains optional, states are required to institute work and training programs for such employable recipients as they do assist.[152] States still wholly control general assistance—its coverage and terms—but the relative importance of the program is dwindling, in large part due to the growth of AFDC-U. Congress, therefore, primarily shapes the

---

[151] This is true even in the short run in high-benefit states. Under the family assistance system proposed by the President, which contemplates a cut-off point at $3,920 in federal income supplement for a family of four, both the "working poor" and those who claim supplementation appear to gain only the "privilege of earning the expense of earning." Such a basic maintenance standard of $3,200, coupled with the allotted $720 allowance for work expenses provided in the President's plan, falls short of what Illinois already considers work expense, assuming that the work-expense allowance is intended to cover Social Security and federal income taxes (totaling $364.69) as well as transportation, carfare, and telephone. (Child care expenses have been omitted from the calculations in this example; given the family situation of many marginal income families, this is unrealistic.) The way in which the new system would mesh with the old is not clear. H.R. 14173, 91st Cong., 1st Sess., introduced October 3, 1969, was not available in time for consideration here.

[152] 42 U.S.C. § 602 (a) (19) (Supp. IV 1968).

choices of needy groups for whom governmental income maintenance is an acknowledged duty.

Even so, the states have considerable voice in determining how
the different categories will be treated. This results from the discretionary authority wielded by the welfare agency, a natural result of program goals. For all the assistance titles, money payment is
but one objective; "service," to the end of self-maintenance, is
another. In AFDC, the strengthening of family life is added; so
too is maintaining "maximum self-support and personal independence."[153] Following these general directions, local welfare officials
determine what services people require, judge what will be good
for them. Money and services, together, are given to enable recipients to be "like other people." If this requires a change in conduct,
the programs provide the services to produce it.

In some cases behavior change is dictated by fiat. In others, services offer an opportunity of which the client may avail himself, at
his option. Whether changes in behavior should be compelled or
stimulated by provision of opportunity (or eliminated as a public
assistance program goal altogether) is a matter on which reasonable
men have differed—and sometimes hotly. Yet it cannot be denied
that "[w]hen government enacts and administers programs dealing
with people, it interferes with personal behavior; indeed, this is usually the intention of the program."[154]

If, for the moment at least, the central "people-changing" purpose of welfare programs is acknowledged, the means for its accomplishment must be determined, a matter of no small importance.
The methods chosen are both measure and mirror of governmental
decency. In welfare programs the stated legislative goals are too
general and inconsistent, and the supporting "consensus" too fragmentary and elusive, to excuse heavy-handed official action.

Separation of income maintenance from services has been identified as one way to curb the dangers of oppressive governmental

---

153 42 U.S.C. § 601 (Supp. IV 1968). These added goals stimulate a host of state
plan requirements not thought appropriate for the adult categories: e.g., provision
of family and child welfare services "for each child and relative" who receives
AFDC "as may be necessary in the light of the particular home conditions and other
needs of such child, relative, and individual," id. at § 602 (a) (14); provision for "the
development of a program for each appropriate relative and dependent child . . .
with the objective of . . . preventing or reducing the incidence of births out of wed-
lock and otherwise strengthening family life," id. at § 602 (a) (15) (A).

154 Handler & Rosenheim, note 147 supra, at 410.

intrusion into poor people's lives.[155] In the light of *Shapiro* this proposal assumes a new dimension. The advocates of separation, drawn from many quarters, rest their case on two main planks. The poor, they say, need money. Poverty alone does not identify personally dependent or incompetent people in need of services. Therefore, public assistance ought to be a money payments program, grounded on objectifiable conditions and administered under nonstigmatizing circumstances. Schemes of negative income taxation, family allowances, and "federalized" public assistance, are examples of the means which have been urged to achieve these ends.

The second major argument relates to services. Some advocates of separation see it as a way to free social services and social "utilities" from the degrading, continuing eligibility process of public aid.[156] They argue that only separation offers hope of protecting the voluntary character of social services offered to financially dependent persons.

What implications does *Shapiro* hold for such proposals? It is necessary first to ascertain the character of social services. And this procedure proves fruitless and frustrating if one deals exclusively with existing statutory definitions and operating programs. These services just grew. They exist; therefore, one presumes, they must be classifiable. But what, save accident, binds together such disparate forms of social provision as "meals on wheels," counseling, adoption service (likely to involve fees set on a sliding scale), and the operation of a sectarian institution for delinquent youth? In short, if one separates income maintenance from services, what are the "services" remaining?[157] What governmental unit shall define

---

[155] *Id.* at 391, 411–12, and authorities cited.

[156] *E.g.,* Kahn, *Social Services in Relation to Income Security: Introductory Notes,* 39 Soc. Serv. Rev. 381 (1965).

[157] Are they mainly casework services? One infers these are the target of concern of some professional social workers who have addressed themselves to the "service delivery" problem. See, *e.g.,* Piliavin, *Restructuring the Provision of Social Services,* 13 Social Work 34 (1968), in which he argues persuasively for a "private entrepreneurial model." Under this model, how would Piliavin handle the "social provisions" of home aid, baby-sitting, "park aunts," etc., which Kahn urges upon us before we extend case services? Kahn, *New Policies and Service Models: The Next Phase,* 35 Am. J. Ortho. 652 (1965). Also see Handelman, *et al.,* The Federalization of Public Assistance: Implications of Structural Change 78 (1969), discussing federal responsibilities for service-funding and standard-setting under an income-maintenance-service-separation scheme. The document, a report to the Social and Rehabilitation Service, HEW, is the product of a student seminar taught by Professor Harold Richman.

them and determine policy? Who shall administer and staff them? How should the statutory services relate to those of voluntary associations? The proposals generate these questions, and many more.

But another point is even more relevant to the *Shapiro* holding. The character and availability of social services influence the extent of income need, in any given community. Thus, social services bear indirectly on income maintenance objectives, staff requirements, and budget. Benefits in kind may push a person just above the line of indigency; yet some of these (like the pre-*Shapiro* categorical assistances) are conditioned on a test of residence.[158] Thus, we confront the question, what implications radiate from *Shapiro* with respect to eligibility conditions surrounding the social services?

States have tried to strike the balance between the public's appetite for in-kind benefits and the resources they command through several means. A state may condition eligibility on proof of poverty, thereby excluding from access to publicly provided service all persons who are better off. Or, if public sentiment disapproves a means-tested approach, the state may instead restrict the number of users by area (identified as "high risk," for example) or by excluding nonresidents from the class of beneficiaries. Are these approaches

---

[158] Examples of residence-related eligibility conditions in service programs, all of which are drawn from Ill. Rev. Stat. (1967) unless otherwise noted, include: care of the mentally ill in state institutions, c. 91½ § 12-7 (it is unlawful to bring into the state for the purpose of hospitalization a person who is mentally ill, c. 91½ § 12-8); admission into the Surgical Institute for Children (the judge must certify that the child has been a resident of the "committing" county for the past year), c. 23 § 2205; care in the state hospital-school and Eye and Ear Infirmary (limited to "residents" of the state), c. 23 §§ 5014, 5017; adoption (petitioners must have resided in the state for six previous consecutive months), c. 4 § 9.1–2. Another section of the act creating a children's department authorizes the giving of service and residential care to nonresidents "provided that no resident of another State shall be received or retained to the exclusion of any resident of this State," c. 23 § 5012. Testimony in *Reynolds* at the trial also indicates the practical difficulty of nonresidents securing services to which they are theoretically entitled; *e.g.*, medical care under the Maternal and Infant Health program; App. in *Reynolds* at 47a–50a; admission into voluntary homes for the aged contingent upon eligibility for OAA, App. at 111a. The more important point is not what provisions are currently on the statute books but the controversy and intractable difficulty surrounding decisions on antipoverty measures. This point is clearly (and elegantly) developed by Rein & Miller, *Poverty, Policy, and Purpose: The Dilemmas of Choice*, in GOODMAN, ECONOMIC PROGRESS AND SOCIAL WELFARE 20 (1966). They outline six different "strategies of intervention" to improve the lot of the poor: "amenities; investment in human capital; transfers; rehabilitation; participation; and aggregative and selective economic measures." *Id.* at 26–27. The Court's opinion in *Shapiro* touches on only one. My question simply is what will be its effect on the others?

vulnerable in view of the *Shapiro* holding? Will it make a difference
to the answer whether federal funds heavily support the social service in question?

Writers who have urged equalization of educational provision,
as well as public assistance, might well contend that uneven distribution of social services is likewise insupportable. This posture
would certainly exacerbate problems with which administrators
already struggle. The nature of the services in question defies the
ready definition or application of an equalization formula. But more
important from the policy perspective is the fact that there is less
agreement on the "common human needs" for services than on a
floor of income or a minimum of public schooling. The case for
local preference and experimentation in services is strong.

V. "Beggars" at the High Table

Shapiro v. Thompson expands the class of public assistance
eligibles. Claimants of aid who would fail to meet durational residence tests are now eligible for the "charity" that is available. But,
when we come right down to it, the level of assistance is the critical
issue today.

This does not destroy the importance of cases like *Shapiro*. I
would like to see all needy persons entitled to some form of income
assistance. Certainly, those who are now entitled should not be im-
peded in claiming welfare payments by arbitrary action. Nor
should state regulations which are out of conformity with federal
law go unchallenged. At the same time, *Shapiro* and other examples
of welfare litigation will be Pyrrhic victories if they deflect attention from the standard of living which assistance payments allow.
To achieve expansion of the eligible class and elevation of benefit
level simultaneously calls for more radical reform than many legislators are willing to entertain.

In this connection the welfare rights movement may yet make
its most lasting contribution. It has already left a mark on public
attitudes toward the poor and secured selected gains for indigents.
It has moved to a new stage of stimulating political consciousness
among welfare recipients. With political power could come a reformulation of welfare objectives and a restructured set of programs offering aid at higher levels.

Meanwhile, *Shapiro* stands as a high-water mark of judicial in-
dignation over a discrimination which betrays the meanness and

inhumanity of public assistance. The traditions of six hundred years have been dealt a mortal blow. I would not wish to obscure the significance of this fact by reason of having emphasized here the limitations of *Shapiro* as "reform" and the many different questions that the opinion generates. Durational residence requirements have, at best, a circumscribed role in welfare policy for mobile, modern America.

The next installment in the welfare story is imminent. Whether it will be written by the courts or the legislatures is uncertain. Since legislatures control the purse, and courts do not, and since innovation is so sorely needed in the welfare field, I hope the legislatures will seize the day.[159] It would be a tragedy were the "beggars," on arriving at the "high table," to find that their plates are empty. *Shapiro* indicates the time for action has come. Like so many other aspects of our national life, the welfare problem must be dealt with now, "ready or not."

---

[159] See Note, *Discriminations against the Poor*, 81 Harv. L. Rev. 435, 442 (1967), commenting on the institutional limitations of constitutional decisions, especially those affecting the alleviation of poverty; Note, *The Constitutionality of Residence Requirements for State Welfare Recipients*, 63 Nw. U. L. Rev. 351, 369–72 (1968); Note, note 5 *supra*, 51 Iowa L. Rev. at 1086–90. But *cf.* Harvith, *The Constitutionality of Residence Tests for General and Categorical Assistance Programs*, 54 Calif. L. Rev. 567 (1966); tenBroek, The Constitution and the Right of Free Movement (1955).

PAUL G. KAUPER

CHURCH AUTONOMY AND THE FIRST

AMENDMENT: THE PRESBYTERIAN

CHURCH CASE

While other objectives are served by the twin religion clauses of the First Amendment and the separation principle derived by implication from them, one fundamental purpose is to insure the freedom of the state from ecclesiastical control and, in turn, the freedom of the churches from governmental control. The two decisions by the Supreme Court in its 1968–69 Term, resting on these clauses, highlight this purpose. The decision in *Epperson v. Arkansas*,[1] invalidating the Arkansas statute forbidding the teaching of the evolutionary theory in public schools, implements the first aspect of this purpose. Government may not manipulate the public school's teaching program in order to sanction and thereby to establish a particular religious belief. The decision in *Presbyterian Church in the United States v. Mary Elizabeth Blue Hull Memorial Presbyterian Church*,[2] holding that a state court may not constitutionally resolve doctrinal matters in disputes involving the use of church property, gives effect to the complementary aspect of this fundamental purpose.

The *Presbyterian Church Case*, because of its effect as a constitutional repudiation of a doctrine widely followed by state courts

---

Paul G. Kauper is Henry M. Butzel Professor of Law, University of Michigan.

[1] 393 U.S. 97 (1968).

[2] 393 U.S. 440 (1969) (hereinafter referred to as the *Presbyterian Church Case*).

in resolving ecclesiastical controversies, makes an important and distinctive contribution to the freedom that may be claimed by churches under the First Amendment. In practical terms, it affords federal constitutional protection to the liberty of the churches to define, develop, and apply their doctrines free from intervention by the civil courts.

The case arose as the result of an attempt by two local Presbyterian congregations to withdraw from the Presbyterian Church in the United States, a church which the Court in the very first sentence of its opinion characterized as "a hierarchical general church organization."[3] The members of the two congregations, supported by their ministers and most of the elders, voted to withdraw and to reconstitute the two local churches as an autonomous Presbyterian organization. The grounds for withdrawal were that certain actions and pronouncements of the general church violated that organization's constitution and were departures from the doctrine and practice in force at the time of affiliation. The claimed violations of and departures from doctrine were summarized by the Georgia Supreme Court:[4]

> . . ."ordaining of women as ministers and ruling elders, making pronouncements and recommendations concerning civil, economic, social and political matters, giving support to the removal of Bible reading and prayers by children in the public schols, adopting certain Sunday School literature and teaching neo-orthodoxy alien to the Confession of Faith and Catechisms, as originally adopted by the general church, and causing all members to remain in the National Council of Churches of Christ and willingly accept its leadership which advocated named practices, such as subverting of parental authority, civil disobedience and intermeddling in civil affairs"; also "that the general church has . . . made pronouncements in matters involving international issues such as the Vietnam conflict and has disseminated publications denying the Holy Trinity and violating the moral and ethical standards of the faith."

---

[3] Id. at 441. "Petitioner, Presbyterian Church in the United States, is an association of local Presbyterian churches, governed by a hierarchical structure of tribunals which consists of, in ascending order, (1) the Church Session, composed of the elders of the local church; (2) the Presbytery, composed of several churches in a geographical area; (3) the Synod, generally composed of all Presbyteries within a State; and (4) the General Assembly, the highest governing body." Id. at 441–42.

[4] Id. at 442 n. 1.

After attempts at conciliation failed, the administrative commission appointed by the general church acknowledged the withdrawal of the local leadership and took over the local church property on behalf of the general church until new local leadership could be appointed. Without making an effort to appeal the commissioners' action to higher church tribunals—the Synod of Georgia or the General Assembly—the churches filed suits in the state trial court to enjoin the general church from trespassing on the disputed property, title to which was in the local churches. The general church moved to dismiss the actions and cross-claimed for injunctive relief in its own behalf on the ground that civil courts were without power to determine whether the general church had departed from its tenets of faith and practice. Denying the motion to dismiss, the trial court submitted the question to the jury on the theory that Georgia law implies a trust of local church property for the benefit of the general church on the sole condition that the general church adhere to its tenets of faith and practice existing at the time of affiliation by the local churches. The jury was instructed to determine whether the actions of the general church "amount to a fundamental or substantial abandonment of the original tenets and doctrines of the [general church], so that the new tenets and doctrines are utterly variant from the purposes for which the [general church] was founded."[5] The jury returned a verdict for the local churches and the trial court thereupon declared that the implied trust had terminated and enjoined the general church from interfering with the use of the property in question. The Supreme Court of Georgia affirmed,[6] and the United States Supreme Court granted certiorari to consider questions raised under the First Amendment.

I. The Implied Trust and Departure-from-Doctrine Standard

Before I turn to the Supreme Court's opinion and its disposition of the case, a brief review of the implied trust rule applied by the Georgia courts is in order.

According to this rule, property contributed to a religious body by its members over the years is impressed with a trust in favor of

---

[5] *Id.* at 443–44.   [6] 224 Ga. 61 (1968).

the fundamental doctrines and usages of the organization at the time the contributions were made, and in a dispute concerning the control of this property, centering on claims of substantial departure from these fundamental doctrines and usages, civil courts will award the control to the group faithful to this trust.[7]

This rule is usually attributed to Lord Eldon's opinion in *Attorney General v. Pearson*[8] decided in 1817. It was built on the foundation of the charitable trust doctrine which had recognized that an express trust for a religious purpose would enjoy the protection that had come to be accorded to charitable trusts generally.[9] But to assert that contributions and gifts to a church—not expressly earmarked as a trust or designated for specific purposes and not made dependent upon observance of specific conditions—created an implied trust in favor of established doctrines and usages was a considerable extension of the charitable trust idea. Indeed, the whole notion of a trust rather than a gift in a case like this is a legal fiction. Moreover, it required a determination of ecclesiastical matters by a civil court. The development and application of this rule in English law was understandable, however, since the inquiry into fundamental doctrine required by this standard was not incompatible with a legal system that featured an established church subject to parliamentary control.

The English rule was not at the outset generally accepted in the New England states, since it was not compatible with the congregational polity and the freedom of a majority of a congregation to determine its doctrine and denominational affiliation. Indeed, reflecting a distrust of hierarchical structure, state constitutional pro-

---

[7] ". . . it is the duty of the court to decide in favour of those, whether a minority or majority of the congregation, who are adhering to the doctrine professed by the congregation, and the form of worship in practice, as also in favour of the government of the church in operation, with which it was connected at the time the trust was declared." App v. Lutheran Congregation, 6 Pa. 201, 210 (1847).

[8] 3 Mer. 353, 36 Eng. Rep. 135 (Ch. 1817). See also Lord Eldon's earlier opinion in Craigdallie v. Aikman, 1 Dow. 1, 3 Eng. Rep. 601 (H.L. 1813).

[9] ". . . if any persons seeking the benefit of a trust for charitable purposes should incline to the adoption of a different system from that which was intended by the original donors and founders; and if others of those who are interested think proper to adhere to the original system, the leaning of the Court must be to support those adhering to the original system, and not to sacrifice the original system to any change of sentiment in the persons seeking alteration, however commendable that proposed alteration may be." 36 Eng. Rep. at 157.

visions assured local control of congregational affairs.[10] The implied trust rule did, however, gain wide acceptance in other parts of the country and it is fair to say that it has generally been adopted as part of the American common law.[11]

In this country the implied trust rule, applied in connection with the departure-from-doctrine standard, has generally been supported on the ground that it assured the stability and integrity of churches as institutional bodies by preventing a majority of a congregation from diverting church property—the result of accumulations of gifts made in good-faith reliance on and furtherance of its particular doctrines and practices—for use in support of fundamentally different doctrines and practices.[12] So viewed it could also be regarded as a means of protecting religious liberty by assuring judicial protection of the religious uses for which property was given.[13]

---

[10] See Note, *Judicial Intervention in Disputes over the Use of Church Property,* 75 HARV. L. REV. 1142, 1149 *et seq.* (1962). The general reluctance of early courts to apply Lord Eldon's rule is best expressed in the following passage from Baptist Church v. Witherell, 3 Paige 296, 304 (N.Y. Ch. 1832): "Neither am I prepared to say that it would be right, or expedient, to adopt the principle of Lord Eldon here, where all religions are not only tolerated, but are entitled to equal protection by the principles of the constitution. Upon Lord Eldon's principle, a society of infidels, who had erected a temple to the goddess of Reason, could not, upon the conversion of nine tenths of the society to Christianity, be permitted to hear the word of life in that place where infidelity and error had once been taught."

[11] For discussions of the history and application of the fundamental-doctrine trust rule, see ZOLLMAN, AMERICAN CHURCH LAW (1933); STRONG, RELATIONS OF CIVIL LAW TO CHURCH POLITY, DISCIPLINE, AND PROPERTY (1875); Casad, *The Establishment Clause and the Ecumenical Movement,* 62 MICH. L. REV. 419 (1964); Duesenberg, *Jurisdiction of Civil Courts over Religious Issues,* 20 OHIO ST. L. J. 508 (1959); Stringfellow, *Law, Polity, and the Reunion of the Church: The Emerging Conflict between Law and Theology in America,* 20 OHIO ST. L. J. 412 (1959); Patton, *Civil Courts and the Churches,* 45 AM. L. REG. N.S. 391 (1906); Note, note 10 *supra;* Note, *Judicial Intervention in Church Property Disputes—Some Constitutional Considerations,* 74 YALE L. J. 1113 (1965); Comment, *Constitutional Law—Freedom of Religion—Judicial Intervention in Disputes within Independent Church Bodies,* 54 MICH. L. REV. 102 (1955).

[12] See Casad, note 11 *supra,* at 452 *et seq.*

[13] "The guarantee of religious freedom has nothing to do with the property. It does not guarantee freedom to steal churches. It secures to individuals the right of withdrawing, forming a new society, with such creed and government as they please, raising from their own means another fund and building another house of worship; but it does not confer upon them the right of taking the property consecrated to other uses by those who may now be sleeping in their graves. The law of intellectual and spiritual life is not the higher law, but must yield to the law of the land." Schnorr's Appeal, 67 Pa. 138, 147 (1870).

The power of a civil court to pass on the question whether a religious body is making substantial departures from the fundamental doctrines necessarily requires the court to identify and appraise both the fundamental doctrines and the substantiality of the alleged departures in order to decide which group in a divided congregation is entitled to control the property.[14] Thus a civil court becomes the judge of religious doctrine. Moreover, by freezing the doctrine and usages on an implied trust basis, the civil courts by their decisions were placed in a position of obstructing further development of doctrinal positions or even of challenging new applications of established doctrine.[15] Obviously, the application of the implied trust rule in connection with the departure-from-doctrine standard constituted a considerable intrusion by an organ of government into ecclesiastical affairs.

Such an intrusion in ecclesiastical affairs seemed all the more anomalous in a country which was increasingly committed to the separation of church and state. At an early date, American courts had developed the common-law doctrine that, like the other organs of government, they had no jurisdiction over purely ecclesiastical matters.[16] These were to be decided according to the internal law of the church and according to the procedures established by the church and the organs it had set up for resolution of internal disputes. In following this general rule the courts were influenced in part by the general doctrines respecting internal affairs of voluntary associations, which rested largely on a contractual theory,[17]

---

[14] See Kniskern v. Lutheran Churches, 1 Sandf. 439 (N.Y. Ch. 1844), for an example of the detailed scrutiny to which this procedure can lead.

[15] See ZOLLMAN, note 11 supra, at 238 et seq.

[16] "I regret that suits relating to ecclesiastical affairs have become common in our courts, and that undefined and mistaken views have been entertained, in relation to the powers of the civil and ecclesiastical tribunals. I think it necessary to repeat, what other Judges have thought it necessary to say, that the civil tribunal possesses no authority whatever to determine on ecclesiastical matters—on a question of heresy, or as to what is orthodox, or unorthodox, in matters of belief. So the ecclesiastical tribunals have no authority, as recognized by the law, to entertain any civil question, or in any manner effect a disposition of property by the decisions of their judicatories." Wilson v. Presbyterian Church of John's Island, 2 Rich. Eq. 192, 198 (S.C. 1846). See also German Reformed Church v. Commonwealth ex rel. Siebert, 3 Pa. 282 (1846).

[17] See Fuller, Note on Chase v. Cheney, 10 AM. L. REG. N.S. 313 (1871); Redfield, Note on Gartin v. Penick, 9 AM. L. REG. N.S. 220 (1870).

in part by their reluctance to intervene in areas of doctrinal dispute where they felt they had no competence,[18] and in part by deference to constitutional ideas respecting the freedom of the churches from governmental control.[19]

But while the civil courts denied their jurisdiction to resolve purely ecclesiastical disputes, they asserted jurisdiction to resolve questions respecting the control and use of property—matters appropriate for determination by the civil courts—where in the case of a schism or controversy competing groups were attempting to control the use of the congregation's property.[20] By thus acquiring jurisdiction over the property issue, the civil courts could not avoid facing in some measure doctrinal disputes which were the sources of the schism.[21] It was in this context then that the courts invoked the implied trust doctrine and awarded the control of the property to the group found to be loyal to the fundamental doctrines to which the church was committed.

The application of the departure-from-doctrine standard could not be considered, however, without regard to the question of church polity. Polity refers to the general governmental structure of a church and the organs of authority defined by its own organic

---

[18] ". . . civil courts, if they should be so unwise as to attempt to supervise their judgments on matters which come within their [ecclesiastical tribunals] jurisdiction, would only involve themselves in a sea of uncertainty and doubt, which would do anything but improve their religion or good morals." German Reformed Church v. Siebert, 3 Pa. at 291.

[19] "Freedom of religious profession and worship can not be maintained if the civil courts trench upon the domain of the church, construe its canons and rules, dictate its discipline and regulate its trials. The larger portion of the Christian world has always recognized the truth of the declaration, 'A church without discipline must become, if not already, a church without religion.' It is as much a delusion to confer religious liberty without the right to make and enforce rules and canons, as to create government with no power to punish offenders." Chase v. Cheney, 58 Ill. 509, 537 (1871).

[20] The source of the distinction is uncertain, but it seems to have received explicit recognition as early as 1846. Wilson v. Presbyterian Church of John's Island, 2 Rich. Eq. 192 (S.C. 1846). It has been said that a refusal to hear cases concerning property rights in which churches are involved would come close to being "a denial of equal protection as well as . . . a violation of first amendment religious rights." Casad, note 11 supra, at 432.

[21] See Kniskern v. Lutheran Churches, 1 Sandf. 439 (N.Y. Ch. 1844); Lutheran Free Church v. Lutheran Free Church, 141 N.W.2d 827 (Minn. 1966); Ashman v. Studebaker, 115 Ind. App. 73 (1944); Cantrell v. Anderson, 390 S.W.2d 176 (Ky. 1965); Hale v. Everett, 53 N.H. 9 (1868); Mt. Zion Baptist Church v. Whitmore, 83 Iowa 138 (1891).

law.[22] Two broad types of church polity are recognized by the courts: (1) the hierarchical and (2) the congregational. In the hierarchical type of church the local congregation is an organic part of a larger church body and is subject to its laws, procedures, and organs according to an ascending order of authority. It does not enjoy local autonomy. Its doctrine is defined by that of the parent body and its property, while peculiarly a matter of local enjoyment, is held for uses consistent with the doctrines and practices of the denominational parent church. A further distinction may be made between two types of polities within the general hierarchical group of churches, namely, (a) the episcopal polity and (b) synodical or associational polity. In churches with the episcopal polity, of which the Roman Catholic and Episcopal churches are good examples, authority is vested at various defined levels in ecclesiastical officers, and the general system may be described as authoritarian in character. In churches with a synodical or associational polity, authority is delegated to elected organs exercising power at various levels and culminating at the top in an elected representative body which constitutes the highest organ of authority. This polity has a democratic base. The Presbyterian Church affords the best example of the synodical polity.

The congregational polity, by contrast to the hierarchical, features local congregational autonomy as its central characteristic. It is premised on the idea that the local congregation is the highest authority in all matters of doctrine and usage. Indeed, congregationalism is in itself a fundamental principle of these churches.[23] The Congregational Church and the Baptist Church are prime examples of churches with a congregational polity. It does not follow that a church with a congregational polity may not be affiliated with a national church body or denomination in order to achieve some purposes in common with other congregations of a like na-

---

[22] For a general discussion of church polity and its implications, see SCHAVER, THE POLITY OF THE CHURCHES (1947).

[23] "Congregational polity acknowledges no ulterior jurisdiction over the local church and refuses to subject the decisions of the local church to the governing authority of a broader assembly. Any association of its churches is refused authority to overrule the power of its local constituents. This polity holds that the presence of Christ by his Spirit, as an authoritative influence, manifests itself principally in the conviction and utterance of the individual believer and that the influence of the believer therefore cannot easily go outside the local church. Authority accordingly is accorded only to the local church." *Id.* at 43–44.

ture. What is important is that it is free to join or to withdraw from such a body, is not subject to any ecclesiastical law or authority of a larger body, and is free to act according to the will of a majority of its members, subject only to the rules and limitations prescribed by the internal law of its own constitution and bylaws.[24]

The usefulness to courts of the distinction between hierarchical and congregational polities in resolving church property issues by reference to the implied trust doctrine is readily apparent. The hierarchical church is less vulnerable to judicial intrusion by virtue of the fact that it has its own general law, procedure, and organs for the authoritative resolution of internal disputes.[25] Moreover, it gives some assurance of the continued institutional stability that may be described as the end object of the implied trust doctrine.[26] On the other hand, in the case of a church with a congregational polity, with the result that the local congregation is autonomous and subject to majority rule, the danger of manipulation by a shifting and impermanent temporal majority so as to cause a deviation from established doctrine and usage is greater and consequently invites greater judicial surveillance.[27]

---

[24] Not all courts have adhered to the notion that a traditionally independent church may freely withdraw from a voluntary association of churches with similar beliefs. These decisions seem hard to justify in light of the asserted independence of such congregations. See Whipple v. Fehsenfeld, 173 Kan. 427 (1952); Western North Carolina Conference v. Tally, 229 N.C. 1 (1948); Sorrenson v. Logan, 32 Ill. App.2d 294 (1954); Reid v. Johnston, 241 N.C. 201 (1954); Huber v. Thorn, 189 Kan. 631 (1962); Church of God v. Finney, 344 Ill. App. 598 (1951).

[25] "The courts, often with legislative sanction, leave controversies within the Roman Catholic Church to be settled by its tribunals in accordance with canon law. ... Members of this church, especially those who enter its priesthood, are fully aware of the wide control which a bishop exercises over property and churches in his diocese, and almost all of them would regard any judicial restraint upon his powers as entirely inconsistent with the underlying principles of their religion." Chafee, *The Internal Affairs of Associations Not for Profit*, 43 HARV. L. REV. 993, 1025 (1930). The same holds true in varying degrees for other hierarchical churches.

[26] The "idea of an implied contract—or 'implied trust' as it came to be called—was clearly a fiction, the true *ratio decidendi* being that doctrinal continuity is the essential characteristic of a church, so that doctrinal innovation works a trust diversion." Note, 75 HARV. L. REV. at 1147.

[27] "Unlike law courts or even ecclesiastical tribunals within associated churches, there is a relatively rapid turnover of membership within churches. Members come and go as they move into and out of the geographical area the church serves. Moreover, the number of members is never fixed as it is in the case of judicial or hier-

In general, even before *Watson v. Jones*,[28] the courts tended to observe a distinction between churches, based on the nature of their polity, in applying the implied trust rule. In the case of congregations that were part of a hierarchical church, courts were inclined to resolve the property questions according to the determination made in accordance with the procedures and by the authoritative organs established by the church.[29] The congregational polity churches, on the other hand, presented a greater problem for the courts, and it was in disputes involving churches of this type that the implied trust rule was frequently invoked and applied, although as previously noted it did not at the outset meet general acceptance in the eastern states where the law exhibited a basic predilection in favor of local congregational rule. Faced with the necessity to decide the issue of property in a dispute turning on doctrinal matters, the courts had the choice of saying that the majority will of the local congregation was the ultimate authority[30] or of intervening to award the property to the faithful minority if the court found that the majority was attempting to commit the congregation to a doctrine or practice found to constitute a fundamental departure.[31] The net result was that the hierarchical church enjoyed a greater immunity from judicial intervention in its affairs than the independent congregation. Ironically, the congregationalists, rejecting ecclesiastical authority and law as a matter of principle, found themselves in greater peril of intrusion into their affairs by an organ of civil government.[32]

---

archical tribunals. It can go up or down as new members are added or removed from the rolls of the church. Accordingly, the 'majority' of a congregational church is necessarily a very ephemeral concept; the group of individuals which comprises the congregation varies over relatively short periods of time as to both identity and number of individuals." Casad, note 11 *supra*, at 446.

[28] 13 Wall. 679 (1872). See text *infra*, at notes 33–59.

[29] American Primitive Society v. Pilling, 24 N.J. Law 653 (1855); First Constitutional Presbyterian Church v. The Congregational Society, 23 Iowa 567 (1867); Roshi's Appeal, 69 Pa. 463 (1871); Schnorr's Appeal, 67 Pa. 138 (1870); State *ex rel.* Watson v. Ferris, 45 Mo. 183 (1869); Sutter v. Trustees of the First Reformed Dutch Church, 42 Pa. 503 (1862); McBride v. Porter, 17 Iowa 203 (1864).

[30] Shannon v. Frost, 42 Ky. 253 (1842).

[31] App v. Lutheran Congregation, 6 Pa. 201 (1847); Hale v. Everett, 53 N.H. 9 (1868); Brunnenmeyer v. Buhre, 32 Ill. 183 (1863).

[32] See Note, 75 HARV. L. REV. at 1157 *et seq.*

II. Watson v. Jones and Its Impact

This was the state of affairs when, in 1872, the Supreme Court handed down its famous decision in *Watson v. Jones*.[33] The case was one facet of extended litigation in several courts involving the control of the property of Presbyterian congregations, where schism had occurred over the slavery issue. This particular case, involving a dispute over control of the Walnut Street Presbyterian Church of Louisville, Kentucky, came before the federal courts as a diversity case at a time when federal courts were still applying a federal common law on the basis of *Swift v. Tyson*.[34] The split in the congregation resulted from a declaration of the General Assembly of the Presbyterian Church, to which the Louisville congregation belonged, that persons who had aided the "rebellion" or who believed that slavery was a divine institution "should be required to repent and forsake these sins before they could be received" as members in a Presbyterian Church.[35] Division and schism resulted from this declaration. In an effort to resolve the controversy the General Assembly, the highest organ of the Presbyterian Church, declared the loyal faction to be the "true" Walnut Street Church. When the division persisted, the loyal group sought injunctive relief to assure its control over congregational property. The opposition group's argument was that the General Assembly's declaration respecting the slavery issue had exceeded its authority, since the constitution of the Presbyterian Church prohibited it from "meddling in civil affairs," and that in turn the Assembly's power to "decide controversies" and to "suppress schismatical disputes" was not exercised within the limits of its constitutional authority. The Supreme Court, with two Justices dissenting on jurisdictional grounds, affirmed the action of the lower court in sustaining the loyal faction and granting it injunctive relief.[36]

---

[33] 13 Wall. 679 (1872).   [34] 16 Pet. 1 (1842).   [35] 13 Wall. at 691.

[36] The Supreme Court acted after the Supreme Court of Kentucky had decided the issue in favor of the nonloyal faction. Watson v. Avery, 66 Ky. 332 (1868). The loyal faction began the suit anew in the federal courts using diversity of citizenship to gain jurisdiction. The Court was sharply criticized for accepting the suit in this fashion. See Zollman, note 11 *supra*, at 285; Redfield, *Note on Watson v. Jones*, 11 Am. L. Reg. N.S. 452 (1872), as well as the dissents of Justices Clifford and Davis.

As is true of many notable Supreme Court opinions, Justice Miller's opinion covered a large field and many of the statements contained in it were dicta which have acquired prestige with the passage of time. In the most important part of his opinion he asserted three categories of cases in which courts are asked to resolve disputes over church property:

1. Cases where the religious institution, according to the express terms of the instrument whereby it receives the property, is "devoted to the teaching, support or spread of some specific form of religious doctrine or belief."[37]

2. Cases where the property is held by a church of congregational or independent polity which "owes no fealty or obligation to any higher authority."[38]

3. Cases where the ecclesiastical body holding the property is "a subordinate member of some general church organization in which there are superior ecclesiastical tribunals with a general and ultimate power of control more or less complete, in some supreme judicatory over the whole membership of that general organization."[39] Here the Court was speaking of the hierarchical polity and made no attempt to distinguish further between episcopal and synodical types.

As for cases falling into the first class, Justice Miller said that the ordinary principles of charitable uses would apply and that neither the majority of the congregation in an independent church nor the higher authority in the hierarchical church could direct the property to uses to which it was not dedicated.[40]

In the second type, where properties have been acquired by an independent or congregational church, and no specific tenet is attached to it, "where there is a schism which leads to a separation into distinct and conflicting bodies, the rights of such bodies to the use of the property must be determined by the ordinary principles

---

[37] 13 Wall. at 722.   [38] *Ibid.*   [39] *Ibid.*

[40] "In regard to the first of these classes it seems hardly to admit of a rational doubt that an individual or an association of individuals may dedicate property by way of trust to the purpose of sustaining, supporting, and propagating definite religious doctrines or principles, provided that in doing so they violate no law of morality, and give to the instrument by which their purpose is evidenced, the formalities which the laws require. And it would seem also to be the obvious duty of the court, in a case properly made, to see that the property so dedicated is not diverted from the trust which is thus attached to its use." *Id.* at 723.

which govern voluntary associations.[41] Here the internal law of the congregation is determinative. If its own rule is that majority vote determines the manner of using the property, this determination must be accepted as final by the individual members and by the courts:[42]

> This ruling admits of no inquiry into the existing religious opinions of those who comprise the legal or regular organization; for, if such was permitted, a very small minority, without any officers of the church among them, might be found to be the only faithful supporters of the religious dogmas of the founders of the church. There being no such trust imposed upon the property when purchased or given, the court will not imply one for the purpose of expelling from its use those who by regular succession and order constitute the church, because they may have changed in some respect their views of religious truths.

Turning then to the third class of case—the one actually involved in *Watson v. Jones*—where the congregation is a member of a church with a hierarchical polity, the Court said:[43]

> In this class of cases we think the rule of action which should govern the civil courts, founded in the broad and sound view of the relations of church and state under our system of laws, . . . is, that, whenever the questions of discipline, or of faith, or ecclesiastical rule, custom, or law have been decided by the highest of these church judicatories to which the matter has been carried, the legal tribunals must accept such decisions as final, and binding on them in their application to the case before them.

Since the Presbyterian Church was found to fall into the third category,[44] the Court held that the action of the General Assembly of the Presbyterian Church in designating the loyal faction of the Walnut Street Presbyterian Church as the true church was determinative of the case before the Court and it affirmed the decree enjoining the dissidents from interference with use of the property.

What was most significant about the opinion was its repudiation of the departure-from-doctrine standard and the correlative implied trust rule. In the case of a church with a congregational polity, its internal law governs and ordinarily this means majority rule.

---

[41] *Id.* at 725.

[42] *Ibid.*

[43] *Id.* at 727.

[44] See note 3 *supra*.

In the hierarchical church, the question is resolved by the authoritative organs of the church in accordance with its established law. If the opinion is taken literally, then neither the action of a majority in a congregational church nor that of an authoritative tribunal in a hierarchical church can be examined and condemned by a civil court on the ground that it results in a substantial departure from fundamental doctrines.[45] The courts will not interpose to insure institutional stability and integrity other than to inquire as to the determination by the organ vested with authority to make the decisive determination.

Watson was decided on the basis of federal common law in a diversity case. The Court's repudiation of the departure-from-doctrine standard appeared to rest primarily on the Court's application of principles derived from the law of voluntary associations[46] and its feeling that courts lack competence to define and interpret fundamental religious doctrines or to identify departures therefrom.[47] But as Mr. Justice Brennan later pointed out in the *Presbyterian Church Case*, the following language that he quoted from the *Watson* opinion also had a "clear constitutional ring":[48]

> In this country the full and free right to entertain any religious belief, to practice any religious principle, and to teach any religious doctrine which does not violate the laws of morality and property, and which does not infringe personal rights, is conceded to all. The law knows no heresy, and is committed to the support of no dogma, the establishment of no sect. . . . All who unite themselves to such a body [the general church] do so with an implied consent to

---

[45] See TORPEY, JUDICIAL DOCTRINES OF RELIGIOUS RIGHTS IN AMERICA 133 *et seq.* (1948); Casad, note 11 *supra*, at 435 *et seq.*

[46] "Religious organizations come before us in the same attitude as other voluntary associations for benevolent or charitable purposes, and their rights of property, or contract, are equally under the protection of the law, and the actions of their members subject to its restraints." 13 Wall. at 714.

[47] "Each of these large and influential bodies . . . has a body of constitutional and ecclesiastical law of its own, to be found in their written organic laws, their books of discipline, in their collections of precedents, in their usages and customs, which as to each constitute a system of ecclesiastical law and religious faith that tasks the ablest minds to become familiar with. It is not to be supposed that the judges of the civil courts can be as competent in the ecclesiastical law and religious faith of all these bodies as the ablest men in each are in reference to their own." *Id.* at 729.

[48] 393 U.S. at 446, quoting 13 Wall. at 728–29. (Bracketed material inserted by Brennan, J.)

[its] government, and are bound to submit to it. But it would be a vain consent, and would lead to the total subversion of such religious bodies, if anyone aggrieved by one of their decisions could appeal to the secular courts and have them [*sic*] reversed. It is of the essence of these religious unions, and of their right to establish tribunals for the decision of questions arising among themselves, that those decisions should be binding in all cases of ecclesiastical cognizance, subject only to such appeals as the organism itself provides for.

Implicit in this language is the idea that the constitutional freedom of the churches includes an immunity to intervention by civil courts to pass on questions of religious doctrine, a domain reserved to the churches.

Justice Miller in writing the *Watson* opinion painted with a broad brush. Not only did the opinion mark a complete rejection of the departure-from-doctrine standard as a basis for judicial intervention through use of the implied trust fiction. It seemed to go all the way in rejecting any judicial examination of the determination by the appropriate authority, however determined and whether applied to a congregational or a hierarchical church. The Court did not distinguish between substantive and procedural matters. Did the case mean that courts could not inquire into questions of jurisdiction, procedure, and fundamental fairness when asked to accept at face value the determination of the ecclesiastical issue by the organ claiming authority to make the determination? On its face the opinion seemed to require such thoroughgoing judicial abstention.

That the Court's sweeping language in *Watson* should not be so literally construed was made clear shortly after *Watson* was decided. At the following Term the Court in *Bouldin v. Alexander*[49] held that the trustees of land given in trust for a Baptist church in the city of Washington could not be removed from their trusteeship by a minority of the church society or meeting without warning, without charges and trial, and in direct contravention of the church rules. The Court said it could inquire whether an attempted act of expulsion of members was the act of the church. "In a congregational church, the majority, if they adhere to the organization and to the doctrines, represent the church. An expulsion of the majority by a minority is a void act."[50]

---

49 15 Wall. 131 (1827).   50 *Id.* at 140.

The opinion in *Bouldin* was written by Justice Strong speaking for a unanimous Court that included Justice Miller. While the case affirmed majority rule in a church with a congregational polity, what was important was the Court's willingness to inquire into the legal authority of the group that had presumed to act for the congregation. Apparently the *Watson* case, not even mentioned in the opinion, was not regarded as relevant. Even more striking was the opinion of Federal Circuit Judge Taft, in *Brundage v. Deardorf*,[51] where he reviewed at length the validity of the adoption of a new constitution by the Brethren Church. Here the case turned on procedural regularity measured by the law of the church. Taft said that nothing in *Watson* required acquiescence in what he termed "an open and avowed defiance of the original compact, and an express violation of it."[52]

Watson stated a rule of federal common law applicable in diversity cases. As such it was not binding on the state courts. It did, however, exercise considerable influence on the state courts, particularly in its treatment of the question of church polity and in the propriety of judicial application of the departure-from-doctrine standard in the case of disputes involving hierarchical churches.[53] The effect of *Watson* was to confirm and strengthen the autonomy of a hierarchical church. It was a different story, however, with congregational churches. Many state courts were not convinced that they should abstain from applying the departure-from-doctrine standard in churches with a congregational polity, where a rule of abstention would permit a temporary majority to impair the insti-

---

[51] 55 Fed. 839 (C.C. N.D. Ohio 1893).

[52] "Even if the supreme judicatory has the right to construe the limitations of its own power, and the civil courts may not interfere with such a construction, and must take it as conclusive, we do not understand the supreme court, in Watson v. Jones, to hold that an open and avowed defiance of the original compact, and an express violation of it, will be taken as a decision of the supreme judicatory which is binding on the civil courts. Certainly, the effect of Watson v. Jones cannot be extended beyond the principle that a bona fide decision of the fundamental law of the church must be recognized as conclusive by the civil courts. Clearly, it was not the intention of the court to recognize as legitimate the revolutionary action of a majority of a supreme judicatory, in fraud of the rights of a minority seeking to maintain the integrity of the original compact." *Id.* at 847–48.

[53] See Note, note 10 *supra*.

tutional stability and continuity of the congregation.[54] They continued to use the implied trust rule and apply the departure-from-doctrine standard in disputes over property, where it was found that the majority was attempting a "fundamental" or radical deviation from established doctrine and usage.[55] Indeed, the *Watson* opinion itself suggested an opening for inquiry into radical or basic departure when it said that no trust would be implied "for the purpose of expelling from its use those who by regular succession and order constitute the church, because they may have changed in some respect their views of religious truth."[56] The phrase "in some respect" plausibly left open a judicial inquiry whether a majority was engaging in a fundamental departure from established doctrine and usage and could furnish a justification for the continued but discrete application of the implied trust rule. Apparently not all the Justices who participated in the *Watson* case were satisfied that it left no further room for the departure-from-doctrine standard in its application to congregational type churches. Justice Strong, in lectures on church law at the Union Theological Seminary during the winter of 1874–75, assumed the continued vitality of the implied trust rule as a matter of common law and attached great importance to it.[57]

The Supreme Court had no further occasion to deal with a problem of this kind until 1929, when it reviewed and affirmed a decision of the Philippine Supreme Court which had dismissed a complaint challenging the refusal of the Roman Catholic archbishop of Manila to appoint petitioner as a chaplain on the ground that he did not satisfy the qualifications established by canon law for that

---

[54] See Note, note 11 *supra*, 74 YALE L.J. at 1118 *et seq.*; sources cited note 45 *supra*.

[55] ". . . in cases of this kind the alleged deviation from the tenets or true standard of faith of the religious denomination ought to be so palpable and unequivocal as to enable the court, from an examination of the historical and doctrinal practices of the church, to say, that in respect of the doctrine in question there has been an essential change and departure therefrom. . . . In other words, before the court will be justified in holding the trust to have been perverted or misused, it must clearly appear that such a change or departure has taken place in the fundamental doctrine that it cannot be said to be the same, or that the denomination, as it existed before the change, is not, in all essential particulars and purposes, identical with that existing afterwards." Kuns v. Robertson, 154 Ill. 394, 415 (1895).

[56] 13 Wall. at 725.   [57] STRONG, note 11 *supra*.

office.[58] Respecting the role of a civil court in the case of a dispute over an ecclesiastical matter, the Court, speaking through Mr. Justice Brandeis, said:[59]

> In the absence of fraud, collusion, or arbitrariness, the decisions of the proper church tribunals on matters purely ecclesiastical, although affecting civil rights, are accepted in litigation before the secular courts as conclusive, because the parties in interest made them so by contract or otherwise.

This case clearly fitted the rules governing hierarchical churches. In no church is the locus of authority more clearly defined than in the Roman Catholic Church. Several points in Justice Brandeis' opinion deserve brief attention. He rested the case for judicial abstention on familiar grounds of civil law. The parties had "by contract or otherwise" made the decision of the proper tribunal conclusive on matters purely ecclesiastical. Perhaps more significant was the proviso "In the absence of fraud, collusion or arbitrariness. . . ." This language did not appear in *Watson*. It could well be construed as limiting the breadth of the *Watson* opinion and sanctioning judicial review for the limited purpose of inquiring into questions of jurisdiction, procedural regularity, and perhaps fundamental unfairness.

III. The Presbyterian Church Case

It was apparent that state courts that continued to follow the departure-from-doctrine standard as a matter of state common law had no intention of abandoning it unless forced to do so by some higher authority. This development was foreshadowed when the Supreme Court, by its interpretation of the Fourteenth Amendment made the free exercise and establishment clauses of the First Amendment applicable to the states.[60] Insofar as the application of the departure-from-doctrine concept in conjunction with the implied trust concept raised questions of undue intrusion by the civil courts into ecclesiastical matters, thereby interfering with the freedom of religious bodies to order their own affairs, the door was now open for invoking the limitations under the First and Four-

---

[58] Gonzalez v. Archbishop, 280 U.S. 1 (1929).

[59] *Id.* at 16.

[60] Cantwell v. Connecticut, 310 U.S. 296 (1940); Everson v. Board of Education, 330 U.S. 1 (1947).

teenth Amendments. Astute attorneys were quick to seize the opening. *Kedroff v. St. Nicholas Cathedral of the Russian Orthodox Church in North America*[61] grew out of a dispute between the Moscow-based general Russian Orthodox Church and the Russian Orthodox churches located in North America over an appointment to St. Nicholas Cathedral in New York City. The Court declared unconstitutional a New York statute that recognized the autonomy and authority of the North American churches which had declared their independence from the general church. The New York courts sustained the validity of the statute and held that the North American Church's appointed hierarchy had the right to use the cathedral. This legislative intrusion into the government and control of the church was held by the Supreme Court to constitute an interference with the free exercise of religion guaranteed by the First Amendment. The Court now began the process of converting the common-law doctrine of *Watson v. Jones* into a constitutional limitation:[62]

> The opinion [in *Watson v. Jones*] radiates . . . a spirit of freedom for religious organizations, and independence from secular control or manipulations—in short, power to decide for themselves, free from state interference, matters of church government as well as those of faith and doctrine. Freedom to select the clergy, where no improper methods of choice are proven, we think, must now be said to have federal constitutional protection as part of the free exercise of religion against state interference. . . .
>
> By fiat [the statute] displaces one church administrator with another. It passes the control of matters strictly ecclesiastical from one church authority to another. It thus intrudes for the benefit of one segment of a church the power of the state into the forbidden area of religious freedom contrary to the principles of the First Amendment.

When later the New York courts attempted to achieve the same result, without the aid of the statute that had been held invalid, the Court in the *Kreshik* case[63] reached the same result.

Kedroff and *Kreshik* went far on the road to constitutional status

---

[61] 344 U.S. 94 (1952).

[62] *Id.* at 116, 119. For critical analyses of *Kedroff*, see Duesenberg, note 11 *supra*; Note, note 11 *supra*, 74 YALE L.J. 1113.

[63] Kreshik v. St. Nicholas Cathedral of the Russian Orthodox Church of North America, 363 U.S. 190 (1960).

for the *Watson* doctrine that organs of civil government should not intrude into the determination of ecclesiastical affairs when deciding a controversy over the control of church property. But these two cases had dealt with a peculiar question—although a very vital one—of ecclesiastical authority. The Court by its decision put its weight behind the traditional established authority. No question was raised about deviation from fundamental doctrine. The implied trust rule was not at issue. *Kedroff* and *Kreshik* dealt with a question of underlying importance in *Watson:* where does ecclesiastical authority reside? But the problem in *Watson* grew out of a congregational schism and did not directly involve the question of control of the central church.

Notwithstanding these limitations, *Kedroff* and *Kreshik* pointed to erosion of the common-law implied trust rule as used to sanction the departure-from-doctrine standard. Commentators also were suggesting that the rule could not withstand constitutional scrutiny.[64] But state courts continued to follow and apply the rule.[65]

It was against this background that the Georgia Supreme Court decided the *Presbyterian Church Case.* Finding that the Presbyterian Church–U.S.A. had made substantial departures from established Presbyterian doctrine and usage, the court declared that the implied trust of the local congregational property in favor of the general body had terminated and it awarded custody of the property to the members and ministers who withdrew from the general church.[66]

---

[64] See PFEFFER, CHURCH, STATE AND FREEDOM (1967); Casad, note 11 *supra;* Duesenberg, note 11 *supra;* Note, note 10 *supra;* Note, note 11 *supra,* 74 YALE L.J. 1113.

See also Northside Bible Church v. Goodson, 387 F.2d 534, 538 (5th Cir. 1967), where the court held unconstitutional an Alabama statute that authorized a 65 percent majority of a local congregation to sever its connection with a parent church and to retain possession and ownership of its local church property free and clear of any trust in favor of the parent church whenever the local group determined that a change of social policies had occurred within the parent church. The court said that the statute "brazenly intrudes upon the very basic and traditional practice of the Methodist Church, and supersedes the processes available within the church structure for the settlement of disputes."

[65] See Cantrell v. Anderson, 390 S.W.2d 176 (Ky. 1965); Holiman v. Dovers, 236 Ark. 211, 236 Ark. 460 (1963); Vogler v. Primitive Baptist Church, 415 S.W.2d 72 (Ky. 1967); Davis v. Scher, 356 Mich. 291 (1959); Huber v. Thorn, 189 Kan. 631, (1962).

[66] The Georgia Supreme Court found that the "General Assembly's declaration that foreordination was no longer necessary for Reformed theology was contrary

The case bears many resemblances to *Watson v. Jones*. The Presbyterian Church—a hierarchical (in this case synodical or associational) church—was again involved. Courts had not generally applied the implied trust rule in cases involving churches of this type. Moreover, just as in *Watson*, where the schism arose over the general church's declaration on the slavery issue, so here the principal source of schism was over the declaration of the national church respecting social issues. The dispute turned on the interpretation and application of the church's doctrine and in a broad sense the dispute was a sociopolitical one. The Georgia Supreme Court could have reached a contrary decision either by finding that the implied trust doctrine was not applicable to hierarchical churches or that in this case there was no substantial departure from fundamental doctrine and usages or that the fundamental doctrine rule was no longer valid.

The Supreme Court's reversal of the Georgia decision marks the demise on constitutional grounds of the departure-from-doctrine rule. In reaching this result the Court dwelt on *Watson, Gonzalez, Kedroff*, and *Kreshik*. Indeed, the Court said that *Kedroff* had converted "the principle of *Watson* as qualified by *Gonzalez* into a constitutional rule."[67] While recognizing that the state has a legitimate interest in resolving property disputes, and that a civil court is a proper forum for that resolution, the Court said:[68]

> [T]he First Amendment severely circumscribes the role that civil courts may play in resolving church property disputes. First Amendment values are plainly jeopardized when church property litigation is made to turn on the resolution by civil courts of controversies over religious doctrine and

---

to one of the basic tenets which has made Presbyterianism significantly different from other denominations. The General Assembly's endorsement of civil disobedience, which would allow a citizen to decide whether or not he will obey the law, is a radical venture into civil affairs. It is absolute defiance of law and order, and is the road to anarchy. Also, the General Assembly's recommendation as to what steps should be taken to secure peace in Vietnam is an entry into diplomatic and military matters beyond the church's function as delineated by its Westminster Confession of Faith and Book of Church Order." 224 Ga. at 77.

In view of the action taken by the Georgia Supreme Court on the remand of the case, see note 71 *infra*, it is important to note that any claim by the Presbyterian Church in the United States with respect to the use of the property owned by the local congregation rested on an implied trust theory.

[67] 393 U.S. at 447.   [68] *Id.* at 449.

practice. If civil courts undertake to resolve such controversies in order to adjudicate the property dispute, the hazards are ever present of inhibiting the free development of religious doctrine and of implicating secular interests in matters of purely ecclesiastical concern. . . . The Amendment therefore commands civil courts to decide church property disputes without resolving underlying controversies over religious doctrines.

As pointed out by the Court, the application by the Georgia court of the departure-from-doctrine standard required two determinations: [69] (1) what the tenets of faith and practice of the Presbyterian Church were at the time of the local congregation's affiliation and (2) whether the general church departed substantially from prior doctrine: [70]

Thus, the departure-from-doctrine element of the Georgia implied trust theory requires the civil court to determine matters at the very core of a religion—the interpretation of particular church doctrines and the importance of those doctrines to the religion. Plainly, the First Amendment forbids civil courts from playing such a role.

To emphasize its point the Court said that since the Georgia courts on remand may undertake to determine whether the petitioner (the general church) is entitled to relief on its cross-claims, the Court found it appropriate to remark that the departure-from-doctrine element of Georgia's implied trust theory "can play *no* role in any future judicial proceedings." [71] The Court then made

---

[69] "This determination has two parts. The civil court must first decide whether the challenged actions of the general church depart substantially from prior doctrine. In reaching such a decision, the court must of necessity make its own interpretation of the meaning of church doctrines. If the court should decide that a substantial departure has occurred, it must then go on to determine whether the issue on which the general church has departed holds a place of such importance in the traditional theology as to require that the trust be terminated. A civil court can make this determination only after assessing the relative significance to the religion of the tenets from which departure was found." *Id*. at 450.

[70] *Ibid*.

[71] *Ibid*. On remand of the case the Supreme Court of Georgia again affirmed the judgment of the trial court in favor of the local congregations. Presbyterian Church in the United States v. Eastern Heights Presbyterian Church; Presbyterian Church in the United States v. Mary Elizabeth Blue Hull Memorial Presbyterian Church, 225 Ga. 259 (1969). Finding that the departure-from-doctrine standard declared unconstitutional by the United States Supreme Court was an essential element of the common-law rule whereby an implied trust resulted in favor of the general

the interesting point that even if the general church in reaching this decision purported to apply the state-fashioned departure-from-doctrine standard, this would not be subject to review by a civil court, since the "First Amendment forbids a state from employing religious organizations as an arm of the civil judiciary to perform the function of interpreting and applying state standards."[72]

What then does the *Presbyterian Church Case* contribute to the body of doctrine respecting the intervention of civil courts in ecclesiastical disputes?

1. It is constitutionally appropriate for civil courts to take jurisdiction of and decide cases that raise questions of control of church property, even though the dispute over control arises from a controversy over ecclesiastical matters.

2. In deciding these cases, the courts are constitutionally prohibited from employing the departure-from-doctrine element of the implied trust rule as a standard for deciding which faction in the congregation or church is entitled to the use and control of the property. This limitation appears to apply regardless of the nature of the church polity. Although the *Presbyterian Church Case* involved a hierarchical church, the Court's adoption of *Watson* as constitutional principle, the rationale of its decision with its emphasis on the freedom of the churches, and the explicit ban on any future use of the departure-from-doctrine standard, all leave no doubt that the Court did not mean to make distinctions turning on the nature of the church polity.[73]

Presbyterian church body, the court held that since a part of the rule had been stricken, the remainder fell with it and that the property in question was therefore no longer subject to an implied trust. Since it was clear that the local congregations held legal title to the property, the court affirmed the original judgment in their favor.

Claiming that the action of the Georgia Supreme Court on the remand in refusing further to apply an implied trust rule in this situation violates the First and Fourteenth Amendments, the Presbyterian Church in the United States has now applied to the United States Supreme Court for review of this action on a writ of certiorari. Presbyterian Church in the United States v. Mary Elizabeth Blue Hull Memorial Presbyterian Church, 38 U.S. LAW WEEK 3092 (1969).

[72] *Id.* at 451.

[73] The question whether a civil court can apply the departure-from-doctrine standard in the case of an express trust remains an open issue. Mr. Justice Harlan, in his short concurring opinion, assumed that its use was permissible in this situation. He stated that he did not read the Court's opinion "to go further to hold that the Fourteenth Amendment forbids civilian courts from enforcing a deed or will which

3. Since the civil courts will continue to decide cases growing out of church disputes where control of property is at issue, the effect of the *Presbyterian Church Case* is to require courts to focus their attention on the locus of authority in the determination of ecclesiastical issues. Where does the power reside in the church structure for passing on the issue and what line of authority must be pursued? Here the distinction made in *Watson* between the congregational and hierarchical polities becomes important. According to *Watson* in the case of the independent or congregational churches, the issue of authority is determined by the usual rules applicable to voluntary associations.[74] The internal rules of the organization are determinative and if they prescribe rule by the majority of the congregation, this becomes the controlling authority subject to any limitations found in its constitution and bylaws. Presumably, then, if a majority of a congregation wish to employ a minister of a different faith or affiliate with a church body with entirely different tenets and practices, a minority loyal to the established tenets and usages of the congregation can no longer invoke a civil court's intervention to support its control of the property.

In the case of a hierarchical church, the authority for determination of the ecclesiastical issue is prescribed by the law of the general church body and binding determinations are made by its ecclesiastical organs in accordance with this law.

The application of this distinction to some well-known church bodies presents no problems. The Roman Catholic, Episcopal, and Presbyterian churches, for instance, are readily identified as hierarchical in the legal sense. The Congregational and Baptist churches are just as easily classified as congregational in their polity. Others are not so easily classified, as evident from the problems courts have faced in attempting to classify the polity of the Lutheran churches in the United States. Clearly hierarchical in the European countries of their origin, the Lutheran churches when established in this country showed a strong bent toward congregational autonomy despite synodical or denominational affiliation. This has led to disagreement between courts on the characterization of the Lutheran

---

expressly and clearly lays down conditions limiting a religious organization's use of the property which is granted. . . . In such a case, the church should not be permitted to keep the property simply because church authorities have determined that the doctrinal innovation is justified by the faith's basic principles." *Id.* at 452.

[74] See *supra* note 46.

polity.[75] The varying results reached respecting the legal characterization of the polity highlights the important point, sometimes
obscured by attention to the constitutional issues raised by the
departure-from-doctrine standard, that civil courts in identifying a
church's polity for legal purposes are necessarily at the same time
passing on an important ecclesiastical question respecting the nature
of the church and its authority. Whether a court's determination
of polity is founded on common knowledge, expert testimony, or
the court's own examination of historical, documentary, and theological sources, it is resolving a legal issue by reference to a standard
that requires a judicial interpretation of ecclesiastical sources.

Even if the issue of polity is readily determined, the sources and
organs of authority may not be so readily ascertained. In the case
of the congregational type of polity, the assumption is that the usual
rules respecting voluntary associations apply and that the question
becomes one of examining the constitution and bylaws to which
members are presumed to subscribe. In many and probably most
instances this may not present difficulties. But an examination of
cases arising from disputes within an independent congregation reveals instances where congregations have no authoritative source
documents, such as charters, constitutions, or bylaws.[76] Where does
authority reside here? Perhaps a court will find some controlling
usage such as rule by a majority of members of the congregation
or by a body of elected trustees or elders, or, as in some cases, it
may simply resolve the question by its own rule that the majority

---

[75] For example, in the context of the same factual dispute the United Lutheran
Church in America was first found to be synodical in character by a federal district
court, Evangelical Lutheran Synod v. First English Lutheran Church, 47 F. Supp.
954 (W.D. Okla. 1942), and then, after the district court was reversed on jurisdictional grounds by the court of appeals, 135 F.2d 701 (10th Cir. 1943), was found to
be congregational in polity by the Oklahoma Supreme Court. First English Lutheran
Church v. Bloch, 195 Okla. 579 (1945).
    Compare Dressen v. Brameier, 56 Iowa 756 (1881); Duessel v. Proch, 78 Conn.
343 (1905); Fadness v. Braunborg, 73 Wis. 257 (1889); Gudmundson v. Thingvalla
Lutheran Church, 29 N.D. 291 (1914); Mertz v. Schaeffer, 271 S.W.2d 238 (St. Louis
Ct. App. 1954); and Rock Dell Norwegian Lutheran Congregation v. Mommsen,
174 Minn. 207 (1928), all of which found the Lutheran Church to be congregational
in polity, with First Evangelical Lutheran Church v. Dysinger, 120 Cal. App. 132
(1931); Harmon v. Dreher, 1 Speers Eq. (S.C. 1843); Wehmer v. Fokenga, 57 Neb.
510 (1899), all of which found the church to be hierarchical.

[76] See, e.g., Evans v. Criss, 39 Misc.2d 314 (N.Y. Sup. Ct. N.Y.Co. 1963); Golden
v. Brooks, 276 S.W.2d 670 (Ky. 1955); Sapp v. Callaway, 208 Ga. 805 (1952).

governs, thus judicially creating a polity for the congregation by reference to well-accepted democratic principles.

4. In a part of its opinion in the *Presbyterian Church Case*, the Court indicated that though actions by authoritative religious organs may not be impugned on doctrinal grounds, courts may make a limited or marginal inquiry to determine the legality of these actions. As previously observed, the opinion in *Watson* taken on its face left no room for any kind of review of the ecclesiastical organ's determination. The eminent and leading authority on American church law, Carl Zollman, sharply criticized this aspect of the judicial abstention rule formulated in *Watson*.[77] In his view this would lead to judicial acquiescence in arbitrary and unprincipled action and abuse of power. Should not a civil court have authority to inquire into the question of jurisdiction of a church organ and the regularity of its actions? Should the question be examined by a court whether a church tribunal followed the procedures prescribed by its own internal law?[78] In the case where affairs of a congregation are determined by a majority of its members, should a civil court inquire whether the meeting was properly called and notice given and whether only properly qualified members took part in the meeting?[79]

---

[77] ". . . a refusal by the courts in a proper case to construe the constitution, canons or rules of the church and revise its trials and the proceedings of its governing bodies, instead of preserving religious liberty, destroys it *pro tanto*. If a person who connects himself with a religious association is to be placed completely at its mercy irrespective of the agreement which he has made with it, the conception of religious liberty as applied to such a case becomes a farce, a delusion, and a snare. Such a conception opens the doors wide for the most odious form of religious tyranny." ZOLLMAN, *supra* note 11, at 237–38; see also *id*. at 281 *et seq*.

[78] Justice Strong, who voted in the majority in *Watson v. Jones*, was not sure of the answer to this question. He stated that "this question is at present a pending one in the country, and opinions differ respecting it." STRONG, note 11 *supra*, at 42. He noted the arguments pro and con, but was careful to conclude that he did not "wish to be understood as expressing any fixed opinion on the subject." *Id*. at 44.

[79] Comparatively little has been written on this subject. Many commentators agree with the following statement written in 1871: "Non-established churches are merely voluntary associations founded on contract. Their constitutions, canons, rules and regulations are the stipulations between the parties. Tribunals may be established by agreement, for the enforcement of discipline, but they are limited by the terms of such agreement and must proceed as therein specified, and substantially in accordance with the law of the land and the principles of justice. They have no 'jurisdiction,' properly speaking, for that implies the existence of a power conferred by the state and vested in functionaries sanctioned for that purpose by the state, but that which for convenience may be so termed, entirely dependent

Courts generally have experienced no difficulty in reviewing actions of membership organizations to see whether they conformed to the organization's internal law.[80] To apply this same degree of review to determination by ecclesiastical organs is simply an application of the neutral principles to which Mr. Justice Brennan referred in the *Presbyterian Church Case*.[81] The truth is that courts, notwithstanding *Watson*, have reviewed actions by ecclesiastical authority to determine legality.[82] This has not been peculiar to state courts. In the *Bouldin* case the Supreme Court reviewed the validity of what purported to be the action of a church, and in the much cited case of *Brundage v. Deardorf*, the federal court scrutinized at length the validity of procedures employed in amending a national church body's constitution.[83]

---

upon the contract, and which never precludes the fullest investigation by the civil courts in a proper case, arising upon the action of such voluntary tribunals, and the administration of such relief as upon the facts appears appropriate and necessary." Fuller, note 17 *supra*, at 314.

[80] See Chafee, note 25 *supra*; Comment, *Developments in the Law—Judicial Control of Private Associations*, 76 HARV. L. REV. 983 (1963). For discussions respecting labor unions, see Summers, *Union Schism in Perspective: Flexible Doctrine, Double Standards, and Projected Answers*, 45 VA. L. REV. 261 (1959); Summers, *The Law of Union Discipline: What the Courts Do in Fact*, 70 YALE L.J. 175 (1960).

[81] "It is obvious, however, that not every civil court decision as to property claimed by a religious organization jeopardizes values protected by the First Amendment. Civil courts do not inhibit free exercise of religion merely by opening their doors to disputes involving church property. And there are neutral principles of law, developed for use in all property disputes, which can be applied without 'establishing' churches to which property is awarded." 393 U.S. at 449.

[82] Some courts will grant review of any ecclesiastical proceeding despite the character of the interest involved: Taylor v. Jackson, 273 Fed. 345 (App. D.C. 1921); Jones v. State, 28 Neb. 495 (1890); Hendryx v. People's United Church, 42 Wash. 336 (1906); Kaminski v. Hoynak, 373 Pa. 194 (1954); Russian-Serbian Holy Trinity Orthodox Church v. Kulik, 279 N.W. 364 (Minn. 1938); Sims v. Greene, 76 F. Supp. 669 (E.D. Pa. 1947).

Others grant review of procedural regularity only when a property interest is at stake: Fussel v. Hail, 233 Ill. 73 (1908); Ramsey v. Hicks, 174 Ind. 428, 434 (1910); State ex rel. Johnson v. Tulane Ave. Baptist Church, 144 So. 639 (La. App. 1932); Shaw v. Harvey, 7 N.E.2d 515 (Ind. App. 1937); Jenkins v. New Shiloh Baptist Church, 189 Md. 518 (1948).

Still others deny review altogether despite the character of the interest: Van Vliet v. Vander Naald, 290 Mich. 365 (1939); *but see* Komarynski v. Popovich, 232 Mich. 88 (1925).

[83] See text *supra*, at notes 51 and 52. For later cases where federal courts undertook a careful review of the procedural regularity of actions taken by church bodies, see Taylor v. Jackson, 273 Fed. 345 (App. D.C. 1921); Sims v. Greene, 76 F. Supp. 669 (E.D. Pa. 1947).

In *Gonzalez* Justice Brandeis said that the decisions of proper church tribunals on matters purely ecclesiastical are accepted in litigation before the civil courts "[i]n the absence of fraud, collusion or arbitrariness."[84] This limiting phrase now assumes new importance. The Court in the *Presbyterian Church Case* said that in *Kedroff* the Court had converted the principle of *Watson* "as qualified by *Gonzalez*" into a constitutional rule.[85] But Mr. Justice Brennan went on to say that the *Gonzalez* exception permits only the narrowest kind of review. It was unnecessary for the Court to elaborate upon these terms, but clearly they leave open an important avenue for collateral judicial review of an ecclesiastical determination. "Arbitrariness" as a standard for review is an indeterminate and flexible term. Much can be poured into it. It is not stretching the limiting phrase of *Gonzalez* to suggest that it permits an inquiry into jurisdiction, regularity of procedure, and basic fairness of the ecclesiastical proceeding and determination. Indeed, the Court's reference in a footnote[86] to the *Bouldin* and *Brundage* cases as instances of the marginal review of ecclesiastical determination offers persuasive evidence that the *Gonzalez* exception will be construed to authorize review of questions going to legality in the strict sense. This suggests a parallel to judicial review of administrative tribunals. In any event it may safely be predicted that future litigation will furnish a rich glossary on "fraud, collusion, or arbitrariness."

What does the *Presbyterian Church Case* contribute to the general body of ideas developed in the interpretation of the establishment and free exercise clauses of the First Amendment? Intervention by a civil court in an ecclesiastical dispute presents a genuine question of church-state relations where it is particularly meaningful to speak of the separation of church and state whether viewed as a principle derived from the twin religion clauses of the First Amendment[87] or as an instrumentality doctrine serving the cause of religious liberty.[88]

It is worth noting that while the Court in the *Presbyterian Church Case* speaks of values protected by the First Amendment, at no

---

[84] 280 U.S. at 16.   [85] 393 U.S. at 447.   [86] 393 U.S. at 447 n. 6.

[87] See Everson v. Board of Education, 330 U.S. 1, 14–15 (1947); Zorach v. Clauson, 343 U.S. 306, 312 (1952).

[88] See Katz, *Freedom of Religion and State Neutrality*, 20 U. CHI. L. REV. 426 (1953).

point in the opinion is it categorically stated that the judicial application of the departure-from-doctrine standard violates either the establishment or the free exercise limitations or both. Indeed, if First Amendment values are the criteria, it may be argued that the decision upholds a general freedom of association distilled from the First Amendment freedoms and that the holding applies equally to prohibit state interference with the internal affairs of any voluntary nonprofit association that serves a charitable purpose. The law respecting voluntary membership associations generally has been developed on the basis of contract, property, and trust law.[89] The general tendency in recent years has been to enlarge judicial review of the action of private membership organizations in the interest of assuring fair treatment of members. In affirming the jurisdiction of civil courts to review religious disputes in order to settle property issues and in saying that courts in applying neutral principles do not thereby establish a religion, the Supreme Court appears to be treating churches like any other voluntary association.[90] Such an interpretation of the case fits into Professor Kurland's thesis that the purpose of the twin religion clauses of the First Amendment is to eliminate the religious factor as a basis for legislative classification.[91] But the underlying substance of the *Presbyterian Church Case* opinion clearly reflects reliance on the religion clauses of the First Amendment and strongly suggests that in the Court's view voluntary religious associations are constitutionally distinguishable from other types of voluntary associations. The Court relied heavily on *Watson*, which contained strong overtones of religious liberty, and on *Kedroff*, which, in converting *Watson* into a constitutional rule, clearly rested on the free exercise clause. A reading of the total opinion seems to make clear, therefore, that when the Court spoke of "First Amendment values," it was referring to values protected by the free exercise and establishment clauses. It is, however, interesting that the Court did not explicitly ground the decision on the free exercise clause as appears warranted by its reliance on *Kedroff*. The ambiguous reference to First Amendment values suggests reliance on both the free exercise and establishment clauses. This is a situation where the two clauses work to the same end.

---

[89] See sources cited in note 17 *supra.*

[90] See note 81 *supra.*

[91] See KURLAND, RELIGION AND THE LAW (1962).

Application of the departure-from-doctrine standard interferes with the freedom of churches to interpret and develop their doctrines; it also requires courts to put the imprimatur of their authority behind a particular set of religious doctrines, thereby raising an establishment issue. Moreover, according to Mr. Justice Black's famous dictum in *Everson,* any interference by organs of government in the affairs of the churches violates the establishment limitation.[92]

The *Presbyterian Church Case* reinforces *Kedroff* on the general proposition that the freedom of religion secured by the First Amendment extends to the churches in their institutional and corporate capacity. By far the greater number of free exercise cases have involved claims of violation of individual freedom, and it is possible that the free exercise clause has its greatest significance in application to individual claims. But the churches as institutions may also stake out some very elementary and basic claims to freedom under the First Amendment. Certainly any notion that the First Amendment freedoms can be invoked only by natural persons has long since become obsolete.

The Court's action in utilizing the First Amendment to condemn the application of a state common-law doctrine that threatened inhibition of free development of religious doctrine by implicating secular organs in matters of purely ecclesiastical concern should not obscure the complexity of the issues involved and the problem faced by the Court in choosing between competing interests. Probably the principal reason why state courts have applied the departure-from-doctrine standard is to protect the expectations of those who have helped to build up congregations by their contributions and other efforts. The departure-from-doctrine standard therefore helped to promote the free exercise of religion. The Court in the *Presbyterian Church Case* made a choice between competing claims to freedom. Moreover, while the Court's decision purported to rest on a constitutionally required abstention of civil organs of government from the determination of ecclesiastical affairs, complete abstention is impossible as long as civil courts undertake to review in any way ecclesiastical determinations that touch on civil rights. When a court intervenes to determine property rights, its decision

---

92 "Neither a state nor the Federal Government, can, openly or secretly, participate in the affairs of any religious organizations or groups and *vice versa.*" 330 U.S. at 16.

necessarily gives support to one faction or another, and it uses the force of governmental authority to support and establish the victorious faction. By the same token the courts cannot be strictly neutral in reaching decisions on these matters.

The Court's language in the *Presbyterian Church Case* is categorical. Civil courts may not interpret religious doctrine in resolving church property disputes. The Court did not presume to weigh the interests served by the departure-from-doctrine standard against the constitutional difficulties resulting from this intrusion of the civil government upon the autonomy of the churches. But balancing is implicit in the resolution of the problem faced by the Court. It is fair to interpret the decision to mean that the legitimate interests served by the application of this standard are not sufficiently important to justify a state-created limitation on the freedom of an ecclesiastical body to be master in its own house in accordance with its established polity.

In conclusion, a word may be said on the practical implications of the *Presbyterian Church Case*. The ground rules for judicial intervention in religious disputes are now being nationalized and the application of these rules will be subject to supervision by the Supreme Court. Churches of both types of polities now may assert a federal constitutional liberty to define and develop their doctrines and to determine their affiliations with other church bodies, free from the hazards of litigation in the civil courts over the departure-from-doctrine issue. Freedom of affiliation is particularly important in this day of the ecumenical movement. The Supreme Court by its recent decision has facilitated the freedom of the churches to further this movement.[93] Parishioners and ministers dissatisfied with the policies adopted and actions taken by churches at the national level and congregations at the local level, where such actions are taken in accordance with the organization's own internal law, may of course withdraw, but in doing so they forfeit their claim to use of the church property.[94]

---

[93] For discussion of the problem prior to the *Presbyterian Church Case*, see the articles by Casad and Stringfellow, note 11 *supra;* also Note, 1967 Wis. L. Rev. 497.

[94] This conclusion assumes that the local congregational property is subject to a trust in favor of the national church body. If a state court may now constitutionally withdraw the entire benefit of the common-law implied trust doctrine in this situation, any interest of the national church body in the use of the property will have to rest either on statutory authority or on the express terms of a deed or trust instru-

A second practical effect of the *Presbyterian Church Case* is that it elevates a religious body's organic law—charter, constitution, and bylaws—to a new level of importance. Values served by the departure-from-doctrine standard, in terms of institutional stability and the expectations of donors, can be achieved by formulations explicitly set forth in the organization's basic documents. Similarly, a church organization, whatever its polity, is in the best position to maintain its autonomy as against the risk of judicial intervention by spelling out in its organic law the locus of authority, the procedure to be followed, and the limitations to be observed.[95] A well-defined organic law—whether or not called ecclesiastical law—is the best assurance of both stability and autonomy. This lesson, emerging from the *Presbyterian Church Case*, should not go unheeded by American churches.

---

ment or of the constitutions of the local congregation or the national church body. See note 71 *supra* respecting the action taken on remand by the Supreme Court of Georgia in the *Presbyterian Church Case.*

[95] See in this connection the following statement from the *Presbyterian Church Case:* "States, religious organizations, and individuals must structure relationships involving church property so as not to require the civil courts to resolve ecclesiastical questions." 393 U.S. at 449.

OWEN M. FISS

GASTON COUNTY v. UNITED STATES:

FRUITION OF THE FREEZING

PRINCIPLE

In the effort to secure a position of equality for the Negro in American society, the predominant strategy of our legal system has been to prohibit racial discrimination. In the recent past, attention has primarily focused on the question: What areas of human activity should be covered by the prohibition against racial discrimination? That question is considerably less important today. With the enactment of the Civil Rights Acts of 1964 and 1968 and the recent reconstruction of the Civil Rights Acts of 1866 in *Jones v. Alfred H. Mayer Co.*,[1] the federal prohibition against racial discrimination, once applicable only to governmental activity, has been applied to major areas of private activity, such as public accommodations, employment, and housing, which were the principal subjects of the coverage controversies. The coverage questions that remain are in many aspects interstitial.[2]

Today the central problem for antidiscrimination strategy is that of enforcement, in both its procedural and substantive guises. The

---

Owen M. Fiss is Associate Professor of Law, The University of Chicago.

[1] 392 U.S. 409 (1968). See Casper, *Jones v. Mayer: Clio, Bemused and Confused Muse*, 1968 SUPREME COURT REVIEW 89; Note, *Racial Discrimination in Employment under the Civil Rights Act of 1866*, 36 U. CHI. L. REV. 615 (1969).

[2] *Compare, e.g.,* Daniel v. Paul, 395 U.S. 298 (1969), *with* Griffin v. Maryland, 378 U.S. 130 (1964) (amusement parks).

substantive question is what conduct violates the prohibition against racial discrimination? The procedural question asks: What legal processes and techniques are most effective and appropriate for preventing and remedying conduct that violates that prohibition? Although the components are interrelated, the substantive one is at least logically prior. The difficulty with that question stems from the unwillingness of the legal system to rule that only overt racial discrimination—such as exclusions and refusals explicitly based on race—violates the prohibition. Instead, it is committed to evaluating apparently innocent conduct to determine whether in fact it violates the prohibition. This evaluation requires the formulation of governing principles.

It is appropriate, therefore, to turn to the rich enforcement experience in the area of voting rights. The richness of this experience derives in part from its age: the prohibition against racial discrimination in voting was an early, specific guarantee of federal law, expressed both by the Fifteenth Amendment and by statute.[3] While coverage questions have arisen, such as those relating to party primaries,[4] challenges to the qualification of registered voters,[5] and private interferences with attempts to exercise the right to vote,[6] they have been resolved at an early stage and with relative speed and ease, certainly as compared with the coverage questions in other fields, such as housing, employment, and public accommodations. The rich enforcement experience may also be attributed to the fact

---

[3] Act of May 31, 1870, ch. 114, § 1, now 42 U.S.C. § 1971(a)(1) (1964).

[4] Smith v. Allwright, 321 U.S. 649 (1944); Terry v. Adams, 345 U.S. 461 (1953).

[5] United States v. McElveen, 177 F. Supp. 355 (E.D. La. 1959), 180 F. Supp. 10 (E.D. La. 1960), aff'd with modifications sub nom. United States v. Thomas, 362 U.S. 58 (1960). The Supreme Court, in a per curiam opinion affirmed the district court judgment insofar as it prohibited the respondent registrar from giving effect to discriminatory challenges. See also United States v. Association of Citizens Councils, 196 F. Supp. 908 (W.D. La. 1961); United States v. Wilder, 222 F. Supp. 749 (W.D. La. 1963).

[6] United States v. Bruce, 353 F.2d 474 (5th Cir. 1965); United States v. Beaty, 288 F.2d 653 (6th Cir. 1961); United States v. Original Knights of the Ku Klux Klan, 250 F. Supp. 330 (E.D. La. 1965). See also the predecessor to 18 U.S.C. § 241, as construed in Ex parte Yarbrough, 110 U.S. 651 (1884) (criminal remedy for private interferences in federal elections); § 131(c) of the Civil Rights Act of 1957, 42 U.S.C. § 1971(c) (Supp. IV 1968) (civil remedy of Government for private interferences in federal elections); § 101(a) of the Civil Rights Act of 1968, 18 U.S.C. § 245(b)(1)(A) (Supp. IV 1968) (criminal remedy for private interferences in all elections).

that the initial legislation following *Brown v. Board of Education*[7]—
the first civil rights act since Reconstruction, the Civil Rights Act
of 1957—authorized general injunctive litigation[8] to be brought by
the United States to enforce the prohibition against racial discrimination in voting. After 1960 that authority was used with some
vigor, and the result was a large body of case law addressed to the
enforcement question. In turn, that litigation—by revealing and
carefully documenting the nature and magnitude of the wrongs and
the inadequacies of the existing remedial tools—was partly responsible for three more major enforcement acts passed by Congress
within the decade: the Civil Rights Act of 1960, the Civil Rights
Act of 1964, and the Voting Rights Act of 1965.[9]

Central to this enforcement experience has been the effort to
determine whether seemingly innocent standards imposed as qualifications for voting violate the prohibition against racial discrimination. In doing so, the enforcement agencies focused on the relationship of such standards to past discrimination that had already ended

---

[7] 347 U.S. 483 (1954).

[8] § 131(c), 42 U.S.C. § 1971(c) (Supp. IV 1968). Although that statute spoke only
in terms of "preventive relief," it was early decided that the injunctive litigation
authorized could be corrective of discriminatory practices as well as preventive.
United States v. Alabama, 192 F. Supp. 677 (M.D. Ala. 1961), *aff'd*, 304 F.2d 583
(5th Cir. 1962), *aff'd per curiam*, 371 U.S. 37 (1962). Prior to 1957, the only statutory
remedy available to the United States for enforcement of voting rights was the criminal prosecution. That remedy was used on occasion, even to challenge ostensibly
innocent qualifications for voting. See, *e.g.*, Guinn v. United States, 238 U.S. 347
(1915). The procedural safeguards of such proceedings, the risk of nullification by
juries, and the fact that the outcome of a criminal prosecution is punishment rather
than correction limited its value as an enforcement device. It could reach only rank,
crude, and dramatic forms of racial discrimination, and was a clumsy tool for the
development of sophisticated answers to subtle enforcement questions. See also
United States v. Louisiana, 225 F. Supp. 353, 356 (E.D. La. 1963), *aff'd*, 380 U.S. 145
(1965); United States v. Mississippi, 229 F. Supp. 925 (S.D. Miss. 1964), *rev'd*, 380
U.S. 128 (1965). In dissent, Judge Brown had indicated a willingness to rely on *In re
Debs*, 158 U.S. 564 (1875), for filling any gaps in the statutory authorization to
conduct general injunctive litigation in voting. And see Voting Rights Act of 1965,
§ 12(d), 42 U.S.C. § 1973j(d) (Supp. IV 1968).

[9] For this relation between the litigation and this enforcement legislation see, Note,
Federal Protection of Negro Voting Rights, 51 VA. L. REV. 1053 (1965); South
Carolina v. Katzenbach, 383 U.S. 301 (1966).

Title I of the Civil Rights Act of 1968 also provided a specific criminal remedy
for forcible interferences with exercises of the right to vote as part of a larger category of federally protected activities.

or was near an end.[10] The agencies recognized that such standards could have a "freezing effect," *i.e.*, could perpetuate past discrimination, and a principle—the "freezing principle"—emerged which invalidates standards that would perpetuate or continue the effects of past discrimination.

I. THE GRANDFATHER CLAUSE CASES

In the classic grandfather clause case, *Guinn v. United States*,[11] the first in which the Court invalidated a law establishing a voting qualification, some recognition was given to the freezing principle. An amendment to the Oklahoma constitution imposed a literacy requirement as a condition of registering to vote. At the same time, it provided an exemption from this literacy requirement for persons who were entitled to vote on January 1, 1866, and for their lineal descendants. The validity of a literacy requirement itself as a qualification for voting was not challenged on Fifteenth Amendment grounds. It was the exemption that was challenged on the ground that it constituted a form of racial discrimination prohibited by the Fifteenth Amendment. The Court found this exemption discriminatory because "on its face [it] was in substance but a revitalization of conditions which when they prevailed in the past had been destroyed by the self-operative force of the Amendment."[12] The literacy requirement was also declared to be invalid, but only on the ground—explicitly recognized by the Court as a question of state law—that it was inseparable from the prohibited exemption. The right to vote granted by state law was not affected.[13]

In *Guinn*, the perpetuation of the past discrimination was patent.

---

[10] Past discrimination may also indicate how serious a risk is created by vesting discretion. Louisiana v. United States, 380 U.S. 145 (1965). It is relevant to the determination of a present need for injunctive relief. United States v. Atkins, 323 F.2d 733 (5th Cir. 1963); United States v. Ramsey, 353 F.2d 650 (5th Cir. 1965). And it may explain conduct that might otherwise be ambiguous, such as Negroes' failure to register. United States v. Dogan, 314 F.2d 767 (5th Cir. 1963). It has also been relevant in voting cases to show that a "discriminatory act" was part of a "pattern or practice" of discrimination. *Ibid.*; Kennedy v. Lynd, 306 F.2d 222 (5th Cir. 1962). See text *infra*, at note 64.

[11] 238 U.S. 347 (1915). See also Myers v. Anderson, 238 U.S. 368 (1915) (Maryland grandfather clause).

[12] 238 U.S. at 364.

[13] The Court made this clear in the companion *Myers* case. 238 U.S. at 382.

The linkage with the past was explicit. No legitimate state interest could be served by an exemption tied so unambiguously to January 1, 1866. The racial contour of the exempted class was as clear as possible, short of explicit use of racial criteria. Conceivably, some whites could not qualify as grandfather electors, and some Negroes might. But it was historical fact that at the point in the past chosen as the criterion, Negroes were excluded from voting because of their race and were therefore outside the class entitled to the exemption.

Residual problems about the grandfather clause confronted the Court. Grandfather voters had obtained discriminatory benefits before the clause had been declared invalid. Although *Guinn* was argued before the Supreme Court in October, 1913, it was not until June, 1915, that the opinion was rendered. In that period of two years, a general election was held. *Guinn* was a federal criminal prosecution against local officials applying the grandfather clause. But it did not inhibit the use of the grandfather clause in the 1914 election, in which whites were registered as grandfather electors and Negroes were subjected to the literacy test. Presumably few Negroes were registered.

Thus, the question arose what to do with the nongrandfather electors who, but for the literacy test, could have qualified as voters at the time of the 1914 election. Oklahoma responded by establishing a short period of registration—twelve days in the spring of 1916—for those who were qualified but who did not vote at the time of the 1914 election. Although no different standards would be imposed on those applicants for registration from those imposed on grandfather electors and although there was a short extension of the time for those who for some exceptional reason, such as sickness, could not register during that twelve-day period, those failing to register during that period would be forever barred from voting.

This 1916 Oklahoma law was not tested until twenty years later. In *Lane v. Wilson*[14] the Court held that denying a Negro the right to vote in the 1934 election on the basis of the 1916 law violated the Fifteenth Amendment. The Court viewed this supplemental registration period as inadequate to correct the effects of past discrimination: "We believe that the opportunity thus given Negro voters to free themselves from the effects of discrimination to which they should never have been subjected was too cabined and con-

---

[14] 307 U.S. 268 (1939).

fined."[15] The disenfranchisement of qualified voters who had not taken advantage of the supplemental registration period was viewed as a means of perpetuating the discrimination effected by the operation of the grandfather clause in 1914. In reaching this conclusion, the Court was not troubled by the fact that "there were probably also some whites who were qualified to vote at the 1914 election who did not vote" and that "they were on the same footing as to registration as were the qualified Negroes."[16] There is language in the opinion of the Court by Justice Frankfurter suggesting that the Court considered the shortness of the supplemental registration period more of a burden for Negroes than for whites, and for that reason a form of unequal treatment.[17]

It also seems likely that the Court built on the insight of *Guinn:* a class was exempt from the requirement to register within the twelve-day period, and past discrimination had excluded Negroes from the class. In *Lane v. Wilson* the exempt class was not simply grandfather electors but also those who had taken advantage of the exemption in the general election of 1914. That did not obscure the racial contours of the exempted class. The Negroes who voted in the 1914 election could do so only after they passed the literacy test. Thus the two opportunities that Negroes qualified by age and residence had for registering—passing the literacy test in 1914 or registering without one in the twelve-day period in the spring of 1916—differed significantly from the two opportunities afforded whites who could register without a literacy test in 1914 or in the twelve-day period in 1916. One had only to assume that those exempted from the literacy requirement in 1914 took advantage of that exemption to conclude that a significant additional opportunity had been afforded whites. The 1916 law not only perpetuated but aggravated past discrimination by permanently disenfranchising Negroes who did not take advantage of the twelve-day period to bring themselves within the exempted class.

In *Lane v. Wilson* the Court did not have to ask whether a requirement—such as literacy—not imposed on earlier registrants

---

[15] *Id.* at 276.   [16] 98 F.2d 980, 984 (10th Cir. 1938).

[17] "The restrictions imposed must be judged with reference to those for whom they were designed. It must be remembered that we are dealing with a body of citizens lacking the habits and traditions of political independence and otherwise living in circumstances which do not encourage initiative and enterprise." 307 U.S. at 276.

could be imposed upon all post-1914 registrants. The litigation, brought by a single Negro, was an action for damages. The immediate effect of the Supreme Court decision was simply to set aside a directed verdict in favor of the election officer who, acting under the authority of the 1916 statute, had denied the Negro plaintiff the opportunity to vote in the 1934 election.[18] Moreover, Oklahoma had not yet indicated that the standard to be applied to the electors qualified as of 1914 but who did not vote at the 1914 election was to be any different from that applied to those who did vote in that election. In fact, it appeared that the standard applied to those who qualified after 1914 was the same as that applied to the 1914 grandfather electors, with no literacy requirement. In *Guinn*, the Supreme Court reached the state law question and held that the Oklahoma literacy requirement in the amendment containing the grandfather clause was inseparable from that clause and fell with it. At the time of *Lane v. Wilson* that literacy requirement had not been resurrected in Oklahoma.

In 1957, however, North Carolina did what Oklahoma apparently did not do. It imposed a literacy test that would exempt those already registered, including grandfather electors, who had taken advantage of the original exemption. In 1902 the constitution of North Carolina was amended to include a grandfather clause almost identical to the Oklahoma one: an ability to read and write the North Carolina constitution was a qualification for voting, with an exemption for grandfather electors if they registered before December, 1908, and with a provision that made such registration permanent. In addition, the North Carolina amendment contained an

---

[18] The record and briefs in the Supreme Court suggest that the wrong was not as personal or individual as the form of the litigation would indicate. Negroes constituted about 30 percent of Wagoner county population. In the twenty years before the trial only two Negroes were registered to vote. Under the 1916 law, apparently thirteen Negroes registered in the county during the twelve-day supplemental period. There were allegations that the shortness and specificity of this supplemental period facilitated the organization and operation of a conspiracy forcibly to prevent Negroes from registering. There was also the suggestion that none of the thirteen who registered in the county during this supplemental period was allowed to cast a ballot. The highly individualized form of this action for damages may be attributable to a desire to avoid the effect of Giles v. Harris, 189 U.S. 475 (1903), which the Supreme Court in *Lane v. Wilson* seemed to assume was still good law, but distinguished *Giles* because it was a suit in equity rather than an action for damages. See text *infra*, at note 151.

indivisibility clause.[19] The implementing statute incorporated the literacy requirement with an explicit exemption for grandfather electors as provided in the 1902 amendment. In 1957 that statute was amended to eliminate any mention of grandfather electors. Instead, it required that all persons "presenting" themselves for registration "be able to read and write any section of the Constitution of North Carolina in the English language."[20]

Before this statute reached the Supreme Court in *Lassiter v. Northampton Board of Elections*,[21] the question whether under its constitution the state legislature had the power to pass this statute was resolved. The state supreme court held—somewhat tortuously—that the 1902 amendment authorized the 1957 legislation imposing the literacy requirement.[22] A 1945 amendment of the state constitution that did no more than declare, "Every person born in the United States and every person naturalized, twenty-one years of age and possessing the qualifications set out in this article, shall be entitled to vote," was construed by the state supreme court to free the 1902 amendment of the indivisibility clause and to incorporate the unchallenged provisions of that amendment, including the literacy requirement, notwithstanding the invalid exemption for grandfather electors. As a result, the state court thought, "the way was made clear for the General Assembly to act."[23]

In *Lassiter*, the Supreme Court went to great lengths to avoid invalidating the North Carolina legislation. If it was not prompted by doctrinal reasons, perhaps it acted to avoid exacerbating the hostile response that had developed after *Brown v. Board of Education*.[24] Or the Court may have been moved by confidence in the new voting legislation which the Court quickly supported in the following Term by validation of the authorizing statutes and the Government's initial efforts under those statutes.[25] Relying on the

---

[19] N.C. Const. Art. VI, §§ 4, 5 (1902). [21] 360 U.S. 45 (1959).

[20] N.C. Gen. Stat. 163–28. [22] 248 N.C. 102 (1958).

[23] 248 N.C. at 110, 112. The state legislature acted after Lassiter had filed suit to declare the literacy requirement invalid. See Lassiter v. Taylor, 152 F. Supp. 295 (E.D. N.C. 1957).

[24] At a special Term, immediately prior to the Term in which *Lassiter* came down, the Court had decided Cooper v. Aaron, 358 U.S. 1 (1958).

[25] United States v. Raines, 362 U.S. 17 (1960) (Civil Rights Act of 1957); United States v. Thomas, 362 U.S. 58 (1960) (Civil Rights Act of 1957). And see Alabama v. United States, 371 U.S. 37 (1962) (Civil Rights Acts of 1957 and 1960); United States v. Alabama, 362 U.S. 602 (1960) (Civil Rights Acts of 1957 and 1960).

Government's concession in *Guinn* and the Court's adoption of that concession,[26] the Court in a unanimous opinion in *Lassiter*, disposed of what it perceived as claims under the Fourteenth and Seventeenth Amendments[27] by holding that legitimate state interests—promoting the "intelligent use of the ballot"—were served by the North Carolina law requiring an ability "to read and write any section of the Constitution of North Carolina in English." That was not, however, the end of the inquiry. For the Court also had to deal with two Fifteenth Amendment claims.

The first Fifteenth Amendment issue arose from the claim that the unfettered discretion vested in the registrars charged with applying this test presented a serious risk of discriminatory abuse and that no legitimate state interest justified exposing Negroes to that risk. No evidence of actual abuse was presented, nor did it seem necessary under the doctrine of *Davis v. Schnell*.[28] There the federal district court had invalidated on a similar risk-of-abuse theory a similar Alabama literacy test, and the Supreme Court summarily affirmed. Although the discretionary elements in the Alabama "understand and explain" test may be more apparent than one couched in terms that the voter "be able to read and write any section of the Constitution of North Carolina in the English language," the discretionary elements in the latter are still large. The registrar had discretion to decide who was to be tested, since all that was required was an "ability" to read and write; the registrar had discretion to determine which section of the constitution was to be

---

26 In *Guinn* the whole of the Court's discussion on the question consisted of a single sentence: "No time need be spent on the question of the validity of the literacy test considered alone [*i.e.*, apart from the grandfather clause exemption] since we have seen its establishment was but the exercise by the State of a lawful power vested in it not subject to our supervision, and indeed, its validity is admitted." 238 U.S. at 366.

27 The Court in *Lassiter* introduced the problem whether the literacy law served a permissible state purpose in these terms: "We come then to the question whether a State may consistently with the Fourteenth and Seventeenth Amendments apply a literacy test to all voters irrespective of race or color." 360 U.S. at 50.

28 81 F. Supp. 872 (S.D. Ala. 1949), *aff'd per curiam*, 336 U.S. 933 (1949). The Supreme Court in *Lassiter* described the theory of *Davis v. Schnell*: "The legislative setting of that provision and the great discretion it vested in the registrar made clear that a literacy requirement was merely a device to make racial discrimination easy." 360 U.S. at 53. Presumably, the Court was not attaching any great significance to "the legislative setting" of the Alabama provision, because—as the Court knew from reviewing the origin of the North Carolina law—the setting of the North Carolina literacy test was equally suspect.

given; the registrar had discretion to determine when the mere pronouncement of a series of symbols was reading, since "reading" entails understanding the symbols; and the registrar had to determine which errors in pronunciation, explanation, or transcription of symbols were so serious as to indicate that the applicant for registration could not read or write.[29] But the Supreme Court was unpersuaded by this range of discretionary elements. Although the Court left open the possibility of subsequent relief upon proof of actual discretionary abuse or misapplication of the test, it was unprepared to invalidate the requirement under the risk-of-abuse theory.

The Supreme Court was also unprepared to deal fully with the second Fifteenth Amendment claim, that which perceived the freezing effect of the literacy test to be applied under the statute. The past discrimination issue, like that in *Lane v. Wilson*, arose from the fact that the grandfather clause stayed in effect longer than it should have. While *Guinn* was decided in 1915, the North Carolina grandfather clause gave grandfather electors an exemption from the literacy requirement which they could—from the terms of the law—take advantage of from 1902 to 1908, and thereafter permanently retain the benefits thereof. The 1957 literacy requirement perpetuated that exemption, since it was not conditioned upon a general registration and applied only to new applicants. As the Supreme Court understood this claim: "Appellant points out that although the cutoff date in the grandfather clause was December 1, 1908, those who registered before then might still be voting. If they were allowed to vote without taking a literacy test and if appellant were denied the right to vote unless she passed it, members of the white race would receive preferential privileges of the ballot contrary to the command of the Fifteenth Amendment."[30]

This claim focusing on the perpetuation of past discrimination was one of the issues the Court refused to decide in *Lassiter*.[31] The

---

[29] *Compare* discussion in United States v. Louisiana, 225 F. Supp. 353, 386–87 (E.D. La. 1963), *aff'd*, 380 U.S. 145 (1965), *with* United States v. Mississippi, 229 F. Supp. 925, 950–51 (S.D. Miss. 1964), *rev'd*, 380 U.S. 128 (1965). See also Dent v. Duncan, 360 F.2d 333 (5th Cir. 1966), a post–Voting Rights Act of 1965 case where Judge Rives described the question, "Can you read or write?" as deceptive because there are "all degrees of the ability to read," and noted that the question "can never set a qualitative standard subject initially to an objective test." *Id.* at 337.

[30] 360 U.S. at 49–50.

[31] It did not deal with the issue of actual abuse of the test, and the theory of

Court justified its refusal on the ground that it had "not been framed in the issues presented for the state court litigation."[32] Perhaps the Court anticipated subsequent proceedings for further fact-finding, although it is not clear what findings of fact it thought essential to the theory. One could be a determination whether a substantial number of grandfather electors actually took advantage of the privilege, even though it might have been fair to infer that they did. Another could have been whether those grandfather electors constituted a significant segment of the electorate, though statistics from the census were cited in appellant's brief on that question. A third could have been whether a substantial number of Negroes were registered by 1957 and whether those Negroes were tested for litracy, even though, once again, it could be presumed from the presence of the grandfather clause statute up to 1957 that the literacy component of the grandfather clause was given its effect on the nonexempt class whenever necessary.[33]

The Court in *Lane v. Wilson* had not paused to find such facts, although they might have been equally relevant there. Perhaps in *Lassiter* there was reason for more caution. All that was at stake in *Lane v. Wilson* was a rule that denied the right to vote to nongrandfather electors on the ground that they failed to register during the twelve-day supplemental period, a rule that did not seem to serve any permissible state interest and had a punitive appearance. But in *Lassiter* what was at stake was a rule that denied the right to vote to nongrandfather electors on the ground that they were unable to read and write, a rule that the Court was prepared to say furthered permissible state interests. Notwithstanding this reluctance to examine the full implications of appellant's concern with the perpetuation of past discrimination, the Court in *Lassiter* did state that this claim of appellant "would be analogous to the problem posed in the classic case of *Yick Wo v. Hopkins*," and the

---

Gaston County v. United States, 395 U.S. 285. See text *infra*, at note 82. And see Katzenbach v. Morgan, 384 U.S. 641 (1966); and the dissenting opinion of Mr. Justice Douglas, in Cardona v. Power, 384 U.S. 672, 675 (1966).

[32] 360 U.S. at 60.

[33] The opinion below made reference to a 1919 amendment to the grandfather clause, which seemed to presuppose the continued operational existence of the literacy test. See also Allison v. Sharp, 209 N.C. 477 (1936); Clark v. Statesville, 139 N.C. 490 (1905); where Fifteenth Amendment challenges to the literacy requirement were rejected.

Court was careful to make it clear that nothing in its opinion "will prejudice appellant in tendering that issue in the federal proceedings which await the termination of the State court litigation."[34]

II. Louisiana v. United States

In the grandfather clause cases the issue of past discrimination was linked to an exemption structured by the explicit terms of the law. In *Guinn* the exempt class was those who were entitled to vote before 1866 and their lineal descendants, and in *Lane v. Wilson* and *Lassiter* the exempt class was those who actually took advantage of the original grandfather exemption. Thus, in each instance, the exempted class of grandfather electors, with its racial exclusionary contours, was provided for and defined by the terms of the law.

In the version of the freezing principle represented by *Louisiana v. United States*,[35] the issue of past discrimination was still linked to exemptions. Unlike the grandfather clause cases, however, the exemption derived from two facts: (1) The standard was to be applied only to new registrants, including both whites and Negroes. (2) This standard was not applied to those previously registered either because it had not existed in the past or, if it had existed, it had not been implemented.

The standard in question in *Louisiana v. United States* was not a read-and-write literacy test; it was a "citizenship test." It was first imposed as a qualification for voting in 1962. The pertinent statute directed the state board of registrars to "prescribe and direct the registrars of voters to propound an objective test of citizenship under a republican form of government."[36] Pursuant to this direc-

---

[34] 360 U.S. at 50. Following the Supreme Court decision, the federal district court, stating that "the cause has now been completely litigated and . . . there are no more questions of law or fact to be determined," dismissed the case. Lassiter v. Taylor, E.D.N.C., Raleigh Div., C.A. 1019, March 3, 1960. The order recited that plaintiff consented to the dismissal, and from a letter dated October 1, 1969, from plaintiff's attorney it appears that this issue was not tendered to the district court, probably owing to a failure to understand that the issue was preserved.

[35] 380 U.S. 145 (1965), *aff'g*, 225 F. Supp. 353 (E.D. La. 1963).

[36] Act 62 of 1962, amending LSA-R.S. § 18:191. In the November, 1962, general election, after the board of registrars adopted a resolution to implement the statute, a similar constitutional amendment to Art. VIII, § 18, was adopted. The district court noted that since 1898 there had been a provision in the state constitution that an applicant "shall be of good character, and shall understand the duties and obli-

tive the state board devised a testing procedure—obviously designed to avoid the reach of *Davis v. Schnell*—whereby an applicant for registration would draw one of ten cards, on each of which there were six multiple-choice questions testing specific knowledge of the theory and structure of government. An applicant was required to answer four of the six questions correctly.

Serious questions might have been raised whether such a test served any legitimate government interest.[37] But the Court was not prepared to treat the citizenship test on those terms because that "test was never challenged in the complaint or any other pleading."[38] Instead, the Court dealt with it in relation to the interpretation test, which in essence required an applicant "to be able to understand and give a reasonable interpretation of any section of the [state or federal] Constitution when read to him by the registrar."[39] In the first part of its opinion in *Louisiana v. United States*, the Court held invalid the interpretation test under the risk-of-abuse theory of *Davis v. Schnell*. The Court, noting that the virtually unlimited discretion vested in the registrars had been exercised to keep Negroes from voting because of their race, affirmed the decree below that had enjoined the use of the citizenship test in part because it would perpetuate the past discrimination attributable to the use of the interpretation test. The Supreme Court said:[40]

---

gations of citizenship under a republican form of government," but apparently that provision had never been applied. 235 F. Supp. at 392.

[37] As Judge Wisdom put it in his opinion in the district court: "Considering Louisiana's unhappy position as the State with the highest rate of illiteracy and the lowest percentage of citizens with a high school education, the citizenship test can be regarded as a step forward only by those in favor of a severely limited representative government of guardians elected by a small, elite electorate." 225 F. Supp. at 392.

[38] 380 U.S. at 154 n. 17.   [39] La. Const. Art. 8, § 1(d) (1921).

[40] 380 U.S. at 154–55. The link between the two tests was not as complete as the Court would make out. The district court found that in the twenty-one parishes where the interpretation test had been applied there was a great disparity in the number of white and Negro voters caused by past racial discrimination. But there was no finding—and the initial sentence of the Court quoted above is careful to avoid attributing one to the district court—that the abuse of the interpretation test was the sole or even primary racially discriminatory conduct that was responsible for the disparities. Various historical forms of racial discrimination were responsible, including registration of grandfather electors, the inhibiting effect of the white primary, and an organized campaign to purge registered Negroes from voting lists. See 225 F. Supp. at 393. In fact, as the Court noted, in 1944 only about 0.2 percent of the registered voters in the state were Negro (Negroes then constituted at least

The court found that past discrimination against Negro applicants in the 21 parishes where the interpretation test had been applied had greatly reduced the proportion of potential Negro voters who were registered as compared with the proportion of whites. . . . Since the new "citizenship" test does not provide for a reregistration of voters already accepted by the registrars, it would affect only applicants not already registered and would not disturb the eligibility of the white voters who had been allowed to register while discriminatory practices kept Negroes from doing so. . . . Under these circumstances we think that the court was quite right to decree that, as to persons who met age and residence requirements during the years in which the interpretation test was used, use of the new "citizenship" test should be postponed in those 21 parishes where registrars used the old interpretation test until those parishes have ordered a complete reregistration of voters, so that the new test will apply to all or to none.

The keynote of the opinion is the declaration that in enforcing the prohibition against racial discrimination the equity court had "not merely the power but the duty to render a decree which will so far as possible eliminate the discriminatory effects of the past as well as bar like discrimination in the future."[41] There is language in the opinion that suggests a purely tactical dimension to the freezing principle—that, like provisions requiring the submission of monthly reports, it is simply one principle governing the chancellor's decision how to make the decree most "effective."[42] There was little sugges-

---

30 percent of the voting-age population), and the registrars began to use the interpretation test only in the mid-1950's, after the decision in *Brown v. Board of Education*. 380 U.S. at 149; 225 F. Supp. at 377–81. The record may provide that explanation for the narrowness of the order. Because initial focus was on the interpretation test, there was some evidence in the record—such as the disparity by race between voting-age population and registered voters—as to the twenty-one parishes that used the interpretation test. 225 F. Supp. at 385 n. 81. With respect to the remaining parishes, there does not seem to be much of a record. The breadth of the order so as to reach all twenty-one parishes where the interpretation test had been used—even where there was no affirmative record of abuse—may be explained either by the willingness of the Court to presume the existence of past discrimination from the spectacular statistical disparities or its willingness to deem the inhibiting effect derived from the mere existence of the interpretation test as sufficient "past discrimination" that would be perpetuated by the citizenship test.

[41] 380 U.S. at 154.

[42] For example, the citizenship test is discussed only in the context of evaluating the district court's decree, along with other facets of the decree. The Court emphasized that it expressed "no opinion as to the constitutionality of the new 'citizenship'

tion of a substantive dimension to the principle that the perpetuation of past discrimination violates the prohibition against racial discrimination and must be corrected by the decree. Yet the Court's language recognized that the new citizenship test was not challenged in the pleadings. In *Louisiana v. United States* the Court spoke not only of the power but of the duty to forbid the application of a standard that perpetuates past discrimination, and the existence of that duty had to be based on the view that the freezing effect violates the prohibition against racial discrimination.

As in the grandfather clause cases, the freezing effect in *Louisiana v. United States* was related to an exemption. A class was exempted from the application of the statute, and it was claimed that currently exempting this class and applying this standard to all others was to perpetuate past discrimination. The racially discriminatory nature of that exemption in *Louisiana v. United States*, however, begins to get blurred because the class exempted consists of all those already registered and, unlike *Lane v. Wilson*, where reliance can be placed on the terms of the law, it cannot be assumed in this context that in the past Negroes had been excluded from that class. The existence of past discrimination thus remained to be established, and the mere disparity in percentage of registered voters was not logically sufficient to establish that. The claim was not that disparity was being perpetuated, but rather that discrimination was being perpetuated, although in many instances the disparity was so overwhelming[43]

---

test," that any "question as to that point is specifically reserved." 380 U.S. at 154 n. 17. It described the impact of the decree as a "postponement." The district court, probably less troubled by the alleged gap in the pleadings, was more direct. "The new tests discriminate against Negroes of voting age by subjecting them to standards to which the registered applicants (most of whom are white) were not subjected." 225 F. Supp. at 396. "Our order forbids enforcement of the citizenship test until Negro applicants can be judged by the same standards used in qualifying those persons already registered." *Id.* at 397.

43 The percentages of voting-age population registered in the 21 parishes as of the end of 1960 were (white and Negro, respectively): Bienville—92, less than 1; Claiborne—86, less than 1; De Soto—89, 1; East Carroll—95, 0; East Feliciana—58, 2; Franklin—92, 9; Jackson—88, 19; LaSalle—100, 26; Lincoln—72, 15; Morehouse—73, 4; Quachita—62, 4; Plaquemines—83, 2; Rapides—68, 17; Red River—100, 1; Richland—80, 6; St. Helena—100, 60; Union—84, 20; Webster—78, 2; West Carroll—84, 1; West Feliciana—80, 0; Winn—94, 42. 225 F. Supp., at 385 n. 81. Similar patterns were present in those cases in which the lower federal courts applied the *Louisiana v. United States* freezing principle. See, *e.g.*, United States v. Logue, 344 F.2d 290 (5th Cir. 1965) (Wilcox County, Ala.; 90 percent to 100 percent, as compared to no Negroes); United States v. Penton, 212 F. Supp. 193 (M.D. Ala. 1962) (Montgomery

that there could be only one inference—that discrimination had to be responsible for it, at least in part. The one ameliorating factor is that under the theory it did not matter whether some Negroes had been included in the exempted class on nondiscriminatory terms. Discrimination would occur if some portion of the Negro population were excluded from registering in the past because of their race. It is perpetuated by imposing the new test upon these victims of past racial discrimination while continuing to exempt the class of persons already registered. This was held sufficient to preclude the application of the new test unless the state conducted a general reregistration, an option that was carefully preserved by the Court. There were valid interests served by not conducting such a reregistration—the interest in minimizing administrative costs as well as the human and political costs of disenfranchising people who had voted all their adult lives but who would be unable to meet the new standard. But these interests were not sufficient to justify failure to take action that would eliminate the wrong of perpetuating past discrimination against a substantial segment of the Negro population.

The logic of this theory and the norm that corrective action by the judiciary extends only to the "victims of a wrong" seem to have dictated that one of the benefits of the remedial order—enjoining the use of the new test until there be a reregistration—should be limited to the Negroes who had been excluded because of their race from the class being exempted. This would be a subclass of the whole class of Negroes eligible to vote in the past. The nullification

---

County, Ala.; 54 percent, compared to 11 percent); United States v. Cartwright, 230 F. Supp. 873 (M.D. Ala. 1964) (Elmore County, Ala.; 89 percent, compared to 8 percent); United States v. Duke, 333 F.2d 759 (5th Cir. 1964) (Panola County, Miss.; almost 100 percent, while only one Negro, who was 92 years old, was registered); United States v. Mississippi, 339 F.2d 679 (5th Cir. 1964) (Walthall County, Miss.; almost 100 percent, compared to no Negroes); United States v. Ward, 345 F.2d 857 (5th Cir. 1965) (George County, Miss.; almost 100 percent, compared to 2 percent); United States v. Ramsey, 353 F.2d 650 (5th Cir. 1965) (Clarke County, Miss.; 83 percent, compared to only 3 Negroes); United States v. Dogan, 314 F.2d 768 (5th Cir. 1963) (Tallahatchie County, Miss.; almost 100 percent, compared to no Negroes); United States v. Ward, 349 F.2d 795, 352 F.2d 330 (5th Cir. 1965) (Madison Parish, La.; 81.4 percent, compared to no Negroes). See also the disparities in 12 Mississippi counties in June, 1962, United States v. Mississippi, 229 F. Supp. 925, at 994 n. 86, where the percent of voting-age whites registered runs from 57 percent to 100 percent, compared to a range of 0–2.9 percent for Negroes.

of the standard, however, was not confined to this subclass, and there are three explanations for that.

The first is an evidentiary one, the enormous difficulties of identifying with any degree of accuracy this subclass, particularly because of its historical dimension and because the records and memories of the past are so often fragmentary and unreliable. The second explanation inheres in the ripple effect of any discriminatory act. The class of victims might go far beyond those Negroes who applied to vote and had been discriminatorily turned away—the only members of the subclass likely to be identified with any degree of accuracy at all. Aside from those turned away, there were those who never applied because, on the basis of what they understood to be the experience of other Negroes, applying to register would be idle formality.[44] There were also those Negroes who did not apply because they did not have the qualifications required by the law on the books[45] but who had other qualifications that the registrar found sufficient for white applicants. And there were those Negroes—some with the paper qualifications and some with only actual qualifications—who did not apply because there were other discriminatory practices that would keep them from casting their ballots, or because they believed there would be little point in voting since others with similar interests were discriminatorily excluded from voting.[46] Recognizing these persons as victims would not only compound the evidentiary difficulties but would expand the subclass to such a size that the margin of overinclusion of a class of all Negroes eligible in the past would likely be of little significance. A third explanation is that because this subclass could not be identified by a finite list of names,[47] there was a need to define it in terms

---

[44] 225 F. Supp. at 393, 397. See United States v. Duke, 332 F.2d 759 (5th Cir. 1964). Not more than 5 or 6 Negroes had applied to register between 1932 and 1959. More than 2,000 had received seven or more years of schooling and 750 had some high school training. See also United States v. Ramsey, 331 F.2d 824, 833–38 (5th Cir. 1964) (dissenting opinion); United States v. Dogan, 314 F.2d 967 (5th Cir. 1963); United States v. Mississippi, 339 F.2d 679 (5th Cir. 1964).

[45] The district court noted that after the announcement of the litigation, the state board of registrars had discontinued the use of the interpretation test or supplanted it with the citizenship test. But the Court proceeded to determine its validity in part because of the inhibiting effect it might have, since it was still on the books. 225 F. Supp. at 382, 384. See note 40 *supra*.

[46] See generally Hamer v. Campbell, 358 F.2d 215 (5th Cir. 1966).

[47] In United States v. Alabama, 192 F. Supp. 677 (M.D. Ala. 1961), *aff'd*, 304 F.2d 583 (5th Cir. 1961), *aff'd per curiam*, 371 U.S. 37 (1962), the district court provided

of a set of criteria. Such criteria would have to be capable of easy application in order to minimize administrative costs and minimize the risk of abuse. No such criteria that would identify the subclass of victims were readily apparent.

While these factors would lead a court delineating the class of beneficiaries away from the limited subclass of victims and, notwithstanding the margin of overinclusion, to the class of all Negroes who were eligible by age and residence to register in the past, the Court did not stop at that point.[48] Instead, the class of beneficiaries of the freeze order was extended to both whites and Negroes who were eligible by age and residence standards during the period of discrimination. This could also be justified. First, there was the understandable desire to avoid injecting a racial distinction into the remedial order. This desire might have been based on the mistaken view[49] that the constitutional prohibition against racial discrimination ordinarily precluded any distinction based on race or on the view that such a distinction would only impair the acceptance of the order in the community. Second, there may have been an unwillingness to exclude whites from this order when the class of all eligible Negroes admittedly had a margin of overinclusion based on an expansive concept of the notion of a "victim." Third, the registration statistics were such that it did not seem there were many unregistered whites left who would have been eligible but for the test. Fourth, there may have been a recognition that even apart from racial considerations, there are elements of arbitrariness in imposing qualifications on some voters and not on others solely because the latter had already registered and the former, for some reason, had

---

a list of names of fifty-four Negroes to be registered by the defendant. But that relief was designed to provide dramatic correction of some type for past discrimination—an immediate, highly visible change—and not to exhaust the relief the plaintiffs were entitled to. Similar individualized relief was given in United States v. Lynd, 349 F.2d 785 (5th Cir. 1965); United States v. Penton, 212 F. Supp. 193 (M.D. Ala. 1962); United States v. Cartwright, 230 F. Supp. 873 (M.D. Ala. 1964). But see United States v. Ward, 345 F.2d 857 (5th Cir. 1965).

[48] The capacity of the Court to expand the class of beneficiaries because of these considerations was enhanced by the fact that the plaintiff was the United States, not any particular individual or segment of the community. See Alabama v. United States, 304 F.2d at 591. See generally United States v. Raines, 362 U.S. 17 (1960).

[49] See generally United States v. Montgomery County Board of Education, 395 U.S. 225 (1969); Brooks v. Beto, 366 F.2d 1 (5th Cir. 1966); Fiss, *Racial Imbalance in the Public Schools: The Constitutional Concepts,* 78 HARV. L. REV. 564, 575–83 (1965).

not. Fifth, there was the recognition that, if the registrars, some of whom are elected and others appointed by elected officials and most if not all of whom are white, were not allowed to apply the test to Negroes, then they would be likely to extend the same privilege to a similar class of whites on their own. Sixth, there was the desire to provide some symmetry to the option that was preserved in the freeze order as an alternative corrective, a complete reregistration of the voters, which would apply to both whites and Negroes.[50] Thus, the order in *Louisiana v. United States*, although rooted in the freezing principle and the duty to eradicate the effects of past discrimination, applied in general terms to all who were eligible to vote during the period of past discrimination[51] and prohibited the imposition of the new citizenship test until the risk of perpetuating past discrimination was eliminated by a reregistration.

The version of the freezing principle represented by *Louisiana v. United States* was also applied by the lower federal courts to old qualifications that had been on the books in the past but not applied to those allowed to register. The past discrimination consisted of excluding Negroes from the class of registered persons, and that discrimination would be perpetuated because, although the registrar was applying or intending to apply the test to all who registered in the future, both whites and Negroes, those already registered would retain their discriminatory exemption. In these cases, two remedial issues not present in *Louisiana v. United States* arose: one related to the alternative of a purge of voting lists and the other to the need to determine what standards could be applied in the future if no reregistration were required.

The alternative of purging the voting lists of persons who did not possess the qualifications purportedly required under the old test would have the distinct advantage of avoiding the costs involved in a general reregistration or in nullifying a voting requirement that was assumed to serve a legitimate state interest. But this was rejected

---

[50] The logic of these last three factors may be to extend the class of beneficiaries to those who become eligible by age and residence during the period after the freeze order is entered. See text *infra*, at notes 80–81.

[51] In paraphrasing the district court decree, the Supreme Court defined the class of beneficiaries as "persons who met age and residence requirements during the years in which the interpretation test was used." 380 U.S. at 155. The district court delineation was, in fact, sharper. It included all who became eligible by age and residence by August 3, 1962, the date the citizenship test was implemented. See notes 40 and 45 *supra*.

as a viable alternative because of the inherent risks and costs of such a purge.[52] Under *Louisiana v. United States*, the plaintiff would have to establish that the standard had not been applied to those registered and, absent an admission, the plaintiff would have to prove this by demonstrating either that individual, identified whites, often a substantial number, who were registered in the past could not have met those standards or that they were not asked to meet them. Thus, the famous "Frdum Foof Spetgh" example.[53] But this proof respecting particular individuals would be suggestive of a more general pattern and an effort to identify everyone so exempted from the requirement could not generally be undertaken. It would consume enormous investigative and judicial resources and, given the gaps and ambiguities of records and memories, would at best afford an unsatisfactory result. It would be impossible for a court to specify a list of individuals to be purged that would be corrective of the past wrong. Nor could administrative costs be avoided by giving the task to local officials. Their past misconduct suggested, at least to the courts and to the victims, that they could not be trusted. The factors that made it difficult for the court to do the job itself would also make meaningful supervision of this selective purge all but impossible.[54]

Having rejected the alternative of a purge and remaining unwilling to order (as opposed to permitting) a reregistration in the

---

[52] United States v. Louisiana, 225 F. Supp. at 396–97; United States v. Duke, 332 F.2d 759, 768 (5th Cir. 1964); United States v. Mississippi, 339 F.2d 679, 682 (5th Cir. 1965); United States v. Ward, 345 F.2d 859 (5th Cir. 1965). Two exceptions were United States v. Ramsey, 321 F.2d 824 (5th Cir. 1964), and United States v. Atkins, 323 F.2d 733 (5th Cir. 1963). Neither case, however, seems to be a persuasive precedent. As the court later said in United States v. Ward, 349 F.2d 795 (5th Cir. 1965), after rehearing there was nothing left to *Ramsey*. In the second *Ramsey* appeal, 353 F.2d 650 (5th Cir. 1965), the option of a purge was clearly foreclosed.

[53] "A white applicant in Louisiana satisfied the registrar of his ability to interpret the State constitution by writing 'Frdum Foof Spetgh.' United States v. Louisiana, 225 F. Supp. 353, 384." South Carolina v. Katzenbach, 383 U.S. at 312 n. 2. See also United States v. Penton, 212 F. Supp. 193, 210–11 (M.D. Ala. 1962) (registrar filled out entire form for a white applicant who had never completed the first grade of school).

[54] In United States v. Ward, 349 F.2d 795, 802 n. 12 (5th Cir. 1965), the court rejected the option of a purge in more doctrinaire terms: "Purging of whites does not correct the federal wrong—racial discrimination—but merely rectifies violations of State law." The court also justified this per se rule in terms of avoiding a conflict with the freeze provisions of the Civil Rights Act of 1960, 42 U.S.C. § 1971(e), which does not explicitly provide for a purge. See text *infra*, at notes 64, 66.

cases involving an old test, the courts had the responsibility to decide what standards could properly be applied to the class of beneficiaries. In *Louisiana v. United States* the Court could merely "postpone" or prohibit the imposition of the new test absent a re-registration, since a new test is one that by definition had not been applied to anyone in the exempt class of those already registered. This was not possible in the old-test cases. In those cases it is possible that the old test was applied to some whites, including those already registered, but not to others, or that, because of the great discretionary elements vested in the registrars, only parts of the test or lax versions of it were given.

This possibility does not preclude the application of the freezing theory to old tests. The theory requires two elements: (1) Negroes had been excluded because of their race from becoming members of the class of persons already registered. (2) The old test had not generally been applied in the past. The second element establishes the existence of the exemption being perpetuated by currently applying the standard. It indicates that the practical impact of the exemption is not de minimis. And, given the striking racial homogeneity of the class of persons already registered, it lends inferential support to the first element, which establishes the racially discriminatory contours of that exemption. Proof that the old test was not generally applied in the past, however, would not be the same as proof that it never had been applied in the past. It is possible that it had been applied sporadically, particularly given the changes in local officials and the varied, complicated political and personal relationships often existing among the registrars, the candidates, and the applicants for registration. A decree so general that it did no more than provide that the registrar continue to apply the standards he had generally applied to whites in the past would not give any meaningful guidance to the registrars and would contain serious risks of abuse.

As a guide in discharging this responsibility, the United States on some occasions has proposed that courts hold the registrar to the past low watermark—the standards "of the least qualified white person who has been registered."[55] Although this low-watermark guide might seem attractive, it is too uncompromising and is not based on the logic of the freeze theory. The standards had to be linked to

---

[55] See, *e.g.*, prayer for relief quoted in United States v. Ramsey, 321 F.2d 824, 825 (5th Cir. 1964).

those applied to a class from which Negroes were excluded, and those applied to the least qualified white person who had been registered in the past do not necessarily meet that requirement. For example, one white person may have been totally relieved of the standards for political or personal reasons unrelated to his race, while the standard generally applied to whites might have been quite different. The courts did not acquiesce in this proposal. In cases involving old tests the courts embarked on the more unstructured task—one allowing great room for unarticulated compromises with the full logic of the freezing principle—of determining what standards were generally applied in the past to those persons allowed to register.

The lower federal courts applied this version of the freezing principle not only to old tests as well as new tests but also to a great variety of types of tests and requirements qualifying persons to vote. It was applied to the requirements that persons wishing to pay the poll tax personally see the sheriff,[56] that the application for registration be filled out without assistance,[57] that an applicant for registration establish his identity, residence, and absence of disqualification by having a registered voter vouch for him,[58] and that an applicant for registration fill out a perfect registration form.[59] It was also applied to the Mississippi versions of the interpretation and citizenship tests.[60] With all these tests and requirements, as with the

---

[56] United States v. Dogan, 314 F.2d 767 (5th Cir. 1965) (requirement not prescribed by state law).

[57] United States v. Lynd, 301 F.2d 818 (5th Cir. 1963), *cert. denied*, 371 U.S. 893 (1963). See also the subsequent order in *Lynd* described in United States v. Louisiana, 225 F. Supp. at 395; United States v. Duke, 332 F.2d 759 (5th Cir. 1964); United States v. Lynd, 349 F.2d 785 (5th Cir. 1965); United States v. Lynd, 349 F.2d 790 (5th Cir. 1965); United States v. Ward, 349 F.2d 795 (5th Cir. 1965).

[58] United States v. Logue, 344 F.2d 290 (5th Cir. 1965); United States v. Hines, 9 RACE REL. REP. 1332 (N.D. Ala. 1964). See also United States v. Ward, 349 F.2d 795 (5th Cir. 1965).

[59] United States v. Penton, 212 F. Supp. 193 (M.D. Ala. 1962).

[60] Question 18 of the Mississippi application form required that the applicant write and copy a section of the Mississippi constitution selected by the registrar; question 19 required that the applicant write a reasonable interpretation of that section; and question 20 required a statement setting forth the applicant's understanding of the duties and obligations of citizenship. United States v. Lynd, 349 F.2d 790, 792 (5th Cir. 1965). The freezing theory was applied to relieve applicants from the requirement of answering questions 19 and 20. United States v. Duke, 332 F.2d 759 (5th Cir. 1964); United States v. Mississippi, 339 F.2d 679 (5th Cir. 1964); United States v. Ward, 345 F.2d 857 (5th Cir. 1965); United States v. Lynd, 349

citizenship test of *Louisiana v. United States,* it was difficult to perceive any significant state interest that would be served by them, particularly since their creation, or imposition after years of nonuse, coincided with increased voter registration drives in the Negro community. Some had an even more tenuous relationship to legitimate state interest than the citizenship test, and in some such instances the freeze order did not preserve the option of a general registration.[61] It was inconceivable that the state would conduct a general reregistration to further the interests served by the nullified test or requirement.

In spite of this breadth of the freezing principle, one voting qualification seemed immune to its logic—the read-and-write literacy test, the test the Supreme Court had said, in *Lassiter,* served a permissible state purpose. The district court in *Louisiana v. United States* carefully avoided applying the freezing principle to such a literacy test, although there was every reason to believe—or if the record was not fully adequate on this score, at least to suspect—that no literacy test had been applied to whites in the past.[62] In other cases, where

---

F.2d 785 (5th Cir. 1965). Following the reversal and remand in United States v. Mississippi, 380 U.S. 128 (1965), and almost contemporaneous with the decision in the *Lynd* appeal, the Mississippi constitution was amended so that the literacy requirement was limited to an ability to read and write and the good moral character requirement that had been added in 1960 was eliminated. United States v. Ramsey, 353 F.2d 650 (5th Cir. 1965). See also United States v. Cartwright, 230 F. Supp. 873 (M.D. Ala. 1964).

61 See, *e.g.,* United States v. Logue, 344 F.2d 290 (5th Cir. 1965).

62 The district court in *United States v. Louisiana* wrote: "No one doubts the broad scope of the State's power to fix reasonable, nondiscriminatory qualifications for voting consistent with the Constitution. Thus, a literacy test bears a reasonable relation to a governmental objective and, if it does not perpetuate past discrimination, is a permissible requirement. . . . Since Louisiana has the highest illiteracy rate in the nation, the State has even more reason than most states to use a literacy test as a spur to improve the level of the electorate. *But the understanding clause, which is an interpretation test of the constitutions, must not be confused with a literacy test or the two treated as peers.* Under Louisiana law, any literacy qualification is met by the requirement that the applicant read to the registrar the Preamble of the United States Constitution. In fact, an applicant need write the Preamble only in his mother tongue, through the dictation of an interpreter if he cannot speak, read, or write English. La. Const. Art. VIII, § 1(c). For good measure, ability to fill out an application form is an additional test of literacy. Moreover, under another statute and provision of the state constitution, until 1960 *all of the time Louisiana had an interpretation test it allowed illiterates to vote.* (LSA-R.S. 18:36). In November 1962 the State carried 37,365 illiterates on the registration rolls." 225 F. Supp. at 385–86. (Emphasis in original.) See *id.* at 357 n. 6, for further discussion of the

the record was clear that no read-and-write literacy requirement had been applied in the past, where the United States specifically requested that the freeze order extend to that requirement, and where the freezing theory was adopted in most emphatic terms, the lower federal courts silently declined—at least until specific congressional assistance arrived—to have the full force of the *Louisiana v. United States* freezing principle reach that requirement.[63]

Legislative assistance soon came. In the Civil Rights Acts of 1960 and 1964, in existence at the time *Louisiana v. United States* was decided, Congress gave recognition to the freezing principle. In Title V of the Civil Rights Act of 1960 Congress provided for a mechanism for a federal court to declare named Negroes qualified to vote in local, state, and federal elections and that any refusal to honor such an order would constitute a contempt of court.[64] This

---

ambiguous nature of the read-and-write literacy test at that time. This test was not discussed in the Supreme Court opinion.

[63] United States v. Duke, 332 F.2d 759, at 762–63, 766 (5th Cir. 1964); United States v. Mississippi, 339 F.2d 679 (5th Cir. 1964); United States v. Ward, 345 F.2d 857 (5th Cir. 1965); United States v. Lynd, 349 F.2d 785, 788 (5th Cir. 1965); United States v. Ward, 349 F.2d 795, 806 (5th Cir. 1965).

For an observation on the limitations of *Lynd* and *Ward*—otherwise read, along with *Duke*, as the strongest adoption of the *Louisiana v. United States* freezing theory—see the subsequent decisions in United States v. Ward, 352 F.2d 300 (5th Cir. 1965); United States v. Ramsey, 353 F.2d 650 n. 20 (5th Cir. 1965).

[64] 74 Stat. 86, 90 (1960), now 42 U.S.C. § 1971(e) (1964). In United States v. Alabama, 192 F. Supp. 677 (M.D. Ala. 1961), aff'd, 304 F.2d 583 (5th Cir.), aff'd per curiam, 371 U.S. 37 (1962), it was decided that even absent this statutory provision, the federal courts could enter similar decrees as part of their general equitable powers. In that case the district court granted such relief to Negroes who were denied the right to vote before the court had entered the finding of a pattern or practice of discrimination, rather than after, as required under the § 1971(e) provision.

The Civil Rights Act of 1960 contained other provisions also designed to perfect the litigative tool authorized in the Civil Rights Act of 1957: (1) A provision, requiring the retention of records relating to applications to vote in federal elections and giving the Attorney General access to those records before the commencement of litigation and on the basis of a written demand. (2) A provision authorizing the appointment of voting referees—similar to masters—to assist in the process of listing qualified voters described in the text. (3) A provision authorizing the joinder of the state as a party defendant even when only the conduct of a local official is involved. For analyses of the problems in the litigative process that gave rise to these provisions see Note, note 9 *supra*.

The Civil Rights Act of 1964 also attempted to perfect the litigative tool in voting by authorizing the Attorney General to request a three-judge district court and providing for expedition of these proceedings, a provision designed to deal with the

statutory provision was applicable in suits brought by the United States under the Civil Rights Act of 1957 where a finding had been made that the discrimination was "pursuant to a pattern or practice" of racial discrimination. For at least one year, or until the court found that the pattern or practice had ceased, a Negro was entitled to an order declaring him qualified to vote if, so the statute provides, he establishes, first, that he is qualified under state law to vote and, second, that since the finding of a pattern or practice he has not been allowed to register. With respect to the latter determination there was no need to show racial discrimination. This provision became applicable only if there was a finding that the state officials had recently engaged in a pattern or practice of discrimination. With respect to the first determination, whether the individual is qualified under state law, the statute provides: [65]

> [T]he words "qualified under State law" shall mean qualified according to the laws, customs, or usages of the State, and shall not, in any event, imply qualifications more stringent than those used by the persons found in the proceeding to have violated subsection (a) [containing the general Fifteenth Amendment prohibition] in qualifying persons other than those of the race or color against which the pattern or practice of discrimination was found to exist.

This section had been viewed as being predicated on or incorporating a freezing principle similar to that of *Louisiana v. United States* and as contributing to the development of the principle. The word "used" looks to the past and has been construed to forbid the use of standards higher than those used in the period for which a pattern or practice existed, rather than just those in the period following the entry of the finding. Moreover, Congress preserved the option of reregistration by providing that the Court order declaring

---

difficulties of delay occasioned by a trial judge refusing to decide. 42 U.S.C. § 1971(g) (Supp. IV 1968). Although the Voting Rights Act of 1965 generally shifted the enforcement process out of the courts, and in that sense expressed a lack of confidence in ever perfecting the litigative tool to the point of making it do the job fully, that act had some minor provisions for improving it, such as authorizing the court to appoint examiners.

[65] 74 Stat. 92 (1960), 42 U.S.C. § 1971(e) (1964). See United States v. Duke, 332 F.2d 759 (5th Cir. 1964); United States v. Ramsey, 331 F.2d 824 (5th Cir. 1964); United States v. Ward, 349 F.2d 795 (5th Cir. 1965); United States v. Ramsey, 353 F.2d 650 (5th Cir. 1965); United States v. Palmer, 356 F.2d 951 (5th Cir. 1966). See Comment, *The Federal Voting Referee Plan and the Alteration of State Voting Standards*, 72 YALE L. J. 770 (1963).

the person qualified "shall be effective as to any election held within the longest period for which such applicant could have been registered or otherwise qualified under State law at which the applicant's qualifications would under State law entitle him to vote."

Unlike the Civil Rights Act of 1960, however, the Civil Rights Act of 1964 is not confined to a litigative context. It provides: [66]

> (2) No person acting under color of law shall—(A) in determining whether any individual is qualified under State law or laws to vote in any Federal election, apply any standard, practice or procedure different from the standards, practices, or procedures applied under such law or laws to other individuals within the same county, parish, or similar political subdivision who have been found by the State officials to be qualified to vote.

Although this provision has been recognized as embodying the freezing principle,[67] the prohibition against applying different standards in the future from those applied in the past is not—at least on the face of the statute—conditioned in any way upon a determination that Negroes were excluded from the class of those allowed to register in the past or that whites were exempted from those standards in the past. That probably accounts for the fact that the provision is limited to federal elections, evoking a broader array of sources of congressional power than just the Fifteenth Amendment. That limitation, of little significance because of the practice of a single registration for state and federal elections, was soon eliminated by § 15 of the Voting Rights Act of 1965.[68] There, Congress amended this section of the Civil Rights Act of 1964 by eliminating the word "Federal."

This amendment was not the only role the freezing principle played in fostering the Voting Rights Act of 1965—the congressional response to a long chain of dramatic events, which included *Louisiana v. United States*, its companion *United States v. Mississippi*,[69] which after pending for almost three years was returned

---

[66] 78 Stat. 241 (1964), 42 U.S.C. § 1971(a)(2)(A) (1964). See 110 CONG. REC. 6750, 8205 (1964), acknowledging the recognition of this principle in existing case law.

[67] United States v. Duke, 332 F.2d 759, 769 (5th Cir. 1964); United States v. Palmer, 356 F.2d 951, 952-53 (5th Cir. 1966); United States v. Cox, 11 RACE REL. REP. 269, 291 (N.D. Miss. 1964, 1965).

[68] 42 U.S.C. § 1971(2)(A) (Supp. IV 1968).

[69] 380 U.S. 128 (1965).

to the trial court for its first evidentiary hearing, and the historic events involving Selma, Alabama.[70] The principle was one of the important justifications for the central enforcement technique provided in the act with regard to voting qualifications: to suspend literacy tests and similar qualifications for voting in all jurisdictions that fell within the coverage formula of the act.[71] Such an enforcement technique could in part be justified on some version of the risk-of-abuse theory—the suspension was necessary in order to eliminate the discretionary elements vested in local registrars by such tests, a discretion which Congress believed had been abused in nearly all of those jurisdictions identified by the coverage formula.[72] Another explanation for the suspension of tests was the freezing theory of *Louisiana v. United States*. In sustaining the suspension provisions, the Supreme Court in *South Carolina v. Katzenbach* ac-

---

[70] The decisions in *Louisiana v. United States* and *United States v. Mississippi* were announced on Monday, March 8, 1965, the day the national newspapers carried photographs of club-swinging deputies riding into a group of Negroes protesting the denial of voting rights in Selma. Then followed the historic march from Selma to Montgomery. See *Williams v. Wallace*, 240 F. Supp. 100 (M.D. Ala. 1965); Marshall, *The Protest Movement and the Law*, 51 VA. L. REV. 785, 787–92 (1965); and President Johnson's address to Congress and the nation on March 16, 1965. For further litigation involving the right to vote in Dallas County and Selma, see *United States v. Atkins*, 323 F.2d 733 (5th Cir. 1963); *United States v. Clark*, 249 F. Supp. 720 (S.D. Ala. 1965); *United States v. McLeod*, 385 F.2d 734 (5th Cir. 1967).

[71] The statutory phrase is "test or device," and is defined in the act to mean "any requirement that a person as a prerequisite for voting or registration for voting (1) demonstrate the ability to read, write, understand, or interpret any matter, (2) demonstrate any educational achievement or his knowledge of any particular subject, (3) possess good moral character, or (4) prove his qualifications by the voucher of registered voters or members of any other class." 42 U.S.C. § 1973b(c) (Supp. IV 1968).

[72] One year earlier, in the Civil Rights Act of 1964, Congress had tried to eliminate some of the discretionary elements. It prohibited the use of "any literacy test as a qualification for voting in any Federal election unless . . . such a test is . . . conducted wholly in writing. . . ." It defined literacy test to include "any test of the ability to read, write, understand, or interpret any matter." The act also provided that no one shall be denied the right to vote in a federal election because of immaterial errors or omissions in the registration process. Finally, the Act of 1964 also attempted to facilitate injunctive litigation by the Attorney General by providing that in such proceedings completion of the sixth grade would create a rebuttable presumption of literacy, comprehension, and intelligence to vote in any federal election. Section 15 of the Voting Rights Act of 1965 eliminated the restriction of these provisions to federal elections; but even before that, the single registration process probably extended their practical significance.

knowledged the congressional recognition of the freezing principle embodied in the Voting Rights Act of 1965:[73]

> Congress knew that continuances of the tests and devices in use at the present time, no matter how fairly administered in the future, would freeze the effect of past discrimination in favor of unqualified white registrants. Congress permissibly rejected the alternative of requiring a complete re-registration of all voters, believing that this would be too harsh on many whites who had enjoyed the franchise for their entire adult lives.

Through the coverage formula the tests would be suspended in those jurisdictions where there was risk of perpetuating past discrimination by imposition of an ostensibly innocent standard.

Viewed as an implementation of the freezing principle, the suspension technique of the Voting Rights Act of 1965 embodied several innovations, some of which were immediately adopted by the courts in the few cases that remained from the early regime where litigation predominated. First, the option of reregistration was eliminated, an option not likely to be utilized anyway. Second, as with the earlier Civil Rights Acts the principle was not confined to suspect tests or qualifications such as the citizenship test. It was clearly applicable to the read-and-write literacy tests of *Lassiter*.[74] After the Voting Rights Act the courts took this same step.[75] Third, the special problem of applying the principle to old tests, namely, determining precisely what standard could be applied in the future by making a determination as to what standards were applied in the past, was eliminated. The tests were suspended in toto.

Fourth, the period during which the tests were to be nullified or suspended was extended to five years. Under case law, the suspension of the test or order enjoining its enforcement generally could be brought to an end by a general reregistration, but it was necessary to prescribe a period of time—the "freeze period"—for which the

---

[73] 383 U.S. at 334. The omitted footnotes referred to H. Rep. No. 439, 89th Cong., 1st Sess. 15; S. Rep. 162, pt. 3, 89th Cong., 1st Sess. 16; Hearings on H.R. 6400 before Subcommittee No. 5 of the House Committee on the Judiciary, 89th Cong., 1st Sess. 17; Hearings on S. 1564 before the Senate Committee on the Judiciary, 89th Cong., 1st Sess. 22–23. See also Dent v. Duncan, 360 F.2d 333 (5th Cir. 1966).

[74] See Dent v. Duncan, 360 F.2d 333 (5th Cir. 1966); United States v. Mississippi, 256 F. Supp. 344 (S.D. Miss. 1966); United States v. Louisiana, 265 F. Supp. 703 (E.D. La. 1966), aff'd per curiam, 386 U.S. 270 (1967).

[75] United States v. Ward, 352 F.2d 329 (5th Cir. 1965); United States v. Ramsey, 353 F.2d 650 (5th Cir. 1965); United States v. Palmer, 356 F.2d 951 (5th Cir. 1966).

test would be suspended or nullified in the likely event that a general reregistration was not held. In the early cases, such as *Louisiana v. United States*, the freeze period was not defined in very specific terms. There the freeze period was to be "until the discriminatory effect of the test [had] been vitiated to the satisfaction of the court."[76] Perhaps for reasons of judicial administration, a minimum number of years was imposed by the court of appeals before the trial court could bring the suspension to an end by finding that the effects of the past discrimination had been vitiated. Initially, this minimum component of the freeze period was set at one year, drawing some guidance from the provision of the Civil Rights Act of 1960 that acknowledged the freezing principle.[77] Then this minimum period was extended to two years, in part to accommodate the large number of persons to be registered under its terms and to avoid frequent resort to the courts,[78] and finally, after the Voting Rights Act of 1965, to five years,[79] the period provided in the statute.

---

[76] 225 F. Supp. at 397.

[77] United States v. Duke, 332 F.2d 759 (5th Cir. 1964). Similar considerations of judicial administration led the Court in *Duke* to prescribe the precise terms of the decree to be entered by the district court on the remand, and indicated—as a forerunner to the uniform circuit-wide school desegregation decree in United States v. Jefferson County Board of Education, 372 F.2d 836 (5th Cir. 1966), adopted *en banc*, 380 F.2d 385 (5th Cir. 1967), *cert. denied*, 389 U.S. 840 (1967)—that it should be the model or standard. See, *e.g.*, United States v. Mississippi, 339 F.2d 679 (5th Cir. 1964); United States v. Ward, 345 F.2d 857 (5th Cir. 1965); United States v. Lynd, 349 F.2d 785 (5th Cir. 1965), all Mississippi cases using the *Duke* decree. This innovation might well have been triggered by the willingness of the trial judges in Mississippi, Judge Cox in the Southern District, and then Judge Clayton in the Northern District (now of the Court of Appeals), to tolerate and defend such rank practices described by the court of appeals in *Duke*, 332 F.2d at 766, which were reflective of the larger syndrome. See Comment, *Judicial Performance in the Fifth Circuit*, 73 YALE L.J. 90 (1963).

[78] United States v. Ward, 349 F.2d 795 (5th Cir. 1965). The Voting Rights Act was signed on August 6, 1965. Louisiana was brought under its coverage the next day. Although this first decision in *Ward* was dated Aug. 11, 1965, it was obviously written before the act became law, and it was not until the second decision, 352 F.2d 329, that full account of the act was taken. It also seems that the two-year period in the first *Ward* decision was designed to give further effect to another innovation made in that decision, namely, extending the class of beneficiaries to all those eligible during this period. Neither the extension of the freeze period from one to two years nor the extension of the class of beneficiaries was specifically requested by the United States.

[79] United States v. Ward, 352 F.2d 329 (5th Cir. 1965); United States v. Ramsey, 353 F.2d 650 (5th Cir. 1965).

The fifth innovation of the act, made almost contemporaneously by the courts, was the expansion of the class to whom the test could not be applied. The benefit of the nullification was made available not only to those who were eligible by age and residence to vote during the period of past discrimination, as in *Louisiana v. United States*, but also to those who became eligible during the freeze period.[80] This innovation, like the others, may be explained by considerations that are not rooted in the freezing theory but that undoubtedly played a role in justifying the suspension under the act, such as the fact that the suspension was also a means of eliminating discretion. It may also be a technique to increase the electorate. But it could be explained by the factors tied to the *Louisiana v. United States* freezing theory that led to the expansion of the class of beneficiaries from the Negro victims, to the class of Negroes eligible by age and residence during the period of discrimination, to the class of all persons—both white and Negro—so eligible.[81] Any distinction based solely on when voters became eligible has tones of arbitrariness. Administrative and political difficulties are avoided by applying one set of qualifications to all voters. And expanding the class to those who became eligible by age and residence during the freeze period would have the greatest symmetry with the one option preserved in the freeze order that would concededly eradicate the effects of past discrimination, a general reregistration.

III. Gaston County v. United States

Nominally, *Gaston County v. United States*[82] involved the same literacy test as *Lassiter*, that of North Carolina. But, by the time this problem once again appeared before the Supreme Court,

---

[80] United States v. Ward, 349 F.2d 795 (5th Cir. 1965).

[81] See note 50 *supra*. The Court in *Ward* assigned two further reasons for this extension: (1) the provisions of the order should be harmonized with the freeze provision of the Civil Rights Act of 1960, otherwise the applicants would take advantage of the more lenient court procedure of the 1960 act, throwing more registration to the courts than on the registrar subject to the freeze order; and (2) not only should the Negroes eligible in the past be compared to the whites previously registered but all Negroes now applying should be so compared. 349 F.2d at 802–03. The latter reason is not particularly persuasive, since there still must be a reason why those Negroes who become eligible to register after the court order should be compared to the whites registered in the past as opposed to those whites who became eligible to register after the court order. See note 54 *supra*.

[82] 288 F. Supp. 678 (D.D.C. 1968), *aff'd*, 395 U.S. 285 (1969).

three significant changes had taken place in the implementation of this law in Gaston County.[83] The first was that the problem of exemptions raised but not decided in *Lassiter* had been eliminated by a general reregistration in the county. Second, administrative action by the board of elections eliminated many of the discretionary elements inherent in a read-and-write literacy test. Third, the law had been suspended in the county by operation of the Voting Rights Act of 1965 because a determination had been made that the county fell within the § 4(b) coverage formula.

The exemptions arising since the reregistration seem, on the record before the Court, to be of little significance, hardly sufficient for invoking *Louisiana v. United States*. For a significant portion of the period in question, fairly complete records of those who attempted to register seem to have been maintained by the board of elections.[84] The evidence established that a relatively small number of white illiterates were registered.[85] There was some proof of a few illiterate Negroes being registered. There was no dramatic disparity by race in the percentages of voting-age population registered.[86] It was the existence of this disparity, among other things,

---

[83] Within the territorial limits of Gaston County there are at least eleven municipalities, including the city of Gastonia, the county seat where about one-third of the population lives. The Gaston County board of elections is generally responsible for the administration of all federal, state, county, and township elections. It has no jurisdiction over registration in the municipalities, where the registration process is handled by separate registrars in each municipality. (It also appears that some of the municipalities, including Gastonia, have their own school systems.) Although there is considerable ambiguity in the record as to the distinction between the county and the municipalities, references to the county have been construed to include only the jurisdiction of the county board of elections, and to exclude the municipalities. This distinction provides the basis of the concurring decision of one of the trial judges. See note 93 *infra*.

[84] See notes 62 and 72 *supra*.

[85] There is no finding as to the precise number. Fifteen registered whites admitted in deposition that they could not read or write; and another fourteen whites said that they were not required to demonstrate literacy. A notebook of registration forms was introduced which, the district court said, indicated that these twenty-nine persons "were not the only whites who were permitted to register although they were incapable of satisfying the literacy requirements of North Carolina law." 288 F. Supp. at 683. The Government's brief put this unspecified number at seventy. Brief of the United States, at 12 n. 6. Thus, at most, one hundred illiterate whites were established as registered, in a county with about 43,000 white voters.

[86] The statistics provided in the record and post-trial brief of the United States are for the county as a whole, including the municipalities. In a sense the most accurate voting statistics by race are those for May, 1966, and June, 1967, for they

that generalized the proof that the test in question was not applied to individual whites and laid the foundation for the conclusion that there was a class exempted from the standard to which Negroes were subjected. At the time of the November, 1964, general election, a time when the literacy test was in effect, about 52 percent of the adult Negro population was registered, compared to about 66 percent of the adult white population. This statistic did not readily lend itself to the theory of a racial class being exempted, a necessary condition for the application of the *Louisiana v. United States* freezing principle.[87]

---

are the contemporaneous count of persons actually registered, thus reflecting intervening purges. The voting-age population base used here is the 1960 census (64,154 whites, 8,365 Negroes) until the 1966 special census figures (69,252 whites, 8,407 Negroes) were available. The statistics of registered voters by race (whites and Negroes, respectively) are: November, 1962—33,162 (51.7 percent), 2,809 (33.6 percent); November, 1964 (general presidential election, following the adoption of a simplified literacy test)—42,376 (66.1 percent), 4,371 (52.3 percent); November, 1966 (general election, following the suspension of the literacy test)—42,898 (61.4 percent), 4,381 (52.1 percent); June, 1967 (date of trial)—43,874 (63.4 percent), 4,388 (52.2 percent). While it appears, on the basis of the above statistics, that the suspension of the test had no appreciable effect on reducing the disparity, that might be attributable to the absence of a general presidential election between the suspension of the test and the trial. However, in a letter from the attorney for the board of elections, dated October 10, 1969, it was stated that the registration statistics at the time of the general presidential election in November, 1968 were: 51,892 (74.9 percent) of the total white voting-age population, compared to 5,172 (61.5 percent) of the total Negro voting-age population. Compare the statistics in *Louisiana v. United States,* note 43 *supra.*

[87] This perhaps explains the gradual evaporation of this theory in *Gaston County.* In the Government's pleading and its trial brief it was the principal theory of discrimination relied on. The district court noted that "[s]ince there is evidence that in the past illiterates have been permitted to register, we could simply find that unless reregistration rolls are purged of all illiterates, Gaston County cannot, under § 101(a) of the Civil Rights Act of 1964, reinstate its literacy test." 288 F. Supp. at 685. But it refused to rest on this theory, since another was available. In the Government's brief in the Supreme Court, the theory emerged as nothing more than a long footnote awkwardly added to the last sentence of text, indicating that it was likely to be either ignored or jettisoned on oral argument. It is not even so much as mentioned in the Supreme Court opinion.

Section 101(a) of the Civil Rights Act of 1964, as amended by the Voting Rights Act of 1965, is cast in more doctrinaire terms, not explicitly linking the exemption to any finding of a pattern or policy of racial discrimination and thus creates no need to prove an exemption to a racial class. See text *supra,* at notes 66–67. That is perhaps in part why the Government in its Supreme Court brief viewed § 101(a) merely "as a statutory bar" to the reinstitution of the literacy test once the suspension of the Voting Rights Act was terminated, rather than as a basis for informing the Court's decision whether the test had been used since the reregistration to dis-

The implementation of the North Carolina literacy test in the county also made this case an inappropriate one to reexamine the holding of the *Lassiter* Court that the test was not invalid under the doctrine of *Davis v. Schnell*. The details of the literacy test administered in the county from the spring of 1962 until the summer of 1964 remain somewhat unclear in the record. There was some evidence that the board, operating under a state court decision limiting some of the more striking elements of discretion,[88] still required an oral reading. In any event, most of the discretionary elements in the test were eliminated by the board in the summer of 1964. In response to the enactment of the Civil Rights Act of 1964,[89] and in time to register for the general election in November, 1964, the board of elections eliminated the oral reading aspect of the test altogether and implemented the writing aspect by printing on a card three of the provisions of the North Carolina constitution— according to testimony, "the shortest provisions"[90]—and requiring an applicant for registration to copy one of the provisions.

It was this test that was suspended by operation of § 4(a) of the Voting Rights Act of 1965, and the Court considered this literacy requirement in the context of a proceeding to terminate the suspension. The determination was made in March, 1966, that Gaston County[91] fell within the coverage formula of § 4(b) of the act.

---

criminate on the basis of race, a decision that had to be made in order to terminate the suspension. It is also significant that the Voting Rights Act requires a measure of substantiality in the discrimination. 42 U.S.C. § 1973b(d) (Supp. IV 1968).

[88] Bazemore v. Bertie County Board of Elections, 254 N.C. 398 (1961). The court declared that writing from dictation was not required under the law; that occasional misspelling and mispronunciation of more difficult words should not count; that it was not an endurance test; and all that was required was "reasonable proficiency."

[89] While the provisions requiring the literacy test to be "wholly in writing" applied in terms only to federal elections, Gaston County apparently had a single registration for all elections. See note 72 *supra*.

[90] The three sections of the North Carolina constitution were Art. IV, § 17; Art. VII, § 8; Art. XIV, § 6.

[91] On August 7, 1965, the day after the Voting Rights Act went into effect, the § 4(b) coverage determination was made on a statewide basis for Alabama, Georgia, Louisiana, Mississippi, South Carolina, and Virginia, and for twenty-six North Carolina counties. 30 FED. REG. 9897 (1965). Two more North Carolina counties were covered on January 4, 1966, 31 FED. REG. 19 (1966), and two on March 2, 1966, 31 FED. REG. 3317 (1966). Gaston County was in the last group of ten North Carolina counties brought within the coverage on March 29, 1966. 31 FED. REG.

Although at the time of the presidential election of November, 1964, the percentage of registered voters was greater than the 50 percent required for coverage, the county was brought within the coverage of the act because fewer than 50 percent of the residents of voting age had actually voted in that election.

Soon after learning of the inclusion of the county and the resulting suspension of the literacy test, in August, 1966, the board of elections commenced a declaratory proceeding against the United States in a three-judge court in the District of Columbia under the § 4(a) termination provision. Under § 4(a), the Voting Rights Act suspension may be terminated whenever the court determines "that no such test or device has been used during the five years preceding the filing of the action for the purpose or with the effect of denying or abridging the right to vote on account of race or color."[92] In applying this standard the Court focused on the

---

5080–81 (1966). See *Voting Rights Act Extension,* Hearings before Subcommittee No. 5, Committee on the Judiciary, House of Representatives, 91st Cong. 1st Sess. on H.R. 4249, Serial No. 3, p. 273 (1969) (hereinafter cited as House Hearings).

[92] This case exposed two ambiguities in the language of § 4(a). The reference to "no *such* test" in § 4(a) has two possible interpretations: (*a*) it is a necessary (and sufficient) condition of a termination that no test meeting the statutory definition of "test or device" had been discriminatorily used during the past five years; or (*b*) it is a necessary (and sufficient) condition of termination that the particular test which was suspended and which would be reinstated on the termination not have been used discriminatorily in the past five years. This question arose because in a sense Gaston County had two literacy tests, one from the spring of 1962 to the summer of 1964 and the other from the summer of 1964 to the suspension in 1966. It was the latter which the county sought to reinstitute. The Court did not resolve this ambiguity. See note 95 *infra.* The implication of the Court's opinion, however, was to choose the second alternative. This seems to be in accord with the general tenor of § 4(d) of the act. See note 87 *supra.*

The second ambiguity derives from the failure to specify the area for measuring the use of the test. This was the basis of a separate concurrence in the trial court by a judge who rejected the freezing principle approach of the majority. He construed this provision of § 4(a) in a geographic rather than a jurisdictional sense. Thus, even though the municipalities are not within the jurisdiction of the plaintiff county board of elections, see note 83 *supra,* they are within the territory of the county and he thought it incumbent upon the county board of elections to prove that the literacy test was not discriminatively used in those municipalities during the past five years. There was no evidence on that issue. The Supreme Court did not mention this as an alternative ground for decision. The argument does derive strong support from the fact that the coverage and suspension aspects of § 4(a) seem to have a territorial dimension. When the § 4(b) certification of the State of Mississippi was made, see United States v. Mississippi, 256 F. Supp. 344, 349 (S.D. Miss. 1966); Allen v. State Bd. of Elections, 393 U.S. 544 (1969); and of Alabama, Had-

problem of past discrimination—not in administration of voting qualifications, but in public education. It held that the imposition of the literacy test violated the prohibition against racial discrimination in voting by perpetuating past discrimination in public education.[93]

This theory relating to the past discrimination in education is dependent on two factual assertions: (1) At the time a significant proportion of the current electorate was in school—the period from 1908 to 1949—the public school system provided inferior and unequal educational opportunities to Negroes. (2) The level and quality of the education was such as to impair the Negroes' chances—as compared to that of whites—to pass the literacy test now. The first assertion establishes past discrimination, and the second is a necessary condition for claiming that past discrimination is being "perpetuated" by imposition of the literacy test or, more specifically by denying or threatening to deny the right to vote to those who do not pass the test.

The trial record supporting these assertions was thin. Neither assertion received much support from the registration statistics by race. As noted, a significant portion of the Negro voting-age population was registered, and the differential between that figure and the proportion of the white voting-age population registered was not so striking as to make racial discrimination the most plausible

---

nott v. Amos, 394 U.S. 358 (1969), the tests were suspended throughout the state. Administrative considerations would seem to extend that to a county certification, although there may be jurisdictional power in a state over all its subdivisions that does not exist in the county with regard to municipalities. These administrative considerations do not seem to be present in a § 4(a) termination, where the locality has all the initiative and where it is possible for the Court to tailor its judgment to terminate the suspension only within the jurisdiction of the plaintiff board of elections rather than the entire county.

93 Mr. Justice Black, author of the Court's opinion in *Louisiana v. United States,* was the only dissenter in *Gaston County.* Mr. Justice Black dissented for "substantially the same reasons he stated in § (b) of his separate opinion in *South Carolina v. Katzenbach.*" His position is not altogether clear.

In *South Carolina v. Katzenbach* his dissent was addressed only to the Court's holding that § 5 was valid. That section established a clearance procedure for new voting laws. *Gaston County,* which was a § 4(a) termination procedure, did not in any way implicate the § 5 clearance procedure.

Nor did the reason Mr. Justice Black articulated in § (b) of his opinion in *South Carolina v. Katzenbach* for believing § 5 to be unconstitutional—that it "distorts our constitutional structure of government"—seem to be applicable to a § 4(a) termination proceeding.

explanation.[94] On the second factual issue there was virtually no evidence in the record.[95] The first factual issue was made easier by the Court's assumption that "most of the adult residents of Gaston County resided there as children"[96] and that evidence concerning past education in Gaston County was all that was needed. The evidence in the record on that issue consisted of four types of statistics that indicated the difference according to race: (1) annual salary for teachers from 1908 to 1949; (2) the number of teachers who received certification in 1919; (3) the valuation of the school prop-

---

[94] In United States v. Texas, 252 F. Supp. 234 (W.D. Tex.), *aff'd on other grounds*, 384 U.S. 155 (1966), a similar theory was advanced for invalidating the poll tax, but the Court refused to apply it because of the existence of comparable statistics. In that case it was asserted that in the past the state had discriminated in education, that discrimination impaired the income-producing potential of Negroes, and the imposition of the poll tax perpetuated that discrimination. While the district court acknowledged the soundness of the theory and found that there was past discrimination in education that left "a substantial proportion of the present adult Negro population as products of its discrimination," the small disparity was fatal in that instance. See note 86 *supra. Cf.* Swain v. Alabama, 380 U.S. 202 (1965). Negroes represented 26 percent of those eligible for jury panels. The jury panels averaged 10 percent to 15 percent Negroes. The Court held that the disparity was not sufficient to make out a prima facie case of discrimination under the doctrine of Norris v. Alabama, 294 U.S. 587 (1935). According to the 1960 census, Negroes constituted 11.5 percent of the voting-age population in Gaston County, including the municipalities. At the November, 1964, election Negroes were 9.4 percent of the persons registered. See note 86 *supra.*

[95] Mr. Justice Harlan rested on two very weak reeds to support this argument. One, a quotation from Bazemore v. Bertie County Board of Elections, 245 N.C. 398 (1961), which he used to show that the literacy requirement was "high." The other, testimony by a Negro minister active in voter registration who "testified that [the literacy] test placed an especially heavy burden on the county's older Negro citizens."

When the state court in *Bazemore* used the word "high," it was referring not to the read-and-write test but rather to what had to be read and written (a section of the state constitution). Moreover, the court in *Bazemore* had placed limitations on the test. And, in any event, *Bazemore* did not address itself to the test being administered in Gaston County after the Civil Rights Act of 1964. See note 92 *supra.* Nor did Mr. Justice Harlan accurately represent the Negro minister's testimony. The word "especially" related to the age and not the race of the applicant, and the thrust of his testimony was that the burden would be as heavy on the county's older white citizens as it was on the county's older Negro citizens.

[96] 395 U.S. 293, n. 9. In that same footnote the Court, perhaps somewhat uneasy with its assumption added: "It would seem a matter of no legal significance that they may have been educated in other counties or States also maintaining segregated and unequal school systems." *Ibid.* There still needs to be a basis for finding that the school systems from which some of the current adult residents of Gaston County came were "segregated and unequal" when they went to school.

erty per pupil and per classroom from 1908 to 1949;[97] and (4) the number of persons over twenty-five years of age in 1960 with no schooling or with four years or less of schooling.[98]

In each instance, the difference by race was striking and substantial, but hardly sufficient to carry the burden. The story told by the statistics was at best fragmentary and incomplete. Its burden was not that the public school system discriminated by making a differential financial input for Negroes but that the training in reading and writing was poorer for Negroes than for whites. The financial issue would be critical for determining correction of a school system; the reading and writing issue would be critical for determining whether the use of literacy tests perpetuated past discrimination. The differential pay may reflect, not an inferior quality of Negro teachers, but that a dual pay structure existed based on racial discrimination or the operation of supply and demand in different markets. The difference in the number who received certificates may reflect, again not an inferior performance by Negro teachers, but merely the absence of appropriate paper credentials or discrimination in the administration of the certification program. Differences in the valuation of the buildings, if they are an indication of the quality of training, may have been attributable simply to the location of these buildings and the impact of racial discrimination on the real estate market. And the difference in the 1960 proportion of the Negro and white over-twenty-five population with little or no schooling need not have been due to the nonavailability of public education or to a negative reaction to poor schools, but to a host of other factors, such as the family structure and the financial need for the children to work.

The existence of these possible alternative explanations of the statistics meant that the statistics hardly told the whole story. Both the district court and the Supreme Court placed considerable stress on the fact that because this proceeding was commenced by Gaston County, it had the burden of proof. But this allocation of the

---

[97] The district court had stated: "The evidence also shows that in the earlier years Negro schoolhouses tended to be constructed of wood whereas white schoolhouses were built of brick, and that in white schools the pupils had desks rather than the benches provided Negro pupils." 288 F. Supp. at 678, n. 18.

[98] In United States v. Texas, 252 F. Supp. 234 (N.D. Tex. 1966), another type of statistic was also used, the number of pupils per teacher. See also cases cited in notes 105 and 112 *infra.*

burden—which had been construed by the Court essentially as one of refuting the evidence of the Government[99]—cannot serve to make the statistical evidence less fragmentary. The Court did not assert that under § 4(a) a suspension should be continued on a finding by the trial court that plaintiff failed to prove no past discrimination in public education which was or would be perpetuated by the imposition of the literacy test. Instead, the Court assumed that the trial court, as a condition of denying the termination, must make an affirmative finding of discrimination in the educational system in the past which was or would be perpetuated by the imposition of the literacy test. Such a finding seems difficult to predicate solely on the fragmentary statistical evidence in the records in this case. The failure of the county to establish that these alternative explanations of the statistics are their actual explanations did not eliminate them as possible alternative explanations.

If the evidentiary gap left by these statistics was ever closed, it was by evidence of the existence of the dual school system in the county for the entire pertinent period. The Court was unwilling to rely on this undisputed fact because that might prove an embarrassment in light of the legislative history and the very existence of the termination option.[100] But the fact of segregated education seems to be the only one that could fill the gap left by statistics and impart credibility to the finding. Even without laying great stress on the perceived effect of segregated education on the quality of educational opportunity afforded Negroes, it was possible to draw certain inferences about the quality of education afforded Negroes under the dual school system.[101] These inferences are either

---

[99] The burden of refutation imposed in *Gaston County* is significantly more difficult than that envisaged in South Carolina v. Katzenbach, 383 U.S. at 332, where the Court said: "South Carolina contends that these termination procedures are a nullity because they impose an impossible burden of proof upon States and political subdivisions entitled to relief. As the Attorney General pointed out during hearings on the Act, however, an area need do no more than submit affidavits from voting officials, asserting that they have not been guilty of racial discrimination through the use of tests and devices during the past five years, and then refute whatever evidence to the contrary may be adduced by the Federal Government. Section 4(d) further assures that an area need not disprove each isolated instance of voting discrimination in order to obtain relief in the termination proceedings. The burden of proof is therefore quite bearable, particularly since the relevant facts relating to the conduct of voting officials are peculiarly within the knowledge of the States and political subdivisions themselves."

[100] See text *infra*, at notes 105–09.

[101] See generally Fiss, note 49 *supra*, at 589–96.

confirmed by the statistics or possible alternative explanations are made less plausible, and the factual assertion concerning past discrimination in education in the county is made all the more credible.

The district court made these findings. The Supreme Court accepted them—though not without protecting itself with an oblique reference to the clearly erroneous rule. The Court reasoned that when a substantial portion of the current voting-age population attended school between 1908 and 1949, "the County deprived the black residents of equal educational opportunities, which in turn deprived them of an equal chance to pass the literacy test."[102] What thus emerges from *Gaston County* is a robust form of the freezing principle. As put in the closing sentences of the Supreme Court opinion: "From this record, we cannot escape the sad truth that throughout the years, Gaston County systematically deprived its black citizens of the educational opportunities it granted to its white citizens. 'Impartial' administration of the literacy test today would only perpetuate these iniquities in a different form."[103]

The reach of this version of the freezing principle cannot be ignored. Even if it were confined to the special § 4(a) termination proceedings of the Voting Rights Act, it would seem to effect a greater change than the Court would have us believe. It will clearly preclude most jurisdictions now within the coverage of the act from effectively seeking termination.[104] Although the Court's opinion minimized any explicit reliance on the existence of the dual school system and emphasized certain statistics of the Gaston County educational system during the first half of this century, it is not unduly speculative to suggest that these statistics could be found in virtually all the covered jurisdictions, almost all of which had

---

[102] 395 U.S. at 291.   [103] *Id.* at 296–97.

[104] Areas now subject to the coverage of the act are Alabama, Georgia, Louisiana, Mississippi, South Carolina, Virginia, thirty-nine counties in North Carolina, one county in Arizona, and one in Hawaii. House Hearings at 273.

One anomaly is the United States' consent to a termination judgment for another North Carolina county, Wake County. D.D.C. Civil Action No. 1198–66, January 23, 1967. This may be explainable by what was obvious throughout the *Gaston County* proceeding, that the theory that viewed the imposition of the literacy test as discrimination because it perpetuated past discrimination in education was an afterthought of the attorneys representing the United States and that the trial court, particularly Judge Wright, gave the theory its prominence. The consent judgment in *Wake County* was entered shortly before the filing of the United States' answer in *Gaston County*, and there was no mention of this particular freezing theory at all in that pleading.

dual school systems at the time of *Brown v. Board of Education.* It was unlikely that the Court was unaware of this. In a school desegregation case from Alabama, there had been findings in the record about the inequalities in public education throughout the state; and the Court had affirmed in a per curiam opinion.[105] In a case involving voting qualifications in Mississippi, the voluminous responses to interrogatories prepared by the United States indicated a similar pattern in that state.[106] In the uniform circuit-wide decree formulated by the Fifth Circuit in *United States v. Jefferson County Board of Education*,[107] the general nature of the alleged special facts of *Gaston County* was implicitly recognized in the requirement that as part of the minimum program required to disestablish the dual school system a remedial education program would have to be provided for those who attended Negro schools in the past.

Although in its brief in the Supreme Court the Department of Justice emphasized the so-called special facts of Gaston County's dual school system and represented that an "all-encompassing rule" was not at issue, but one requiring a case-by-case adjudication,[108] it was subsequently more candid. On June 26, 1969, three weeks after the Court's decision in *Gaston County* the Attorney General appeared before the House Judiciary Committee and stated: "Evidence in our possession indicates that almost all of the jurisdictions in which literacy tests are presently suspended did offer educational opportunities which were inferior."[109] Given the allocation of the burden of proof by the Court in *Gaston County*, that it is up to the local jurisdictions to refute that "evidence" in the Attorney Gen-

---

[105] Lee v. Macon County Board of Education, 267 F. Supp. 458 (M.D. Ala. 1967), *aff'd sub nom.*, Wallace v. United States, 389 U.S. 215 (1967).

[106] See United States v. Mississippi, 229 F. Supp. 925, 990–93 (S.D. Miss. 1964), *rev'd*, 380 U.S. 128 (1965).

[107] 372 F.2d 836, 891–92, 900 (5th Cir. 1966), adopted *en banc*, 380 F.2d 385 (5th Cir.), *cert. den.*, 389 U.S. 840 (1967).

[108] Brief for the United States, p. 30 n. 21.

[109] Statement of Attorney General John N. Mitchell before Subcommittee No. 5 of the House Judiciary Committee on H.R. 4949, June 26, 1969. House Hearings, 218–27. To make the linkage between that "evidence" and the dual system clearer, the Attorney General added: "Furthermore, I believe that the *Gaston County* decision would continue to suspend existing literacy tests . . . in those areas outside of the seven states covered by the 1965 Act where publicly proclaimed school segregation was prevalent prior to 1954. This would include all or part of Florida, Arkansas, Texas, Kansas, Missouri, Maryland, the District of Columbia, Kentucky, and Tennessee." House Hearings at 222–27.

eral's possession, the inevitable effect of the *Gaston County* freezing principle is an "all-encompassing rule" making § 4(a) termination unavailable to virtually all covered jurisdictions.

The *Gaston County* principle reaches beyond the § 4(a) termination proceeding. The Court did not attempt to limit the principle to invalidating or suspending voter qualifications already suspended by operation of the statute. Instead, it emerged from the opinion as a sufficient basis for further action of the nature taken in the Voting Rights Act, namely, for congressional suspension of literacy tests that still remain in effect. As such, this version of the freezing principle would be much more encompassing than the theory focusing on the risk of abuse in light of past discriminatory disenfranchisement and the freezing theory of *Louisiana v. United States*.[110] Unlike the other theories, this theory for suspension does not seem to be regionally confined. Accordingly, *Gaston County* immediately became the basis for the Attorney General's request for a nationwide suspension of literacy tests, reaching the thirteen states outside the South that have literacy tests.[111] The litigation concerning the unequal quality of education in the areas outside the South may not have as yet been as rich as the school or voting litigation in the South.[112] But the census statistics concerning number of years of school completed by race indicate a disparity similar to that relied on in *Gaston County*,[113] and for the Attorney General the

----

[110] See text *supra*, at notes 72 and 73.

[111] According to the Attorney General's testimony, Alaska, Arizona, California, Connecticut, Delaware, Hawaii, Maine, Massachusetts, New Hampshire, New York, Oregon, Washington, and Wyoming are the states outside the South that have literacy tests, and Idaho has a good character requirement. House Hearings at 223.

[112] See, *e.g.*, *In re* Skipwitch, 14 Misc.2d 325 (N.Y. Dom. Rel. Ct. 1958); Hobson v. Hansen, 269 F. Supp. 401 (D.D.C. 1967), *aff'd sub nom.*, Smuck v. Hobson, 408 F.2d 175 (D.C. Cir. 1969); Horowitz, *Unseparate but Unequal—the Emerging Fourteenth Amendment Issue in Public School Education*, 13 U.C.L.A. REV. 1147 (1966); Rousselot, *Achieving Equal Educational Opportunity for Negroes in the Public Schools of the North and West: The Emerging Role for Private Constitutional Litigation*, 35 GEO. WASH. L. REV. 698 (1967).

[113] According to the Attorney General's testimony: "In the Western states, 3.5 percent of the white males have only a fourth grade education as opposed to 10.6 percent of the Negro males over 25 years of age; in the North Central states, 3.1 percent of the white males have only a fourth grade education as opposed to 14.6 percent of the Negro males; and in the Northeast, 4.2 percent of the white males have only a fourth grade education as opposed to 8 percent of the Negro males." House Hearings at 224. These statistics compare favorably with the same ones in

migration statistics tell the rest of the story that seems to be required by *Gaston County*. As emphasized in the Attorney General's testimony several weeks after *Gaston County*:[114]

> The Bureau of the Census estimates that, between 1940 and 1968, net migration of nonwhites from the South totaled more than four million persons.
>
> Certainly, it may be assumed that part of that migration was to those Northern and Western states which employ literacy tests now or could impose them in the future; and that, as was true in Gaston County, the effect of these tests is to further penalize persons for the education they received previously.

This theory seems all the more plausible because the Court in *Gaston County* stated that it would be of no legal significance if some of the adult residents of Gaston County received their past unequal education in other states and counties, because the differential rate of registration in Gaston County could probably be duplicated in many other regions of the country.[115]

As broad a thrust as the *Gaston County* version of the freezing principle might have in its statutory context, whether it be the special § 4(a) termination proceeding or a nationwide expansion of the Voting Rights Act by further congressional action, this is not the limit of its utility. True, the standard applied was a statutory one—"used . . . with the purpose or effect of denying or abridging the right to vote on account of race or color." But this statutory phrase essentially expresses the general prohibition against racial discrimination, which is made applicable to voting in the Fifteenth Amendment.[116] Mr. Justice Harlan, the author of *Gaston County*,

---

Gaston County, although the comparable figure in the South is somewhat more striking. The Attorney General said: "[I]n the South, 8.5 percent of the white males over 25 have only a fourth grade education as opposed to 30 percent for Negro males." *Ibid.* He based these statements on Bureau of Census, Current Population Reports, Series P-20, No. 182 (1969); Educational Attainment: March 1968, table 3.

114 House Hearings at 223. The footnote omitted refers to Bureau of Census, Current Population Reports, Series P-23, No. 26 (July 1968). Social and Economic Conditions of Negroes in the United States, p. 2.

115 See note 86 *supra*. It nevertheless appears difficult to obtain percentage statistics on the racial disparity of registered voters.

116 In litigation that might be brought where the literacy tests were not suspended by virtue of the operation of the Voting Rights Act of 1965 but based instead on the self-operative provisions of the Fifteenth Amendment or 42 U.S.C. § 1971(a) it might well be argued that certain considerations of fairness—relating to such

dissented in *Morgan v. Katzenbach*,[117] indicating his belief that congressional power to invalidate state laws under the appropriate-legislation clause of the Fourteenth and Fifteenth Amendments is limited to those instances where the judiciary has determined or would be prepared to determine that the laws violated the self-operative, general prohibitions of the initial clauses of those amendments. The identity between this statutory phrase and the general antidiscrimination prohibition is also made clearer by the paraphrasing of the statutory phrase in *Gaston County* and *South Carolina v. Katzenbach;* the frequent use of that particular phrase throughout the statute; the previous use of the standard in litigation that immediately preceded the legislation; the role that the principal litigator, the Department of Justice, had in drafting the legislation; the legislative history of the act; and the formulations of the prohibition against racial discrimination in other cases.

The statutory phrase "purpose or effect" has no special limiting significance.[118] It was used simply to distinguish the ways in which an apparently innocent test could violate the prohibition. A test with a racially discriminatory purpose is one that could serve or further no legitimate state interest, but instead could serve only as a means of preventing Negroes from voting because of their race. A test with a racially discriminatory "effect" is one that might serve some legitimate state interest, such as the read-or-write literacy test, but the test through its operation—inevitable or actual—discriminates against Negroes on the basis of race. Nor does the Court's reliance on the legislative history of the Voting Rights Act—which seems in any event overstated[119]—have the effect of confining the

---

questions as who is likely to have knowledge of the facts, who has the resources needed to uncover the facts, and whose view of the facts comport with widely shared beliefs—should lead the court to shift a substantial part of the burden of proof to the defendant, this time the locality that imposed the test. See Chambers v. Hendersonville City Board of Education, 364 F.2d 189 (4th Cir. 1966).

[117] 384 U.S. 641, 659, 666–68 (1966).

[118] See Louisiana v. United States, 380 U.S. 145 (1965), *aff'g* 225 F. Supp. 353 (E.D. La. 1963); Smith v. Texas, 311 U.S. 128 (1940); United States v. Dogan, 314 F.2d 767 (5th Cir. 1963); United States v. Atkins, 323 F.2d 733 (5th Cir. 1963); South Carolina v. Katzenbach, 383 U.S. at 326; Sellers v. Trussell, 253 F. Supp. 915, 917 (M.D. Ala. 1966); Meredith v. Fair, 298 F.2d 696 (5th Cir. 1962); Hawkins v. North Carolina Dental Soc., 355 F.2d 718 (4th Cir. 1966); Note, *Developments in the Law—Equal Protection*, 82 HARV. L. REV. 1065, 1099–1101 (1969).

[119] The *Gaston County* freezing principle emerges from the Supreme Court opinion as an independent, alternative justification for the central enforcement

principle to the interpretation of a peculiar statutory phrase, divorced from the general prohibition against racial discrimination. The pertinent statements in the legislative history may have informed the Court's judgment in applying the statutory standard. But, to be sure, they could do so only on the premise that the statutory standard is identical with the Fifteenth Amendment prohibition against racial discrimination. One statement relied on by the Court was that of the Attorney General:[120]

> The impact of a general re-registration would produce a real irony. Years of violation of the 14th amendment right of equal protection through equal education, would become the excuse for continuing violation of the 15th amendment right to vote.

The other statement relied on is that of twelve of the sixteen members of the Senate Judiciary Committee:[121]

> [T]he educational differences between whites and Negroes in the areas to be covered by the prohibitions—differences which are reflected in the record before the Committee— would mean that equal application of the test would abridge 15th amendment rights.

As a principle to guide the application of the general prohibition against racial discrimination, the version of the freezing principle that emerges from *Gaston County* should be placed on a continuum with those of the grandfather clause cases and *Louisiana v. United States*. There are, however, two interrelated innovations.

First, the *Gaston County* principle is not linked, as were the earlier cases,[122] to the problem of exemptions. Past discrimination does not result in the creation of a class from which some Negroes have been excluded and which is now exempt from the application of the standard. Instead, past discrimination relates to the distribution of government services—public education—and allegedly impairs the ability of Negroes compared with that of whites to satisfy a stan-

---

technique of the Voting Rights Act of 1965, *i.e.*, test suspensions. It is hardly supported by the legislative history.

[120] 395 U.S. at 289. Hearings on S. 1564 before the Senate Committee on the Judiciary, 89th Cong., 1st Sess., 22 (1965).

[121] Quoted in 395 U.S. at 290; S. Rep. No. 162, 89th Cong., 1st Sess., pt. 3, at 16 (1965).

[122] But see *Hamer v. Campbell*, discussed in note 127 *infra*.

dard to be applied to all. Some whites might not have the ability to pass the test and some Negroes do have the ability; but it is the factual premise of the *Gaston County* theory that at least a substantial proportion of those Negroes without this ability do not have it because of discrimination in the past against Negroes.

This departure from the traditional concern with exemptions has in turn two further consequences for the principle. It increases the evidentiary burden involved in establishing the causal links involved in the concept of perpetuation. What must be demonstrated to establish the freezing effect is not only that there was racial discrimination in the past but that this past discrimination was of such a nature originally and has so persisted during the intervening years that the imposition of the challenged test will be a perpetuation of that discrimination. Account must be taken of the significant possibility that over the years the disabling quality of the original discrimination has been dissipated or reinforced by a great number of factors and experiences, and, as a result, the disability may have disappeared or lost its racial contours. With *Louisiana v. United States*, however, as long as the local registrars persisted in refusing to register Negroes because of their race and the Negroes generally remained unregistered, as was invariably the case up to the filing of the complaint, and sometimes after, the exemption and its racial contours remained; and thus the freezing effect was clear.

The absence of a connection in *Gaston County* with exemptions also means that certain remedies are no longer available to correct the freezing effects: suspension for a limited number of years or reregistration. In the courts, the freezing principle of *Louisiana v. United States* prohibited the enforcement of the test but generally, or at least nominally, gave the local officials the option of avoiding or terminating that prohibition at any time and instituting the test, provided they conducted a reregistration. The costs of a reregistration were some measure of the importance local officials attached to the test. Moreover, even if this option of reregistration was not exercised, the nullificaton of the standard was limited to a relatively short period of years, just enough to give the otherwise nonexempt class the same opportunities as the exempt class. Hence the use of the words "suspension" or "postponement." Under the *Gaston County* version of the freezing principle, however, if it is not tied to the special termination proceeding of § 4(a) but governs the interpretation of the Fifteenth Amendment self-operative prohibition,[123] the nullification takes on an air of permanency. Short of instituting a remedial education program for persons educated in the past, which admittedly is not inconceivable, it is hard to see how or when the effects of the past discrimination in public education—which may be reinforced by other consequences of its own making, such as unemployment—are ever to be dissipated so that the literacy test could be imposed without freezing those effects.

The second innovation of the *Gaston County* version of the freezing principle is that it is freed from any requirement that the past discrimination be in the same area as the perpetuating act. The past discrimination in *Gaston County* did not occur in the qualifying of persons to vote, as was true in the grandfather clause cases and *Louisiana v. United States*, but in public education. By so sensitizing the principle to discrimination in areas of human activity other than voting and thus making it a two-dimensional theory, the potential of the freezing principle is magnified considerably. This is particularly true because the second dimension—public education—seems to play such an important role in our society, and the effects of past discrimination in education may be perpetuated by standards and conduct in areas not related to voting but also covered by a prohibition against racial discrimination.

This new two-dimensional quality of the freezing principle also has the effect of blurring the identity between the past discriminator and the perpetuator and changes the nature of the evidentiary inquiry. In *Guinn* there was not much of an issue of identity between the past discriminator and the perpetuator, since, presumably, the state legislature was responsible for the past discrimination and its perpetuation. With regard to *Louisiana v. United States* there was only slightly more of an issue. While the past discriminators differed from the perpetuators in name and person, sufficient identity was established by emphasizing the identity of the office and the fact that

---

[123] Unless the present act is extended, an issue currently before congressional committees, regardless of the discriminatory nature of the test, those covered jurisdictions will be able to obtain a § 4(a) termination five years after they were brought within the coverage of the act, for no test would have been used for five years. Section 4(a) also provides that the district court is to retain jurisdiction of the action for five years after judgment and is to reopen the matter upon motion of the Attorney General alleging discriminatory use of a test or device. The Attorney General stated that even if the Voting Rights Act were not extended, and literacy tests reintroduced, in light of *Gaston County* and the evidence in his possession he would "be obliged to move, shortly after reintroduction of the literacy test, to have the test suspension reimposed in the seven covered States." House Hearings at 222.

the officeholder has little personal stake in the qualifications imposed on voters.[124] In *Gaston County* the concern with past discrimination in public education and present discrimination in voting qualifications either eliminates a requirement of identity between the past discriminator and the perpetuator or finds it satisfied: (1) by the interrelationships of different government units or officers; (2) by the appropriateness of evaluating one entity's behavior in terms of its effect on the wrongs of another, if the second has power to correct those wrongs or avoid the perpetuation of them in a different form; or (3) by the fact that whatever costs there may be to the corrective action—administrative costs or costs in terms of the quality of the electorate—will be spread throughout the entire community. Although different governmental entities may be involved in this two-dimensional freezing theory, both entities speak for the same community.

There is a suggestion in a footnote in *Gaston County* that the identity between the discriminator and the perpetuator can be even further attenuated in the remark that it was of "no legal significance" which counties or states were responsible for inferior and unequal education. But the force of this suggestion is unclear, since it is made on the assumption that a substantial portion of the present adult population of the county had been educated in the county education system. Instead of saying that it will hold Gaston County responsible for the past discrimination of another county or state, it might be saying that the standard is discriminatory simply on the basis of its impact on Gaston County–educated Negroes. Just as the theory does not require that the past discrimination be of a quality to impair the chance of every Negro to pass the literacy test, the presence in the electorate of some Negroes who were educated elsewhere does not defeat the theory. What is critical is that in the

---

124 See, *e.g.*, United States v. Mississippi, 339 F.2d 679 (5th Cir. 1964), where in the course of the appellate proceedings the notorious Registrar Wood of Walthall County, see United States v. Wood, 295 F.2d 772 (5th Cir. 1961), died, and the freeze order was issued against his successor.

In United States v. Duke, 332 F.2d at 770, the court of appeals said that the "state's presence was essential to the granting of complete relief." But it made that remark in justifying the joinder of the state. It is clear that a federal court can enjoin a local official from enforcing a statewide law in his jurisdiction without making the state a party, particularly when its action is predicated on abuse of that statute by a local official. See 28 U.S.C. § 2284(2) (requiring notice to the governor or Attorney General if the injunctive suit involves the enforcement, operation or execution of state statutes or state administrative orders).

past there was discrimination against Negroes in their education in the county—by a substantially related government institution—and that discrimination is being perpetuated by the imposition of the test on some significant segment of the same class of Negroes.

Finally, this two-dimensional quality radically changes the nature of the evidentiary inquiry required to establish past discrimination —a necessary condition for the application of the principle. In *Guinn* the past exclusion was judicially noticeable and confirmed by the choice of dates in the statute. In *Louisiana v. United States* an inquiry was undertaken to determine whether Negroes had been excluded from registering and what standards were applied to those who were registered in the past. This inquiry was a significant one. But the evidentiary inquiry called for by the *Gaston County* version of the freezing principle is significantly more ambitious. Two things are required. First, an assessment of the quality of education that is not satisfied simply by proof of the segregated character of student attendance patterns. Second, an evaluation of that education, as well as all the other factors responsible for the level of an adult's present ability. The staggering proportions of such an inquiry, assuming it is possible, are clear even when the interest is limited to the present educational system or that of the recent past.[125] But those dimensions are magnified when one has to reach further into the past to evaluate the education received by significant segments of the present electorate, and then go perhaps even deeper.[126]

IV. The General Contours of the Freezing Principle

The freezing principle is applicable in evaluating apparently innocent standards to determine whether they violate the prohibi-

---

[125] Judge Wright, the author of the trial court opinion in *Gaston County*, was no doubt aware of this. See his opinion in Hobson v. Hansen, 269 F. Supp. 401 (D.D.C. 1967), *aff'd sub. nom.*, Smuck v. Hobson, 408 F.2d 175 (D.C. Cir. 1969).

[126] When one ambiguity with the 1960 statistics concerning the disparity in the proportion of all Negroes and whites with four years or less of schooling was pointed out—that this might not be attributable to the inferior educational opportunity provided Negroes but to other factors, such as "economic necessity"—the district court raised the specter of an earlier historical inquiry: "Gaston County would, of course, also have to show the economic necessity was not itself the result of segregated education of the Negro parents." It is conceivable at that point that the inquiry may get easier because one is back to the cardinal past discrimination—slavery.

tion against racial discrimination because of their actual or inevitable effects. To understand the theoretical role that the freezing principle plays in this evaluation, two types of voting standards should be distinguished: past-required-act standards and content standards.

Past-required-act standards require that some particular act have been done by the applicant in the past. The time when the act was done is as important to the standard as that the act was done. In such a context the risk of the freezing effect is clear, and the freezing principle has particular force. Under it the claim could be made that: (1) past discrimination either prevented the applicant from performing the required act when it was required or made it entirely excusable not to do the act then; and (2) to disqualify a person from voting for not doing the required act would perpetuate past discrimination. The relief sought could be either to relieve the applicant from doing the required act or, more modestly, relieve the applicant from having failed to act at the time it was required. In the latter instance the decree would require the registrar to accept *nunc pro tunc* performance of the act.[127]

These past-required-act standards have not been a significant barrier to Negro voting and thus have played a minor role in the litigation and legislation. Moreover, the freezing effect of such special standards is so easily perceived that no sophisticated doctrines need be developed to account for it.

With the standards that have been the subject of concern in the

---

[127] In Hamer v. Campbell, 358 F.2d 215 (5th Cir. 1966), the court had occasion to apply the freezing principle to this special type of standard. The registrar of Sunflower County had engaged in a pattern or practice of discrimination in the registration process. The court entered an order enjoining the registrar from such discrimination in the future. The order also contained a freeze provision. Because of the short time between that order and the scheduled elections, two types of past-required-act voting-qualification standards were challenged on the basis of their freezing effect in subsequent proceedings in the district court: (1) a requirement that an elector register four months prior to the general election—a cutoff date that expired two months before the initial federal court order; and (2) a requirement that poll taxes must be paid for the two preceding years. The district court denied relief, and before the appellate court acted, the local elections were held, in which these two standards were imposed. The court of appeals set aside the election, ordered that new cutoff dates for registration be set, and ordered that nonpayment of the poll taxes for the preceding two years would not be ground for disqualification if the applicant now tenders poll tax for the two preceding years. See also United States v. Dogan, 314 F.2d 767 (5th Cir. 1963) (actual discrimination in acceptance of poll tax); § 10(d) of Voting Rights Act of 1965, 42 U.S.C. § 1973h(d) (Supp. IV 1968). *Cf.* Lane v. Wilson, 307 U.S. 268 (1939).

grandfather clause cases, in *Louisiana v. United States*, and in *Gaston County*, the freezing effect is more subtle. With content standards, such as the literacy test, the essence of the requirement is doing the act or having the ability required by the standard, not doing the act at some particular point of time. Thus, a freezing effect can be present and take at least two forms: (1) granting an exemption and (2) requiring performance when the chance of success is impaired by a disability for which government is responsible.

In grandfather clause cases and *Louisiana v. United States* the critical flaw in the operation or application of the standard consisted of the fact that a class was exempted from it. Without regard to considerations of racial discrimination, past or present, the exemption—itself a distinction, classification, or form of unequal treatment —can be invalidated under general guarantees of equal treatment if the interests served by it do not justify it.[128] Wholly apart from the racial dimensions of the claim, a serious question is whether any exemption from a voting qualification standard can be justified. With this perspective, the special role of the freezing principle is to relate the exemption to the prohibition against racial discrimination, to perceive the discrimination even though the standard is to be applied to both whites and Negroes who are not already registered. Attention is focused on the past and how the class now exempt was constituted. If it is determined that in the past Negroes were excluded from the class exempted, something admittedly violative of the antidiscrimination prohibition, the present exemption can be conceptualized as "the perpetuation of past discrimination" and a heavier burden of justification is required of the interest served by granting the exemption or not taking action that would eliminate that exemption (*e.g.*, reregistration). If that interest is of insufficient magnitude to justify the perpetuation of the past discrimination by the granting of the exemption, then the exemption

---

[128] See Carrington v. Rash, 380 U.S. 89, 95 (1965) (invalidation of Texas law disenfranchising servicemen stemmed in part from exemption of another group of likely nonresidents, students, from similar treatment). See generally Rinaldi v. Yeager, 384 U.S. 305 (1966) (exemption for unsuccessful appellants who were merely fined, as opposed to those imprisoned); Skinner v. Oklahoma *ex rel.* Williamson, 316 U.S. 535 (1942) (exemption for embezzlers from statute providing for sterilization of habitual criminals). This past Term the Court formulated the balancing test in these terms: "In determining whether or not a state law violates the Equal Protection Clause, we must consider the facts and circumstances behind the law, interests which the State claims to be protecting, and interests of those who are disadvantaged by the classification." Williams v. Rhodes, 393 U.S. 23, 30 (1968).

cannot be given or the exemption must be extended to those excluded from that class and, for practical considerations, often to others.

The other, and perhaps more subtle, type of effect of these standards, such as that involved in *Gaston County*, is the impairment of the chances of success attributable to certain disabilities. The test is a "heavier burden" on a class. Once again with this effect, like the exemption, it is not a necessary condition of invalidating an ostensibly innocent standard that its differential impact be linked to past discrimination. The differential impact may be such as to offset any legitimate interest served by the standard and thus constitute a prohibited discrimination under more general guarantees of equal treatment. In *Harper v. Virginia Board of Education*,[129] for example, the payment of a poll tax was invalidated on this differential-impact theory: as a qualification for voting the poll tax cast a heavier burden on the poor than on the rich, and the legitimate state interest served by this law was not sufficient to justify the unequal treatment. This theory, which focuses on the differential impact without regard to historical or causal explanations, should be as sufficient a basis for establishing a violation of the prohibition against racial discrimination as it is for establishing a violation of the less clearly recognized prohibition that forbids discrimination against a less well-defined class, the "poor." The racial contours of this differential impact could be predicated on such statistics as the disparity by race of the number of years of schooling (without regard to the causal explanation for that disparity). Under this theory, apparently innocent standards that placed a heavier burden on Negroes would be evaluated on the basis of a balancing process between the harm—denial of the right to vote or the risk of being denied that vote—and the interest served by the standard.

Assuming the general availability of such a theory,[130] the added function of the freezing principle is to structure and facilitate this

---

[129] 383 U.S. 663 (1966).

[130] See also Draper v. Washington, 372 U.S. 487 (1963); Lane v. Brown, 372 U.S. 477 (1963); Douglas v. California, 372 U.S. 353 (1963); Griffin v. Illinois, 351 U.S. 12 (1956). See Fiss, note 49 *supra*, at 588–89. In his opinion for the Court in *Gaston County* Mr. Justice Harlan clearly preserved his disassociation from the pure differential-impact theory by stating: "We have no occasion to decide whether the Act would permit reinstatement of the literacy test in the face of racially disparate educational or literacy achievements for which a government bore no responsibility." 395 U.S. at 293 n. 8.

balancing process between the harm and the legitimate interests. Once again, attention is focused on the past. This time the purpose of such a historical inquiry is not to determine the racial contours of an exempted class, as in the grandfather clause cases and *Louisiana v. United States*. Instead it is to seek the historical or causal explanation for the heavier burden and to determine whether it is attributable to a disability that is due to past discrimination by government. If it is determined that past discrimination is to some significant degree responsible for this disability and hence the heavier burden, then rejecting Negroes for not meeting that standard can be classified or conceptualized as "the perpetuation of past discrimination." This conceptualization in turn imposes a heavy burden of justification on the interests furthered by the standard. It requires compelling interests. If they are not present, the standard is held to violate the prohibition against racial discrimination. In *Gaston County* the Court in one sense did not have to consider the remedial consequences of that judgment, for the standard was already suspended by operation of a statute based at least in part on other theories. More generally, the remedial consequence could be similar to that of *Harper* and the post–Voting Rights Act application of *Louisiana v. United States*. Rather than leading to a more tailored decree enjoining the enforcement of the standard only against the direct victims of the past discrimination, the inhibiting effect of the standard and practical considerations, in fashioning a remedy, could result in a blanket decree totally enjoining the enforcement of the standard until it no longer poses the risk of perpetuating past discrimination.

Thus, stated more generally, in both the exemption and disability situations, the special office of the freezing principle is to structure and facilitate a balancing process between the effect of a seemingly innocent standard—disenfranchisement or the risk of disenfranchisement—and the legitimate interests served by that standard. That principle operates in two steps. If the effect of imposing the standard would be to perpetuate past discrimination, that is, have a "freezing effect," then a heavier burden of justification is imposed upon the legitimate interests served by that standard. If that burden cannot be sustained, the application of the standard violates the prohibition against racial discrimination.

While the freezing principle appears as a means of facilitating and structuring the balancing process, there are several difficulties with its use that must be noticed. First, the evidentiary difficulty of reconstructing the past limits the capacity to classify the effects in question as the "perpetuation of the past." The second difficulty—a more normative one—requires the principle to have a margin of flexibility so that even after the evidentiary difficulties are overcome and the determination is made that the standard perpetuates past discrimination, it is possible to accommodate compelling state interests.

The difficulties inherent in attempting to reconstruct the past should not go unnoticed. These evidentiary difficulties place a genuine strain upon the legal system, particularly the judicial component. Under *Louisiana v. United States* theory it was necessary to establish both that there was a substantial class of Negroes excluded from the class of those already registered because of their race and, where the challenged standard had been on the books for some time, that the standard was not in fact imposed upon those already registered. This factual inquiry was made manageable because great reliance was placed on the striking racial disparities existing in the percentages of voting population registered, coupled with general familiarity with the social setting. The more vigorous proof—usually unavailable because of inadequate records and memories—concerning the experiences of particular individuals was confirmatory of the natural inferences from this disparity, and the disparity had the effect of generalizing the experience to a class. Similarly, the evidentiary responsibility in *Gaston County* was made manageable because the evidentiary requirements were not very exacting, nor could they have been. An inquiry into the nature of the public educational system during the past half-century and a determination of the quality of education provided Negroes and the effect it had on their present abilities to qualify borders on the hopeless. The evidence is likely to consist of nothing more than old surveys and reports, at best containing fragmentary and ambiguous statistics,[131]

---

[131] In *Gaston County* the Negro principal of the Negro high school testified for the county that, however bad the schools had been, they were of sufficient quality to enable the Negroes to pass the county's literacy test. But his testimony was dismissed by the district court on the ground that it was "unpersuasive," as the "mere contemporary conclusions from an interested witness," and on the ground that the witness came to Gaston County and started teaching there in 1932 and "his knowledge therefore dates only from that time." 288 F. Supp. at 668 n. 19. The word "only" is startling, when one realistically reflects on the witnesses usually competent to testify on these questions.

although in *Gaston County* these gaps appeared to be filled by inferences drawn from the existence of the dual school system during that period. Moreover, under both *Louisiana v. United States* and *Gaston County* types of theories, difficulties remained in identifying the victims of the past wrong.

The evidentiary inquiry to reconstruct the past need not, of course, be so difficult. There might well be various ameliorating factors and devices:[132] admissions, either from the lips of a witness or in records generously preserved from an earlier time when admissions of discrimination were less unfashionable; the fact that the alleged discrimination was in the recent past rather than the distant past; the existence of judicial findings of discrimination contemporaneous with the wrong; the fact that the discrimination may be quite easily perceivable even from the current perspective;[133] and the formulation of per se rules based on commonly shared empirical insights or the natural inferences from readily ascertainable facts, such as statistically demonstrable racial disparity or an open policy of maintaining a dual school system. The point is not, however, that the evidentiary burden is impossible, precluding any use of the principle, but rather that the evidentiary difficulties in reconstructing the past—if not the imagination and investigative resources of the litigators and the patience of the trial judge—will limit the role that the freezing principle can properly play in the effort of the legal system to evaluate apparently innocent standards. The judicial component of our legal system should be particularly sensitive to preserving this limitation. Because of its authoritarian, nonrepresentative nature as an institution, it is in no small measure dependent for its moral posture upon the integrity of its fact-finding processes.

---

[132] One basis for placing time limits on the inquiry, namely, that predicated on the date when the past discrimination became "illegal," would not serve as much of a limitation in voting since that past discrimination is—at least now—likely to have been "illegal" under one of the century-old constitutional guarantees, if not the Civil Rights Act of 1866. *Cf.* United States v. Dogan, 314 F.2d 767 (5th Cir. 1963). In any event, as a bar to considering past discrimination, it would seem artificial, since the inquiry is whether certain present conduct violates the legal prohibition against racial discrimination, not whether the past conduct did. As Judge Wisdom pointed out in *United States v. Louisiana*, in *Guinn* the past discrimination—not allowing Negroes to vote before 1866—was not at the time it occurred "illegal." 225 F. Supp. at 394. Whether the past discrimination was "illegal" at the time it occurred might nevertheless be appropriate to consider in determining the strength of the normative force to be given to the conclusion that the present conduct perpetuates the past discrimination.

[133] See United States v. Ward, 349 F.2d at 801.

Even if the past can be reconstructed so that it could be established that past discrimination is being perpetuated, there are other factors that limit the force of the principle. These are the factors that deprive the past wrong of some of its moral force and thus make it sometimes permissible to say, as Judge Wisdom, one of the most sensitive judges, said, "This is a product of the past. We cannot turn back the clock."[134]

Part of the pressure in society to forget the past no doubt generates from either those who discriminated or those who have little or nothing to gain from the correction of past discrimination. As such, these pressures express nothing more than the assertion of self-interest. These assertions of self-interest will have to be confronted and will make the correctional task more difficult. But they are not a sufficient basis for the legal system—if it is to be a just system—to retreat from the task. They, like other forms of resistance, govern the choice of tactics for accomplishing that task, not the commitment to do so. There are other reasons to forget the past, and to the extent that these reasons are generally acknowledged as valid by the victims of the past wrong—as well as others in society—they are severed from considerations of self-interest and begin to supply a basis for a moral climate that sometimes makes it permissible to forget the wrongs of the past without suffering blame, reproach, or guilt. It is this moral permissibility of forgetting the past that will place a strain upon the legal system committed to a version of the freezing principle that is so absolute it would make the perpetuation of any past discrimination automatically a sufficient basis for invalidating the standard and coercing corrective action. It is a strain quite unlike and of a much more serious character than that attributable to the pressure rooted in self-interested resistance, for in this instance the morality of the corrective enterprise is thrown into question.

There are several general reasons that could have this significance. First, owing to the inherent evidentiary difficulties of reconstructing the past and the causal relationship between the past wrong and the present effect, even if the "past wrong" and its "perpetuation" were established, there would inevitably be error in identifying the victims of the past wrong. Either the concept of "victim" will be arti-

---

[134] Whitfield v. United Steelworkers of America, 263 F.2d 546, 551 (5th Cir. 1959). Compare his opinion in Local 189, United Papermakers and Paperworkers v. United States, No. 25956, 5th Cir., July 28, 1969.

ficially restricted or there will be a margin of overinclusion in the class receiving the benefits of the corrective action. Second, the sheer passage of time, as well as the two-dimensional quality of the *Gaston County* freezing theory, means that one person or entity—the perpetuator—would in part be held responsible for the wrongs of another. This element of vicarious responsibility is likely to drain the concept of the force it would otherwise have, particularly when the passage of time between the past wrong and the perpetuation afforded the victims some opportunity to use self-help to correct the discrimination, thus casting some responsibility on the victims themselves for its perpetuation. Third, if the perpetuation of the past discrimination were to be an automatic basis for invalidating ostensibly innocent standards, change—some of which might otherwise be desirable, such as raising standards—will become more costly. Starting from a recognition of how widespread discrimination was in the past, instituting a change would generally have to be accompanied or preceded by action—such as a general reregistration or a remedial education program—that would eliminate the risk of perpetuating past wrongs. Such costs might be not only a tax upon the change but also a diversion of resources from other purposes that might generally benefit the community more. Fourth, the past plays such a pervasive role in determining an individual's ability or qualification and is so filled with "wrongs" that any principle committing the legal system to invalidating every standard that perpetuates past discrimination is likely to compromise another moral tenet—that each person should be judged on the basis of his individual ability. To some extent this norm of judging each on the basis of his ability holds the individual generally responsible for his own present ability or qualification without constantly making readjustments for the historical or causal explanation for the present level of ability or qualification. Such constant readjustments would make the principle administratively unworkable, given the pervasiveness of past wrongs and the likelihood of their continuing effect, and would deprive it of some of its motivational force as a prod to self-improvement. This is not obscured by the moral acceptability and administrative feasibility of giving a cripple a shorter distance to run in a handicap race. Such disability is dramatic and easily perceivable. The handicapped person may run one or two races, but he is not thought to be a full participant in the competitive system to which the other runners belong. Fifth, the disruptive and dislocative quality of correc-

tive action is particularly magnified when it is predicated on conduct that reaches far into the past and upon which further conduct
and action are likely to have been built.

Considered separately, each of these factors might have only
limited applicability to voting qualifications. Considered collective-
ly, they have the force of making it morally permissible sometimes
to forget the past. The conclusion of perpetuated past discrimination demands a very high degree of justification to avoid invalidation of the standard under the antidiscrimination prohibition. But
it does not necessarily require invalidation of the standard or other
corrective action by the legal system. There must be the further
normative judgment that there is no compelling interest that would
justify failure to take action necessary to eradicate the freezing
effect. Thus the freezing principle has a margin of flexibility that
enables it to accommodate these compelling considerations, which
can present themselves with varying degrees of intensity in various
situations.

This margin of flexibility is analytically consistent with the antidiscrimination prohibition. The conduct that concededly violated
the prohibition—the discrimination—occurred in the "past," and it
remains to be decided that the standard that perpetuates past discrimination presents a current occasion for corrective action by the
legal system. Thus, while the Court in *Louisiana v. United States*
spoke of the duty to eliminate the freezing effect, it realized that
this duty—perhaps like all legal duties—had limits. It is the duty of
the equity court to render a decision "which will so far as possible
eliminate the discriminatory effects of the past." In the context of
the legal system and particularly the equitable component, the concept "so far as possible" primarily guards against, not physical impossibilities, but normative impossibilities that would be involved in
the corrective action. More generally, however, this margin of
flexibility is not likely to be openly acknowledged, but instead the
interests it might otherwise protect are likely to be silently accom-
modated in the finding that the claimant has not adequately established past discrimination, or in the specifics of the relief, given the
considerable range of alternatives open to the court nominally
committed to eliminating the freezing effect. For example, even
under the *Louisiana v. United States* theory, a court has considerable latitude in deciding precisely which old standards can be imposed in the future, with what degree of vigor, and what the

appropriate class of beneficiaries is. The logic of the freezing principle provides no inexorable rules for these determinations. Guided
only by concerns of fairness, account is likely to be taken of compelling state interests. Thus, while the Court of Appeals for the
Fifth Circuit repeatedly formulated the *Louisiana v. United States*
freezing principle in the most absolute terms, it quietly refused—
perhaps overcrediting *Lassiter*'s declaration that the read-and-write
literacy test served a permissible state purpose—to apply the principle so as to invalidate that test in toto, even though there was no
doubt that a class with racially discriminatory contours had been
exempted.

There is likely to be a more open recognition of this margin of
flexibility inherent in the freezing principle when the principle is
applied to voting activity other than the qualifying of persons to
vote. What is needed to bring this element of flexibility out into
the open is the presence of compelling interests that might be more
easily perceivable than those that purportedly justify voting qualifications. Then the refusal to conclude that the conduct or standard
with the freezing effect violates the antidiscrimination prohibition
would be more clearly understood not to imply a lack of commitment to enforce the antidiscrimination prohibition. Such a compelling interest was present when attempts were made to set aside
elections because of the freezing effect.[135] In *McGill v. Ryals*,[136]
the freezing principle was used as the predicate for a claim for relief that would declare certain local officers to be elected illegally
and to schedule an election for those officers several years earlier
than would occur under the ordinary operation of state law. It was
alleged that these officers were elected at a time when Negroes
were excluded from voting because of their race, and that allowing
these officials to continue in office would perpetuate past discrimination. The three-judge district court decided the case on the basis of
the pleadings. The court was prepared to assume that the plaintiffs
could, after an evidentiary hearing, reconstruct the past discrimination and establish that the continued occupancy of the elected

---

[135] See Hamer v. Campbell, 358 F.2d 215 (5th Cir. 1966); Bell v. Southwell, 376
F.2d 659 (5th Cir. 1967). See also Mississippi Freedom Democratic Party v. Democratic Party, 362 F.2d 60 (5th Cir. 1966), refusing to postpone an election so as to
enable additional Negroes to register before the election and thus overcome the
effects of the past discrimination.

[136] 253 F. Supp. 374 (M.D. Ala. 1966), *app. dism.*, 385 U.S. 19 (1966).

offices by the incumbents was a form of perpetuating that discrimination. The court also made it clear that it thought it had the power to afford this type of relief and provided reminders of how vigorously the court had been committed to the eradication of the effects of past discrimination. But recognizing the community's interest in avoiding uncertainty in election results, the disruptive impact that the requested relief would have upon "planning and the orderly administration of public affairs," and that "in time" opportunities would present themselves for "easing" this effect of past discrimination, the court granted a motion to dismiss the complaint. The appeal to the Supreme Court was dismissed "for want of jurisdiction because the case was not appropriate for a three-judge court." But, significantly, the Court did not provide an order that would have preserved the plaintiff's right of appeal to the court of appeals, which might have been appropriate, since neither the court below nor the appellees had questioned the appropriateness of the three-judge court. There was a dissent by Mr. Justice Douglas stating that he thought a three-judge court was properly convened but that he would affirm the judgment below.

Nor could the district court's decision in *McGill v. Ryals* be understood as reflecting an ambivalence toward the freezing principle or a view that it was inapplicable beyond the voting-qualification situation or was anything but a recognition of the margin of flexibility in the principle, even once the freezing effect was established. Four weeks after its decision in *McGill v. Ryals,* in the inevitable next case, *Sellers v. Trussell,*[137] the principle was applied in the same general context. There the principle was used as a basis for invalidating a state law that not only perpetuated but in a sense aggravated past discrimination in another Black Belt county—Bullock County—by extending the term of office of the incumbent county commissioners from four to six years. Two of these commissioners were elected in 1962, when 100 percent of the whites of voting age were registered, compared to fewer than 0.2 percent of the Negroes of voting age. The court concluded that the compelling interests involved in *McGill v. Ryals* were not present, or if they were, to a lesser degree, and that the law violated the Fifteenth Amendment prohibition against racial discrimination in voting. As the Court said in *Sellers v. Trussell,* "The Act freezes into office

---

[137] 253 F. Supp. 915 (M.D. Ala. 1966) (alternative basis for decision was § 5 of the Voting Rights Act of 1965).

for an additional two years persons who were elected when Negroes were being illegally deprived of the right to vote. Under such circumstances, to freeze elective officials into office is, in effect, to freeze Negroes out of the electorate."[138]

Within these general contours, the freezing principle plays a role not dissimilar to the theory that assigns a special role to the right to vote because it is allegedly "a fundamental right, preservative of all rights."[139] This precious-right theory, which played some role in *Harper* as a supplement to the differential-impact theory of that case, can be used in connection with general prohibitions against discrimination, such as that of the Equal Protection Clause, as well as the more specific prohibition against racial discrimination, such as that of the Fifteenth Amendment. Its function is to require a very high burden of justification of any standard that denies the right to vote. As such, its function is quite similar to that of the freezing principle in evaluating putatively innocent state laws, but it does not supplant that principle. Although it would not be useful to speculate whether there are any differences in the weight of the burden of justification cast by the freezing theory as opposed to the precious-right theory, there are other reasons that make the freezing principle of some significance, notwithstanding this precious-right theory. First, the freezing principle is available to those who do not subscribe to the precious-right theory, and that no doubt accounts for the fact that Mr. Justice Harlan—who has steadfastly refused to subscribe to the precious-right theory as an adjunct to the guarantee of equality—wrote the opinion in *Gaston County* for a near unanimous Court with no mention of the fact that what was at stake was a "precious right." Second, the freezing principle is able to deal with an offsetting constitutional value present in the voting-qualification area that makes it difficult to place a heavy burden of justification on the standards qualifying persons to vote simply because the right to vote is at stake. The latitude of the states in setting voting qualifications, as opposed to most other general activity that falls within the reserved powers of the state,

---

[138] 253 F. Supp. at 917.

[139] See Reynolds v. Sims, 377 U.S. 533, 562 (1964); Harper v. Virginia Board of Elections, 383 U.S. 663, 667, 670 (1966); Wesberry v. Sanders, 376 U.S. 1, 17–18 (1964); Carrington v. Rush, 380 U.S. 89, 96 (1965); Yick Wo v. Hopkins, 118 U.S. 356, 370 (1885); Williams v. Rhodes, 393 U.S. 23, 30–31 (1968). But see McDonald v. Board of Election Comm'rs, 394 U.S. 802 (1969).

has some specific constitutional recognition. The Constitution specifically allows states to set standards for the election of federal officials and thus clearly implies that it has a similar power for state officials.[140] It is true that this latitude or power is specifically circumscribed by certain constitutional prohibitions, but the freezing principle is directly rooted in one of those specific prohibitions, that against racial discrimination, rather than simply in the fact that voting is involved.

Third, as an independent principle for guiding the application of the prohibition against racial discrimination, and one that *Gaston County* does not in any way tie to any alleged unique importance of voting, the freezing principle has greater potential for expansion and application in other areas of human activity, such as employment, housing, and education. As a principle linked to the prohibition against racial discrimination rather than to the activity (voting), it functionally resembles the suspect-classification theory. That theory treats any racial classification, among a select group of classifications, as inherently suspect, and thus once again requires a heavy burden of justification to avoid the conclusion that it violates the prohibition against racial discrimination.[141] The suspect-classification theory is of limited utility in guiding the application of the antidiscrimination prohibition to seemingly innocent standards. By definition, such a standard does not contain explicit racial classification as is envisaged by the suspect-classification theory. There may be a situation, and perhaps *Guinn* was one, where the racial classification is thinly veiled and the Court is prepared to say that the surface innocence is just a disguise; but that seems to be the unusual, less problematic situation.

Finally, the freezing theory, which makes disqualifications suspect because they perpetuate past discrimination, may rest on more realistic assumptions than that which makes these standards for voting suspect because the right to vote is allegedly "preservative of all rights." The fact of the matter is that while the right to vote may be a necessary condition for full participation in the political

---

140 See the dissent of Mr. Justice Harlan in Katzenbach v. Morgan, 384 U.S. at 660–61.

141 See Hirabayashi v. United States, 320 U.S. 81 (1943); Korematsu v. United States, 323 U.S. 214 (1944); McLaughlin v. Florida, 379 U.S. 184 (1964); Loving v. Virginia, 388 U.S. 1 (1967); McDonald v. Board of Election Commissioners of Chicago, 394 U.S. 802 (1969). See also Note, note 118 *supra*, at 1087–1131; Fiss, note 49 *supra*, at 576–77.

process, and its general availability critical on a theoretical level for that process to become meaningful, unfortunately it is too often the case that it is not preservative of all other rights, particularly from the individual's perspective. Sometimes it is not even preservative of itself, as emphasized in the post-Reconstruction wave of disenfranchisement.[142] That preservative role is dependent on a great number of other factors, such as the short-run self-interest of the majority and the number of persons with similar interests, and these factors often make the right to vote quite meaningless. Thus, under the precious-right theory a role is claimed for the right to vote that does not readily accord with some of our experiences and sense of reality, and this is often manifested in claiming that other rights—education, employment, and then housing—are basic rights. On the other hand, the freezing theory is more realistic in that it finally enables the Court—*Lassiter* notwithstanding—to confront the read-and-write test on its own terms. These terms were perceived in *South Carolina v. Katzenbach*, when the Court said:[143]

> Meanwhile beginning in 1890, the States of Alabama, Georgia, Louisiana, Mississippi, North Carolina, South Carolina, and Virginia, enacted tests still in use which were specifically designed to prevent Negroes from voting. Typically, they made the ability to read and write a registration qualification and also required completion of a registration form. These laws were based on the fact that as of 1890 in each of the named states, more than two-thirds of the adult Negroes were illiterate while less than one-quarter of adult whites were unable to read or write.

In a footnote the Court gave a historical or causal explanation for this disability that directs the inquiry to the central, dominating past discrimination—slavery: "Prior to the Civil War, most of the slave States made it a crime to teach Negroes how to read or write."[144]

There is a special attractiveness to a principle that satisfies accepted criteria for a legal principle and at the same time is capable of dealing with the validity of a law on terms that accord with a

---

[142] See generally Mills v. Green, 159 U.S. 651 (1895); Giles v. Harris, 189 U.S. 475 (1903); Giles v. Teasley, 193 U.S. 146 (1904); Williams v. Mississippi, 170 U.S. 213 (1898); United States v. Texas, 252 F. Supp. at 243. In United States v. Louisiana, 225 F. Supp. at 374, the court supplied the following statistics to show the disenfranchisement brought about in that state by the grandfather clause adopted in 1898: January 1, 1897: number of Negro voters, 130,344; white voters, 164,088. March 17, 1900: Negro voters, 5,320; white, 125,437.

[143] 383 U.S. at 310–11.   [144] *Id.* at 311 n. 10.

reality. Although in one sense it is perhaps fortunate that the *Gaston County* freezing theory was not advanced and thus not in any way foreclosed in the early literacy test cases, including the 1959 decision in *Lassiter*, in another sense it is surprising that it took so long to emerge if the observation of *South Carolina v. Katzenbach* is accurate. Its full emergence might have been, however, in some subtle way conditioned, not only upon a constant whittling away of the literacy test through other doctrines and upon the presence of the proper trial record, but also upon a general societal acceptance of *Brown*. Lawyers and judges are, of course, not blind to what they see as men, but sometimes they do not know how, or believe it appropriate, to say what they see.

V. Conclusion

The freezing principle emerged in evaluating standards by which to qualify persons to vote and the general contours of the principle have been sketched in that context. The natural, inevitable thrust of its logic extends to other areas covered by the prohibition against racial discrimination.[145] In these areas the risk of perpetuating past discrimination might be more acute and more generalized than in voting, where the freezing principle might be considered limited because of the constantly recurring opportunity to register,[146] the regular and frequent occurrence of elections, and the

---

[145] In areas other than voting, consideration of past discrimination has been relevant for some for answering not only the enforcement questions but also the coverage question. See note 10 *supra*. For example, present, admittedly discriminatory conduct has been viewed by some as a "relic" or "badge" of slavery, thereby eliminating any state action requirement by bringing the conduct within the self-operative provisions of the Thirteenth Amendment or at least within the grant of congressional power of that admendment. See Jones v. Alfred H. Meyer Co., 392 U.S. 409 (1968); Note, *The "New" Thirteenth Amendment: A Preliminary Analysis*, 82 HARV. L. REV. 1294 (1969).

[146] See United States v. Palmer, 356 F.2d 951 (5th Cir. 1966), where, following the district court decision in *United States v. Louisiana*, the registrars in East and West Feliciana parishes stopped registering persons altogether, and the Court, recognizing that this would most acutely perpetuate past discrimination (*i.e.*, the exclusion of Negroes from the class of those already registered), enjoined the registrars from failing to register or to slow down the registration process. See also United States v. Atkins, 323 F.2d 733, 745 (5th Cir. 1963), where the Court prohibited the registrar from not allowing rejected applicants to reapply, and thought "as long as there is the ability to reapply, it is unlikely that within this zone [of practices permitted by Alabama law] there would be any freezing effect so great as to amount to an injustice."

presence of special political incentives in voting for organizing self-help measures to correct the effects of the past. By comparison, the other areas are characterized by a general absence of decisions and by conduct having a mark of permanence, such as constructing a school, acquiring seniority rights in employment, and choosing a residence, a job, or a trade. This is not the occasion to judge the appropriateness of extending the principle to these other areas, but two striking aspects of the enforcement process in voting that might be responsible for the emergence of the freezing principle should be noted. Both underscore the fact that this has been the analysis of what many regard as a success story.[147]

The first is the lack of any ambivalence in recent years about the correctness of the antidiscrimination prohibition in voting and a vigorous commitment to the enforcement process. This may be due to a commonly shared belief in the unique importance of the right to vote. More realistically it seems to be due to the utter lack of justification for racial discrimination in voting. Voting is a government activity that leaves little room for personal associational interests which have—at least at certain points in our history—justified the refusal to extend the antidiscrimination prohibition to other areas of human activity and are responsible for resistance to and complications in the enforcement of that prohibition in covered areas. Extending the vote to those who are disenfranchised does not involve the reallocation of a scarce opportunity or resource, and the cost of this action is small to each individual who is franchised and to the community. Whatever costs are said to exist are difficult to defend on grounds consistent with democratic values concerning representative government or widely shared experiences. For example, we generally know too much about the nature of our own voting decisions to believe seriously the claim that the integrity of the electoral process will be impaired by dispensing with a requirement to read and write a section of a constitution as a qualification to vote. In addition, our notions of representative government may reflect an affirmative value in encouraging total participation in elections. The principle of "one man–one vote" reflects not only an ideal distribution of representatives so as to equalize voting pow-

---

[147] See U.S. CIVIL RIGHTS COMMISSION, POLITICAL PARTICIPATION 222–56 (1968), giving registration statistics in jurisdictions covered by the Voting Rights Act of 1965. The Attorney General said, "Since 1965 more than 800,000 Negroes have been registered in the seven States covered by the act." House Hearings at 221.

er but also the democratic ideal that each man should have a vote. These factors might be present to varying degrees in other areas, but in voting they have coalesced to give additional moral impetus to the enforcement process. This is in part reflected in the fact that the prohibition against racial discrimination in voting has been a very specific constitutional guarantee for almost a century.

The second notable aspect of the enforcement process in voting —perhaps in part due to the general societal commitment to the process—is that the separation-of-powers doctrine has had a very special meaning in this context. The doctrine has not been used as a mere basis for resolving jurisdictional disputes. It does not emphasize the separation of the powers, but their existence. The enforcement process in voting has been a collective enterprise in which each branch has used its distinctive powers and facilities fully and inventively, and the exercise of power by one branch has been respected, supported, and built on by the others.[148]

The importance of this interplay to the strength of the enforcement enterprise and the emergence of the freezing principle is part of the message of *Guinn v. United States, Louisiana v. United States,* and *Gaston County v. United States.* It is also vividly illustrated by *Giles v. Harris,*[149] a case at the turn of the century when organized efforts to deprive Negroes of the franchise they had enjoyed since Reconstruction reached a crescendo. Giles, who brought the suit on behalf of himself and "about 5000 Negroes" in Montgomery, Alabama, alleged that whites had been permanently registered in the recent past under lax standards; that Negroes, including himself, were, because of their race, excluded from registering at the time whites were registered; and that in the future more severe standards would be required to qualify to vote. The theory—so strikingly similar to that of *Louisiana v. United States*— was that the continued exemption of whites from the higher standards imposed on Negroes would perpetuate past discrimination. In an opinion by Justice Holmes, the Court reached out to declare that "it seems impossible to grant the equitable relief which is asked."[150] Unwilling to stop at the ground or decision that "the tra-

---

[148] See generally Katzenbach v. Morgan, 384 U.S. 641 (1966); South Carolina v. Katzenbach, 383 U.S. 301 (1966).

[149] 189 U.S. 475 (1903).

[150] *Id.* at 486. The first Justice Harlan, noting that the case involved "questions of considerable importance" and that it was submitted to the Court without oral

ditional limits of proceedings in equity have not embraced a remedy for political wrongs,"[151] the Court articulated two further grounds. The first, making little sense, was predicated on the view that there was inconsistency in the two claims to have "the whole registration scheme of the Alabama Constitution" declared void and to register as a qualified voter; the Court said that it could not resolve one claim without the other.[152] The second ground, and clearly the more important, candidly reflected a sense of the loneliness and helplessness of the judiciary in, as Justice Holmes described it, "a new and extraordinary situation":[153]

> The bill imports that the great mass of the white population intends to keep the blacks from voting. To meet such an intent something more than ordering the plaintiff's name to be inscribed upon the lists of 1902 will be needed. If the conspiracy and the intent exist, a name on a piece of paper will not defeat them. Unless we are prepared to supervise the voting in that State by officers of the court, it seems to us that all that the plaintiff could get from equity would be an empty form. Apart from damages to the individual, relief from a great political wrong, if done, as alleged, by the people of a State and the State itself, must be given by them or by the legislative and political department of the government of the United States.

Sixty years later, in *United States v. Alabama*,[154] a voting suit brought in the name of the United States under the Civil Rights Act

---

argument, paused on certain jurisdictional problems which led him to believe that the Court should not decide the merits. But "to avoid misapprehension" he briefly added that on the facts alleged "the plaintiff is entitled to relief in respect of his right to be registered as a voter." *Id*. at 494, 504.

[151] *Id*. at 486.

[152] Persistent Giles also instituted an action for damages of $5,000 and applied for a writ of mandamus to compel the registrars to register him. The state court then denied relief on grounds quite similar to that of Justice Holmes: If the constitutional provisions were void under the Fifteenth Amendment, the board of registrars appointed under it would be a "nullity" (not liable for refusing to register him and could not be compelled to register him), and if they were valid, these registrars acted validly. The Supreme Court thought these were adequate, independent state grounds and dismissed the writs of errors in both cases. Giles v. Teasley, 193 U.S. 146 (1904).

[153] 189 U.S. at 486, 488.

[154] 192 F. Supp. 677 (M.D. Ala. 1961), *aff'd*, 304 F.2d 583 (5th Cir.), *aff'd per curiam*, 371 U.S. 37 (1962).

of 1957, which postdated the decision in *Gomillion v. Lightfoot*,[155] the Court of Appeals for the Fifth Circuit not only understood the kind of equitable relief Justice Holmes had found incomprehensible but, more importantly, realized that, at least in voting, the era of *Giles v. Harris* had come to an end. What "*Giles* itself envisaged"[156] had been done. On a petition for certiorari, and without plenary consideration, the Supreme Court unanimously affirmed in a one-sentence per curiam.

---

[155] 364 U.S. 339 (1960).

[156] 304 F.2d at 592.